Principles and Practice of Sex Therapy

PRINCIPLES AND PRACTICE OF SEX THERAPY

Second Edition

Update for the 1990s

Edited by

SANDRA R. LEIBLUM
RAYMOND C. ROSEN

THE GUILFORD PRESS
New York   London

© 1989 The Guilford Press
A Division of Guilford Publications, Inc.
72 Spring Street, New York, NY 10012

Printed in the United States of America

This book is printed on acid-free paper.

Last digit is print number: 9 8 7 6 5 4 3

Library of Congress Cataloging-in-Publication Data

Principles and practice of sex therapy: update for the 1990s
    edited by Sandra R. Leiblum, Raymond C. Rosen.
        p.   cm.
    Includes bibliographies and index.
    ISBN 0-89862-389-8
    1. Sex therapy.   I. Leiblum, Sandra Risa.   II. Rosen, Raymond.
1946–
    [DNLM: 1. Psychosexual Disorders—therapy.   2. Sex Counseling.
WM 611 P9572]
    RC557.P75   1989
    616.85′83—dc20
    DNLM/DLC
    for Library of Congress   89-7458
                                                        CIP

Contributors

STANLEY E. ALTHOF, Ph.D., Director of the Male Sexual Health Center, University Hospitals of Cleveland, Cleveland, Ohio; Department of Psychiatry, Case Western Reserve University School of Medicine, Cleveland, Ohio.

BERNARD APFELBAUM, Ph.D., Director of the Berkeley Sex Therapy Group, Berkeley, California.

JUDITH V. BECKER, Ph.D., Department of Psychiatry, College of Physicians & Surgeons of Columbia University, New York, New York.

ENID H. CAMPBELL, Ph.D., Department of Psychology, Trenton State College, Trenton, New Jersey.

VIRGINIA GRAFTON-BECKER, Psy.D., Department of Psychiatry and Behavioral Sciences, University of Washington Medical School, Seattle, Washington.

JULIA R. HEIMAN, Ph.D., Department of Psychiatry and Behavioral Sciences, University of Washington Medical School, Seattle, Washington.

ARNOLD A. LAZARUS, Ph.D., Department of Psychology, Graduate School of Applied and Professional Psychology, Rutgers University, New Brunswick, New Jersey.

SANDRA R. LEIBLUM, Ph.D., Department of Psychiatry, and Co-Director of the Sexual Counseling Service, College of Medicine and Dentistry of New Jersey—Rutgers Medical School, Piscataway, New Jersey.

BARRY W. McCARTHY, Ph.D., Department of Psychology, American University, Washington, D.C.

ARNOLD MELMAN, M.D., Department of Urology, Montefiore Medical Center and Albert Einstein College of Medicine, Bronx, New York.

MARGARET NICHOLS, Ph.D., Director of the Institute for Personal Growth, New Brunswick, New Jersey.

LAWRENCE A. PERVIN, Ph.D., Department of Psychology, Livingston College, Rutgers University, New Brunswick, New Jersey.

RAYMOND C. ROSEN, Ph.D., Department of Psychiatry, and Co-Director of the Sexual Counseling Service, College of Medicine and Dentistry of New Jersey—Rutgers Medical School, Piscataway, New Jersey.

LESLIE R. SCHOVER, Ph.D., Center for Sexual Function, The Cleveland Clinic Foundation, Cleveland, Ohio.

R. TAYLOR SEGRAVES, M.D., Ph.D., Department of Psychiatry, Cleveland Metropolitan General Hospital, Cleveland, Ohio; Department of Psychiatry, Case Western Reserve University Medical School, Cleveland, Ohio.

LEONORE TIEFER, Ph.D., Departments of Urology and Psychiatry, Montefiore Medical Center and Albert Einstein College of Medicine, Bronx, New York.

JOHN P. WINCZE, Ph.D., Department of Biology and Medicine, Brown University, Providence, Rhode Island.

To my son, Jonathan Leiblum Kassen, who gives meaning to my life.

Sandra R. Leiblum

To my mother and father for their constant support and encouragement.

Raymond C. Rosen

Foreword

It is difficult to believe that only two decades have passed since the publication of Masters and Johnson's groundbreaking volumes on human sexual response and human sexual inadequacy. These books challenged many shibboleths about human sexuality and the treatment of sexual problems.

It was in 1980 that Leiblum and Pervin published the first edition of *Principles and Practice of Sex Therapy*, setting forth the major developments in clinical practice and research since Masters and Johnson's breakthrough. This present volume updates the advances of the last decade in the theory and practice of sex therapy.

In the last 10 years, monolithic theories and modalities have become increasingly integrated into theoretically eclectic formulations and technically opportunistic treatments. Values and ethical issues have become more and more prominent in our field.

Sex therapy has also profited from the explosion in medical and psychological information. Gynecology, psychiatry, endocrinology, urology, psychology, social work, education, physiology, anatomy, radiology, anthropology, sociology, and other disciplines have contributed to our field and to our understanding of sexual behavior.

Increasingly, assessment has become multidisciplinary. Psychological, systemic, medical, cultural, and ethnic perspectives have become important in evaluating clinical data and determining appropriate treatments. The recognition of multiple etiological factors is reflected in several chapters and in the overall conceptualization of this new edition of *Principles and Practice of Sex Therapy*.

In the last several decades, we have witnessed a "sexual revolution," which endorses female sexual enjoyment and entitlement, as well as male. This went hand in hand with women's struggles for equality at home and in the workplace. The sexual revolution was followed by a reactionary backlash, reinforced by reactions to the high divorce rate, noninvolved sex, the confusion between sexual freedom and license, and the fear of AIDS. These factors have contributed to the recent leveling off of the divorce rate and, most recently, to a modest decline. A possible return to longer marriages makes it increasingly important to determine how to maintain sexual viability and interest over a lengthy monogamous period and to handle creatively problems of reduced sexual desire.

Both the male's susceptibility to erectile dysfunction and the female's ability to achieve orgasm have always been sensitive to psychological and interpersonal factors. However, with respect to erectile failure, it has become increasingly apparent that organic changes and their interplay with psychological and interpersonal factors are important. Advances in methods of studying the blood supply to the penis and evaluating the efficiency of the penile venous valves to entrap blood have made major contributions to our understanding of many erectile problems. The promise of vascular surgery, regrettably, has not been fulfilled, however, and our ability to diagnose these problems has outstripped our ability to successfully treat them.

Other changes have characterized the practice of sex therapy over the last decade as well. The dysfunction we describe as lack of sexual desire remains puzzling. We know that there are many etiological determinants to this difficulty. Boredom, loss of sexual attraction, iatrogenic factors, pituitary tumors, change of sexual orientation, etc., are all possible etiological factors. Pharmaceutical companies are engaged in research for the magic substance that will stimulate the area in the hypothalamus, or elsewhere, that will produce desire and arousal. More research is clearly needed in dealing with this "hydra!"

The current edition of *Principles and Practice of Sex Therapy* is welcome. It summarizes the major theoretical and clinical advances in the field of sex therapy in a scholarly and relevant manner. The chapters are uniformly excellent and demonstrate the growing maturity in a field that is fundamental to the health and happiness of individuals, couples, families, and society. As a subspeciality that no one discipline can claim as its own, sex therapy has been quietly consolidating and expanding. Research rather than opinion marks its advances. The editors and authors of the current volume have done a fine job. They have provided us with a dynamic update of the state-of-the-art and science of sex therapy!

Clifford J. Sager, M.D.

Preface

It is nearly a decade since the publication of the first edition of *Principles and Practice of Sex Therapy*, and the field of sex therapy has changed dramatically in that time. Not only has our patient population aged and changed (along with ourselves!), but approaches to assessment and treatment have become increasingly sophisticated and comprehensive. Our clients nowadays complain far less frequently of early ejaculation and orgasmic inability and are experiencing, instead, greater difficulty achieving and maintaining erections, dealing with the sexual sequelae of medical illnesses and procedures, and sustaining sexual interest in the partner relationship. Over the last 10 years, the emphasis placed on sexual spontaneity and activity has been replaced by a sense that caution and care must be exercised in dealing with sexual matters. Interestingly, more couples are requesting sexual counseling because of too little sexual passion rather than too much. In fact, low desire problems have come to dominate media interest and private concern.

The issues and treatment approaches dominating the practice of sex therapy at the present time are strikingly different from those that occupied theorists and clinicians a decade ago. Sex therapy has matured. New societal concerns have surfaced that greatly influence the research and clinical practice in our field. The presence of AIDS has influenced—directly and indirectly—many aspects of our treatment. The increasing medicalization of sex therapy, a trend that began in the late 1970s, has mushroomed. Pharmacological and surgical interventions are becoming ever more popular.

In reviewing the 1980 edition of *Principles and Practice of Sex Therapy*, we realized that many of the chapters had become dated. We recognized the importance of including chapters on topics that had been omitted and of updating and revising the coverage on more "traditional" problems such as early ejaculation and anorgasmia. Consequently, the present volume contains ten entirely new chapters, including ones on sexuality and chronic illness, sex and aging, sexual assault, and two state-of-the-art presentations on assessment and treatment of erectile failure. Several new contributors present their unique approaches to the evaluation and treatment of sexual difficulties. We gratefully acknowledge the outstanding contributions of

Judith Becker, Julia Heiman, Barry McCarthy, Arnold Melman, Margaret Nichols, Leslie Schover, R. Taylor Segraves, Leonore Tiefer, and Stanley Althof. Our other outstanding contributors Bernie Apfelbaum, Enid Campbell, Arnold Lazarus, Lawrence Pervin, and John Wincze (from the first volume) have revised and updated their presentations for the present book.

Our goals have remained largely unchanged. As with the first edition, we aim to present the major conceptual and clinical approaches to the treatment of sexual dysfunctions. We specifically invited clinicians who represent a variety of theoretical perspectives to highlight our observation that no one conceptual approach has dominated the field, and that theoretical eclecticism is pervasive and entrenched. We consider this a necessary and inevitable stage in the development of the field.

We requested that our contributors illustrate their treatment approaches with in-depth case illustrations, including both successful and not-so-successful cases. We continue to believe that there frequently is a major disparity between theory and practice. It is far easier to discourse knowledgeably about how treatment might proceed; it is quite different to accomplish one's treatment goals with one or two unique and, often, conflicted individuals who may (or may not) want to modify their sexual behavior. In real-life practice, treatment plans are continually modified to fit the changing life circumstances presented by particular clients, and the exigencies of each particular clinical situation.

Finally, we invited our contributors to identify those factors that they believe contribute to therapeutic success or failure with specific problems and patients. Discussions concerning such factors remain the basis for ongoing research in the broader field of psychotherapy and behavior change. It is often difficult, if not impossible, to determine the critical change agents in treatment. Why does the same intervention appear to work well with one client while fail miserably with another? What patient variables are prognostically related to more or less favorable outcomes? While post-hoc formulations may work well for some cases, we often remain perplexed about the critical etiological factors in others. Nevertheless, we believe such speculation to be essential if our field is to advance.

In reading through this volume, one is certain to be impressed by the growing sophistication of clinical conceptualization and exposition. Sex therapists have become increasingly comprehensive in their assessment and treatment approaches. Few clinicians nowadays prescribe simple behavioral exercises or "cook-book" approaches as remedies for complex problems. Interpersonal and systemic concepts currently dominate discussion, along with surgical, physical, and pharmacological interventions.

We wish to thank our authors for their remarkable open-mindedness in sharing their thoughts and methods, their disappointments, and their triumphs. We are greatly indebted to them for their honesty and willingness to examine their work critically and to receive our editorial feedback graciously. We also wish to thank our editor and friend, Seymour Weingarten, for his support and encouragement throughout this volume. Special appreciation is due to our loyal and devoted secretary, Agnes Bertelsen. Those extending cheer, support, and patience throughout the many months of this process are particularly deserving of our gratitude and affection. In particular, we have long appreciated the support and wisdom of our friends, Marian Dunn, John Gagnon, Daniel Goldberg, Kathryn Hall, Monica McGoldrick, Larry Pervin, Barbara Rabinowitz, Raul Schiavi, Patricia Schreiner-Engel, Susan Shaffer, and George Soules.

Contents

Introduction: Sex Therapy in the Age of AIDS

Sandra R. Leiblum and Raymond C. Rosen

The decision to update and revise this second edition of the *Principles and Practice of Sex Therapy* was prompted by several factors. It is now 20 years since Masters and Johnson published *Human Sexual Inadequacy* (1970), the landmark book that radically changed the manner in which sexual problems were conceptualized and treated. Prior to Masters and Johnson, psychotherapists tended to view sexual difficulties as indicative of long-standing psychopathology and therapy focused on resolution of intrapsychic conflict. Masters and Johnson challenged this view and provided a novel conceptual and clinical approach to the treatment of sexual difficulties. Their emphasis on anxiety, specifically performance anxiety, as the basic ingredient in all sexual dysfunctions was regarded by many experienced therapists as too simplistic. The suggestion that re-education procedures could reduce or eliminate the debilitating performance anxiety and pave the way for "natural," problem-free sexual activity was considered overly optimistic by many. Nevertheless, few therapists could convincingly challenge the results that Masters and Johnson achieved in their work with the 790 patients who sought treatment in St. Louis. Erectile difficulties, ejaculation problems, and anorgasmia were seemingly successfully resolved during an intensive 2-week period with the assistance of a dual sex therapy team and a focus on active relearning utilizing sensate focus and other directive techniques.

Now, nearly two decades later, the optimism and enthusiasm that accompanied Masters and Johnson's pioneering work has abated. Sexuality, generally, is viewed with greater uncertainty and suspicion, and few clinicians are claiming *miraculous* 2-week cures for chronic problems. In fact, most sexual problems are currently considered the net result of a complex interaction among physical, psychological, and interpersonal factors. Increasingly, clinicians are admitting to feeling "baffled" about the etiology and treatment of the sexual complaints greeting them. It is ironic that Masters and Kolodny's most recent volume, *Crisis: Heterosexual Behavior in the Age of AIDS* (1988), has a markedly different emphasis from their earlier works celebrating sexuality. Masters, as well as other sex therapists, is now preaching sexual caution and restraint. The increased awareness of the dangers as well as the delights of sexuality are dominating popular consciousness and cooling the sexual climate.

In thinking about the evolution of the field since the publication of the first edition of *Principles and Practice of Sex Therapy*, we realized that societal attitudes toward sexuality and treatment methods designed to overcome sexual dysfunction have changed considerably. Sexual attitudes in an age of AIDS are markedly different from those of the previous "Age of Aquarius"! This chapter highlights the major shifts in sexual beliefs and behavior over the last two decades and demonstrates how these changes have contributed to changes in the practice of sex therapy. Additionally, we update some of the latest technological, pharmacological, and conceptual approaches to the assessment and treatment of sexual disorders.

THE SEXUAL LIBERATION MOVEMENT

The decade of the 1960s marked the growth and development of the so-called "sexual liberation movement." This movement was spurred, in part, by changes in birth control technology occurring in the 1950s that helped separate sexuality from procreation. The pill made sexual spontaneity possible and helped pave the way toward recreative rather than procreative sex. Advances in birth control options were accompanied by several other societal changes: the increasing activism, autonomy, and assertiveness of women, the ready availability of legal abortion, and the free-wheeling "flower and drug" cultures of the 1960s, which emphasized the abandonment of all authoritarian and restrictive limitations to personal freedom. Finally, the proliferation of popular magazine articles and media events devoted to sexual enhancement set the stage for the leap into sexual liberation.

It was during the 1970s that the gay liberation movement entered its decade of greatest visibility. Following the attack in 1969 of Greenwich Village drag queens against police who were harassing a gay bar called the Stonewall Inn, gay men and women became increasingly political. "Sex was part and parcel of political liberation," Shilts (1987) points out, and sexual anonymity, promiscuity, and commercialization flourished. The gay liberation movement of the 1970s spawned a business of bathhouses and sex clubs, which permitted the rapid spread of venereal disease, hepatitis, and enteric disorders (Shilts, 1987). In 1980, Governor Edmund G. Brown, Jr. issued a proclamation honoring Gay Freedom Week throughout the state of California, and hundreds of thousands of marchers and spectators came to participate and revel in the Gay Freedom Day Parade. Tragically, their celebrations during these riotous days helped spread the deadly HIV virus, although the connection between the strange and dreadful illnesses that appeared during the following years and the means of its transmission evaded scientific investigation for several years.

It should be noted that although gays were the most visible and outspoken proponents of casual sex, even middle-class heterosexuals enjoyed ample opportunities for extramarital and casual sexual experimentation in bars and private clubs across the northeast and west coasts during the early and mid-1970s. Swinging clubs announced their parties in local newspapers, and the growing availability of video cassette players provided easy access to the visual depiction of unconventional and titillating sexual behaviors for all.

It was only in the late 1970s that consternation about the consequences of the sexual liberation movement began to be actively expressed. Objections to the increasing portrayal of violence against women in the visual media as well as the ready availability of child pornography were raised by feminists and social activitists across the United States. The publicity afforded to reports of child sexual abuse in seemingly sacrosanct places such as schools and churches created a heightened awareness of the incidence and prevalence of sexual coercion generally and led to a crackdown on the availability of both "soft" erotica and "hard-core" pornography. The report of the Attorney General's Commission on Pornography (1986) represented a significant about-face from the earlier President's Commission on Obscenity and Pornography (1976). The earlier report tended to be tolerant of pornography and sanguine about its long-term effects. The Meese Commission, on the other hand, expressed strong concern about the role of pornography, particularly violent pornography, in undermining "the values underlying the family unit" (p. 29). The committee noted that "despite the absence of clinical evidence linking Class III materials to anti-social behavior, several correlational connections are disturbing . . ." (p. 28). In part, the sentiments expressed in the Meese report reflected the antisexual climate of the Reagan years, and in part, they reflected genuine and realistic anxiety about the consequences of unbridled and unpoliced pornography. In the zeal to remove violent pornography from newsstands and other public places that followed the publication of the Meese report, all pornography became suspect.

Other factors contributed to the retreat from the sexual permissiveness of the 1970s. Concern about the staggeringly high rates of unplanned and often unwanted teenage pregnancies alarmed social activists and led to the reopening of the debate about the availability of birth control and abortion for minors. The Reagan administration proposed measures that would severely limit the activities of organizations like Planned Parenthood to provide contraceptive information to minors without parental consent. The increase in sexually transmitted diseases was similarly alarming. In the early 1980s, the growing number of herpes cases captured the attention of the public. *Time* magazine (August 2, 1982) entitled its article on herpes "The New Scarlet Letter," implying that individuals diagnosed with herpes were social lepers. The article went on to conclude that fear of herpes had drastically altered the dating and sexual behaviors of the singles population. In fact, there was a significant upsurge in all sexually transmitted diseases over the decade, and sexually active singles became increasingly concerned about the potential consequences of unprotected sexual relations. Not only were singles, along with separated and divorced individuals, uneasy about acquiring venereal diseases, but more and more women were becoming painfully aware of the dangers of pelvic inflammatory disease for future fertility.

Nevertheless, it was probably the realization that the deadly HIV virus was transmitted by blood and sexual contact that had the greatest impact on society's attitude toward sexuality in the 1980s. The horror of AIDS and the fear of its transmission put the final nail in the coffin of casual sex. As Margery Nichols notes in Chapter 10, sex began to be seen as dangerous by heterosexuals as well as by gays. Hell and brimstone messages suggesting that sex can be lethal and that semen might be toxic dulled the ardor of even the most outspoken advocates of sexual spontaneity. Nowadays, casual sex with anonymous partners is considered akin to a game of Russian roulette, and few individuals are willing to place their bets on unprotected sex. The threat of AIDS has radically altered the sexual life styles of gay men and has impacted on the heterosexual community as well. "Safe Sex" is dominating the consciousness of all sexually active single individuals. Professional organizations are devoting large portions of their programs to AIDS workshops, educational forums, and counselor training, just as sex educators are receiving mandates from boards of education that had traditionally been reluctant to provide sex education. "Family relations" courses are being offered in many educational institutions formerly hostile to them. Even the Surgeon General's office, albeit belatedly, is actively involved in providing public education about the health risks associated with activities that heretofore were rarely mentioned in public forums. Dating clubs for those individuals who can "prove" their HIV-negative status have formed in large cities, and individuals are more likely to seek sexual histories from prospective partners than to seduce them willy-nilly into bed. Books on AIDS are appearing daily and often confuse the public with contradictory messages. For some individuals, "safe sex" involves watching soft-core films on video, whereas others in long-standing relationships, are motivated to seek resolutions for chronic sexual problems.

Prostitution is becoming less popular, adolescents are engaging in less frequent coital experimentation, and sexually active individuals are avoiding partners with histories of bisexuality and intravenuous drug use. Regrettably, there is evidence of an increase in harassment and crimes against homosexuals (*New York Times*, July 3, 1988). In a report issued by the National Gay and Lesbian Task Force, a Washington-based lobbying group, antigay incidents increased 42% between 1986 and 1987, and the tide appears to be rising. Interestingly, hostility toward homosexuals is increasing at a time when there is evidence of greater acceptance of homosexual rights in legal affairs. Antidiscrimination laws have been passed, and openly gay candidates have attained political office. Nevertheless, it is not uncommon for individuals suspected of leading gay life styles to be the victims of both covert and overt hostility and even violence.

Sexuality has, once again, become a force that needs channeling and control, an activity that must be approached with condoms and caution. In many respects, marital and sexual therapy is more sought after than ever, but new and perplexing ethical and moral issues have become the subject of debate and controversy. For instance, dealing with the confidentiality issues involved if one learns that one partner in a marriage is HIV positive but refuses to inform his partner has surfaced as a not uncommon issue in couples' therapy. What is the responsibility of the therapist in preserving the confidentiality of one partner versus protecting the health of the other? What is the therapist's responsibility if a wife complains that her husband is behaving in a sexually (or physically) inappropriate or coercive fashion with either her or her child? Does one report such behavior to the appropriate authorities or deal with it exclusively as a couple issue? In many respects, the practice of sex therapy is both more challenging and more difficult than ever before in its brief history.

CHANGES IN SEX THERAPY PRACTICE

Four major trends have characterized the practice of sex therapy over the last decade: (1) a trend toward greater "medicalization" or appreciation of the role of biological factors in sexual dysfunctions, (2) an increasing emphasis on pharmacological intervention, particularly in the treatment of erectile dysfunctions but in other sexual dysfunctions as well, (3) greater attention to the dilemmas posed by desire disorders and inhibitions in the experience and expression of sexual interest, and (4) a therapeutic focus that relies more on interpersonal systems concepts and object-relations theories.

The "Medicalization" of Sex Therapy

In the last 10 years, there has been a growing emphasis on physical as opposed to psychological contributions to sexual difficulties. In part, this trend was influenced by the publication of Spark, White, and Connolly's (1980) study entitled "Impotence is not always psychogenic" in the *Journal of the American Medical Association*. These authors screened 105 men with erectile failure and reported that 37 had abnormal steroid hormone levels suggestive of disorders of the hypothalamic–pituitary–gonadal axis. They recommended routine hormonal screening for all men with erectile problems and argued that neither a history of occasional early morning erections nor sporadic successful intercourse excluded a hormonal basis for erectile dysfunction.

This study stimulated considerable controversy among clinicians who argued that it contained, a priori, a sample of men at high risk for endocrine disorders, which was nonrepresentative of the population at large. Nevertheless, sex therapy clinics began to move toward establishing more comprehensive vascular, hormonal, and neurological procedures for men referred with erectile problems. As Tiefer and Melman discuss in Chapter 8, the evaluation of erectile disorders has become quite sophisticated technologically, and there is growing awareness that organic factors may be implicated in a large proportion of cases with erectile dysfunction.

Contributing to this trend has been the increasing age of many patients reporting for sex therapy as well as the incidence of concomitant medical disorders. The mean age in our clinic has increased from the early 30s to the mid-50s over the past decade, in part reflecting the large number of elderly men requesting nocturnal penile tumescence evaluation (Rosen, Leiblum, & Hall, 1987).

Paralleling the increased awareness of the role of vascular and endocrinological factors in the etiology of impotence has been the increasing involvement of urologists and other medical specialists in the management of erectile and other sexual dysfunctions. More than ever before, physicians have become involved in assessing and treating complaints of erectile failure. We should note, however, that most physicians receive no formal training in sex therapy and are not well informed about the latest developments in the field. At times, they attempt treatments without sufficient assessment of the presenting problem. For example, a female-to-male transsexual who was recently evaluated in our clinic indicated that he had been receiving testosterone injections for 3 years for treatment of his "impotence." In fact, he did not have a penis and had never received a physical examination from the urologist!

Many physicians rely on assessment instruments that have questionable validity, such as portable devices for evaluating nocturnal penile tumescence. As recently discussed by Schiavi (1988), such devices do not assess the presence or absence of REM sleep and thus are susceptible to both false-positive and false-negative errors. There is evidence that some physicians routinely prescribe medications (e.g., testosterone, yohimbine) for erectile dysfunction without adequate knowledge of the research findings concerning their use. On the other hand, some centers have developed productive collaborative arrangements between physicians and sex therapists in which the expertise of each contributes to optimal evaluation and treatment. As Tiefer and Melman discuss in their chapter, such interdisciplinary relationships are clinically essential and mutually productive.

During the past decade, physicians have also become increasingly aware of the sexual concomitants of disease and illness (Schover & Jensen, 1988). Sexual medicine has become a specialized area for interdisciplinary study, and inquiry about sexual function is becoming more routine in the initial medical work-up of patients (Bachmann, Leiblum, & Grill, 1989). The sexual sequelae of every condition from diabetes to arthritis, dialysis to hypertension, are being investigated and are receiving increasing coverage in the medical literature. Regrettably, however, male problems continue to occupy the major attention of practitioners and researchers alike. For example, a 52-year-old female stroke victim complained that her neurologist blushed and changed the subject when she complained about her lack of orgasms. It is unlikely that he would have been as surprised and uncomfortable if a similarly aged male patient had inquired about erectile insufficiency or lack of ejaculation. Women's concerns generally are relegated to "back-burner" status, although this situation is slowly changing as greater numbers of female researchers enter the field and investigate such topics as the sexual impact of PMS, hypertension, menopause, etc. Overall, there is greater acknowledgment that both men and women can enjoy physical intimacy whether old or young, healthy or infirm. The chapters on sex and aging and sex and chronic illness in the present volume are testimony to the wider net that sex therapy embraces in this context.

Finally, concerns about AIDS have alerted all health professionals to the importance of sexual inquiry for patients undergoing a wide variety of medical or surgical procedures, from artificial insemination with donor semen to blood transfusion. Physicians who, heretofore, were loathe to inquire about the sexual intimacies of their patient's lives are finding that failure to include such inquiry may leave them liable to criticism of inadequate treatment or even the potential of a malpractice suit.

Pharmacological Interventions

The search for a quick "fix" for sexual problems has been evident throughout medical history. As Rosen (1983) has noted, as long ago as 2000 B.C., Egyptian papyri contained specific potions for curing impotence. The Romans put their faith in a concoction made from the testicles of a bull. In more recent times, seemingly more scientific "brews" have been used in treating erectile failure, but to date, none has proven reliably effective. The last decade, however, has witnessed a remarkable upsurge in the use of pharmacological interventions for assessing and treating erectile failure. In particular, the use of self-administered or physician-administered intracavernosal papaverine or papaverine plus phenotolamine has gained widespread acceptance, and several other antidepressant (e.g., Welbutron®) and antianxiety drugs are under investigation in urology and sex therapy clinics across the country (Turner et al., 1988). What is particularly noteworthy about these recent developments is the willingness of clinicians to prescribe these drugs for men with psychogenic erectile failure. In the past, "physical" interventions were reserved for men with demonstrable organogenic dysfunction. Surgical implants, for example, tended to be reserved exclusively for men with clear-cut organic impotence. Nowadays, there is greater willingness to treat long-standing and refractory "psychogenic" problems with physical interventions. Stanley Althof in Chapter 9 notes that psychotherapy has its limitations and that for some men with chronic erectile failure, autoinjection or other pharmacological approaches to therapy may be indicated.

The search for the perfect aphrodisiac has also been a consistent theme throughout recorded history. Humankind has always been intrigued by the possibility of whetting sexual appetite through the use of magical and powerful potions that, once ingested, would unleash passionate and lusty behavior. For some time now, both clinicians and investigators have been experimenting with the administration of exogenous testosterone for both men and women as a means of stimulating sexual desire and arousal. Much of this work is anecdotal, and the few controlled studies by Bancroft (1983) and others have yielded inconclusive results concerning its efficacy. In the last decade, the pharmaceutical industry has supported extensive research to investigate various medications for overcoming sexual desire deficits. Welbutron®, an antidepressant drug, has attained considerable attention as a "modern-day aphrodisiac," but its efficacy continues to be hotly debated (Lief, 1988). More recently, a new dopamine agonist compound is under investigation in sex therapy clinics across the country. Although it is too early to state with any certainty whether an effective drug will be found, it is reasonable to expect that the search for a drug to stimulate desire will continue.

Pharmacotherapy has also become prominent in the treatment of sexual aversion and phobias. Helen Singer Kaplan, in particular, is a strong advocate for the use of psychopharmacological agents for these problems. In her recent book, co-edited with Donald Klein (1987), Kaplan suggests that the new antipanic medications have added an additional "dimension" to the established ones of psychodynamically oriented sex therapy and behavioral prescriptions for overcoming sexual panic states and intense separation anxieties. In particular, she recommends the use of tricyclic antidepressants, such as imipramine (Tofranil®), desipramine (Norpramin®), amitriptyline (Elavil®) and nortriptyline (Aventil®) (Kaplan, 1987, p. 86). For those patients who do not respond to these medications or who cannot tolerate their side effects, Kaplan recommends MAO inhibitors. She strongly suggests that various drug treatments be attempted until the "right" medication for overcoming the patient's panic disorder is found, "even when a patient is difficult to medicate" (p. 87). Kaplan suggests that until the debilitating anxiety can be reduced, psychotherapy will be ineffective. Although she acknowledges that the best treatment for sexual aversion is a combination of medication and sex therapy, she is, perhaps, the most vocal advocate of the judicious use of medication in sex therapy. Although the long-term efficacy of these treatments is yet to be demonstrated in methodologically well-controlled studies, the reliance on medication is clearly indicative of a growing trend in sexual therapy.

Finally, antiandrogenic drug treatments have gained widespread acceptance as a means of controlling the compulsive, antisocial sexual behavior of paraphilics (Berlin & Meinecke, 1981). In this country, sex offenders have been increasingly treated with Depo-Provera®, a treatment sometimes referred to as "chemical castration" in view of the drug's effects in diminishing both sexual desire and arousal. Despite a variety of ethical, clinical, and research questions, this pharmacological approach offers potential advantages compared to incarceration or other forms of aversive sexual behavior control. Most authors recommend that antiandrogenic therapy be combined with ongoing psychotherapy to ensure lasting behavioral changes.

We, like many sex therapists, have concerns and questions regarding the use of some of the newer pharmacological interventions in the treatment of sexual disorders. First, the scientific evidence supporting the use of these treatments continues to be sketchy and problematic. For those pharmacological interventions, such as papaverine, where there is some evidence of short-term efficacy, the long-term impact on sexual and physical health remains to be established. Second, it is all too easy to become invested in achieving technically satisfactory performance while ignoring the importance of the emotional interaction. The strength of the relationship, rather than the strength of the erection, is critical. As Althof notes in Chapter 9, the penis is connected to the heart, and it is often the heartfelt emotions that should become the focus of treatment. Although drugs may assist in enhancing desire or arousal, they can do little to overcome deep-seated animosities, resentments, or relationship conflicts. In desire problems, particularly, identifying and addressing the problems in the partner relationship may prove more efficacious in the long run than finding the right pill. Relationship therapy rather than pharmacological therapy may be what the doctor should order!

Emphasis on Desire Disorders

Desire disorders have occupied a position of increasing importance in contemporary sex therapy. In most sex therapy centers, complaints of desire discrepancies, as well as deficient or excessive sexual interest, are common (LoPiccolo, 1988; Kilmann, Boland, Norton, Davidson, & Caird, 1986). Early in the decade, attention was focused on inhibited sexual desire, that is, on those individuals who seem devoid of sexual appetite, whether in fantasy or reality. Such patients rarely engaged in masturbation, infrequently initiated sexual overtones, and derived little satisfaction from their sexual interactions. Although some patients, particularly men, seem to display a madonna–prostitute dynamic with respect to their partners, others seem never to have found sex compelling or particularly enjoyable. These cases challenged traditional Masters-and-Johnson-type formulations, which emphasized performance anxiety and negative conditioning as the major deterrents to sexual expression, and provided ripe ground for investigation into the psychodynamic and interpersonal aspects of these patients' lives. In one sense, desire disorders prompted the necessity for more inclusive theoretical approaches. They forced clinicians and theorists to think more broadly about sexual behavior and emphasized the importance of integrating biological, intrapsychic, and interpersonal determinants (Leiblum & Rosen, 1988).

Toward the mid-1980s, reports of sexual "addiction" or hyperactive sexual interest began appearing (Carnes, 1983; Quadland, 1985; Mattison, 1985). Clinicians presented case reports highlighting individuals who seemed "driven" by sexual urgency. Although a number of these cases were paraphilic or homosexual individuals, others presented as heterosexuals who were distressed by their "compulsive desire" for orgasmic release, either through frequent masturbation or intercourse. Therapy was sought because these sexual cravings were so insistent as to be distracting, or, more commonly, these individuals were referred by their partners who complained that they were "oversexed." Nevertheless, a closer examination of many such cases suggested that the majority were either instances of deviant arousal or were reactions to disturbed and conflictual marital relations, with the sexual "symptom" an indication of more basic relationship maladjustment. Although there was some discussion about designating hypersexuality as a discrete diagnosic entity in DSM-III-R, the consensus was that there was insufficient evidence at present to justify this inclusion. In fact, most recently, the identification of sexual addiction and sexual compulsion as a diagnosis has been challenged as being conceptually flawed, subjective, value-laden, and an example of "pseudoscientific codifications of prevailing erotic values rather than bona fide clinical entities" (Levine & Troiden, 1988, p. 349).

Nevertheless, complaints involving desire are often the most perplexing and prevalent cases facing practitioners today. As we indicate in Chapter 2, the etiology of these cases is quite diverse, as are the clinical approaches needed for intervention. Some progress has been made in articulating the role of androgens in stimulating sexual appetite (Bancroft, 1983; Segraves, 1988), but the role of biological factors generally is incompletely understood (Lief, 1988). Treatment approaches include cognitive–behavioral, psychodynamic, interpersonal, and systems-interactional perspectives, and it is clear that little consensus has emerged about either theory or practice with these problems. As yet, no single conceptual or clinical approach has "cornered the market" in terms of accounting for the complexity of case presentations or varieties of outcome.

Greater Reliance on Systemic and Object-Relations Theory

Prior to Masters and Johnson's focus on treating the "couple" as the "client," the primary modality for treating sexual problems was long-term "individually" oriented psychoanalytic psychotherapy. Following the publication of their landmark book *Human Sexual Inadequacy* (1970), however, sexual therapy began to rely primarily on short-term behavioral interventions for treating a wide range of sexual dysfunctions. Sensuality training exercises were routinely prescribed, and treatment tended to proceed in a stepwise fashion of increasingly genital and physically intimate exercises. Techniques of successive approximations were more popular than investigations of the psychodynamic contribution to problems. "Symptom-removal" short-term, directive therapy became the norm.

During the late 1970s and early 1980s, it became apparent that such approaches, although effective in some cases, were not useful for all individuals or types of problems. Desire difficulties, for example, did not respond readily to short-term behavioral prescriptions. Clinicians bemoaned the lack of "techniques" for resolving these and other increasingly complex cases. It became apparent that systemic issues play a considerable role in creating and maintaining difficulties with desire and arousal and that more complex and sophisticated interventions are needed to address the power and intimacy issues often operative in such cases. Similarly, intrapsychic difficulties such as deficiencies in attachment, dependency, and commitment seemed to be critical issues for many individuals displaying chronic low sexual desire. In such cases, behavioral or pharmacological interventions were clearly secondary to resolving the underlying psychodynamic conflicts. A number of prominent clinicians in the field of sex therapy espoused either an object-relations or ego-analytical approach to treatment (Scharff, 1982, 1988; Kaplan, 1979, 1988; Apfelbaum, 1984, 1988.)

Over the last decade, sex therapy has become more intensive and often more protracted, as therapeutic orientations have shifted toward systemic and object-relations approaches. Therapists of all theoretical persuasions are paying greater attention to couple and family issues as "sexual genograms" are used to identify relevant figures from the past who may mirror or model certain critical attitudes and assumptions about masculinity and femininity, sexual values, and appropriate gender role behaviors. Workshops in these approaches are proliferating. It is likely that the next decade will witness an even greater cross-fertilization of ideas between sexual and system-oriented therapists.

OTHER DEVELOPMENTS IN THE FIELD

In addition to these four major trends, several minor changes characterize the current practice of sex therapy. In the early 1980s, at the time of publication of the first edition of *Principles and Practice of Sex Therapy* (Leiblum & Pervin, 1980), group therapy approaches for female anorgasmia, early ejaculation, and a variety of couples' problems were popular. In fact, our own clinic was actively engaged in organizing, conducting, and researching the usefulness of such time-limited sex therapy groups (Leiblum & Eisner-Hershfeld, 1977; Leiblum, Rosen, & Pierce, 1976; Mullen & Rosen, 1979). Over the last decade, however, group treatment approaches for these dysfunctions have declined markedly, in part because of difficulties in recruiting appropriate participants for such groups and in part because of the complexity of patients and problems presenting to most clinics today. There appear to be far fewer preorgasmic women, probably because of the existence of self-help books and "instructional" articles in popular women's magazines. Women's sexual enhancement groups continue to be offered, although with much less frequency than a decade ago. In some clinics, women's enhancement groups are focusing on the sexual needs and concerns of older climacteric women rather than on their younger anorgasmic counterparts. Incest survivor groups are increasing and appear to be useful adjuncts to individual and family therapy in dealing with the long-term sequelae of sexual coercion.

The use of sexual surrogates in sex therapy, although always controversial, has generally been abandoned over the last several years. For example, in the first edition of *Principles and Practice of Sex Therapy*, Apfelbaum presented a treatment model for male sexual dysfunction that extensively utilized "body-work therapists," who worked actively with a primary therapist in planning and implementing treatment. Nowadays, medical, legal, and ethical concerns have rendered the use of surrogates in sex therapy untenable in most centers.

Along with the increasing complexity of many cases, the boundary between sex therapy and psychotherapy or couples' therapy is frequently blurred. Often, the focus on the sexual "symptom" must be delayed until weeks or months of exploration of other intimacy or relationship issues has occurred. As the chapters in the current volume illustrate, few authors are advocating technique-based approaches to the treatment of specific dysfunctions. In particular, chapters on female anorgasmia (Heiman & Grafton-Becker), erectile dysfunction (Althof), and sexual desire disorders (Rosen & Leiblum), among others, illustrate the growing breadth and eclecticism in the field.

SEX THERAPY IN THE AGE OF AIDS

Reflecting on the omnipresent specter of AIDS, we are struck by the magnitude of its impact on all aspects of sex therapy and sexuality generally. First, efforts to check the spread of AIDS have highlighted the inadequate data base that currently exists for understanding sexual practices and determining standards for sexual conduct. For example, norms for universal age-related changes in sexual function are unknown at present. For example, we wonder how typical it is for a 65-year-old married man to be able to complete coitus on only 25% of his coital encounters. Or how characteristic is it for newly postpartum women to experience a lack of sexual interest? The Kinsey studies (1948, 1953) remain the only large-scale population studies documenting the sexual practices of Americans. Because our information base for understanding sexual behavior is so outdated and limited, there remain many questions about the incidence of sexual practices that might compromise our health or increase the likelihood of disease transmission. On the positive side, the existence of the AIDS epidemic has challenged NIH and other governmental funding agencies to develop and execute large-scale population-based studies of sexual behavior.

Indirectly, the presence of AIDS has prompted heterosexual monogamous couples to find new ways of maintaining sexual intimacy and satisfaction over a lifetime. We are no longer living in a culture in which sexual partners are routinely "traded in" when sexual interest has waned. Couples are increasingly committed to monogamy despite the wish for the passion and intensity that characterize a new relationship. How do we teach couples in today's society ways of sustaining sexual desire over a lifetime when novelty and the attractions of youth have waned?

We may also ask what impact the specter of AIDS will have on the sexual values, comfort, and spontaneity of today's young adults. Earlier generations experienced anxiety and concern about unplanned pregnancies, and indeed, the worry for certain individuals may have been so great that celibacy was chosen over sexual involvement, and procreational anxiety dulled sexual passion. It may be that denial will dominate fear in the years to come and that young adults will be disproportionately represented in the dreadful statistics documenting the dissemination of the HIV virus. Unfortunately, adolescents have an unshakable belief in their own immortality, and campus ecology or street culture continues to make drugs and alcohol easily available and seductive. On the other hand, with sane and sound sex education, it is possible that young adults will continue to celebrate and explore their sexuality in ways that do not compromise their health. It is up to us as sex educators and therapists to help young people find new ways to become responsible sexual citizens.

Although the threat of AIDS will not affect the majority of long-term heterosexual or homosexual monogamous couples, concerns about earlier sexual practices or experiences do intrude on current sexual comfort. Past experiences with prostitutes or casual sexual partners lead to anxiety and questions about the advisability of being tested for the presence of the HIV virus. Sex therapists will need to counsel individuals and couples about the benefits and risks of undergoing AIDS testing and whether or not to use condoms with their long-term sexual partners. It behooves sex therapists to maintain up-to-date information on the most current research and CDC recommendations about AIDS.

For adults who become newly single as a result of separation, divorce, or widowhood, and for single adults generally, the importance of direct and explicit sexual communication is evident. No longer can personal discomfort or disinclination be viewed as a valid reason for avoiding sexual discourse. Women, as always, need to be vigilant about protecting themselves against the dual risks of sexually transmitted diseases and unwanted pregnancies. They must take the initiative in discussing and, if necessary, demanding and providing condoms in sexual exchanges. Sexual assertiveness has traditionally been difficult for women, and sex educators and therapists need to suggest sound models of taste and tact coupled with firm but feminine ways for accomplishing self-protection. Men, too, need to take greater sexual responsibility. As Dr. June Osborn, Dean of the Michigan School of Public Health, has noted (1988), we are living in an era when "people are playing a dreadful version of Russian roulette where the bullet can take from 5 to 10 years to reach its mark." As sex therapists, we must endeavor to prevent such games from being played.

What about the impact of condoms on sexual exchange? The complaints about loss of seductiveness, spontaneity, and sensation are omnipresent and real for many individuals. For example, a recent patient of ours, a 59-year-old married man who was HIV positive from blood transfusions received 6 years earlier during triple bypass surgery, complained that he was unable to adjust to using condoms. He would lose his arousal (and erection) as soon as he tried to place one on. How can such individuals, who have not used condoms for years or are resistant to their use, be helped? It behooves both condom manufacturers and sex educators and therapists to find ways of making condoms acceptable and sensual so that they will be regularly employed during sexual exchange for high-risk populations.

Finally, sex therapists and educators must embrace a philosophy of prevention rather than providing treatment alone in the next decade. We can no longer afford to see the victims of sexual ignorance or misinformation only after the fact, since for some it will be too late. We must become better facilitators of behavior change and more adept at integrating a variety of approaches to our clinical armamentarium. We must become more knowledgeable about the impact of disease and drugs on sexual function. We must teach some individuals how to eroticize safe sex, how to say "no" when they are sexually disinterested, and how to make virginity and abstinence acceptable choices for more individuals. We must also find effective sexual and nonsexual ways to encourage and sustain intimacy over a lifetime and to overcome sexual boredom. While preaching caution, we must avoid fearmongering, since sexuality will always be a positive and life-affirming force that warrants celebration. We have our work cut out for us!

REFERENCES

Apfelbaum, B. (1984). Ego-analytic sex therapy: The problem of performance anxiety. In R. Segraves & J. Haeberle (Eds.), *Emerging dimensions of sexology*. New York: Praeger.

Apfelbaum, B. (1988). An ego-analytic perspective on desire disorders. In S. Leiblum & R. Rosen R. (Eds.), *Sexual desire disorders* (pp. 75–104). New York: Guilford Press.

Attorney General's Commission on Pornography. (1986). *Final report.* Washington, DC: U.S. Department of Justice.

Bachmann, G., Leiblum, S., & Grill, J. (1989). Brief sexual inquiry in gynecologic practice. *Obstetrics & Gynecology, 73*(3), 425–427.

Bancroft, J. H. (1983). *Human sexuality and its problems.* New York: Churchill Livingstone.

Berlin, F. S., & Meinecke, C. F. (1981). Treatment of sex offenders with antiandrogenic medication. *American Journal of Psychiatry, 138,* 601–607.

Carnes, P. (1983). *Out of the shadows: Understanding sexual addiction.* Minneapolis, MN: CompCare Publications.

Kaplan, H. (1979). *Disorders of sexual desire.* New York: Brunner/Mazel.

Kaplan, H. (1987). *Sexual aversion, sexual phobias, and panic disorder.* New York: Brunner/Mazel.

Kaplan, H. (1988). Intimacy disorders and sexual panic states. *Journal of Sex and Marital Therapy, 14* (1), 3–12.

Kilmann, P. R., Boland, J. P., Norton, S. P., Davidson, E., & Caird, C. (1986). Perspectives on sex therapy outcome: A survey of AASECT providers. *Journal of Sex and Marital Therapy, 12,* 116–138.

Kinsey, A. C., Pomeroy, W. B., & Martin, C. E. (1948). *Sexual behavior in the human male.* Philadelphia: W. B. Saunders.

Kinsey, A. C., Pomeroy, W. B., Martin, C. E., & Gebhard, P. H. (1953). *Sexual behavior in the human female.* Philadelphia: W. B. Saunders.

Leiblum, S., & Ersner-Hershfield, R. (1977). Sexual enhancement groups for dysfunctional women: An evaluation. *Journal of Sex and Marital Therapy, 3,* 139–152.

Leiblum, S., & Pervin, L. (Eds.). (1980). *Principles and practice of sex therapy.* New York: Guilford Press.

Leiblum, S., Rosen, R., & Pierce, D. (1976). The group treatment format: Mixed sexual dysfunctions. *Archives of Sexual Behavior, 5,* 313–321.

Leiblum, S., & Rosen, R. (1988). Conclusion: Conceptual and clinical overview. In S. Leiblum & R. Rosen (Eds.), *Sexual desire disorders* (pp. 446–458). New York: Guilford Press.

Lief, H. (1988). Foreword. In S. Leiblum & R. Rosen (Eds.), *Sexual desire disorders* (pp. vii–xiii). New York: Guilford Press.

LoPiccolo, J., & Friedman, J. M. (1988). Broad-spectrum treatment of low sexual desire: Integration of cognitive, behavioral and systemic therapy. In S. Leiblum & R. Rosen (Eds.), *Sexual desire disorders* (pp. 107–144). New York: Guilford Press.

Masters, W., & Johnson, V. (1970). *Human sexual inadequacy.* Boston: Little, Brown.

Masters, W., & Kolodny, R. (1988). *Crisis: Heterosexual behavior in the age of AIDS.* New York: Grove Press.

Mattison, A. M. (1985). *Group treatment of sexually compulsive gay and bisexual men.* Paper presented at the Annual Meetings of the Eastern Region of the Society for the Scientific Study of Sex, Philadelphia, PA.

Mullen, S., & Rosen, R. C. (1979). Self-administered masturbation training in the treatment of primary orgasmic dysfunction. *Journal of Consulting and Clinical Psychology, 47,* 912–918.

Osborn, J. (1988). *The overview on AIDS and its impact*. Paper presented at UMDNJ–Robert Wood Johnson Medical School, Piscataway, NJ.

President's Commission on Obscenity and Pornography. (1970). *Report of the Commission on Obscenity and Pornography*. New York: Random House.

Quadland, M. C. (1985). Compulsive sexual behavior: Definition of a problem and an approach to treatment. *Journal of Sex and Marital Therapy, 11*, 121–132.

Rosen, R. C. (1983). Clinical issues in the assessment and treatment of impotence: A new look at an old problem. *Behavior Therapist, 6*, 81–85.

Rosen, R. C., Leiblum, S. R., & Hall, K. S. (1987). Etiological and predictive factors in sex therapy. Paper presented at the 1987 Annual Meeting of the Society for Sex Therapy and Research, New Orleans, LA.

Scharff, D. E. (1982). *The sexual relationships: An object-relations view of sex and the family*. London: Routledge and Kegan Paul.

Scharff, D. E. (1988). An object-relations approach to inhibited sexual desire. In S. Leiblum & R. Rosen (Eds.), *Sexual desire disorders* (pp. 45–74). New York: Guilford Press.

Schiavi, R. (1988). NPT in the evaluation of erectile disorders: A critical review. *Journal of Sex and Marital Therapy, 14*, 83–88.

Schover, L. R., & Jensen, S. B. (1988). *Sexuality and chronic illness: A comprehensive approach*. New York: Guilford Press.

Segraves, R. T. (1988). Hormones and libido. In S. Leiblum & R. Rosen (Eds.), *Sexual desire disorders* (pp. 271–312). New York: Guilford Press.

Shilts, R. (1987). *And the band played on*. New York: St. Martins Press.

Spark, R., White, R., & Connolly, P. (1980). Impotence is not always psychogenic. *Journal of the American Medical Association, 243*, 750–755.

Turner, L., Althof, S., Levine, S., Risen, C., Jursh, E., Resnick, M., and Bodner, D. (1988). *Self-injection of papaverine and phentolamine in the treatment of psychogenically impotent men*. Paper presented at the Society for Sex Therapy and Research Annual Meeting, New York.

Desire Disorders

I

2

Assessment and Treatment of Desire Disorders

RAYMOND C. ROSEN AND SANDRA R. LEIBLUM

During the past decade, sexual desire disorders have assumed an increasingly prominent role in both the theory and practice of sex therapy. In addition to being among the most prevalent and perplexing sexual complaints facing practitioners nowadays, desire problems present a theoretically challenging "new frontier" for the field. In fact, there is little agreement among the experts concerning the role of physiological, intrapsychic, and interpersonal determinants of libido. Although research efforts in recent years have focused on the role of hormones in particular, the results have been inconsistent and ambiguous overall.

Clinically, desire disorders are among the most intriguing of sexual problems. As illustrated by the numerous case examples in the present chapter, special skill is required to assess the multitude of factors potentially contributing to this common complaint. In order to simplify the process of evaluation, we have developed a clinical decision-making model in which primary and secondary low desire are differentiated, as well as a variety of individual and systemic issues. For example, it is important to assess past medical and psychiatric histories in addition to early experiences of sexual abuse and coercion. The relationship between inhibited desire and other sexual performance difficulties also warrants careful attention. Problems of hyperactive sexual desire and sexual aversion are also briefly addressed.

Given the complexity of etiological factors involved in most cases, we have recommended a flexible and individualistic approach to treatment. Individual psychotherapy or couples therapy is frequently indicated, with conventional sex therapy techniques (e.g., sensate focus) playing a relatively minor role. We have also proposed the use of script modification or negotiation techniques, particularly for use in desire discrepancy cases. Although considerable interest has recently been expressed in the use of pharmacological agents, we have yet to be convinced of the value of this approach for individuals with chronic or situational low desire. As illustrated by the detailed case studies presented, relationship conflicts are perhaps the most central and pervasive issue for treatment.

How successful are current treatment approaches for problems of desire? Although estimates of outcome vary considerably from one center to another, we have generally found these cases among the more difficult and demanding to treat. Where partners display major differences in intrinsic levels of desire, compromise may be the optimal outcome. Finally, in the absence of adequate follow-up studies to date, it is unclear to what extent treatment gains can be maintained over time.

Raymond C. Rosen, Ph.D., is Professor of Psychiatry and Co-Director of the Sexual Counseling Service at Robert Wood Johnson Medical School. He has written extensively on human sexuality and sex therapy and is co-author of Patterns of Sexual Arousal: Psychophysiological Processes and Clinical Applications (1988, with J. G. Beck) and co-editor of Sexual Desire Disorders (1988, with S. R. Leiblum).

Sandra R. Leiblum, Ph.D., is Professor of Clinical Psychiatry and Co-Director of the Sexual Counseling Service at Robert Wood Johnson Medical School. She is widely known for research and writing in the field of sexuality and is co-editor of Principles and Practice of Sex Therapy (1980, with L. Pervin) and Sexual Desire Disorders (1988, with R. C. Rosen).

HISTORICAL OVERVIEW

Beginning with the publication in 1970 of *Human Sexual Inadequacy*, Masters and Johnson described a novel conceptual framework for an understanding of sexual dysfunction and provided a short-term, directive approach to be used in the treatment of these problems. Classification of male and female dysfunctions was based on their four-stage sexual response cycle model, as described in the 1966 book, *Human Sexual Response*. According to this model, male problems of erection and ejaculation were given primary emphasis, as were problems of arousal, penetration, and orgasm in women. The importance of their contributions cannot be overemphasized, as Masters' and Johnson's diagnostic system provided a quantum leap forward from the earlier psychodynamic formulations of female "frigidity" and male "impotence." It was deficient, however, in at least one major respect—a lack of attention to problems of sexual desire.

This omission in the Masters and Johnson system was independently identified in the mid-1970s by Harold Lief (1977) and Helen Singer Kaplan (1977). Lief, in particular, noted that a substantial proportion of patients presenting for treatment at sex therapy clinics at that time could not be adequately diagnosed according to the categories provided by Masters and

Johnson. Lief therefore proposed that the diagnosis of "inhibited sexual desire" be added to the nosology of sexual dysfunction and suggested that the diagnosis be applied to those patients who chronically failed to initiate or respond to sexual stimuli. Based on her theoretical critique of the Masters and Johnson sexual response cycle formulation, Kaplan (1977) recommended the adoption of a triphasic model of sexual response with desire as the first and most fundamental component of sexual arousal. Kaplan further suggested that a growing number of treatment failures in sex therapy could be attributed to a lack of therapeutic focus on problems of "hypoactive sexual desire." To meet this need, Kaplan espoused a more psychodynamic approach to desire problems, suggesting that such difficulties were symptomatic of long-standing intrapsychic conflicts, particularly in the areas of intimacy and emotional control.

Within a short span of time, sexual desire disorders began to dominate theoretical discussions within sex therapy. This was reflected first in the 1980 revision of the *Diagnostic and Statistical Manual* of the American Psychiatric Association (DSM-III), which included "Inhibited Sexual Desire" as a separate diagnostic entity. According to the DSM-III, this dysfunction was defined as "persistent and pervasive inhibition of sexual desire" (p. 285). In the same year, the first edition of *Principles and Practice of Sex Therapy* was published, which included separate chapters by L. LoPiccolo (1980) and Zilbergeld and Ellison (1980) on assessment and treatment of desire disorders. These chapters reflected at least three major themes in early clinical approaches to sexual desire: (1) the heterogeneity of etiological and developmental determinants, which can result in a deficiency of desire; (2) the importance of assessing and treating couple conflicts, which often impede desire; and (3) the need for an eclectic treatment approach in which a variety of interventions might be used depending on the exigencies of each particular case. Cautious optimism was expressed at the time regarding the potential outcome of treatment in these cases.

In the intervening years, theoretical models and clinical treatment approaches have proliferated, just as the number of desire cases presenting for treatment has markedly increased. J. LoPiccolo and Friedman (1988), for example, report that in the years 1974–1976 roughly 32% of couples evaluated at the Stony Brook center were given a primary diagnosis of low sexual desire. By 1982, this number had jumped to 55%, with approximately equal numbers of males and females presenting with the problem. Recent findings from our own clinical sample (Rosen, Leiblum, & Hall, 1987) indicate that approximately 40% of patients in sex therapy treatment receive a diagnosis of inhibited desire, although we have found that women are still more likely than men to be given the diagnosis. It is possible, however, that inhibited desire is obscured in some male patients by overriding concerns regarding erectile failure. Similar findings have been reported in a national survey of 289 sex therapists (Kilmann, Boland, Norton, Davidson, & Caid, 1986), in which desire discrepancy problems were observed in 31% of

couples presenting for treatment. Recent European studies (Hawton, Catalan, Martin, & Fagg, 1986) have reported high rates of inhibited desire in
female patients (37%) but much lower rates in males. This finding can, of
course, be interpreted as indicating that European men are less likely to
acknowledge the problem than their American counterparts.

In response to the evidence of increasing clinical demand, a variety of
treatment approaches for problems of desire were advanced in the late
1970s and early 1980s. Helen Singer Kaplan (1979), for example, continued
to advocate a psychoanalytically based treatment model in her influential
book *Disorders of Sexual Desire*. In contrast, Schover and LoPiccolo (1982)
reported a relatively high success rate within a cognitive–behavioral orientation to the problem. Our own approach drew on sociological script theory
in dealing with problems of desire discrepancy (Gagnon, Rosen, & Leiblum, 1982), whereas Regas and Sprenkle (1984), Verhulst and Heiman
(1988), and others have recommended family-systems approaches to desire
disorders. An interest in pharmacological intervention for inhibited desire
also began to emerge in the 1980s as Bancroft and Wu (1983) and Sherwin,
Gelfand, and Brender (1985) described the positive outcome of androgen
replacement therapy in this regard. More recently, pharmaceutical companies and independent researchers have begun to experiment with antidepressant agents and dopamine-agonist drugs as a potential means of enhancing desire (Segraves, 1988).

We have attempted to represent the remarkable breadth and variety of
current treatment approaches in our recent volume, *Sexual Desire Disorders*
(Leiblum & Rosen, 1988). Included are chapters on psychodynamic and
object-relations perspectives, cognitive–behavioral and systems approaches, and desire disorders in various special populations. The interested
reader may wish to consult this source for a complete survey of the area.
The present chapter focuses on our current clinical approach to conceptualization and treatment of these problems with particular emphasis on the
need for an integrated, multidimensional approach in most cases.

DEFINITIONAL AND DIAGNOSTIC ISSUES

Desire disorders are among the most difficult of the sexual dysfunctions to
define or diagnose. Whereas earlier approaches, such as Kinsey's (1948;
Kinsey, Pomeroy, Martin, & Gebhard, 1953), had relied on frequency measures of sexual behavior, numerous authors have recently commented on the
need for inclusion of a *subjective component* in the definition of sexual
desire. This point has been cogently argued by Lief (1988) as follows:

> Sexual desire is an extraordinarily complicated aspect of human life, and it
> requires a multifaceted approach to its understanding . . . One cannot sim-
> ply count sexual outlets, as Kinsey did. A person could conceivably mastur-

bate 20 or more times a week, but lack desire to have sex with a partner, or a person could have sex 20 times a month with a partner, yet never once truly desire it. (p. vii)

In some cases a lack of desire is manifested by a failure to *initiate* sexual expression, whereas for others, it is the lack of *responsivity* to initiation that characterizes the disorder. To some extent this distinction is influenced by gender biases, as failure of initiation is more likely to be associated with low desire in men, whereas lack of responsivity is frequently viewed as evidence of low desire in women. Although historically women have been assumed to have more modest levels of desire and to require more deliberate efforts for arousal (Leiblum & Pervin, 1980), these assumptions have been challenged in recent years by feminists and sex therapists alike. It is certainly more difficult for men to "mask" sexual disinterest, since sexual initiation is typically the male perogative, and sexual avoidance or erectile difficulties are readily apparent. Overall, it is more likely that men and women experience generally similar levels of desire and that differences reported in prevalence rates of desire problems between men and women reflect different socialization experiences and societal norms. One male-female distinction is worth noting, however. As observed by Kinsey et al. (1953), desire is experienced more continuously by men across the life cycle, whereas for women, sexual desire is more variable, depending on hormonal, interpersonal, and other contextual determinants.

Inhibited desire can be global, in the sense that the individual lacks interest in any or all sexual activity, or the problem may be situational, with lack of desire only for a particular partner or activity. Certainly, sexual desire involves the presence of a *subjective feeling state* (Leiblum & Rosen, 1988), which can be triggered by either internal or external cues and which may or may not result in overt sexual behavior. The frequency of occurrence and intensity of this subjective state can vary enormously, with some studies reporting rates as high as several hundred times per day (Lief, 1988), whereas others report little or no awareness of spontaneous interest in sex (Garde & Lunde, 1980). Unfortunately, there are no normative data currently available on the incidence or frequency of sexual desire in the population at large.

A key diagnostic issue is the distinction between inhibited or hypoactive desire as the *primary diagnosis*, versus loss of sexual interest secondary to other medical, psychiatric, or sexual dysfunction conditions. DSM-III-R emphasizes this point in defining the exclusion criteria for hypoactive desire as: "Occurrence not exclusively during the course of another Axis I disorder (other than a sexual dysfunction), such as Major Depression" (1987, p. 285).

Sexual desire is also affected by a wide range of physical diseases as Schover emphasizes in her chapter on chronic illness effects (Chapter 12). Many chronic illnesses, from cancer to heart disease, as well as many of the drugs used in the treatment of these conditions, can either temporarily or chronically impair sexual interest. Finally, it is important to distinguish low desire that is experienced as secondary to a specific performance difficulty (e.g., erectile dysfunction, dyspareunia), since treatment of the primary problem may directly alleviate the lack of desire. The reverse situation, in which a desire disorder is the primary problem but is masked by a performance inadequacy, is equally important to assess. The following case vignette underscores this clinically relevant distinction:

Mrs. O, a 32-year-old married homemaker, was referred to our service with the presenting complaint of primary orgasmic dysfunction. She and her husband had been married for 6 years and have a 2-year-old son. At the time of the evaluation, both husband and wife expressed frustration with the state of their sexual relationship. This frustration led to increasingly strained and infrequent sexual encounters. During the course of her pregnancy, intercourse had been discontinued altogether. Although it initially appeared that her lack of interest in sex was related to the presenting complaint of primary anorgasmia, her subsequent lack of progress in therapy indicated that this was not the case. Despite the fact that an intensive program of guided self-stimulation exercises was successful in permitting Mrs. O to achieve orgasm, her interest in sex with her husband showed little change and, if anything, declined over the course of treatment. It became painfully clear to both partners that Mrs. O's inability to achieve orgasm at the outset of therapy had little or no bearing on her more fundamental lack of desire.

Our current diagnostic terminology is ambiguous and unclear in certain key respects. For example, whereas DSM-III had used the label of "inhibited sexual desire" for problems of low desire, more recently, DSM-III-R has substituted the terms Hypoactive Sexual Desire Disorder and Sexual Aversion Disorder. The term "sexual apathy" has also been recommended by Apfelbaum (1988). Although the phrase "hypoactive desire" was substituted for "inhibited" in order to avoid earlier psychodynamic connotations, the newer term is awkward and no less ambiguous. In making the diagnosis, DSM-III-R specifically advises clinicians to consider "factors that affect sexual functioning, such as age, sex, and the context of the person's life" (p. 285). This leaves the door open for a great deal of subjective judgment on the part of the evaluating clinician. In contrast, sexual aversion disorder is defined as a much more specific diagnosis that refers to individuals with "persistent or recurrent extreme aversion to, and avoidance of, all or almost all, genital sexual contact with a sexual partner" (p. 285). Interestingly, this latter diagnosis is applied almost exclusively to female patients. It is also unusual for patients who present clinically with problems of low desire to show such extreme aversion to sexual touch.

Despite the continuing controversy regarding diagnostic criteria and terminology, clinicians appear to be utilizing the diagnosis of desire disorder with greater frequency in recent years. On the positive side, this may reflect a growing awareness and acknowledgment of the role of emotional and interpersonal factors in sexual dysfunction. Also, as we have noted in Chapter 1 of the present volume, there is increasing pressure in our society for couples to maintain a high level of sexual interest in their primary relationship. This has had a negative effect, according to Apfelbaum (1988), in raising performance pressures and creating potentially unrealistic sexual expectations for many individuals. In our experience, the diagnosis of low or inhibited desire needs to be judiciously applied, with careful considera-tion paid to the possible iatrogenic effects of labeling an individual in this way. Furthermore, because sexual desire problems almost always present in the context of a couple's relationship, the clinician needs also to consider the possible role of the "high-desire" partner in defining the problem as well as the likelihood that symptoms of low desire may reflect problems of intimacy, power, or territoriality in the relationship (Verhulst & Heiman, 1988).

Although much of the focus to date has been on problems of inhibited desire, there is also evidence of a growing interest in excessive or hyperac-tive desire. Our experience has been that individuals with excessive desire usually present clinically as paraphilic disorders, and it is typically the specific object or direction of sexual interest (e.g., young children, S–M activities) rather than the high drive per se that motivates treatment in these cases. Furthermore, the definition of hyperactive desire is even more con-troversial than low desire, with little or no agreement among clinicians regarding the symptoms or criteria to be used in making such a diagnosis. Certainly there are numerous individuals with persistent and pressing sexual appetites who may be at the high end of this continuum of sexual drive but who have no difficulty with the choice of partners or outlets. On the other hand, some individuals with high drive seem to use sex to satisfy their needs for conquest, tension relief, and success without the need for commitment and intimacy.

Case Example

Arthur T is a highly successful 55-year-old chief executive officer in a large, international firm. He is an energetic and charming individual who enjoys the company of women as well as work. Throughout his career, he has had a series of casual affairs, although one was serious enough to lead to the breakup of his marriage. Nevertheless, he realized that sex was an insuffi-cient base on which to build a life-long relationship and ended this relation-ship after 2 years. Strong sexual urges for women other than his wife continued to occupy his attention, and he found it convenient to develop casual affairs with "professionals." He enjoyed the sexual variety and excite-ment these encounters provided, and he sought treatment at the behest of his wife only when he became unable to perform sexually with her. Interest-ingly, with partners other than his wife, both his desire and his erections continued to be strong.

A MULTIDIMENSIONAL ASSESSMENT MODEL

Current assessment approaches for desire disorders typically include consideration of a wide range of possible biological, intrapsychic, and interpersonal contributions. Whereas different authors have emphasized one or another of these dimensions (cf. Leiblum & Rosen, 1988), we have argued instead for an integrated and comprehensive assessment approach with particular emphasis on interpersonal and systemic factors (Rosen & Leiblum, 1987). In developing this approach, we have drawn heavily on the conceptual model of sexual desire recently proposed by Levine (1984, 1988). According to Levine's model, sexual desire can be conceptualized as incorporating at least three critical dimensions: (1) a biological drive component based on neuroendocrine mechanisms and evidenced by "endogenous or spontaneous manifestations of genital excitement" (Levine, 1988, p. 24); (2) a cognitive or attitudinal component, which the author refers to as "sexual wish," that typically reflects the mores or expectations of the peer group and society—among adolescents, for example, high drive may be associated with a wish for limited sexual activity or even abstinence, whereas older adults may aspire to frequent sexual activity despite declining levels of drive; (3) the affective or interpersonal components of desire, subsumed under the category of "sexual motive" and characterized by the willingness to engage in sex; according to Levine, this is the most important factor.

Although biological drive and sexual wish need to be evaluated in each case, we concur with Levine that psychological motivation, or "sexual willingness," is the core clinical factor and the most important element to assess in most instances. Certainly, we have encountered individuals whose sexual desire is diminished by the effects of physical illnesses, pharmacological agents, or other biological causes. Similarly, we always take great pains to assess unrealistic expectations or beliefs regarding the "sexual script" (Rosen & Leiblum, 1987). On the other hand, the majority of cases treated to date cannot be accounted for by either of these factors in isolation. Rather, we see increasing numbers of individuals for whom the willingness to engage in sex had been diminished or lost because of self-esteem or personal adequacy problems, conflict in the partner relationship, or problems related to intimacy, trust, and territoriality (cf. Verhulst & Heiman, 1988). The role of performance anxiety, or the pressure to be sexual that many individuals experience, has also been emphasized by Apfelbaum (1988) and others.

For individuals in a long-standing intimate relationship, there is usually little sympathy for the individual who is sexually disinterested. He or she feels little entitlement *not* to experience sexual desire, and this constant pressure to be sexual frequently destroys desire. Even if the initial cause of the desire problem were unrelated to relationship issues, the ongoing demand to be sexually available is a burden that impedes spontaneous desire.

Unfortunately, many partners are not tolerant of their partner's lack of sexual interest. Many view it as a sign of personal inadequacy and become depressed or upset. Others become angry and insistent that their partner should "try" harder to be sexually available.

Past psychiatric history is another key area for assessment in light of the frequently reported association between depression and diminished desire (e.g., Schreiner-Engel & Schiavi, 1986). In one recent study, these authors demonstrated that a majority of patients with inhibited desire had a past history of at least one episode of major depression. Moreover, the first depressive episode in this study nearly always preceded or accompanied the onset of low desire. We have similarly observed a subclinical depressive state, manifested primarily by poor self-esteem, negative self-evaluation, and general anhedonia in many of these individuals. For example, one recent patient commented that: "Other than work, I can't think of anything that excites me much these days." Clearly, it is important to evaluate the extent to which loss of sexual interest in these cases can be attributed to an overall loss of interest in sensory pleasure or sensual exchange. The negative effects of depression on low desire may be directly mediated by biological (i.e., neurotransmitter or endocrine) changes, or depression may indirectly interfere with interpersonal functioning or self-esteem in these individuals. The relationship among physical illness, depression, and low desire can be subtle and complex in some instances as illustrated by the following case vignette.

Mr. P is a 42-year-old, twice-married accountant who had undergone a series of operations for severe inflammatory bowel disease culminating in a total colectomy and ileostomy. Despite the relatively positive effects of surgery on the patient's overall health, he showed little interest in resuming sexual relations with his wife and was unresponsive to her advances. Additionally, on the few occasions that intercourse was attempted, the patient experienced difficulty in attaining an erection. Further testing (including NPT evaluation) indicated that the erectile difficulty was psychogenic in origin and that the patient's lack of desire was primarily the result of the nonspecific psychological effects of surgery. As with other ileostomy patients (Alterescu, 1981), Mr. P seemed to be experiencing a chronic, low-grade depression coupled with a very negative body image, particularly in regard to wearing a pouch. He refused to accept that his wife was genuinely interested in having sex with him and felt that she was initiating solely out of a sense of pity.

Other important etiological factors include a past history of sexual abuse or trauma, which may be associated with either hyper- or hypoactive sexual desire in some cases. As noted by Becker (Chapter 11), loss of desire is among the most common sequelae reported among survivors of sexual assault. Possible reasons for low desire in these individuals include chronic fears of vulnerability or loss of control, inability to establish intimate relationships, or a conditioned aversion to all forms of sexual contact. Sexual trauma may have a negative impact on a partner's sexual desire as well as on that of the victim. In one recent case, the husband, on learning that his wife's first sexual experience was a brutal rape, became inhibited in expressing his own sexual passion for his wife. When he experienced sexual desire, he would try to distract himself. He reported that he would often have images of what his wife experienced at the hands of her rapist, and he was filled with rage at the perpetrator as well as tenderness toward his wife. He wanted to protect her, so he shielded her from his own "animal" passion. She complained that he avoided sex and that when he did become engaged, he would try to "get it over with as soon as possible." It was clear to the therapist that at least part of his problem with sexual desire was his identification with his wife and need to protect her from what he believed were the "baser" sexual appetites.

Conflicts around sexual preference or identity are another important area to assess, as individuals with conflicts—overt or covert—about sexual orientation often display desire deficits. Repressed homosexual attractions are especially problematic in this regard, since they frequently cause guilt and shame, even if expressed only in the individual's fantasy life. Rather than experience the self-condemnation that accompanies homosexual imagery, the individual tends to avoid partner-sex altogether.

Case Example

Mr. and Mrs. G are a gray-haired, distinguished couple in their early 50s. During the initial evaluation, Mrs. G tearfully exclaims that a "part of her life has been missing for the past 10 years." On further inquiry, it is revealed that Mr. G, who is a deacon in the local church and a "pillar of the community," has harbored an exclusively homosexual orientation throughout their married life. This was first manifested in his late teens, at which time he had sought psychotherapy. At the advice of his therapist at the time, Mr. G had married in his early 20s to "work it out." Throughout the early years of their marriage, he had succeeded in functioning sexually only through the use of extensive homosexual fantasies. His sexual preference had been completely hidden from his wife until the death of his mother and a subsequent period of depression about 10 years ago. Since that time, he had gradually revealed his homosexual feelings in a piecemeal fashion to her, only fully acknowledging the extent of it following an individual therapy session about 2 years ago. During the past 10 years, the frequency of their sexual contacts has also declined markedly, as he now feels unable or unwilling to function sexually through the use of fantasy.

LoPiccolo and Friedman (1988) have identified a number of additional factors that may be etiologically important in specific cases. These include an "overdose" of religious orthodoxy during early upbringing, an obsessive–compulsive personality style with an aversion to bodily contact or fluids, fear of loss of control over sexual urges or fears of pregnancy, and the "widower's syndrome." This refers to the common situation encountered by the older, widowed male, who is expected to be quickly and easily responsive with a new sexual partner, often before the grieving process has been resolved. Finally, a host of relationship factors have been implicated, ranging from a simple boredom to deep-seated hostility or distrust.

In order to simplify the process of assessment for these and other factors, we have developed a flow-chart model for evaluation of desire disorders in individuals and couples. This model is illustrated in Figure 2.1.

Key features of this assessment model are the distinction made between primary (global) and secondary (situational) low desire, the emphasis placed on medical and psychiatric screening, the differentiation of low desire secondary to sexual performance problems, and the separate evaluation of couples or script issues in each case. As can be seen, sex therapy is frequently indicated as an adjunct, if not the primary form of treatment, in cases where other forms of medical or psychiatric intervention are required. Finally, the model emphasizes the importance of a multidimensional approach to assessment, with specific attention to potential medical, psychological, and interpersonal determinants of the problem.

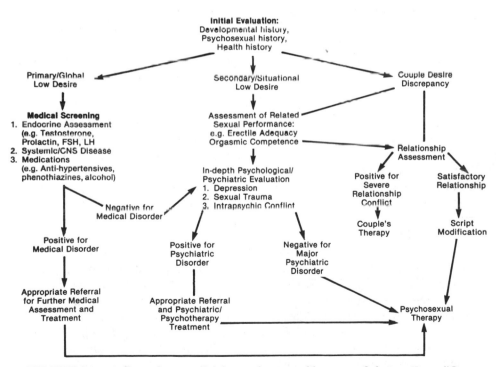

FIGURE 2.1. A flow-chart model for evaluation of low sexual desire. From "Current Approaches to the Evaluation of Sexual Desire Disorders" by R. C. Rosen and S. R. Leiblum, 1987, *Journal of Sex Research*, 50, p. 152. Copyright 1987 by the *Journal of Sex Research*. Reprinted with permission.

CURRENT TREATMENT APPROACHES:
LIFTING THE ROADBLOCKS TO DESIRE

The current clinical focus on increasing sexual desire has led to several significant changes in the practice of sex therapy generally. First, since problems of desire are intrinsically subjective or psychological complaints, as opposed to the more overtly physiological dysfunctions such as erectile dysfunction or vaginismus, clinical interventions have tended to become more psychological in response. As noted earlier, Kaplan (1977) advocated more traditional psychodynamic treatment approaches for problems of desire. Similarly, other authors, such as Scharff (1988) and Levine (1988), have argued convincingly for the role of individual psychotherapy, including object-relations therapy and psychoanalysis, in treating individuals with chronic desire disorders. We, too, have often found it necessary to explore in some depth the early childhood experiences and memories of individuals with chronically inhibited desire. Both of the cases discussed below are examples of this approach. An important consequence of this trend, however, is that the line between sex therapy and psychotherapy has become increasingly arbitrary and potentially irrelevant.

Other therapists have responded to the challenge with a greater emphasis on cognitive–behavioral or systemic–interpersonal treatment approaches. Thus, Lazarus (1988) recommends that we approach "the kaleidoscopic heterogeneity of desire dysfunctions" with a more broad-spectrum, but nonetheless directive, treatment approach. Guided compromise is the key to success in many instances according to Lazarus. In the same vein, we have described a variety of ways in which the "sexual script" can be enhanced or modified to achieve greater harmony of sexual needs (Rosen & Leiblum, 1988). Treatment from a sexual scripting approach requires assessment of each partner's performative (actual) and ideal (covert) script with sufficient detail obtained so that script negotiation can occur. Such an approach also invites an exploration of factors other than sexual frequency, rather than a focus on frequency, as the major or only therapeutic goal in these cases.

We have found it especially important to consider the degree of complexity, rigidity, conventionality, and satisfaction of both the overt script and the ideal script. Another advantage of this approach is that it tends to defuse "blaming" of the low-desire partner and to focus attention on the role of the high-desire partner in maintaining the problem. Following a detailed assessment of current and ideal scripts, we typically attempt a process of compromise and renegotiation toward a more mutually acceptable and satisfying repertoire of sexual exchange. The second case study presented below illustrates key aspects of this approach.

Other cognitive–behavioral approaches have been recommended as either adjuncts or primary forms of intervention in these cases. For example, LoPiccolo and Friedman (1988) have described several "cognitive restructuring" procedures that they have found to be useful components of treatment. Unrealistic or irrational beliefs are confronted (e.g., "If I allow myself to enjoy sex, it does not mean that I will lose all control"), and a variety of coping or positive self-statements are prescribed:

> For patients whose low drive is related to family-of-origin issues, coping statements differentiating the sexual partner from the opposite-sex parent are useful. For example, for a low-drive woman whose father was an alcoholic, a useful coping statement is "My husband is not like my father. I deliberately picked a man whom I can trust, who is dependable, and who is not an alcoholic." We often have our patients write 15–20 such coping statements on cards and ask them to spend some time every day reading and elaborating on the coping statements. (p. 134)

LoPiccolo also draws on transactional analysis techniques for encouraging patients to adopt the "playful child" role in sexual interactions, as opposed to the "judgmental parent" or "frightened child" roles that these individuals may be accustomed to playing. This author further recommends specific behavioral interventions designed to "prime the pump" of the low-desire partner. Included here are techniques such as keeping a desire checklist for identifying situations or conditions that may elicit desire, taking fantasy "breaks" during the day for rehearsal of specific sexual fantasies, and increasing exposure to explicit books, magazines, and videos. LoPiccolo also advises increasing the level of physical intimacy generally, including more frequent hugging, kissing, hand-holding, etc. Although there are certainly instances in which these interventions are helpful and appropriate, we have also treated patients who experienced such recommendations as coercive and threatening. Clearly, therapists are advised to tailor the use of such interventions to the needs of each particular case.

A systemic or interactional approach to treatment has also been advocated as a necessary component in many cases. Issues in the couple's relationship are critical to explore in therapy; as Schwartz and Masters (1988) have recently observed, "frequency of sexual desire and behavior becomes both a mirror and a manifestation of intimacy in the relationship." Among the various couple's issues to be addressed in treatment, Verhulst and Heiman (1979, 1988) particularly recommend dealing with territorial interactions (e.g., "I feel you're invading my space when you touch my body"), dominance and "ranking-order" communications (e.g., "I always feel 'one-down' in our sexual relationship"), and attachment interactions (e.g., "It's difficult for me to trust you when my feelings are hurt"). One woman, for example, was enraged by what she perceived as the power differential in her relationship with her husband. He was a physician who, by virtue of his superior income, made the final decision regarding all major purchases. He bought boats and cars without taking her considerations or objections into account. He said "It's my hard-earned money and I'll spend it the way I want to." Whereas she had tolerated this attitude for many

years, over time, her increasing anger as well as developing sense of self-
esteem had enabled her to ventilate her rage. Although she now verbalized
her anger, she found it difficult to experience or express any sexual desire
for him. Too many years of passive compliance with his sexual overtures, as
well as suppressed rage at his interpersonal style, had buried her desire. She
was receptive to being held or caressed but refused all forms of genital sex.
Whereas he was receptive to caressing her, he complained about her "little
girl" demands and wanted more genital intimacy. They presented for treatment at this juncture.

Seductions rituals are also important in long-standing relationships.
Apfelbaum reports that many patients have lost or abandoned the "gentle
art of seduction." Partners may be better able to demand sex but less able to
excite it. According to Verhulst and Heiman (1988), seduction rituals are
important as a means for coordinating the sexual rhythms of individual
partners:

> Lack of attention to *seduction* can also affect the development of a couple's
> low sexual activity and lack of desire. As we are using the term, seduction
> refers to the maneuvers employed by one partner to evoke feelings of
> desire in the other. In other words, seduction is an attempt to establish the
> interactional fit of corresponding sexual desire. (p. 251)

In each of the cases described below, the desire problem was inextrica-
bly associated with dissatisfaction with other aspects of the relationship. In
both cases, adequate levels of desire were manifest during early stages of
the relationship and were eroded by increasing conflict over time. Conversely, our most notable successes have been associated with successful conflict resolution between couples.

Finally, a number of authors have recently advocated the use of pharmacological or hormonal agents for treatment of low desire. In general,
attempts to enhance desire pharmacologically or hormonally have met with
disappointing results. Based on his comprehensive review of drug effects on
desire, Segraves (1988) concluded that the perennial "search for libido
enhancers" has too often led to erroneous and misleading results. The
evidence is much stronger, according to Segraves, for drug-induced suppression of desire in individuals being treated with antihypertensive or
psychotropic medications. It should be noted, however, that several controlled clinical trials are currently evaluating the effects of antidepressant
and antianxiety drugs as direct or indirect treatment for low desire (Klein,
Mendels, Lief, & Phillips, 1987; Crenshaw, Goldberg, & Stern, 1987). Certainly it has been shown that tricyclic antidepressants can have a positive
effect on desire in clinically depressed individuals (Thase et al., 1986). It is
not clear, however, to what extent these enhancing effects are mediated by
the nonspecific impact of the drugs on overall physical or psychological
well-being. On the other hand, there is mounting evidence that suppression

of desire in sexually compulsive males is readily accomplished via the use of antiandrogenic agents (Berlin & Meinecke, 1981) and is currently the treatment of choice for many of these individuals. Overall, it seems that pharmacological interventions are of more value in cases of hyperactive than inhibited desire.

CASE STUDIES

The following two cases were selected for presentation as representative of the complex psychological and interpersonal issues confronting clinicians in this area. Our treatment approach was decidedly eclectic in both cases and involved a highly individualized combination of behavioral, psychotherapeutic, and systems interventions. In both instances, imbalances and conflicts in the couple's relationship were a major focus of treatment, with family-of-origin issues being viewed as important. Individual and conjoint therapy sessions were also used on an ad hoc basis as the therapists attempted to work at several levels simultaneously. If nothing else, these cases illustrate the complexity and challenge of most cases of inhibited desire. Although neither case can be viewed as an outright success or failure, we will consider factors contributing to a somewhat more satisfactory outcome in the first case.

Case 1: Successful Outcome

James and Diane O'Neil presented as a handsome, articulate, and urbane couple in their mid 40s. James was of Irish descent and had lived in the United States for the past 11 years, whereas Diane was Jewish and had been born and raised in Jersey City. Diane was 2 years older than James and had been previously married for 9 years. She had two daughters from her first marriage, the younger of whom (Jill) still lived with the O'Neils. Despite a great deal of mutual respect and admiration for one another, the couple described the 4 years of their marriage as tense and stormy with increasing sexual conflict and distance in the relationship. The major difficulty, it seemed, was that James felt little interest in any form of intimate or sexual contact and experienced intermittent erectile difficulties on the very few occasions in recent months in which sex had been attempted.

During the course of several initial conjoint and individual sessions, it became apparent that the sexual problems of this couple had begun soon after marriage. Prior to marriage, the O'Neils had enjoyed a passionate and sexually active courtship, with frequent encounters, mutual initiation, and a rich and varied sexual script. The frequency and quality of their sexual interactions diminished dramatically almost from the night of the wedding, and Diane described the honeymoon as "just short of a total disaster" in terms of the lack of sexual initiation and frequent arguments between them.

James began to withdraw from all forms of physical and sexual contact as he threw himself totally into work and household projects over the months that followed. Occasional efforts to discuss the problem had typically erupted into heated arguments, which James usually terminated by withdrawing into angry silence or storming from the house. Diane expressed increasing frustration and anger at the time the couple entered therapy and was considering separation if their difficulties could not be resolved soon.

Background History

The first and most striking issue in this case was the enormous gap in sociocultural backgrounds and relationship histories that the O'Neils presented with. They were certainly aware of some of these differences and reported that part of the initial attraction to one another was based on these differences. For James, Diane's ability to express her emotions in a direct and straightforward manner was a welcome relief from the often distorted and covert emotional communication patterns in his family of origin. On the other hand, Diane was strongly attracted by her husband's European gentility, perfect manners, and dry sense of humor. She described her first husband, Fred, as an abusive alcoholic from a working-class neighborhood in Jersey City who had been emotionally and occasionally physically abusive to Diane and their two daughters. After several bitter and fearful years of struggle, she had finally succeeded in divorcing him a year before she and James had met. The difference between her first and second husbands was "like night and day," according to Diane, as James was a perfect gentleman with an outstanding career as a sales executive. Ironically, sex had always been intense and physically satisfying with Fred, as opposed to the great frustration in her current marriage.

In contrast, James had grown up in a rural village in Northern Ireland, of Irish–Catholic, working-class parents. He was the second of three sons and described himself as his mother's favorite. Because of the special attention he had received from his mother, he believes that his father rejected and resented him throughout his childhood. He felt driven to prove himself worthy of his mother's love and left home early to work, attend night school, and finally, to receive a Master's degree from an English university. His father mocked his efforts at self-improvement, stating only that James would probably never talk to them again after going to college. At the age of 28, he had received an employment offer from a large U.S. company and had left Great Britain to "seek his fortune abroad." He remains very attached to his mother, returning at least once a year to Ireland to spend time with the family. He also provides financial support for his parents and recently bought them a new house on the coast of Ireland. Sex was an entirely taboo subject in his household when he was growing up, and James describes his father as a "totally asexual man." Although he always felt much closer to his mother, he also describes her as very dirty and unclean, with disgusting personal habits such as leaving her used tampons in drawers around the house. He also resents the way in which she allowed herself to be dominated by his father.

After coming to the United States, James entered into a series of brief and superficial relationships with a number of partners, including a series of "one-night stands." Although he enjoyed the sexual conquest aspect of these relationships, he began to experience loneliness and a sense of emptiness in his life. He also suffered a major business failure in his early 30s and returned to England for a period of time. Prior to meeting Diane at the age of 35, his longest period of involvement in a relationship had been about 1 year, and he had experienced no desire for children or a family of his own.

The couple were introduced by a close friend of Diane's and had dated for 3 years prior to getting married and enjoyed frequent and mutually satisfying sex during this period. In addition, Diane had welcomed James' help with her two daughters, both of whom were described as difficult children. Shortly before getting married, he had moved into her house from her first marriage, where the couple has since continued to live. He had also begun working for a new company and was rapidly promoted to an executive sales position. Children were not possible for the couple, since Diane had received a tubal ligation prior to her divorce. James expressed no regrets in this regard.

Problems began to emerge on the couple's honeymoon trip to England and Ireland. Diane had not met James's parents previously and found them to be "extremely strange and uncommunicative people." When she complained to her husband about her difficulties in relating to his mother, he became defensive, distant, and angry. In turn, James felt acutely aware of the cultural differences between them and found himself reacting to Diane as a brash and crudely outspoken "Yank." Several heated arguments had ensued, with little yielding on either side. Even after their return to the United States, the couple reported mounting tension and distance in the relationship.

In the intervening 4 years, James has dedicated himself tirelessly to his new job, describing himself as a "true workaholic." He travels frequently for days or weeks at a time and typically returns home in a state of physical and mental exhaustion. He states that he is now on the point of a "major breakthrough" at work and can't afford to let up for some time. He perceives Diane as becoming more and more emotionally intrusive and wishes she would "back off" at times. Although he acknowledges her complaint of emotional and sexual unavailability on his part, her constant pressuring only makes matters worse. Diane reports that James has been drinking more frequently, is distant and critical to her and her daughters, and is completely unapproachable regarding their sexual difficulties. On recent occasions when she has approached him sexually, he has usually responded that he is "too tired" or "not in the mood." At the outset of therapy Diane felt rejected and humiliated, tearfully expressing her fears that her second marriage was about to end in divorce, "just like the first."

Clinical Formulation

Inhibited desire in this case can be viewed as secondary to a number of interpersonal, intrapsychic, and systems issues. The rapid onset of the problem during the course of a honeymoon visit with James's parents was a strong indication of the importance of parental relationship issues. Whereas sociocultural and ethnic differences had been minimized during the courtship phase of the relationship, while the couple had been living in suburban New Jersey, these differences became glaringly apparent during the honeymoon visit with his parents in Ireland. James's intense ambivalence toward his mother caused major difficulty in his responding to tensions between her and Diane, leading Diane to feel rejected and abandoned. On the other hand, the critical rejection that he continued to experience from his father provoked James to work harder than ever to achieve power and success in his career. Whereas Diane had initially been attracted by her husband's reserved European style, compared to the abusive treatment she had received from Fred, she began increasingly to view him as emotionally distant and aloof, "just like his father." Her efforts to reach out to him, however, were perceived by James as evidence of her overbearing and pushy "New York Jewish style."

Although James had experienced occasional erectile failure in the past few years and had reported some degree of performance anxiety, these difficulties were viewed as secondary to his more basic problem of low desire. He continues to find his wife physically attractive and claims not to be affected by their difference in age. A recent physical examination and hormonal assessment had proven negative, although his increased drinking over the past 2 years was viewed as a contributing factor. Neither partner had engaged in extramarital activity to date, although both had considered the possibility on occasion. Rather, they reiterated their love for each other and commitment to the marriage.

Treatment

In keeping with the complexity of issues in this case, treatment interventions were introduced at a number of levels. At first, James and Diane were each seen individually for a number of sessions to deal with specific individual issues. James's drinking pattern was evaluated, and suggestions were made for bringing this under control. It was pointed out to him that drinking was a particularly sensitive issue for Diane, in view of the problems this had caused in her first marriage. In response, James made a commitment to limit his drinking at home to a minimum and was able to honor this commitment throughout the period of treatment. On the other hand, the therapist adopted an extremely supportive position regarding James's work ambitions and pressures and agreed to assist him in gaining more support and understanding from Diane in this area. In fact, Diane felt justifiably proud of her husband's business accomplishments but had not been sufficiently vocal about her feelings. The therapist agreed with James that work should be his major priority for at least the next year or two and adopted the somewhat strategic position that he should not "hold back" at all in his commitment to his career. He responded, predictably, by suggesting that some compromises might be worked out. In this vein James offered Diane the opportunity to accompany him on several forthcoming trips.

Several individual therapy sessions were also focused on resolving key family issues for both partners. In James's case, it was pointed out that in his efforts to prove himself superior to his father he was in fact becoming more like him in many ways. Specifically, his father was perceived as a distant and unloving figure, which was precisely the way in which Diane and the girls were beginning to view James. Also, the hostile, critical, and seemingly asexual relationship between his parents was being recapitulated in his own marriage. The manifest differences between Diane and his mother were emphasized, particularly in regard to their emotional styles. These sessions elicited intense feelings of anger and sadness in James, leading to a recommendation of further individual psychotherapy following the conclusion of sex therapy for the couple.

Individual sessions with Diane focused on her deeply ingrained feelings of emotional vulnerability developed during the course of her first marriage and negative earlier relationship with her mother. She was the younger of two siblings and felt that her older brother had always been preferred. Her father had died when she was 14, and she recalls feeling abandoned and fearful at the time. She had become pregnant and married in high school, largely motivated by a desperate desire to leave home. The traumatic aftermath of her first marriage was also explored, along with her subsequent difficulty in trusting relationships. She was strongly encouraged to develop alternative ways of achieving security and independence (e.g., through work and a number of close friendships) and to avoid the role of "pursuer" in the marriage.

Following the initial individual sessions with James, he had invited Diane to accompany him on business trips to Florida and the Bahamas. The couple reported that both of these trips had been highly enjoyable, with "some of the best sex in years," along with a renewed feeling of closeness in the relationship. Despite these early success experiences, progress in therapy was sporadic and unpredictable for several months thereafter. In fact, it is our experience generally in such cases that periods of forward progress may be followed by lengthy periods of relative inactivity. Therapy during this phase consisted of a number of conjoint sessions to explore possible reasons for the decline in James's sexual interest and other issues in the relationship. Over time, the strategy of encouraging greater independence in Diane appeared to pay dividends, as James reported feeling "surprised and impressed" at her lack of pressure on him during this period. His work situation had reached a crescendo, with a takeover of the company by an outside group. Diane was able to provide emotional support to James during this time, and he reciprocated by inviting her again on an extended business trip. Although it was not as successful as their earlier trips, the couple did succeed in enjoying several mutually satisfying sexual encounters.

After 8 months of individual and conjoint therapy sessions, both partners felt relatively satisfied with their progress in treatment. James's erectile difficulties had been largely resolved, and he experienced far less performance pressure than previously. Although Diane continued to express a higher and more consistent desire for sex than her husband, increasing periods of time were noted when the couple were "in synch." The quality of their sexual encounters had improved markedly, and James's initiations were much appreciated by his wife. Both had achieved greater understanding of the origins of this problem, and James indicated a willingness to continue individual therapy regarding family-of-origin issues.

Commentary

It is vitally important in such cases for therapists and clients alike to strive for realistic and attainable goals. Given his family background and relationship history, it is likely that James will always experience some difficulty with emotional and sexual intimacy. Her traumatic first marriage and unhappy childhood have also left Diane with a deep sense of emotional vulnerability. Furthermore, considering the enormous sociocultural differences in their backgrounds, periods of tension and distance are likely and inevitable in the marriage. The O'Neils are also a typical dual-career suburban family with all the associated stresses and strains of jobs, children, and other household demands. Periods of sexual inactivity should be viewed as necessary and predictable, provided that some outlets for emotional or sexual intimacy are maintained. Differences in sexual appetite levels need also to be made explicit and better understood, as couples are encouraged to negotiate a manageable compromise regarding their different levels of desire. The case also illustrates the need for flexibility in the format of therapy, as individual and conjoint sessions were interspersed throughout, just as a variety of early developmental, family-of-origin, and couple's communication issues were addressed throughout.

Case 2: A Partially Successful Case

The Sharps were a hip, intelligent, and active couple in their mid-30s who came to the Sexual Counseling Service requesting help for their faltering sex life and related marital distress. Alice Sharp was particularly distraught and felt guilty, angry, and upset at the constant sexual pressure she felt her husband, Bill, placed on her. "He won't leave me alone," she exclaimed. "He can't keep his hands off me, and it's driving me crazy! I don't want to be touched. I just want to be left alone!"

The Sharps were seen individually and together, and their accounts of the sexual problem were quite consistent—they both dated the onset of the problem to the time of pregnancy with their first and only child, Tiffany. Prior to that time, they had enjoyed regular, frequent, playful, and gratifying sexual relations. They concurred that Bill had the stronger sex drive and was always initiating affectionate and sexual contact. Alice tolerated his attentions without difficulty and was readily arousable during sexual contact with him.

After being married for about 2 years, the Sharps had decided to have a child. Alice became pregnant without difficulty, and she and her husband devoured every available book about childbirth and child development and, at the same time, devoured all the food and drink they could consume. They passed the 9 months in a shared orgy of rich meals and excited anticipation over the upcoming event. In fact, they each gained more than 50 pounds during this period but were not particularly troubled by this. Bill said he still found his wife attractive, and Alice was so "into the pregnancy," that it didn't matter." Sex, however, became something of a problem. The bigger she became, the less sexually desirous (or desirable) Alice felt, and she began increasingly to reject Bill's sexual overtures. He would plead with her for physical contact, and she would occasionally consent to his giving her a back rub or body rub. Eventually, Bill's begging for sex became part of their sexual script and an integral part of Bill's sexual arousal. Prior to this time, he had privately enjoyed fantasies of a slave–master relationship in which he played the slave. Now, he found himself acting out his fantasies with the cooperation of his wife. Alice said she "played along" with Bill's fantasies since they involved little active participation from her. In the scenario, she would refuse to have sex with Bill, he would plead and beg, she would "order" him to massage her or perform oral sex, which he would do while he masturbated himself to orgasm. According to Alice, they engaged in this "master–slave" scenario both during the pregnancy and for several years afterwards. She commented: "Eventually, it did kill something. I lost respect for him."

Following the birth of their daughter, life continued to be enjoyable for the Sharps. Bill worked at two jobs to support his growing family, and Alice remained at home with her daughter and continued to prepare gourmet meals. After a while, this idyllic domesticity grew boring to Alice—she wanted to work, socialize with other adults, and achieve some independence from Bill. At this time, she became very involved with performing as the lead singer in a small band. She said music had always been the passion of her life—the "call of the wild" and the promise of performing in public inspired her to shed her excess weight. She achieved a slim, svelte figure, which she adorned in tight, sexy clothing when she performed. Bill also lost weight. Although Bill's sexual attraction to her increased during this time, Alice's interest in Bill waned further. She began to find his sexual approaches and incessant pleas for sex distasteful and avoided him more and more. This only served to enhance his wish for sexual intimacy and affirmations of love from Alice.

The friction between them grew, erupting often into angry outbursts. Alice felt smothered by Bill. She took a job at an all-night video store where she worked from 5 a.m. to 1 p.m. while her mother minded her daughter. She returned home to prepare dinner and to spend a little time with her daughter, but then, when Bill came home from work, she would often leave for rehearsals with her band or performances at local clubs. Bill would babysit for Tiffany or accompany Alice to her performances. However, both staying home and going out posed a problem for Bill: If he babysat, he would begin to feel angry and upset that his wife was not at home with him; if he went with her to the clubs, he felt jealous and insecure about the attention she received from men in the audience. He was also angry about the enthusiasm his wife showed for performing and interacting with the band at all times and at any hour and at the animosity she showed toward him for making sexual overtures or for complaining about her lack of availability.

At the time the Sharps contacted our service, they had already separated once and were on the verge of a second separation. Alice felt that she could no longer "take" the constant sexual pressure she was under.

Past History

Bill was the younger of two sons born to abusive and neglectful parents. He describes his father as volatile, explosive, and physically abusive, a man "who would fly into rages at the slightest provocation." Nevertheless, throughout his childhood and adolescence, Bill longed for recognition and affection from his father. Bill's mother was a remote and cold woman. She shouldered the major burden of supporting the family and fought constantly with her husband. Bill says she was so puritanical and "frigid" that "she would not undress if a dog was in the same room with her." He remembers his childhood as having been miserably unhappy: He had felt alone, abandoned, and unloved most of the time. Adding to his distress was the development at puberty of a severe skin condition that resulted in unsightly boils and blemishes on his face and back. Although possessed of a bright native intelligence, he was undisciplined and angry and hated the nuns at the parochial school he attended. He remembers baiting them until they rebuked him. On one occasion, a nun slapped him. In high school, he turned to drugs, was eventually suspended from school, and then enrolled in a Jesuit school. At around the same time, he began using and selling drugs. In fact, Bill and Alice both had smoked marijuana regularly until Alice became pregnant.

Despite his "punk" appearance and stormy personal history, Bill was a genuinely warm, likable, and intelligent person. He became embarrassed and apologetic when discussing his outbursts with Alice, although he admitted that it "drove him crazy" when she was "sexy to everyone" but him. He acknowledged feeling lonely and dependent on Alice and admitted that she was the more socially adept and gregarious of the pair.

Alice had grown up in an equally abusive home, although in her case, her father was an alcoholic. Like Bill, she was the younger of two children. Her mother was depressed for much of the time and, in fact, made a suicide attempt when Alice was pregnant. Alice remembers being left on her own a great deal. She disliked her father intensely—he couldn't do anything right— and remembers that her mother "was dominant and took care of everything." When her father was drunk, he would occasionally make affectionate overtures to Alice, which disgusted her. Her brother, who was 8 years her senior, married and left the house when she was a teenager. When she was 14, she became pregnant and told her mother, who accompanied her when she went to have an abortion. Immediately afterwards, however, her parents left for a vacation in England, leaving Alice to fend for herself. She went through a year of depression but eventually found a new boyfriend and moved in with him. When she was 18, they bought a house together. Alice acknowledged that although she had initially enjoyed sex with her boyfriends, she would eventually lose interest. Music was more satisfying to her than sex, although she admitted that she felt she was not "normal."

When Alice first met Bill, her current relationship was on the decline, and she was attracted to Bill's thoughtful, caring ways; after knowing him for only 2 weeks, she allowed him to move in with her. They were both tired of "running around" and felt a basic sympathy for each other, sharing recollections and stories of their abusive and neglectful childhoods. Sexual relations occurred often and were gratifying until the pregnancy.

Clinical Formulation

It was clear that Alice and Bill's difficulties stemmed in part from their early developmental experiences. They both were seen to be projecting onto their partners unresolved feelings toward parents of the opposite gender. For Alice, Bill was reminiscent of her inadequate, demanding father, who was ineffectual and dependent on her mother. When Bill beseeched Alice for sex, she began to feel contemptuous and disgusted (much as she did toward her father's drunken affectionate overtures), and she either played the haughty femme, "Mistress Alice," who ordered Bill around (the way her mother had ordered her father around), or else she avoided him entirely. At this time in her life, she wished to fulfill her adolescent fantasy of becoming a successful musical performer. She finally had the time and resources to do this, and she resented Bill's emotional and sexual demands. Instead of desiring home and hearth (which had never been fulfilling for her), she craved stimulation and excitement.

Bill, on the other hand, had been severely neglected by both his mother and father. He longed for attention. He was willing to accept it in any form, positive or negative. Alice's deprecating comments or commands only increased his ardor, since they were reminiscent of his early adolescent years when sexual excitement had occasionally been paired with physical punishment. Moreover, his masturbatory fantasies often involved humiliation and sexual abuse.

Unlike Alice, Bill yearned for a stable and traditional home life. He recalled the first 3 years of his marriage as being the happiest time of his life. He loved cooking and staying home with his wife and daughter.

Treatment

Following the evaluation sessions, the therapist acknowledged the distress that both of the Sharps were experiencing and suggested that the problem be viewed in terms of the couple's relationship, rather than being seen as caused by either one of them individually. Their expectations from marriage were not unreasonable but did clash with their individual aspirations and goals. Although they certainly loved each other, it was difficult to find a way in which each of them could feel fulfilled without the other feeling deprived. Periods of peace were followed by periods of tension. Both Bill and Alice would feel pushed to their limits and would erupt with rage and accusations. In many ways, their home life resembled that of their respective childhoods—with the atmosphere ringing with feelings of hurt and anger, rejection, and loneliness. In conjoint therapy sessions, the specific ways in which each projected aspects of his own parental relationships onto the other partner were identified and discussed. In individual sessions, more intensive exploration was conducted into early childhood feelings and memories. Following such therapy sessions, the marital tension would dissipate noticeably, and the Sharps would enjoy several weeks of companionship and harmony.

Behavioral assignments were sparingly given. For instance, it was suggested that they spend at least one weekday and one weekend evening together, during which time they could "have fun" in whatever way they chose. Ensuring that there was a modicum of private time together helped reassure Bill that Alice did, in fact, value him and alleviated some of the guilt Alice felt about going to rehearsals and clubs on other nights. Bill was encouraged to find other ways of entertaining himself so that he was not quite so dependent on Alice. He decided to enroll in night school for a business degree, which gave him a source of stimulation and gratification. Getting the attention he needed from school diminished his need for attention from Alice. As his sexual demands on Alice became less frequent, she became somewhat more receptive about engaging in sexual activities with him. Although she did not feel intrinsic "desire," she did want to please Bill and could derive pleasure from sexual encounters once she relaxed.

The sexual script was discussed in detail, and Bill acknowledged that the slave–master script had become a "turn-off" for Alice. Alice recognized that when Bill became too active, on the other hand, she also resented it. They eventually agreed that sex was more mutually gratifying when she initiated encounters and when the couple spent more time in mutual foreplay. Therapy sessions began to be spaced over 2- to 3-week intervals as marital relations improved. By this time, each partner felt better understood and appreciated by his mate, although both recognized that conflicts would continue around the amount of private and couple "time" each needed. Although their sexual fequency was still less than Bill desired, when sex did occur, it was more reciprocal and mutually gratifying.

Although therapy in this case was not an unqualified success, the outcome achieved with the Sharps is characteristic of that typically achieved with cases involving inhibited desire or desire discrepancy. The partner who desires greater sexual frequency rarely gets as much as he or she wishes, but the marital atmosphere is improved. Sex, when it occurs, can be more satisfying to both. The person with low desire finds sex less anxiety-producing and aversive and, to the extent that he or she feels understood and accepted, can accept sexual contact without feeling either coerced or guilt-ridden.

CONCLUSION: OUTCOME ISSUES IN THE TREATMENT OF DESIRE DISORDERS

Notwithstanding the general view that desire problems are complex and difficult to treat, we have obtained successful outcomes in many of these cases. Even in those instances involving global or long-standing sexual inhibition, we have found that considerable gains can be made (in either the sexual or nonsexual aspects of the relationship) through sex therapy or psychotherapy. In unsuccessful cases, however, it is not always possible to identify, except in the most speculative or *post hoc* fashion, the cause of the difficulty or the factors responsible for treatment failure.

How successful is the treatment of desire disorders? Clearly there is considerable variability in outcome from one sex therapy center to another. In a recent random survey of sex therapists and counselors, for example, Kilmann et al. (1986) reported that problems of desire required the greatest number of treatment sessions and that fewer than 50% of clients reported a successful treatment outcome for their desire difficulty. On the other hand, Schover and LoPiccolo (1982) had earlier reported outcome data comparable to those achieved for other sexual dysfunctions such as premature ejaculation and anorgasmia. It should be noted, however, that this latter study included only a very brief (3-month) follow-up period and that only modest gains were achieved at the conclusion of treatment. Rather than a "life of sexual ecstasy," most couples reported some limited increase in initiation and greater responsivity to the partner's sexual advances.

In contrast, LoPiccolo and Friedman (1988) have recently reported that positive outcome is generally achieved with their present multidimensional treatment model, which involves the combined use of experiential/sensory awareness exercises, insight, cognitive restructuring, and behavior therapy. Schwartz and Masters (1988) have also reported that desire problems are as likely to be successfully resolved as are the other sexual dysfunctions. Apfelbaum (1988) goes so far as to state that: "We find cases of low sexual desire among the easiest to treat and have not had a failure case of this type in which treatment was pursued to its conclusion" (p. 102). However, he goes on to qualify this statement by indicating that he has noted a sizeable number of treatment dropouts. Also Apfelbaum indicates more equivocal outcome when it is the female partner that has the higher drive level.

Two separate aspects of treatment outcome need to be addressed. First, the number of treatment sessions required for therapy (treatment duration) must be differentiated from the ultimate success or failure achieved (treatment outcome). Most therapists would acknowledge that desire problems require a greater number of treatment sessions than other dysfunctions. Even in our own center, where a short-term cognitive–behavioral treatment approach is encouraged, most cases involving desire problems require longer treatment (Rosen & Leiblum, 1987). Similar results were obtained in the Kilmann et al. (1986) study. It should not be assumed, however, that the number of sessions is positively correlated with treatment success.

Given the variability in reported outcome rates with this problem, it is important to consider what factors are associated with treatment success or failure. For example, we have recently observed higher success rates when the identified patients were males and when patients presented with concomitant sexual dysfunctions, most notably erectile dysfunction. Clearly, then, the presence of specific performance difficulties in addition to inhibited desire does not constitute, in and of itself, a significant impediment to successful outcome.

It is worth noting that a significant proportion of successfully treated cases in our center involved couples with fairly serious degrees of marital distress. We have frequently observed, however, that the degree of *commitment* to the marriage is an important predictor of success, despite the presence of substantial areas of conflict or disagreement. Successfully treated patients are also noted more frequently to be committed to the therapy process, although this is true for most areas of psychotherapy or couples' therapy.

An interesting question in this regard is the possible value of traditional sex therapy techniques, such as sensate focus, in the treatment of desire disorders. According to Schwartz and Masters (1988), these techniques are applicable and useful in *all* cases of inhibited desire. LoPiccolo and Friedman (1988) have similarly advocated the use of such techniques in most cases. Other therapists, including Rosen and Leiblum (1987), recommend these techniques only when other performance difficulties are involved. As

Apfelbaum (1988) has repeatedly cautioned, to prescribe sexual exercises for an individual who complains of sexual apathy or aversion may exacerbate the already existing subjective experience of sexual demand. Apfelbaum has identified "response anxiety," or the pressure to engage in and enjoy sexual exchange, as constituting the primary cause of all desire disorders. Accordingly, he would find the prescription of sensate focus exercises for these individuals to be countertherapeutic.

What factors contribute to unsuccessful outcome? Some of the salient issues that have been identified in this regard are the presence of major secrets in the marital relationship, a history of chronic alcoholism or drug abuse, religious orthodoxy, a history of depression, organogenic erectile dysfunction, and significant body image concerns. It is worth noting that in many instances it is simply not possible to identify the apparent causes of treatment failure. Clearly, more research is needed before we can specify which factors are likely to predict outcome in these cases.

Overall, it appears that most cases of inhibited desire present the clinician with a challenging and complex set of clinical issues. As we have emphasized throughout this chapter, desire problems are frequently related to early developmental experiences, personality issues, and a wide range of couples' conflicts. We have emphasized the value of a multidimensional treatment approach, incorporating biological, psychological, and interpersonal elements. Little attention has been given to date to the problems of sexual aversion of hyperactive desire. Finally, pharmacological approaches to the treatment of low desire have met with little success to date, although we anticipate increasing efforts in this direction in the years to come.

REFERENCES

Alterescu, V. (1981). Sexual functioning following creation of an abdominal stoma. In D. G. Bullard & S. E. Knight (Eds.), *Sexuality and physical disability: Personal perspectives* (pp. 23–24). St. Louis: C. V. Mosby.

American Psychiatric Association. (1987). *Diagnostic and statistical manual of mental disorders* (3rd ed., rev.). Washington, DC: Author.

Apfelbaum, B. (1988). An ego-analytic perspective on desire disorders. In S. R. Leiblum & R. C. Rosen (Eds.), *Sexual desire disorders* (pp. 75–106). New York: Guilford Press.

Bancroft, J., & Wu, F. C. W. (1983). Changes in erectile responsiveness during androgen therapy. *Archives of Sexual Behavior, 12*, 59–66.

Berlin, F. S., & Meinecke, C. F. (1981). Treatment of sex offenders with antiandrogenic medication: Conceptualization, review of treatment modalities, and preliminary findings. *American Journal of Psychiatry, 138*, 601–607.

Crenshaw, T. L., Goldberg, J. P., & Stern, W. L. (1987). *Pharmacologic modification of psychosexual dysfunction.* Unpublished manuscript.

Gagnon, J. H., Rosen, R. C., & Leiblum, S. R. (1982). Cognitive and social aspects of sexual dysfunction: Sexual scripts in sex therapy. *Journal of Sex and Marital Therapy, 8*, 44–56.

Garde, K., & Lunde, I. (1980). Female sexual behavior: A study in a random sample of 40-year-old women. *Maturitas, 2*, 240–255.

Hawton, K., Catalan, J., Martin, P., & Fagg, J. (1986). Prognostic factors in sex therapy. *Behaviour Research and Therapy, 24*, 377–385.

Kaplan, H. S. (1977). Hypoactive sexual desire. *Journal of Sex and Marital Therapy, 3*, 3–9.

Kaplan, H. S. (1979). *Disorders of sexual desire.* New York: Brunner/Mazel.

Kilmann, P. R., Boland, J. P., Norton, S. P., Davidson, E., & Caid, C. (1986). Perspectives of sex therapy outcome: A survey of AASECT providers. *Journal of Sex and Marital Therapy, 12*, 116–138.

Kinsey, A. C., Pomeroy, W. B., & Martin, C. E. (1948). *Sexual behavior in the human male.* Philadelphia: W. B. Saunders.

Kinsey, A. C., Pomeroy, W. B., Martin, C. E., & Gebhard, P. H. (1953). *Sexual behavior in the human female.* Philadelphia: W. B. Saunders.

Klein, K., Mendels, J., Lief, H., & Phillips, J. (1987, March). *Drug treatment of inhibited sexual desire: A controlled clinical trial.* Paper presented at the annual meeting of the Society for Sex Therapy and Research, New Orleans.

Lazarus, A. A. (1988). A multimodal perspective on problems of sexual desire. In S. R. Lciblum & R. C. Rosen (Eds.), *Sexual desire disorders* (pp. 145–167). New York: Guilford Press.

Leiblum, S. R., & Pervin, L. A. (Eds.). (1980). *Principles and practice of sex therapy.* New York: Guilford Press.

Leiblum, S. R. & Rosen, R. C. (Eds.). (1988). *Sexual desire disorders.* New York: Guilford Press.

Levine, S. B. (1984). An essay on the nature of sexual desire. *Journal of Sex and Marital Therapy, 10*, 83–96.

Levine, S. B. (1988). Intrapsychic and individual aspects of sexual desire. In S. R. Leiblum & R. C. Rosen (Eds.), *Sexual desire disorders* (pp. 21–44). New York: Guilford Press.

Lief, H. I. (1977). Inhibited sexual desire. *Medical Aspects of Human Sexuality, 7*, 94–95.

Lief, H. I. (1988). Foreword. In S. R. Leiblum & R. C. Rosen, (Eds.), *Sexual desire disorders* (pp. vii–xiii). New York: Guilford Press.

LoPiccolo, L. (1980). Low sexual desire. In S. R. Leiblum & L. A. Pervin (Eds.), *Principles and practice of sex therapy* (pp. 29–64). New York: Guilford Press.

LoPiccolo, J., & Friedman, J. M. (1988). Broad-spectrum treatment of low sexual desire: Integration of cognitive, behavioral, and systemic therapy. In S. R. Leiblum & R. C. Rosen (Eds.), *Sexual desire disorders* (pp. 107–144). New York: Guilford Press.

Masters, W. H., & Johnson, V. E. (1966). *Human sexual response.* Boston: Little, Brown.

Masters, W. H., & Johnson, V. E. (1970). *Human sexual inadequacy.* Boston: Little, Brown.

Regas, S. J., & Sprenkle, D. H. (1984). Functional family therapy and the treatment of inhibited sexual desire. *Journal of Marital and Family Therapy, 10*, 63–72.

Rosen, R. C., & Leiblum, S. R. (1987). Current approaches to the evaluation of sexual desire disorders. *Journal of Sex Research, 23,* 141-162.

Rosen, R. C., & Leiblum, S. R. (1988). A sexual scripting approach to problems of desire. In S. R. Leiblum & R. C. Rosen (Eds.), *Sexual desire disorders* (pp. 168-191). New York: Guilford Press.

Rosen, R. C., Leiblum, S. R., & Hall, K. S. (1987). *Etiological and predictive factors in sex therapy.* Unpublished manuscript.

Scharff, D. E. (1988). An object relations approach to inhibited sexual desire. In S. R. Leiblum & R. C. Rosen (Eds.), *Sexual desire disorders* (pp. 45-74). New York: Guilford Press.

Schover, L., & LoPiccolo, J. (1982). Effectiveness of treatment for dysfunctions of sex desire. *Journal of Sex and Marital Therapy, 8,* 179-197.

Schreiner-Engel, P., & Schiavi, R. C. (1986). Life-time psychopathology in individuals with low sexual desire. *Journal of Nervous and Mental Disease, 174,* 646-651.

Schwartz, M. F., & Masters, W. H. (1988). Inhibited sexual desire: The Masters and Johnson Institute treatment model. In S. R. Leiblum & R. C. Rosen (Eds.), *Sexual desire disorders* (pp. 229-242). New York: Guilford Press.

Segraves, R. T. (1988). Drugs and desire. In S. R. Leiblum & R. C. Rosen (Eds.), *Sexual desire disorders* (pp. 313-347). New York: Guilford Press.

Sherwin, B. B., Gelfand, M. M., & Brender, W. (1985). Androgen enhances sexual motivation in females: A prospective, crossover study of sex steroid administration in the surgical menopause. *Psychosomatic Medicine, 47,* 339-351.

Thase, M. E., Reynolds, J. R., Jennings, D. E., Sewitch, L. M., Glanz, E., Frank, E., & Kupfer, D. J. (1986, June). *Alterations of noctural penile tumescence in depressed men.* Paper presented at the annual meeting of the Sleep Research Society, Columbus, Ohio.

Verhulst, J., & Heiman, J. (1979). An interactional approach to sexual dysfunction. *The American Journal of Family Therapy, 7,* 19-36.

Verhulst, J., & Heiman, J. R. (1988). A systems perspective on sexual desire. In S. R. Leiblum & R. C. Rosen (Eds.), *Sexual desire disorders* (pp. 243-270). New York: Guilford Press.

Zilbergeld, B., & Ellison, C. R. (1980). Desire discrepancies and arousal problems in sex therapy. In S. R. Leiblum & L. Pervin (Eds.), *Principles and practice of sex therapy* (pp. 65-104). New York: Guilford Press.

Female Sexual Disorders

II

3

Orgasmic Disorders in Women

JULIA R. HEIMAN AND VIRGINIA GRAFTON-BECKER

Although not as prominent a sexual problem as it once was, failure to achieve orgasm continues to be a major complaint of many women. In the history of sexuality, anorgasmia may be considered a relatively new disorder, but in recent decades there has been a remarkable concern about female orgasmic responsivity. The manner, method, and ease of orgasmic attainment has received wide publicity, and the woman who does not regularly achieve orgasm feels deficient, deprived, and often depressed.

In their chapter on orgasmic disorders in women, Heiman and Grafton-Becker note that the ultimate causes of orgasmic difficulties are not known with any real certainty, although most orgasmic problems are undoubtedly the net result of several variables. Anatomic and physical factors, sociocultural factors, and psychological determinants are all involved in the genesis and maintenance of orgasmic problems. Treatment approaches are similarly varied. Psychoanalytic, object-relations, cognitive–behavioral, and systems theory all offer conceptual approaches for treating these problems.

Heiman and Grafton-Becker favor a systems orientation to orgasmic problems in which a couple learns to recognize that their relationship consists of intricate patterns. The couple automatically constructs these patterns and in turn is constructed by them. Couple interactions occur on symbolic, affect-regulated, and sensory levels. Sometimes the levels function independently, but often they interact with each other within each individual and between partners. A systems orientation enables therapists to formulate and treat the orgasmic problem in interactional rather than technique-oriented terms. The patient is not the anorgasmic woman but, rather, the sexual relationship.

The authors suggest helping the couple understand why and how the symptom may make sense on both an individual and interactional level. What does having an orgasm mean to the woman? To her partner? What solution does the problem offer to the couple? Does the woman have a sense of ownership over her body? Does she want to attain an orgasm primarily to satisfy a partner or to satisfy herself? Can the couple communi-

cate directly about sensual preferences? These and similar issues become
the treatment focus.

Heiman and Grafton-Becker present a multifaceted and comprehensive approach to working with orgasmic problems in the context of the
couple system. Such a model accurately reflects current realities. Moreover,
their case vignettes vividly illustrate how complicated the presentation,
treatment, and outcome or orgasmic dysfunction can be.

Julia R. Heiman, Ph.D., is Professor of Psychiatry and Behavioral
Sciences at the University of Washington Medical School in Seattle, Wash-
ington and the author of several books on sexuality including Becoming
Orgasmic: A Sexual and Personal Growth Program for Women (1976, with
L. LoPiccolo & L. LoPiccolo, and 1988, with J. LoPiccolo).

Virginia Grafton-Becker, Psy.D., is a Post-doctoral Fellow in Psychiatry
and Behavioral Sciences at the University of Washington Medical School.

———————

Cultures of Western societies have historically been far more interested in
the outcome of a woman's sexual behavior, pregnancy, than in her sexual
responsiveness. Out-of-control and wanton sexual behavior implied child-
bearing with possibly unknown fathers. Societies, especially societies based
on paternal lineage and economic privilege, are very uneasy with this level
of chaos. Their response has been to create rules and regulations as well as
images about good and bad sexual behavior.

It is not surprising therefore that women's sexual responsiveness is a
recent concern, for all practical purposes one that begins at the turn of the
20th century. The preceding century had been imbued with values we now
call Victorian. With respect to sexuality, this meant that women, especially
"good" women such as wives, were to be "pure" and asexual and, in fact,
respected for their lack of sexual response. Prostitutes abounded, and prostitution was big business during the 1800s in part because sex had become
the equivalent of an illegal drug and in part because any sign of "impurity"
led women in one direction.

One of the core factors separating the more traditional from the more
modern views of sexuality is the degree to which sexual problems were seen
as needing control and inhibition as opposed to needing stimulation and
facilitation. It is clear that excessive sexual activity was thought in the 19th
century to require therapeutic and social controls, whereas inhibited or lost
sexual behaviors and feelings became the concern of the superficially more
prosexual 20th century (see Robinson, 1970, for further discussion of tradi-
tionalists versus modernists). As we now look back, there are some interesting constructs to examine about orgasmic problems in women.

One can, for example, see Sigmund Freud's work on women as being on
the cusp of this dialectic, although Freud's concepts are clearly more Victorian

than modern. He presented a categorization of female orgasm based on personality maturity. Clitoral orgasms were superficial and immature, whereas vaginal orgasms were authentic and adult. Although irritating to those who disagree with this distinction, the anatomically based distinction of different orgasms represented an important initial transition from Victorian values: It recognized the presence and power of female orgasm without abandoning the cultural paradigm of procreative sex as more valued and correct.

Contemporaneous with Freud's work was that of Havlock Ellis. Ellis not only suggested that women's responses were equivalent to men's but that women were probably more sexual than men. He saw women's sexuality as more mysterious and more massive. Women not only had a clitoris, but they also had a womb that gave them a large and diffuse sexual anatomy with which to respond. Ellis said very little about female orgasm. He did see women as innately passive beings who required both the courtship and driving interest of the male to elicit female sexual response.

A different perspective came from Alfred Kinsey, who prepared the way for a new look at female orgasms. Kinsey did not distinguish between anatomic types of orgasms in women. He did use orgasms as one of the several markers of human sexuality. He was quite impressed with the fact that the females of other species did not seem to experience orgasm (we have since found several primates for whom orgasm does seem to occur). For Kinsey, this fact seemed to make humans, women in particular, rather unique. Kinsey counted orgasms, among other sexual behaviors, with equal seriousness and commitment for men and women. An indirect outcome of his survey research was that orgasm frequency became one of the variables that made up a person's, a group's, and a society's sexual demographics. It was also Kinsey who noted, much to the distress of readers in the 1950s, that a woman was more likely to be orgasmic during masturbation than during sex with a partner.

Masters and Johnson's view was that all female orgasms were the result of the same neurophysiological process of response and that women's orgasms were more similar than dissimilar to male orgasms. Masters and Johnson published this information in 1966 when the atmosphere promoting sexual equality was more vociferous than in the previous decade. Women were claiming legal rights and, especially, reproductive rights. Reliable contraceptives were available. The "right" to orgasm made sense in this context, and it was Masters and Johnson's *Human Sexual Inadequacy* in 1970 that proposed a plan for making orgasm possible to women who never or rarely experienced them. Masters and Johnson offered a nonpathological model for cure: remove the anxiety, and the natural expression of sexual response will appear. As modest as this model was, it probably would not have been accepted in 1900. Masters and Johnson required the data of Kinsey's work as well as a different cultural environment to be heard.

In sum, the fact that we recognize and treat orgasmic problems in women is, in part, a cultural accident. One hundred years ago we would not have done so. Therefore, we must view with caution the attempts to diagnose problems attaining orgasm. Women can have orgasm with the appropriate stimulation in about the same amount of time as men; when they do not, it may be because of personal history, current relationship issues, or simply lack of education and information about sexual matters. In other words, orgasm problems are signs, not syndromes, and they may say more about a woman's sociocultural and interpersonal contexts than her individual psychological functioning.

Problems with orgasm are usually divided into the categories of primary and secondary or situational. Primary anorgasmia refers to women who have never had an orgasm; secondary refers to women with orgasmic infrequency. Although this chapter discusses both types, it focuses more on secondary orgasmic problems, as these are more common and typically more difficult to treat (Arentewicz & Schmidt, 1983; Heiman & LoPiccolo, 1983; Kaplan, 1974; Masters & Johnson, 1970).

How common are problems with orgasm? The incidence of orgasm problems, as of other sexual problems, is difficult to estimate because of the paucity of random samples. Kinsey's work, now 50 years old, was one of the largest and most random. He reported that by their mid-30s 10% of women remained incapable of orgasm (Kinsey, Pomeroy, Martin, & Gebhard, 1953). Other figures range from 50% almost or never orgasmic (Hunt, 1974) to under 10% (Garde & Lunde, 1980). A study from Holland indicated that 33% of the women were dissatisfied with their orgasm pattern (Frenken, 1976). Gebhard (1978) reported that 60% of wives considered themselves to have a problem achieving orgasm. In terms of clinical populations, between 20% (Bancroft, 1983; Heiman & LoPiccolo, 1983) and 90% (Arentewicz & Schmidt, 1983; Masters & Johnson, 1970) report arousal and orgasm problems. It is important to keep in mind that orgasmic problems do not always cause sexual distress. A nonrandom sample of happily married couples was studied by Frank, Anderson, and Rubinstein (1978). In this study, 63% of the women reported arousal and orgasm problems even though they were happily married, and 85% of them reported that they were satisfied with their sexual relationship.

DETERMINANTS OF FEMALE ORGASM

Although much theorizing has been directed toward understanding what factors contribute to women's orgasmic capacity, little can be stated conclusively.

Some anatomic and physical factors have been proposed as interfering with female orgasm. For example, there is inconsistent evidence that diabetes, spinal cord injury, and hormonal imbalance may influence orgasm in women. One study found that providing testosterone plus counseling helped women's sexual responsiveness more than diazepam (an anti-anxiety

medication) plus counseling (Carney, Bancroft, & Mathews, 1978). However, more recent research comparing testosterone and a placebo found no
differences (Whitehead, Mathews, & Kellett, 1981; Bancroft, 1983). In
general, there does not seem to be one common physical pathway or even a
constellation of physical factors that automatically determine whether a
woman will have orgasm problems.

Strength and tone of the pubococcygeus (PC) muscle has been proposed as a contributing factor to orgasm capacity (Kline-Graber & Graber,
1978). However, correlation between PC muscle tone and orgasmicity is
low. Probably PC muscle strength is idiosyncratically related to orgasm in
some women.

Essentially, the problem remains that too little is known about the
neurophysiological basis of human orgasm in men or women. In addition,
compared to men, there is even less research on women with various
diseases, medications, injuries, and surgeries.

In spite of assumptions about the impact of religion, education, age,
social class, and other sociocultural factors, few convincing results have
emerged in research (e.g., Kinsey et al., 1953; Hunt, 1974). Women's orgasmic response per sexual contact does seem to decrease as the marriage
increases in age. In addition, better-educated women with fewer religious
and moral constraints may be somewhat more orgasmic. However, none of
these variables shows consistent interactions, and thus none should be pre-
sumed to be a determinant of orgasm capacity.

Perhaps most surprising is the infrequency with which psychological
factors are consistently related to orgasmicity. Even an event as dramatic as
sexual abuse does not necessarily produce orgasm problems, although such
problems are higher in an abused than in a nonabused sample (Tsai, Feld
man-Summers, & Edgar, 1979; Norris & Feldman-Summers, 1981). The
most complete investigation of personality and background variables as
they relate to female orgasm is still that of Fisher (1973). Fisher's most
consistent finding was that anorgasmic women often had experienced their
early love objects, especially fathers, as undependable and tended to experience later objects similarly. These women therefore had an increased need
to control situations involving high arousal that held a potential for loss of
control. Although no one has replicated Fisher's findings, his results have
been clinically useful. In fact, the theme of early abandonment by an
important male figure occurs in both of the cases we present below.

Anxiety has been hypothesized to be the major interference with orgasm (Kaplan, 1974; Masters and Johnson, 1970). However, there may be
different types of anxiety associated with women with different orgasm
patterns. Women who get aroused but cannot experience orgasm except
with a vibrator may have a different anxiety process than women who never
get aroused and are never orgasmic. Anxiety may be modified by other
emotional states such as anger, disgust, and guilt in influencing different
orgasmic patterns.

In summary, there are no consistent empirical findings that support a constellation of factors separating orgasmic from nonorgasmic women. We suggest that the reason for this is that the labels orgasmic, nonorgasmic, or situationally orgasmic are too global and will never yield reliably discriminating factors. We might find more satisfying results if patterns of orgasmicity and nonorgasmicity were developed based on early-history factors plus personal (medical and psychological) factors plus relationship factors. Certainly our own clinical experience is consistent with the view that there are more differences among women with orgasm problems than there are similarities.

TREATMENT APPROACHES: THEORETICAL AND APPLIED ELEMENTS

This section provides a brief overview of the three major theoretical and treatment approaches to inhibited female orgasm: psychoanalytic, cognitive–behavioral, and systems theory. Only the most salient features of each method are examined, since the focus of this chapter is on an approach that includes elements of each of these theories.

Psychoanalytic Approaches to Inhibited Female Orgasm

Theoretical Elements

From a psychoanalytic point of view, the usual purpose of sexual behavior is pleasure and orgasm. An alternate function of sexual behavior may be a defense or a symbolic means of expressing internal conflicts (Cohen, 1978; Rosen, 1982). Traditionally, sexual dysfunction has been viewed as a symptom that expresses a pathological process in personality development; a developmental arrest is thought to result from castration fantasies, guilt over wishes for gratification with father, and unconscious fears (see papers by Bergler [1944] and Fenichel [1946] in Faulk, 1973). More recently, "maturity" from clitoral to vaginal orgasm is no longer seen as a goal; the focus has shifted from a debate about physiological origins of orgasm to the experienced psychological differences between vaginal and clitoral orgasm. Implications are that the capability to experience orgasm and pleasure during sexual intercourse is intrinsically related to the woman's capacity to relate intimately to another person.

From the perspective of object-relations theory, an individual's capacity to relate to another is innate, begins at birth, and is in part determined by her or his ability to form an internal representation of the other. Later, both the negative and positive attributes of the caretaker are internalized, and these engender the capability for relatedness in later life. Tolerance of the ambivalence brought about by recognizing a loved one's faults contributes to a person's ability to maintain trust and intimacy with another.

Newer formulations about female psychological development have emphasized the relationship with the mother as critical to adult heterosexual functioning (Jordan, 1985; Stiver, 1984; Surrey, 1983). Emotional proximity of mother and daughter helps to create an identity of self that is determined, in part, by relatedness to others (Surrey, 1983; Jordan, 1985). Thus, rather than being a pathologically dependent syndrome, as it is often labeled, the reliance of women on relationships is a normal part of self-definition (Stiver, 1984).

The pitfalls of the reliance on relationships for self-definition, in terms of adult sexual functioning, are that intimate relationships may be threatening because they recreate a feeling of merging with the mother, similar to the preverbal, undifferentiated experience between the infant and mother. Sexually intimate relationships may recreate the demand of having to meet another's emotional needs, previously the mother's, currently the spouse's. Since women's identities are intrinsically tied to others, they are especially vulnerable. Clear boundaries with an internal sense of separateness are necessary to enable one to tolerate intimacy, and so conflicts with closeness may result in hostility and anger directed against the male, an inability to trust, and inhibited orgasm. A woman needs to feel secure enough in her self-identity to experience pleasure in the physical "taking-in" of the other, without fears of merger, abandonment, or loss of self.

Several defenses, the ego's unconscious means of managing anxiety, are pertinent to orgasm dysfunction. *Denial*, often a form of minimization of an event or physical sensation, is a common coping mechanism. For example, a woman in treatment presented a "perfect relationship" in which she could not obtain orgasm; however, her live-in partner severely limited her household budget, made it clear that the relationship was temporary, and refused to make love with her except on special occasions such as her birthday. Clearly, she had denied the negative aspects of this relationship that were contributing to her sexual problems. *Repression*, the complete removal from consciousness of an experienced feeling, allows an individual to continue life when events are too stressful to tolerate. Frequently, trauma, such as childhood physical or sexual abuse, is the precursor of repression. *Projective identification*, unconsciously projecting one's feelings onto a significant other, is another way of dealing with unacceptable feelings or impulses. For example, a nonorgasmic woman uncomfortable with her own desire to control others may see and interact with her husband in a way that identifies whatever he does as controlling. She unconsciously provokes his controlling behavior, thus confirming her expectations (Kernberg, 1987; Scharff & Scharff, 1987).

Therapeutic Applications

In psychoanalytical psychotherapy, the emphasis is not on symptom removal but on working through conflicts that lead to the symptom. The symbolic content and functional utility of the symptom are explored

(Cohen, 1978). Other central features include uncovering and reclaiming the memories of early childhood experience and relationships, interpreting and working through the resistance to change in therapy, and attending to the transference and countertransference aspects of the therapeutic relationship. Treatment is focused on the patient–therapist dyad, with longer and more frequent sessions than with other approaches. Variations of traditional treatment have combined individual and couple treatment and added sex therapy (Kaplan, 1974; Levay, Weissberg, & Blaustein, 1976; Segraves, 1986). However, sex therapy has caused concern, since it requires an alteration of the therapist's neutrality to an investment in the patient's recovery of sexual function (Rosen, 1982; see also Dickes & Strauss, 1979; Weissberg & Levay, 1981, for other therapist issues).

Outcome data are sparse, restricted primarily to clinical reports. Dynamic therapy improves overall life satisfaction more than the sexual dysfunction (Frances & Kaplan, 1983). Long-term recovery of sexual functioning is fostered by a combination of the in-depth psychodynamic treatment and specific symptom removal (Obler, 1982; Frances & Kaplan, 1983).

Cognitive–Behavioral Approaches

Theoretical Elements

Cognitive–behavioral therapists depend on learning theories to help explain the origins of orgasmic problems. Sexual behavior may become aversively conditioned because of accompanying pain or fear. Anxiety and fear may interfere with relaxation, prevent arousal, and inhibit orgasmic response (cf. Barlow, 1986). Lack of adequate reinforcement for sexual thoughts and behaviors can also lead to negative expectations of sexual events, an impaired attitude toward sex, extinction of sexual desire, and avoidance behaviors. Related to anorgasmia are other common attributions: poor self-image, feeling "different" from others, and feeling incapable of communicating sexual desires (Kuriansky & Sharpe, 1981; Cotten-Huston & Wheeler, 1983). The latter may be caused by a lack of assertiveness or impaired communication skills (Kuriansky, Sharpe, & O'Connor, 1982).

Therapeutic Applications

The goals of cognitive–behavioral therapy are to promote cognitive change, shift attitudes, reduce anxiety, increase orgasmic frequency, and increase the connection between positive feelings and sexual behaviors (Ellis, 1975; Fichten, Libman, & Brender, 1986; LoPiccolo & LoPiccolo, 1978).

Cognitive–behavioral therapy works with individuals, couples, or groups. Variables such as sex of therapist, single therapist versus a co-therapist team, and spacing of sessions have been demonstrated not to influence sexual and marital outcome measures. (Ersner-Hershfield &

Kopel, 1979; Heiman & LoPiccolo, 1983; LoPiccolo, Heiman, Hogan, & Roberts, 1985). The hallmarks of behavioral therapy are the prescription of privately enacted behavioral exercises, the results of these "debriefed" in treatment, and new prescribed exercises tailored to meet the client's needs. Treatment is generally brief, averaging about 15–20 sessions. The therapist is an educator/facilitator who defines and assesses the problem and then prescribes learning situations to remedy it.

Directed masturbation (DM) is most frequently used with primary anorgasmic women. The procedures include a period of education and information followed by visual and kinesthetic self-exploration of the woman's body. This procedure has been successful in a variety of modalities, including minimal therapist contact of four sessions at monthly intervals and the viewing of a film and reading matter (Morokoff & LoPiccolo, 1986). DM is used in group, individual, and couple's therapy. Generally, most studies report fairly high success rates, with greater than 80% of women being able to experience masturbatory orgasm after completion of therapy, and a lower percentage, 20–60%, able to have orgasm with their partner. Most women report increased enjoyment and satisfaction of coital activities, a more relaxed attitude to sex and life, and increased acceptance of their bodies (Ersner-Hershfield & Kopel, 1979; Leiblum & Ersner-Hershfield, 1977; Nairne & Hemsley, 1983; Riley & Riley, 1978; Wallace & Barbach, 1974).

Group treatment fosters an environment that normalizes each woman's perception of her condition (Mills & Kilmann, 1982). Groups emphasize sharing, assertiveness, self-touch, and masturbation (Barbach, 1974; Kuriansky & Sharpe, 1981) as well as education, relaxation, reading, and prescribed sexual activity (Mills & Kilmann, 1982).

There has been some criticism of the group format and DM because of its emphasis on autocrotic technique and response (Barbach, 1974; Wakefield, 1987) and because these experiences may not transfer into partner-related activities (Wakefield, 1987; Kuriansky & Sharpe, 1981). Wallace and Barbach (1974) reported that 87% of 22 women were orgasmic with partners; and Ersner-Hershfield and Koppel (1979) reported that, of their clients successful in reaching orgasm, 82% of 22 transferred this to partner-related activities. However, Schneidman and McGuire (1976) found 80% of women under 35 years to be orgasmic with partners at 6-month follow-up compared to 60% of the older women. Other studies have indicated that orgasm during intercourse did not improve significantly from pre- to post-treatment (Libman et al., 1984; Fichten et al., 1986; Kilmann, Mills, et al., 1986). Additional studies have indicated lower success rates for orgasms with partners, especially for secondary anorgasmia. They range from 30% (Spence, 1985) to 66% (Weiss & Meadow, 1983). The problem is partly one of definition in that partner-related activity can mean masturbation in front of the partner rather than coitus. Couples need to be educated that additional stimulation is normal for many women to experience orgasm during coitus (Hoch, Safir, Peres, & Sopher, 1981; Kaplan, 1974; LoPiccolo &

Stock, 1986). Directed masturbation and eventually partner stimulation may be positively incorporated into the desired outcome of orgasm with a partner during coitus.

Another recent controversy has been the effectiveness of Kegel exercises (contraction of the pubococcygeus [PC] muscle) in producing orgasm. Roughan and Kunst (1981) found no difference in orgasmic frequency among groups who used Kegel exercises, relaxation training, or attention control, although the PC group had increased muscle tone. These findings have since been supported by Trudel and Saint-Laurent (1983) and Chambless et al. (1984). Tensing the vaginal musculature has been found to be less arousing than use of fantasy on both physiological and subjective measures of arousal; however, tensing plus fantasy was most arousing (Messe & Geer, 1985). These results suggest that Kegel exercises have arousal enhancement value; however, it is also possible that they facilitate orgasm by increasing women's awareness and comfort with their genitals.

Consideration of the specific type of anorgasmia, primary or secondary, is important to treatment planning. Directed masturbation is most effective in treating primary anorgasmia, and the success rate is at least 80–90% (Riley & Riley, 1978; LoPiccolo & Stock, 1986). The success rate of secondary anorgasmia treatment ranges from 10% to 75% (Fichten et al., 1986; Kilmann, Boland, Sjortus, Davidson, & Caid, 1986; Kilmann, Mills, et al., 1986; Kuriansky et al., 1982; Mills & Kilmann, 1982). Generally younger, emotionally healthier, and more happily married women have a higher probability of success (Schneidman & McGuire, 1976; Libman et al., 1984; LoPiccolo & Stock, 1986). LoPiccolo and Stock (1986) suggest a combination of marital and sex treatment. Several studies have shown an increase in sexual and relationship satisfaction without a significant improvement in the presenting sexual symptom (Everaerd & Dekker, 1982; DeAmicis, Goldberg, LoPiccolo, Friedman, & Davies, 1986; Hieman & LoPiccolo, 1983; LoPiccolo et al., 1985).

Systems Theory

General systems theory claims to offer a new paradigm to account for multifactoral phenomena. In medicine, it has been applied primarily to those illnesses, psychosomatic conditions for example, for which the traditional linear-causal model of disease is inadequate (Brody, 1973; Engel, 1980). In psychotherapy, a systems approach has been primarily developed within family and marital therapy.

Systems theory has not been applied to understanding and treating orgasmic problems in women. Its application to sexual problems has been restricted to general dysfunctions or inhibited sexual desire (Heiman, 1986; Verhulst & Heiman, 1979, 1988; Weeks, 1987). Systems theorists themselves tend to view symptoms such as anorgasmia rather suspiciously, even as a smokescreen produced by a distressed dyad in order to divert all parties from more essential marital problems (Whitaker & Keith, 1981). Sexuality is a particularly sensitive subject for family therapists, many of whom broke away from psychoanalytic positions where sexuality was considered part of the core structure of individual development (cf. Weeks & Hof, 1987).

Masters and Johnson have been described as taking a systems perspective. However, in spite of seeing the couple as "the patient" and using the couple to treat the sexual problems, the conceptualization of sexual disorders was focused on individualistic etiological factors. The heart of Masters and Johnson's approach, sensate focus with its gradual increase of sexual stimuli, can easily be conceptualized as a generic systems intervention; the sexual relationship is a patient overwhelmed with anxiety, and each member of the couple helps put "the patient" at increasing ease. However, Masters and Johnson never claimed to be systems theorists (or behaviorists, although their techniques, as we have mentioned, are often viewed as emerging from that school). Part of their program's effectiveness is that they devised a treatment that worked very well for most symptomatic, nonphysically based sexual problems. One could call it a "universal prescription" (cf. Selvini-Palazzoli & Viaro, 1988).

Whereas family therapists have eschewed sexual dysfunctions, sex therapists have typically ignored family issues. Reasons for this go beyond the scope of this chapter, although one issue to keep in mind is the relative youth of each specialty. Family therapy, as already mentioned, was initially too infused with psychoanalytic rebels to consider sex as only a symptom. Sex therapists, in their own reaction against the past and affirmation of the cultural and reproductive freedom of the 1960s, felt compelled to align with "sex for pleasure" rather than "sex for reproduction." At times, this position became almost imperious and may have contributed to their continued isolation from family therapists who treat the consequences of reproductive sex by adults or acting out teenagers as common and important issues.

Only recently has a book stressing the integration of sex and marital therapy been compiled (Weeks & Hof, 1987). Interestingly, this book makes no mention of orgasm, erection, or ejaculation in the index, nor could any references to these be located in case examples. The integration may have begun; however, a gulf still remains.

Theoretical Elements

Before we can discuss sexuality, there are several key systems concepts that must be considered. Living systems are composed of mutually interacting components. They have boundaries, yet they are open and constantly interchanging information with their environment (von Bertalanffy, 1968; Miller, 1978). Each person is a system and is part of subsystems within a family; the family is embedded in a sociocultural context, yet another system.

The systems principle of *emergent qualities* states simply that a system, such as the couple, is more than the sum of its parts. Relationships therefore have properties of their own, beyond the properties that people bring to it. We try to impart this to couples early in treatment to help them begin to see that there are more issues than "one against the other," to decrease the sense that there is one patient and one nonpatient, and to build a general nonjudgmental working alliance. For example, we might suggest to a woman, "Isn't it interesting that you are a competent, assertive person in your relationship with your co-workers, even your boss, but you feel inadequate and dependent around your husband." And to her husband we might suggest, "Others seem to experience you as easygoing and generous, and yet you feel resentful about sharing time with your wife." With periodic reminders and examples, couples begin to see that the relationship currently has as much, if not more, power over them than they have over the relationship.

A relationship can be described in many ways. In sexually troubled relationships, there are often problems with flexibility or adaptability, with cohesion or the regulation of distance and closeness, and with commitment. Giving the relationship a diagnosis, sometimes with an explanation to the couple as to what the diagnosis means, can be an useful first step in shifting away from an individual problem focus.

Other important theoretical elements to consider include *homeostasis*, the system's self-regulating process that maintains stability; *morphogenesis*, the capacity to change and adapt; and *circularity* or circular causality, meaning that a change in one element influences the other elements.

The above general principles can be incorporated into a systems perspective of sexual dysfunction. The following is an outline of a theoretical model presented in greater detail elsewhere (Verhulst & Heiman, 1988). In sexual problems, different types of interactions are exchanged between the two people involved. One level, *symbolic interactions*, refers to the exchange of words, ideas, symbolic gestures, and other representational cognitive features. This symbolic level needs to be considered as abstracted and detached from the affective tone of speech. A simple example is that two people need to come from a similar enough cultural background for each to have a similar interpretation of such symbols as presenting flowers, making eye contact, and even use of the word "marriage." These are not issues of agreement but issues of shared understanding of meaning.

A second level, *affect-regulated* interactions, is the focus on the interacting expressions and perceptions of affect, exclusive of the symbolic level just described. Affect-regulated interactions are coordinated by the affective states of the participants and are expressed through autonomic responses, movements, postures, facial expressions, gestures, and the affective component of speech. Affect-regulated interactions predominate in sexual interactions because of sexuality's emphasis on desire, arousal, and nonverbal communication. In an earlier paper, Verhulst and Heiman (1979) described four different types of "affect-regulated interactions" that can steer a couple toward or away from a sexual context of meaning: attachment, exploratory, territorial, and ranking-order interactions. Attachment interactions focus on establishing, preserving, and intensifying the affiliative bond between individuals. Exploratory interactions focus on familiarity through sensory contact. Territorial interactions focus on the acquisition, management, and defense of ownership over material and psychological possessions. Ranking-order interactions focus on the acquisition and defense of social position and status, with dominance and submission issues often the visible evidence. Affect regulation patterns can both enhance and detract from sexual interactions.

A third level of interactions are *sensate exchanges*, referring to the sensory pattern, neurophysiological responses, and motor reflexes that each partner elicits from the other. Masters and Johnson's (1970) work was particularly aimed at coordinating the sensate stimulation while decreasing physiological anxiety and the influences of affective and symbolic interactions.

The above three levels—symbolic, affective, and sensate—can function somewhat independently but also are constantly interacting with each other within each individual. Additionally, they comprise subsystems. Each level requires some type of interactional fit between individuals or there will not be a connection on that level.

Therapeutic Applications

The therapist uses systemic theory as a process tool to formulate the problem in interactional terms rather than as a technique-specific intervention medium. The therapist will notice interactional patterns according to his or her own sensitivities, those sensitivities being constructed from past experiences. For example, when a couple comes in complaining of nonorgasmic sex, one therapist may focus more on the issues of territoriality, whereas another may focus on intimacy. The patterns the therapist notices must overlap with the patient's experience. Otherwise the therapist only treats his or her own image of the problem or, in effect, treats the therapist. The overlap between therapist and patient has been called "resonance" or "intersection" by Elkaim (1986) and also "interactional fit" by Verhulst and Heiman (1988). Because there are many simultaneous interactional patterns that can be the focus of a couple's interaction, there can be many therapeutic roads to follow. The therapist's role is usually an active and directive one in which exercises may be suggested in or out of the session.

In most cases, a systemic approach will emphasize that the patient is the sexual relationship in order to decrease the individual focus and to increase the involvement of both partners in possible solutions. The therapist may need to question why a given person is the symptom carrier—what especially within the relationship helps to maintain this person in the chosen role?

There is not enough written about the systems approach to treatment of sexual problems to estimate therapy length and success. In general, therapists from this perspective aim toward brief rather than long-term treatment and emphasize the integration of treatment interventions and treatment vacations of several months (e.g., Heiman, 1986; Sanders, 1988).

Other Treatments

Other treatments of orgasm dysfunction have had variable successes. Pharmacotherapy with bupropion hydrochloride has not proven effective at increasing specific sexual behaviors (Crenshaw, Goldberg, & Stern, 1987). Renshaw (1980) cautions that 30% of the improvement from drug treatments may be due to placebo effect. Sex education and bibliotherapy have shown promising results. For example, Kilmann et al. (1983) found significant increases in orgasmic frequency and decreases of sexual anxiety in secondary anorgasmia after 4 hours of sex education in 1 week. Similar findings occurred for Jankovich and Miller (1978), who reported that seven of 17 primary anorgasmic females had orgasm in the week following an audiovisual presentation designed to educate health care providers. The content included anatomy and physiology of sexual response and a film on intercourse. Hahn (1982) found that videos on masturbation coupled with a programmed manual were sufficient for increasing orgasm and improving body image. Minimal therapist contract appears to be effective in conjunction with self-help manuals that outline exercises for women to try on their own (Tripet Dodge, Glasgow, & O'Neill, 1982; Morokoff & LoPiccolo, 1986). For a motivated primary anorgasmic woman who does not have major conflicts in her primary relationship, reading appears to be an adequate intervention. Finally, hypnotherapy used adjunctively to sex therapy has been reported to be useful for individuals and couples. Hypnosis can uncover buried material, as the hypnoanalytic approach proposed, or it can be a vehicle for allowing people to experience themselves differently (Araoz, 1982; Beigel, 1972; Cheek, 1976; Stewart, 1986).

INTEGRATED THEORY AND PRACTICE

When actually faced with the complaint of inhibited orgasm, how does the therapist combine the theoretical and empirical information already discussed? Although there is no formula, there are important elements that require attention during assessment and treatment.

Assessment: Elements and Issues

It is crucial and revealing to track closely what happens in the first 15 to 30 minutes of the first visit (we recommend videotaping if at all possible, especially if a couple is present). During this period, the person or couple should do most of the talking. Both content and context are important. In terms of content, it is important to pay attention to how the couple or individual presents the initial description of the problem. "I don't like sex," "I find sex humiliating," "My wife doesn't enjoy sex," "He thinks I should have an orgasm," are useful entrees into how the lack of orgasm is experienced by the woman and her partner. Their thoughts on the problem's origins and maintenance as well as their ideas on how connected or disconnected sex is to other aspects of their lives are all important. Contextual factors draw attention to certain elements. For example, the structure of the first therapeutic session communicates several messages. Does the woman come without a partner because she does not have one, does not want one, does not want her partner to know, or has more than one partner?

The affect (individual and relationship) surrounding the expression of the problem is also important. Common affects are sadness, self-denigration, anger or irritability, anxiety, and depression. An apparent lack of affect or detachment is very frequent in nonorgasmic women, who often seem somewhat removed from their search for this unknown entity that they have been missing. The therapist also develops an initial sense of the relationship's emotional climate: tense, relaxed, full of territorial and ranking-order interactions, resentment, or hostility. One also draws from the nonverbal messages, including posture, mannerisms, eye contact, verbal–nonverbal contradictions, and the general energy level of the couple. Nonverbal categories can help reveal conflicts and fears over and above the words expressed about the problem.

In terms of content the therapist first needs a carefully detailed problem description. Both partners should be evaluated in terms of level and frequency of desire, arousal, orgasm, and the degree of satisfaction (see Schover, Friedman, Weiler, Heiman, & LoPiccolo, 1983, for further details). A woman who gets aroused but is not orgasmic will usually need a different therapeutic intervention than the woman who is never aroused. In addition to the above categories, one must ask whether pain in sex occurs or has occurred. As a natural lead-in to more historical material, it is important to know whether the sexual symptoms are global or situational and whether they have been lifelong or are intermittent problems.

Therapists vary in the amount of time they devote to history taking. Masters and Johnson's (1970) sex histories lasted some 5 hours over 3 days and were very thorough but not very interactional. Some of the cognitive–behavioral and the systems (e.g., strategic family therapy) subgroups focus minimally on historical factors, believing that a current focus is essential if the past is not going to continue invading the present. Masters and Johnson accomplished the same goal by using an extensive, evocative history-taking session, culminating in a roundtable discussion with therapists and patients present. This effectively drew a line between the past(acknowledging the contribution of historical factors) and the present (doing sex-therapy exercises). A newer twist to history taking is the sexual genogram (Bergman & Hof, 1987) in which couples are taught the basics of making a genogram and then sent home to construct one including three generations of their family with an emphasis on sexual, gender, and intimacy issues across the different generations.

Although a detailed history taking is not absolutely essential, it has many valuable features, especially with anorgasmic women. If a partner exists, it usually makes good sense to include him for the history and treatment. Furthermore, it can be very informative to do a history in the presence of the partner—the reactions of both individuals to the material and process cannot be captured in individual interviews. We use assessment sessions to obtain content, as an opportunity to establish a therapeutic relationship, and to develop an understanding of the symbolic, affective, and sensory aspects of the problem. The content of the sex history varies (see Masters & Johnson, 1970; LoPiccolo & Heiman, 1978). Areas of special importance include formalized overt and covert treatment of sexuality and affection in the family of origin with special attention to the role of the parents toward each other and the children, early sexual experiences, adolescent development, losses, especially of early male and female figures, affects associated with sexual ideas and experiences, and degree of enjoyment of sensual experiences. Information is obtained concerning the parents' attitude towards sex and the perception of the parental relationship. A straightforward and nonthreatening approach is, "What did you learn about how men and women relate to each other from your parents' relationship?" Direct questions about past sexual and/or physical abuse and the degree of coercion throughout the sexual history are important. Given the prevalence of these events for women, combined with the cultural inhibitions against disclosing, patients often delay sharing this critical information, even when it is conscious memory, until treatment is advanced.

The therapist must assess whether the orgasm problem is secondary to a physical or biochemical disorder. Psychotropic medications have been reported to impair orgasmic function (Nurnberg & Levine, 1987; Pohl, 1983; Segraves, 1985). Monoamine oxidase inhibitors, used in the treatment of depression, have sexual dysfunction side effects more often than their well-know hypertensive side effects (Nurnberg & Levine, 1987). Decreasing the dosage has been effective in returning orgasmic capacity in some cases (Nurnberg & Levine, 1987). Tricyclic antidepressants inhibit orgasm because of their serotonergic effects on the adrenergic fibers of the sympathetic nervous system (Aldridge, 1982; Segraves, 1985). Cyproheptadine, a serotonergic receptor antagonist, has been used to reverse the inhibiting effects of antidepressants (Riley & Riley, 1986). Clomipramine, used to treat severe obsessive–compulsive disorders, is also an α-adrenergic blocking agent, preventing the sympathetic nervous system activation required for orgasm. In a blind comparison of clomipramine with placebo, 96% of the previously orgasmic patients developed anorgasmia (Monteiro, Nashirvani, Marks, & Lelliott, 1987). Quirk and Einarson (1982) effectively switched two clomipramine patients to desipramine and lowered the dose of the third, restoring orgasmic function. Current medications should be checked to see if their onset coincides with the sexual problem. Use of prescription as well as nonprescription drugs and alcohol should be assessed, as any drug that affects the vascular or central nervous system may affect sexual functioning. A dosage or class change may be possible.

Back problems or nerve damage problems can interfere with orgasm and should be considered in cases in which the woman has noticed a change, can tolerate long periods of intensive vibratory stimulation, or has a lack of sensation of any kind in her genital area. Sexual dysfunction has been reported in the early stages of multiple sclerosis, often in conjunction with bladder and bowel problems (Lundberg, 1980), as well as in diabetic women who have peripheral neuropathy (Jensen, 1985). Abdominal surgeries that cut vascular tissue and lymph nodes may interfere with autonomic nervous system functioning and inhibit orgasm (Wise, 1983). Hysterectomy with or without oophorectomy has been reported to inhibit the experience of orgasm in 33–46% of women who undergo the procedure (Zussman, Zussman, Sumley, & Bjornson, 1981). Additionally, some women have decreased orgasmic response during pregnancy and post-partum (Ryding, 1984).

An evaluation of current depression is also important. Undiagnosed depression may be behind the presenting symptom of infrequent orgasm in a woman, expecially if she reports low sexual desire as well. Seasonal depression may also require diagnosis, although sexual symptoms have rarely been reported with this disorder (Rosenthal & Wehr, 1987). Women are less likely than men to present a sexual complaint masking a clinical depression because of sex differences in acknowledging depressive symptoms. Many women with orgasmic problems have subclinical depressive symptoms (e.g., low self-esteem and sleeping and appetite problems).

In the early phase of treatment, it is important to listen with questions rather than to commit to a particular explanation about the problem and its solutions. Even in the course of assigning homework, the attitude is more experimental and probing than confirmatory. This does not mean that the therapist is passive and uncertain; rather she or he continuously tests hypotheses instead of interpreting and explaining.

With this in mind, an important job of the clinician is to study with the clients why the symptom makes sense, and what function it has on an individual and interactional level. Understanding the function of the sexual symptoms is critical in determining therapeutic interventions and managing therapeutic impasses. A natural place to begin is to ask women what having orgasms means to them. For example, "What would it mean if you had no more orgasm difficulties?" Reactions to this question are varied: "I would feel powerful," "I would be vulnerable," "I would be close to my partner," "Extremely sexual." Usually these meanings are conflicted—desired and feared, sought and avoided—by both the woman and her partner. A couple who believes that the woman's orgasms will make them feel closer may be singing silent praise to the symptom bearer who does them both the service of preventing closeness. The symptom bearer is an important and valuable role. For example, a patient responded to the question about her reaction to having the orgasm problem resolved with the comment, "Well, then Paula would be *the* relationship." This was an important remark from a 39-year-old single woman involved with a female lover 2,000 miles away and for whom being in a committed relationship signaled the beginning of the end of her life. For this patient, in some sense being orgasmic was being connected to death, a not infrequent association for patients.

An assignment we frequently give after the first session, particularly when the problem seems entrenched, is to think about what the problem does for the couple. It is a good sign if the couple can come up with a response. The symptom then stops being the enemy and, instead, heralds the beginning of a solution.

The therapist's role is to listen to what the person says or cannot remember, omits, glosses over, or emphasizes in order to help frame or reframe the picture into one that helps explain why the sexual problem exists and has served a protective function. To a woman whose view of orgasm is loss of control and whose family background is explosively physically violent and alcoholic, we might begin the therapy by agreeing that it makes sense not to ever have orgasms, especially around others. This hypothesis would be proposed to the couple. A therapeutic issue then becomes whether orgasm can mean something besides loss of control.

The power of past patterns is sometimes more striking when each partner hears the other discuss earlier events. Interactional patterns and themes begin to surface, and therapists can begin to weave an initial systems understanding of the problem with the couple. We have recently seen two couples in whom the partners experienced childhood and adult sexual abuse. Lack of sex was the primary issue, with lack of female orgasm being a secondary concern. A therapeutic dilemma in certain cases of abuse is whether to see each person individually, which might make it possible to obtain more information but could leave the therapist vulnerable to inclusion in the systemic proclivity to keep sexual secrets or repress them. One solution is to meet partners separately but to tell each person that the purpose of the sessions is to find another way besides secrets and forgetting to protect each of them. The first session often ends with an urging to accept the wisdom of the ways things are and a suggestion that things can also safely be different.

Standardized assessment can also be useful. We include formalized assessment routinely: the Spanier Dyadic Adjustment Scale (Spanier, 1976), which examines relationship factors including consensus, satisfaction, cohesion, and affectional expression; a medical history form; the Brief Symptom Inventory (BSI) (Derogatis, 1977), which assesses psychiatric symptoms; the Life Experiences Survey—Abridged & Revised (adapted from Sarason,

Johnson, & Siegel, 1978); and a sexual history form (Heiman & LoPiccolo, 1983; LoPiccolo et al., 1985), which asks about specific sexual behaviors.

Treatment: Elements and Issues

Treating inhibited orgasm initially requires a decision of format: Would this woman or couple benefit most from an individual, couple, or group setting? The outcome data are not very helpful in making this decision. If the woman has an ongoing partner, especially a spouse, no current affairs, and no history of sexual or physical abuse, it is likely she will benefit from couple's therapy, especially if her desire is to have orgasms with that partner. Women-only groups are valuable if the woman is anorgasmic, without a partner, and focused on orgasm as the goal. Women in tentative relationships, hopeless marriages, with a history of abusive relationships, may benefit from individual treatment, at least for a period of time.

Symbolic Issues

The initial symbolic issue to explore is the meaning of the orgasm for the woman and her partner. The woman might say "Our sexual relationship would be more complete if my orgasm were part of it," whereas her partner's response might be, "If she had orgasms, our marriage would be perfect." The woman in this situation may find it difficult to begin to change if it means that (1) she is the only obstacle between their current situation and a "perfect" relationship, and (2) he will not acknowledge the problems that she experiences in the relationship after she becomes orgasmic. To understand the couple's images of orgasm, one often asks about images of relationships, sexual behaviors, and having children. The therapeutic task is to use this material to help understand, on a symbolic level, why orgasm must be difficult. Assignments can complement this process as we will show shortly.

Affect

Many anorgasmic women do not feel that their body belongs to them. Or, if they do have a sense of ownership, their body image is so negative that they wish their bodies would belong to somebody else. This issue can take many forms. For example, women may report that they find their bodies ugly and their genitals disgusting. They may try to make their bodies "look better." However, since appearance standards are derived from social norms, conforming to these norms implies that society is at least co-owner of women's bodies. Alternatively women may report feeling nothing when their body, expecially their genitals, is touched. These examples of disconnectedness are also examples of historical and current territorial themes. The woman may feel that any partner who touches her touches something she does not like, cannot feel, and/or does not own. This gives the partner ownership with a sense of burden and responsibility when sex does not go well. How crucial is a sense of bodily ownership to orgasmic responsivity? No one knows. It depends on what is missing from the woman's sense of self when she is involved in a relationship. Some sense of ownership over her own body does seem to be important for the woman whose orgasm evades her. It seems especially useful as a healing approach for women with histories of abuse—those women who have had experiences of having their bodies invaded territorially. The masturbation program (LoPiccolo & Lobitz, 1972; Hieman & LoPiccolo, 1988) was used successfully for many women as a means for women to claim their bodies and sexual sensations. It is difficult to share what does not feel like yours to give in the first place.

Ranking-order interactions commonly present in the form of "I want to have orgasm for my partner," or "I do everything I can to try to please her so that she will get aroused." The message is that one person is in charge of trying to get the interaction to move in a particular direction. This is not necessarily a problem, as all kinds of status hierarchies are successfully used by couples, including those in which one person dominates the other. However, with a sexual problem such as inhibited orgasm, one person's steering the other to obtain orgasm rarely works. A man recently reported that he was constantly trying different forms of stimulation in order to get his wife closer to orgasm. As a result, he was irritated, she was distracted, and each felt inept. Using sensate focus as a medium, the therapist had the couple focus on the touching he enjoyed giving (rather than touching they thought would get her aroused) and on her initiating tender caressing if she felt pressured. The ranking-order interaction was thus corrected with an exploratory–attachment interaction that helped to resexualize the couple's experience.

Sensate Exchanges

Women and their partners often have difficulty facilitating and moderating arousal and are unable to communicate about the stimulation they want during the sexual activity. Many women do not know what is arousing or are committed to a restricted arousal pattern. Often partners feel out of tune with each other. For example, the male may ejaculate too quickly. Greater sensate exchange for the woman thus can overstimulate the male, increasing the nonorgasmic woman's sense of being left behind. The interaction will need to be slowed down, perhaps by excluding ejaculation for a while or introducing attachment interaction patterns such as nongenital tender stroking.

There are other sensate patterns, however. Recently, we saw a woman who was having an affair for the past 2 years with a man she had decided not to "commit to" because of a clash in values. Ann was a 34-year-old divorced nurse with one daughter. She had been raised in an authoritarian

Calvinist family. Although orgasmic in masturbation, she never had experienced an orgasm with a partner. Her masturbation pattern began as a young girl, when she would urinate as part of her masturbation ritual. She no longer urinated during masturbation, although she did occasionally urinate with her boyfriend during high arousal. For her, urination was connected with "total relaxation." Her sensate exchange pattern was in tune with her boyfriend, even to the point of "letting go." However, orgasm was not the result. She enjoyed sex with her boyfriend more than masturbating. Her experience of the difference between masturbation (and here we can see an interaction with the symbolic and the affective levels) was that masturbation was connected to what she called her erotic, pornographic, genital center. It was not connected to what she called her "heart center."

The major effort of four sessions of therapy was (1) to appreciate her current pattern, as it allowed her both to enjoy mutual sex and to sequester orgasm, which was her most private but value-conflicted area within her relationship with a partner of conflicting values; and (2) to let her read *Becoming Orgasmic* as preparation for eventual merging of orgasm and partner sex. Interestingly, Ann left therapy feeling good about herself although not orgasmic with her partner. Ann is an example of someone whose sensate exchange pattern reflected difficulties in the symbolic–affective interaction level with respect to sex and her relationship with her boyfriend.

CASE EXAMPLES

We have selected two cases that differ in several respects including the presence or absence of a partner in the therapy sessions, amount of attention given to the historical material, and the degree of change in the presenting symptom. Both cases have successful and unsuccessful elements, and both cases involve some degree of change.

Case 1. Carole: The Unconscious Orgasm

Session 1

Background. Carole was a 61-year-old woman, married for 34 years, with two daughters in their early 30s. Her husband was semiretired. Carole was a writer and had published several books. She was tall and slim and looked younger than her age. Carole had given up on making her marriage work. After a steadily decreasing sexual frequency early in their marriage, her husband had stopped having sex with her when she was 35. He told her it was "animalistic." On the last occasion she initiated sexual contact, he had said, "Get away from me. I'll have a heart attack." He had no history of cardiovascular problems. Carole remained in the marriage initially because of the children and more recently because of financial repercussions. She felt her husband had been depressed for years. One daughter had made two serious suicide attempts. The other daughter worked as a deep-sea diver.

Carole, an only child, grew up in a physically abusive family setting. Her father seriously beat her mother, leaving her with cuts, black eyes, and bruises. He was physically abusive with Carole, and he once threw her down a flight of stairs. After 8 years, her mother divorced her father. Life was not easy. Carole remembered when her mother had to cut up a wooden chair in order to have firewood to burn. Her mother never remarried and often spoke ill of men, saying such things as "Never let them touch you" and "They only want one thing."

The patient began a 2-year affair in her late 30s. As it was winding down, at age 40, she reported having had her first orgasm, which began while she was asleep and continued as she became fully awake, with "waves" of feelings. This was her only reported orgasmic pattern at the time she entered therapy; it occurred approximately once a week. In her current affair, with a married family friend, she did become very aroused. Asked how she experienced sexual arousal, she described it as feelings between her chest and her belly. Her breasts were not sensitive, and her genitals (which she misheard three times as "gentle") were "not very noticeable."

A turning point in her life was a rape that occurred when she was 46. The rapist was a construction worker whom she had seen the day before the rape. He came to her door during the day, forced her into a room, and raped her from the rear. She thought he was going to kill her; yet at the end of the rape, with him still behind her, she kissed his gloved hand. The rapist was picked up the next day in the neighborhood. The man had previous theft and molestation convictions, and he was sent to prison. The patient stated, "I sent him to prison for 5 years." Twelve years after this incident, Carole, who had subsequently moved to another state, received a call to testify in a rape–murder case involving the same man who had raped her. There were distinct parallels in the incidents that were 12 years apart. The murdered woman lived within two blocks of Carole's previous residence; she also had the same first name Carole. Another conviction occurred. Over the years, Carole retained a continual sense of having, "sent him [the rapist] away," as if it were her act more than his that put him in prison.

The therapist asked her in what sense she felt guilty about "sentencing this man." Carole related it to feeling responsible for driving her father away when she was six, in spite of his abusiveness. She remarked that issues with her father may also be related to her inability to leave her husband.

Carole had also experienced multiple medical problems, including a brain tumor at age 21, three knee surgeries, and thyroid problems. She sporadically used medications for anxiety, sleep, and pain when she began therapy. Previously, she had briefly taken antidepressants without much benefit. She had not discussed the rape with her psychiatrist.

On the Spanier Dyadic Adjustment Scale, Carole obtained a score (50) far below the mean for divorced couples. She scored near the mean for psychiatric outpatients on the hostility and depression scales of the BSI.

Therapeutic Response. One of the striking aspects about Carole's situation was the fact that she offered orgasm as the symptom she wished to change. It appeared that the orgasm problem was both a meaningful and somewhat safe message that she might want new ways to manage her memories and terrors. The future held little promise. Her marriage seemed dead. She faced another imminent knee surgery, which symbolized the theme of "no power but full responsibility" over a body that others do painful things to (the rapist, the medical profession) or withhold pleasurable things from (her husband). Thus, several paradoxical issues became immediately clear: Carole's sexual pattern was perfect for someone with a history of missing, unpredictable, denying, or aggressive male figures—solitary orgasms and enjoyable sex within an affair. A shift in orgasm capacity might not be the isolated change that Carole seemed to be asking for. An agreement was made to explore whether there were ways for her orgasmic pattern to broaden. It was agreed that conscious solo orgasms would be the first goal.

The therapist-patient interaction seemed disjointed during the first session. Carole talked quickly and skittishly, darting among subjects as if too nervous to land. Little affect was apparent as Carole discussed her life. Empathy on the part of the therapist increased Carole's tendency to change the topic or offer a quick explanation. Carole seemed to want something to happen quickly, and the therapist felt powerless to move quickly.

Sessions 2–6 over the Next 4 Months

Carole began Session 2 by wandering a bit before giving the therapist two of her books of short stories, books that recorded her reactions to the rape. The session was spent discussing the impact of the three important men in her life: the rapist, to whom she felt somewhat wedded, with their destinies permanently entwined; her father, who had abused and abandoned her and whom she felt some responsibility for "driving away"; and her current lover, whom she never felt certain of seeing again each time they met. Carole felt her father was the most critical person in her life. Her last visit with him as a child occurred when she was 8, after her parents had divorced. She returned home from her visit disheveled and crying but did not know why. There was no evidence of sexual abuse. She did not see him again until she was in her 20s, just before she had surgery for a brain tumor suspected to be cancerous. She was not expected to recover fully.

Two levels of therapy were focused on: the symbolic level in sessions (the meaning of orgasm, trust issues with men) and the sensate experiences outside of sessions (self-touching, arousal stimulation). The therapist monitored how the affective level intertwined in both contexts. The affective level seemed to infuse Carole's writing but was missing from her sensate experiences. When asked what having an orgasm with her lover might mean, Carole said "vulnerability, the openness to be hurt." Based on the rationale that expanding orgasm opportunities was her territory and within her control, Carole was asked to read several chapters of *Becoming Orgasmic* (Heiman & LoPiccolo, 1988), and to try as many of the experiences suggested as possible. She was told not to use a vibrator because of the distance she already experienced from her body, especially her genitals.

In Session 3, the therapist discussed Carole's writing. The therapist noted that Carole's writing had no anger directed toward the rapist; she responded, "No, it's just sadness." When pressed as to how she dealt with anger and fear, she could not say. She seemed to connect violence with anger and thus could not easily recognize her own anger. However, she was quite hostile toward her husband for his lack of sensitivity and support about the rape and throughout her life with him.

Carole could not say why she needed to keep writing about the rape. The therapist suggested that doing so gave the experience back to her, as something she could create, mold, control, and even put in its place. Carole neither accepted nor rejected this possibility and seemed to feel accused of writing too much on the topic. Continued homework with *Becoming Orgasmic* focused on developing conscious fantasy and noticing small arousal differences.

During the session, Carole recalled that when she was about 5 she was thrown down the steps by her father, an incident her mother confirmed, apparently because Carole had gone to her parents' room and had opened the bedroom door.

In Session 4, Carole became impatient about her slow progress in reaching orgasm and mentioned that one of her daughters had the same orgasmic pattern. She also talked about her mother's "veiled" sexuality. The theme was that women's sexuality must be very private in this family.

In Session 5, Carole complained that her mind wandered during the exercises in *Becoming Orgasmic*. 'What should I think about?" The session also wandered. She mentioned that her father, a magazine journalist, had not wanted her mother to go out of the house or to be photographed by others. She mentioned that one of her daughters was scheduled to come to Seattle next month from Montana for treatment of psychiatric symptoms. Carole said she liked male genitals; they seemed "right, more complete, not missing anything," but she could not go further with associations to this. She was experiencing knee pain. Of her male lover she said, "I'm going to keep this one," but she constantly felt, "This is the last time; he will disappear now." Orgasm was again discussed as vulnerability: "I must protect myself from another loss." The therapist assigned her 20 minutes of meditation a week on the following sentence: "Could anything else other than lack of orgasm protect me?" After asking this question of herself, it was suggested she observe any physical signals, images, or words that came to her attention. These signs did not have to make any sense; she just needed to notice them.

Session 6, 1 month later, focused on her relationship with the men at an East Coast maximum-security prison to which she had been invited for a reading of her work. During her reading, she almost cried when she felt she was not being accepted, understood, heard, or liked. She asked, "Did I do this to be liked?" She had been getting more aroused during self-stimulation but had been interrupted several times by noises and phone calls. She did not attempt the meditation assignment, nor did she feel she had made any progress. The therapist encouraged practice on *Becoming Orgasmic* exercises and suggested she try a vibrator.

Session 7

This session followed 6 weeks after the prior session with two intervening cancellations. Carole discussed her daughter's 2-week psychiatric hospitalization. In a family interview, the psychiatrist called Carole the family "enabler." She seemed pleased with the recognition.

Several new revelations occurred in this session. Carole mentioned her lover's name for the first time. He had said, "I guess we are getting committed." She had a "strange feeling" in response and could not discuss the emotional side but could say, "Committed means you're going to work on something" and alluded to feeling trapped. She also spoke of her husband in more depth. She disliked him but felt (indeed) trapped and sorry about his situation. He had had two suicide attempts in college after a broken affair and had been "depressed, drinking, and dependent" throughout most of their marriage. Carole had tried to save him.

Late in the session Carole mentioned that she had not had her usual orgasmic pattern while her daughter had been hospitalized, but the pattern had returned. In addition, she was twice able to bring on an orgasm in the morning, while awake, by clenching her thighs, although not using a vibrator (it didn't work), or touching herself. This was her first "conscious" orgasm. She described it as a "faded black and white photo" compared to her usual "full color" orgasm. In session, she suddenly remembered having conscious orgasms while petting in the car of a boyfriend when she was about 22.

The therapist noted that it may have been important for her not to enjoy a conscious orgasm, to keep that experience "dim." The therapist suggested that she had done a great deal and might need to keep things at the right speed for her. It was agreed to take a break and perhaps meet again after her knee surgery.

Commentary

Carole's situation and the therapy process have been described in some detail in order to allow a greater appreciation of the complexity of treatment. Other theoretical orientations might have followed different threads and have constructed a different treatment for Carole. The psychodynamic material is rich and obvious. Similarly, her traumatic conditioning with men, sex, and violence easily fits a cognitive–behavioral perspective.

Therapy focused on Carole's accepting and studying the experience of her body as being "unsafe" and uncared for by men as well as exploring the theme of "lost men." Carole believed that men were driven away, not by their bad or even vicious behavior, but by women. In her life, relationships between men and women were marked by physical and emotional distance.

Outside of therapy, the primary focus was on the sensate exercises, the conscious noticing of her body's arousal. Her adeptness at metaphor and symbol made her an evocative and interesting writer, yet writing was no longer therapeutically productive in that her work "rewrote" and controlled the experience too much. It seemed as if her writing served as a defense, controlling the overwhelming emotions (anxiety, guilt, fear) she had about her prior traumatic experiences. It is possible that her lack of orgasms with men was a parallel effort to control emotional response.

Was this case a success? The lack of orgasm symptom improved, and Carole "remembered" and revealed to the therapist that she had had such experiences before. These memories broke new ground and opened up a new sphere of consciousness, one that was somewhat anxiety provoking and that may have changed the meaning of orgasms for her.

Carole made increased efforts to examine several issues of great emotional importance. At Session 7, she was pleased with her effort, although rather disappointed with the "black and white" orgasm outcome. She also felt she needed a break. She was writing more about her mother. She was still not at ease with herself and the world, although she was strong and capable. She had very little support except for contacts made through her writing. She remained convinced that she had been responsible for the loss and violence of her father. Carole said she would return. We suspect not, at least for a while. She began to find that nonsexual feelings about her husband and her lover were also disturbing her. At this point, we would rate Carole's case as symptomatically improved and deserving of more therapeutic work if and when she becomes ready.

Case 2. Erica and Dan: Sex as a Psychosomatic Sign of a Troubled Relationship

Sessions 1 and 2 (2 Months Apart)

Erica and Dan came to the first session presenting Erica's disinterest in sex as the problem (only in Session 3 did the orgasm problem get mentioned).

Erica cried frequently. She wanted to want sex and did not see how she could feel the way she used to feel with Dan. Dan arrived 40 minutes late for the session. They were an attractive couple; he appeared younger than she did. Both had attended college, and currently worked at sales jobs.

Background. Erica was 35; Dan was 38. They had been married for 7 years and had 2½-year-old twin daughters. Their family histories were quite different. Erica was the youngest, with two older brothers, in a Catholic family. Her father had died of a heart attack when she was 12; her mother died slowly from breast cancer when Erica was 14–17. Her mother's death was extremely hard on Erica, as she had had to take care of her mother, including the administration of morphine shots. Erica married her first boyfriend when she was 20. He told her, and she believed him, that she had to get married because "no one would want a nonvirgin." The marriage ended after 6 months because he physically assaulted her and sexually coerced her when he drank.

Dan's parents were alcoholic and had been divorced for many years. Dan also had a younger sister who recently quit her job after 17 years of work. The family suspected she had a drug problem. No further history was gathered from Dan until later sessions.

The sexual problem had existed for about 3½ years, just preceding the pregnancy. Their overt reaction to the sexual problem was quite different. When asked what would happen if the sexual problem did not improve, Erica was tearful and predicted the loss of the relationship. Dan minimized its effects, saying "I'll accept it," although he acknowledged feelings of rejection around sexual issues.

Several relationship issues were raised by Erica: (1) Dan was "always" late; (2) knowing his mother was still an alcoholic, Dan still drank one to three drinks per day with drunken nights about once a month; and (3) her lack of sexual interest was related to what she perceived as Dan's constant criticism of her.

Although Dan listened to all the problems Erica mentioned, he did not react directly and therefore did not seem highly invested in any of them. His primary focus was wanting sex between them to improve.

On the standardized forms, the Dyadic Adjustment Scale showed Erica to be far more unhappy (77 vs. 108) and within the divorced range compared to Dan's being in the happily married range. Erica's BSI was elevated on the hostility scale; Dan had no elevations. Erica reported orgasm less than 25% of the time during any type of partner sex. She never masturbated. She desired sex less than once a month.

At the end of the second session, the therapist focused on territoriality and ranking-order interactions as the areas of tension. Everything belonged to everyone, and therefore, neither Erica nor Dan felt they had anything, that is, time or space, for themselves. Erica could only be defensive, not assertive, whereas Dan was frequently assertive, which Erica took to be domineering. Hence, their communication never went anywhere: Dan kept pressing his points, and Erica eventually gave in. Each interpreted a "difference of opinion" in different ways. Erica thought Dan was calling her "wrong," and Dan thought that she should just be able to see his point.

The therapist thought that these issues needed to be addressed along with the sexual ones. It was clear that the territorial and ranking-order interactions were preventing Erica's sexual feelings from emerging.

The home exercises suggested after session 2 were (1) to decide who owns what in the household space and what is common territory and (2) to permit themselves to be affectionate without sex for the following 2 weeks. This session closed with a request for each to tell the therapist what they appreciated in the other. They did this with ease and revealed complementary features about what they valued in each other. The therapist mentioned that they had chosen one another for their differences; yet it was those differences that were now causing distress.

Sessions 3–7

Session 3, a month later, began with Erica saying, "I'm no better, he is." The territoriality assignment had been done, but the affection-without-sex assignment had been avoided. Erica expressed resentment and anger toward Dan, apparently borne out of the style they had of disagreeing. A disagreement would typically begin to feel like a standoff that would always result in Erica giving in by saying, "All right, I'm wrong. I must be wrong." She was almost phobic about expressing anger. When asked about her early experience with anger and fights, she had only one clear memory of a bad fight between her parents. When she was 10, Erica's drunken father had hit her mother. Her mother said that she would leave him if he ever did that again. Erica watched, frightened, feeling trapped, and feeling as if she could not breathe—the same feeling she experienced with her husband when he started to pressure her to see his viewpoint.

The session focused on communication styles and conflicts. Major disagreements occurred over money. Dan saw her as spending money too easily; she saw him as frugal. Money to him meant security; to her, it meant freedom. The difference between them seemed greater because of the couple's general discomfort about differences and their communication pattern. Family-of-origin issues around money were discussed to make sense of their current styles. The communication issue was also worked with, attending to basic communications techniques of "I" statements, reflection, and verification. Sending clear messages without expecting agreement was practiced. Interestingly, it was in this session that Erica revealed several secrets her family had kept. One was that her father had had a previous wife who had died in childbirth, something that Erica learned by overhearing an aunt talking at a family gathering. When Erica had asked her mother about this, her mother denied that Erica's father had ever previously been married. In addition, Erica had had a sister who had died in infancy before Erica was born. No one discussed this in her family.

The assignments given were (1) to foster affection without sex and be affectionate only when each desired or felt good toward the other and (2) to do one activity (1–2 hours) alone, apart from one another, and to discuss it.

The couple returned for Session 4 without having done the assignments but were getting along better. There had been a family crisis. Dan's sister had given birth, and his mother had been on a drinking binge ever since. They both felt uneasy about not trying the assignments. Dan also asked Erica why she had not read a marriage advice book she had bought several months earlier. The therapist asked her if it would make a difference if she could choose one chapter to read. Erica reported having that same feeling of not being able to breathe, "like the air is being sucked out of me," that she had experienced periodically while fighting with Dan, when she felt pressured to give in to him. She denied being angry. The therapist thanked her and asked her if she could keep a close watch on whenever she had the sensation and let the therapist and Dan know. The message was that it was an important signal about her feelings, and we could not ignore it.

The assignment was to talk together for 30 minutes a week and simply note how it went and to spend 1½ hours together doing something both enjoyed.

Dan and Erica returned 3 weeks later for Session 5, with Erica having requested an emergency appointment. Erica was concerned about Dan's drinking. He periodically drank too much and returned late, and then arguments would ensue during which he would make insulting remarks to her. There was an attempt to clarify what the most troublesome aspects of Dan's drinking were for both of them. The therapist pushed for Dan to have some time away from responsibility without drinking, since Dan used alcohol partly to escape time. It was agreed that Dan would let Erica know when he needed some hours "off," and during that period, he would keep his limit to three beers. Both felt that this would work well. During the discussion, the communication was direct and less encumbered with attack and defense statements. No assignments were given, but it was suggested that the couple complete prior assignments or develop their own. They planned two practical chores that each would take responsibility for but would also require the other's assistance.

In Session 6, 3 weeks later, the couple reported less tension and success in following the drinking rules. Erica said that Dan was more aware and considerate. During the session, the theme of feeling appreciated was raised, and different ways of expressing appreciation were mentioned. Again, the assignment of (1) talking and (2) touching without sex was made, this time limiting each to 40 minutes per week.

In Session 7, the couple reported they had spent 10 to 20 minutes talking together each week but had not made any sexual progress. Erica said that she had felt sexual feelings for Dan while they were out dancing and had wanted to go to a motel, but they had to get back to the babysitter. The therapist interpreted this as a sign that Erica did have sexual feelings, which was reassuring even if the feelings had not been acted on.

Erica then expressed her conflicts about motherhood, being married, and being sexual. She could not imagine being both sexually active and being a good mother conjointly. She feared that if her attitude did not change she would end up being divorced and without her children.

Erica's patterns of sensitivity were discussed. For example, she consistently called herself "bad." This pattern of negative self-appraisal was discussed in terms of what she wanted to transmit to her children. She recalled that one of her twins often said, indeed, as frequently as Erica herself did, "I'm a bad girl, I'm stupid," which bothered Erica very much. A second pattern for Erica involved her tendency to concentrate on how much further she had to go rather than on small, positive changes. Relatedly, little mistakes were seen as big failures. A third issue was that Erica never thought of sex positively. Whenever she thought about sex, she chastised herself for not engaging in it more often and then felt guilty. Several suggestions were made as to how she could change this: They involved using a stop technique and developing brief 10-second positive sexual fantasies that she could also stop. Finally, the couple's "different styles" were addressed. By using examples the couple brought in of Dan's neatness and Erica's disorganization, the therapist developed a cross-cultural metaphor to help them to appreciate the positive and negative aspects in both patterns and their combined value for their children. A trip to Canada was planned. The therapist advised against sex. The next session was to be the last because of lapsing insurance.

Session 8

The couple had sex in Canada and said it was "okay." They had had a wonderful week. Dan was worried that Erica would not want to continue growing sexually; he said she did not seem interested in sex. He pushed a bit for more therapy for Erica. The therapist suggested that they both take some time to get used to the changes that had already occurred. It had been helpful to know that reducing the hostility and irritability in the relationship made it more pleasant. However, things were still changing, and it would take a while for Erica's sexual feelings to be expressed. They would not return to the old pattern, but additional change might be slow. The couple felt good about themselves as they left although Dan was a bit worried. Some posttherapy suggestive statements were made about the importance of appreciating small improvements, as well as the importance of practicing positive feelings about sexuality.

Commentary

This couple is in many ways a familiar one. Money was a central issue in the relationship, since they both worked, were therefore both tired, and had almost no free time. Both partners were devoted to their children, to the exclusion of themselves as a couple or one another individually. Parenting had replaced sexual interactions for them as ways of caring. Their mode of staying involved with one another consisted of focusing on each other's style and pushing the other to see or do small tasks in his or her own way in order to feel a sense of having some impact on the other's life, if only by some form of nettling. Territorial and ranking-order interactions predominated; attachment interactions were minimal. Investment in and coming to treatment began to be a type of attachment interaction that devoted time and energy to them.

How does one revive sexual satisfaction in a marital relationship? What role does lack of orgasm play in this particular constellation of circumstances? In this case there were a number of choices. The focus on marital issues first was centered around the predominant interaction problems seen in the therapy session. It became clear that the couple's inability to process and communicate around "differences" was increasing their tension. Erica's smoldering anger precluded sexual interactions. Decreasing the marital interaction problem was a necessary but not sufficient condition for improvement of the sexual problems. Although sex did not behaviorally improve to the couple's satisfaction, Erica was able to acknowledge increasingly positive sexual feelings in the last two sessions. It appeared that an inroad had been made, but it would still take effort to increase the sexual interactions between the two.

What about orgasm? Erica had never presented this as a core problem for herself. Dan thought she might enjoy sex more if she had orgasms. The therapist took a neutral position but let them know that if this was a central concern there were therapies available. With some couples, it might make sense to attempt to achieve the orgasm first. But for Erica, this would be one more thing she had to do for Dan, one more ranking order she had to submit to as well as a territorial interaction. That complex pattern of reacting had to be addressed first; otherwise her orgasm would have felt to her as if it belonged to Dan.

As we reviewed this case, we wondered why the therapist did not confront the couple more on all of their incompleted assignments, even the apparently low-pressure discussion assignments. Unlike their use in classical sex therapy, assignments here were used primarily as an assessment probe. Had they been done, the couple would have been given further assignments; when they were not done, the reasons, both emotional and practical, were explored. Also, prescribing assignments that are not done can still lead to revelations and changes for the couple. Eventually Dan complained that Erica was not really committing herself to change. At that point, it became clear that Dan was as frightened of change as Erica, since he had not done his assignment either. Nevertheless, both of them devised other ways to change. Most notable were Erica's reduction in negative self-thoughts and talk, her interpretation of Dan's communication, and Dan's treatment of alcohol and time. In addition, the theme of different roles in their relationship was handled with greater ease. It was particularly important for Erica and Dan to focus on differences because it was precisely their complementarity that had attracted them to one another initially. It would have been a mistake to try to reduce their differences as opposed to help them communicate more clearly and effectively about them.

In terms of success of therapy, we can say that there was no change in the major symptoms (her desire, her orgasm), although Erica's sexual dissatisfaction did decrease slightly. She expressed an increase in sexual feelings. Dan did not change sexually. In fact, he managed to escape much scrutiny regarding his role in the sexual problem. The relationship became more satisfactory to both partners, and they now felt as though they were different players but on the same team. After about 3 months of integrating these changes, another 7 to 10 sessions of therapy focusing on both of their sexual feelings, behaviors, and interactions would be appropriate.

CONCLUDING COMMENTS

Orgasm problems in women can be examined from a framework that uses a systems approach to integrate cognitive behavioral and psychodynamic elements. The result is a flexible and comprehensive approach. This is particularly useful when dealing with complex cases such as situational anorgasmia.

Applying a systemic perspective is not always easy. Readily available techniques do not currently exist, although certain therapists have developed specific models for developing assignments in families or couples (e.g., Elkaim, 1986; Selvini-Palazzoli and Viaro, 1988). Another difficulty for the systems therapist is that most people automatically think of sex as a quality "in" the individual rather than a dynamic "between" the couple or even created by interactions across a lifetime. It is a particular challenge not to abandon the systems approach when faced with a person who has a more unusual sexual pattern—therapeutic frameworks have usually reacted by labeling the person rather than the interactional fit.

Difficulties notwithstanding, systemic thinking has several specific strengths when applied to human sexual patterns: (1) it supports a view of sexuality as a socially constructed quality subject to lifelong revision; (2) it has a capacity to routinely reduce or diffuse the blame individuals experience about the sexual problem; and, (3) it clearly can integrate sexuality with other interactional patterns ongoing in the relationship. Although it is not a theory proposing perfect solutions, systemic thinking offers a perspective from which to develop and implement new solutions.

REFERENCES

Aldridge, S. A. (1982). Drug induced sexual dysfunction. *Clinical Pharmacy, 1*, 141–147.

Araoz, D. L. (1982). *Hypnosis and sex therapy.* New York: Brunner/Mazel.

Arentewicz, G., & Schmidt, G. (1983). *The treatment of sexual disorders.* New York: Basic Books.

Bancroft, J. (1983). *Human sexuality and its problems.* New York: Churchill Livingstone.

Barbach, L. G. (1974). Group treatment of preorgasmic women. *Journal of Sex and Marital Therapy, 1*(2), 139–145.

Barlow, D. H. (1986). Causes of sexual dysfunction: The role of anxiety and cognitive interference. *Journal of Consulting and Clinical Psychology, 54*(2), 140–148.

Beigel, H. G. (1972). The use of hypnosis in female sexual anesthesia. *Journal of the American Society of Psychosomatic Dentistry and Medicine, 19*(1), 4–14.

Bergman, E. M., & Hof, L. (1987). The sexual genogram—assessing family-of-origin factors in the treatment of sexual dysfunction. In G. R. Weeks & L. Hof (Eds.), *Integrating sex and marital therapy* (pp. 37–56). New York: Brunnel/Mazel.

Brody, H. (1973). The systems view of man: Implications for medicine, science, and ethics. *Perspectives in Biology and Medicine, 17*(3), 71–92.

Carney, A., Bancroft, J., & Mathews, A. (1978). Combination of hormonal and psychological treatment for female sexual unresponsiveness: A comparative study. *British Journal of Psychiatry, 132*, 339–346.

Chambliss, D. L., Sultan, F. E., Stern, T. E., O'Neill, C., Garrison, S., & Jackson, A. (1984). Effect of pubococcygeal exercises on coital orgasm in women. *Journal of Consulting and Clinical Psychology, 52*(1), 114–118.

Cheek, D. B. (1976). Short-term hypnotherapy for frigidity using exploration of early life attitudes. *American Journal of Clinical Hypnosis, 19*(1), 20–27.

Cohen, S. J. (1978). Sexual interviewing, evaluation, and therapy: Psychoanalytic emphasis on the use of sexual fantasy. *Archives of Sexual Behavior, 7*(3), 229–241.

Cotten-Huston, A. L., & Wheeler, K. A. (1983). Preorgasmic group treatment: Assertiveness, marital adjustment and sexual function in women. *Journal of Sex and Marital Therapy, 9*(4), 296–302.

Crenshaw, T. L., Goldberg, J. P., & Stern, W. C. (1987). Pharmacologic modification of psychosexual dysfunction. *Journal of Sex and Marital Therapy, 13*(4), 239–253.

DeAmicis, L. A., Goldberg, D. C., LoPiccolo, J., Friedman, J., & Davies, L. (1986). Three-year follow-up of couples evaluated for sexual dysfunction. *Journal of Sexual and Marital Therapy, 12*(1), 215–228.

Derogatis, L. (1977). *SCL-90-R: Administration, scoring and procedures manual.* Baltimore: Clinical Psychometrics Research.

Dickes, R., & Strauss, D. (1979). Countertransference as a factor in premature termination of apparently successful cases. *Journal of Sex and Marital Therapy, 5*(1), 22–27.

Elkaim, M. (1986). A systematic approach to couple therapy. *Family Process*, 25(1), 35–42.

Ellis, A. (1975). The rational–emotive approach to sex therapy. *Counseling Psychologist*, 5, 14–21.

Engel, G. L. (1980). The clinical application of the biopsychosocial model. *American Journal of Psychiatry*, 137(5), 535–544.

Ersner-Hershfield, R., & Kopel, S. (1979). Group treatment of preorgasmic women: Evaluation of partner involvement and spacing of sessions. *Journal of Consulting and Clinical Psychology*, 47(4), 750–759.

Everaerd, W., & Dekker, J. (1982). Treatment of secondary orgasmic dysfunction: A comparison of systematic desensitization and sex therapy. *Behaviour Research and Therapy*, 20, 269–274.

Faulk, M. (1973). "Frigidity": A critical review. *Archives of Sexual Behavior*, 2(3), 257–265.

Fichten, C. S., Libman, E., & Brender, W. (1986). Measurement of therapy outcome and maintenance of gains in the behavioral treatment of secondary orgasmic dysfunction. *Journal of Sex and Marital Therapy*, 12(1), 22–34.

Fisher, S. (1973). *The female orgasm*. New York: Basic Books.

Frances, A., & Kaplan, H. S. (1983). A case of inhibited orgasm: Psychodynamic or sex therapy? *Hospital and Community Psychiatry*, 34(10), 903–917.

Frank, E., Anderson, A., & Rubinstein, D. (1978). Frequency of sexual dysfunction in "normal" couples. *New England Journal of Medicine*, 299, 111–115.

Frenken, J. (1976). *Afkeer van seksualiteit*. Deventer: Van Loghum Slaterus (English summary: pp. 219–225).

Garde, K., & Lunde, I. (1980). Female sexual behavior. A study in a random sample of 40-year-old women. *Maturitas*, 2, 225–240.

Gebhard, P. H. (1978). Factors in marital orgasm. In J. LoPiccolo & L. LoPiccolo (Eds.), *Handbook of sex therapy* (pp. 167–174). New York: Plenum.

Hahn, M. M. (1982). Vicarious treatment of primary sexual dysfunction. *Dissertation Abstracts International*, 43, 249B.

Heiman, J. (1986). Treating sexually distressed marital relationships. In N. S. Jacobson & A. S. Gurman (Eds.), *Clinical handbook of marital therapy* (pp. 361–384). New York: Guilford Press.

Heiman, J. R., & LoPiccolo, J. (1983). Clinical outcome of sex therapy: Effects of daily v. weekly treatment. *Archives of General Psychiatry*, 40, 443–449.

Heiman, J. R., & LoPiccolo, J. (1988). *Becoming orgasmic: A sexual and personal growth program for women* (revised and expanded edition). New York: Prentice-Hall.

Heiman, J. R., LoPiccolo, L., & LoPiccolo, J. (1976). *Becoming orgasmic: A sexual growth program for women*. Englewood Cliffs, NJ: Prentice-Hall.

Hoch, Z., Safir, M. R., Peres, Y., & Sopher, J. (1981). An evaluation of sexual performance—comparison between sexually dysfunctional and functional couples. *Journal of Sex and Marital Therapy*, 7(3), 195–206.

Hunt, M. (1974). *Sexual behavior in the 70s*. Chicago: Playboy Press.

Jankovich, R., & Miller, P. R. (1978). Response of women with primary orgasmic dysfunction to audiovisual education. *Journal of Sex and Marital Therapy*, 4(1), 16–19.

Jensen, S. B. (1985). Sexual dysfunction in younger insulin-treated diabetic females. *Diabetes and Metabolism*, 11, 278–282.

Jordan, J. (1985). *Empathy and self boundaries. Work in progress, 16.* Wellesley, MA: Stone Centers Working Papers Series.

Kaplan, H. S. (1974). *The new sex therapy.* New York: Brunner/Mazel.

Kernberg, O. F. (1987). Projection and projective identification: Developmental and clinical aspects. *Journal of the American Psychoanalytic Association, 35*(4), 795–819.

Kilmann, P. R., Boland, J. P., Sjortus, S. P., Davidson, E., & Caid, C. (1986). Perspectives of sex therapy outcome: A survey of AASECT providers. *Journal of Sex and Marital Therapy, 12*(2), 116–138.

Kilmann, P. R., Mills, K. H., Bella, B., Caid, C., Davidson, E., Drose, G., & Wanlass, R. (1983). The effects of sex education on women with secondary orgasmic dysfunction. *Journal of Sex and Marital Therapy, 9*(1), 79–87.

Kilmann, P. R., Mills, K. H., Caid, C., Davidson, E., Bella, B., Milan, R., Drose, G., Boland, J., Follingstad, D., Montgomery, B., & Wanlass, R. (1986). Treatment of secondary orgasmic dysfunction: An outcome study. *Archives of Sexual Behavior, 15*(3), 211–229.

Kinsey, A. C., Pomeroy, W., Martin, C., & Gebhard, P. (1953). *Sexual behavior in the human female.* Philadelphia: W. B. Saunders.

Kline-Graber, G., & Graber, B. (1978). Diagnosis and treatment procedures of pubococcygeal deficiencies in women. In J. LoPiccolo & L. LoPiccolo (Eds.), *Handbook of sex therapy* (pp. 227–240). New York: Plenum.

Kuriansky, J. B., & Sharpe, L. (1981). Clinical and research implications of the evaluation of women's group therapy for anorgasmia: A review. *Journal of Sex and Marital Therapy, 7*(4), 268–277.

Kuriansky, J. B., Sharpe, L., & O'Connor, D. (1982). The treatment of anorgasmia: Long-term effectiveness of a short term behavioral group therapy. *Journal of Sex and Marital Therapy, 8*(1), 29–43.

Leiblum, S. R., & Ersner-Hershfield, R. (1977). Sexual enhancement group for dysfunctional women: An evaluation. *Journal of Sex and Marital Therapy, 3*(2), 139–151.

Levay, A., Weissberg, J., & Blaustein, A. (1976). Concurrent sex therapy and psychoanalytic psychotherapy by separate therapists: Effectiveness and implications. *Psychiatry, 39,* 355–363.

Libman, E., Fichten, C. S., Brender, W., Burstein, R., Cohen, J., & Binik, Y. B. (1984). A comparison of three therapeutic formats in the treatment of secondary orgasmic dysfunction. *Journal of Sex and Marital Therapy, 10*(3), 147–159.

LoPiccolo, L., & Heiman, J. (1978). Sexual assessment and history interview. In J. LoPiccolo & L. LoPiccolo (Eds.), *Handbook of sex therapy* (pp. 103–112). New York: Plenum.

LoPiccolo, J., Heiman, J., Hogan, D., & Roberts, C. (1985). Effectiveness of single therapists versus co-therapy teams in sex therapy. *Journal of Consulting and Clinical Psychology, 53,* 287–294.

LoPiccolo, J., & Lobitz, W. C. (1972). The role of masturbation in the treatment of orgasmic dysfunction. *Archives of Sexual Behavior, 2*(2), 163–171.

LoPiccolo, J., & LoPiccolo, L. (Eds.). (1978). *Handbook of sex therapy.* New York: Plenum.

LoPiccolo, J., & Stock, W. E. (1986). Treatment of sexual dysfunction. *Journal of Consulting and Clinical Psychology, 54*(2), 158–167.

Lundberg, P. O. (1980). Sexual dysfunction in female patients with multiple sclerosis. *International Rehabilitation Medicine, 3*(1), 32–34.

Masters, W., & Johnson, V. (1966). *Human sexual response.* Boston: Little, Brown.

Masters, W., & Johnson, V. (1970). *Human sexual inadequacy.* Boston: Little, Brown.

Messe, M. R., & Geer, J. H. (1985). Voluntary vaginal musculature contractions as an enhancer of sexual arousal. *Archives of Sexual Behavior, 14*(1), 13–28.

Miller, J. G. (1978). *Living systems.* New York: McGraw-Hill.

Mills, K. H., & Kilmann, P. R. (1982). Group treatment of sexual dysfunctions: A methodological review of the outcome literature. *Journal of Sex and Marital Therapy, 8*(4), 259–296.

Monteiro, W. O., Noshirvani, H. F., Marks, I. M., & Lelliott, P. T. (1987). Anorgasmia from clomipramine in obsessive–compulsive disorder, a controlled trial. *British Journal of Psychiatry, 151,* 107–112.

Morokoff, P. (1978). Determinants of female orgasm. In J. LoPiccolo & L. LoPiccolo (Eds.), *Handbook of sex therapy* (pp. 147–166). New York: Plenum.

Morokoff, P. J., & LoPiccolo, J. L. (1986). A comparative evaluation of minimal therapist contact and 15 session treatment for female orgasmic dysfunction. *Journal of Consulting and Clinical Psychology, 54*(3), 294–300.

Nairne, K. D., & Hemsley, D. R. (1983). The use of directed masturbation training in the treatment of primary anorgasmia. *British Journal of Clinical Psychology, 22,* 283–294.

Norris, J., & Feldman-Summers, S. (1981). Factors related to the psychological impacts of rape on the victim. *Journal of Abnormal Psychology, 90,* 562–567.

Nurnberg, H. G., & Levine, P. E. (1987). Spontaneous remission of MAO-I-induced anorgasmia. *American Journal of Psychiatry, 144*(6), 805–807.

Obler, M. (1982). A comparison of hypnoanalytic/behavior modification technique and a cotherapist-type treatment with primary orgasmic dysfunctional females: Some preliminary results. *Journal of Sex Research, 18*(4), 331–345.

Pohl, R. (1983). Anorgasmia caused by MAOIs. *American Journal of Psychiatry, 140*(4), 510.

Quirk, K. C., & Einarson, T. R. (1982). Sexual dysfunction and clomipramine. *Canadian Journal of Psychiatry, 27,* 228–231.

Renshaw, D. C. (1980). Pharmacotherapy and female sexuality. *Modern Problems of Pharmacopsychiatry, 15,* 145–157.

Riely, A. J., & Riley, E. J. (1978). A controlled study to evaluate directed masturbation in the management of primary orgasmic failure in women. *British Journal of Psychiatry, 135,* 404–409.

Riley, A. J., & Riley, E. J. (1986). Cyproheptadine and antidepressant-induced anorgasmia. *British Journal of Psychiatry, 148,* 217–218.

Robinson, P. (1970). *The modernization of sex.* New York: Harper & Row.

Rosen, I. (1982). The psychoanalytic approach. *British Journal of Psychiatry, 140,* 85–93.

Rosenthal, N. E., & Wehr, T. A. (1987). Seasaonal affective disorders. *Psychiatric Annals, 17,* 670–674.

Roughan, P. A., & Kunst, L. (1981). Do pelvic floor exercises really improve orgasmic potential? *Journal of Sex and Marital Therapy, 7*(3), 223–229.

Ryding, E.-L. (1984). Sexuality during and after pregnancy. *Acta Obstetrica et Gynecologica Scandinavica, 63,* 679–682.

Sanders, G. (1988). Of cybernetics and sexuality. *Family Therapy Networker, 12*(2), 38–42.

Sarason, I. G., Johnson, J. H., & Siegel, J. M. (1978). Assessing the impact of life changes: Development of the Life Experiences Survey. *Journal of Consulting and Clinical Psychology, 46*, 932–946.

Scharff, D. E., & Scharff, J. S. (1987). Objects relations theory and family therapy. In D. E. Scharff & J. S. Sharff (Eds.), *Object relations family therapy* (pp. 43–64). Northvale, NJ: Jason Aronson.

Schneidman, B., & McGuire, L. (1976). Group therapy for nonorgasmic women: Two age levels. *Archives of Sexual Behavior, 5*(3), 239–247.

Schover, L. R., Friedman, J. M., Weiler, S. J., Heiman, J. R., & LoPiccolo, J. (1982). Multiaxial problem-oriented system for sexual dysfunctions. *Archives of General Psychiatry, 39*, 614–619.

Segraves, R. T. (1985). Female orgasm and psychiatric drugs. *Journal of Sex Education and Therapy, 11*(2), 69–71.

Segraves, R. T. (1986). Implications of the behavioral sex therapies for psychoanalytic theory and practice: Intrapsychic sequelae of symptom removal in the patient and spouse. *Journal of the American Academy of Psychoanalysts, 14*(4), 485–493.

Selvini-Palazzoli, M., & Viaro, M. (1988). The anorectic process in the family: A six-stage model as a guide for individual therapy. *Family Process, 27*, 129–148.

Spanier, G. B. (1976). Measuring dyadic adjustment: New scales for assessing quality of marriage and similar dyads. *Journal of Marriage and Family Therapy, 38*(7), 15–28.

Spence, S. H. (1985). Group versus individual treatment of primary and secondary female orgasmic dysfunction. *Behaviour Research and Therapy, 23*(5), 539–548.

Stewart, D. A. (1986). Hypnoanalysis and orgasmic dysfunction. *International Journal of Psychosomatics, 33*(3), 21–22.

Stiver, I. (1984). The meanings of dependency in female–male relationships. *Work in progress*, 83-07. Wellesley, MA: Stone Center for Developmental Services and Studies.

Surrey, J. (1983). Self-in-relation: A theory of women's development. *Work in progress*. Wellesley, MA: Stone Centers Working Papers Series.

Tripet Dodge, L. J., Glasgow, R. E., & O'Neill, H. K. (1982). Bibliotherapy in the treatment of female orgasmic dysfunction. *Journal of Consulting and Clinical Psychology, 50*(3), 442–443.

Trudel, G., & Saint-Laurent, S. (1983). A comparison between the effects of Kegel's exercises and a combination of sexual awareness, relaxation and breathing on situational orgasmic dysfunction in women. *Journal of Sex and Marital Therapy, 9*(3), 204–209.

Tsai, M., Feldman-Summers, S., & Edgar, M. (1979). Childhood molestation: Variables related to differential impact on psychosexual functioning in adult women. *Journal of Abnormal Psychology, 88*, 404–414.

Verhulst, J., & Heiman, J. R. (1979). An interactional approach to sexual dysfunction. *American Journal of Family Therapy, 7*, 19–36.

Verhulst, J., & Heiman, J. R. (1988). A systems perspective on sexual desire. In S. R. Leiblum & R. C. Rosen (Eds.), *Sexual desire disorders* (pp. 243–267). New York: Guilford Press.

von Bertalanffy, L. (1968). *General systems theory*. New York: Brazillier.

Wakefield, J. C. (1987). The semantics of success: Do masturbation exercises lead to partner orgasm? *Journal of Sex and Marital Therapy, 13*(1), 3–14.

Wallace, D. H., & Barbach, L. G. (1974). Preorgasmic group treatment. *Journal of Sex and Marital Therapy, 1*(2), 146–154.

Weeks, G. R. (1987). Systematic treatment of inhibited sexual desire. In G. R. Weeks & L. Hof (Eds.), *Integrating sex and marital therapy* (pp. 183–201). New York: Brunner/Mazel.

Weeks, G. R., & Hof, L. (Eds.). (1987). *Integrating sex and marital therapy*. New York: Brunner/Mazel.

Weiss, L., & Meadow, R. (1983). Group treatment for female sexual dysfunction. *Arizona Medicine, 9*, 626–628.

Weissberg, J. H., & Levay, A. N. (1981). The role of resistance in sex therapy. *Journal of Sex and Marital Therapy, 7*(2), 125–130.

Whitaker, C. A., & Keith, D. V. (1981). Symbolic experiential family therapy. In A. S. Gurman & D. P. Kniskern (Eds.), *Handbook of family therapy* (pp. 187–225). New York: Brunner/Mazel.

Whitehead, A., Mathews, A., & Kellett, J. (1981, July). *Psychological and hormonal factors in the treatment of sexually unresponsive women*. Paper presented at the annual meeting of the British Association for Behavioral Psychotherapy, Bristol.

Wise, T. N. (1983). Sexually dysfunction in the medically ill. *Psychosomatics, 24*(9), 787–805.

Zussman, L., Zussman, S., Sunley, R., & Bjornson, E. (1981). Sexual response after hysterectomy–oophorectomy: Recent studies and reconsideration of psychogenesis. *American Journal of Obstetrics and Gynecology, 140*(7), 725–729.

4

Dyspareunia: A Multimodal Psychotherapeutic Perspective

ARNOLD A. LAZARUS

The complaint of dyspareunia (pain or discomfort during intercourse) is most often viewed as a female dysfunction associated with specific organic or medical etiology (e.g., vaginitis, endometriosis). Certainly, such physical causes are common and need to be carefully evaluated in each case. There are many instances, however, in which no specific organic factor can be identified, and psychotherapy or sex therapy becomes the treatment of choice. Although dyspareunia is far more common in women, the problem is occasionally reported by male clients and may similarly be associated with either physical or psychogenic determinants.

Lazarus, the orginator of multimodal therapy, identifies three general classes of factors that may contribute to psychological dyspareunia: developmental, traumatic, and relational. He notes that almost 50% of cases seen in recent years have presented with unsatisfactory or unhappy relationships. It is the attempt to perform sexually without accompanying desire or arousal, according to Lazarus, that results in dyspareunia in many instances. Given the complexity of psychological factors that may contribute to this problem, the author recommends a comprehensive, multimodal approach to assessment in each case. Although each of the seven areas addressed in this approach can be relevant, it is particularly important to assess the role of sensation and imagery. Lazarus also cautions against assuming a simple one-to-one relationship between specific etiological factors and current dysfunction. In fact, several detailed case studies are presented to illustrate the complex interplay between psychological determinants and symptoms of dyspareunia.

A wide variety of treatment interventions can be applied to this condition. Although traditional behavior therapists relied heavily on systematic desensitization, Lazarus recommends this technique only when the problem is associated with a circumscribed sexual phobia. Instead, he makes extensive use of imagery techniques, rational–emotive cognitive restructuring, and relationship interventions. Traditional sex therapy techniques, such as sensate focus, are also recommended in some instances. In addition. Lazarus raises the provocative question of whether sexual mismatches between mates may be a prime consideration in psychogenic dyspareunia rather than specific traumatic or developmental factors. And if so, what are the ethical and treatment implications?

Arnold A. Lazarus, Ph.D., is Distinguished Professor of Psychology in the Graduate School of Applied and Professional Psychology, Rutgers University. He is a prolific and engaging writer and author of many books in clinical psychology, including Marital Myths (1985) and Mind Power (1988).

Dyspareunia—painful intercourse or coital discomfort—is often a medical problem. (*Dys-* is a prefix used to signify ill, difficult, bad, painful, or disordered. *Pareunia* is derived from the Greek and refers to "lying beside in bed." Freely translated it means "badly mated.") In general, gynecological and urological disorders must be ruled out or fully treated before psychotherapeutic measures are applied. In some instances, however, nothing more than the routine use of a lubricating cream or jelly is indicated.

The varieties of dyspareunia are many, ranging from mild postcoital genital irritation to searing, ripping, fulminating pain during intromission or intercourse. In women, common organic reasons for coital discomfort include infections of the vagina, lower urinary tract, cervix, or fallopian tubes (caused, for example, by trichomonas, coliform bacteria, or mycotic organisms), endometriosis, surgical scar tissue (e.g., following episiotomy), ovarian cysts, and tumors. Pain during sexual activity may also signify an anatomic defect (e.g., retroverted uterus) and congenital or structural abnormalities. Postmenopausal dyspareunia is fairly common and is clearly attributable to estrogen deprivation in most cases. Estrogen-replacement therapy (ERT) alleviates the symptoms associated with lack of vaginal lubrication. In this chapter, emphasis is on the treatment of "psychogenic dyspareunia"—that is, sexual pain or discomfort when organic causes have been ruled out or fully treated.

Usually, the complaint of painful intercourse is made by a woman, but men may also suffer from dyspareunia. Some males experience acute pain, often testicular and/or in the glans area of the penis, immediately after ejaculation. If there is infection in the prostate, the bladder, or the seminal vesicles, ejaculation may produce intense burning or itching sensations. Of course, any inflammation such as urethritis or prostatitis can render genital stimulation unpleasant or painful. Anatomic deformities of the penis, congenital or as the result of direct trauma, can occasion pain during sexual activity. Nevertheless, in the past 30 years, I have treated about four or five men for "functional dyspareunia," compared to dozens of women. Hence, this chapter is devoted to the latter.

Over 10 years ago, Abarbanel (1978) listed more than 100 diseases and disorders of the genitourinary tract and the reproductive organs that can produce dyspareunia. Thus, when a woman complains of persistent sexual discomfort, the first step is to try to exclude or mitigate organic pathology. Although psychological interventions may play a role regardless of the etiology, it is imperative that organic factors be excluded or that competent medical consultants determine that they cannot be remedied by somatic intervention. When physical disorders have been found absent or have been treated and pain is still present, primary psychological factors may then be considered. These fall into three main categories:

1. Developmental factors (e.g., an upbringing that invested sex with guilt and shame, religious taboos that aroused ambivalence and confusion, misinformation that engendered tension and anxiety).
2. Traumatic factors (e.g., rape or other sexual assaults, violent defloration, sexual abuse in childhood).
3. Relational factors (e.g., resentment and antagonistic feelings towards one's sexual partner, a lover's sexual clumsiness, insufficient foreplay and arousal, personal upsets and anxieties).

It is worth noting that in a few instances, the problem was largely a matter of situational factors (e.g., fears of being overheard, anxiety that children might walk into the room).

In reviewing my last 20 cases of female dyspareunia, I was curious to determine how many of these women attributed their sexual problems to developmental, traumatic, or relational factors. Three clients ascribed their problems to traumatic events (childhood molestation); five came from puritanical backgrounds that viewed sex in a pejorative light, investing it with guilt, sin, shame, and fear; three had a homosexual orientation while enduring heterosexual marriages. The remainder (almost 50%) were all in unhappy and unsatisfactory relationships. I wonder how my patient sample compares with dyspareunia sufferers at large. It would not surprise me if it were true that after ruling out organic factors, about half the women who suffer from dyspareunia are simply having sexual intercourse with the wrong man!

It is important to draw a distinction between those women who suffer from coital distress and who genuinely wish to overcome the problem and those who use real, imagined, or fabricated pain as a deliberate distance-creating device. In dysfunctional marriages, it is not uncommon for women to complain of pain during sex as an excuse to avoid frequent or further contact with their husbands. In these instances of *pseudodyspareunia*, the mainstay of therapy is to examine the viability of the marriage, to unravel the games, and to teach authenticity in place of passive–aggressive tactics (Fay, 1988).

Relatively little attention has been directed to the treatment of psychological dyspareunia (cf. Lazarus, 1980). Apart from scattered case histories, the literature on sex therapy and psychotherapy continues to gloss over numerous strategic and tactical procedures for treating this distressing condition. Perhaps such neglect is partly attributable to the fact that most problems of sexual dysfunction have not responded impressively to psychodynamic, Rogerian, or other conventional psychotherapies. Psychogenic dyspareunia, like many sexual dysfunctions, requires problem-focused, reeducative methods. Very few benefits are likely to accrue from focusing on intrapsychic forces. This does not imply a superficial, mechanical, or simplistic approach. The psychological treatment of dyspareunia calls for an appreciation of the impact of imagery and cognition, the network of interpersonal processes, and the associated range of affective, sensory, and behavioral responses. Hence, a multimodal approach will be advocated.

WHAT IS MULTIMODAL THERAPY?

Although numerous writers use the terms "multimodal," "multidimensional," "multiform," and "multifactorial" interchangeably, my use of *multimodal* has remained separate and distinctive since its introduction into the clinical literature (Lazarus, 1973). There are now scores of publications (books, monographs, articles, chapters, and reports) here and abroad, specifying that multimodal assessment places primary emphasis on a thorough and comprehensive assessment of behavior, affect, sensation, imagery, cognition, interpersonal relationships, and biological factors. The acronym BASIC IB is derived from the first letters of these seven discrete yet interactive modalities. By changing "B" to "D" for drug therapy (since most psychiatric interventions at this level call for neuroleptics, antidepressants, and anxiolytic agents), the convenient mnemonic BASIC I.D. emerges. (The "D" modality goes beyond drugs or pharmacological intervention and also includes nutrition, hygiene, exercise, and all physiological and pathological inputs.) What separates multimodal therapy from the many varieties of multifaceted and multidimensional orientations is the level of systematic attention devoted to each area of a client's BASIC I.D.

The multimodal emphasis is pluralistic. It is assumed that most clients are troubled by a multitude of specific problems that should be dealt with by a broad spectrum of specific treatments. Another assumption is that durable results are usually in direct proportion to the number of different modalities addressed, that lasting change calls for a variety of techniques, strategies, and modalities. Using the sevenfold multimodal framework as a template for a thorough problem-focused assessment, multimodal practitioners have developed several diagnostic instruments and procedural tactics. These are beyond the scope of this chapter, but the interested reader will find that a few selected references can provide most of the essential details (Brunell & Young, 1982; Kwee & Lazarus, 1986; Lazarus, 1986, 1987, 1989). For present purposes, it is sufficient to understand that multimodal therapy calls for a precise tailoring of the therapeutic climate to fit each client's personal needs and expectancies. The use of the Multimodal Life History Questionnaire (Lazarus, 1981/1989)[1] is one of the major means of achieving meaningful problem identification. This 12-page inventory addresses routine background information, followed by a "Modality Analysis of Current Problems" via behavior, affect, sensation, imagery, cognition, interpersonal relationships, and biological factors.

At the very least, a multimodal assessment would address the following issues:

1. *Behavior.* Are there deficits and shortcomings in sexual technique?
2. *Affect.* Is guilt, anger, fear, or shame a primary or contributary factor? Are feelings of love and physical attraction absent or present?
3. *Sensation.* Because dyspareunia presents as a sensory complaint, this modality requires a detailed initial assessment (see below).
4. *Imagery.* Are there intrusive images (negative mental pictures such as disapproving parents, being mutilated, or flashbacks to childhood humiliations) that disrupt sexual enjoyment? Is there a poor or distorted body image?
5. *Cognition.* Do negative self-statements, dysfunctional beliefs, and misinformation (e.g., this is sinful, I will be punished, I am not entitled to pleasure) play a role in undermining sexual participation and enjoyment?
6. *Interpersonal.* What is the personal climate between the partners in sexual and nonsexual settings? How do they communicate and relate specific sexual desires?
7. *Drugs (biological).* Is there evidence of improper hygiene? Is the client on any medication that tends to diminish vaginal lubrication? Has a physician ruled out organic pathology?

The sensory modality calls for special scrutiny in terms of the pain and discomfort—its location, type, frequency, intensity, and duration. Does the pain or discomfort occur before, during, or after arousal? Is the onset gradual or sudden? How often does it occur? Is the pain mild, moderate, or severe? Is the discomfort persistent or does it lessen at times? Is it related to coital position? Are there episodes of pain or "twinges" that are especially severe? If so, when and under what circumstances? Is most of the discomfort felt only at intromission? Does pain increase, remain the same, or decrease with deeper penetration? Is orgasm a trigger for pain? Is the discomfort always in the same place? Where exactly does it occur? Does a lubricant tend to reduce the discomfort?

[1]The Multimodal Life History Questionnaire is obtainable from Research Press, Box 3177, Champaign, IL 61821.

Dyspareunia is not a unitary or monosymptomatic problem. A woman whose coital pain stems from guilt and shame vis-à-vis all erotic stimuli is very different from someone with excessive performance anxieties. The subjective sensations of pain are personal and individual—they may arise from diverse objective factors. Consider a woman whose problems of dyspareunia were related to fears of pregnancy, compared to someone who had never experienced sexual discomfort prior to the AIDS epidemic. Evidence of a traumatic etiology calls for a different treatment process than would be the case with a couple in whom painful intercourse was a product of marital strife. A brief example should illustrate how a multimodal assessment brings significant features into clear focus.

MULTIMODAL FACTORS

One of my clients was firmly convinced that the pain she experienced during intercourse stemmed entirely from her fear of erotic sensations. She had been educated in a Catholic convent and attributed her problems to a misguided nun who had instilled the belief that "genital pleasures pave the way to hell." She had seen a psychiatrist who felt that she had fully rejected these ideas "intellectually," but that a "conditioned response" nevertheless persisted that signaled guilt and fear whenever she felt herself becoming aroused. After the Multimodal Life History Questionnaire had been administered and a Modality Profile of her BASIC I.D. had been completed, the simple-minded conditioned-reflex hypothesis gave way to a matrix of specific and interrelated problems:

1. *Behavior.* There was evidence of rigid, constricted, and sabotaging reactions in sexual and nonsexual settings. For example, she assiduously avoided all situations that might draw public attention to herself (crowds, restaurants, dinner parties, sports, games, and so forth), and she adamantly refused to use a lubricant to try and ease her sexual discomfort.

2. *Affect.* She tended to bottle up her feelings and keep them well under control, and admitted feeling "annoyed and frustrated much of the time."

3. *Sensation.* Dyspareunia was present during any form of penile insertion ("It is just very uncomfortable rather than truly painful"). Most of the discomfort centered around the labia minora and the vaginal outlet. She also reported feeling generally tense and suffered from frequent headaches. She was completely nonorgasmic. Dysmenorrhea also constituted a problem, and she was often bedridden during the first 8 hours of her menstruation.

4. *Imagery.* Loss of control was a central theme in this modality. She had memories of a film depicting inmates of a mental institution losing control during sexual (mainly masturbatory) frenzies.

5. *Cognition.* Perfectionism and a host of categorical imperatives ("shoulds" and "musts") tended to characterize much of her thinking.

6. *Interpersonal.* She tended to be more of a "taker" than a "giver." A girlish rather than a womanish quality rendered her uncomfortable in adult-to-adult interactions. Her husband seemed inclined toward paternalistic overprotection.

7. *Drugs (biological).* Medical examinations revealed no organic pathology except for a mild, labile, anxiety-related hypertension.

One cannot overstate the need for adequate assessment procedures. Catch-all terms—conditioned response, fear of losing control, passive-aggressive personality, narcissistic disorder—are too often used as central explanatory constructs. These labels need to be broken down into their component parts. If therapists want to achieve successful and durable outcomes, it is necessary to ferret out the subtle network of antecedent events, ongoing behaviors, and their consequences in each area of malfunction.

In the field of psychotherapy, it is too easy to leap to unfounded conclusions. The fallacy of arguing from a temporal sequence to a causal relationship is particularly widespread. Two events may coexist, be correlated, but they need not be causally connected. A case history may reveal that a patient with dyspareunia had experienced no discomfort prior to an extramarital relationship. To assume that there has to be a causal connection between the love affair and the subsequent dyspareunia is fallacious. Only a comprehensive inquiry will establish whether the extramarital liaison contributed substantially, moderately, or insignificantly to the development of later coital discomfort. If psychotherapists would remain extremely cautious and tentative about ascribing causes to various antecedent events, less biased and more accurate assessments might be forthcoming. Let us consider a case in point.

The Case of Mrs. J

Mrs. J, a 24-year-old woman, was married for 2 years. A bright, attractive, and vivacious law student, she had dated many men prior to marriage, but she was a virgin until her engagement. Sexual intercourse was always uncomfortable at best and often extremely painful. The pains were described as "pressure, at times a throbbing like a toothache, and sometimes a sort of cutting sensation as if something is tearing inside." She could not localize the discomfort, and lubricating jellies were of little help. She was prone to cystitis, but there were no other medical problems according to her gynecologist, who added that although her vagina was "small and tight," it was nevertheless within normal limits.

I met with Mrs. J and her husband, a young, hard-driving, and already successful accountant. He seemed to be a considerate and proficient lover, a fact that his wife confirmed. "We have a fabulous relationship," she stated, "but sex has never been good." Mrs. J sometimes climaxed with prolonged clitoral stimulation. "Even with a vibrator, it takes me about 15 minutes to come!" she complained.

Her history, however, was replete with psychological trauma and conflict. An only child, she was aware that her father "played around," and she witnessed bitter scenes between her parents, which eventually culminated in an acrimonious divorce when she was 10 years old. Her father had not contacted her in the ensuing 14 years, and she did not know if he was alive or dead. Her reaction to this abandonment involved a good deal of self-recrimination. She felt that she must have disappointed him in some fundamental way.

After the divorce, her mother had a succession of boyfriends, one of whom persuaded the patient to perform fellatio when she was 12 years old. She informed her mother, who blamed her and punished her for being too seductive. This incident was related with considerable emotion, a mixture of confusion, self-blame, and resentment toward her mother. In general, Mrs. J lacked adequate self-acceptance and self-worth. She was prone to guilt and far too ready for self-deprecation and self-negation.

What bearing did these specific factors have on her current sexual performance and lack of enjoyment? Theorists of many different persuasions could readily create a mosaic in which her dyspareunia would be an obvious manifestation of these background factors. In the absence of further data, I assumed that the psychic scars left by paternal abandonment, compounded by the father's own sexual indiscretions, had probably colored her own present sexual outlook. In addition, I theorized that the unsatisfactory mother–daughter relationship (poor modeling, ambivalent identification, unexpressed hostility) had also played a role. And she reported feeling "terrified when that man made me suck him." In attempting to account for her sexual dysfunction, I drew on theories that were not fanciful or farfetched. Yet, as shall be seen, none of the foregoing factors and events seemed especially relevant when more compelling information emerged.

Therapy was directed at a cognitive and affective re-evaluation of specific dysfunctional beliefs. I challenged her catastrophic self-talk, searched for benign hypotheses to account for some of the variance (e.g., "What other reason, apart from your own shortcomings and failures as a child and as a daughter, could have led your father to keep away from you?"), and pointed out several irrational and illogical conclusions. The affective modality was tackled mainly through an analysis of specific feelings surrounding each area of distress by means of desensitization: "Let's picture a scene going back in time. . . . You are about 7 or 8, and your parents are arguing. . . . Picture that scene vividly, relax, and try to feel calm and indifferent." We also used the empty-chair technique: "Imagine that those two chairs next to you are not empty but that your mother and father are sitting in them. Now I want you to try and really see them, imagine they are really there. . . . What do you want to say to either one or both of them?" The client also used imagery techniques wherein she pictured herself confronting her parents and expressing her feelings.

From time to time, Mrs. J's husband came to the sessions. He was supportive and sympathetic to our therapeutic endeavors, but he did ask to see me alone and confided that he had decided to have an affair with his receptionist. At one of our joint sessions he expressed impatience with the therapy. Atypically, Mrs. J erupted and directed unbridled anger at him, and a heated argument followed. This led me to explore the basic feelings between them much more closely, but Mrs. J insisted that apart from minor annoyances that sometimes flared into heated arguments the basic tenor of their relationship was one of love, caring, and mutual respect.

About 6 months later, after some 24 sessions, we had made considerable headway concerning Mrs. J's self-blame, self-confidence, and self-acceptance, but no improvement was evident in her sexual responses. Once or twice she reported feeling "less discomfort," but no sustained carryover ensued. On one occasion, a prolonged sensate-focus interaction followed by cunnilingus produced two orgasms within a few minutes of each other, but intromission was only "less painful" rather than pleasurable.

I began to question whether some medical disorder had been overlooked. The usual psychological factors associated with dyspareunia were not present—there were no religious conflicts, no apparent fears of rejection, no undue guilt, no heightened fear of pain or erotic stimuli, no specific fear of failure, no sexual myths or fallacies—and the patient had come to terms with many affect-laden issues out of her past. It was about this time that a perplexed Mrs. J confessed that she had gone to bed with one of her classmates, "a dynamic, Aryan-looking young man" for whom she had felt "a sneaking attraction" since first seeing him. "It really was on impulse," she explained. "We had kidded around for a couple of months, and lately he started coming on strong. . . . I just decided to go along with it out of curiosity." For the first time ever, she reported having experienced vigorous penile thrusting *without any pain or discomfort whatsoever*. During a "repeat performance" the following day, she claimed to have achieved "an intense orgasm."

It transpired that although Mrs. J loved her husband, she had never felt *physically* attracted to him, a fact that she had tended to downplay, ignore, and deny. During our initial assessment interview, she claimed to be "turned on to him." There was nothing about her husband's appearance that displeased her. She considered him "pleasant to look at, well built, masculine, and cuddly," but she had never experienced a "surge of excitement" or an autonomic thrill as was true in response to some other men. ("I guess deep down I've always known that there was a lack of chemistry, but I hated admitting it to myself or to anyone else. . . . I thought it might develop with time because I truly love him.") She ventured that because she was "small and tight inside," perhaps she had to be fully aroused in order to avoid discomfort.

At this juncture, therapy seemed to provide a crutch that enabled Mrs. J to experiment. She had sexual relations with the senior partner of a law firm where she had worked during the summer and enjoyed the experience without discomfort, but coitus with a different classmate proved unsatisfactory and painful. "I'm in touch with a definite pattern," Mrs. J now declared. "For me, sexual chemistry means a certain look that's difficult to put into words, but physically it seems that the guy must be tall and slimly built, with blue eyes and light-colored hair and skin. I'm just not the Burt Reynolds type." Her husband was relatively tall and slim, but his eyes were brown, and he had a medium complexion with dark hair.

Earlier in the therapy, I had asked her to conjure up erotic fantasies during sex to determine whether this would decrease coital discomfort, but she reported no success with this method. Since pursuing extramarital activities, however, she discovered that she was able to have pain-free intercourse with her husband "when I really get into imagining that he is somebody else." She, had been extremely careful to prevent her husband from discovering any of her affairs, and he, in turn, had been most discreet about his own extramarital activities.

Mrs. J and her husband continued seeing me for another 4 months. It became more and more obvious that they were in a deteriorating relationship. Approximately 2 years later, they divorced, and each remarried within 6 months. The patient reported that dyspareunia was no longer present.

Commentary

The case of Mrs. J raises many issues—procedural, professional, and ethical. But my reason for presenting this clinical vignette was mainly to emphasize how readily one may be misled into assuming that causal links exist when, in fact, only tenuous connections may be present. When Mrs. J described the type of man to whom she felt sexually attracted, my first question was, "Do you recall how your father looked and how he was built?" She remembered her father as "pleasant-looking, of average height and build with curly reddish–brown hair, and gray–green eyes, I think." But what conclusion could we draw if her father had been tall, slim, blond, and blue-eyed, or short, fat, and dark? It seems far too glib and fatuous to infer that she was embroiled in a secret search for a father figure or that there was some "reaction formation" at work!

Perhaps the most parsimonious explanation is that the patient's background rendered her deficient in self-esteem and failed to provide her with subjective security and a sense of autonomy. Consequently, her marriage choice was predicated more on matters of security, dependency, and protection than on attraction, male–female involvement, sexual compatibility, and mature emotional reciprocity. Thus, although the various antecedent events may have contributed indirectly to the dyspareunia per se, none of them could be regarded as specific causal agents. Was she incapable of marrying a nurturant man who would provide love and security, as well as sexual and erotic pleasures? Did her background predispose her to select a mate whom she found physically nonerotic, or was this aspect fortuitous? We have no answers for these questions, only speculations. But it is simplistic to conclude that Mrs. J's marital sexual discomfort was entirely a function of insufficient or inadequate sexual attraction or arousal. Whatever the case, the role of various antecedent events remains entirely speculative. Nevertheless, therapeutic progress ensued by dwelling on a variety of situational and specific problems rather than searching for underlying and cohesive causal themes. The therapy probably facilitated the eventual outcome—an amicable divorce and a successful second marriage.

During couples' therapy in general or sex therapy in particular, how should a therapist deal with disclosures of extramarital affairs? Although there are no hard and fast rules that pertain to all relationships, in most instances, it is a serious error to recommend that our clients make their dalliances known, that they confess and "come clean." Dire consequences can ensue (see Lazarus, 1985). If an extramarital liaison interferes with therapy, I will see the client individually and emphasize that unless or until he or she is genuinely committed to working on the marriage, therapy might best be discontinued. It is not the therapist's place to tell the other partner "the truth," nor should advice be given to the client to "own up." Confidences concerning an *affaire d'amour* are best kept extremely private.

AN EXAMPLE OF
COMPREHENSIVE PSYCHOTHERAPY

Multimodal assessment is predicated on the assumption that the more a person learns in therapy, the less likely he or she is to relapse afterward. This negates the search for a panacea or a single overriding therapeutic modality. To the extent that interactive problems in behavior, affect, sensation, imagery, cognition, interpersonal relationships, and biological functioning are systematically explored, the diagnostic process is likely to be thorough. And to the extent that therapeutic intervention remedies whatever deficits and maladaptive patterns emerge, treatment outcomes are likely to be positive and long-lasting. At the same time, "idiosyncratic perceptions" have to be considered. People do not respond to some *real* environment but rather to their *perceived* environment. The personalistic use of language, semantics, expectancies, and selective attention must be factored into the therapeutic process. The next case history addresses some of the foregoing points and also emphasizes the importance of "imagery" in assessment and therapy.

The Case of CS

CS, a 29-year-old married female computer programmer, experienced pain-ful intercourse on her honeymoon. Premarital sex with a former fiance had occasioned no difficulties. Her husband, however, for religious reasons, had refused to engage in sexual intercourse until after the wedding, although they had frequently indulged in mutual masturbation to orgasm. After the honeymoon, her discomfort during sexual intercourse grew more severe and prolonged ("Sometimes I would feel sore and sensitive for days after-wards!"), and over the next 2 years their sexual practices were limited only to oral–genital stimulation.

Gynecological and other medical examinations revealed no pathology, but an iatrogenic problem arose when a physician questioned her too pointedly about possible lesbian tendencies. She obsessed over the idea and finally consulted a psychiatrist who managed to reassure her and who also led her to conclude that her problems were not based on any generalized underlying hostility toward men. Nevertheless, the psychiatrist did pro-claim that she resented her husband for adopting complete premarital control by refusing to consummate their relationship before marriage ("It seems that I am punishing him now by refusing to let him enter my body").

CS and her husband were referred to a "sex clinic" where they were seen by a male and female co-therapy team who prescribed a graduated sensate focus (Masters & Johnson, 1970). Despite verbal disclaimers from the therapists, the couple experienced this treatment as an implicit demand to conform and perform, and they emerged feeling like "foolish failures." A family friend referred CS to me for a consultation.

Initially, there was a paucity of relevant information in each modality. The main behavior was coital avoidance; her affect included some anger, anxiety, and guilt; in the sensory mode, she alluded to sharp pains with each penile thrust; but as we explored imagery, a number of significant facts came to light.

> THERAPIST: I want you to close your eyes, relax, and imagine as vividly as you can that you and your husband are having intercourse and that you feel no pain. [It is often informative to begin with a picture of the avowed treatment goal.]
>
> CLIENT: Do I feel *anything*?
>
> THERAPIST: That's up to you.
>
> CLIENT: (*Closes her eyes for about 30 seconds*) I see it happening, and I feel nothing.
>
> THERAPIST: Now try to imagine that you do feel good sexual feelings. There's no discomfort but a very pleasant massaging and erotic pleasure.
>
> CLIENT: (*Opens her eyes after about 10 seconds*) No, I can't picture that. Right off, I got the idea "That's dangerous!" "Keep away!" I

can picture that with other men, but not with my husband. I can masturbate to images of being in bed with other men. . . . It's got something to do with my husband.

THERAPIST: How about imagining that you are not yet married to him. It is premarital sex you are having with him. Can you picture that and allow yourself to experience pleasant sexual feelings?

CLIENT: You want me to try that fantasy now?

THERAPIST: Would you mind?

CLIENT: Oh, no. I don't mind. (*Closes her eyes for about 30 seconds*) That's amazing! (*Opens her eyes*) That's really peculiar. I can do it. I can see it. It was really strange. I had no problem. . . . As long as we're not married it's all right.

THERAPIST: I wonder what there is about being married that makes such a tremendous difference?

CLIENT: I don't know. . . . Perhaps it's all connected to trust.

As we explored this issue more fully, an interesting superstition emerged, one that is at variance with a common cultural norm. Like many women, CS believed that men often leave after sexual seduction or "conquest." ("My mother would say that the way to keep a man is not to give in to him sexually.") Some women believe that if they submit sexually before marriage they will lose their partner, but after marriage, sex cements the bond. CS, however, seemed to have the opposite point of view. "I know it's completely irrational," she protested. Yet every image involving the scene of coital activity with her husband invariably elicited a theme of rejection and abandonment.

The foregoing information was obtained during an initial 90-minute consultation. Since the client and I had established good rapport, we decided to continue working together. Given her pervasive and specific fears of rejection and abandonment, and in view of her proclivity for mental imagery, I decided to embark on a course of therapy using coping imagery and images of mastery (Lazarus, 1984; Zilbergeld & Lazarus, 1988). The *coping imagery* involved a series of vignettes in which her husband left her but she could, nonetheless, picture herself coping with the desertion, the loneliness, and the humiliation. It took about eight weekly therapy sessions, reinforced with homework assignments in applying coping-imagery exercises, before she was able to picture the "rejection-from-husband" scenes without feeling devastated. Throughout these same sessions, *images of mastery* (Zilbergeld & Lazarus, 1988) involved specific pictures in which she saw herself meeting other men, taking the initiative, dating, and finding specific outlets to offset the loneliness and abandonment. The rationale is that if one has no options, no alternatives, the risk is overwhelming. The terror of attachment and loss is somewhat mitigated by the image of personal survival even under such adverse circumstances. One is then more likely to take the chance of entering into a deeply intimate nondefensive relationship.

Therapy also dealt with numerous irrational cognitions along the lines of Ellis and Harper (1975) and Ellis (1989). For example, CS oversubscribed to the idea that approval from significant others was a dire necessity, that divorce was an insurmountable stigma, and that marriage was a form of ownership. These ideas were parsed, challenged, and thoroughly refuted. During the therapy, I had requested to meet with CS's husband in order to gain an appreciation of the dyadic factors in their marriage. He had refused to see me and insisted that he had no need or desire for therapy. But after some 3½ months of treatment, when CS suggested that they might attempt to have "proper intercourse," her husband was impotent. I met with him alone for two sessions and then saw the couple together for two sessions.

The year before meeting CS, her husband's first attempt at intercourse (with a prostitute) was a failure. His consequent performance anxiety was part of the reason he had insisted on postponing sex and only consummating their relationship after marriage. As he became more and more comfortable with CS during their courtship, his anxieties abated, and on their honeymoon, he had no sexual difficulties. CS, however, complained of pain and discomfort, and gradually he found his potency becoming affected by her lack of ardor and by his own guilt for inflicting pain on her. Their mutual decision to avoid intromission and to focus exclusively on oral–genital sex while CS sought medical and psychological treatment restored his potency. My assessment of the husband revealed no relevant psychopathology or immediate problems other than those outlined above. Consequently, I saw the couple together and described a sensate-focus regimen that they could practice at home in their own time, at their own pace. I emphasized the critical importance of avoiding any performance demands. He was not to pressure her, and vice versa. Since I detected some reluctance and ambivalence in both parties, I decided to "side with the resistance" by commenting that it would probably take at least 6 months before they would have potent and pain-free sexual relations. Therapy was discontinued at that point, and CS promised to inform me "if and when we succeed" and to consider returning for additional therapy if more than 6 months elapsed.

About 3 weeks later, she called to say that they had been avoiding all sexual contact. We had a three-way telephone conversation, and I decided to apply the usual paradoxical procedure of promoting the desired response by prohibiting it (Fay, 1978): "May I suggest that you start practicing and sensate-focus exercises, but do not even attempt intercourse until you double-check with me, and I give you the go-ahead." Less than a month later, CS called to report that they had had intercourse twice in one day. When her husband first moved into position for possible insertion, CS had said, "Wait! Arnie told us that we have to check with him first." Her husband answered, "To hell with Arnie!"

Minor setbacks and temporary relapses occurred during the course of the next several months, and a few "booster sessions" were administered. These consisted mainly of some "pep talks" that reinforced the nondemanding aura of sexual togetherness. A specific follow-up inquiry 18 months later revealed a sustained and satisfactory level of sexual, social, and interpersonal adjustment.

Commentary

The foregoing case shows that singularity of thought is a great impediment to learning and therapeutic progress. Psychological processes are multi-leveled and multilayered. The need for pluralism cannot be overstated. Even in CS, a woman whose problems were relatively straightforward, a person without undue guilt, raging conflict, or traumatic upheavals, the problem of dyspareunia was nonetheless convoluted. The multimodal assessment showed that her problems were not the upshot of a punitive attitude toward her husband, nor the result of sensual anxieties. Nor were they "all connected to trust." Instead, even this rather uncomplicated case revealed a coalescent mixture of some of the foregoing factors in addition to superstitions, fears of rejection and abandonment, response deficits, irrational ideas, elements of "resistance" (Lazarus & Fay, 1982), and performance fears. Imagine trying to treat these same features in a borderline personality with a history of religious indoctrination plus the aftermath of incest and perhaps a tinge of paranoia! Instead of searching for a panacea, postulating unitary constructs, or looking for unimodal solutions, we seek a new awareness of the multifaceted nature of psychological problems encompassing (1) specification of goals and problems, (2) specification of treatment techniques to achieve these goals and remedy these problems, and (3) systematic measurement of the relative success of these techniques.

A brief elaboration of the techniques of coping imagery and images of mastery might lend substance to this commentary. The use of these imagery methods is based on a fundamental assumption, namely, *that we are often unable to perform in reality that which we cannot achieve in fantasy.* A person who, for instance, wishes to quit smoking and says, "I can't picture myself stopping!" will, in all probability, remain unable to give up the habit. An impotent man who is unable to imagine himself obtaining and maintaining an erection in the presence of a sexual partner needs to achieve this mental picture before he can hope to effect a satisfactory real-life adjustment. In the foregoing case, given CS's overwhelming vulnerability to rejection and abandonment, especially from her husband, it was necessary to replace her parasitic attachment with a mature and self-sufficient response pattern. To achieve realistic mental pictures of oneself coping rather than disintegrating in the face of abandonment and aloneness is an essential precursor to the emotional risk taking that comes with any deep attachment.

The words "I can't," together with the defeatist images that accompany this proclamation, are responsible for a great deal of human limitation and suffering. When CS stated, "I can't make it in life without my husband," it was necessary for her to acquire a repertoire of mental images depicting herself coping with or without him. In her case, the view of her husband as "emotional oxygen" was undermining her capacity to relax and enjoy having sexual intercourse with him. I introduced the coping-imagery procedure in the following way:

"Let's imagine that a UFO lands from a galaxy outside our solar system and whisks away your husband. You will never see him again. We can but hope that he will have a happy life wherever he is headed, but here you are on earth without him. Now you can decide to kill yourself because your life support is gone. But don't do that. Instead, let's see how you can manage to cope and survive and even end up smiling again and being happy."

I elicited from her a series of images wherein she saw herself leaning on friends, keeping very busy, and eventually recovering from the loss. Thereafter, in subsequent sessions, I introduced more realistic pictures of rejection (e.g., "Imagine that he has found another woman!"), and we worked through a similar series of coping reactions.

Images of mastery pave the way for various skills that add confidence to the probability that one will cope in the face of adversity. In the case of CS, she had to see herself mastering the art of meeting new men, dating, conversing, and relating. At first, she pictured herself being awkward, inept, shy, making stupid remarks, and failing to impress. Gradually, this gave way to images where she could see herself being charming, seductive, witty, and relaxed. The assumption behind these tactics is that a healthy or happy marriage is not based on desperate, last-chance, clinging attachments. In a worthwhile marriage, one remains with one's spouse not because one has to but because one desires to. An awareness of one another's "high market value" vis-à-vis members of the opposite sex engenders self-respect and mutual respect (Lazarus, 1985).

Again, it must be emphasized that CS's successful sexual and interpersonal adjustment called for a broad range of interventions. The essence of effective therapy seems to be the capacity to persuade our clients to do different things and to do things differently.

A Less Successful Case

Let us now turn to a case wherein the outcome was less than positive. Initially, LC, a 36-year-old surgeon, and his wife KT, a 32-year-old attorney, consulted me about "parenting skills" regarding their 3-year-old daughter about whom they each held different ideas concerning discipline. Whereas the father was *laissez-faire* in attitude, the mother favored "very strict routines." LC and KT were both immaculately dressed and extraordinarily attractive. It was soon clear that KT tended to be obsessive–compulsive and found rigid structure and clear-cut order necessary for her own peace of mind. She called her husband "a slob," and LC countered that he was "really quite tidy" but that KT's low tolerance for disorder rendered her "tough to live with." The initial attempt was to find some middle ground that might

be acceptable to them vis-à-vis child discipline and daily living. At the end
of the session, KT remarked that they also had sexual problems, and she
scheduled an appointment to see me individually.

It transpired that KT had always found sex with LC "uncomfortable
and somewhat bland." They had been married for 5 years. Premarital
relationships were "acceptable," but compared to her previous lovers, LC
"was never up to par." When asked for specific details, KT was evasive but
stated that she had made her feelings of discontent fully known to LC, who
had subsequently become even less arduous. After the birth of their daughter, KT began to experience "unbearable pain and zero pleasure during
intercourse." She added, "Despite the pain, displeasure, resentment and
tension, we battled on for a year or so. But for the past couple of years, I
have called a halt to sexual intercourse. . . . If my husband wants relief, I
will masturbate him." Had she been medically and gynecologically examined? "Yes, very thoroughly."

KT offered the following information: "When I was a teenager I knew
exactly what I wanted to do and what I wanted to get out of life. My friends
were all having 'identity crises.' They were pondering over what they
wanted to be when they grew up. But I had no doubts whatever. I wanted
to be an attorney; I wanted to marry a doctor; and I wanted a child—
preferably a girl. Now I am 32, and I have achieved all that. LC and I are
viewed as the perfect couple. To outsiders it seems idyllic. But for the past
few years, I have been asking myself if this is all there is to life. I'm very
bored. Surely there must be more. . . . Now I am having an identity crisis!"

KT met LC when he was completing his surgical residency, and they
became engaged shortly thereafter. Interpersonal difficulties were evident
immediately. KT resented the time that her fiance spent at the hospital. "I
became even more angry when we were first married. Instead of spending
time with his new bride, LC elected to be at the hospital. . . . Even worse,
when he was in the operating room I couldn't reach him at all. There he was
ostensibly saving the lives of complete strangers, but if I, his own wife,
needed him, he was unavailable." I pointed out that in addition to the
dyspareunia, there appeared to be a wide range of resentments, unfulfilled
expectations, dyadic struggles, and temperamental differences, all of which
might or might not have a bearing on the sexual problem. "Where do we
start?" I asked. "Do you want me to do your job for you?" she countered. I
recommended that they be treated as a couple. "If we upgrade your relationship in general, introduce some simple sensate focus exercises, and
develop a successful *modus operandi* concerning such issues as tidiness,
your daughter's routines, and the development of quality time between LC
and you, we'll see where that leads. How does that sound to you?" KT
found this broad description acceptable.

Two conjoint sessions followed. The first one did not go well. KT
availed herself of the opportunity to castigate LC, and he became a whip-
ping boy for all her discontents. I pointed out that she was behaving like a

prosecuting attorney, not a wife. LC remained stoic in the face of the abuse being heaped on him until KT made disparaging remarks about his mother. "Keep my family out of this!" he snapped. My attempts to convey the importance of assertive versus aggressive communications were overshadowed by KT's apparent desire to express her anger. She riled on. "I wanted to marry a doctor not a butcher. As far as I'm concerned, what LC does for a living is carve up meat. He might as well work in a delicatessen. Imagine liking blood and guts. As far as I'm concerned, it's not dignified or refined. As a lawyer, I have to use my head. I'm not a manual laborer. When people ask LC what he does for a living, I hate it when he tells them he is a surgeon. I keep telling him to say he is a doctor. After all, he actually did go to medical school before becoming a butcher." When LC was asked how he felt about KT's disdain for his line of work he stated, "I don't care. I enjoy what I do, and I think it's important."

The second conjoint session focused on compromise, on negotiation, and on other constructive ways of handling their differences constructively. I interceded whenever KT became destructively critical and modeled positive and supportive ways of conveying frustration, anger, and disappointment. When discussing their specific sexual transactions, both LC and KT expressed opposition to using sensate-focus exercises. KT referred to them as "locker room not bedroom activities." I recommended a procedure that they found acceptable. "KT, if you use a vibrator and bring yourself to orgasm, you may find that you become sufficiently relaxed and vaginally distended so that painless intercourse might ensue, especially if you also use a lubricant." The next conjoint session was scheduled 2 weeks later, allowing sufficient time for the couple to try different sytles of communication as well as the prescribed sexual procedure. KT came to the session alone. "LC couldn't get away from the hospital," she explained.

The prescribed sexual tactic had been attempted only once. "It still hurt like hell!" KT declared. And then she added: "There's something you have to understand. LC is very large. He's hung like a horse. I've never found intercourse especially pleasurable with him; it has always been uncomfortable at best." She then confided that she had been having an affair for the past year with an architect. "Bill is older—he's almost 40. He is considerate and knows how to treat a woman. He takes no crap from me. With him, sex is terrific. He was married for a few years in his 20s, got divorced, and has remained single. He wants me to divorce LC and marry him. I've given it serious consideration, but if you want to know the truth, Bill couldn't earn one 10th of what LC makes a year, no matter how successful he became. Have you any idea how much money LC makes? True, if Bill and I got married, I could work full time, and between us we'd make a decent living. But I'd hate to have to get into that cut-throat rat race, busting my ass. I like working part time and still having plenty of money."

KT described her lover as "active and exciting," whereas her husband was "passive and dull." "All he does is perform his butchery, attend meetings at the hospital, and slump in front of the TV." I was quite blunt with KT at this juncture and pointed out that I felt sorry for LC. "The poor sucker is in a loveless, sexless marriage but has to foot most of the bills." KT pensively remarked, "Oh, I think I sort of love him in my own peculiar way." She then requested that I have a man-to-man talk with LC with a view to modifying his passivity. "Obviously," she added, "what I told you about Bill is strictly *entre nous.*"

The session with LC first dwelled on why he found the marriage sufficiently rewarding to remain in it. "I love KT," he explained, "and besides, I take my marriage vows seriously—for better or worse. . . . When KT gets off my back she can be very engaging." LC stated that on observing the marriages of his friends and colleagues, he did not see any that were substantially superior to his. He embroidered the view that women are by nature "clinging, picky, bitchy, petty, needling, nasty, ball-busting." He stressed, "It's in their DNA!" Attempts to persuade him that his misogynistic generalizations were false fell on deaf ears.

The next topic was his passive rather than assertive stance with KT. "There's no point in saying anything to her," he protested. "She's a lawyer. She can argue anyone to death. I've taken that tack. Believe me, it goes nowhere." As the session continued, it became clear that LC and KT had no significant common interests, pursued few meaningful activities, and endured a relationship that was almost totally devoid of the mutual caring, sharing, companionship, emotional support, and happy collaboration that most people look for in marriage.

Did LC have any love, sex, or companionship extramaritally? "I wouldn't think of it! As I already said, I take my marriage vows very seriously. . . . I would never sue for divorce. If KT instituted divorce proceedings I would not oppose her, but I would not be the one to initiate or instigate a divorce." How interested was he in making a concerted effort to upgrade the quality of the marriage? "I think the wounds run too deep," he answered. What was this so-called "love" for KT and his intense devotion to "marriage vows" that kept him in such an arid relationship? Was there evidence of more basic insecurities, or a sense of underentitlement? Did LC derive so much gratification from his work that other desires paled into insignificance? Answers to such questions require time, commitment, and a level of rapport that was not present, and perhaps not possible, between LC and me. This made me question whether a female co-therapist might prove helpful, or if the couple should be referred elsewhere.

KT called for an appointment and announced: "I think you got through to LC. He has stopped taking any crap from me. For example, on Saturday night we went to a restaurant, and when I started to complain that we would have to wait too long, he said I should leave if I didn't like it, but that he was staying. I liked that. I stayed, and when we finally got seated we had quite a romantic dinner." During the rest of the session KT elected to dwell on issues pertaining to her mother and sister. When I started constructing a genogram, she snapped: "I'm not going to waste time on going over my background. I spent over 2 years doing that with a psychiatrist, and it achieved less than nothing!"

The next two appointments were canceled. LC was very busy at the hospital, and KT had undertaken a child custody case and was "up to my ears in paperwork." She stated, "We'll be back in touch as soon as work pressures ease up."

Commentary

Working with this couple was interesting and challenging but not very gratifying. It is difficult to determine how I might have proceeded differently and been more effective. Perhaps a co-therapist should have been enlisted. Should I have been more confrontative, or was I in fact too intrusive? Would a more highly targeted treatment focus have produced a better outcome? Significantly, I was unable to work multimodally. When they were asked to complete the Multimodal Life History Questionnaire, they were "too busy" (often a poor prognostic sign). My attempts to unravel their hidden agendas provided speculative notions rather than clinical data. It is always easy for therapists to claim their clients were not "really motivated" or were invested in some form of stasis, but as Lazarus and Fay (1982) have underscored, these are often employed as convenient rationalizations whereby clinicians dismiss their own incompetence.

In retrospect, it might have been advisable not to enter into the sexual arena until their overall relationship had been addressed in greater detail. It will be recalled that they had not mentioned their sexual difficulties initially but had focused on child-rearing differences and on KT's desire for structure. If more time had been given to developing a *unity of togetherness* (e.g., better ways of budgeting their time, tactics for acquiring effective negotiation skills, agreement to make compromises and concessions, development of common recreational outlets, and the pursuance of other mutual interests), the viability of the relationship might have been tested, and better-informed choices and decisions might have been forthcoming.

THE USE OF SYSTEMATIC DESENSITIZATION

Many years ago (Lazarus, 1963), I had pointed out that "where specific or reasonably clear-cut fears inhibit sexual pleasure, systematic desensitization is the method of choice." Whereas this statement, in my present judgment, is probably accurate, over the years I have found relatively few cases in whom specific clear-cut fears were present without a variety of secondary anxieties and interpersonal difficulties. Nevertheless, as some of the cases in this chapter have shown, some form of habituation or desensitization through imagery may play an important role in the treatment of dyspareunia. There are instances that seem to call for more elaborate, precise, and systematic desensitization tactics. A typical example of this formal technique appears below.

The Case of Mrs. A

Mrs. A, aged 24 years, had been married for 2½ years, during which time she claimed to have had coitus on fewer than two dozen occasions. She always experienced violent dyspareunia during intercourse. She could tolerate little more than casual kissing without anxiety. The background to her problem was clearly one of puritanical upbringing, in which much emphasis had been placed on the sinful qualities of carnal desire. Mrs. A's husband had endeavored to solve their difficulties by providing his wife with books on sex techniques and practices. Mrs. A had obligingly read these works, but her emotional reactions remained unchanged. She sought treatment of her own accord when she suspected that her husband had developed an extra-marital attachment.

It took three to four sessions for Mrs. A to feel at ease with me. During several diagnostic interviews, sufficient rapport was established for us to develop the following 21-item hierarchy. The list was generated from the client's self-report:

1. Dancing with and embracing husband while fully clothed.
2. Being kissed on cheeks and forehead.
3. Being kissed on lips.
4. Sitting on husband's lap, both fully dressed.
5. Husband kissing neck and ears.
6. Husband caressing hair and face.
7. Shoulders and back being caressed.
8. Having buttocks and thighs caressed.
9. Contact of tongues while kissing.
10. Embracing while semiclothed, being aware of husband's erection and his desire for sex.
11. Breasts being caressed while fully clothed.
12. Naked breasts being caressed.
13. Oral stimulation of breasts.
14. Caressing husband's genitals.
15. Husband's fingers being inserted into the vagina during precoital loveplay.
16. Manual stimulation of the clitoris.
17. Having intercourse in the nude under the bed covers.
18. Having intercourse in the nude on top of a bed.
19. Having coitus in the nude in a dining room or living room.
20. Changing positions during intercourse.
21. Having intercourse in the nude while sitting on husband's lap.

After Mrs. A had been taught the basics of deep muscle relaxation, the desensitization procedure commenced by having her picturing, as vividly as possible, the easiest image (item 1). Thereafter, step by step, through guided imagery, she proceeded to picture more and more difficult items. Variations in brightness of lighting played a prominent part in determining the client's reactions. After four desensitization sessions, for instance, she was able to visualize item 8 (having her buttocks and thighs caressed) without anxiety if this was occurring in the dark. It required several additional treatments before she was able to tolerate this imagined intimacy under conditions of ordinary lighting.

Mrs. A received three desensitization sessions a week over a period of about 3 months. When item 5 on the hierarchy had been successfully visualized without anxiety, Mrs. A "seduced" her husband one evening and found the entire episode "disgustingly pleasant" and experienced only slight discomfort. Thereafter, progress was extremely rapid, although items 20 and 21 proved slightly troublesome, and each required over 20 presentations before the criterion (a 30-second exposure without anxiety or anticipated discomfort) was reached. A year later, Mr. and Mrs. A both said that the results of therapy had remained "spectacularly effective."

Commentary

When specific fears, feelings of guilt, and phobic reactions are predominant, systematic desensitization is probably one of the most effective techniques. Generally, this procedure is only one element in a broad-spectrum treatment regimen. Most cases call for cognitive restructuring, social skills training, relationship enhancement, an affective expression in which guided imagery can play a significant role. This chapter has tried to show that dyspareunia is not a unitary disturbance but, like most psychological problems, involves a wide range of idiosyncratic variables.

CONCLUSION

Although there are many organic diseases and dysfunctions of the genitourinary tract that result in dyspareunia, when these have been ruled out or fully treated and pain still persists, primary psychological factors ("psychogenic dyspareunia") come into play. In this regard, although traumatic factors (e.g., sexual assaults or sexual abuse) and developmental issues (e.g., an upbringing that invested sex with shame and guilt) may be significant in certain instances, the majority of clients are likely to reveal relational conflicts—unhappy and unsatisfactory relationships. Nevertheless, a thorough psychodiagnostic evaluation that examines salient behaviors, affective responses, sensory inputs, mental images, cognitions, interpersonal relationships, and biological considerations (multimodal assessment) is recommended.

Therapeutic progress is more likely to be achieved by remedying a variety of situational and specific problems than by searching for cohesive and underlying causal themes. Case vignettes were selected to underscore the dangers of confusing causal and correlational factors and to point out the need to avoid singularity of thought in favor of multileveled and multi-layered processes. At the same time, the importance of avoiding needless complexity was also emphasized. In treating most cases of psychogenic dyspareunia, therapists must be well versed in the application of relationship enhancement, cognitive restructuring, and social skills training.

Acknowledgment. My special thanks to Allen Fay, M.D., for his constructive criticisms.

REFERENCES

Abarbanel, A. R. (1978). Diagnosis and treatment of coital discomfort. In J. LoPiccolo & L. LoPiccolo (Eds.), *Handbook of sex therapy* (pp. 241–259). New York: Plenum Press.

Brunell, L. F., & Young, W. T. (Eds.). (1982). *A multimodal handbook for a mental hospital: Designing specific treatments for specific problems.* New York: Springer.

Ellis, A. (1989). Rational-emotive therapy. In R. J. Corsini & D. Wedding (Eds.), *Current psychotherapies* (pp. 197–238). Itasca, IL: Peacock.

Ellis, A., & Harper, R. A. (1975). *A new guide to rational living.* Englewood Cliffs, NJ: Prentice-Hall.

Fay, A. (1978). *Making things better by making them worse.* New York: Hawthorne Books.

Fay, A. (1988). *PQR: Prescription for a quality relationship.* New York: Multimodal Press.

Kwee, M. G. T., & Lazarus, A. A. (1986). Multimodal therapy: The cognitive-behavioral tradition and beyond. In W. Dryden & W. Golden (Eds.), *Cognitive-behavioral approaches to psychotherapy* (pp. 320–355). London: Harper & Row.

Lazarus, A. A. (1963). The treatment of chronic frigidity by systematic desensitization. *Journal of Nervous and Mental Disease, 136,* 272–278.

Lazarus, A. A. (1973). Multimodal behavior therapy: Treating the BASIC ID. *Journal of Nervous and Mental Disease, 156,* 404–411.

Lazarus, A. A. (1980). Psychological treatment of dyspareunia. In S. R. Leiblum & L. A. Pervin (Eds.), *Principles and practice of sex therapy* (pp. 147–166). New York: Guilford Press.

Lazarus, A. A. (1981). *The practice of multimodal therapy.* New York: McGraw-Hill. (Updated paperback edition, Baltimore: Johns Hopkins University Press, 1989).

Lazarus, A. A. (1984). *In the mind's eye: The power of imagery for personal enrichment.* New York: Guilford Press.

Lazarus, A. A. (1985). *Marital myths: Two dozen mistaken beliefs that can ruin a marriage or make a bad one worse.* San Luis Obispo, CA: Impact Publishers.

Lazarus, A. A. (1986). Multimodal therapy. In J. C. Norcross (Ed.), *Handbook of eclectic psychotherapy* (pp. 65–93). New York: Brunner/Mazel.

Lazarus, A. A. (1987). The multimodal approach with adult outpatients. In N. S. Jacobson (Ed.), *Psychotherapists in clinical practice* (pp. 286–326). New York: Guilford Press.

Lazarus, A. A. (1988). Multimodal therapy. In R. J. Corsini & D. Wedding (Eds.), *Current psychotherapies* (pp. 503–544). Itasca, IL: Peacock.

Lazarus, A. A., & Fay, A. (1982). Resistance or rationalization? A cognitive–behavioral perspective. In P. L. Wachtel (Ed.), *Resistance: Psychodynamic and behavioral approaches* (pp. 115–132). New York: Plenum Press.

Masters, W. H., & Johnson, V. E. (1970). *Human sexual inadequacy.* Boston: Little, Brown.

Zilbergeld, B., & Lazarus, A. A. (1988). *Mind power: Getting what you want through mental training.* New York: Ivy Books.

5

The Treatment of Vaginismus: Success and Failure

SANDRA R. LEIBLUM, LAWRENCE A. PERVIN,
AND ENID H. CAMPBELL

In the 10 years since the first publication of Principles and Practice of Sex
Therapy, *the theory and treatment of vaginismus have changed very little.
The major goal of treatment is the elimination of the spasmodic reflexive
contraction of the muscles controlling the vaginal entrance, typically
through a series of gradual approximations with the insertion of increasingly
larger dilators (or fingers).*

*It is important to determine the "real" motivation for seeking treatment,
since often the desire for a child is more intense than the desire to accomplish successful intercourse. Although some therapists wonder whether to
recommend conception through artificial insemination using husband's
semen, this is not a wise idea since the penetration problem remains and
may be masking real ambivalence about parenthood.*

*Despite the high degree of agreement concerning treatment approaches,
treatment is not effective for all vaginismic women. The woman (and her
partner) may be quite ambivalent or fearful about tolerating and dealing with
the anxiety that therapy necessarily entails. Determining which factors predict
success and failure in a variety of cases is important, since failure is always
discouraging and humiliating for the woman and her partner. In this chapter,
we report on the treatment of three cases with varying outcomes. What is
apparent in these case vignettes is the variety of women, partner relationships,
and sexual enjoyment found in women with vaginismus. The factor most
predictive of successful outcome appears to be the nature of the supportive
factors that permit the toleration of the anxiety about change. Moreover, the
therapeutic alliance formed between therapist and client is important, as well.
The implication for sex therapy generally is that techniques, however effective and well-conceived, rarely facilitate a cure in the face of ambivalent
motivation and a noncongruent patient–therapist relationship.*

*Sandra R. Leiblum is Professor of Clinical Psychiatry and Co-Director
of the Sexual Counseling Service at the University of Medicine and Dentistry of New Jersey—Robert Wood Johnson Medical School. Lawrence A.*

Pervin is Professor of Psychology at Rutgers University. Enid H. Campbell is Professor of Psychology at Trenton State College.

Vaginismus is a perplexing and frustrating problem. The woman who experiences the involuntary, spasmodic contraction of the pubococcygeus and related muscles controlling the vaginal opening cannot have intercourse, but may be quite capable of becoming sexually aroused, lubricating, and experiencing multiple orgasms. Virgin wives and their partners often report a rich sexual repertoire. However, when the wife senses or fears that her vagina is going to be "penetrated," the muscles tighten so that intercourse becomes impossible. What is so striking in so many of these cases is the number of years the couple tolerates the difficulty before seeking treatment, whether because of ambivalence about resolving the problem or for other reasons. Often, it is the desire to have children that ultimately propels the couple to seek assistance. Although vaginismus is considered to be relatively rare, it is likely that it exists to a far greater degree than is statistically reported. Furthermore, many women experience partial vaginismus on intermittent sexual occasions. Often such difficulties seriously interfere with sexual comfort and satisfaction but are not deemed sufficiently disturbing to warrant treatment.

HISTORICAL OVERVIEW

Vaginismus was first described in the scientific literature in 1834 by D. K. Huguier, who compared the involuntary spastic constriction of the circumvaginal musculature to the spasms of the anal sphincter as a result of painful fissures. The term "vaginismus" was coined by an American gynecologist, J. Marion Sims. In an address to the Obstetrical Society of London in 1862, he said:

> From personal observation I can confidentally assert that I know of no disease capable of producing so much unhappiness to both parties of the marriage contract and I am happy to state that I know of no serious trouble that can be cured so easily, so safely and so certainly. (Quoted in Drenth, 1988, p. 126)

Sims advocated complete excision of the hymen, a Y-shaped incision of the introitus as far as the perineum, a transection of part of the sphincter muscle, and the use of a glass bougie to be worn for 2 hours twice daily for a few weeks. Today, such treatment is unthinkable. Not only is it ineffective because the fear underlying the symptom is never addressed, the basic contraction of the circumvaginal muscles will remain.

Nineteenth-century writers assumed that there was a predisposition to the condition. Faure and Sireday (1909) observed that the condition was more common in arranged marriages. First intercourse was often traumatic in these instances and was exacerbated by the women's ignorance and, perhaps, by her spouse's lack of empathy. Although the major cause of the penetration phobia was different for each woman, there was some recognition of the psychosomatic nature of the problem by these early authors (Drenth, 1988).

THEORETICAL EXPLANATIONS OF AND APPROACHES TO VAGINISMUS

Psychoanalytical Explanations and Approaches

Psychoanalytic views generally conceive of vaginismus as a rejection of the female role, a resistance against male sexual prerogative, a defense of the woman against her father's real or fantasized incestual threats, and a warding off of her own castration images (Drenth, 1988). Musaph (1977), a Dutch physician, suggests that the woman unconsciously says to herself, "Now this big, dangerous instrument is going to penetrate me; there will be bleeding wounds; I will suffer unbearable pain and my revenge will be terrible" (quoted in Drenth, 1988, p. 127).

Currently, traditional psychoanalytic therapists advocate an exploration of the unconscious fears and ambivalence underlying the problem. Other psychoanalytically oriented therapists believe that a more active behavioral approach is needed in order to overcome the high anxiety accompanying the symptom. Kaplan (1974), for example, rejects the psychoanalytic view of vaginismus as a conversion symptom expressive of the woman's hostility toward men and her unconscious wish to castrate them in revenge for her own castration. Rather, she suggests a multicausal concept of vaginismus as a conditioned response to any adverse stimulus associated with intercourse or vaginal entry: "Vaginismus occurs when a negative contingency becomes associated with the act or fantasy of vaginal penetration" (p. 417). The aim of treatment, then, is the extinction of the conditioned vaginal response. This is accomplished through the insertion of graduated rubber or glass catheters until a catheter the size of an erect penis is inserted without pain or discomfort. Often the patient's or partner's finger is used rather than a catheter. Then, the woman is instructed to guide her husband's penis into the vaginal opening while remaining in control throughout. When the phobic element remains strong, it is treated through the use of systematic desensitization. Here, the patient repeatedly imagines the feared stimuli while deeply relaxed. In sum, the conditioned vaginismic response is treated through the insertion exercises, and the phobic element is treated with systematic desensitization. The essential element, as in cognitive–behavioral treatments, is to repeatedly expose the woman, both in imagery and in actuality, to the feared situation while keeping anxiety at a minimum and providing reassurance and support. No specific recommendations are made concerning the woman's partner since this depends on the particular dynamics of each case. Kaplan suggests that successful outcome is achieved in virtually all cases, although on occasion, success may be followed by the husband reporting problems of erectile failure or premature ejaculation.

Cognitive–Behavioral Explanations and Approaches

Learning theorists generally view vaginismus as a conditioned fear reaction, a learned phobia. Reinforcing the conditioned fear response is the cognitive belief that penetration can only be accomplished with great difficulty and may result in pain and discomfort. In order to overcome the avoidance of intercourse, it is necessary to challenge both the cognitive and phobic elements.

Masters and Johnson (1970) view vaginismus as an involuntary reflex "due to imagined, anticipated, or real attempt at vaginal penetration" (p. 250). They refer to it as a psychosomatic illness and discuss a variety of etiological factors including a response to male sexual dysfunction, the psychosexually inhibiting influence of religious orthodoxy, a prior sexual trauma, a response to a homosexual identification, and/or a secondary response to dyspareunia. They also emphasize the importance of acknowledging the contribution of the male partner: "Interestingly, the syndrome has a high percentage of association with primary impotence in the male partner, providing still further clinical evidence to support procedural demand for simultaneous evaluation and treatment of both marital partners" (p. 252). A recent case seen at the Robert Wood Johnson Medical School Sexual Counseling Center highlights the importance of treating both partners. The couple, a religiously orthodox Italian-Catholic pair, were raised by "old-world" parents. Moreover, the wife's mother strongly reinforced traditional beliefs. She rebuked her daughter if she wore red nail polish—"You look like a whore"—or purchased sheer lingerie. Sex was never discussed, and modesty was strictly enforced. The fact that the maternal mother lived with the couple complicated the situation, but neither husband nor wife felt comfortable about asking her to leave.

In taking a history, the couple related that they were both virgins at marriage and had not been successful in accomplishing any sort of penetration during the 5 years of their life together. The wife, a 33-year-old ecologist, initiated the request for treatment only after she had completed her master's degree and decided that the time had finally come to directly address the sexual problems in her marriage. Both she and her husband concurred in assigning the "cause" of their difficulty to the husband's inability to sustain erections. It was only in interviewing the husband alone that it became apparent that his erectile failure had begun only after he had made repeated, unsuccessful attempts to penetrate his wife during intercourse on their honeymoon. She had displayed such anxiety and discomfort with genital contact following the initial intercourse "catastrophe" that they both had avoided all sexual intimacy for the next 6 months. In fact, both husband and wife experienced high degrees of sexual anxiety. He blamed himself for his sexual incompetence and erectile difficulties, and she felt inadequate as a woman and as a lover. Neither wanted to expose their perceived inadequacies to a therapist. It was clearly important that both of them be seen—both individually and together—during treatment.

In their approach to treatment, Masters and Johnson start with a demonstration of the existence of the involuntary nature of the vaginal spasm or contraction. They consider it important that both partners understand that the response is involuntary and reflexive rather than intentional. Beyond this, the main element of treatment is the use of Hegar dilators in graduated sizes to enable the woman to allow penetration by an object the size of a penis. The use of the dilators is initiated and conducted by the husband with the wife's physical control over verbal direction of the exercises. Masters and Johnson reported that they had seen 29 cases in 11 years and were successful with each case once the cooperation of the partners in the dilation therapy was obtained.

Other Explanations and Approaches

Drenth (1988), a Dutch sex therapist, suggests that there are women who dislike or fear genital intercourse but who are interested in having a biological child. With these women, traditional treatment with dilators or systematic desensitization is likely to end in failure. Drenth suggests that artificial insemination with the husband's semen, performed at home by the couple themselves might be a possible treatment alternative although he acknowledges that a successful outcome is not always achieved with this intervention.

Despite the differences in these conceptual models and treatment options, a number of salient points emerge:

1. There is obvious agreement concerning the nature of the vaginismic response, but it is alternatively described as a psychosomatic disorder, a phobia, a conditioned response, or a conversion reaction.
2. There are no accurate statistical figures concerning the incidence of vaginismus. Although most authors view it as uncommon, others suggest that it may be more widespread than we suspect.
3. A variety of etiological factors can give rise to the symptom, ranging from a specific traumatic event to an underlying psychodynamic conflict. Most likely, the vaginismic response is overdetermined and is multicausal in nature. However, most authors agree that the husband is important in maintaining, if not causing, the problem.

4. Regardless of the etiological hypothesis, most authors believe that the treatment of choice is the gradual insertion of objects into the vagina (e.g., fingers, tampons, dilators) of increasing size under conditions of relaxation and patient control. Systematic desensitization can also be helpful, particularly in treating the phobic elements. Views concerning the husband's participation in treatment vary from recommending full involvement at every stage of treatment, to inclusion once the wife has started to make progress, to a varied response depending on the particular dynamics of the case.

6. Most authors view the prognosis as good. For the most part, failures tend not to be discussed, although recently Drenth (1988) has suggested that couples may not truly desire sexual "consummation" but rather enter treatment primarily in order to accomplish a pregnancy. In these instances, he suggests, intercourse should not be considered the primary treatment goal and success should not be defined exclusively in terms of vaginal penetration.

Because treatment outcome can be quite variable, several case studies will be presented with varying outcome. We will then discuss some of the patient and treatment characteristics that contribute to treatment outcome.

CASE 1: SUCCESS

The first case involves a white couple in their mid-20s. The intake evaluation indicated a severe penetration phobia and vaginismus. She reported having been in psychotherapy for over a year, with little benefit concerning the vaginismus problem. Although the couple had an active sex life, and she was able to have orgasms through masturbation and oral sex, intercourse had not occurred during the 4 years of their marriage. The specific reason for contacting the Sexual Counseling Service at Robert Wood Johnson Medical School at this time was the wish to begin a family. A discussion of the treatment program follows, with a summary of major techniques and events presented in Table 5.1.

In the first session with a co-therapy team, the couple appeared to be friendly, nervous, highly motivated, and very affectionate toward one another. The wife was girlish, immature, and somewhat hysterical. The husband was more realistic in describing their problems and was protective (almost paternal) toward his wife. He tended to make decisions for both of them, and she instinctively turned to him for advice and decisions. At the time they came for help, she was unemployed and experienced acute gastrointestinal symptoms without any discernible physical cause. The husband believed it would be good for her to have a child to keep her occupied. Very early in the discussion, the wife centered attention on a new source of anxiety and a new obsession. Each was given a confidential

TABLE 5.1   Case 1: Treatment Sessions and Progress

Session		Techniques employed and progress noted
1–3		History-taking.
4–12	(6 joint sessions and 3 individual sessions with wife and female co-therapist)	Emphasis on relaxation, desensitization, self-control: Kegel exercises, progressive relaxation training, fantasy exercises, finger insertion, viewing of film of intercourse, interpretation of defensive nature of obsession, scheduling of gynecological exam. Husband is able to insert his finger into wife's vagina.
13–15		Discussion of gynecological exam, successful intercourse experiences, and issues of contraception and pregnancy.
16		Follow-up session. Intercourse and general sexual relationship are reported to be very satisfactory. Wife is pregnant.

questionnaire to be completed at home, and before mailing out her husband's questionnaire, she looked at the section on extramarital affairs and was distressed to read that her husband had had extramarital intercourse once, a number of years ago, with someone he met in a bar after drinking heavily. Even though he had otherwise been devoted and faithful, her preoccupation with and distress over this event led to severe sleeping and eating difficulties. Although there was some brief discussion of her background and the couple's marital relationship, her anxiety about what had happened and fear that her obsession would remain with her for the rest of her life dominated the initial session.

The sex history was taken in an individual session with the female cotherapist. The wife again began with her current upset and obsession. She was having problems of diarrhea, vomiting, and general agitation. In terms of background, she was the elder of two sisters. Mother was described as insecure, dependent, and fearful of her husband. She would not get a job because menstrual difficulties led her to spend one week a month in bed. Father was described as a large, strict, strong man with a booming voice. Though never hit by him, she was terrified of him. Father and mother had to marry because mother was pregnant. The patient had received a Catholic upbringing but had attended public schools. Sex was not talked about at home, and what she learned about sex came from friends. At age 7, she and a friend had been molested by the uncle of a neighborhood friend. She could not recall any of the details except that her father raged about it and threatened to tear the man apart. Growing up, she was generally fearful and felt that father put her down in everything she did. The patient's family was critical of "trashy" people in the neighborhood who were sexually active. Generally, the patient had tried to please the parents, father in particular, and related to her husband in a similar fashion. At age 14, she had inserted a tampon against her mother's advice and was so anxious about it that she had to go to a physician to have it removed. She reported that while sex (other than intercourse) with her husband was generally pleasurable, she had fears during oral sex that her husband's tongue would rip her apart. She felt that her vagina was not big enough and that his penis was huge.

The male co-therapist met with the husband individually to get some of the details of his background and to determine his perception of the problem. He was the eldest of three children, with a younger brother and sister. He had been raised in a Catholic family and had attended parochial school until high school. His parents were described in positive terms, and he reported feeling closer to his mother than his father. Sex was discussed openly in his home. He had started masturbating at age 14 and reported no feelings of guilt about it. He had had limited sexual experience prior to meeting his wife but reported no earlier difficulties. He contrasted his home and himself with his wife's family and her personality. He viewed his wife as overly attached to her father. When they were first married, she was reluctant to move away and defended her father strongly whenever anything critical was said about him. He saw his wife's father an "an animal" with enormous arms and hands who was idealized and feared by his daughter. She would never smoke in his presence or be seen having any physical contact with a boy, including holding hands. He described great love for his wife and wondered whether part of the problem was that he had never tried hard enough to have intercourse. He avoided this because of fears of hurting her, particularly in terms of tearing some of the muscles of her hymen. He was puzzled about why his wife had this problem, particularly since her unmarried sister was sexually active. He wondered whether perhaps her difficulties were related to her trauma at age 7, and noted that the girl she was with at the time, who also was molested, was now a lesbian.

The early sessions tended to focus on the wife's obsession with her husband's extramarital experience. Despite much support by the therapists and repeated reassurances by her husband that he had been otherwise faithful and did not feel that this would occur in the future, she continued to be preoccupied with this episode. This was about where matters stood after three sessions with them as a couple and a session with each individually. At this time, it was decided to have her begin Kegel exercises and relaxation training. Additionally, some individual sessions with the wife and female co-therapist were scheduled to avoid going along with the possible defensive-avoidance aspects of her obsession while still giving her considerable support and reassurance.

The next five sessions consisted of three joint sessions and two individual sessions limited to the female co-therapist and wife. The results were mixed, but there was evidence of some progress. For example, she continued to do the Kegel exercises but often found it easier to tighten her pelvic muscle than to relax it. She followed the directions concerning the progressive relaxation training but continued to find that thoughts of her husband's sexual experience intruded. In the individual sessions, the therapist interpreted her obsession as a way of distracting herself so that she would not fully experience her fear concerning intercourse. In addition, there was discussion of her fears of pregnancy and of her almost complete dependence on her husband. Although she hoped to have a family, the main initiative in this area was coming from her husband. She did not feel ready for the responsibility of parenthood and did not want to make the mistakes with her children that she felt had been made with her. No decision had been reached concerning contraceptive devices, so that this was another source of anxiety for her. The therapist helped her to recognize her right to determine when she was ready to be a mother and which kind of contraceptive device was preferable.

Three other developments of significance took place during these five sessions. First, after the therapist suggested that the wife try inserting her own finger into her vagina, she asked her husband to do so. At first, she felt a tightening of her vaginal and abdominal muscles as he approached. The importance of relaxation, lubrication, some sexual arousal, and her control over when and how far his finger was inserted was emphasized. Again, her own responsibility in this area was stressed. Progress began to be made, and during one of these efforts she recalled the details of the traumatic molestation at age 7. The event involved the man putting his finger into her vagina and it hurting her. She felt relief about being able to recall this experience. The second significant incident involved the couple viewing the film *Free* demonstrating intercourse. Her response to the film was that it looked like fun, but she was not sure that she could feel that way herself. There was some discussion of her tendency to be pessimistic and to put herself down. The third development involved scheduling an appointment to see a gynecologist. The goal was to better familiarize both of them with her vagina and to discuss various contraceptive alternatives.

The 11th and 12th sessions consisted of one joint session and one individual session with the wife. During these sessions, she began to look more at her family's attitude toward sex and how often sex was negatively valued. Also, fantasy exercises were practiced in conjunction with relaxation. In the course of one fantasy exercise, she reported feeling aroused when imagining having intercourse with her husband while his friends watched. The fantasy exercises were also used to prepare and desensitize her for the upcoming gynecological examination. Finally, she received considerable support in handling pressures from her husband to move toward intercourse and to avoid using contraceptives.

She arrived for the 13th session excited to report that following the gynecological examination, her husband had been able to insert his penis almost completely. While not in pain, she told him to stop since she was afraid. When he withdrew, he noticed some blood and was reluctant to continue. She felt very aroused and wanted to resume their efforts, but her husband's anxieties prevailed. She reported being pleased but disappointed that her husband's response was not more enthusiastic. At this session, she also reported that the examination with the gynecologist had gone extremely well. The gynecologist, who had been contacted by the sex therapists and was sensitive to the patient's difficulties, took great care to explain everything that he would be doing. His supportive manner, perhaps in conjunction with the preparatory fantasy exercises, permitted a full pelvic examination, which had previously been impossible. The gynecologist reported that her hymen was still intact but that there was no need for him to perforate it since it would not be a barrier to intercourse.

In the course of the next two sessions, the couple reported striking progress. They succeeded in having intercourse three times and felt very optimistic. The husband ejaculated quickly the first time but reported no subsequent difficulties. Although still somewhat apprehensive, she was delighted with her progress. They were not using any birth-control devices, since the husband was against them, and the wife was unable to assert herself in this area. For the most part, she remained quite dependent on him. She found herself occasionally bothered by the idea of her husband's extramarital experience, but the idea was slowly fading into the background. Since they were quite delighted with their progress and optimistic about the future, therapy was terminated after the 15th session, with a follow-up visit scheduled for a month later.

In the follow-up visit, the couple reported continued pleasure in their progress. They were enjoying intercourse approximately three times weekly. They were not using contraceptive devices and, although she hoped that she would not become pregnant immediately, she was receptive to the possibility. She volunteered to help other women with a similar problem. Although clearly pleased with the outcome, both husband and wife were uncertain about the factors that were critical to the success of the treatment. A follow-up call 8 months later found the couple to be getting along well and the wife pregnant. She said she was pleased and was particularly happy that she had experienced no nausea or other physical discomfort in the first 5 months of her pregnancy. Their sexual relationship was described as excellent, although recently the husband had become concerned that the fetus might be injured during intercourse. She was not worried, and, in fact, had been able to reassure him.

CASE 2: PARTIAL SUCCESS

The second case involves another white couple in their mid-20s, married for 5 years with a child 2 years old and the problem of vaginismus since marriage. A summary of the treatment program for this case is presented in Table 5.2.

TABLE 5.2   Case 2: Treatment Sessions and Progress

Session	Techniques employed and progress noted
1–3	History-taking.
4	Discussion of treatment plan; husband refuses participation.
5–12	Kegel exercises, genital self-examination, guided fantasy exercises with relaxation, her control over insertion of husband's finger and penis. Partial penetration is possible, but full intercourse is problematic.
13	Session with couple to discuss sensate focus.
14–16	Husband refuses sensate focus and further participation. Wife continues Kegel exercises, fantasy with overcorrection; dilators of increasing size are utilized. Success at intercourse is erratic. Patient feels that vaginismus problem is gone and that problem now is husband's attitude and differing sexual desires.
17	10-week follow-up. Situation remains unchanged. Wife is pleased with results; husband is moderately satisfied.

The wife was first seen at a community mental health center. She came for treatment at the insistence of her husband, who threatened to leave unless she got some help with her problem. Although she resented his labeling her as the problem, and believed that his lack of warmth contributed to it, she felt pressure to comply with his ultimatum. She was seen for four sessions at the mental health center prior to being referred to the Sexual Counseling Service. These sessions had focused mainly on educational matters and had included an individual session with the husband. The wife appeared to have great difficulty in talking about herself and failed to complete a body-exploration assignment because she was reluctant to touch herself. The husband left his session early to attend a sporting event. He felt that it was his wife's problem, though he might "consider" joint therapy sessions if it would be of help.

At the Sexual Counseling Service, the treatment program was conducted by a male therapist. The husband behaved in a hostile and denigrating manner during the sessions, and the wife seemed frightened, timid, and depressed. The husband felt frustrated and disgusted and reported that she seemed indifferent to sex and influenced by "some religious thing." He felt angry at himself for having put up with her for so long, that he had "wasted" 5 years of his life and "was not about to waste 5 more." She cried during the initial session and felt embarrassed, mistreated, and misunderstood. Apparently, their child had been conceived through some semen entering her vagina during an attempt at intercourse without penetration. There were frequent arguments and little communication or understanding. He felt that there must be something wrong with her vagina, which he compared to a "nostril," and that chances of therapy working were about zero. She was not sure what was wrong and gave therapy a 50–50 chance for success.

In the individual history-taking session with the wife, she had difficulty talking about herself and had to be repeatedly prompted for what little history could be obtained. She came from a close-knit, religious family of four. Her father had almost become a priest and was described as quiet and generous. Her mother was strict and outspoken. Sex had not been discussed at home. She had attended public schools except for 2 years at parochial school, which she described as uneventful. She had had no premarital sex experience. She enjoyed kissing but not anything else and had had relatively little contact with men prior to meeting her husband at age 16. She did not masturbate until after the birth of her child. She recalled having had gynecological examinations during her pregnancy but did not associate them with pain. She also recalled the doctor telling her that she was a virgin. She recalled little about childhood and could identify no significant experiences that might relate to her current difficulties. At present, she felt that sex was a chore and that she could do without intercourse, though she did enjoy closeness and physical warmth. She had no difficulty lubricating and had orgasms easily during occasional masturbation and foreplay. Her only explanation of her vaginismus problem was that someone must have told her that it hurts because she had such a fear of pain. In addition, she noted that while she could insert her small finger into her vagina, her husband's penis seemed "so big and I'm so small."

In the individual history-taking session with the husband, he reported that he was not sure that he still loved his wife, that she had humiliated him by taking him for a fool, and that now she was being a phony in being nice to him. He was the eldest child in a family of six. Father was an alcoholic who had been nasty and punishing—"like a sergeant in the army." Mother was described as religious and a martyr type—"I'll slave so you can do this." Sex had been taboo at home, and he recalled his father cutting a picture of a nude woman out of the newspaper so that the children would not see it. He started masturbating at age 15 but stopped, for unknown reasons, at age 16. He had had little experience with girls and felt awkward in making sexual advances. He had met his wife when he was 17 and felt attracted to her. They had little sexual contact prior to marriage, and the difficulties became apparent immediately after the wedding. He reported no erectile or ejaculatory difficulties. He felt that extramarital affairs were "all right" but had not had any. He felt that his wife should have become a nun and that the only things keeping him home were the child and the cost of separation and divorce. Although he ascribed the problem to his wife, he acknowledged some "hang-ups" and expressed a fear that intercourse might cause physical pain to his wife.

In addition to these evaluation sessions, therapy consisted of 12 sessions and a follow-up visit 10 weeks after termination. In the first conjoint therapy session, treatment possibilities were discussed. Despite an explanation of the involuntary nature of his wife's response, the husband continued to feel bitter and duped, suggesting that treatment proceed without him. There was discussion of the bind he was putting his wife in by giving her an ultimatum and then telling her that if she made progress it did not mean much because she only wanted his paycheck. He continued to be unwilling to become involved in the sensate-focus exercises, since he felt that they would be giving her what she wanted—physical closeness but no "sex." While distressed by his anger, the wife was willing to work independently on the problem.

The early sessions focused on the use of the Kegel exercises, genital self-examination, insertion of penile-shaped objects into her vagina, and fantasy exercises to reduce anxiety and associate pleasure with intercourse. Her initial efforts at the Kegel exercises were half-hearted, but once she was asked to keep a record of them, she did them faithfully and dutifully brought in her detailed record each week. She had a great deal of initial difficulty in examining her genitals with a mirror. She reported feeling tense and fearful of self-injury. She perceived her genitals as "ugly" and recalled her mother telling her that the body is ugly. The patient realized that she communicated the same message when she told her daughter that it is dirty to touch her genitals. She also had a great deal of difficulty inserting her finger into her vagina. She was tense, inserted her finger briefly, and quickly retracted it. If she rotated her finger at all, she experienced pain and found it much easier to rotate her body while leaving her finger stationary. Gradually, she began to feel more comfortable and reported experiencing an orgasm when removing her finger, but little real pleasure. In order to develop the association between having an object in the vagina and pleasurable sensations, she was asked to insert her finger into her vagina during masturbation. At this point, she began inserting a lubricated tampon. This was a new experience for her, since she had never used a tampon except once in adolescence, when she inserted one and then had difficulty removing it. Finally, desensitization was begun, in which she would imagine inserting her finger, a tampon, and then her husband's penis. She had difficulty in developing fantasies generally but especially with imagining inserting her husband's penis.

Despite the therapist's recommendation that they refrain from attempting intercourse, such efforts were continued at the husband's insistence. By the end of 4 weeks of exercise, he was able to achieve partial penetration and he felt that she was making some progress. This pleased her, but she continued to want him to ejaculate quickly and also continued to fear that his large penis could not entirely fit into her vagina.

During the next four sessions, she continued her Kegel and insertion exercises. She was surprised when she had an orgasm with her husband's finger inside her vagina. She continued her fantasy exercises in conjunction with relaxation both during the sessions and at home on her own. She found that her revulsion was diminishing. Efforts at intercourse, however, remained problematic. Only partial penetration was possible, and she would insert his penis at the point of ejaculation "to get it over with." She discussed the possibility of sensate-focus exercises with him, but he continued to refuse to participate.

The husband was invited to attend another session to maintain contact with him and secure his perceptions of his wife's progress. He reported an improvement in their sexual relationship—his penis could now enter about halfway and on one occasion entered completely. The possibility of sensate-focus exercises was again recommended as a means of satisfying his wife's needs for greater warmth and communication. Despite the fact that he was only interested in full penetration and increasing the frequency of intercourse, he agreed to attempt these exercises. Since they felt that they had little privacy, there was discussion of putting their child to bed earlier so as to have more evening time to spend together.

The efforts at sensate focus proved to be a failure since the husband resisted all attempts to become involved. One positive outcome of this effort, however, was that it became apparent that they could arrange to be in bed together when their relationship was going well. During the final three sessions, she continued the Kegel and fantasy exercises and began using dilators of increasing size. In the fantasy exercises during the therapy sessions, an effort was made to overcorrect for her fears that her vagina was too small for her husband's large penis; that is, she was asked to imagine herself as possessing an almost cavernous vagina which could incorporate a penis without any difficulty whatsoever. She was gradually able to insert a dilator the size of a penis, though her efforts were erratic. Success at intercourse also remained erratic. At one point, she felt that her husband just wanted to "jump in" and she tightened up. He felt that she had no interest in sex and again threatened to leave. Just prior to the final session, they attempted intercourse with almost complete entry and with some pleasure for her. Interestingly enough, as she made more of an effort to initiate intercourse, she found that her husband was "tired" and not really interested in daily intercourse after all. At the time of termination, she felt that while full penetration was not routine, the vaginismus problem itself was gone and that what remained was the problem of his attitude and their differing sexual desires.

At the follow-up session 10 weeks later, the situation remained fairly stable. They reported having intercourse two to three times weekly, occasionally with full penetration and at times with approximately two-thirds penetration. He felt that this was satisfactory, although he desired sex more frequently and wanted to engage in oral sex. She felt that things were fine, although she still objected to oral sex. He continued to be denigrating toward her, comparing her unfavorably with a television actress, and she continued to tolerate his hostility and her own resentment. She reported to be quite pleased with treatment, while he was "somewhat satisfied." The wife was contacted by phone 6 months after termination and reported that the situation had remained relatively the same as at termination and, at times, better.

This case may be viewed as an illustration of partial success, both because of continued difficulties with consistent full penetration and because of the continued difficulties in working out a mutually satisfactory sexual and martial relationship.

CASE 3: FAILURE

The third case represents a complete *treatment* failure. The patient, a 25-year-old black social worker, had been separated from her husband for 18 months. Although she and her husband had been married for 5 years, penetration had never been accomplished, and she remained a virgin. At the time she sought assistance, she was dating an older man who was gentle and caring toward her. She felt hopeless about her condition and feared his discovering that, although she had been married, she was still a virgin. It was under this impetus that she went to the local health maintenance organization and requested a hymenectomy. Since her fear of intercourse and penetration was so pervasive that she could not even tolerate a gynecological examination, they referred her for psychotherapy. Disappointed with their decision, she reluctantly called the Sexual Counseling Service.

During the first session, she displayed considerable anxiety and despair about her condition. She related with detachment to the female clinician and provided minimal information. The patient was the elder of two sisters and had grown up in a lower-middle-class family. She described her mother as unaffectionate and cold, saying that her mother also had sexual difficulties. In fact, according to the patient, her mother also had vaginismus and had difficulty tolerating full penetration to the present day. Her mother had given her and her sister repeated warnings about maintaining ones' virginity at all costs; the stigma of being an unwed mother was posed as a constant threat. She began menses at age 12 without difficulty but was not told the facts of reproduction until she was 14 years old. She recalled that her sex-education teacher warned the girls that intercourse "would hurt" and that her girlfriends substantiated this message. The patient said that she always feared intercourse, expecting to experience great pain.

She met her husband-to-be when she was a freshman in college. He was the first person she dated, and she went out with him for 4 years until their marriage. Although her husband dropped out, and she had academic difficulties, she continued and graduated from college. Both her husband and his parents resented the fact that she had succeeded in school whereas he had not. Although the couple attempted sex on numerous occasions, it was always unsuccessful. She enjoyed foreplay and affectionate closeness but panicked whenever he attempted penetration. Eventually, he gave up trying. The marriage was punctuated by a host of difficulties, both financial and interpersonal, and her husband alternated between anger at her and depression. It was he who finally decided to leave the marriage, which he did without much warning. She reacted to her husband's departure with considerable despondency, feeling responsible for the marital breakup.

During a second history-taking session, she reported that she had attempted masturbation only a few times during her adolescence. She did this by rubbing a blanket between her legs but felt so guilty that she ceased. She also reported that on the few occasions when she went for a gynecological examination, she became so anxious that she broke into tears and would not allow an internal examination. In view of her enormous anxiety, a relaxation program was started. She was instructed in the method of progressive relaxation and asked to practice it twice daily. Further, she was told that following her relaxation exercises, she should take a hand mirror and visually explore her genitals.

On the third session, she reported that she felt "silly" doing the relaxation exercises and had not practiced them. She also reported feeling "hopeless" about overcoming her problem. She had seen her boyfriend several times during the week and, although she enjoyed his company, she refrained from becoming physically involved with him since she could not bear the humiliation of his discovering that she was a virgin. In order to secure his cooperation and support for the rest of treatment, the therapist advised that the boyfriend be told directly of the patient's fears of intercourse. She refused, saying that it was "impossible." The rationale of practicing self-stimulation was explained to her and it was emphasized that with her self-stimulation exercises, she would have total control over her body and need continue only as far as she felt comfortable. The various myths and fallacies regarding masturbation were discussed, and she agreed to experiment with tactual exploration at home.

She returned the following week, saying that she could not complete the assignment. She had, however, become involved in "necking" with her boyfriend and felt more relaxed with him. She again expressed concern about going further, since he would *then* discover that she was a married virgin. In light of her refusal to share her sexual concerns with him, and her wish that she might have a hymenectomy, the pros and cons of such a procedure were explored. The therapist agreed to speak with her gynecologist and to recommend surgical removal of the hymen. The patient was told to contact her gynecologist directly for an appointment. She refrained from doing so for 2 weeks following the referral and, when she did, the doctor said that it was not necessary. Following that visit, she was successful in inserting her small finger into her vagina.

During the fifth session, she reported this success but expressed discouragement about treatment. She did not view her ability to insert her finger into her vagina as indicative of improvement, had ceased masturbating, and had not told her boyfriend of her sexual fears. Further, she had attempted intercourse with him unsuccessfully and her panic about penetration was fully reinstated. The therapist pointed out to her that she was sabotaging her treatment program by not following therapeutic instructions—she did not practice relaxation or masturbation at home but went ahead with an activity that the therapist had explicitly told her she was not ready to attempt. The patient agreed, saying that she had given up most activities soon after she started, and rationalized her lack of commitment to treatment by saying, "It's very difficult." She asked whether hypnosis might be used to overcome her problem. The therapist pointed out that her wish to have the problem hypnotized away might reflect her unwillingness to take responsibility for touching her own body. She reluctantly agreed with this interpretation.

The patient missed the next two sessions and, when she reappeared, said that she had not made any progress. Her tone indicated that she blamed the therapist for this. She felt that the therapist, who was white, failed to understand her cultural inhibitions against sexual activities such as masturbation or oral sex, and said that she was worried about the confidentiality of her sessions. She was reassured on the latter point, and the session was devoted to working on the transference issues. At the end of the session, she was invited to join a women's sexual enhancement group as an adjunct to her treatment. She refused, saying that she could not discuss her problems in a group. The therapist urged her to continue the relaxation exercises, provided reassurance that she was not alone in her problem, and indicated that her problem could be resolved if she would commit herself to the treatment effort. Since she was still dating her boyfriend, the possibility of using his penis as a substitute for her own fingers was discussed. She indicated that she preferred this to masturbation and was instructed to guide his penis around her clitoris and labia minora as a means of erotic arousal.

She returned to the next (seventh) session and indicated that she did not want to continue treatment. She had not followed through on any of the suggestions from the previous sessions and felt that improvement was hopeless. Termination was mutually agreed upon, with an open invitation to recontact the Sexual Counseling Service in the future.

Although the formal therapy effort was a total *treatment* failure, the patient was, in fact, successful in resolving the vaginismus problem! Ten months after treatment had been terminated, the patient was contacted as part of a standard follow-up from the Sexual Counseling Service. The patient indicated that she had overcome the problem with the assistance of her boyfriend 4 months after therapy had been terminated. She eventually told him that she was a virgin, and "much to my surprise, just as you predicted, he did not view it as a major problem." Together, they continued penetration efforts and currently were enjoying intercourse about four times weekly without difficulty. When asked what had enabled her to finally overcome her phobia, she replied, "I wanted to love him in a total and complete way." She indicated that she felt secure and cared for in the relationship and had finally recovered from her attachment to and depres-

sion over the loss of her first husband. She added that she "had no idea" of
why she could "let it happen within this relationship" and not in her first.
The patient still does not masturbate ("I don't need to and don't care to"),
although she now finds masturbation acceptable for others.

DISCUSSION

We shall now return to some of the issues raised at the start of this chapter
and review them in light of these three case illustrations as well as observations from other cases. In proceeding with this discussion, it may be useful
to focus on three questions:

    1. What are these women and their partners like?
    2. What factors seem to be important in the etiology of vaginismus?
    3. What factors play a role in the success or failure of treatment?

The Women and Their Partners

Beyond the common symptomatology, it is clear that there is great diversity
among these women and their relationships to their partners. Even in terms
of the problem itself, one sees considerable heterogeneity. A pelvic examination is possible with some and not with others; in the second case, the
woman had even experienced the birth of a child.[1] Despite this experience,
she viewed her vagina as too small for her husband's penis and, until
therapeutic intervention, found intercourse impossible because of the tightening of her vaginal muscles. The three cases presented also illustrate the
wide diversity of other aspects of the sexual experience. In the first case, the
couple was able to engage in and enjoy a wide variety of sexual practices
other than intercourse. This was not true for the other two cases. Two of the
women were able to experience arousal and orgasm with little difficulty,
whereas the third was quite sexually inhibited.

    Table 5.3 presents relevant patient characteristics. In addition, one can
note the strong dependency that existed in the first two women and that is
frequently seen in others. Both women preferred to stay at home and relied
heavily on their husbands and/or parents to make decisions. While almost
nothing is known about the husband in the third case, the husbands in the
first two cases provide some interesting contrasts. Both husbands were
somewhat naive sexually, although neither had a specific sexual dysfunction. Both husbands showed a fear of injuring or causing pain to their wives
and demonstrated a remarkable tolerance for abstinence from intercourse,
although each responded quite differently to the wife's difficulty and ef-

---

[1]Other cases of such impregnation with only shallow penetration have been reported in relation
to the problem of vaginismus (Fertel, 1977).

TABLE 5.3 Patient Characteristics

Case	Age (yr)	Religion	Years married	Educational level	Previous psychotherapy	Referral source
1	Wife: 24 Husband: 25	Roman Catholic Roman Catholic	4	High school graduate High school graduate	18 mo individual psychotherapy (wife)	Gynecologist
2	Wife: 25 Husband: 25	Roman Catholic Methodist	5	High school graduate High school graduate	None None	Social worker
3	Wife: 25	Episcopalian	3[a]	College graduate	None	Gynecologist

[a]Patient had been divorced for 18 months when seen for treatment.

forts at change. Fertel (1977) has commented on the observation that husbands of "virgin wives" are often overly considerate, weak, and passive–dependent. Their lack of persistence in insisting that their spouse attempt to overcome the phobic avoidance of intercourse is said to express their own fears about the aggressiveness of sex and serves as an unconscious collusion in maintaining the problem. Whereas there is some evidence to support such an interpretation in the first two cases (e.g., the sexual naiveté and fears of injury to the spouse), they also were quite different in their individual histories and reported attitudes toward sex.

In sum, amid some similarities is striking diversity in the nature of the women, the nature of their husbands, and the relationships between them.

Factors Important in the Etiology of Vaginismus

The etiology of vaginismus remains a perplexing question. The literature reports a wide variety of factors contributing to vaginismus, including past sexual trauma, psychological and social factors in the family of origin, physical pain (dyspareunia), and conditions in the present such as the partner's erectile problems or the woman's hostility toward her partner. A specific childhood sexual trauma was found only in the first case, in which the wife was molested by a man at age 7. From her description, the trauma was at least equally a result of her father's response to the event as it was a result of the event itself.

Religious orthodoxy was not a consistent theme in these three cases, although in each case there was considerable evidence that sex had been treated as a taboo area. More striking than religious orthodoxy were the rigid and restrictive attitudes toward sex in all three families of origin. The disgrace and dishonor of an out-of-wedlock pregnancy was an important theme. Perhaps of even greater significance was the fact that all three women reported that their mothers were sexually anxious and inhibited. Whereas such a pattern appears striking, it is equally obvious that many women with such backgrounds do not develop this problem. Indeed, the ability of the sisters in all three cases to have intercourse clearly indicates that other factors must also be involved.

One problem in understanding the etiological factors involved in cases of vaginismus is often the brevity of treatment and minimal detail obtained concerning varied aspects of the individual's psychological functioning. Much of the richness of detail obtained in long-term, dynamic psychotherapy is not available for consideration. For example, in the cases presented, little is known about the women's feelings toward their bodies other than their difficulty in touching and examining their genitals. This can be contrasted with the material gained from two other patients seen in long-term individual psychotherapy. Both experienced frequent situational vaginismus and inhibition in touching and examining their genitals. Beyond this, however, there was considerable additional material indicating negative feelings, at times including revulsion, toward their vaginas. One patient talked of feeling that she was damaged, incomplete, and had a hollow, empty space inside her. Both reported fantasies of the vagina functioning similar to a mouth and also reported early feeding difficulties in which they would shut their mouths tight and prevent feeding as a means of expressing rage and gaining control.

To summarize, the cases presented fit with the impressions of other clinicians that many factors play a role in the development of vaginismus and that no single etiological pattern emerges as definitive. Thus, the etiology of vaginismus remains somewhat of a mystery, fortunately one that is not necessary to solve to be of help to most patients with this sexual dysfunction.

Factors Influencing the Course of Treatment

In this section, we come to what is perhaps the most critical concern of this chapter: an explanation for the varying degrees of success among the three cases. In accounting for the differences, we can consider aspects of the patients such as motivation to change, quality of the partner relationship, and general sexual comfort, as well as relationship factors. Discussion of each of these variables follows. A summary of these factors in relation to each of the patients is presented in Table 5.4.

All of the women displayed considerable ambivalence about confronting their problem, and, as has been noted, each came to treatment because of some external pressure. Of the three, the first woman stood to gain the most from achieving successful intercourse. She enjoyed a stable, loving relationship with her husband, found other sexual activities enjoyable, and, although experiencing somewhat conflicting feelings, did wish to become a mother. In the second case, sex generally was devalued, and the woman found the rewards of motherhood mixed. In the last case, there was little motivation to conquer the vaginismus throughout her marriage, and the patient entered treatment more out of humiliation at being a divorced virgin wife than out of a wish to enjoy sexual or interpersonal intimacy.

Motivation to change clearly involves both the quality of the relationship with the partner and more general potential for meaningful interpersonal relationships. In the three cases, there appears to be a positive relationship among degree of improvement, marital satisfaction, and generally satisfactory interpersonal relationships. For example, on the Locke–Wallace Marital Adjustment Test (Locke & Wallace, 1959), the husband and wife in the first case had scores of 116 and 127, respectively, whereas the corresponding scores for the second case were 63 and 97 (low score = high dissatisfaction). The first couple enjoyed an affectionate and mutually caring relationship (albeit one of dependency on her part and overprotectiveness on his), whereas the second couple was locked into a hostile, withhold-

TABLE 5.4 Patient Characteristics Relevant to Treatment Progress

Case	Marital satisfaction (Locke–Wallace score)[a]	Ability to masturbate to orgasm	Sexual repertoire		Previous trauma	Other symptoms	Completion of assignments	Treatment outcome
			Noncoital sex with partner					
1	Wife: 127 Husband: 116	Yes	Oral-genital, mutual masturbation		Yes	Gastrointestinal, obsession	High	Success
2	Wife: 97 Husband: 63	Yes	Mutual masturbation		No	Headaches, depression	Moderate	Partial success
3	Divorced	No	Nongenital caressing		No	Depression	Very low	Failure

[a]High score = marital satisfaction.

ing marriage. The husband's refusal to attempt the sensate-focus exercises because they would give his wife what she desired is indicative of the hostility he expressed toward, and perhaps engendered from, his wife. Although the third woman had a caring male friend, she was fearful of intimacy generally and during therapy refused even to tell him of the treatment effort. Since she was still in the early phases of her relationship with her boyfriend, she still felt distrustful and dubious about making a complete therapeutic commitment.

Finally, in relation to patient characteristics, let us consider general sexual comfort. The three cases presented suggest that the extent to which the vaginismus is part of a more generalized sexual inhibition is relevant for predicting the outcome of treatment. In the first two cases, both women were able to masturbate to orgasm and were orgasmic with partner stimulation as well. The third woman, on the other hand, was inhibited sexually in all respects. Comparing the first two women, it is clear that the first was able to engage in a greater variety of sexual practices with greater pleasure. These varying degrees of general sexual comfort and discomfort were important not only because they were associated with other aspects of the partner relationship but also because they were related to the ease with which the patient could undertake the various assigned exercises.

Turning to the treatment process itself, the cases presented would appear to support the view that the deconditioning of the reflexive vaginal response is an important therapeutic ingredient. In the first case, dilators were not used, but there were successful efforts on the part of the husband to insert his finger into his wife's vagina. Additionally, the skillful handling of the gynecological examination was followed by a significant improvement in tolerating penetration.[2] The relaxation training and fantasy exercises also appeared to be critical ingredients in the successful treatment of this case, which began with such difficulty. In the second case, the gradual insertion into the vagina of objects of increasing size under relaxing conditions and the supplementary use of fantasy were also instrumental in treatment success. In this case, the Kegel exercises seemed useful in directing the patient's attention to self-control and in heightening her awareness of bodily sensations. In both the first and second cases, the observation of films and encouragement of fantasy appeared to serve a permission-giving and guilt-reducing function.

While these treatment techniques clearly are important, they occur in the context of a patient–therapist relationship. All of the procedures emphasized above require the active cooperation of the patient. The patient's attitudes toward herself and her difficulty, toward her partner, and toward

[2]In addition to a preliminary gynecological examination being essential, at times, such a visit during treatment can be used in desensitizing patient anxieties, in increasing patient sophistication regarding the anatomy of the vagina, and in remedying any medical problem that may have developed during the course of treatment (e.g., infection).

the therapist thus become important aspects of the treatment. In other words, in sex therapy we must be sensitive to the issues of transference and resistance. In short-term therapy, the therapist relies on the positive feelings of the patient to give weight and credence to the educational and prescriptive program and to overcome minor resistances. These positive feelings appeared to be present in the first two cases but absent in the third.

In all three cases, there was evidence of resistance to treatment and change. The nature of the resistance and the extent to which it interfered with treatment varied. In the first case, resistance primarily took the form of psychosomatic symptoms and the obsession with the one occasion of marital infidelity. In the second case, there were periodic failures to comply with homework exercises. In the third case, resistance took a general form of rebellion and aggressive withdrawal—appointments were missed, exercises were skipped, and intercourse was attempted despite the therapist's advice. The basis for the resistance in terms of the avoidance of anxiety and maintenance of the status quo was apparent in all three cases. What appeared to be different were the supportive factors that would permit the overcoming of the resistance. We are speaking here of the positive feelings toward the therapist and the relationship factors operating to increase motivation for change. In the third case, the therapist was, perhaps, insufficiently understanding of the patient's need to move more slowly and to gain greater trust in her relationship with her boyfriend before complying with therapeutic instructions. Although her accusations that the therapist failed to accept her sociocultural inhibitions against masturbation may be seen, in part, as a resistance against assuming responsibility for her sexual satisfaction, they also underscore the need for the therapist to be fully cognizant of the patient's fears and worries about "giving up" a dysfunction. In retrospect, it seems obvious that both the patient's distrust of "psychotherapy" from the professional establishment and her lack of security in her relationship with her new boyfriend contributed to the treatment failure.

We have come full circle in discussing the factors contributing to varying degrees of success in the treatment of vaginismus. These factors involve motivational inducements for change coming from within the person and from the surrounding interpersonal environment, as well as the quality of the alliance that is formed with the therapist and the ways in which resistances are met and handled. Although related to one another, these form distinctive elements that contribute toward the final outcome.

CONCLUSION

Most therapists report good success in treating vaginismus. For the woman who has succeeded in overcoming her anxieties, there is an affirmation of herself as an adult woman, relief from long-standing feelings of shame, and freedom to decide on motherhood. Where the marital relationship is good, both partners are jubilant that they no longer have a shameful secret that makes them seem different from others. It would appear, however, that sex therapy is not always completely successful in the treatment of vaginismus and that many cases never come to the attention of sex therapists. As we have seen, partial success may occur in some cases and complete failures in others. We have tried to understand the reasons for these varying degrees of success, and more work remains to be done in this area. Beyond this are the cases in which improvement in the partner with the presenting problem is followed by the development of a problem in the spouse. There have been reports of such developments, but they did not occur in the two successful cases presented, and the frequency with which they do occur remains to be determined. Finally, although discussion has focused on the treatment of primary vaginismus in what have been called "virgin wives," these may represent only a small proportion of the population with difficulties. Whereas vaginismus as generally seen in sex therapy may be a relatively rare phenomenon, many more women report having had similar experiences during periods of stress and marital difficulty. When viewed in this broader context, vaginismus may be found to be much more common than previously reported in the literature.

Acknowledgment. The case material in this chapter was originally published in 1980 in "The Treatment of Vaginismus" (pp. 171–191) by S. R. Leiblum and L. A. Pervin from *Principles and Practice of Sex Therapy* (edited by S. R. Leiblum and L. A. Pervin). It is reprinted here with the permission of The Guilford Press.

REFERENCES

Bezemer, W. (1987, June). *Vaginismus: A woman's problem?* Paper presented at the 8th World Congress for Sexology, Heidelberg.

Drenth, J. J. (1988). Vaginismus and the desire for a child. *Journal of Psychosomatic Obstetrics and Gynecology, 9*(2), 125–138.

Ellison, C. (1972). Vaginismus. *Medical Aspects of Human Sexuality, 8,* 34–54.

Faure, J. L., & Sireday, A. (1909). *Traité de gynecologie* (3rd ed.). Paris: Octave Doin.

Fenichel, O. (1945). *The psychoanalytic theory of neurosis.* New York: W. W. Norton.

Fertel, N. (1977). Vaginismus: A review. *Journal of Sex and Marital Therapy, 3,* 113–121.

Fuchs, K., Hoch, Z., Paldi, E., Abramovici, H., Brandes, J. M., Timor-Tritsch, I., & Kleinhaus, M. (1973). Hypnodesensitization therapy of vaginismus: *In vitro* and *in vivo* methods. *International Journal of Clinical and Experimental Hypnosis, 21,* 144–156.

Kaplan, H. S. (1974). *The new sex therapy.* New York: Brunner/Mazel.

Locke, H. J., & Wallace, K. M. (1959). Short marital adjustment and prediction tests: Their reliability and validity. *Marriage and Family Living, 21,* 251–255.

LoPiccolo, J., & LoPiccolo, L. (Eds.). (1978). *Handbook of sex therapy.* New York: Plenum Press.

Masters, W. H., & Johnson, V. E. (1976). *Human sexual inadequacy.* Boston: Little, Brown.

Musaph, H. (1977). Vaginismus. In H. Musaph & A. A. Haspels (Eds.), *Dyspareunia: Aspects of painful coitus.* Bohn, Utrecht.

Male Sexual
Disorders

III

6

Cognitive–Behavioral Strategies and Techniques in the Treatment of Early Ejaculation

Barry W. McCarthy

Premature ejaculation continues to be a highly prevalent, frequently misunderstood, and sometimes debilitating male sexual dysfunction. Sex researchers since Kinsey have disagreed strenuously on how to define premature ejaculation. Even today, there is little consensus in the field on the causes or etiology of this common male disorder. Accordingly, McCarthy begins this chapter with a thoughtful review of the key definitional and diagnostic issues. The term "early ejaculation" is preferred since it is intrinsically less pejorative and value-laden than "premature ejaculation," and the author draws our attention at the outset to the role of situational factors and expectations in defining the problem. He argues that it is not possible, as others have suggested, to establish an absolute definition of early ejaculation. For example, previous attempts to specify a given time period or number of thrusts during intercourse need to be qualified by the age of the individuals, the circumstances of sexual contact, and the expectations of each partner. It is the extent to which early ejaculation interferes with subjective satisfaction, according to McCarthy, that is essential to the diagnosis of the problem.

Why does early ejaculation continue to play such an important role in the sexual experience of most American males? Noting that few systematic studies have been conducted on this important topic, McCarthy nevertheless offers a number of tentative explanations. He discusses the role of masturbation, for example, which is viewed as contributing indirectly to the problem via the expectations that it should be conducted in a manner that is "penis-focused, goal-oriented, rapid, and intense." Early experiences with partner sex can also foster early ejaculation, as many adolescent males function autonomously and without much need for sexual stimulation from their partners. High levels of sexual excitement in combination with high

141

anxiety, in many instances, lead naturally to rapid ejaculation. McCarthy also cites recent research indicating that some males may have constitutionally lower thresholds for orgasms, thus predisposing them to problems of early ejaculation. Finally, he distinguishes between primary and secondary early ejaculation, with the latter condition referring to individuals who once had control of ejaculation but no longer do so. Secondary early ejaculation is more likely to be associated with relationship conflicts and is sometimes indicative of the male being intimidated by a sexually or emotionally demanding partner.

In this chapter, McCarthy offers a cognitive–behavioral approach to the treatment of early ejaculation. The three major components of this approach are (1) challenging the self-defeating cognitions of the male, (2) establishment of a cooperative partner relationship, and (3) introduction of specific behavioral techniques for improving ejaculatory control. The author emphasizes that behavioral interventions should be introduced concurrently *with cognitive approaches, in order to integrate fully the separate components of the treatment program. Behavioral techniques are described in detail, and the central concept of* successive approximation *is clearly enunciated. A number of valuable script modifications are also included, such as guided masturbation, oral stimulation, and changing positions of intercourse. In the detailed case presentations, McCarthy illustrates the critical importance of relationship factors in determining the clinical outcome in most cases.*

Other unique aspects of this chapter are the discussion of ejaculatory control techniques for single males and the emphasis on a psychoeducational approach to sexuality for prevention of early ejaculation in future generations. Key elements in this approach are the emphasis on similarities between male and female sexual needs, development of more accepting attitudes toward masturbation, and the substitution of nondemand, pleasure-oriented focus in partner sex, as opposed to the more typical goal-oriented approach of most males. The author concludes with the suggestion that by changing sexual attitudes and expectations in this way, men are also better prepared to deal with sexual difficulties commony associated with aging.

Barry W. McCarthy, Ph.D., is Professor of Psychology at the American University in Washington, D.C. He is the author of numerous articles, chapters, and books on various aspects of sexuality, including Sexual Awareness *(1984, with E. McCarthy) and* Male Sexual Awareness *(1988).*

Recent sex therapy research and intervention have focused on the complex male problems of erectile dysfunction, inhibited sexual desire, and paraphilias. Surprisingly little work has been done on the most common male sexual dysfunction, early ejaculation. In other male sexual dysfunctions, the man's desire or ability to be sexual with a partner is prevented, or there is a major impairment. In early ejaculation, the male does experience desire, arousal, orgasm, and a sense of satisfaction. So unless the partner has objections, the sexual relationship simply proceeds. An alternative explanation for the lack of research and therapeutic attention to the problem of early ejaculation is the mistaken notion that it is a simple dysfunction that is well understood and easily treated. From this viewpoint the only therapeutic challenge is dealing with resistance, secondary gain, or an underlying dynamic agenda.

Viewing early ejaculation as an uninteresting male dysfunction that is easily treated by "mechanical" behavioral techniques is a major conceptual and therapeutic misconception. This chapter presents a cognitive–behavioral approach to conceptualizing and treating early ejaculation. There are several reasons to carefully conceptualize, assess, and treat the problem of early ejaculation. First, it represents a major manifestation of the male performance orientation to sexuality generally and orgasm specifically. Secondly, it is one of the most common male dysfunctions, especially frequent among younger males. Third, it is a precursor to other male dysfunctions, especially erection problems and inhibited sexual desire. Fourth, early ejaculation interferes with female sexual response and can be a major source of conflict and misunderstanding in a couple's relationship. Fifth, if the younger male learns lessons about pleasure, comfort, and working together as a couple through developing ejaculatory control, these learnings can serve to inoculate him against subsequent sexual problems as he ages.

"Do-it-yourself" techniques to cure early ejaculation often have iatrogenic effects in causing erection dysfunction, couple sexual dissatisfaction, and eventually inhibited sexual desire. Techniques such as wearing two condoms, using a desensitizing cream, biting his tongue, or thinking aversive thoughts (such as how much money he owes) can be harmful in two ways. These techniques serve to reduce arousal and can cause erection difficulty rather than lead to ejaculatory control. Secondly, the man is isolating himself from his partner, which leads to further emotional alienation and can destroy the couple's bond.

Early ejaculation is a complex problem that can undermine a male's and a couple's sexuality. However, if properly formulated and treated, the attitudes and techniques he learns can help build a solid foundation for functional and satisfying sexuality throughout a person's life. A cognitive–behavioral model of assessment and treatment will facilitate this task.

DEFINITION

How early is too early? Is the measurement an objective or subjective one? Is it a couple or an individual issue? Some researchers have attempted to utilize a time criterion—such as 1 or 2 minutes of intercourse thrusting. Others have emphasized a movement criterion—inability to maintain ejaculatory control with more than 20 seconds of rapid thrusting. Masters and Johnson (1970) emphasized the importance of the couple dimension by defining early ejaculation as the male ejaculating before the female was orgasmic at least 50% of the time. Others emphasize the element of voluntary control by proposing a definition of the problem based not on time, movement, or partner response but on the male's sense of voluntary control over the ejaculation process. The disagreement over definition is reflected in the terms used to describe the dysfunction—"premature ejaculation," "rapid ejaculation," "involuntary ejaculation," and "lack of control." In traditional sexuality texts, this dysfunction was usually placed under the category of "impotence." The term "early ejaculation" is preferred because it is the most descriptive and the least pejorative and value-laden. The term "learning ejaculatory control" is preferred because it emphasizes the voluntary learning process and has the positive connotation of learning a new skill.

The assessment/definition that is most clinically useful focuses on the couple's subjective evaluation and elements of pleasure and satisfaction rather than strictly a performance criterion. Since the major assessment technique in cognitive–behavioral sex therapy is the detailed sex history, an early ejaculation dysfunction would be revealed by asking both partners about the role of ejaculation in the sexual interaction. When the male ejaculates before intromission, at the point of intromission, within two to five thrusts, or before 30 seconds, almost all couples will identify this as early ejaculation. But what if the male ejaculates between 1 and 2 minutes or can thrust slowly for 5 minutes but can only perform three rapid thrusts before he ejaculates? These situations constitute a significant percentage of early ejaculators. In these cases subjective evaluation, sexual satisfaction, and a sense of voluntary control are crucial. There are some couples whose sexual style is to engage in highly arousing multiple-stimulation pleasuring scenarios where the woman is orgasmic and then have quick, intense intercourse with the male ejaculating in a minute of short, rapid stroking. If both partners enjoy this scenario and are sexually and emotionally satisfied with it, an iatrogenic dysfunction could be created by labeling this a sexual dysfunction. On the other extreme are males who present for therapy stating that they seek ejaculatory control so that their partner may become orgasmic with intercourse. In interviewing the couple, the clinician learns that the woman's orgasmic pattern is usually with cunnilingus but that she or he feels inadequate because she's not having the "right" kind of orgasm. She reports enjoying intercourse, and he engages in intercourse thrusting that may last from 7 to 10 minutes. Other couples engage in manual stimulation to the woman's orgasm and find this a satisfactory sexual scenario.

It is impossible to develop a totally objective measure of early ejaculation. Understanding the ejaculatory pattern in a couple's sexual relationship means carefully assessing each partner's pattern of arousal and orgasmic response, their sexual style, expectations regarding sexual satisfaction, the time between intromission and ejaculation, the pattern of intercourse thrusting, the woman's orgasmic response pattern and preferences, and the man's sense of awareness and voluntary control over the ejaculatory process. It is important to assess motivations and expectations carefully. Is the man's interest in better ejaculatory control to increase his pleasure and make sex more enjoyable for them as a couple, or is it to prove something to the woman or have her be orgasmic during intercourse so he feels like a successful lover? Are their expectations about intercourse and the role of orgasm during intercourse reasonable or unrealistic performance demands? Is the focus on ejaculatory control to give and get more pleasure, or is it a performance demand?

INCIDENCE

Having discussed how difficult it is to assess the problem of early ejaculation, let us examine the best estimates of the incidence of the problem. Approximately one in four males has an unsuccessful first intercourse experience, and the most common cause is ejaculation before the penis is in the vagina (McCarthy, 1988). The great majority of males report early ejaculation in their initial intercourse experiences, so that the phenomenon of early ejaculation is an almost universal male experience. Among young adult males, approximately 50% complain of early ejaculation, and approximately one-third of adult males report they ejaculate more rapidly than they would like (Frank, Anderson, & Rubinstein, 1978). There is evidence that early ejaculation is also a problem in homosexual couples. Taken together, these reports indicate that early ejaculation, however defined, may be the most commonly experienced male sexual dysfunction, especially in younger males. Since lasting cognitions and skills concerning sexuality are formed in adolescence and young adulthood, the experience of early ejaculation may be particularly powerful

CAUSES OF EARLY EJACULATION

The great majority of males have their first orgasmic experience during either masturbation or a nocturnal emission (wet dream). Masturbation is experienced by over 90% of young males, typically between ages 10 and 14. Masturbation is usually practiced in an intense, rapid, and goal-oriented manner. The adolescent male focuses only on penis stimulation and is intent on reaching orgasm and the associated few seconds of intense pleasure. Young males who engage in "circle jerks" view the boy who ejaculates the fastest and the farthest as being the most masculine. Basically, the messages about sexuality are all too often that it is penis-focused, goal-oriented, rapid, and intense. These cognitions and behaviors are antithetical to the process of ejaculatory control.

This is not to say that masturbation is the cause of early ejaculation or that masturbation is a negative sexual behavior. The opposite is true. Body self-exploration, genital self-exploration, and learning about sexual responsiveness via masturbation can be a positive, integral aspect of male sexuality. Learning about erections and ejaculations through masturbation is healthy for the young man and can help him in later adult functioning with a partner. The problem is not with masturbation per se, but in the attitudes and behavior that can accompany the masturbation. Anxiety, guilt, and embarrassment about masturbating and/or fear of being discovered are potentially injurious. Young males could benefit from seeing masturbation as natural, positive, and healthy behavior that serves as an excellent means of learning about their body and the sexual response cycle. Rather than masturbating in a rapid, penis-focused, goal-oriented manner, the male could approach masturbation in a slower, more sensual, whole-body, and pleasure-oriented way. Exercises to change male attitudes and behavior regarding masturbation are presented by McCarthy (1988) and Zilbergeld (1978).

In partner sex, young males learn to function autonomously; that is, they are able to experience desire, erection, and orgasm without needing stimulation from their partners. Since they need so little, the "foreplay" time is spent on arousing the woman so she is ready for intercourse. The man resists the woman stimulating him because he worries he'll get too excited and ejaculate too rapidly, perhaps even before intercourse. Thus, the male learns to associate high levels of sexual excitement with high anxiety about early ejaculation. This combination of high excitement and high anxiety leads to early ejaculation. The majority of males begin their sexual lives as primary early ejaculators.

As they become more comfortable with the sexual situation and partner, most males gradually learn ejaculatory control by a process that is undermined. One could hypothesize that there are several components in this process: (1) a regular rhythm of being sexual; (2) increased comfort with practice; (3) a more give-and-take "pleasuring" process rather than goal-oriented foreplay; (4) allowance of more time for the variety of sensations in the sexual experience; (5) greater intimacy and security resulting in increased sexual comfort; (6) partner encouragement for a slower, more tender, rhythmic sexual interchange; and (7) shift of intercourse positions and/or thrusting movements. Which of these components are necessary or sufficient for learning ejaculatory control has not been demonstrated.

A large number of men do not go through this gradual change process to gain better ejaculatory control. The pattern of early ejaculation becomes a regular part of their sexual relationship. There is research evidence (Strassberg, Kelly, Carroll, & Kircher, 1987) that some males are hypersensitive to penile arousal and are predisposed to developing early ejaculation. They believe the orgasmic threshold for early ejaculations is lower for some men, who thus require less physical stimulation to reach orgasm. Other males simply do not regard it as a problem and enjoy rapid, intense orgasms. Some couples develop a pattern of engaging in a quick intercourse where he rapidly ejaculates and then having a second, longer intercourse. In relationships where the woman's sexual needs are considered nonimportant, the male "getting it over with as quickly as possible" may be viewed as showing consideration for the partner. A new "sophisticated" pattern is for the male to use manual or oral stimulation to the woman's orgasm, and then have rapid intercourse. A variant on that theme is to follow early ejaculation with the use of manual or vibrator stimulation to the woman's orgasm.

Kaplan (1974) and Perelman (1980) have focused on the main cause of early ejaculation as being the male's lack of awareness of the premonitory sensations before ejaculation. For most young men "orgasm" and "ejaculation" are experienced as the same phenomenon. Although they do occur almost simultaneously, they are different processes. Ejaculation is an element in the orgasmic response. It is possible to have an orgasm without ejaculation (for example retrograde ejaculation after prostate surgery or "dry orgasm" as a side effect of medication). It is also possible to have a partial ejaculation without the accompanying sensation of orgasm (the sensation of "dripping"). In males, the orgasmic experience is a two-phase process, consisting of the emission phase and the ejaculatory phase. At the point of ejaculatory inevitability (which approximately correlates with the emission phase), the orgasm is no longer a voluntary response (which is not true of female orgasm). In other words, if the male passes the point of ejaculatory inevitability (roughly 1–3 seconds before the start of ejaculation), even if his child walks in or the telephone rings and he is sexually turned off, he will still ejaculate. Thus, a key element in learning ejaculatory control is to identify the point of ejaculatory inevitability.

Some men develop secondary early ejaculation, which refers to the syndrome in which the male once had ejaculatory control but no longer does. Although less common than primary early ejaculation, this phenomenon demonstrates other possible causes for early ejaculation. Perhaps the most common cause is low frequency of intercourse. It is hard to gain or maintain ejaculatory control when intercourse frequency is less than once every 2 weeks. Early ejaculation can also be a sign of relationship stress. For example, the male who ejaculates early is expressing anger at his partner and cheating her of sexual pleasure. This is a popular clinical hypothesis of systemic-oriented therapists, but there is little empirical evidence that it is a frequent cause of early ejaculation. Other relational causes can be anxiety over intimacy and lack of comfort in the sexual relationship. As the woman becomes more interested or demanding sexually, the male might become intimidated and ejaculate rapidly. Another factor is that the woman's sexual arousal can be highly stimulating to the man and result in early ejaculation.

There are also situational causes for early ejaculation. These can include stress, anxiety about being sexual with another partner, or concern over erectile functioning. Although it is quite rare, early ejaculation can also be symptomatic of a neurological disease such as multiple sclerosis. The most common pattern is for early ejaculation to be a primary sexual dysfunction caused by psychological, learning, and relationship factors.

A COGNITIVE–BEHAVIORAL MODEL OF TREATMENT

There are three focuses in a cognitive–behavioral approach to the treatment of early ejaculation: (1) challenging self-defeating cognitions about sexuality and the role of the woman and replacing them with facilitating cognitions about not only ejaculatory control but also the role of sexuality and intimacy in his life; (2) learning the behavioral skills of identifying the point of ejaculatory inevitability, utilizing the stop–start technique, and alternating intercourse positions and thrusting movements; and (3) establishing a cooperative, intimate relationship that facilitates sexual functioning and emotional satisfaction for both people. The primary goal is to teach ejaculatory control, and the secondary goal is to help the male (and the couple) develop the cognitions, behaviors, and emotional intimacy that will inoculate them against future sexual problems.

The cognitive–behavioral strategy is to emphasize learning new attitudes and skills that not only address the ejaculatory control issue but generalize to the entire sexual relationship. A prime cognition is focusing on increasing the man's confort and pleasure and deemphasizing the concept of performing for the woman. Many men (and couples) misconstrue the reasons for learning ejaculatory control as helping the woman to be orgasmic with intercourse. This performance criterion puts additional pressure on both the man and woman.

The second major cognitive restructuring component is to reframe learning ejaculatory control as a couple task rather than the man viewing this as solely his responsibility. The partner is viewed as integral to the change process. There is an involvement and learning for the partner, rather than her view of the therapy as a passive and mechanical experience to help him. Cognitions about being a cooperative sexual couple and giving rather than performance are crucial. The man learns to view the experience as integrating intimacy and sexuality. These cognitions and this view of pleasure and intimacy challenge the male's double standard and autonomous standard of sexual performance. It is sad, but true, that this approach is more inviting and acceptable to the woman than the man. Yet, it is just this broad-based approach to sexuality that will serve to inoculate against future sexual problems as the man and the relationship age.

A common mistake cognitive therapists make is to emphasize cognitive changes before doing the behavioral exercises. Clinical experience indicates that cognitive change in males is facilitated by engaging in the behavioral exercises simultaneously so that the cognitive and behavioral changes reinforce each other. The danger for the male is to become defensive as he is confronted with his traditional cognitions. The man does not trust or respect the cognitions he is being encouraged to adopt. The more the therapist avoids the ejaculatory issue and exercises, the higher the male's anxiety. The therapist cannot become so enamored with secondary goals and making other changes that he forgets the primary goal of developing ejaculatory control. Cognitive changes and secondary goals are facilitated by integrating them into the behavioral exercises.

The behavioral exercises for ejaculatory control are discussed in detail by McCarthy and McCarthy (1984). Before focusing on the actual ejaculatory control exercises, it is highly advised that the couple have at least two experiences with the nongenital sensuality exercises and with the nondemand genital pleasuring exercises. The rationale given to the couple is that this establishes a solid base for their sexual relationship. A secondary benefit is that many couples find this a very pleasurable and bonding experience. The male learns that nondemand pleasuring can be of value to him, and this reduces some of the performance pressure he feels. The woman finds not only that can she be an involved partner but that she is more open and responsive to him than she might have been for months or years.

A central concept in the ejaculatory control exercises is that of successive approximation. The first exercise involves nonintercourse stimulation (manual stimulation at first and oral stimulation if comfortable) with a focus on learning to use the "stop–start" technique and discriminate the point of ejaculatory inevitability. The concept of the "stop–start" technique was originally introduced by Semans (1956) and then was displaced by the "squeeze" technique of Masters and Johnson (1970). However, at present, most clinicians use the stop–start technique because it is easier to teach to couples and more acceptable to them than the squeeze technique. Some males engage in masturbation exercises (Zilbergeld, 1978) during the early part of the program during which the couple is practicing the nondemand exercises. The advantage is that the male practices the discrimination task and the stop–start procedure in an environment where he feels greater control and has more privacy. It also serves as a motivator because he realizes he can learn ejaculatory control by himself and may become enthusiastic about transferring that to partner sex. Masturbation also serves as an orgasmic outlet during the nondemand couple pleasuring week or weeks.

Most couples find the first exercise relatively easy and successful. Identifying the point of ejaculatory control is usually not difficult. However, a problem can occur when the male tries to push the limits too far. He is encouraged to tell his partner to stop well before the point of inevitability.

Most couples communicate by the male simply saying "stop," although others will use a code word such as "now," "hit it," or another idiosyncratic word or phrase. Other couples prefer a nonverbal signal. The exact technique or word is unimportant. What is crucial is that it is a clear signal, readily received, and acted on. Inevitably the male will have at least one experience where he signals too late and ejaculates. Rather than becoming angry or feeling like a failure, he is encouraged to enjoy the ejaculation and to see it as a learning experience in identifying the point of ejaculatory inevitability. Typically the exercises end with an orgasmic experience for both partners. It is crucial that the woman's preferences and desires be given equal importance. A valuable lesson for males is that the woman can be orgasmic with manual or oral stimulation and that many women find this easier and their preferred manner of reaching orgasm. The male can begin to view intercourse in the context of the pleasuring experiences rather than as the prime or only way of being sexual. Intercourse is best viewed as part of the pleasuring process, not separate from it.

Once the stop–start technique is practiced and mastered in nonintercourse sex, the focus shifts to practicing these techniques during intercourse. The intercourse position utilized is woman on top. Most males have learned early ejaculation in the man-on-top position, using short and rapid stroking. The "quiet vagina" exercise is a very different experience when the woman guides intromission and engages in minimal movement. The male is told to make no movements; he simply enjoys the feeling of intravaginal containment. If at any time the male feels himself approaching the point of ejaculatory inevitability, he can signal her to stop moving. If he still feels as if he is going to ejaculate, he can request that she disengage from intercourse and lie next to him. Even if it is necessary to interrupt numerous times, the couple is encouraged to proceed with this nondemand intercourse for 10 to 15 minutes. During the exercise, the male is encouraged to enjoy massaging and touching his partner while engaging in intercourse. Rather than proceeding to orgasm with short, rapid strokes, the woman can control the pace of thrusting in the female-on-top position, using longer, slower stroking, and eventually the male proceeds to orgasm with this type of stroking. Most males report this as a very positive and motivating experience of prolonged intercourse.

As the ejaculatory control exercises continue to be practiced, there is a gradual introduction of different kinds of thrusting and intercourse positions. The therapist needs to reinforce the concept that ejaculatory control skills are a matter of incremental learning. Typically, the male wishes to rush the process and focus on improved performance instead of maintaining the nondemand pleasure orientation. The most difficult position in which to maintain ejaculatory control is the male-on-top position with fast, short thrusting. Most males do desire to have intercourse in the male-on-top position, but if they want ejaculatory control in that position, they need to utilize longer, slower stroking and be willing to stop and/or slow down or pause during coital thrusting.

An important element is learning to set aside time to be a sexual couple. Males have an unrealistic expectation that sex can be easy and automatic. Neither a sexual relationship nor ejaculatory control can be taken for granted; both require continued awareness and attention (which is true of any behavioral change). With continued practice and change, the man and couple become involved in a positive feedback cycle that takes ejaculatory control out of the realm of a problem and into being a positive part of the sexual relationship. Learning to value intimacy and set aside the time to be a sexual couple builds on and reinforces the secondary goal of changing the male's attitudes toward sexuality and an intimate relationship. This helps to maintain and generalize the gains achieved in sex therapy.

BILL AND MARGARET

Sexual problems that last longer than 6 months are not likely to remit spontaneously. However, most males do not seek sex therapy for ejaculatory control until the problem of early ejaculation is behaviorally overlearned and entrenched in the couple's relationship. This was the case with Bill and Margaret, a couple in their late 20s who had been married for 2 years. Margaret was 27 and the owner of a hair-styling studio. Bill was 29 and a legislative lobbyist for a financial institution. This was a first marriage for both. They had had a rather tumultuous dating relationship before marriage. Margaret had been in individual and group therapy for 1½ years at a university counseling center before dropping out of school to enroll in a hair-styling program. During their dating period, Margaret re-entered individual therapy, and Bill, who had never participated in therapy, attended five conjoint sessions. That therapist helped Bill and Margaret deal with issues in their relationship and increased their commitment to marrying. However, the therapist made an incorrect assumption in stating that with increased intimacy and the commitment of marriage, the ejaculatory control problem would disappear. Although this can happen with some couples, it is the exception rather than the rule.

Margaret saw the early ejaculation as a symbol of lack of love and caring on Bill's part. As the problem continued over the next 2 years, Margaret became increasingly frustrated and withdrawn. She demonstrated her displeasure by resisting his sexual advances, and their intercourse frequency decreased from three to four times per week to once every 10 days. A sexual and marital crisis was precipitated by Margaret's belief that Bill was acting more isolated and distant when they did have intercourse. When they talked about their sexual relationship, it was usually in bed after intercourse, and the communication quickly broke down into tears, anger, and accusations. Bill was on the defensive and handled the sexual issue by avoiding talking to Margaret, which frustrated her even more.

Unbeknownst to Margaret, Bill had attempted a "do-it-yourself" technique to gain better control. He had bought a desensitizing cream he'd read about in a men's magazine and applied it to the glans of his penis 20 minutes before initiating sex. He also masturbated the day before couple sex. During intercourse he tried to keep his leg muscles tense and think about sports as a way of keeping his arousal in check. Bill was unaware that Margaret felt emotionally shut out during the sex. Bill was becoming more sensitized to his arousal cycle and was worrying about erection. He was not achieving better ejaculatory control, and he was enjoying sex less. The sexual relationship was heading downhill, and miscommunication and frustration were growing. If they had allowed this trend to continue for 1 or 2 more years, it is likely that Bill would have developed an erection problem, and both would be experiencing inhibited sexual desire and avoidance.

If at all possible, especially with a married couple, it is highly recommended that the first session be conducted with the couple together. The more Bill and Margaret are able to view the ejaculatory control process as a cooperative couple task, the greater the probability of success. Having the first session together allows the therapist to meet both partners and set a tentative therapeutic agenda. In the case of Bill and Margaret, it was important to confront them with their self-defeating conceptualization of the problem. Margaret's ultimatum was that if Bill did not gain ejaculatory control and fulfill her sexual needs within 3 months she would take it as a symbol of lack of caring for her and would separate. The therapist responded that this was an unworkable contract. It increased Bill's performance anxiety and was antithetical to the concept of working together as an intimate, cooperative team. As often happens, the woman's resentment and frustration and the man's embarrassment and avoidance become entrenched over time and interfere with the therapeutic plan. The initial assessment interview is to evaluate whether a couple is appropriate for sex therapy or whether the major focus should be on marital or individual therapy. The decision to pursue sex therapy with Bill and Margaret was based on how disruptive to the relationship the early ejaculatory problem appeared and the clinician's evaluation that although the marital bond of respect, trust, and intimacy was badly strained, it was still intact.

After the initial couple session, individual sex history sessions are scheduled. Obtaining sexual histories individually is necessary if the clinician is to get an honest report as well as uncover any hidden agendas or secrets. At the start of the sex history the client is told "I want to hear about your sexual development, both strengths and problem areas. I'd like you to be as truthful and frank as possible. At the end of the session, I'll ask if there's anything you do not want shared with your partner. I'll respect that, but I need to know what these things are so that I can understand what is happening and be of help to you."

Margaret came in first for the history. The special elements from a cognitive–behavioral viewpoint to focus on in a sex history are cognitions about the self as a sexual person, the role of sexuality in the relationship, the importance of orgasm at each sexual opportunity, the role of guilt and blame, and how negative sexual experiences (past and present) have been dealt with. The behavioral skills to focus on include comfort talking about sexuality and especially being sexually assertive, skills around nondemand touching, multiple stimulation, including oral stimulation, and skills around being orgasmic. The sexual history is conducted in a semistructured, chronological framework, moving from lower-anxiety to higher-anxiety items.

Margaret had two secrets that she had never shared with Bill. Although she found it easier to be orgasmic with manual stimulation, she had been orgasmic during intercourse with a married man she'd had an affair with a year before meeting Bill. Margaret expressed ambivalent feelings about that relationship. She felt that the man was a very sophisticated lover, and she had been highly aroused and orgasmic with him. Yet, the relationship had been a manipulative one. He'd been emotionally abusive to Margaret, and the relationship had ended when he accused Margaret of giving him herpes and berated her. In fact, it was probably he who gave Margaret the herpes. Margaret was only experiencing herpes outbreaks two or three times a year, but when they did occur, she was flooded with negative feelings about herself, sexuality, and relationships. She initially saw Bill as a loving, stable man who would help rid her of negative feelings concerning sexuality. Instead, he continually disappointed her with the early ejaculation. Bill knew about the herpes but not about her sexual history and strong negative feelings.

The second secretive area was that Margaret did not enjoy his performing cunnilingus after he had ejaculated. This pattern had developed during the past year as Bill's compensation for his early ejaculation. Initially, Margaret found it arousing and was orgasmic, but now it had become a "turn-off." She believed Bill did not enjoy giving oral stimulation because he was in contact with his own semen (Margaret was right—when Bill was individually questioned about this technique, he reported he did it out of guilt rather than pleasure). Margaret felt that she was being mechanically serviced so she could have an orgasm. This caused her to feel further alienated from Bill and the sexual experience. Margaret gave permission to share these secrets with Bill at the feedback session.

Toward the end of the session, we carefully reviewed Margaret's cognitions concerning the meaning of the early ejaculation. Margaret began to become aware of how much excess meaning and symbolism Bill's ejaculation held for her. Not only did she take it very personally, but she believed that neither of them were deserving of good sexual feelings. Margaret accepted the concept that it was a couple task to develop better ejaculatory control and a more satisfactory sexual style. This concept was more acceptable because she realized it did not mean that she was the cause of the early ejaculation, nor did it symbolize her sexual unworthiness or his lack of commitment or any of the other negative values she had imbued it with.

Margaret left the session with more hope for successful solution and an agreement to drop her ultimatum about better performance or divorce.

Bill was clearly nervous as he approached the sex history interview. He started out by saying that he thought that the problem really was all his and that although he loved Margaret, he didn't blame her if she left him. Bill felt like a total failure, thought that his "do-it-yourself" techniques had not worked, and was immensely relieved to hear that no matter what the ad said, those techniques did not work for most males. Bill had found the assigned reading (McCarthy, 1988) on the male attitude toward intercourse and on the success rate with ejaculation control somewhat reassuring, but he had labeled himself as more severely dysfunctional than other males.

Bill was terribly embarrassed about his secret concerning masturbation, which he engaged in on a twice-daily basis. From adolescence on, Bill had used masturbation as his primary means of stress reduction. For him, masturbation was a humiliating secret (he believed married men should not masturbate). The manner in which he masturbated undoubtedly contributed to the early ejaculation pattern. Bill focused only on his penis, using rapid strokes with the goal of ejaculating as quickly as he could. This was both to prevent himself from being discovered (he usually masturbated in the bedroom or bathroom—sometimes with Margaret in the house—and he would also masturbate while sitting in the stall at the men's room at work) and from a desire to "get it over with" as soon as he could and forget about it. Bill's view of his masturbation was very negative, and he strove to keep it a brief, isolated part of his life. In a literal sense, he followed the Biblical injunction "let not thy right hand know what thy left hand doeth." By confining the pleasure to a few seconds of orgasm, he minimized his pleasure and thereby appeased his sense of guilt.

When Bill heard that using self-exploration/masturbation exercises to help him learn ejaculatory control would be part of the therapeutic program, he was incredulous. He was given bibliotherapy to change attitudes toward masturbation (McCarthy, 1988) as well as instruction to practice a slower, more aware method of masturbation to facilitate ejaculation control (Zilbergeld, 1978). Bill reduced the frequency of masturbation by only masturbating when he felt sexual desire and using nonsexual anxiety-reduction techniques to deal with stress. As the therapy progressed, Bill continued these exercises and gained greater comfort and good ejaculatory control with masturbation. This served as a major motivator to continue toward better control with partner sex—he realized now it was a goal he had the skills to reach.

As a lobbyist, Bill was very skilled at presenting his case, being optimistic, and arguing his points. When it came to his personal and sexual life, Bill was inhibited, unsure of himself, and had a particularly low sexual self-esteem. As an adolescent, Bill remembered being very interested sexually, but very unsure around girls. He had adopted the role of being the girl's "good buddy" and would participate in social and athletic activities in groups rather than one-on-one dating. His sexual outlet was secretive. Bill's first intercourse at 19 was perceived as a failure because he ejaculated before he could insert his penis in the woman's vagina. He then tried desperately to insert because the young woman urged him to, but he was in the refractory period (a phenomenon Bill did not understand), and so he did not get a firm erection and felt doubly humiliated.

Bill dealt with his sexual anxiety and early ejaculation by avoiding the issue and by being very socially and politically active with a large number of friends and interests. Most of his sexual contacts were one-night stands or short affairs where he did not talk about the sexual functioning. By the time he had met Margaret, his pattern of early ejaculation and avoidance of talking about sexual issues was well entrenched. Margaret was a stylish, ambitious, and energetic person—all characteristics Bill found very attractive. He saw her as someone who would be amenable to his socially active life style and would make few intimacy or sexual demands on him. They had had a roller-coaster dating relationship with a lot of fun and exciting times intermixed with fights and emotionally explosive scenes about being attracted to other people and not paying enough attention to each other. Bill wanted to marry and have children, and it was he who had pushed aside Margaret's doubts and resistance.

Bill was expecting a major change in himself, Margaret, and the relationship with marriage. He was looking to "settle down" and have a more conventional, less party-oriented life. The act of marriage itself typically does not produce change, however. Ideally, marriage is a process where the partners exert positive influence over one another, and the marriage allows each person to bring the best out in himself or herself. Bill was disappointed that this positive process was not occurring between himself and Margaret. Rather than directly confronting her with his dissatisfaction, he handled it indirectly by making hostile and denigrating comments about her. She, in turn, focused more and more on her sexual dissatisfaction and blamed it entirely on him and the early ejaculation problem.

In cognitive behavioral sex therapy, the feedback session is crucial. There are three major foci in the feedback session: (1) give the couple an understanding of the problem that is acceptable to them and focuses toward couple problem solving and away from guilt and recrimination; (2) set a positive expectancy for change based on a model of working together as an intimate team to build a comfortable, functional, and satisfying sexual style; (3) increase commitment toward the sexual exercises in a manner that promotes gradual learning and views roadblocks (problems) as a learning cue, not as a reason to blame or give up. With Margaret and Bill, key concepts included setting a positive expectancy that if they approached ejaculation control as a cooperative team instead of using ultimatums and avoidance, the prognosis was excellent. Although the focus would be on learning ejaculation control, secondary goals would be to improve their communication, assertiveness, and problem-solving skills to put the relationship on a more positive and solid footing. Margaret was challenged to become an active, involved participant rather than being there just to help Bill. There were lessons to be learned about sexuality and being a marital partner that Margaret could benefit from.

Each was sensitized to a psychological "trap" they were at risk to fall into and thus sabotage treatment success. For Bill, the trap was avoidance rather than directly dealing with an issue, and for Margaret, it was to blame and demand rather than assume personal responsibility to help solve the problem.

The first 2 weeks of the sex therapy exercises are crucial both for diagnosis and for development of a base for the change process. Bill and Margaret did well with the nondemand, nongenital and genital pleasuring exercises. They utilized the structured exercises to develop a rhythm of three to four sexual experiences per week. Each became comfortable in initiating. Margaret learned to make requests instead of demands, and Bill learned to slow down and to give and receive tender, sensuous touches; and together, they developed a more intimate and secure bond. Meanwhile, Bill was engaging in masturbation exercises and reporting 10 to 12 minutes of ejaculatory control. In the couple's therapy sessions, Bill became more comfortable discussing explicit sexual issues, and together the couple created their own sexual vocabulary (i.e., penis was called "ringer," the exercises were called "get together time," and intercourse was called "getting it on"). Margaret surprised Bill and herself by being relatively nondefensive when he would confront her with negative or immature behavior patterns. They engaged in an attraction exercise (McCarthy & McCarthy, 1984) in which each partner revealed all the personal, interpersonal, and sexual characteristics they liked and found attractive about the spouse and then made three specific requests for change that would make the spouse more attractive. This exercise had a positive impact in reestablishing a sense of personal value and attractiveness.

Once the prohibition was lifted on intercourse, Bill and Margaret began to reexperience some of the old patterns and problems. Bill had good ejaculatory control by himself and with manual and oral stimulation but was clearly intimidated by intercourse. Margaret reported feeling closer to Bill and more responsive and orgasmic with him then ever before, so the regression with intercourse was unexpected and exasperating. In retrospect, the therapist had erred by not preparing the couple better to deal with problems that might arise with intercourse. Both the couple and the therapist become too caught up in the momentum of positive change and were reluctant to tamper with it by increasing awareness of possible pitfalls.

The "quiet vagina" exercise went well the first time, but the second time, as Margaret engaged in faster, more rhythmic movement, Bill did not signal to stop until too late; as Margaret was moving to break the coital connection, he ejaculated on her. He was embarrassed and apologetic (not an appropriate response), and although she verbalized that it was okay, she was clearly put off. The return to the "trust" position and gentle caressing was a sham—Margaret remained cold and uninvolved. Rather than talking about it or calling for a consultation or additional appointment, the tension and frustration built over the next 3 days. Bill alternated between being apologetic and avoidant. Margaret didn't want to fall into the trap of blaming Bill, but she was very put off by the way he handled this incident.

As the therapist went to meet them in the waiting room, he was aware this would be a difficult and challenging session. Instead of allowing the couple to play out their self-defeating pattern, the therapist structured the session as one to deal positively with sexual problems and directly confront the self-defeating patterns of the past. Margaret was quite responsive to this approach and took responsibility for her negative behavior. In retrospect Margaret wished she had told Bill that the timing had not worked, that she didn't enjoy his ejaculating on her thigh, and either asked to be caressed by Bill or to be involved and receptive in the trust position. Bill was confronted with the fact that although he had made good progress in ejaculatory control techniques, when there was a problem he reverted to his old way of thinking and avoiding. Margaret's frustration came less from the early ejaculation and more from his avoiding and not dealing with her or the feelings. He could have expressed his responsibility at not signaling sooner. Bill could have simply enjoyed the ejaculation instead of kicking himself. He could have reached out to Margaret and been open to her requests rather than apologizing and avoiding her. Instead of the sexual experience being viewed as neutral or mildly negative, it had turned into a very negative experience, which threatened to set off a major regression.

The therapist pointedly said to Bill and Margaret that this was a lapse from which much could be learned, and they had a choice to treat it as such or allow it to turn into a major relapse. They were encouraged to return to the intercourse exercise and practice slower movements and signaling to stop well before necessary. Bill was cautioned not to stretch the limits—to signal 10 times if needed. Margaret was encouraged to continue to focus on the pleasuring experiences and to allow herself to be orgasmic before intercourse began.

In learning ejaculatory control, as with other sexual dysfunctions, the issue is not to avoid problems but to have a learning and coping set so that the couple are brought together as an intimate team. One element in an ongoing sexual relationship is the ability to be flexible and not to overreact to a mediocre or negative experience. Even in couples who do not complain of sexual problems, at least 10% of their sexual interactions will be unsatisfactory (Frank et al., 1978). Couples who continue to enjoy sexuality are able to laugh or shrug off their unsuccessful experience and go back to being sexual the next day. In sex therapy, it is important to learn how to think about these experiences, learn coping skills, and communicate in an empathic, problem-solving manner.

Bill and Margaret continued to make progress in gaining ejaculatory control through intercourse. As with many couples, the progress was not as rapid as they would have liked or as dramatic as in the first 2 weeks. To promote a sense of learning, Bill and Margaret would have a special focus for each exercise session. There was an emphasis on building a more positive couple sexual repertoire rather than just reversing the early ejaculation problem. Bill especially enjoyed experimenting with multiple-stimulation scenarios. He enjoyed giving Margaret pleasure with manual and oral stimulation and was particularly aroused when she stimulated him as he was stimulating her. Bill learned that multiple stimulation enhanced his pleasure during intercourse and that it contributed to ejaculatory control. When intercourse included kissing and breast caresses, it made the experience a slower, more involving one. Margaret found this way of having intercourse much more emotionally fulfilling than the old system of doing nothing but rapid thrusting.

Sex therapy need not end abruptly. After weekly sessions for 16 weeks, the next two sessions were scheduled for every other week. At the last session, Bill and Margaret set goals for what they would accomplish over the next 6 months and how they could maintain and generalize their hard-earned gains in sex therapy. They decided to keep the time they regularly came for therapy to do something as a couple and communicate about their emotional and sexual relationship. They agreed to set aside couple time at least every other week to make sure they continued to nurture their marital bond. Sexually, they planned to maintain the rhythm of being together two or three times a week, to continue slower thrusting, to utilize multiple stimulation during intercourse, and to practice pausing or slowing down rather than stopping movement.

At the 6-month follow-up, Bill and Margaret reported greater confidence in their marital and sexual relationship. During the interim, one of Margaret's sisters had been diagnosed as having cancer, and Margaret appreciated both Bill's concern for her sister and his empathy for Margaret's emotional need to talk things out. Margaret felt that Bill had really "been there" for her and that his concern was genuine. Bill felt that much of what he had learned in sex therapy about being more aware of himself and his feelings, taking a more active and responsive role, working toward a goal with gradual steps, and being more emotionally and sexually expressive had generalized to other situations. He reported feeling more confortable and satisfied with sexuality in the marriage generally and with ejaculatory control specifically. He regretted that he still did not have very good control in the male-on-top position using short, rapid stroking, but he accepted that as a reality. Their once-a-month "quickie" intercourses when Margaret was not interested in an involved scenario utilized the male-on-top, short rapid thrusting, although Bill now found this less satisfying then he had in the past. Six months after the follow-up interview, Bill and Margaret were sent a follow-up therapy evaluation questionnaire. Margaret filled one out for both of them and reported that the greatest satisfaction is that they felt like a more solid and more intimate couple.

Clinical Observations

There were at least three factors that promoted a positive therapeutic outcome for this couple. The destructive nature of their blaming, avoidance, and ultimatum interaction was successfully confronted, and over time, they developed as an intimate team working together to learn ejaculatory control and improve sexual satisfaction. Second, they made rapid progress initially, which reinforced a positive expectation of change. When they ran into problems, they did not regress to self-defeating patterns but successfully problem solved as a couple. Third, they were consistent in using the ejaculatory control exercises. The combination of learning new cognitions, developing sexual skills, and working as an intimate team is a powerful antidote to early ejaculation.

This case demonstrates that conducting successful sex therapy for early ejaculation is not simply a mechanical procedure that can be easily performed by an unsophisticated and uninterested paraprofessional technician. One of the major mistakes clinicians make in conducting sex therapy for early ejaculation is to treat the couple in a noninvolved way and assign homework tasks routinely. The therapist gets more involved in the therapy only when there is a difficulty or resistance. This has the effect of reinforcing the couple for having problems in the sex therapy (McCarthy, 1985). The sex therapist needs to employ a variety of skills including assessment, individual therapy, couple therapy, sex therapy, sexual functioning, giving and processing homework tasks, dealing with cognitive distortions, and teaching emotional intimacy and sexual expression. Successful sex therapy for ejaculatory control requires an attentive, involved therapist who focuses the couple on the ejaculatory control issue and at the same time is cognizant of individual and couple issues that can be utilized to help develop greater self-awareness, sexual expression, and emotional intimacy.

SUCCESSFUL SEX THERAPY FOR MALES WITHOUT PARTNERS

The percentage of males suffering from early ejaculation is probably greater for those who do not have an ongoing relationship than those who do. Males without a regular partner are even more distressed by the problem of early ejaculation because they are fearful of being rejected and/or humiliated by a new partner. A common trap for these males is to have transitory, noninvolving relationships so they can avoid dealing with the woman about early ejaculation. Treatment for males without partners focuses on two issues: (1) increasing comfort with sexuality and learning ejaculatory control techniques via masturbation and imagery and (2) helping the male choose an appropriate partner to integrate sexuality and ejaculatory control into the relationship.

Males with early ejaculation often are not very knowledgeable or comfortable about sexuality. After the initial sex history, the client is given bibliotherapy to provide information and change attitudes toward sexuality in general and male sexuality specifically (McCarthy, 1988; Levine & Barbach, 1983). He is encouraged to practice a different way of thinking about and engaging in masturbation to make it a slower, more pleasure-oriented experience. Eventually, he engages in a series of masturbatory and fantasy exercises to learn the skills of ejaculatory control (Zilbergeld, 1978). In addition, he is taught deep muscle relaxation and breathing techniques to monitor and control his anxiety. The therapist can utilize guided imagery techniques while the client is relaxed to help him rehearse sexual scenarios. Most therapists prefer simply to talk to the client about the benefits of approaching sexuality from a more comfortable, pleasure-oriented perspective.

In discussing partner sex, de-emphasizing the "performance for the woman" orientation is stressed. The male is encouraged to choose a woman with whom he is comfortable, attracted to, and trusts will work with him as his sexual friend in developing a functional and satisfying sexual relationship. This is a new concept for almost all males. The more typical pattern is to play the "macho" role in initiating a relationship. The male is encouraged to avoid singles bars and their version of the sexual game.

Choosing an attractive woman is important, but in addition he is encouraged to pick someone he can emotionally relate to. Many males fall into the trap of choosing a woman to whom they aren't attracted so they have a reason to not be aroused, or choosing a woman who is so attractive that they feel intimidated. The trust factor is particularly important. Males with sexual problems feel particularly vulnerable to the woman's evaluation of them. They deal with this vulnerability by being defensive and avoidant, which serves to exacerbate the sexual difficulty. The male is strongly advised to be more self-disclosing and assertive. He is encouraged to choose a woman who he believes to be psychologically sensitive and trustworthy. By that we mean a woman he can talk to about the sexual problem and who will work with him in developing a more functional and satisfying sexual style. At a minimum, it is crucial that he not choose a woman who will reject and/or humiliate him because of the sexual problem.

The concept of choosing a woman who will be a "sexual friend" in resolving a sexual problem needs to be carefully discussed with the single male because it is so different from his typical cognitions and behavior concerning women. In addition, extensive behavioral rehearsal is utilized to teach the male skills to self-disclose about and discuss the early ejaculation. A typical verbal scenario is "I do like and care about you. I would like us to develop a relationship that is involving and enjoyable. I'm sexually attracted to you and care about your sexual feelings and needs. I have learned a pattern of early ejaculation, and as I get more comfortable I will develop better ejaculatory control. It's a gradual process, and I want you to be my sexual friend in understanding the process and working with me. You didn't cause this problem, and it's not a reflection of my feelings about you, but I do need your help and support in gaining better ejaculatory control. I want our emotional and sexual relationship to be satisfying for both of us."

On occasion, I have had consultations with the couple and in some instances engaged them in couple's sex therapy. However, in general, the intensity of a sex therapy contract is not appropriate for a new relationship, as it can telescope and intensify issues that will cause a new, tenuous relationship to break up. A more appropriate therapeutic strategy is to encourage the male to enjoy the developing relationship, to be more honest and self-disclosing about ejaculatory control, and to provide additional clarification and support to the partner as needed. Perelman (1980) has advocated use of male-only groups in the treatment of early ejaculation. These can be of value, but unlike female sexuality groups, male sexuality groups have proven hard to organize. The factor that seems to be a major inhibition is the reluctance of males to disclose sex difficulties to other males. An individual cognitive–behavioral approach to males without partners has shown a great deal of clinical utility and needs to be investigated empirically.

AN UNSUCCESSFUL COUPLE TREATMENT CASE

Follow-up studies by De Amicis, Goldberg, LoPiccolo, Friedman, and Davies (1985) and Hawton, Catalan, Martin, and Fagg (1986) indicate that early ejaculation can be a difficult problem to treat, and especially to maintain treatment gains with. For successful treatment of early ejaculation, and especially if those gains are to be maintained and generalized, it is crucial to change cognitions about sexuality, learn the behavioral skills of ejaculatory control, and develop an intimate, cooperative emotional and sexual relationship.

Don and Angelica are an example of a couple who learned the basic ejaculatory control skills but whose problems with the cognitive and intimate components negated their sexual changes. They had been married 4 years. It was Don's second marriage and Angelica's first. The referral was from Angelica's therapist who had treated her for depression and low self-esteem. The individual therapist believed that her disappointment and frustration concerning early ejaculation was a major contributing factor to the depression.

Don was 38 years old, a litigating attorney, and a partner in a law firm. He had a son from his previous marriage who visited him once a month and who stayed with him for 2 weeks during the summer. Don had been in couple's therapy during his first marriage, and after it broke up, he had been in individual and group therapy for over a year. Don and Angelica had engaged in 15 sessions of premarital counseling. Interestingly, during all those therapy contracts the problem of early ejaculation had barely been mentioned, much less dealt with. Don hated to be confronted with negative feedback, and he used the litgator's ploy of "the best defense is a good offense." He was a reluctant sex therapy client, claiming that he had no complaints about the marriage or sex. The one issue he identified as problematic was the decision of whether to have children.

Don was the older of two children. His parents had remained married until his father died when Don was 8 years old, and his mother had never remarried. Don recalled his parents' marriage as "all right," but with a good deal of conflict and said he couldn't imagine they were a very sexual couple. Don reported masturbating at 11, beginning intercourse at 18, and being quite sexually active throughout college, law school, and up to the point of his first marriage. He adamantly stated that no one had complained about his early ejaculation, and he considered himself a sophisticated lover. Two years into his first marriage, he and his wife began to have conflicts about sexuality, and there was a precipitous decline in intercourse frequency from four times a week to once a month. Don used masturbation as his primary sexual outlet and had a number of affairs both before and after the separation. Don reported that by the time he met Angelica he was ready to commit to a serious relationship. He saw sex as one of the primary positive forces of his relationship with Angelica. Don conceptualized ejaculatory control and the sex therapy as something he would do for her.

Angelica was 32, a convention planner for a prestigious hotel chain, and 2 years before had won an award as one of the best-dressed women in Washington. She was a very competent professional who traveled at least a week a month for her job and was used to things working right for her. She was quite agitated at the state of her marriage and the role of sex in her life. Angelica was an emotionally expressive person who felt frustrated by Don's avoidance of issues. She had had innumerable internal conversations with herself about whether there was a problem and whether Don was to blame or she was the problem (Don subtly reinforced the latter view). Angelica used the pill but wanted to start a family soon and was agitated about Don's ambivalence about children.

Angelica was the third of five children. She remembers her parents' marriage as stormy but loving. She had grown up with a lot of open affection and strong emotional expression. Angelica started dating at 15, had her first intercourse when she was 19 and away at college, and had her first orgasm through masturbation at 22. Being orgasmic was now easy for Angelica, and her pattern was to be orgasmic with manual or oral sex in the pleasuring/foreplay period. Angelica saw herself as sexually liberated and sophisticated. When Don came into her life, she felt that he was the kind of solid, mature man she wanted to marry. She was attracted to him physically, saw him as successful, and since he had one child, she had assumed he was capable and motivated to have more. Angelica was sensitized to infertility problems because this had occurred with one of her best friends as well as two of her siblings. Initially, sex with Don was frequent, exciting, and experimental (especially with respect to positions and techniques for oral sex). Angelica was aware of the early ejaculation problem, but she naively assumed it would go away with time. The first year of the marriage had been exciting although a bit rocky, but the second year had been highly frustrating, which resulted in the individual therapy and now the couple sex therapy.

From the initial couple assessment, individual sex histories, and conferences with Angelica's therapist and the therapist who had conducted the premarital counseling, it was evident that this was a complex couple who had the potential to develop major relationship problems. However, this is not how they saw themselves. Don was especially resistant to examining other psychological and couple dynamics and wanted to focus the therapy solely on the ejaculatory control issue. The therapist emphasized the importance of Don learning ejaculatory control for himself.

The first 2 weeks of the sex therapy exercises went quite well. Don was an intelligent, competitive person who took the stance that once he could identify a problem he could overcome it. The masturbation exercises went especially well, and Don was pleased that he not only mastered the stop–start process but was able to engage in self-stimulation for 15 minutes before ejaculating. The couple exercises also were progressing satisfactorily. The couple found that identifying the point of ejaculatory inevitability with manual stimulation and signaling the start–stop was reasonably straightforward. Both enjoyed engaging in genital pleasuring and being orgasmic with manual and oral stimulation. In fact, they were very experimental and expressive sexually those first 2 weeks and were clearly having fun with the exercises.

Don and Angelica had a major nonsexual argument between the third and fourth week. They only did one exercise, which was far from pleasurable, and Don experienced his earliest ejaculation, although it was still better than before therapy began. Angelica refused to participate in the quiet vagina exercise because she felt angry at Don and emotionally disconnected from him. The argument revolved around a disagreement between Angelica and a female friend; Angelica strongly felt that Don was not supportive of her. The therapist tried first to work around this issue by getting a commitment from Don to discuss the issue with Angelica in a nonsexual situation (with clothes on over coffee sitting in the kitchen). In exchange, Angelica would initiate the quiet vagina exercise on a different day.

At the next session, Angelica reported that Don had kept his agreement, but not the spirit of it. She still felt misunderstood and unsupported by him, and he felt it was more important to make his point and be right than to be empathetic with her. She did go ahead with the quiet vagina exercise, and the first time it went extremely well, with her controlling the thrusting. Intercourse lasted over 10 minutes, and he reported enjoying intravaginal ejaculation. She said it was an excellent experience but repeated she did not believe she would be orgasmic during intercourse.

The next practice with the quiet vagina was significantly more problematic. Don was suggesting faster movement, and Angelica told him not to try to control her. They argued during the intercourse; Don began moving at his rhythm and ejaculated. Angelica did not enjoy the experience, more because she was angry at Don than by the early ejaculation. Don pushed hard in the therapy session to talk about why Angelica was not more aroused with intercourse. He questioned whether she would ever be orgasmic during intercourse no matter what he did. This set off a power struggle accompanied by name calling. Don's main goal was to prove he was right and to blame Angelica. Her main goal was to ward him off and not let herself be dominated or abused by him. The concept of working together as a team to gain ejaculatory control and to increase pleasure was lost in the fray. The anger was high at the end of the session, so Don and Angelica were advised not to attempt further exercises but, rather, to talk over the kitchen table and to engage in nondemand pleasuring exercises.

As the therapist went to the waiting room to invite the couple in for the next session, it was evident that there was a frostiness in their relationship, and he geared himself for a difficult session. The therapist was shocked and confused when Don made the pronouncement that the ejaculatory control problem was now resolved. They had practiced twice with Don controlling movement and reported excellent control when Angelica did not move and fairly good control when she moved slowly. Don stated, and Angelica nodded agreement, that they understood the technique of ejaculatory control and the process of change. At this point, Angelica starting making a different point, but Don cut her off. He reported they had talked with clothes on in the living room but could not agree on what to do next. The therapist stated that he wanted to understand each person's views of the progress and the impasse and purposefully turned to Angelica and asked for her perception of the issues. As Angelica talked, Don interrupted several times, usually with sarcastic, put-down comments. Although he was assured he'd receive ample time to state his perceptions, it was clear that he had no interest in listening to or understanding Angelica. Angelica said she was pleased with the ejaculatory control progress, but she felt more dominated and pressured than ever with Don. Sex was not a loving act between them. Don's reaction varied between being angry and blaming to being emotionally overcontrolled and distant.

In the ensuing 3 weeks, the gradual exercise approach gave way to a series of sexual experiences some of which were physically satisfying and others of which served as an impetus for anger, blaming, and emotional isolation. This emotional and sexual roller coaster was reflected in the therapy sessions themselves. Angelica and Don were not an intimate team working together on ejaculatory control and developing a sexual style; rather, they were like antagonists increasingly involved in a destructive power struggle.

Don announced this would be their last session because they had learned what they needed to learn, and it was up to Angelica to stop being defensive and put it into practice. The therapist was confrontive with them, saying he did not accept that assessment of progress or Don's statement of the present problem. An alternative therapeutic strategy was proposed, which was to see each person individually and explore perceptions and feelings about sex and power in their relationship. The rationale was that in individual work there would be less defensiveness and greater opportunity to break the impasse. Don was opposed to the suggestion, saying they had all the tools they needed to work this out on their own. The therapist left the option open for couple consultation and/or individual therapy, and the sessions were terminated.

There was no contact from either person, and after 6 months the post-therapy assessment questionnaire was sent to Don and Angelica. Only Angelica returned hers. She said the ejaculatory control problem was moderately better, especially when they worked on doing the stop–start. However, sex was less frequent, and she found it less enjoyable. Angelica had returned to individual therapy to "sort out things for me personally."

In retrospect, this case illustrated two major issues in doing sex therapy for ejaculatory control. A crucial element is developing the concept of the intimate team working together, which broke down with Don and Angelica. The second is that change in cognitions, especially about the male's sexual and emotional expression, is just as important as the behavioral exercises. These cognitive changes were unacceptable to Don. In hindsight, Don might have benefited from three or more individual sessions before beginning the sex therapy program. He saw the psychological domain as his weak point and Angelica's forte, which greatly exacerbated his defensiveness once the sex therapy program became difficult. An alternative strategy, once they had difficulty and had gotten off track, would have had the therapist act more quickly and efficaciously to confront the self-defeating power struggle. When ejaculatory control does not succeed, it is more likely to be a difficulty in maintaining motivation and completing the program than it is with the exercises per se. When couples regress after successful treatment, it is usually because they did not set up a maintenance and generalization program, and/or the cognitive and intimacy skills necessary to maintain long-term changes in a sexual relationship were not adequately attended to.

PREVENTION OF EARLY EJACULATION AND A BROADER VIEW OF EJACULATORY CONTROL

In understanding the process of early ejaculation and effectively intervening, one wonders if it would be possible to adopt a psychoeducational approach that could prevent this problem. One of the major reasons to treat early ejaculation effectively is that the "do-it-yourself" techniques often cause more serious problems of erectile dysfunction, inhibited sexual desire, female sexual dysfunction, and dissatisfaction with the couple's relationship. The concept of the man and woman working together as an intimate team challenges the view of the young man as an automatic and autonomous sexual performer.

Early ejaculation is a multicaused phenomenon. A common theme is the rapid, intense, orgasm orientation learned by males in both masturbatory sex and partner sex. A psychoeducational approach to sexuality that stresses awareness, comfort, and a pleasure orientation would be in the best interest of men and women alike. Most males see those characteristics as being "feminine" rather than "masculine." A positive approach to life-long sexual functioning emphasizes that there are many more similarities than differences sexually and emotionally between men and women (McCarthy, 1988). Concepts of taking time for sexuality, nondemand touching, and pleasure orientation are characteristics that are in the best interest of the man, the woman, and the couple. The man also needs to change his attitudes about masturbation. Masturbation can be viewed as a normal, healthy way to experience sexual pleasure and orgasm with an emphasis on building comfort and prolonging the experience by exploring a variety of sensations and feelings.

A crucial element in prevention and in developing a satisfying sexual relationship is for the man and woman to become respectful, trusting and intimate partners. This means that the man is willing and able to communicate sexual feelings and requests to his partner. So often unsuccessful attempts to treat early ejaculation come from the man trying to do it on his own by reducing arousal instead of increasing comfort. The key concepts in ejaculatory control involve a gradual approach to increasing awareness and comfort and viewing sexuality as an intimate team experience. These concepts not only facilitate ejaculatory control but set a solid basis for an ongoing, satisfying sexual relationship. The attitudes and experiences young males often develop during partner sex are maladaptive for ongoing sexual relationships, especially after age 30. The intense performance orientation and the avoidance of the woman's stimulation make the man vulnerable to sexual problems as he ages. The earlier in his life that he learns to view sexuality as a comfortable, cooperative, pleasure-giving, and pleasure-receiving experience, the better. It will not only facilitate ejaculatory control but will serve to inoculate the man against sexual problems as he ages and promote sexual functioning and intimacy in an ongoing relationship.

REFERENCES

De Amicis, L., Goldberg, D., LoPiccolo, J., Friedman, T., & Davies, L. (1985). Clinical follow-up couples treated for sexual dysfunction. *Archives of Sexual Behavior, 14,* 467–489.

Frank, E., Anderson, C., & Rubinstein, D. (1978). Frequency of sexual dysfunction in normal couples. *New England Journal of Medicine, 299,* 111–115.

Hawton, K., Catalan, J., Martin, P., & Fagg, J. (1986). Long-term outcome of sex therapy. *Behaviour Research and Therapy, 24,* 665–675.

Kaplan, H. S. (1974). *The new sex therapy.* New York: Brunner/Mazel.

Levine, L., & Barbach, L. (1983). *The intimate male.* New York: Doubleday.

Masters, W., & Johnson, V. (1970). *Human sexual inadequacy.* Boston: Little, Brown.

McCarthy, B. (1985). Use and misuse of behavioral homework exercises in sex therapy. *Journal of Sex and Marital Therapy, 11,* 185–191.

McCarthy, B. (1988). *Male sexual awareness.* New York: Carroll and Graf.

McCarthy, B., & McCarthy, E. (1984). *Sexual awareness.* New York: Carroll and Graf.

Perelman, M. A. (1980). Treatment of premature ejaculation. In S. R. Leiblum & L. A. Pervin (Eds.), *Principles and practice of sex therapy* (pp. 199–233). New York: Guilford Press.

Semans, J. (1956). Premature ejaculation. *Southern Medical Journal, 49,* 352–358.

Strassberg, D., Kelly, M., Carroll, C., & Kircher, J. (1987). The psychophysiological nature of premature ejaculation. *Archives of Sexual Behavior, 16,* 327–336.

Zilbergeld, B. (1978). *Male sexuality.* Boston: Little, Brown.

7

Retarded Ejaculation: A Much-Misunderstood Syndrome

BERNARD APFELBAUM

Bernard Apfelbaum is widely regarded as one of the most innovative and creative theorists in the field of sex therapy. In the following chapter he challenges existing clinical accounts of retarded ejaculation as the result of inhibition of orgasm in the male and presents instead a radical reformulation based on the concept of "autosexuality" in the retarded ejaculator. Acknowledging that retarded ejaculation is a relatively rare clinical phenomenon, Apfelbaum suggests that it is crucially important in revealing current biases in the field. For example, he points out that coital anorgasmia in the female, which he equates with retarded ejaculation in the male, is commonly dealt with by focusing on the negative feelings of the woman toward her partner and by relieving her of performance pressures during intercourse. In contrast, most sex therapy manuals recommend the use of guided stimulation techniques for progressively increasing the level of arousal in the retarded ejaculator. These procedures, according to Apfelbaum, produce enormous performance pressure for the patient and border on sexual coercion.

The account of retarded ejaculation presented in this chapter begins with the author's observation that some males appear able to achieve erections sufficient for intercourse despite a relative absence of subjective arousal. These "automatic erections" are taken as evidence by both the male and his partner that he is ready for sex and capable of achieving orgasm. Instead, these individuals frequently experience detachment, performance anxiety, and hostility or resentment toward their partners. The retarded ejaculator is described as "the workhorse of sexual relationships," as he provides constant erections and a compulsive focus on the sexual gratification of his partner. Most female partners, in fact, report multiple orgasms during intercourse with these men. This is in marked contrast to the conventional view of the retarded ejaculator as withholding pleasure or satisfaction from his partner. Apfelbaum argues further that retarded ejaculation may represent one end of a continuum, ranging from those who strongly prefer stimulation by a partner to those who, like the retarded ejaculator, are more responsive to their own stimulation. Most of these individuals, he points out, are likely to avoid partner sex altogether and may thus never enter treatment.

Not surprisingly, Apfelbaum is highly critical of conventional sex therapy approaches to retarded ejaculation. These typically assume that the ejaculatory reflex in the male is "blocked" or "inhibited," requiring increasing levels of stimulation by the female partner. Most sex therapists treat retarded ejaculation in a manner analogous to vaginismus, he notes, rather than approaching it in a similar fashion to female coital anorgasmia. Rather than increasing the performance demands on the patient, Apfelbaum suggests we consider a counterbypassing strategy. This involves encouraging the male to express openly his lack of arousal and feelings of distance or hostility from his partner rather than denying or "bypassing" such feelings. The goal of therapy is to focus awareness of the patient's fundamental lack of arousal and to overcome the powerful performance demands these individuals typically experience. It is only then, according to Apfelbaum, that real progress can be made.

Bernard Apfelbaum, Ph.D., is the Director of the Berkeley Sex Therapy Group. He is the author of numerous articles and chapters in the field of sex therapy.

At one time all the sexual disorders were thought of as symptoms of severe personality disturbances. Long-term therapy was thought to be indicated, and even with extended treatment, the prognosis was considered poor. With the development of the field of sex therapy, this diagnostic assessment has been revised for most of the sexual disorders. The most conspicuous exception is retarded ejaculation (RE).

I propose that the pessimism about treating RE is a consequence of diagnostic and therapeutic misunderstandings of such magnitude and direction as to suggest a pronounced clinical bias. This bias can be seen as intrinsic to both psychoanalytic and behavioral approaches but also as reinforced by easily misunderstood clinical features of RE.

If we correct for this bias, RE is as treatable in brief sex therapy as are the other sexual disorders. This hypothesis is difficult to confirm with certainty because of the clinical rarity of this condition (1–2% of most clinical populations). The actual incidence of RE in all likelihood far exceeds its clinical incidence. Masters and Johnson's (1970) sample of 17 was the largest reported as of the first edition of the present volume. Our sample was then 12, with 10 of these being treated cases. Partly as a result of the impact of the first edition, our sample is now 34. Kaplan's (1974) original statement that her sample size was too insignificant to report has as yet not been revised.

Because RE is rare, it is of only limited clinical interest. However, it is of special interest just because of its rarity: The way it is understood and treated is more revealing of underlying clinical assumptions than is the case for the other sexual disorders, since these biases are less constrained by data and experience.

To begin with, the generally accepted treatment approach to RE uniquely exposes the limitations of the "dysfunction" conception. This conception leads the clinician to expect that the most rapid treatment results will be gained if performance problems are taken as the therapeutic point of entry. However, it is this focus that has partly been responsible for the difficulty treating RE, since, as I will try to demonstrate, this syndrome is a case of a performance symptom that masks a subtle and specific desire disorder. The radical simplification of diagnosis by dysfunction, that is, by performance symptom, has obscured the key diagnostic signs of RE.

DIAGNOSTIC ISSUES

What Is Retarded Ejaculation?

A clue to diagnostic ambiguities in the standard conception of RE is to be found in the diagnostic label itself. In actual practice, "retarded ejaculation" is used to refer to male coital anorgasmia. All causal conceptions and treatment strategies are directed only to the inability to have specifically coital orgasms. At most treatment facilities, RE is seen because the partner wants to be impregnated. Hence, the stress is on not ejaculating rather than on not being coitally orgasmic, a clue to one source of bias in the understanding and treatment of RE. This disorder typically is looked at from the partner's point of view rather than the patient's.

Clearly, if this disorder were simply one of a difficulty reaching orgasm, but orgasm and ejaculation nevertheless did occur, pregnancy would not be an issue. In the typical case, the man will never have experienced a coital orgasm. Yet, the term "retarded ejaculation" equally clearly would seem to refer to a slowness to ejaculate, a meaning even more directly suggested by "delayed ejaculation," an alternate label in use. However, only Kaplan (1974, p. 317) mentions that the term can be used in this sense, and she does not discuss this interpretation of RE further; as is true of all other writers, her discussion is focused exclusively on coital anorgasmia. Interestingly, slowness to ejaculate is not discussed in the literature.

"Partner anorgasmia" might be an apt term for this condition, since the retarded ejaculator has difficulty reaching any kind of orgasm with a partner, although it sometimes is possible, with difficulty, for him to be orgasmic with manual or manual-plus-oral stimulation, since heavy and prolonged friction can be applied in a way that is not possible in coitus.

In addition to the ambiguity of the diagnostic label, there is an ambiguity in the way it is customarily applied. All men who are unable to have coital orgasms are diagnosed as retarded ejaculators (as long as coital orgasm is not prevented by premature ejaculation or erection problems). This thus includes men whose anorgasmia is specific to coitus, as well as men who do not have coital orgasms because they have difficulty reaching orgasm in general.

Men who have difficulty reaching orgasm in general are like women with primary anorgasmia. These women do not have coital orgasms since they do not have any kind of orgasm; it would make no sense to include them with women who are easily orgasmic in general and whose anorgasmia is specific to coitus. Yet this is exactly what is done with men, a practice that is all the more puzzling in view of the fact that no one has attempted to justify it; indeed, it has yet to be noted at all.

As we shall see, the whole focus of the standard treatment approach is on vaginal containment. The capacity to masturbate to orgasm is simply assumed and, indeed, is essential to the standard behavioral treatment of RE. The question of whether the man may also have difficulty masturbating to orgasm is never raised. Men who have difficulty with masturbatory orgasms require quite different treatment than men who are specifically coitally anorgasmic, but there is as yet no discussion of such cases.

What makes this of importance is that it is only when masturbatory anorgasmia is removed from consideration that the features of RE, that is, of specifically coital anorgasmia, appear. I propose that the key diagnostic sign of RE is that only the patient's *own* touch is erotically arousing, and his basic sexual orientation is "autosexual" (masturbatory) rather than heterosexual or homosexual. This is the critical differential diagnostic cue. Patients with RE invariably report enjoying masturbation more than sex with a partner. If a man has had difficulty with masturbation that is not simply episodic, then RE should be ruled out.

Thus, diagnosis by dysfunction has grouped together men who are coitally anorgasmic but who enjoy masturbation, and for whom it is even their primary sexual orientation, with men who are coitally anorgasmic but who masturbate only with difficulty and who, in general, experience little sexual pleasure. The true retarded ejaculator could never develop masturbatory anorgasmia.

Retarded Ejaculation as a Desire Disorder Specific to Partner Sex

Diagnosis by dysfunction has obscured one desire disorder, masturbatory anorgasmia, by classifying it as retarded ejaculation. It also has obscured another desire disorder that is specific to true retarded ejaculation, a desire disorder that appears only when a partner is present but that is masked by the presence of facile and sustained erections.

We are accustomed to thinking that any loss of desire or erotic arousal would be reflected by a loss of erection. Not only does the retarded ejaculator not lose his erection, but a hitherto overlooked feature of this condition is the presence of erections that almost suggest priapism. They are sustained far beyond the ordinary range, but, strangely enough, this almost seems to be a consequence of *lack* of erotic arousal rather than of a high level of arousal.

This quasi-priapism helps account for the repeated and rather startling finding that the retarded ejaculator's partners often are coitally multiorgasmic despite his coital anorgasmia. Still more surprising, these sustained erections are present even when the patient admits feeling sexually repelled by or angry at his partner.

I have no adequate explanation for this phenomenon, although it is reminiscent of the rare reports of men who have been successfully raped by women, that is, who have had sustained erections under stress. It has been speculated that a contributory factor is the total lack of performance anxiety, even of performance intention. In any case, sexual functioning at low levels of arousal or even accompanied by aversion is clinically familiar if theoretically unaccounted for as yet. It is as if the retarded ejaculator's excitement (erection)-phase functioning is out of phase or out of "sync" with his level of desire and erotic arousal.

Performance Implies Arousal

Perhaps the most striking illustration of the effect on the clinician of the RE patient's sustained erections is the fact that *partner-specific* RE is considered a clinical condition. This is a fully accepted diagnostic practice, even though one might ask why, if a man is coitally anorgasmic with only one partner and not others, it is not assumed that something is going on with this particular partner that is causing the problem, rather than that he is suffering from a sexual disorder. This is, in fact, exactly the logic that is applied when a man has an erection problem with one partner but not with any others.

If a patient has erection problems with one particular partner and not with others, it is common for the man himself to leap to the conclusion that he has an erection problem, almost invariably then to be reassured by the clinician that being functional with other partners rules that out. But if the patient has sustained erections and is merely coitally anorgasmic with one particular partner, more likely than not he will be diagnosed as a retarded ejaculator, especially if he is married and if his wife wishes to be impregnated.

If, as is true of partner-specific erection difficulties, partner-specific RE is not necessarily a disorder, this further clouds the diagnostic picture, since a man who experiences RE with only one partner will not show the other critical signs of RE, that is, long-sustained erections and a preference for masturbation.

The clinician may also be influenced by the fact that although "no man can will an erection," in Masters and Johnson's famous phrase, most men (and women) can will orgasms. An orgasm can be produced by heavy and sustained friction despite the total absence of erection or even erotic arousal, a practice common among men who suffer from severe chronic erectile dysfunction.

The Retarded Ejaculator as a Malingerer

Because it is easy to assume that the retarded ejaculator is aroused and should be able to have coital orgasms, he typically is seen as a kind of malingerer. What makes this an almost unavoidable impression is that the retarded ejaculator often *acts* like a malingerer. He may confess, although only privately, that he is unwilling to impregnate his partner or that he is repulsed by his partner and enjoys denying her the satisfaction of seeing him have coital orgasms.

But if he is angry at his partner and wants to reject her, why does the RE patient choose such surreptitious means? Why does he not simply refuse to have intercourse with his partner if he is repulsed by her? If he does not want to impregnate her, why has he entered treatment with her to find a way to conceive? An obvious answer is that he feels guilty about wanting to say no to his partner or is afraid she will get angry or retaliate. If this is the case, shouldn't he be helped to be able to say no directly or at least to express his reluctance?

This alternative is nowhere mentioned in the literature and is not considered in either standard sex therapy or in psychoanalytic therapy, as we shall see. Masters and Johnson (1970) even report that of the 14 men suffering from RE who came to treatment with their wives, "three men offered dislike, rejection, open enmity for their wives *as sufficient reason* [italics added] for failure to ejaculate intravaginally" (p. 120). If these men believed they had sufficient reason not to ejaculate, from whose point of view was their not ejaculating a disorder? Clearly, from their wives' point of view and, apparently, from Masters' and Johnson's point of view as well. Despite this reluctance, the RE patient is expected to be coitally orgasmic and in standard sex therapy even is so aggressively pushed to perform that I consider it to be reminiscent of sexual abuse.

One of Masters and Johnson's (1970) RE patients was a man "who should not have been seen in therapy, as there really was no specific ejaculatory dysfunction. This was only a case of a man's complete rejection of the woman he married" (p. 134). Here is a man who was so completely rejecting of his wife that Masters and Johnson thought it inappropriate of him to have entered treatment with her, yet when the treatment outcome was that he did not become coitally orgasmic, Masters and Johnson rated the case as a *failure* and recommended divorce "to the wife." (She did not take the recommendation.)

This advice was a significant departure from the position of neutrality (rather than advocacy) that Masters and Johnson, alone among sex thera-pists, recommend (Apfelbaum, 1985). Aside from the question of whether a therapist is ever in a position to recommend divorce, Masters and Johnson's statement that they recommend divorce not to the couple but to the wife suggests that there is something about the RE patient that causes therapists to lose their neutrality.

This example deserves further consideration. The patient apparently made it clear that he did not want to have coital orgasms with his wife and that, further, it was unlikely that he wanted to have intercourse or perhaps any kind of relationship with her at all. Masters and Johnson even add that this was a case of partner-specific RE: "He was consistently involved with other women outside of marriage with, of course, no ejaculatory difficulty." Yet it was thought of as a treatment failure if, despite this, he was not coitally orgasmic with her.

Now, this patient did consent to enter treatment with his wife and did present with the complaint of retarded ejaculation. Therefore, it could be argued that he did want to be coitally orgasmic with her. Although this does raise some question about how "complete" his rejection was of his wife, it looks as if his willingness to enter treatment was itself the symptom, repres-enting guilt or fear about being more openly rejecting of his wife. If this is true, the treatment objective should not have been for him to be coitally orgasmic with his wife but for him to be able more directly to reject her.

What this example seems to indicate is that the clinician takes the wives' point of view that these men should not be so rejecting and should want to be coitally orgasmic. This bias makes not wanting to be coitally orgasmic a "dysfunctional" attitude and can even lead, as we shall see, to the interpreta-tion that the RE patient is withholding the correct or "functional" attitude of wanting to be coitally orgasmic with his partner. Hence, he should be more giving. This normative bias makes more understandable the typically unem-pathic treatment of the retarded ejaculator.

TREATMENT ISSUES

The retarded ejaculator is the object of what is by far the most aggressive attack on a symptom to be found in the field of sex therapy. The use of a coercive strategy with RE has even gone so far as to include such an unceremonious procedure as electroejaculation by electrical stimulation of the prostate with an anal probe (adapted from the procedure used to collect bull semen and as yet unreported in the literature but attributed to British behaviorists). The standard procedure for treating the retarded ejaculator is to use a demand strategy in which he begins to masturbate with his partner, who then takes over and is required to stimulate his penis in an aggressive and forceful way and suddenly switches to intromission near the point of ejaculatory inevitability.

The idea behind this strategy is that the orgasm reflex has been inhibited and that heavy stimulation will break the "spell." No attempt is made to reconcile this reflex conception with the picture of the retarded ejaculator as a kind of malingerer. The patient who, in Masters and Johnson's words, speaks of his "open enmity" and offers it "as sufficient reason" for his lack of coital orgasms can hardly be thought of as suffering from a subcortical inhibition. This makes it appear that the reflex conception serves as justification for a treatment approach that the clinician wants to apply quite independently of whether it in fact fits the case.

Indeed, one must wonder at the *furor therapeuticus* that grips the clinician who employs this coercive strategy with a man who has apparently made it clear that he is repelled by his wife and wants to reject her, or at least does not want to impregnate her. This approach to patient care reveals a normative bias and a potential for coercion inherent in standard sex therapy practices.

The contrast between the way men and women are treated emerges quite sharply in this regard. For example, Masters and Johnson use the high-pressure, performance-demand strategy with RE, that is, with male coital anorgasmia, but with female coital anorgasmia they take special pains to avoid even the slightest hint of coercion and place special stress on the need to avoid all performance demands (Williams, 1977).

Indeed, the treatment for RE that I will be advocating is entirely consistent with Masters and Johnson's treatment of *female* coital anorgasmia. I propose that Masters and Johnson's insights into female coital anorgasmia are especially relevant to the male version, in that the RE patient is suffering such an intense performance demand that he must perform regardless of his reluctance.

I am suggesting that the performance pressure felt by the RE patient is overlooked in part because he simply is expected to perform, but I should emphasize that this expectation is strongly reinforced by the man's sustained erections, whereas the clinician is less likely to look with suspicion at the coitally anorgasmic woman's disorder, since she does not manifest such a seemingly obvious orgasmic readiness. Therefore, any attempt to correct the clinical bias against the retarded ejaculator must establish that the RE patient's erections are indeed out of "sync" with his level of desire.

BEYOND DYSFUNCTION

Automatic Erections

The automatic erections that I have claimed are pathognomonic of RE are evident from our own cases, but I will begin with case illustrations taken from Masters and Johnson (1970) and Kaplan (1974) to demonstrate that the evidence for this diagnostic cue has been there all along, although its significance has been overlooked.

Masters and Johnson (1970) note in passing that "the incompetent ejaculator [their diagnostic term] can maintain an erection indefinitely during coital sex play, with mounting, and not infrequently for a continuum of 30 to 60 minutes of intravaginal penile containment" (p. 128). They might well have added that he can maintain an erection even under extremely adverse conditions: They report that one patient was married to a woman "whom he found totally objectionable physically." Yet "he was able to perform coitally with his wife from an erective point of view"—this despite the fact that "after penetration he was repulsed rather than stimulated by her demanding pelvic thrusting" (p. 120). In the case of the man who was rated a failure and whose wife was advised to divorce him, he "was so physically repulsed by his wife that, *although erections were maintained*, he rarely reached sufficient levels of sexual tension to approach ejaculation [italics added]" (p. 121). (Note Masters and Johnson's recognition that in this case, at least, the man did not reach orgasm because he was not sufficiently aroused.) In both cases, we find what amounts to a prescription for "impotence," but instead we find extraordinary "potency."

I can only surmise that all these clinicians believe that the RE patient's erections are long-sustained simply because they are not terminated by orgasm. This, in fact, is the typical RE patient's own belief. Many retarded ejaculators believe, reasoning from their own experience, that there is nothing unusual about their erections and that any normal erection would continue indefinitely unless terminated by orgasm.

In case the reader is still tempted to share this belief, a few striking examples from our own work may be convincing. One of our patients complained that with a sustained full erection he could not gracefully decline to go on to penetration. He seemed genuinely to dread these erections and puzzled over why they were so persistent since he dreaded having them. Another RE patient said that after extended periods of thrusting, his back gave out before his erection did. We (Apfelbaum, 1977) have reported on one RE case in which, during the treatment, the patient learned to urinate through his erect penis. His erection was unaffected.

I should note here that we do not find evidence of automatic functioning in every published case of RE. However, this variable has not been assessed in each case, and the examples given of automatic functioning by retarded ejaculators are among the most dramatic examples of this response style to be found in the literature. Furthermore, almost all of the cases treated by us have evidenced this characteristic. There are some published cases in which the patient was also diagnosed as having an erectile dysfunction (Razani, 1977), and Masters and Johnson reported that some of their RE patients eventually did have erection problems. I take these to be mixed conditions.

Case 1: An Automatic Performer

One of the three cases presented by Kaplan (1974, pp. 321–323) provides a striking example of the retarded ejaculator as an automatic performer. This patient had suffered a spinal cord injury that badly impaired the sensitivity of his penile skin. He was afraid his wife would leave him if she knew he could not reach coital orgasms, and so he faked it for the first 4 months of his marriage. Sexual contact left him "very frustrated and upset," ending in his secretly masturbating. "He was frantic in his attempts to overcome his dysfunction and tried to have intercourse at least once every day." Later in the marriage "he had continued to insist compulsively on daily sex." Evidence for his continuing to have sustained erections despite his panic, drivenness, and lack of desire is the fact that in the "system of lovemaking" they had worked out, "they would have intercourse until she climaxed," and then "she would stimulate him to orgasm manually" even though "stimulation was often very prolonged and tedious." Here is a prescription for the inhibition of erection, and again, the opposite is the case.

Autosexuality

The case cited above is of interest because the numbing of this patient's penile skin mimics the condition that I have proposed to be present in the intact retarded ejaculator. In other words, here we have a case of demonstrable penile numbness leading to RE. This may also be a case in which the RE patient's autosexuality has been overlooked, making his organic impairment appear to be the sole case of his RE. A close reading of the case report indicates that, despite this organic impairment, he may have been a true retarded ejaculator by my definition. His penile numbness may have affected him only when he was with his wife. We are not told whether this patient had equal difficulty masturbating. We only know that "he would wait for her to fall asleep, at which point he would masturbate in the bathroom" (p. 322). This appears to suggest that even this patient could masturbate relatively easily. Only manual stimulation by his wife is described as "often very prolonged and tedious." In other words, it may only have been with his wife that he needed the additional sensitivity he had lost because of his injury.

Case 2: Trying to Include the Partner

The retarded ejaculator is much more responsive to his own hand than to his partner's. This phenomenon deserves more attention than it can be given here. One example, of a couple married 4 years, can serve to illustrate what the retarded ejaculator goes through when trying to include a partner. The husband was able to masturbate easily in his wife's presence. He could also reach orgasm, although with some difficulty, through manual stimulation by his wife, but only if he held his testicles himself. In couple sex therapy they were encouraged to see whether he could taper off self-stimulation while increasing his wife's participation. He was unable to reach orgasm unless he used at least three fingers of his own, whereas the maximum number of his wife's fingers that could be simultaneously included was two. If this ratio were reversed, with her fingers outnumbering his, his erection was unaffected, but he was unable to reach orgasm. Unfortunately, our information stops there, since this was a failure case (largely a consequence of a conflict between the co-therapists).

The Autosexual Orientation

It is as if this patient's genitals were numb to his wife's touch, although not to his own. In this regard, I think that the retarded ejaculator falls at one end of a continuum. Suppose a survey were to be done and men were asked how they ranked penile stimulation by their partner's hand (heterosexual and/or homosexual) versus their own hand. My prediction is that we would find two relatively distinct groups, each having a clear preference for one hand or the other—and each assuming that all men are like themselves. This prediction is based on the finding that in our body-work therapy (see below) about 35% of all patients say that they prefer manual stimulation by their own hand rather than the body-work therapist's. Of course, we do not often find the rigid exclusiveness characteristic of the retarded ejaculator, but the difference is clear in these men's minds. They will often say, as if it is obvious, "How could anyone else know how to do it better than I? After all, I've been doing it for years."

It is evident that this is just what a retarded ejaculator such as the husband described directly above would say if he could. He cannot because he feels so totally discredited. He just feels that he should enjoy his partner more. The RE patient will rarely say how much he enjoys masturbation in contrast to heterosexuality and/or homosexuality. However, if Women's Lib and Gay Lib were to be followed by Masturbators' Lib, he might go on at length extolling the relative joys of masturbation—how one is completely freed from the hassle of a demanding partner, is free to enjoy oneself in any way, is free to lose oneself totally by devoting oneself to a favorite fantasy.

Of course, there is no Masturbators' Lib; there is only the new freedom to masturbate, *not* to prefer masturbation to sex with a partner. And the retarded ejaculator appears to be the least of the liberated in this regard. His position is typically wholly undermined, and he can only doggedly pursue the coital orgasm or, at best, can reap whatever rewards are his due as the workhorse of sexual relationships.

His position is so undermined that he has no way to report it to the clinician, and the clinician is not predisposed to recognize a masturbatory sexual orientation. Thus, Masters and Johnson (1970) only note that for 14 of their RE cases, "masturbation had been the major form of sexual tension release" (p. 129). (Apropos of my argument above, the remaining "three of the 17 men had never been able to masturbate to ejaculation before therapy," thus obscuring the true RE patient's autosexuality.) Kaplan (1974) does not even provide such a summary statement. However, it is clear that in each of her case examples, perhaps even in her one case of organic impairment, the patient at least had no difficulty in masturbation.

To offer a perspective on those with an autosexual orientation, I should note that retarded ejaculators must be only a small part of this group, since many of those whose primary orientation is autosexual will not have automatic erections, whereas others may but probably escape being retarded ejaculators because they have "automatic" orgasms or orgasms with effort as well. Of course, the largest group of autosexuals may be those who make no effort to have an orgasm with a partner, including those who avoid partners altogether to simply pursue their solitary masturbatory ways.

CAUSAL CONCEPTIONS
OF RETARDED EJACULATION

My Own View

My own explanation of RE begins with the observation that, for reasons yet unknown, some people are highly reactive genitally even when erotic feeling is minimal or absent. Just as there are men who have automatic erections, there are women who lubricate easily, even copiously, when they have hardly begun to experience passion. There also are those who are bored by orgasms, though they still have them, and even those who are sexually aversive but still respond with erection or lubrication and orgasm.

I think of the retarded ejaculator as being a member of this genitally reactive group. He is inhibited by the touch of a partner, but this is easy to avoid, and, like many men, he may turn himself on by handling his penis himself, shutting out the partner mentally and going on to intromission. However, he cannot continue to stimulate himself and inevitably must experience partner (vaginal) stimulation of his penis during penetration and thrusting. This automatically orients him to his partner, and he experiences a compulsion to satisfy her and a detachment from himself that blocks orgasm. This is exactly what happens to women in coitus who feel compelled to monitor and cater to the male ego.

In the presence of a partner, the retarded ejaculator's penis is relatively insensate or numb because it is out of phase with his level of erotic arousal. If we think of arousal as accelerating over the course of the response cycle (and I am not sure we should), the RE patient's sexual response to a partner does not show this interdependency of erotic and physical reactions. In this sense, he has what might be called "premature" erections. If the standard view is that the retarded ejaculator should have coital orgasms, my view is that he should have an erectile dysfunction.

The retarded ejaculator's erect penis with a partner is like a flaccid one: Because the typically correlated erotic feelings are absent or minimal, his erect penis does not amplify sensation in the usual way. This is why he cannot have coital orgasms. During intromission, he is less able to stimulate himself, and he does not get enough stimulation from his partner. Like a man with a chronic erection problem, he gravitates toward heavy friction in the effort to reach orgasm. His situation is exactly analogous to that of women who, as has recently been recognized, do not necessarily experience adequate physical stimulation during coitus but need focused and reliable manual or oral stimulation.

It is apparently easy to be drawn into the RE patient's scale of values. Although by the RE patient's standard he is depriving and punishing his partner, we should remember that in reality she is likely to be multiorgasmic. After all, what he is depriving her of is his own orgasm. Depriving the partner of his own pleasure must be seen as a rather mild form of "rejection" or "open enmity," *especially considering that this rebellion never includes refusing or even shortening coitus, much less denying the partner her multiple orgasms.* We have to take account of the scale of values by which such a subtle deprivation is considered to be an indication of rejection or open enmity. It seems to me that the retarded ejaculator's exaggerated view of his negative reactions is a measure of the yoke of conscientiousness under which he labors, that is, is evidence of a compulsion to *satisfy* the partner that the patient has no way to recognize on his own.

The necessity to satisfy a partner can be so taken for granted by the patient that he is only aware of the times when he inwardly balks. Any hesitation to devote himself to the partner's satisfaction can seem to him like a serious transgression. Thus, his admissions of enmity, repulsion, and wishes to frustrate his partner must be understood as confessions of a guiltily experienced aversion generated by feeling trapped, especially in coitus.

It also seems to me that it is this compulsion to please the partner that creates the resentment and impulse toward sexual sabotage that some retarded ejaculators acknowledge. The RE patient's compulsive, genitally focused style can make the partner feel that there is nothing she can do for him. Add to this that he finds her touch unexciting, even oppressive, and it is easy to see how she could fall into a passive role. Since he has no sense of consciously choosing this style, his experience of sex is of a continuous demand for performance. This can create a potential for feeling used, but he typically takes his role so much for granted that he has no way to feel entitled to experience himself as being used. Instead, he has flashes of disgust and/or hatred toward his partner.

He also feels disgusted at his own ejaculate, as expressed by his fear of soiling his partner with it. I take this as a sign of his turned-off state. When people are in a sexual situation but not aroused, they often have disgust reactions that disappear when they are aroused.

As for the fear of impregnating the partner, it may be that the reason this fear is featured so prominently in discussions of this syndrome is that RE comes to most clinician's attention only because of the female partner's wish to conceive, another bit of evidence that RE is looked at from the partner's point of view. In any event, I suggest that too much is made of this, since RE (in anal intercourse) is found in gay men and may even have a higher incidence in these men.

Depth Explanations

Fenichel (1945) offers a one-sentence comment on RE that can still serve to summarize the psychoanalytic view: "It may express unconscious fears about dangers supposed to be connected with the ejaculation (castration, death), or strivings, anal (retaining) or oral (denial of giving), sadistic or masochistic in character" (pp. 172ff). In other words, Fenichel here summarizes two causes of RE: (1) a fear that ejaculation will mean castration or death and (2) an unwillingness to "give" (anal retentiveness, oral sadomasochism).

The first of these two causes is based on the symbolic implications of a coital orgasm. Thus, Ovesey's (1971) conception of RE is as follows:

> [It] results from the patient's misconception of sexual intercourse as an act of masculine aggression in which the penis becomes a weapon of destruction. The patient then fears murderous retaliation from the woman, just as he does from men.
>
> [Retaliation from men is a feared consequence because] successful completion of the act is unconsciously equated with victory over male competitors in which the defeated male is killed, castrated, and homosexually subjugated. (p. 12)

In short, the retarded ejaculator appears to believe that no one wants him to have a coital orgasm. If this is so, why then does he not simply choose not to have coital orgasms? Why, instead, can he not be a thankful nonejaculator? Or, better put, why does Ovesey not consider this question?

As I see it, these repressed fantasies are generated by the retarded ejaculator's compulsion to enter into coitus. His penis is, in effect, not his own: he loses it. He has no way to conceptualize this, and so he has highly symbolic fantasies, and even these are repressed. In simple terms, the psychoanalytic view is that the fantasies are the cause of an unconscious aversion to coital orgasms. My view is that these fantasies represent, in exaggerated form, the feelings that the retarded ejaculator is already having. His is the mentality of the trapped: He is already castrated. (It is generally true of classical psychoanalytic explanations that they reverse the causal sequence in this way since they treat fantasies as ultimate explanations rather than as symptoms of repressed affect.)

No matter how horrible for the retarded ejaculator are his unconscious fantasies, what many analysts are likely to miss is that the retarded ejaculator is unable to have a good reason to dislike sex with a partner. He has no way to feel entitled to complain about feeling turned off by a partner's demands.

Thus, the fantasies Ovesey describes clearly reveal the guilt-ridden world of the retarded ejaculator, feeling at risk and on trial in sex. However, I think that if Ovesey were familiar with what we might call the politics of RE, he might be less convinced of the intepetation that the retarded ejaculator fears punishment for ejaculating and be more likely to interpret these fantasies as representing the fear of being punished for not ejaculating.

The second causal conception summarized by Fenichel (1945) is that the retarded ejaculator is unwilling to "give." Despite their formidable abstruseness, psychoanalytic formulations are, at bottom, based on the familiar, if superficial, impression that the RE patient wants to deprive his partner and thus is withholding his own orgasm from her. We look in vain for any effort by psychoanalytic theorists to make this explanation plausible. It simply fits the classical psychoanalytic assumption that symptoms are unconsciously gratifying, meaning as applied to the RE patient that he unconsciously wants to be anorgasmic.

Unfortunately, retarded ejaculators are typically accused of not wanting to "give" by their partners, just as premature ejaculators are typically accused of being inconsiderate by their partners. Yet, paradoxically the RE patient *cannot* be withholding, cannot *stop* giving. As Masters and Johnson (1970) note of their relatively large sample: "Although only three men constrained their ejaculatory processes to frustrate their wives [Master and Johnson mean that only three men confessed to this motive], many more were accused of this motivation by their partners" (192ff). The retarded ejaculator's own belief that he is withholding is widely endorsed, understandably by his partners and less justifiably by most therapists.

In all of my cases, however, the retarded ejaculator is a classic example of the partner who is unable to take, to be selfish, or, as the current jargon has it, to be responsible for his own satisfaction. It is only when he is alone that he can enjoy his own sensations without worrying about the partner's satisfaction. In fact, I am tempted to say on behalf of the retarded ejaculator, "How much *more* can you give?" He is the workhorse of sex, as I have put it earlier, doing the work of 10.

This misinterpretation of motive is by far the most damaging and disturbing misunderstanding of RE. Indeed, the damge inflicted by this misinterpretation is not limited to confounding the patient's conflicts. It also intensifies his guilt-ridden confusion over who his orgasm is for. Sex therapists and most other therapists are especially clear on this point with the anorgasmic woman. They insist that her orgasm is for her. In Barbach's well-known phrase, it is "for yourself." Thus, no one suggests that the anorgasmic woman is withholding her orgasm from her partner, and if she does give an indication that she is trying to have an orgasm for him, this attitude is quite likely to be questioned.

However, it appears that no one hesitates to endorse an RE patient's guilty belief that it is his partner who suffers from his not having an orgasm. Those therapists who confront him with the interpretation that he is withholding (see discussion of Kaplan's formulation below) show no concern about the implication that if being coitally anorgasmic means that you want to withhold from your partner, then it must be your partner that your orgasm is for.

This is exactly what the RE patient himself believes and is one way of explaining why he does not have coital orgasms. Almost all therapists are well aware of the fact that what prevents many women from being orgasmic is their belief that their partner is the one who is deprived if they are not orgasmic. In other words, it indeed is difficult to have an orgasm for someone else.

I would even venture to suggest that since the RE patient believes it is so abusive of him not to have a coital orgasm for his partner, he might even feel it would be more abusive of him to have a coital orgasm *for himself*. If he is so unable to be selfish that he feels he is depriving his partner by not having an orgasm, it might well feel even more selfish to have an orgasm just to please himself. This may be the best way to look at Ovesey's interpretation that the retarded ejaculator fears punishment for being coitally orgasmic.

A common rejoinder to this argument has been that the retarded ejaculator's orgasm, or at least his ejaculation, *is* for his partner if she wishes to conceive, and therefore it makes sense to think that by withholding it he is punishing *her*. This argument implies that a man would not be a retarded ejaculator with an infertile partner or would be cured if his partner became infertile, an absurd possibility. I find this point especially interesting because this willingness to risk absurdity would appear to reveal the general bias against the retarded ejaculator.

I should here consider Kaplan's psychodynamic formulation (her reflex conception is discussed below), since in the revised edition of her *Illustrated Manual of Sex Therapy* (Kaplan, 1987) it has been reprinted unchanged. It recapitulates the standard explanations that I have just considered:

> Two conflicts do emerge with predictable frequency when treating the retarded ejaculator, namely: fear of involvement with the woman, and related conflicts centering around hostility and sadistic impulses toward women. During the course of treatment with these couples, it is often revealed that the man is really "holding back" psychologically as well as physiologically with his orgasm. Frequently also a great deal of hostility to women is evident of which the man is unaware. The patient must often be confronted with this hostility. (p. 151)

First, one wonders on what grounds Kaplan can say that the two conflicts she identifies "emerge with predictable frequency," a statement originally published in 1975, when a year earlier (1974, p. 336) she declined to state the number of RE cases she had treated, only saying that her experience "has been too limited to be statistically significant." Where the two conflicts emerge with predictable frequency is in the literature, a case of persuasion by authoritative repetition rather than by an appeal to clinical data.

The classical psychoanalytic formulation continues to be repeated. In their column of advice to readers, "Keeping Fit in Bed," Shore and Shore (1987) inform the public that retarded ejaculators are "overcontrolled," listing the causes of overcontrol as guilt over sexual activities, fear of pregnancy, "pressure placed on the man to hold off ejaculation for longer and longer periods of time," conflict with a partner, lack of interest in or dislike of a partner, and difficulty in letting go and giving up some control."

The only new contribution to this list is "pressure . . . to hold off ejaculation," the assertion that in trying to delay orgasm the retarded ejaculator somehow overshoots the mark and gets stuck there. This does not explain how he manages to be so successful where legions of men fail. One can only conclude that, in explaining RE at least, clinicians are constrained only by the limits of their imagination.

Behavioral Explanations

The chief behavioral explanation of RE is that it is an inhibited reflex and that the causes of this inhibition are irrelevant to its treatment. This interpretation of RE is evident just from the diagnostic labels used by Masters and Johnson and by Kaplan. For Masters and Johnson, it is "ejaculatory incompetence," a label that has not achieved currency probably because only Masters and Johnson can keep in mind what it means—that the reflex and not the person is incompetent. Kaplan heads her chapter in *The Illustrated Manual of Sex Therapy* (1987): "Retarded Ejaculation—Ejaculatory Overcontrol." She (1974) offers the clearest and most revealing statement of the reflexogenic interpretation of RE:

> Clinical evidence suggests that all the traumatic factors . . . can result in retarded ejaculation. It may be speculated that the mechanism by which these various factors impair the ejaculatory reflex involves an involuntary, and unconscious, conditioned inhibition. According to learning theory, the ejaculatory response has become inhibited because of its association with a painful contingency. The response is blocked just exactly as though the patient anticipated punishment by an electric shock each time he ejaculated or even had the impulse to ejaculate.
>   The precise nature of the original painful contingency becomes irrelevant when it is considered in this conceptual context. (p. 327)

Kaplan goes on to propose that RE is similar to "constipation, which results from inhibition of the defecatory reflex, globus hystericus, which is due to an inhibited swallowing reflex, and spastic colitis due to impaired peristalsis" (p. 327). Kaplan has not said how her reflexogenic conception can be reconciled with her psychodynamic one, making it difficult to know how far she takes her parallel between RE and constipation. She undoubtedly does not mean to suggest that constipation is a hostile act in which the retarded defecator deprives someone else by withholding his feces.

Also, Kaplan's diagnostic conception makes no distinction between masturbatory and coital anorgasmia. The true retarded ejaculator's orgasmic "inhibition" is specific to one particular context. Constipation is not. It seems unlikely that this formulation would be put so definitively if Kaplan were to recognize that the retarded ejaculator is easily orgasmic in masturbation.

Kaplan does not acknowledge the way that her reflexogenic formulation is difficult to reconcile with her psychodynamic one. The idea that the RE patient has associated orgasm with a painful contingency and hence is afraid of it, is different from the idea that the RE patient has "conflicts centering around hostility and sadistic impulses toward women." The first idea is that he avoids coital orgasm out of a fear of being punished; the second idea is that he avoids coital orgasm as a way of punishing his partner.

Of course, both ideas take as self-evident what is actually an assumption, that in the RE patient orgasm is blocked rather than that his level of arousal is insufficient.

THE TREATMENT OF RETARDED EJACULATION

The Demand Strategy

The reflex conception treats RE much as if it were a male version of vaginismus. At least that is the metaphor: Where muscles should be responsive, they are locked in a clonic spasm. This makes it instructive to compare the treatment of vaginismus with the treatment of RE. A major difference from the treatment of vaginismus (Masters & Johnson, 1970, pp. 129ff) is that the spasm is "forced" abruptly in the case of RE rather than gradually as in the case of vaginismus: the female partner is encouraged "to manipulate the penis demandingly," so as "to force ejaculation." Once this has been achieved, she is to manipulate her partner nearly to orgasm and then to execute "rapid intromission." (This is what Kaplan calls the "male bridge maneuver.") If orgasm does not follow, she is to "demandingly" manipulate the penis, "quickly" reinserting.

Masters and Johnson's treatment of *female* "RE," that is, of female coital anorgasmia, is, of course, strikingly different. Their whole point with women is precisely to avoid the demand pressure that they impose on men. Whereas with men, Masters and Johnson advise a demanding style of pelvic thrusting, in the case of female coital anorgasmia, their advice is just the opposite: coitus is to be performed "without any concept of a demanding thrusting pattern."

With a man, the female partner is advised to force ejaculation. With a woman, the male partner is advised that she should have "the opportunity to express her sexual responsivity *without any concept of demand for an endpoint (orgasmic) goal*," [italics added] and that a "forceful approach will not contribute to facility of response." With men, the objective is to build up sensation almost before they realize it; with women, Masters and Johnson warn that if "a high level of biophysical tension is reached before the psychosocial concomitant has been subjectively appreciated, the woman experiences too much sensation too soon and finds it difficult to accept" (Masters & Johnson, 1970, pp. 304, 307, 309).

Because Masters and Johnson rarely mention subjective arousal, they nowhere state that the female with "RE" is not aroused, but it is apparent from their treatment strategy that this is how they view it. The nondemand strategy may have been seen by Masters and Johnson as required only when the process of arousal is blocked. What they consider blocked in RE is the orgasm reflex, not the process of erotic arousal. No one has ever suggested that female coital anorgasmia is a case of reflex inhibition. Thus, unlike the treatment of male coital anorgasmia, there is no sense of the clinician working in opposition to the patient's responses.

Consistent with their etiological conception (above), Shore and Shore (1987), in their advice column, recommend the usual demand strategy. They call it a seven-step program, the steps (slightly abridged) consisting of masturbation with partner present; partner stimulating manually to orgasm; then stimulating orally to orgasm; then orally preceded by a period of penetration; then penetration when close to orgasm. If this "strategy" does not work, they assert that the problem is "deeply ingrained . . . and may require extensive counseling." Shore and Shore do not even raise the possibility that a treatment program employing such direct pressure to perform can create performance pressure.

From my perspective, what we have here is a program presented to the public that is, in effect, designed to create performance pressure and hence likely to fail, with the retarded ejaculator being advised that this failure will mean that his problem is deeply ingrained and may require extensive counseling.

One might expect that given Masters and Johnson's revolutionary insight into the role of performance anxiety (Apfelbaum, 1985), such misguided efforts might be avoided. However, the Shores can hardly be faulted, since, by turning the demand strategy that Masters and Johnson themselves employ into a self-help program, they have only made more obvious why the general conclusion has been that RE is deeply ingrained and may require extensive counseling.

Kaplan introduces a somewhat different note into the treatment of RE. Recall that in discussing what she calls the patient's "holding back," she argues that the motive for this withholding is "a great deal of hostility toward women . . . of which the man is unaware." She then adds that "the patient must often be confronted with this hostility."

Those familiar with Kaplan's (1979) treatment of desire problems will recognize her heavy reliance on authoritative persuasion, which she refers to as confrontation. My impression is that in those cases (Apfelbaum, 1988) this approach has an effect that can also be seen in her treatment of retarded ejaculation. The patient's guilt is reinforced: There is no way that the retarded ejaculator can defend himself against the charge that he wants to withhold and that he is ungiving.

The retarded ejaculator's enslavement to his partner's demands (as he conceives of them) is of heroic proportions. Another way to put this is to say that he is extremely conscience-ridden, and thus is unable to be selfish. He chronically experiences himself as not giving enough and is all too ready to agree that it is his partner who suffers from his not having coital orgasms.

Any man who felt freer to be selfish and thus to be clear about what is in his own interest and what is in his partner's interest would find Kaplan's interpretation baffling at best, since he would have no trouble realizing that he is actually the one who is deprived by his not having orgasms. He would have the ability to remember that in fact his partners were often multiorgasmic (as I noted above), hardly the picture of sexual deprivation.

On these grounds I cannot avoid the conclusion that Kaplan's confrontations must have the effect of further intensifying the conscientiousness that the retarded ejaculator suffers from. (She does not report success rates with this disorder, as I have indicated. Kaplan [1979, p. xvi] makes any one published reference to outcome rates, reporting a "provisional" combined dropout and failure rate of 30% for all conditions treated at her facility, by far the largest reported in the literature.)

Effects of the Standard Strategy: An Alternative View

My way of understanding how the standard (demand) strategy succeeds with RE when it does is to see it as an accommodation to the retarded ejaculator's need for rough, heavy stimulation. Unlike many premature ejaculators whose penises are exquisitely sensitive to touch, the penis of the retarded ejaculator is insensitive. In Kaplan's case discussed earlier, the patient's penis was seriously numbed by a spinal cord injury. His wife used a rough leather glove to stimulate him manually, and he used a towel to masturbate with. Similarly, in the intact retarded ejaculator, penile numbness is overcome by rapid and heavy stimulation.

My explanation does not account for why, at least at other treatment centers, a single experience of coital orgasm or even, as Masters and Johnson report, the experience of some of the ejaculate entering the vagina can result in successively easier coital orgasms. Our cases have not shown this all-or-none responsiveness. The first coital orgasm has not led, by itself, to dramatic changes. (Similarly, Kaplan [1974, pp. 332ff] reports both "stable" and "unstable" results.) This has also been true of vaginismus in our population: We have only seen cases of intermittent vaginismus, so there was no "spell" to break.

In this treatment model, no distinction is drawn between RE and masturbatory anorgasmia, which makes the results difficult to evaluate. My guess is that "stable" results are more likely with masturbatory anorgasmia, paralleling the prognostic difference between primary and coital female anorgasmia (for a primary anorgasmic woman, to experience one orgasm can mark a qualitative change).

When the treatment of RE *does* have an all-or-none outcome, however, it does appear as if a spell has been broken, directly confirming the conception of RE as an inhibited reflex. My alternative interpretation of this treatment effect is that what gets broken is not a spell but a set. The retarded ejaculator's sexual set is to satisfy the partner. In the strategy recommended by Masters and Johnson and by Kaplan, the partner is helped to overcome her feeling that there is no way to do anything for him. She is brought out of her withdrawal and transformed into a singlemindedly aggressive partner, determined to "*give*" no matter how unreinforcing it is for her. The result is that what I have characterized as the retarded ejaculator's numb response to the partner's touch is overcome, although we cannot tell from published reports of the results of this approach whether coitus and coital orgasms become as exciting as masturbatory orgasms for the male, and whether the partner's touch comes to rival the patient's own.

A serious drawback of this strategy appears in its effect on the patient for whom it fails. When it succeeds, it undoes the patient's oppressive compulsion to satisfy the partner. When it fails, it seems likely that its effect is to strengthen this compulsion. The patient's own belief that he should be having coital orgasms has now been supported not only by the therapist's authority but by the belief that his partner is now doing everything humanly possible for him. As a result, he would feel even less entitled to feel used, even though he would be all the more convinced that if he were to have a coital orgasm, it would be his partner's and not his own: It would be the prize that she had worked so hard to produce and that he owed her for her efforts.

Although I will not discuss the non-sex-therapist's strategy for treating RE since there is not a strategy specific to RE, from my vantage point there is not much difference between the psychodynamic therapist's approach and the behavior therapist's approach to RE. In effect, the patient is treated as if he must overcome feeling used and resentful. The patient's unconscious aversion to coital orgasm is treated as irrational and groundless.

The Counterbypassing Strategy

As I see it, the retarded ejaculator not only should not have a coital orgasm, he should not have an erection. The functionalist model makes such a formulation sound odd only because the phenomenon of functioning with inadequate erotic arousal has been conceptually overlooked, although it is familiar to everyone.

The standard sex-therapy approach begins with the assumption that the RE patient does not experience performance anxiety since his anxiety is believed to be associated with *having* coital orgasms rather than with *not having* them. If those using the standard approach were to see the retarded ejaculator as not aroused and as driven by a performance compulsion, they would be unlikely to use their present strategy. They would be more likely to use a strategy such as the one Masters and Johnson use to treat female coital anorgasmia.

In the treatment of female coital anorgasmia, Masters and Johnson's goal is to train the woman to be in control of her sexual context. During penetration in the female-astride position, the male partner is to remain passive while she meditatively regulates thrusting movements, learning to attend closely to her own sensations and to not cater to her partner. She learns, in effect, to take possession, not just of her body, as it is sometimes put, but of her sexual relationship. However, this can be difficult to accomplish with couples whose basic rapport is not up to the Masters and Johnson standard. The woman cannot as easily shed her insecurity about ignoring her partner, and the man plays a passive role only in the sense of biding his time. In such a couple, these tensions cannot be bypassed.

Such a couple can still reach the same objective by switching to what I call *counterbypassing*, an expressive technique in which the woman is helped to verbalize her worries about her partner's impatience. However, a merely expressive technique in the style of bioenergetics or Gestalt therapy is of limited value unless the woman's worries are validated, that is, unless she is helped to feel entitled to them by virtue of recognizing that her worries are valid. This is not at all difficult to do, since the therapist always has the choice of picking up either her sensitivity (resulting from childhood experience, later trauma, guilt, inhibition of assertiveness, etc.) or the external reasons that her sensitivity is engaged.

In the instance just described in which a woman may be worried about her partner's impatience, the therapist might demonstrate that the partner was, in fact, impatient and that his impatience was perhaps the result of a fear of being turned-off and losing his erection if he is too passive. Having her reactions validated is a form of endorsement that helps give the woman a way to feel more as if a sexual encounter is for *her*.

Such a counterbypassing strategy raises the specter of precipitating and inconclusive and interminable therapy. However, I would argue that this only happens when an expressive or uncovering approach *has the same objective* as a bypassing approach, that is, to extinguish negative feelings. Thus, RE can be seen as the outcome of "an unconscious refusal to ejaculate" (as an anonymous journal consultant put it in response to a manuscript submitted by one of my colleagues). The implication is that this is an inappropriate response and even that it is repressed because it is inappropriate. However, as I see it, the patient must be helped to make a *conscious* "refusal to ejaculate." It is the attempt to get the patient to give up his refusal that can result in an interminable or at least extensive uncovering therapy.

I think of counterbypassing as a more direct way to break the retarded ejaculator's compulsive sexual set and as less likely to reinforce this set when it fails. This means introducing the idea to the RE patient that he is the kind of person who may need to be erotically aroused before he can have a coital orgasm. Although he may protest that he *is* aroused, it should be easy for him to recognize how much more aroused he is in masturbation than he is with a partner. This should be discernible as he is well aware of how coitus feels like drudgery. He can then be introduced to the next idea, which is that he does not feel entitled to complain about his experience with a partner (this is not hard to demonstrate even to the RE patient who begins by confessing that he is repelled by his partner).

The therapist can then present the view that anyone might feel left out, ignored, or used when he is getting very little out of sex at the same time that his partner is multiorgasmic. Because the patient invariably expects to be treated as if he is abnormal for not having coital orgasms, this strategy can be immediately relieving. A complaining assignment can then have equally immediate results, as Case 3 (to come) illustrates.

Effect of the Counterbypassing Strategy

Because the RE patient is unable to make a good case for himself, he is seen as willfully withholding (consciously or unconsciously), as depriving and ungiving. We have found that to interpret the problem in just the opposite terms, as an inability to take and as symptomatic of excessive conscientiousness, is almost invariably relieving to the patient, even in the first hour. Also, although less invariably, the patient can immediately acknowledge that his long-sustained erections are relatively numb.

This kind of relief is not anticipated by behavioral outcome criteria. Especially given the highly unflattering interpretations of RE generated by standard approaches, the therapist knows that to say anything about these interpretations of RE would only be to alienate or depress the patient. This underlies the therapist's assumption that insight therapy cannot be effective in a few counseling hours because the patient can only be gradually exposed to the idea that he wants to deprive and punish women. There is the exception: Helen Kaplan does advocate early confrontations of this type, but her objective is not relief or even insight as such. She uses such interpretations as a way of discrediting or invalidating resistance to assignments in order to elicit from the patient the kind of dedication that her treatment requires, that is to elicit from the patient the motivation to work at conjuring up fantasies and at bypassing any need for contact with the partner.

I am suggesting that the standard insights into RE mimic the RE patient's superego dictates, his negative self-talk, and so are not of much use to the sex therapist except as a way of compelling compliance with the therapeutic regimen. The alternative insights that I am proposing, on the other hand, can undermine superego dictates and negative self-talk and hence can be of immediate therapeutic value.

This effect suggests an additional outcome criterion, the experience of relief gained by the therapist's offering a different perspective. This is the perspective in which the patient is seen as trying too hard to have an orgasm for the partner. We will inform the patient that many women have now realized that they can't have an orgasm for their partners, but that it is a hard lesson for men to learn, since everyone simply assumes that there is no such thing as a man trying to have an orgasm for his partner. This is especially true, we add, since most therapists, both sex therapists and others, think of the retarded ejaculator as withholding his orgasm from the partner. We point out that women who have the same problem, that is, who are coitally anorgasmic, are never thought of as withholding their orgasms from the partner.

It usually is easy to determine that these patients especially enjoy masturbation and that sex with a partner is, by contrast, something of a trial. Again, their naive assumption is that any man enjoys masturbation and also that any man is more excited by his own hand than by his partner's. Making them aware of their own sexual style puts their lack of coital orgasms in context for them. It also can be clarifying for these men to realize that the ways they are turned off by a partner only make sense in view of their proclivity to be accommodators and to be givers rather than takers (to have trouble asking for favors, to be self-reliant, etc.).

It also can be relieving for the RE patient to be educated regarding his erections. Some retarded ejaculators know that they have unusually sustained erections because they have had experienced partners who told them so. As I noted above, many retarded ejaculators think that erections are terminated by orgasms and the only reason other men do not have such sustained erections is that they have orgasms.

A simple way to capture the whole picture for the RE patient, having established that he has relatively numb (premature) erections with a partner, is to say that the therapeutic objective is for him to have enjoyable erections with a partner and to not proceed to penetration unless this objective is met.

In this regard we also make it clear to the patient that working at generating orgasms by heavy friction will quickly lead to diminishing returns and that he should keep the contrast with his orgasmic experience in masturbation, in which little friction is neccessary to reach orgasm, constantly in mind in evaluating his level of responsiveness with a partner.

Typically it is possible to establish these insights rapidly in an hour or two since they are either already familiar to the patient—he has just not seen their relevance—or they are instructive in a way that immediately fits the patient's experience.

In weighing these recommendations for brief counseling with the RE patient, it is essential to bear in mind the fact, as I noted at the outset, that the actual incidence of RE in all liklihood far exceeds its clinical incidence. The RE patient is less motivated for treatment than is the premature ejaculator and far less motivated than the man with an erection problem. Correspondingly, the minority of retarded ejaculators who do come to a treatment facility, even who come in of their own accord rather than being brought in by a partner, are typically not motivated for more than brief counseling.

Case 3: An Illustration of Counterbypassing

It is unfortunate that most of our RE cases were treated in individual body-work sex therapy, since this therapeutic approach has not been applied outside our center. It is a revision of Masters and Johnson's surrogate-partner program in which the substitute-partner concept is discarded in favor of the use of paraprofessional staff members who function both as co-therapists in the therapy sessions and as body-work therapists in sessions comparable to those in which couples carry out their assignments (for further procedural details, see Williams, 1978, Apfelbaum, 1984). The principles of treatment we have developed in individual body-work sex therapy are also used by us in couple sex therapy, and I will draw these parallels.

One advantage in presenting material from the treatment of patients in individual body-work sex therapy is that I have much more information available about the cases, since the body therapist serves as a participant/observer.

The application of this strategy to RE can be quickly illustrated through the case of a Canadian architect, age 36, who requested body-work sex therapy at his second wife's urging. (Although she was an American citizen, an outstanding legal problem made it risky for her to re-enter the United States for sex therapy, and she also had concerns about confidentiality that made it difficult for her to obtain couple sex therapy in her area.) In her telephone contact with us, she complained that her husband was "turned off," a unique perception in my experience from the partner of an RE. He said that he gradually became turned off while thrusting but went on in the hope of becoming aroused again, although he never did. He described the typical retarded ejaculator's automatic erection, mentioning that once when he was hospitalized after a sports accident, he had been tormented by having erections when being washed by the nurses. No matter what stratagem he tried, he was unable to avoid having continuous erections during this process. However, he said that he was otherwise grateful for his constant erections because his partners never had to know how turned off he was.

He had read the first edition (1975) of Kaplan's *The Illustrated Manual of Sex Therapy* and had perfected the bridge maneuver with his wife. Using it, he was able to reach coital orgasms about 50% of the time but found it tedious and unrewarding.

Although this patient was only seen for 1 week of body-work therapy, he was quick to learn counterbypassing. He felt liberated with unusual suddenness when he was coached to express the components of his performance anxiety while being stroked by the body-work therapist. He got "high"—and this feeling turned into sexual excitement—when he told her how he hated sex, how it was an ordeal, a job, how he had to just put himself through it, measure up, and how afraid he was that the body therapist would feel insulted by his expressing these feelings. This is the kind of turning point we look for. Out of this can come an insight, a body insight as well as a cognitive one, about what has been turning the patient off and what it will take to arouse him again.

The insight is what I (Apfelbaum & Apfelbaum, 1985) have called the "ego boost" necessary for erotic arousal, which can be more powerfully generated by partner acceptance of negative feelings than by the standard "sex hype" that has the same goal.

When such a turning point is reached, it is not unusual for the patient and the therapists to feel that the job has been done. In contrast, one *performance* success is much more likely to be experienced as a random event, a fluke, and performance anxiety is intensified.

When the body-work therapist went on to manual stimulation, the patient became aroused by talking about how little he was getting out of it and how frustrating it was going to be for her, as well as by talking about how "the electric feelings" came and went. He enjoyed this so much that he could not wait to try it out on his wife and so returned home before we could go further. The questionnaire follow-up on this case was ambiguous, but it is offered only as a brief illustration of our strategy before we go on to a more extensive case presentation.

Case 4: A Successful Course of Treatment

Background

Frank, 20, a college student, complained of being unable to have a coital orgasm. He was unusually experienced sexually for his age, having had two 2-year relationships and several other briefer ones. He described himself as obsessed with sex and masturbated frequently and easily (two to three times daily), becoming aroused by intricate and extensive fantasies. His principal fantasy was of being a male prostitute (heterosexual) who aggressively "raped" women at their request.

He was concerned enough about not having coital orgasms to have investigated artificial insemination in the event that his problem continued into marriage. However, after several counseling hours, it became clear that his primary complaint was that the reality of his sexual experiences never matched his fantasies. Although this in itself is not unusual, it became clear that he got very little satisfaction from his sexual encounters. Furthermore, his continuing sense of sexual frustration and ubiquitous sexual fantasies were seriously undermining his ability to concentrate, threatening a loss of scholarships and making it necessary for him to consider interrupting the career line he had planned. He was unambivalently devoted to his field and had no history of previous work inhibitions.

Sexual contact with women was a proof of masculinity for him and a way of satisfying them, but masturbation was far more enjoyable. He was able to reach orgasm with a partner through manual stimulation, but only if he could call up his fantasies. However, he found it very difficult to maintain a fantasy in the presence of a partner, and when he did reach orgasm by this means, it did not seem worth the effort. He had not experienced fellatio, and his lack of interest in it seemed consistent with his interest in being an aggressive "phallic" partner as in his fantasies.

His actual sexual role was, as in his fantasies, the compromised form of passivity, represented by being aggressive on demand. A clue to this was his report that his partners were all easily orgasmic. They apparently were assertive and freely able to control their sexual contacts with him. His account also suggested that they encouraged rather than disliked the long-sustained coital thrusting toward which Frank was inclined. He shyly admitted that he was regularly told that he was a great lover, and this seemed based solely on his no-frills approach to thrusting and his reliable and sustained erections. He was a partner who could be easily controlled and safely ignored.

His background was white, middle class, stable, suburban, and sexually liberal. Both parents were alcoholics, although this apparently did not interfere with their duties and was not out of place in their social circle. He saw himself as the sexual adviser of his 15-year-old sister, who, he proudly recounted, was already sexually active and experienced.

He came to us wanting a "surrogate" in response to the December 1972, *Newsweek* cover story that widely popularized sex therapy. He had been in once-a-week psychotherapy for a year and reported that although he now had some insight into his problem, nothing had changed. The insight was that he was afraid of losing control and was unable to "give."

Initial Treatment Findings

He did not have a current partner and had to make a 400-mile round-trip commute from his campus, which limited partner availability. Although the much higher fees for body-work sex therapy as compared with couple sex therapy put him under pressure to work out an arrangement with a partner, he was unable to accomplish this. We offered to reduce the fee in exchange for his seeing a body-work therapist in training, and he agreed. He was seen in once-a-week sessions, a practice that we subsequently discontinued. His was one of the cases that persuaded us that daily sessions could have shortened treatment by perhaps a third from the 18 sessions he was actually seen.

Although Frank was frightened of seeing a surrogate, he was somewhat reassured when he was told that she would not be a surrogate but a body-work therapist (BT) who worked as a co-therapist with me as the review therapist and that we worked one session at a time rather than on the basis of a fixed number of sessions. It was apparent from the first body-work session that, as Frank had reported, he had the automatic erections that I have suggested are characteristic of RE. Whereas full erections lasting as long as a half hour are uncommon, Frank's erections would last almost the entire body-work period, which could be as long as 2 hours out of a 2½-hour session. The BT reported that it was not until the 10th session that she saw Frank's penis in a flaccid state.

As Frank had previously reported, his level of arousal was not at all commensurate with his "excitement-phase" functioning. He claimed to feel nothing and said that his penis felt numb. This was corroborated by the way the BT felt: She found herself feeling bored and aimless. Perhaps because this was her first case and it also was early in the development of our treatment model, we let ourselves entertain the possibility of penetration, a relatively infrequent event in any approach to sex therapy with surrogates (Apfelbaum, 1984) and one that not only happens rarely in body-work therapy, but one that in no other case has been done for more than a few minutes. Furthermore, given our present understanding of RE, it is clear that although the symptom is most noticeable in coitus, this partner-specific desire disorder can only be treated outside of coitus, as will be apparent from this case.

When the BT felt aroused, she decided to take the previously agreed-upon option of penetration and felt some relief at this. But, as we later realized, she responded as his partners had in that she felt relieved of the stress of Frank's tension, only to discover in the review session that he had not enjoyed it and, further, that he was recriminating himself for not being as aroused as she was. Despite this, thrusting went on for almost 2 hours. The result of such "premature" functioning has typically been the prolongation of treatment (calling into question the widespread belief in the relieving effect of performance successes). This event is another indication that our treatment of this case represents an early model.

The Necessity for a Focus on Level of Arousal

In order to keep treatment brief, we have found it necessary to monitor closely the patient's level of arousal and to make it the focus of our efforts. It eventually became evident to us that it is easy to do too much body work, that is, to outstrip what the patient can encompass and to move him into functioning that is relatively autonomous from feeling. Masters and Johnson have already pointed out that this can easily happen with women (see above). With this recognition, we have increasingly centered on events that occur early in the body work and, as I have noted, now rarely find it necessary to go on to penetration.

Frank was a clear case in point. We found that when he was involved in coitus, he felt isolated, passive, and helpless. At this point, Frank invoked the interpretations that he had been given in his previous therapy: These ideas were that he needed to learn to lose control and to be more willing to "give." We pointed out that he condemned himself with these interpretations, whereas in reality, he was being left out by the BT when she withdrew from him into a sexually aroused state. Yet, he criticized himself rather than criticize her.

In the review session following their engaging in coitus, the BT reported being shocked at having lost track of how "turned off" Frank had been. She said that she had just "tripped out" in a way that she had never thought possible for her. She had had this done to her many times by men but had never thought that she could herself be an "oppressor," as she put it. This was a climactic event for Frank, suggesting to him that at least part of his problem was that he "gave" *too* much and that, in contrast to his partners, he was not *in* control at all.

It began to dawn on Frank that he had no way to withdraw into sensation the way the BT had just done and the way his partners had also done. I pointed out that this dependency did offer an increased potential for intimacy but that for this potential to be realized would require him to develop communication skills that others could get by without.

Inappropriateness of the Reflex Model

As I have indicated, the generally accepted strategy with RE in couple sex therapy is to increase sensation in a forceful and goal-directed way. This strategy is even more difficult to apply in body-work sex therapy than it is in couple sex therapy. As in the cases reported by Masters and Johnson and by Kaplan, Frank required his partners to work hard at stimulating him manually for him to reach orgasm. The BT was unwilling to do this. She reported that if she had felt more aroused, it might have been possible to become more vigorous in stroking Frank, but as it was, it just seemed too dreary. The relationship seemed too tense, and Frank already seemed under too much pressure.

As the three of us investigated her reaction further in review sessions, the BT also realized that as matters then stood, to work on physically arousing Frank would make her feel used. This fascinated Frank, and he questioned her at length about it. He had never felt entitled to feel used, as had just been demonstrated by the climactic incident in which he had been, as we had put it, *taken advantage of* by the BT during coitus. We used this way of describing what she had done for its shock value, since he, of course,

considered such moral language to be, at best, quaint. However, it communicated with a deep vein of feeling in him. If he had felt anything in his
previous sexual contacts, it would have been to feel used, but he had had no
cognitive structure to accommodate such a feeling.

This brings up the question of whether the partner in couple sex therapy
should be encouraged to take the risk of being seen as rejecting, a risk the BT
can take because her responses are likely to be seen by the patient as having a
clinical rationale. The demand strategy used with couples in the standard
approach to RE requires more subordination of the partner's needs than does
the treatment of any other sexual disorder. She must aggressively stimulate
the patient, either manually or orally, until he comes close to ejaculatory
inevitability. This typically requires heavy, prolonged, and uninterrupted
application to the task, followed by rapid intromission, also executed by the
partner. Thus, it is in Kaplan's (1974) chapter on RE that she raises the
problem of the effect on the partner of being required, as Kaplan puts it, to
"service" her husband. Kaplan warns that this may be a lot to expect of the
partner unless the relationship is "good enough":

> If the woman is mature enough to withstand temporary frustration without
> hostility, and if the couple's relationship is good enough to make her
> generosity psychologically rewarding, treatment can proceed smoothly
> under these conditions.
>   However, the wife's intrapsychic conflicts and consequent marital
> discord may be evoked by the man's progressive improvement and the fact
> that she is required to "service" her husband. (p. 332)

"Generosity" may not be the most accurate word for the spirit with
which the partner carries out her assignment. She can hardly avoid feeling
obliged to comply. The alternative is to sacrifice the patient's chance to
overcome his symptom. Add to this the fact that the female partner is
usually the one who brings the patient into treatment and we have what
amounts to a contractual obligation on her part.

This is not to say that the partner necessarily resents this obligation, at
least at first. However, recall that most of the partners in Masters and
Johnson's sample experienced "a real concept of personal rejection" and a
level of frustration "beyond comprehension." Some were rejected by their
husbands as physically unappealing, but probably for most of them, it was
their husband's unresponsiveness that they took as a rejection. (Unlike the
therapist and the patient himself, the partner cannot avoid recognizing that
the retarded ejaculator is not aroused by her.)

This treatment strategy depends on the partner being "mature enough,"
as Kaplan puts it, and on the couple's relationship being "good enough" for
the partner to stand further frustration and feelings of rejection. More than
that, it depends on the partner's ability not just to tolerate such feelings but
not to communicate them unduly by the way she stimulates the patient. It is
easy to imagine her being a bit too aggressive—or not aggressive enough.

Furthermore, even when the partner succeeds, she is modeling conscientiousness for the patient, an unfortunate reinforcement of his sex-at-
work philosophy. As for the virtues of a nondemand approach, Masters and
Johnson themselves have written the text. Thus, the BT ideally models a
resistance rather than a submission to sexual demands, and this would be my
objective with the patient's partner as well. She can be helped to have *her*
complaints about the patient's unresponsiveness and about his lack of joy.
He can then be helped to express his side of it—"But I'm doing it all for
you"—something she undoubtedly has never realized and would then insist
was not at all what she wanted. This is how their compulsive set would
begin to break down.

Psychogenic Arousal

With respect to our present case, when the BT first said that she found
herself reluctant to do manual stimulation, Frank was unbelieving. At first
he thought it was a pose or a trick, but when he decided it was a reaction she
really was having, he accused *her* of being unwilling to give. This gave him
a chance to watch her cope with the same accusations that had been flung at
him by one of his partners and offered as an interpretation by his previous
therapist. To his surprise, the BT responded that she did not know why he
wanted her to stroke him so vigorously, even though she could understand it
intellectually. To condense this three-way discussion: Frank acknowledged
that he did not know that a person needed reasons to do things and that he
had always just done what he thought he was supposed to do. The BT was
able then to say that she found little to respond to in him and that if she had
not *known* that he was obsessed with sex, she would have thought that he
had no interest in it.

This seemed to liberate Frank to be critical of the BT for the first time.
He told her that she just did not turn him on, and then, suddenly, he felt a
surge of sexual feeling. This was the turning point in the case. Much like the
turning point noted in Case 3, it was an example of becoming aroused by
counterbypassing. At first, Frank was disturbed by it. He had reported it to
the BT at the time and to both of us in the review session with some
embarrassment, thinking that it must be abnormal to feel aroused by a
complaint, especially by the complaint that he was turned off. We reassured
him that this had become a familiar occurrence to us and encouraged him to
go further in this direction. At this point, he reported more sensation in his
penis, although this soon disappeared as he reacted with renewed performance anxiety. He then responded with despondency, and we helped him
to articulate this through our technique of script construction. The patient is
instructed to review his experience with the body therapist, and then they
both construct and shape a list of statements that he can subsequently use to
identify and make contact with what he is experiencing. Frank's list included such lines as: "I am afraid of feeling hopeless"; "I'm afraid there is

something really wrong with me"; "I'm afraid you're going to give up on me"; and, in a different vein, "I just don't know what you want."

In reaction to saying these lines, especially the first one, Frank again experienced sexual feelings (for more detailed examples of this, see Apfelbaum, 1984). Simultaneously, he no longer had his automatic erection, and it rarely appeared in the subsequent sessions. Although he still had erections quickly, they were typically accompanied by erotic feeling, and when his mood shifted, at moments that were usually clearly distinguishable, his degree of erection reflected this. For example, whenever he lapsed into compliance, he now would lose some, or all, of his erection. These shifts all took place during genital stroking, and the body work was confined to this during the remaining sessions.

Uncovering Residual Performance Anxiety

During this period, signs of pelvic tension were noted that related to what he was experiencing. He and the BT also located tension in his pubococcygeus muscle, which then reminded him of past difficulties urinating in public men's rooms.

Although Frank was now noticeably more relaxed, he still had not reached orgasm, our goal for the genital stimulation. He then reported that his masturbatory fantasy had changed: Instead of being paid to "rape" women, they now paid him to do female-superior coitus. It was just as aggressive, but now the women did most of the moving. He revealed that he had begun trying to fade his fantasy women out of the fantasy and to bring the BT into the fantasy just before orgasm in the hope of associating her with erotic feeling.

A Complaining Assignment

We felt fortunate that in Frank's spontaneous self-assignment of stimulus fading we had stumbled on a clue that he still felt it was up to him to generate erotic feeling. We said that this feeling of responsibility was the last hiding place of his performance anxiety and then gave him a complaining assignment to do during the genital stroking. While it was going on, it was his responsibility not to get aroused but to complain about what the BT was doing. He found himself enjoying saying, "I'm not feeling anything." When the BT jokingly responded, "Well, I'm doing the best I can," he felt close to orgasm but only reached it when he said, "This really feels mechanical."

This was Frank's only orgasm during the treatment period. Although this might be a minor event if the standard strategy had been used, what happened in this instance was a "spontaneous" orgasm, that is, one that occurred without heavy and deliberate stroking, something Frank had not experienced with a partner before. With this experience of orgasm, the whole treatment approach was then reinforced and internalized. Generalization to a partner was to be expected, since this orgasm made sense to Frank. He could easily see what was arousing about his exchange with the BT.

Indeed, I would not expect an "accidental" orgasm to generalize. Thus, if Frank had had a coital orgasm during his earlier episode of coitus with the body therapist, I would not expect this to affect his sexual responsiveness with other partners or, for that matter, with the BT herself. Nothing would have happened to change his sexual set. Regardless of the source of stimulation, what is needed is a "spontaneous" orgasm, that is, one that happens as an outcome of peak arousal rather than of prolonged and intense local stimulation. This is what is likely to generalize to coital orgasms, as it did in Frank's case. The coital specificity of RE is not dynamically meaningful; what is dynamically meaningful is the retarded ejaculator's insensitivity to a partner's touch in contrast to his own.

In the next session, Frank tried to repeat the series of events that had led to an orgasm, but, as usually happens, it had become a formula, and, to his disappointment, neither he nor the BT felt aroused.

He then had a sudden financial setback and had to interrupt the treatment. His father's alcoholism had finally cost him his job, and his father had borrowed Frank's savings on a short-term loan to get started in a business venture. It failed, and Frank could not afford further treatment or to return to school.

Treatment Effects

I saw Frank again 5 years later. He was now in his last year of a professional school and reported that although his sexual "obsessions" no longer interfered with his work, his sexual experiences had been only partly satisfying. He reported now being able to have an erection without assuming that this required him to go on to penetration and also being able, at least at times, to stop the action when he felt out of contact. He appeared to retain awareness of his dependency on psychogenic stimulation and reported being able to tell his partner when he was turned off. He claimed to have coital orgasms easily when he felt aroused, although this was not often. It was difficult to evaluate this claim, since he knew this was what I wanted to hear, and he was still essentially the same person, someone whose first impulse is to satisfy the other.

For such a person, changing partners can be a solution, and it became clear that Frank had made a truly inspired choice. He apparently had instinctively shied away from the enthusiastic performers who would have reinforced his sexual compulsions and, instead, had a 3-year relationship with a woman who was not coitally orgasmic. This did help reverse his order of priorities, but he found toward the end of that relationship that he did not *want* to have coital orgasms, although he was somewhat less reluctant about having extravaginal orgasms. He was disturbed about not wanting coital orgasms, and it was for this reason that he wanted to resume body-work therapy. However, I thought what he needed was some reassurance and a redefinition of the problem.

Fear of Being Exploitive

Bearing in mind that what makes a retarded ejaculator is *having to have coital orgasms*, my strategy was to help Frank stay with his reluctance rather than to help him overcome it. True to type, Frank thought that he should not feel this reluctance, seeing it as unmanly of him to be so squeamish and foolish as well, to feel that he was using his partner if she were not equally orgasmic, since she reassured him that she enjoyed it when he had coital orgasms.

Given our sexual norms, it is all too easy for the clinician to share Frank's concern and to believe that he should be helped to overcome his ambivalence. However, in accordance with my conception of the pathogenesis of RE, my expectation is that an intervention of this kind would have led to a recurrence of Frank's RE.

I congratulated Frank on being able to acknowledge his ambivalence about having coital orgasms, since to experience sex as exploitive could at that time (the present-day awareness of sexual abuse was then lacking) make one feel unenlightened. I told him that I thought RE is created by having to deny and overcome this ambivalence, and that when the feeling of being exploitive returns (from repression), it does so in concretized form as a fear of soiling or impregnating.

I also suggested that needing his partner to have coital orgasms reflects the retarded ejaculator's inability to "take." I reminded him of what I have here called the "climactic" incident with the BT in which we said that *we* thought he had been used by her, and I suggested that on this basis, his worry might be at least partly iatrogenic. He agreed but added that this had made him realize how he had always felt used and how he could hardly imagine it otherwise, even in his masturbatory fantasies.

Now that he could have coital orgasms, he worried that his partner would feel used just as he had, although she might not be aware of it, or if she were aware of feeling this way, she might be just as skilled as he had been at concealing it. He then realized that this worry resolved into his being afraid that she had to like everything, just as had been true for him. This turned his attention to the possibility of helping her, or a future partner, to be freer to have her dislikes, by doing a better job of expressing his own.

TWO FAILURE CASES

Case 5: A Missed Arousal Deficit

Two failure cases are of interest. The first patient was 23, unmarried, and a college dropout who drove a cab in a midwestern city. He was the only retarded ejaculator we have seen who bragged openly about his sustained erections and about how capable this made him as a sex partner. This was a 1-week body-work therapy case, a patient who, like other retarded ejaculators, had an erection in the first session, could masturbate easily on day 3, but, unlike other retarded ejaculators, in the fifth session reached his first coital orgasm (he was, like Frank, an early case). He then terminated, feeling he could no longer justify the expense of continued treatment.

His coital orgasm might best be thought of as what I earlier called an "accidental" orgasm, in that the therapists saw no evidence that the patient's sexual set had changed in any way. It was a relatively joyless experience, and the therapists believed that he had never really been aroused and that he was relieved to terminate before his "turned-off" state had been exposed. My impression is that such a performance success is experienced by the patient as a fluke that he is afraid he will never be able to repeat. I have not found the "one good experience" to be reassuring unless it is accompanied by an increase in sexual pleasure.

This patient has not returned. We now might treat this case differently, having learned to resist the pressure to go ahead with the body work when the patient is not aroused. However, this can be a difficult determination to make and to be done effectively requires an experienced co-therapy team.

Case 6: A Failure to Relieve Performance Anxiety

The second failure case was a man of 43, never married, and a tutor in the humanities at a British university; he had just completed a 7-year analysis. As in the previous case, he was proud of his sustained erections (although not as openly), advertised in British swinger-style magazines, and maintained current sexual relationships with over 30 women. He nevertheless found masturbation more satisfying and had never come close to a coital orgasm. He had only reached orgasm four times with a partner, all with the same partner, by masturbating and then switching to fellatio only at the point of ejaculatory inevitability.

He was a highly urbane man who made the memorable comment, "Girls just don't have the touch" (the comparison being with himself, not with men). What he seemed most attracted to in women was neatness, cleanliness, quietness, and decorum. He denied that this suggested that he did not see women as sex objects. In the body-work sessions he was cool and impersonal, but our efforts to reflect this back to him were interpreted by him as a sign that the BT was disappointed.

Some work was done with muscle relaxation, and this led to somewhat greater responsiveness. He said that he had never enjoyed manual stimulation of his penis before, but he (perhaps correctly) attributed it all to the use of Albolene™ (our preferred genital lubricant). His defensiveness continued, and he became difficult to control in the body-work sessions. Contrary to our advice, he would keep his eyes closed when stroked and also would make thrusting movements. However, we were able to get him in touch with some of the components of his sexuality.

He said that it felt like a sacrifice to penetrate a woman, as if he had given them a part of himself, but at the same time it was an honor to be allowed this act of chivalry. He also said that he was afraid that if he reached orgasm, he would be "under a woman's dominion." (I see the presence of this fear as a symptom of his low level of arousal in the face of the pressure he felt to perform; cf. *vagina dentata* fantasies as a reflection of the experience of feeling trapped in coitus, discussed above.) He was able to recognize, seemingly for the first time, that he felt no warmth from women and that he wanted to be held more than he wanted to reach orgasm.

Despite his gaining these insights, we lost control of the therapy. The BT felt incapacitated, and this proved difficult to present properly to the patient. He felt at fault and became alarmed when, for the first time, his erections were no longer firm. When the typical 2-week limit was reached, he was obviously relieved to have a pretext for termination. Although we were only guardedly optimistic, we encouraged him to continue, saying that we thought his case might simply be long term (3 or 4 weeks). He did not continue and, despite his expressed intention to return, probably will not.

I do not think that a more aggressive BT or the use of the standard technique of vigorous manual stimulation and rapid intromission would have been any more effective in this case. He may have been most like the relatively content nonclinical retarded ejaculators who have elaborated their symptom into a life style and, as I speculated earlier, may represent the majority of men with this disorder.

CONCLUSIONS

Retarded ejaculation is thought of as difficult to treat because, uniquely among the sexual disorders, the standard interpretations have not been revised and still reflect early psychodynamic thinking. The retarded ejaculator is thought of as hostile and withholding, and his inability to have coital orgasms is seen as a refusal that must be aggressively overcome in sex therapy.

What should have alerted clinicians to the inadequacy of this interpretation is the well-known fact that the retarded ejaculator does not merely have difficulty reaching orgasms in coitus; his coital anorgasmia is absolute. Even to experience coital orgasm once in the course of treatment constitutes a major breakthrough. It is difficult to imagine a hostile act being carried out so unwaveringly.

In my view, what accounts for this consistency is simply that the retarded ejaculator is never sufficiently aroused to reach orgasm in intercourse. This is the same consistency shown by the woman who is coitally anorgasmic.

However, the absolute lack of male coital orgasm is accounted for in the standard view by offering a second explanation, that RE is a reflex inhibition. Putting these two explanations together, it appears as if the retarded ejaculator refuses to be coitally orgasmic (the dynamic explanation), evidently not realizing that he could not be orgasmic even if he changed his mind (the reflex explanation).

Although no one has put it that whimsically, it is difficult to reconcile the two standard explanations since the dynamic explanation is based on the idea that the retarded ejaculator refuses to be orgasmic because he wants to punish the partner, whereas the reflex explanation is based on the idea that he is afraid *he* will be punished if he is orgasmic.

I propose that the two explanations simply exist side by side with no attempt to reconcile them because they both justify aggressively attacking the retarded ejaculator's reluctance. Given the dynamic interpretation that retarded ejaculation represents a *refusal*, the therapist feels justified in aggressively overcoming this refusal rather than helping the retarded ejaculator to feel less self-condemnatory about it, that is, to be able to refuse more directly.

The reflex explanation helps buttress this justification. Sex therapists can think of themselves as trying to break a spell, since they would, of course, not want to think of themselves as trying to break the patient's will. In other words, the two standard explanations are a disguised expression of disapproval.

Even sex therapists who are sensitive to the role of performance anxiety and who recommend a scrupulous avoidance of performance demands in the treatment of coitally anorgasmic women, recommend an intensely demanding regimen in the treatment of coitally anorgasmic men. To explain this discrepancy requires a recognition of hitherto masked features of RE as well as of a normative bias in the way clinicians react to socially deviant attitudes.

Among those diagnosed as retarded ejaculators, that is, as suffering from coital anorgasmia, are men who also have difficulty masturbating. This has masked the pronounced autosexual (masturbatory) orientation that emerges as a critical diagnostic cue for RE once men who have difficulty masturbating are excluded. This autosexual orientation is manifested by masturbatory facility and enjoyment and a loss of desire in partner sex.

An additional reason why therapists are not disposed to help the retarded ejaculator to refuse to be coitally orgasmic is that, much as once was true for homosexuality, autosexuality is not acceptable as a bona fide orientation.

The loss of desire in partner sex has also been masked by the retarded ejaculator's quasi-priapic erections. Because the retarded ejaculator mani-

fests unusually sustained erections in partner sex, it has been assumed that
he must be fully aroused and therefore that his disorder is specific to the
orgasm phase. Although the retarded ejaculator's erections are long-sustained, they are insensate to such an extent that the behavioral objective
with the retarded ejaculator should not be for him to have coital orgasms
but should be for him to have enjoyable erections with a partner. The
retarded ejaculator is not likely to report his lack of desire with a partner
because, just as is true for the coitally anorgasmic woman, he focuses on his
partner's enjoyment rather than his own.

Although the cues that reveal the retarded ejaculator's partner-specific
desire disorder are masked, this alone does not account for the standard
misinterpretations of RE. Some retarded ejaculators make plain their aversion to the partner, but it is discounted. In effect, the retarded ejaculator is
treated as if he should want to have coital orgasms. No consideration is
given to the possibility that he needs to be better able to refuse to have coital
orgasms and to refuse coitus and that he may have good reason to do so.

Recognition of the retarded ejaculator's desire disorder specific to
partner sex makes it clear that he does in fact have good reason to refuse
coitus. However, he believes that he should be enjoying partner sex, and he
typically is in full agreement with the clinician that he should be having
coital orgasms. The use of a demanding treatment regimen is congruent
with the retarded ejaculator's conscientious approach to sex and reinforces
the performance pressure he already feels.

The way the retarded ejaculator is disapproved of is reminiscent of the
once-popular disapproving attitude taken against "frigidity." Most sex therapists now have a secure grasp on the insight that the "frigid" woman is not
withholding and that her problem is quite the opposite, that she is too
preoccupied with pleasing the partner. She is told that she needs to learn to
please herself. The retarded ejaculator can benefit from the same insight,
but he is not likely to be presented with it. He needs to realize that he cannot
have an orgasm for someone else, yet he still is thought of as withholding his
orgasm from his partner.

This psychodynamic bias that originally was directed against "frigidity" and all the sexual disorders and still affects the way retarded ejaculation
is thought of is based on the assumption that symptoms gratify unconscious
wishes. Therefore, the patient is not seen as authentically suffering from a
symptom. Only those around him or her are seen as suffering. They are the
ones who need to be rescued, not the one who is symptomatic.

The possibility that patients are authentically suffering has been
granted, at least by behavioral and cognitive therapists and by ego-analyti-
cally oriented psychodynamic therapists, but this dispensation has not yet
been extended to the retarded ejaculator. He is still viewed with suspicion.
Hence, the standard treatment of retarded ejaculation continues to be
unempathic.

REFERENCES

Apfelbaum, B. (1977). Sexual functioning reconsidered. In R. Gemme & C. C. Wheeler (Eds.), *Progress in sexology* (pp. 93–100). New York: Plenum Press.

Apfelbaum, B. (1984). The ego-analytic approach to individual body-work sex therapy: Five case examples. *Journal of Sex Research, 20,* 44–70.

Apfelbaum, B. (1985). Masters and Johnson's contribution: A response to "Reflections on sex therapy," an interview with Harold Lief and Arnold Lazarus. *Journal of Sex Edcuation and Therapy, 11,* 5–11.

Apfelbaum, B. (1988). An ego-analytic perspective on desire disorders. In S. Leiblum & R. Rosen (Eds.), *Sexual desire disorders* (pp. 75–104). New York: Guilford Press.

Apfelbaum, B., & Apfelbaum, C. (1985). The ego-analytic approach to sexual apathy. In D. C. Goldberg (Ed.), *Contemporary marriage handbook* (pp. 439–481). Homewood, IL: Dorsey Press.

Fenichel, O. (1945). *The psychoanalytic theory of neurosis.* New York: W. W. Norton.

Kaplan, H. (1974). *The new sex therapy.* New York: Brunner/Mazel.

Kaplan, H. (1979). *Disorders of sexual desire.* New York: Brunner/Mazel.

Kaplan, H. (1987). *The illustrated manual of sex therapy* (2nd ed.). New York: Brunner/Mazel.

Masters, W. H., & Johnson, V. E. (1970). *Human sexual inadequacy.* Boston: Little, Brown.

Ovesey, L. (1971). Inability to ejaculate in coitus. *Medical Aspects of Human Sexuality, 5,* 121.

Razani, J. (1977). Ejaculatory incompetence treated by reconditioning anxiety. In J. Fischer & H. L. Gochros (Eds.), *Handbook of behavior therapy with sexual problems* (Vol. 1, pp. 312–326). New York: Pergamon.

Shore, D., & Shore C. (1987). Keeping fit in bed. *Penthouse Forum, 17*(2), 54–56.

Williams, H. H. (1977, March). *An unnoted inconsistency in Masters and Johnson's use of nondemand techniques: Retarded ejaculation.* Unpublished paper presented at the California State Psychological Association Convention, Los Angeles.

Williams, M. H. (1978). Individual sex therapy. In J. LoPiccolo & L. LoPiccolo (Eds.), *Handbook of sex therapy* (pp. 477–483). New York: Plenum Press.

8

Comprehensive Evaluation of Erectile Dysfunction and Medical Treatments

LEONORE TIEFER AND ARNOLD MELMAN

*Complaints of erectile dysfunction have assumed ever-increasing promi-
nence in sex therapy clinics around the country. Tiefer and Melman accordingly begin this chapter with a detailed discussion of factors that appear to
contribute to the dramatic rise in the number of cases of erectile dysfunction
in recent years. Among these are the increased expectations for sexual
function in the later years, women's rising expectations for sexual gratification, and the explosion of information about causes and treatment of erectile
dysfunction presented in the popular media. Although the public is inun-
dated with information, common misconceptions about erectile dysfunction continue to abound, as most males, for example, still conceive of sexual
arousal in purely mechanistic or biological terms. For this and other reasons,
compliance is a major problem in the treatment of erectile dysfunction. The
authors note that only 30% of patients evaluated in their center were found to
follow through on treatment recommendations!*

*Based on a wealth of clinical experience, Tiefer and Melman have
developed a systematic and comprehensive approach to evaluation of erectile dysfunction. This approach incorporates a thorough physical examination; nocturnal penile tumescence (NPT) testing; endocrine, vascular, and
neurological evaluation; and separate interviews with both the patient and
his partner. These interviews are used for detailed assessment of the history
of the problem as well as exploration of the couples' attitudes and expectations for treatment. Numerous case vignettes are included in the chapter to
illustrate the complexity of medical and psychological issues to be evaluated
in each case.*

*Because psychological approaches to treatment are presented in detail
in Chapter 9 (Althof), this chapter focuses primarily on the use of medical or
surgical interventions. Intracorporeal injections have come to be widely
used in recent years, and the authors cautiously evaluate the potential risks
and benefits of this approach. Various forms of penile vascular surgery and
prosthetic implants are also considered in detail. Based on their own follow-*

up study, Tiefer and Melman conclude that surgical implants produce
satisfactory results in some, but not all, areas of function. They also report
no significant differences in satisfaction levels between different types of
implant. Finally, they emphasize that a surgical implant can be as important
to the patient's self-esteem as his sexual function, as is nicely illustrated in
the concluding case presentation.

Leonore Tiefer, Ph.D., is Clinical Associate Professor of Urology and
Psychiatry at the Albert Einstein College of Medicine and at Montefiore
Medical Center. She has published widely in the field of sexuality, including
both empirical and theoretical studies from animal mating behavior to
social constructionist theory.

Arnold Melman, M.D., is Professor and Chairman of Urology at the
Albert Einstein College of Medicine and at Montefiore Medical Center. He
has conducted extensive research on the physiology and pharmacology of
male erection.

Concern over male sexual performance and particularly over penile erections has been part of every culture in every age (Strage, 1980). This
"cultural demand for effectiveness of sexual performance" (Masters &
Johnson, 1970, p. 159) rests on an enduring social connection between
masculinity and sexual function.

> An impotent man always feels that his masculinity, and not just his sexual-
> ity, is threatened. In men, gender appears to "lean" on sexuality . . . the
> need for sexual performance is so great. . . . In women, gender identity and
> self-worth can be consolidated by other means. (Person, 1980, pp. 619, 626)

Although current incidence and prevalence figures for erectile dysfunction are not available, the Kinsey survey in the 1930s and 1940s reported that
erectile dysfunction increased directly as a function of age, with 25% of their
male sample "completely" impotent by age 65, 55% by age 75, and 75% by age
80 (Kinsey, Pomeroy, & Martin, 1948). A more recent report by Martin (1981)
on married men only indicated that about a third of the 60 to 79-year-old
group had difficulty with erections, and an additional 15% were sexually
inactive and thus unsure of their potency. Although more is now known about
the psychology and physiology of erections than in the 1940s, there is still a
dearth of useful epidemiological data to guide our normative assumptions.

Although concern over impotence is not new, additional contemporary
factors fuel public interest in evaluation and treatment (D'Emilio & Freedman, 1988): (1) the rising importance of sexual function in personal life
(Schmidt, 1983); (2) the relatively new expectation that sexual function is a
lifelong capacity, not normally diminished by middle or older age (Masters
& Johnson, 1970); (3) women's increased expectations for sexual satisfaction
(e.g., Barbach, 1975; Heiman, 1983); (4) decreased media censorship of

sexual topics and subsequent media explosion of primarily medicalized information (Tiefer, 1986); (5) recent changes in professional codes of ethics to permit physician and other health care provider advertisements; and (6) disproportionate growth of professional literature on impotence in contrast to other sexual problems (Elliott, 1985).

Whatever the prevalence, and whether or not the disorder is increasing, there does seem to be an increasing demand for evaluation and treatment of erectile dysfunction. Sex therapists currently report informally that their clientele consists preponderantly of erectile disorder cases. Moreover, the evaluation and treatment of erectile dysfunction has become a thriving subspecialty within urology. In recent years, erectile dysfunction evaluation centers have appeared in urology departments and group practices, supplementing or replacing the sexuality dysfunction clinics formerly located in psychiatry settings. This development has occurred because of the growth in knowledge about organic contributions to erectile dysfunction, media news and talk show promotion of the new technologies, aggressive campaigning by urologists and penile prosthesis manufacturers, and the fact that locating erectile dysfunction centers in a traditional medical department offers a face-saving environment for many men who feel that coming to a psychiatry setting is humiliating (Segraves, Schoenberg, Zairns, Camic, & Knopf, 1981).

The new urology-based settings, however, require a new, multidisciplinary evaluation design. Whereas psychiatrists are presumably trained in both medicine and psychology, that is not true for other medical specialists. In the urology-based setting, we and others have found that the most effective arrangement involves separate evaluations for the medical and psychosocial components of sexual dysfunction by a urologist (A.M.) and a psychologist (L.T.) (Melman, Tiefer, & Pedersen, 1988). Unfortunately, the need for a multidisciplinary evaluation is not yet widely shared. Many surgeons see the utility of psychological evaluation limited to "the exclusion of patients at risk of becoming psychotic or suicidal, developing chronic psychogenic pain, or initiating inappropriate malpractice suits" (Schover & von Eschenbach, 1985, p. 58). Moreover, although our previous work has shown the importance of interviewing the patient's sexual partner during the evaluation for both appropriate diagnosis and treatment referral (Tiefer & Melman, 1983), we know from our own patients' previous medical encounters that even this step into the psychosocial reality of the sexual dysfunction is still infrequently taken.

COMPREHENSIVE EVALUATION

Smith (1988) has recently described the interaction between psychological and biological events in successful male sexual functioning as one wherein "each physiologic event interacts with a psychologic event in a positive feedback loop, each phase leading to the next in a chain of events" (p. 42).

Without giving priority to either the biological or psychosocial (and always presuming the absence of inhibiting or distracting psychobiological events), she describes how sexual drive aroused by a potential sexual situation (that is, by imaginal or sensory stimulation and attraction) produces afferent stimulation to the brain. Intrabrain events (with awareness of erotic stimulation) then in turn produce efferent stimulation to the genitals and some reinforcing short-acting hormonal events (with further erotic awareness). These, then, result in genital vasodilation and penile corpus cavernosal filling (with heightened arousal), penile blood trapping and maintained erection (with further sexual activity and maintained arousal), orgasm (with positive memories and sensations), and, finally, physiological detumescence (with relaxation and positive evaluations).

Evaluating the occurrence of the many components of this sequence, pinpointing the loci of any disruptions, and speculating about their causes require familiarity with the complete spectrum of human sexual physiology and psychology. Erection is, truly, at least a sensorymotorneurohormonal-vascularpsychosociocultural interpersonal event! The result of contemporary specialist training is that neither the urologist nor the psychologist alone is capable of an exhaustive evaluation.

The importance of a comprehensive evaluation not only for correct diagnosis but for appropriate treatment planning, including, if necessary, referral, must be underscored. The recent development of a medical treatment for erectile dysfunction far less invasive than implant surgery, penile injections of papaverine (see discussion below), creates the temptation to bypass complex intrapsychic or interpersonal issues. Why bother worrying about the complex psychosocial spectrum when we have available a "harmless" and "easy" medical treatment that may provide relief? Yet research suggests that both preliminary and continuing psychosocial evaluation must be undertaken even with this "simple" treatment in order to forestall misuse, misunderstanding, and premature dropout (Althof et al., 1988). The treatment of erectile problems teaches us again and again how the complexities of patient's lives, relationships, and personalities influence how they utilize even the simplest medical treatment. And, of course, as we discuss below, this "simple" medical treatment, like so many others, turns out not to be harmless or carefree at all. The psychosocial aspects of erectile function simply cannot ever be bypassed in favor of an exclusively biomechanical model of sexuality.

PURPOSES OF THE EVALUATION

Patient's Purpose versus Professional's Purpose

An unanalyzed assumption in most health care discussions is that the patients' and the professionals' goals are the same, presumably to make the best (i.e., most accurate) evaluation of the problem and to follow through with the most appropriate treatment. The assumption is made that both patients and providers are rational and "open-minded" about the causes of the problem and will go wherever the data direct in terms of evaluation and treatment.

But this assumption is foolish for two reasons. First, we cannot assume that health care providers from different specialties perceive sexual problems similarly (Byrne, 1986). Trained to look at different parts of the elephant, to cite the old parable, sexologists from different specialties will be likely to prioritize dysfunction etiologies and treatments from their own area of expertise.

Second, we must discard the assumption that patients and professionals see erectile disorders similarly. Some writers have mentioned in passing that men would frequently "prefer" to have a physical rather than a psychological or interpersonal cause identified for their problem. Masters and Johnson (1970), for example, claimed that

> . . . for many years, the pattern of the human male has been to blame sexual dysfunction on specific physical distresses. Every sexually inadequate male lunges toward any potential physical excuse for sexual malfunction. (p. 187)

In the chapter on erectile problems of a well-known text on sex therapy, we find the same claim: "In our culture, men with sexual dysfunction find it considerably more acceptable to blame it on physical disability than on psychologic disability" (Reckless & Geiger, 1978, p. 299).

Some social psychologists would identify men's "blaming" their dysfunction on medical causes as the use of a physicalistic "attribution bias" (Harvey & Weary, 1985), and they might speculate that this serves as a psychological defense, a face saving maneuver to preserve masculine self esteem (Tiefer, 1986). Men with such a bias may slant their behavior throughout the comprehensive evaluation, first by influencing the type of health care provider they seek out (Segraves et al., 1981) and later by causing them to omit relevant information during the initial history-taking, to refuse the participation of their sexual partners, to stonewall during the interview with the psychologist, and even to reject any nonmedical treatment recommendation. A firm insistence by the treatment team on the routine conduct of the evaluation (including psychological interviews with both patient and partner) will usually produce compliance with the evaluation, but it may not affect the patient's original goals and may not affect ultimate compliance with treatment recommendations.

We analyzed the results from 99 questionnaires completed by men who had been evaluated at least 18 months previously for erectile dysfunction and discovered that only 30% had followed through with the treatment recommendation made at the end of the evaluation (Tiefer & Melman, 1987). This lack of compliance probably relates to many factors, but prospective research is needed to identify its relationship to patients' preevaluation expectations and wishes.

Determine Nature and Extent of the Problem

An obvious purpose of the erectile dysfunction evaluation is to answer the nonobvious question, "What is the patient's problem?" It is certainly not always the case that the patient coming for an erectile dysfunction evaluation *has* a problem with erections!

> *Case 1: Mr. DT.* A 58-year-old separated Vietnamese immigrant with a history of hypertension, referred from his primary physician and group plan urologist, anxiously reported potency difficulties over the past 2 years with all casual partners, reduced morning erections, and no erections to previously effective erotic films. Painstaking interview finally clarified that he had erectile problems only on the second or third intercourse attempt of each of these casual encounters, a pattern that he utilized because sexual opportunities were so infrequent since his emigration. He acknowledged that this point had not been raised with previous interviewers.

> *Case 2: Mr. MS.* A 56-year-old married executive presents a complaint of less rigid erections over a period of 1–2 years as well as health problems of irregular heartbeat and recurrent urinary infections. The patient mentions less frequent intercourse, but, separately, his wife reflects that for 17 years she was the primary initiator of intercourse. She acknowledged that this has changed recently because of her increasing independence in work and reduced interest in trying to stimulate her husband's low sexual interest.

Part of the difficulty in identifying the nature of the problem occurs because the sexual languages used by patients and by sexologists differ. Current professional terminology is derived from Masters and Johnson's (1966) physiological sexual response cycle model together with Kaplan's (1979) additions and modifications and is codified in the American Psychiatric Association's (1987) diagnostic manual, which becomes more elaborate with each revision. "Male erectile disorder" is currently defined in that manual as either of the following:

> (1) persistent or recurrent partial or complete failure in a male to attain or maintain erection until completion of the sexual activity;
> (2) persistent or recurrent lack of a subjective sense of sexual excitement and pleasure in a male during sexual activity. (1987, p. 294)

This disorder is to be distinguished from lack of desire, sexual aversion, delay in or absence of orgasm, premature ejaculation, or genital pain in conjunction with intercourse, the other sexual dysfunctions listed for men in the diagnostic manual. Very few patients complain of a disorder with definition 2, or at least very few find their way to our unit. It is the performance, not the experience, that worries our patients.

Although the response cycle model implies a sequence of relatively distinct psychophysiological experiences, many men become confused when asked whether they suffer from difficulties with desire or erection. Sometimes this confusion can be traced to the patient's wishes, as discussed above, for a simple physical explanation and treatment, and any discussion that seems to "pry" into the details implies doubt regarding the patient's own explanation. In other cases, the patient seems not to have encoded sexual experiences in terms of a sequence of separable events, and it takes patient (and time-consuming) discussion for distinctions to be communicated.

Patients frequently use the terms "desire," "erection," "ejaculation," etcetera, very differently from professionals, and it is essential to check and double-check through the use of synonyms and descriptive phrases (i.e., for ejaculation using words like "coming," "discharging," or concrete descriptive phrases like "the part of sex where the feeling is strongest and the fluid comes out of the penis") to make sure communication and not miscommunication is occurring. As with Case 1 above, we have seen numerous cases where the patient's "incorrect" use of "impotence" was misunderstood by several professionals prior to our evaluation.

Determine Etiology(ies) of the Problem

Why is this person having an erectile problem? Most professionals and almost all patients perceive sexual problems as being caused by *either* organic *or* psychological causes. Thus, every man without a significant history of physical illness seems prepared to behave defensively during history taking, inevitably saying at some point, "You're asking these questions because you think it's all in my head, right!" This polarization is played out over and over again in clinical work, even though lip service is often paid to combinations of causative factors. In fact, psychological interviews are often used to "rule out" psychogenic etiologies in the mind of the referring physician.

> Conceptually, most of the research suffers from the flaw of attempting to categorize the patients into discrete, nonoverlapping categories of organic *or* psychogenic failure. Yet, many cases, and *perhaps the majority of cases, involve both organic and psychogenic erectile factors* in the genesis of erectile failure. (LoPiccolo, 1985, p. 221, emphasis added)

There is an unfortunate tendency to feel that the etiological problem has been solved whenever *any* organic condition has been identified, with the assumption that this condition must be causing the dysfunction. This tendency is growing as the literature identifies more and more physical problems related to erectile disorders. Drawing such a conclusion is unwarranted, however, since a physical condition may exist and even be severe and long-standing, and the patient still have psychogenic erectile dysfunction.

Case 3: Mr. GS. A 67-year-old married, retired office worker has had diabetes and hypertension since 1972, both treated with oral medication. He reports erectile problems for the past 2 to 3 years, and comes from his group internist and urologist fully expecting surgery. Careful interview reveals that he can stimulate himself to full erection in the shower, and he also admits that his wife's dental problems and offensive breath odor have reduced his sexual interest in recent years.

Case 4: Mr. JT. A 45-year-old married subway motorman has had hypertension since 1968 and has taken Inderal® since 1977. He had a minor stroke in 1973 and a heart attack in 1983. He reports erectile problems for 5 to 10 years, although his wife says it's been more recent. They both report that *several* physicians have told them that his problems are the result of his medications and that "either you have happy sex and die, or you take the medications and live." The couple has avoided sexual activity for the most part (both are working at two jobs), although the husband believes that men need to satisfy women in order to keep relationships. He is very concerned that his 39-year-old wife is losing respect for him. The full medical work-up reveals that he is capable of normal long-lasting erections.

Case 5: Mr. NB. The patient is a 39-year-old, never-married lawyer who has had insulin-dependent diabetes since 1974. He has consulted numerous doctors for various sexual problems, including rapid ejaculation, diminished sensations, and erectile problems, *all of which* began during masturbation in 1971, a week after he failed the bar exam. He has rigid morning erections, and comprehensive testing resulted in a psychogenic diagnosis.

We have seen many patients who came for a second opinion after a penile prosthesis was suggested for their "organic impotence" who indeed turned out to have organic disease, usually diabetes, but who had clear-cut psychogenic erectile problems anyway.

The second reason for resisting the temptation towards dichotomous thinking is that a physical condition that exists may contribute to erectile problems without being their primary cause.

Case 6: Mr. AS. A 55-year-old married salesman had been diagnosed as having atherosclerosis following a pudendal angiogram and was referred for internal iliac angioplasty. He reported erectile difficulties for 3 years and denies morning erections. Detailed interviewing suggested the onset and maintenance of the problem were associated with the wife's evolving parkinsonism and the anxious husband's reaction. His penile blood pressure was normal, although nocturnal erections were brief and not rigid. Our conclusion was that the patient's sexual difficulties resulted from a mixture of psychogenic and organic factors.

Our impressions about etiology are expressed in a five-category system: (1) purely organic, (2) primarily organic, (3) primarily psychogenic, (4) purely psychogenic, (5) unknown. Over the last 8 years, almost 1,400 patients have been thoroughly evaluated in our Center for Male Sexual Dysfunction. Approximately 15% resulted in an "unknown" etiology diagnosis. Of the rest, 55% were diagnosed as psychogenic or primarily psychogenic, with the remainder as organic or primarily organic (Melman et al., 1988). This is most definitely not to be taken as normative for all men with erectile disorders, however, since these patients hardly represent a random sample of men with erectile disorders. In fact, most of these patients were referred by primary care physicians because of suspected organic impotence. Moreover, in our center, those men whose obvious purely psychogenic impotence could be determined during the initial interview based on the urologist's initial brief history are usually referred directly for sex therapy without completion of the full comprehensive evaluation.

The above percentages, with the majority of cases being "psychogenic" or "primarily psychogenic," are therefore based on a sample where both patient and referring professional felt there was significant reason to suspect organic impotence. The importance of this cannot be overemphasized. The patient's beliefs about the causes of his problems must be verified by a variety of empirical tests and until then must be considered as much a statement of his wishes as anything else. Moreover, there is obviously a dearth of sophisticated knowledge about the psychophysiological nature of sexual function among referring physicians.

Treatment Planning

Treatment planning must be based on a full understanding of the patient's sexuality. It is a false impression that the type of treatment recommended depends simply on the type of problem the person has, particularly on its etiology; for example, organic impotence requires a penile prosthesis, psychogenic impotence requires sex therapy, etcetera. This type of formulaic recommendation treats sexual problems as mechanical malfunctions and neglects the fact that sexuality is an expression of a complex personality and, usually, of a relationship. In our opinion, responsible treatment recommendations must cohere with other aspects of that personality and relationship. This is why treatment planning begins during the evaluation rather than after the outcome of the evaluation has been determined.

As mentioned earlier, our questionnaire follow-up of 99 patients who completed the comprehensive evaluation 18 to 48 months previous to that time showed that more than half had failed to follow through on *any* treatment recommendation, and only 30% had complied with the treatment recommendation made at the end of the evaluation (Tiefer & Melman, 1987). This suggests the importance during the evaluation of the team's understanding enough about the patient's/couple's outlook, expectations, and resources to recommend a treatment that will be psychosocially acceptable as well as medically appropriate. The need for such understanding underscores the role of multiple interviews and points to another reason why the interview of patients' sexual partners is so crucial. In a previous study (Tiefer & Melman, 1983), we found that wives' interviews altered treatment recommendations based on patients' interviews in 58% of the 40 cases reviewed. This was usually because information about the partner's sexuality or psychology signaled the need for additional treatment considerations or a different approach, although in four cases, the partner revealed highly significant information about the patient that he had withheld.

Case 7: Mr. AB (from Tiefer & Melman, 1983). A 58-year-old accountant reported no sexual problems in a first marriage, which ended with his wife's sudden death in 1982. He had not been able to achieve intercourse with his new fiance despite a close relationship with mutual sexual desire during the last 18 months. He has had diabetes for 10 years, and the comprehensive work-up resulted in an organic diagnosis and a penile prosthesis recommendation. An interview with the patient's fiance, however, revealed that she was not at all dissatisfied with the status quo and may even have chosen the patient in part because of the lack of sexual intercourse in the relationship. Preoperative joint counseling was recommended to explore issues of mutual motivation for surgery.

Evaluating patients with sexual problems requires a diversified medical and psychosocial treatment referral network of the sort provided by a multidisciplinary evaluation team, since subspecialty differences known in one discipline (e.g., involving different types of couple therapy appropriate for couples with different styles or backgrounds) will often be completely unknown to another.

We refer many patients and couples for sex therapy and choose referrals to professionals who practice a sophisticated blend of marital and sex therapy or whose individual treatment is informed by thorough training in human sexuality. Referred cases include those without organic pathology; with some organic but primarily psychogenic etiology; with organic etiology but too much immaturity, couple conflict, or ambivalence to be able to embark on medical treatment that would renew their sexual function; or with other serious psychological problems. Because many patients come to us with a confident expectation that their problem is straightforwardly physical, their shock at hearing that we are not going to proceed with medical treatment can be tempered by stressing the utility of sex therapy as a conservative intervention for all sexual problems. We tell patients that, during sex therapy, they will either improve or not improve, and that if after they give the therapy enough time there is no improvement, they are welcome to return for further evaluation. We hear later that many of these cases (although probably not as many as we would like) undergo very useful psychotherapies.

Therapeutic and Educational Purposes

Participating in an evaluation for a sexual problem can have numerous therapeutic benefits. Knowing that patients and their partners have rarely spoken candidly or at length to any knowledgeable, nonjudgmental persons about their problems, we intend the evaluation to be an affirming experience. Concerns are treated respectfully, patients are addressed in language they will understand, written materials are shared, confidentiality is emphasized, numerous areas of life related to sexuality (and stress) are examined, and topics are approached in a minimally threatening order. In this atmosphere, many patients have commented on the relief they experience in finally confronting their troubling problem.

Many couples have become estranged from each other because of an erectile problem, especially one neglected by the man for years. The fact that the patient is participating in the comprehensive evaluation is evidence that he is willing to begin to confront the problem. Sometimes this can provide an opportunity for a reconciliation and a chance to begin the type of collaboration the couple will need to stay with whatever treatment they pursue as well as to renew their sexual life together. As we interview members of the couple separately, we take the opportunity to emphasize the potentially positive meanings of the gesture being made by each member of the couple (e.g., generosity, hopefulness, caring).

We are no longer surprised when a patient reports that he has regained his erectile function during the course of the evaluation (which, for scheduling reasons, usually takes place over a period of several weeks).

> *Case 8: Mr. MK.* A 72-year-old married, retired investor who is healthy despite a heart attack 14 years ago reported erectile problems for the past 2 to 3 years, which resulted in cessation of all sexual activity for the past few months. No masturbation or morning erections were reported. Following the sleep center testing, and prior to coming for his appointment to hear the test results, the patient and his wife had had normal intercourse three times and reported that they felt the problem was cured. They were congratulated, but the message was communicated that sometimes rapid relief is short-lived and that they should return if dysfunction returned.

Because there is so much media misinformation about male sexuality, usually consisting of oversimplified reports of "new treatment breakthroughs," we increasingly need to take time during the evaluation to provide accurate information. This often disappoints patients who had thought a simple solution was going to be available to them, and sometimes they are doubtful and suspicious about the accuracy of *our* information! Careful interviewing is occasionally necessary to distinguish mere misinformation (almost universal) from evidence of poor judgment, overvalued ideas, obsessions, or true delusions, all of which can be present when men are talking about erectile problems.

Case 9: Mr. JC. A 33-year-old, never-married lawyer developed numerous sexual complaints during his first sexual relationship 4 years ago. He had had no prior difficulties in masturbation. Careful history taking revealed that prior to undergoing the comprehensive evaluation, the patient had over 15 physician contacts, including repeated hormonal testing, electromyography, corporal cavernosography, a penile vein ligation, repeated sperm counts, and a computerized tomography (CT) scan. Some of these tests had produced positive results, and the patient had been self-injecting human chorionic gonadotropin for 7 months. There had been no improvement in spontaneous or masturbatory erections, and the patient had not had a sexual partner. The patient's obsessive overconcern with details of genital appearance and function, long history of compulsive masturbation, social reclusiveness, and anxious, pressured interview manner had all been dismissed as physiological testing and varied treatments proceeded. In light of the failure of the many medical interventions, we tried to persuade the patient to accept a referral for psychotherapy. Although he was impressed with the thorough review of his previous care, and seemed at times responsive to the logical discussion of its implications (namely, that he had some emotional problems related to sexual function that he'd neglected and that ought to be addressed), the patient's obsession with a medical solution seemed to persist.

Case 10: Mr. JW. A 39-year-old, never-married messenger was referred by a urologist who had treated him with testosterone (brief improvement) and penile injections of papaverine (two out of three injections successful) when the patient began insisting on a penile prosthesis. Interview revealed an obsessed and irrational man who, prior to the treatments, had been able to have daily intercourse normally, but who wished to be able to have intercourse two and three times daily, since "once is never satisfying." His woman friend of 5 years confirmed his pattern and wishes and also confirmed his stories of violent and abusive agitation when his potency failed. He had been hospitalized once on a psychiatric ward following such an episode. Again, a calm discussion of the implications of the evaluation test results (i.e., physically normal function) seemed not to affect the patient's attitude or wishes.

DESIGN OF THE COMPREHENSIVE EVALUATION

Medical Tests

In our clinic, the medical part of the comprehensive evaluation typically consists of the following:

- Initial interview, history, and examination
- Two nights of sleep testing with nocturnal penile monitoring (including Rigiscan) and visual sexual stimulation
- Hormone assays (testosterone, estradiol, prolactin)
- Glucose tolerance testing
- Pelvic arterial and venous function tests
- Pelvic sensory–motor function tests

Initial Interview and History by the Urologist

The patient is first interviewed and examined by the urologist, and a history focused on medical contributions to sexual difficulties is obtained. The patient's definition of the problem as "impotence" is questioned to determine whether he is referring to changes in libido, retarded or premature ejaculation, or lengthy post-ejaculatory periods as contrasted with changes in ability to attain or maintain erectile rigidity.

Special attention is paid to possible interactions of organic and psychogenic factors. For example, a man started on medication for diabetes may have an episode of erectile failure and, perhaps prepared by patient literature for diabetics that usually discusses erectile problems, be so frightened that he reports total absence of erection, stops all attempts at sexual activity, and believes he is impotent. This conclusion may be supported by the behavior of his primary physician, who, hearing that he has erectile problems as well as diabetes, may communicate the conviction that the sexual problems are organic. A complete list of prescription and nonprescription drugs is compiled because of the ever-growing number of medications known to affect erection, emission, ejaculation, and orgasm (Wein & Van Arsdalen, 1988).

History taking frequently focuses on situational elements of the problem such as erectile failure with some partners and not others or with some sex activities and not others. Questions are raised about middle-of-the-night and awakening (morning) erections. Basically, the interviewer looks for intermittency in erectile function rather than evidence of complete nonfunction.

Physical Examination

With few exceptions, positive findings during physical examination can only suggest possible etiologies for the erectile dysfunction, but they do direct the physician to more specific system evaluation. Gross observations of gait and skin direct attention to possible neurological disease, contributory medications, drug abuse, endocrine deficits, or nicotine abuse. General and local blood pressure abnormalities imply possible small blood vessel disease. Head and neck examination may suggest atherosclerosis, pituitary tumor, diabetic complications, or thyroid abnormalities. Chest examination may suggest abnormal estrogen production. Abdominal examination may produce evidence of arterial or liver abnormalities.

Various medical reasons for erectile dysfunction can be suggested during examination of the penis, testicles, rectum, and internal organs, including cancers, infections, abnormalities of the internal genitalia, or neurological problems. Some patients who complain of unusual penile curvature have plaque deposits, which can be felt during penile examination. They can be tentatively diagnosed as Peyronie disease, but a more accurate diagnosis of this disorder can be made by requesting that the patient masturbate to create an erection that the physician can observe or, alternately, the patient can mail Polaroid® photographs of his best erection.

Endocrine Tests

Patients with diminished desire, with or without erectile failure, may have a reduction in plasma testosterone or an elevation in prolactin or estradiol, all of which have been related to male sexual dysfunction. The evaluation can be made with blood tests done by most commercial laboratories. In our long experience, reduced plasma testosterone is not clinically relevant unless the levels are below 100 to 200 ng/dl, a lower level than is often published. The reasons that the generally accepted lowest level of normal may not be accurate may relate to the pulsatile release of testosterone from the testis and the need for repetitive sampling. Also, clinical experience has shown a lack of response to hormone treatment unless the plasma levels are below 200 ng/dl.

> *Case 11: Mr. AA.* A 28-year-old engaged accountant reported both diminished libido and increased difficulty obtaining erections over the past 9 months. He denied illnesses or any conflict with his fiancee, although it was she who insisted he investigate the cause of the problem. Physical examination revealed severe bilateral testicular atrophy. Two years earlier he had undergone bilateral hernia surgery and had suffered bilateral injury to the testicular blood flow. Although the surgery had resulted in a law suit, no one had suggested any testosterone alteration. Plasma testosterone was found to be 58 ng/dl, a nearly castrate level. The patient responded to monthly testosterone injections administered by his fiancee. The couple was advised that the injury had rendered him sterile, and the couple subsequently married. A satisfactory outcome was achieved when the wife became pregnant through artificial insemination (donor).

> *Case 12: Mr. LW.* A 58-year-old writer sought treatment for a 4-year problem of diminished libido and total erectile failure. The patient appeared to have underactive pituitary function. He indicated that 12 years previous to that time he had undergone radiation treatment for a pituitary tumor and was taking steroid replacement only. Plasma testos-

terone was 45 ng/dl, a reflection of his primary pituitary failure. The patient's wife was instructed to administer monthly testosterone, and the patient responded with normal erections.

Frequently, patients with excess prolactin (a pituitary hormone) report many and varied symptoms of malaise in addition to loss of libido and erectile dysfunction. Hormone levels usually reveal both elevated prolactin and diminished testosterone. Treating the testosterone deficit without reducing the prolactin overproduction with surgery, radiation, or oral bromoscriptine will not reverse the libido and erectile problem.

Alcohol abusers, patients taking digoxin, and men with adrenocortical tumors may have elevated plasma estradiol. Such hormone excess may cause decreased libido and is best treated by removing the cause, or with oral testosterone.

Nocturnal Penile Tumescence (NPT) and Visual Sexual Stimulation

Recognition that regular spontaneous penile erections occur during sleep was first reported by Olenmeyer, Brilmayer, and Hullstrung (1944). Fisher, Gross, and Zuch (1965), and Karacan, Goodenough, Shapiro, and Starker (1966) first suggested nocturnal penile monitoring (the use of NPT) as a test for erectile dysfunction, and the inclusion of NPT testing has become standard in such evaluations.

However, there are two pitfalls in interpreting NPT results. The first is that the mercury strain gauges used in most labs measure circumference, that is, penile tumescence, but not penile rigidity. Circumference measures alone do not provide adequate evidence that a man is capable of coitus. In the past, to evaluate rigidity, an observer had to be present to measure the best angle of any erections or to estimate the hardness or buckling pressure of the penis. However, there are now new technologies to measure rigidity (see below).

The second caveat is that NPT testing assumes that all normal men have four to five erections of 10 to 15 minutes duration nightly. Schiavi and Schreiner-Engel (1988), however, studied men over age 60 who claimed to be capable of coitus and found that they had fewer nocturnal erections than were expected. It may be that aging reduces nocturnal erections without reducing erections from sexual stimulation. Schiavi and Fisher (1982) had also reported that 20% of young, potent men had "abnormal" NPT results when measured in a sleep laboratory.

Methods devised to allow at-home NPT testing include stamp-ring testing and the Snap-Gauge® (Dacomed, Minneapolis, MN). The stamp test, in which a man places a circle of stamps tightly around his flaccid penis and checks to see in the morning whether the ring has broken, presumably by nocturnal erection, seems an inexpensive alternative to formal testing, but Marshall, Earls, Morales, and Surridge (1982) demonstrated that it is not sufficiently reliable to establish a clinical diagnosis. The Snap-Gauge measures penile rigidity with three plastic elements imbedded in a band surrounding the penis, each of which breaks at a particular rigidity. Independent evaluation has shown inconsistent results. Condra et al. (1986) reported that 5 of 19 men did not break all bands despite achieving full erection, and that some men broke all bands with less than their fullest erection.

The Rigiscan® (Dacomed, Minneapolis, MN), a computer-driven portable device, measures both penile tumescence and rigidity. We have determined that a 60% rigidity reading on the Rigiscan's 0–100% scale corresponds to a 90 mm Hg pressure in the penile corpora cavernosa (the parts of the penis that fill with blood during erection), the least pressure needed for erection. We measure erections (with both the Rigiscan and a conventional mercury strain gauge) over a two-night test period to increase the probability that a patient will be relaxed enough to sleep well. However, even so, patients occasionally report nocturnal or morning erections at home without having such erections in the sleep laboratory.

During one of the sleep laboratory nights, after signing a consent form in the privacy of their sleeping room, patients are shown both an educational film with explicit sexual activities and a commercial X-rated film. Patients are informed that masturbation is optional. Any rigid erection is timed and noted. This Visual Sexual Stimulation Test occasionally offends patients, and it is worthwhile taking adequate time for preparation (make sure patients realize that showing erotic films is routine and has a diagnostic purpose) and, if possible, choosing a film compatible with the patient's own fantasies.

The sleep laboratory technician photographs any rigid erection that occurs during sleep or while the patient watches the films. Such photographs provide graphic evidence of erectile competence that neither the Rigiscan nor the plethysmograph printouts do, evidence that often helps persuade a disbelieving patient that his penis did, in fact, become erect during the night.

Arterial Measures

The bilateral arterial inflow of the penis is derived from the pudendal branches of the internal hypogastric artery. Classically, three paired branches (dorsal, cavernous, and urethral) have been described, and one ought to be able to measure blood pressures (normal, elevated, or subnormal) in all of these vessels. However, multiple variations of the normal penile vasculature are common, and the technician may not to be able to detect the full number of penile blood vessel measures.

The standard method of measuring penile arterial pressure has been to compare arm artery pressure to either the highest penile pressure or the mean of all vessels in which systolic pressures can be elicited. A score is calculated from the Penile–Brachial Index (PBI) of the mean penile artery pressure divided by the mean brachial artery pressure. A PBI ratio of <0.6 is thought to be diagnostic of vasculogenic erectile dysfunction. Metz (1986) reported a mean PBI in a group of sexually functional men (median age 54) to be 0.86 ± 0.08. Reduced PBI accuracy is caused by variation in penile artery supply or penile size (occasionally making measurement difficult even with a small cuff) or by a variety of functional or technical difficulties.

For further diagnostic accuracy, we measure whether penile blood pressure changes after pelvic exercise. Such a change might indicate a "pelvic steal syndrome," wherein the penile vessels do not adequately trap the blood if there is muscle demand elsewhere in the body. A patient with this syndrome might give a history of losing his erection with movement prior to or during intercourse.

There are ways to study the penile arteries that allow simultaneous visual imaging and measurement of blood flow. Their principal advantage may be to measure the ability of the corpus cavernosal arteries to dilate in response to direct injections of substances that induce a "pharmacological erection," a recent development in the medical treatment of erectile dysfunction. Virag, Legman, Zwang, and Dermange (1979) were the first to report that papaverine hydrochloride, a drug that causes relaxation of the smooth muscle of the corpora cavernosa, can create this pharmacological erection. Papaverine seems particularly effective for the treatment of patients with neurological deficits such as spinal cord injury, diabetes mellitus, or multiple sclerosis, but there has been tremendous publicity about the new technique, and patients with every sort of erectile dysfunction are coming to their physicians requesting "the injections."

Papaverine is commercially available, but it has not yet been approved by the FDA or by the manufacturer for intrapenile injection because of reports of prolonged, painful erections that have to be treated as medical emergencies. There may also be some worry about scarring and liver changes with long-term use. However, with education, and by using the procedures of proper informed consent, papaverine can be used for evaluation and treatment purposes. Treatment is discussed below.

As an evaluation device, injections of papaverine can help determine the normality of the penile arteries, since normal arteries are reported to double in diameter after papaverine injection (from 0.5–0.7 to 1.0–1.2 mm). Abnormal arterial dilation may suggest various organic problems including atherosclerosis, but no conclusions can be drawn from this one test.

Case 13: Mr. DP. A 61-year-old man complained of losing his erection after a few seconds of coitus, a history consistent with a pelvic steal syndrome. He had no specific risk factors. No penile artery flow could be heard, and there was no change in penile artery diameter after papaverine injection. Making the assumption of a vasculogenic erectile disorder, the physician advised the patient to return to the office in a week's time to plan therapy. At that time the patient reported that he had developed a rigid erection lasting 3 hours after leaving the laboratory on the day of the papaverine test. Moreover, he had had intercourse three times that weekend with rigid, long-lasting erections.

It is possible that the papaverine had had a therapeutic effect, but it was more likely that the patient's erectile failure had been related to anxiety. The case also illustrates the axiom that *no one test by itself can establish a diagnosis of organic erectile failure.*

Michal, Kramar, Popsichal, and Hejhal (1977) first suggested that surgery involving the penile arteries was a potential cure for erectile dysfunction caused by vascular disease. Techniques were developed to search for blockages of the penile arteries responsible for decreased blood flow to the corpora cavernosa. However, with the exception of that done in the case of pelvic trauma following injury, the results of arterial bypass surgery have been disappointing. The most common cause of arterial blockages, atherosclerosis of the penile arteries, usually recurs following any surgery.

Venous Incompetence

When the penis is erect, external pressure will not cause it to detumesce, implying the presence of an internal valve mechanism for trapping blood in engorged spaces. If the trapping mechanism fails, maximal internal pressure will be limited, and it will be impossible to achieve or maintain penile rigidity. The realization that penile erection is dependent on both adequate arterial inflow and containment of blood has spurred the development of tests that measure the dynamic changes of erection, and these are now an integral part of the erectile dysfunction workup.

Cavernosography, an x-ray technique in which contrast material is injected into the corpora cavernosa and visualized, was the first technique for observing the adequacy of the outflow mechanism. A more recent procedure called dynamic cavernosography added to this visualization a measurement of the rate of flow of saline into the corpora cavernosa needed to create an artificial erection. Currently, papaverine is used to create an erection for cavernosographic measurement (Mueller & Lue, 1988). We discuss penile vein surgery for the treatment of "venous leaks" below.

Penile Sensitivity and Nerve Conductivity

As discussed in greater detail in Chapter 9, this volume, men lose penile sensitivity as a concomitant of normal aging. In the office, there are devices with which one can measure a patient's sensitivity threshold to vibration. However, although a patient may show a significant decrease in penile sensation, this test alone will not definitively identify the cause of erectile failure and is probably of use only to document (or dispute) patient's claims of reduced penile sensitivity.

Glucose Tolerance Testing

Diabetes mellitus is known to be related to the type of peripheral nerve and vascular damage that contributes to erectile dysfunction. Although many patients come to us diagnosed with diabetes, the rest believe they do not have the disease, often on the basis of rudimentary blood glucose tests. We conduct a fasting glucose tolerance test, measuring blood glucose before and at 1- and 2-hour intervals after the patient ingests a heavily sugared drink, on all patients not known to have diabetes. In addition, we have patients' blood assayed for indications of longer-term glucose function (the glycosylated hemoglobin measure). Based on these tests, we have found many patients to have borderline or frank diabetic indications, and they are referred back to their physicians for further evaluation, treatment, and stabilization before continuing with the erectile evaluation.

Summary of Medical Evaluation

The medical history, physical examination, physical tests, and nocturnal observations and measurements are designed both to search for and to rule out medical causes for the erectile dysfunction. As emphasized above, no one physical test is sufficient (as in "Oh, you have abnormal penile blood pressure—that's why you are having trouble") to indicate organic etiology, even if some organic pathology is detected. Many patients have erections despite compromised physical function. Indications of normal functioning (e.g., rigid nocturnal erections, good PBI) are useful in ruling out various sources of pathology. However, since the group of patients we see has a median age of 55, we find few with a completely clean bill of health. Making conservative and judicious inferences is more the task.

Psychological Assessment of Patient and Partner

In addition to the medical aspect, the comprehensive evaluation includes a 45-minute to 1½-hour interview with the psychologist, with the patient's primary sexual partner scheduled for a separate 30-minute to 1-hour interview. The goal in these interviews is not necessarily to take comprehensive psychological, psychosocial, and relationship histories but rather to uncover individual, interpersonal, and situational issues relevant to diagnosis and treatment and to lay appropriate groundwork for treatment compliance. Justification for the partner interview and for the relationship of interviews to later compliance is based on our follow-up research and has been discussed earlier.

The patient interview with the psychologist covers the issues listed below, in the order listed, as much to build rapport within the session as to accumulate information in the most logical way. Years of experience have shown, for example, that inquiring about the number and dates of all marriages at the outset of the interview communicates to the patient that the interviewer is seriously interested in detail and in sexual context as well as in performance factors. Much can be learned from the patient's style (both defensive and cognitive) in handling the early questions that will help in the asking of later ones. The interview begins with a reminder of confidentiality, a pledge that no information will be communicated to the partner or anyone other than the urologist without the patient's express consent (the same pledge is made to the partner).

Beginning with name (to determine ethnicity), age, and history of marriage(s) (did they end in divorce or death?), the interview proceeds to name and age of primary sexual partner, ages of any children, and identities of all persons living with the patient. Relevant specifics of the patient's life may begin to emerge here, for example, that the primary partner is not the wife, or that the patient is recently widowed after a long marriage, or that there may be a history of infertility in the marriage. A question about sexual orientation will be asked here, as routinely as possible, although many patients disbelieve that this is a routine question.

Next come a series of educational and employment questions, with some effort being made to gauge the patient's intellectual function, identification groups, stability, and some sources of stress. Asking about a man's work usually gives him a chance to speak at length on a self-esteeming topic; this often builds rapport and offers details of character as well as cognitive style.

Making a transition from the background information to the present problem, the next question will be about the referral source (sometimes a recent media story—always a clue that the patient comes with certain expectations), which gives clues about compliance and initiative, urgency of the problem, and whether the patient is coming at his wife's behest.

Next follows the section on health history, including surgeries, hospitalizations, chronic illnesses, history of ulcers or other psychosomatic conditions, current and recent medications (prescribed or over the counter), any genital trauma or abnormalities (even an adolescent or childhood history is often most relevant to adult feelings of sexual inadequacy), use of cigarettes, alcohol, or recreational drugs.

Finally, we begin to discuss the patient's sexual problem and history, including onset and course of the difficulty, clear and detailed description of the difficulty, description of any prior sexual difficulties, recent frequencies and conduct of all sexual acts and all partners, masturbation, ejaculation, and orgasm, desire, fantasies, and all previous sexual treatments. The detailed nature of these inquiries cannot be overemphasized, since it is in this section of the interview that misunderstandings about the nature of the problem or about other aspects of the patient's sexuality are revealed. Politeness and the communication of genuine interest in the patient in the earlier parts of the interview have usually established the necessary rapport for this detailed inquiry to succeed.

A great deal of information has by now accumulated in passing about the patient's personality and about the current relationship, and at this point questions are asked to complete the picture in these two domains. Questions are asked to detect relationship discord, partner illness, sexual conflicts, advantages of sexual symptom, history of somaticization, possible hypochondriasis, past individual or couple psychological treatment, major stressors, meaning and priority of sex in the relationship, and why the patient is coming for help at this particular time.

Finally, if this topic has not yet emerged, questions are specifically asked about the patient's expectations concerning the outcome of this evaluation and the course to be pursued afterwards. A sense will have developed of the flexibility of the patient's cognitive functioning so that the interviewer knows whether and how to address misinformation and inappropriate expectations.

The interview with the partner is organized to corroborate important facts and dates provided by the patient, to learn about the patient's character and coping style from the partner's point of view, to assess contributions to the problem by the partner, to learn what types of treatments will be acceptable to the partner, and to mobilize the partner toward compassion and cooperation.

TREATMENT OF ERECTILE DYSFUNCTION

In a feedback session following the comprehensive evaluation, the urologist and psychologist present the patient/couple with all the results and impressions developed to date, and a plan of therapy (or further evaluation, if the etiology is still unclear) is recommended. If the dysfunction is primarily caused by intrapsychic or interpersonal factors or seems an outgrowth of deficient education or sexual technique, or the patient/couple is so agitated or confused that we feel medical treatment without prior psychological intervention would be inadvisable, the couple or patient will be referred for the appropriate psychotherapy, couple therapy, sex therapy, or sexual counseling. These approaches are dealt with in Chapter 9, this volume. The remainder of this chapter deals with treatment recommendations when a primarily organic problem is present and the patient/couple seems able to deal appropriately with biomedical interventions, or, occasionally, when sex therapy has failed, and the couple is a good candidate for medical treatment.

No Medical Treatment: Sexual Technique Expansion

Some couples unwilling to undertake further treatment may be able to utilize suggestions about nonintercourse sexual techniques, that is, oral, manual, or vibrator stimulation and satisfaction. For some older patients/ couples, those with chronic, debilitating disease, or for men whose partners may be opposed to invasive interventions, the introduction of sexual options may fulfill their needs. If these suggestions come from "medical authority," the permission to bypass earlier taboos (and their residual anxiety and conflict) may be sufficient to allow for meaningful experimentation.

Endocrine Treatment

Primary hormonal abnormalities such as abnormally low testosterone (related to primary testicular failure or to hypothalamic or pituitary dysfunction) is best treated with monthly intramuscular administration of 200 to 400 mg of a preparation of testosterone in oil. Clinically significant hyperprolactinemia is caused by prolactin-secreting tumors of the anterior pituitary gland. Treatment is either oral bromocriptine, radiation, or surgical removal of the pituitary. Increased estradiol caused by adrenal gland tumors is treated with adrenalectomy. Increased estradiol related to alcohol abuse may respond to decreasing alcohol intake and oral testosterone.

Other Medical Treatments

Yohimbine, an α_2-adrenoceptor antagonist initially derived from the bark of the yohimbehe tree, has long been thought to enhance penile erection, and we frequently find that patients referred to us have taken yohimbine for several months, usually without any benefit. Recent double-blind research has shown no significant increase in erection of men with organic erectile dysfunction taking yohimbine over those taking placebo (Morales, Condra, Owen, Fenemore, & Surridge, 1988).

Smoking, alcohol, and drug abuse are often related to erectile dysfunction. Cigarette smoking in men with atherosclerosis is damaging, and patients can occasionally be persuaded that their penile blood pressure is being diminished by the constricting effects of nicotine on blood vessels. But we have not had any more luck than others in convincing patients to stop abusing various substances.

In addition to the papaverine discussed above, there are other drugs available for intracorporeal injection that will cause penile rigidity, including phentolamine, prostaglandin E_1, and vasoactive intestinal polypeptide (VIP). The penile injection program can be offered to all men with irreversible erectile dysfunction, but its utility for men with psychogenic dysfunction is more problematic. It is tempting to offer such therapy to the man who wants a quick fix and refuses psychogenic treatment. However, two factors indicate that this course is unwise (Sidi, 1988). The first is that this treatment is not without risk: There is the possibility of permanent penile scarring as a result of priapism or of a local reaction from the needle or drug or of infection or liver damage. The second is that ongoing research (Althof et al., 1988) suggests that patients with psychogenic impotence not infrequently drop out from and are dissatisfied with autoinjection therapy. At the very least, such patients should be in concurrent sex or marital therapy.

To use papaverine in intracorporal injection therapy, it is necessary to obtain a signed informed consent, which includes the statement that Lilly laboratories disclaims the use of papaverine for this purpose. Proper dosage using the minimal amount of the drug to effect penile rigidity for under 4 hours must be determined in the office. There will be dosage variations among patients based on their penile neurological and vascular status. Once it has been determined that a patient responds adequately to intracorporal injections and the proper dose has been established, patients and partners are instructed on proper injection technique. Some urologists have developed teaching aids such as videotapes and narrated slide presentations to assure complete patient education (Duffy, Sidi, & Lange, 1987). Depending on patient competence and proximity to the office, the drugs can be dispensed in multidose vials or in prepared syringes with 27- or 30-gauge needles. Intermittent examination of the corpora and liver chemistries must be obtained before dispensing a new supply of the drug.

Vacuum constriction devices are a nonsurgical, noninvasive alternative treatment for psychogenic and organic erectile dysfunction. The penis is placed in a tube in which a vacuum is artificially created, blood rushes into the sinusoidal spaces, and a constricting band is placed at the penile base. There have been several such devices manufactured over the past 70 years, and they continue to be popular (Witherington, 1988). Problems with these devices include numbness caused by the tourniquet and the unwieldy and mechanical method of producing the erection. To date there have been no studies of the long-term effects of using this device on penile tissue, but their long history and lack of known negative effects require that they be included in treatments mentioned to patients.

Surgery

Severe penile curvature resulting from Peyronie disease can be corrected with an operative procedure that can be done on an ambulatory basis under local anesthesia.

The evolution of microvascular arterial surgical correction of pudendal and penile artery defects has proceeded in stages and is still undergoing much experimentation. As mentioned above, the surgery is most successful in limited cases where the arterial lesion is localized and the bypass is placed into normal vessels. Balloon angioplasty dilation of certain pelvic arteries should be an ideal treatment for erectile failure secondary to isolated lesions, but in our evaluation of over 1,400 patients with erectile dysfunction, only two were candidates for angioplasty, and dysfunction recurred in both within a year.

In their description of surgery to correct penile venous leaks, Ebbehoj and Wagner (1979) created an entirely new area of evaluation and treatment of erectile dysfunction. Unfortunately, the ability to diagnose such corporal incompetence has not been matched by surgical success in procedures to treat the defect. In a recent review, Lewis (1988) reports an "excellent" result ("ability to have erections sufficient for vaginal intercourse for patient and partner satisfaction [p. 118]") in only 24% of his cases. The reasons may be related to the difficulty in reaching the source of the deficit with current surgical methods, or that new leaks develop in other areas of the penis with time.

The development in 1947 of the first penile prosthetic implant (initially, a rigid, nonreactive plastic rod) revolutionized the medical approach to erectile dysfunction. The ability to offer patients a concrete solution further stimulated the development of diagnostic methods and resulted in the movement of urologists into the field of male sexual dysfunction. Over recent decades, numerous manufacturers have produced variants on two basic penile implant models: (1) the semi-rigid or malleable device, consisting of a pair of rods that do not change in length or girth implanted into the corpora, creating a permanent erection that can be bent up or down against the body, and (2) the multicomponent hydraulic inflatable device, allowing for both tumescence and detumescence as saline is pumped in and out of the penile rods. The hydraulic device requires the more extensive surgery, since the complete implant consists of the cylindrical rods in the penis, the reservoir of saline in the abdomen, the valve to effect tumescence and detumescence in the scrotum, and tubes to connect these components. Manufacturers of penile implants are very active, and a number of new models are under development or have recently been introduced. This makes it difficult to conduct adequate evaluation research on any particular model.

We have recently completed a long-term (1 to 4 years post-implant) follow-up study of prosthesis recipients and their partners (Pedersen, Tiefer, Ruiz, & Melman, 1988; Tiefer, Pedersen, & Melman, 1988). Although almost all the patients did have regular sexual intercourse, it was not as frequent as they had expected. The primary benefit of the prosthesis seemed to be to repair the patient's wounded masculine self-esteem. There were no significant differences in satisfaction between the two types of prosthesis: There was more concern about concealment with the semi-rigid model and more concern about malfunction with the inflatable one. Most patients reported satisfaction with the prosthesis (normal orgasm, female reports no difference from normal) despite a variety of disappointments (penis usually shorter than preoperatively and intercourse positions may be limited) and difficulties (postoperative recovery is more painful than expected, especially for diabetics, and pumping may continue to be difficult for years). Partners were less happy overall and seemed to have a more realistic assessment of the mechanical contributions of the prosthesis. Nevertheless, acknowledging the psychological asset of the prosthesis, partners, too, felt the choice had been a good one.

The choice of surgical or medical treatment is very individual, involving numerous personal issues in addition to the medical and technical ones.

Case 14: Mr. NC. A 61-year-old entertainer was evaluated for erectile dysfunction. The patient suffered from insulin-dependent diabetes mellitus, and the evaluation pointed to this condition as the cause of his organic erectile deficit. All the various treatments were described and discussed. The patient believed that because he had to wear tight costumes, he was not a candidate for the semi rigid prosthesis. The inflatable devices were described, and the patient revealed extreme anxiety over having to manipulate his scrotum because of unpleasant childhood experiences related to his genitals. He rejected psychotherapy for this anxiety and eventually elected to try intrapenile injection therapy. To date (less than 6 months has passed), this has been a successful choice.

As part of the informed consent for the prosthesis, the mechanical failure rate of the inflatable models (as high as 50% in one series) must be mentioned. The risk of immediate postoperative infection is 1%. The patient must be informed that should he have an implant removed at some future date, he will no longer be capable of any erection, since the cavernosal tissues can no longer respond. This is one of many reasons why a penile implant should be considered the "court of last resort" in the treatment of erectile disorders.

CONCLUSION

Our development of the comprehensive evaluation has taken place over a number of years of working closely together and seeing hundreds of patients. We have learned to support each other despite differences in our orientation toward sexuality and sexual dysfunctions. Patients are relieved to find that they are in a situation where nothing is being sold to them and where their individuality is respected. The key to our evaluation is keeping an open mind about the sources of sexual difficulties and paying attention to the potential contribution of every physical and psychosocial factor.

As knowledge of sexual physiology becomes more sophisticated, we can predict that there will be further technological developments in the medical evaluation of erectile disorders. New generations of medical and surgical treatments will inevitably emerge. In the same way, our increasing sophistication with sex therapy will continue to enrich and expand our understanding of the intrapsychic, interpersonal, and self-reinforcing mechanisms at work in the psychological generation and maintenance of erectile disorders. A comprehensive, multidisciplinary approach to impotence evaluation, which seems like a good idea now, will shortly become an absolute necessity if the true complexity of these problems is to be adequately understood and treated.

COMPREHENSIVE CASE PRESENTATION

Mr. AP, a 32-year-old, white, Jewish (Orthodox), divorced man, first came to our attention in 1982. He was a successful businessman despite having had severe diabetes since the age of 16, which was currently causing hypertension and deteriorated renal function. He had developed retinopathy and, following four laser operations, had been completely blind for the past 2 years. The patient was clearly depressed over his physical condition. At the time of the initial consultation, there were no other findings, and a comprehensive evaluation was recommended. However, the patient failed to set up an appointment for the remainder of the tests until late in 1983, over a year later.

In 1983, his situation was unchanged except that he was threatened with the imminent loss of his job. This factor, among others, had prompted his return, since he feared the loss of extensive medical benefits. The psychological evaluation indicated that the patient's marriage (divorced in 1981, after 12 years of marriage and two sons) had been stormy and sexually unsatisfactory. It seemed that religious ties were the only reason the marriage had continued. The patient reported that his wife had never enjoyed sexual relations and that he had turned to prostitutes once or twice per week for the last decade. He also reported frequent masturbation and volunteered that some of his "sexual hangups" had to be caused by the negative influence of his intrusive and critical mother. This woman had examined his genitals frequently throughout childhood and had brought him to a physician at age 12 because she felt his testicles were too small. The physician gave him some medication which the patient believes was a placebo.

The parental influences, plus his Orthodox background, had given the patient the feeling that sexual pleasure and abandon are inappropriate with "nice" partners. Thus, although he had learned from prostitutes that a certain type of prolonged, intense stimulation could result in an erection sufficient for intercourse (although not really normal), he had been unwilling to have his postmarital dating partners stimulate his penis in this way. The patient had recently been dating a woman with diabetes who was also blind. He spoke warmly of her and felt sometimes that he loved her, but he also indicated various ambivalent feelings about her; for example, he asked if she was "strange-looking" as a result of her eye surgeries. However, it was partly as a result of her encouragement that the patient had returned to complete his evaluation. The psychological evaluation concluded that issues of possible psychological conflict plus the obvious depression indicated a diagnosis of primarily organic origin, but with significant psychological factors.

The patient had very little erectile activity during the two NPT nights and attained only a 30% erection while listening to the sound tracks of the sexual films. However, his Penile–Brachial Index was 0.84 before exercise and 0.81 afterwards, indicating no significant vascular abnormalities. His hormones were all normal. His overall diagnosis was organic dysfunction secondary to diabetes.

We discussed the results with the patient in December 1983, and he decided to have an inflatable penile prosthesis implanted. He declined therapy or a referral for the depression. His renal function was declining further, and it was thought that he might soon have to go on dialysis. However, this was not a contraindication for surgery. His woman friend was supportive of the surgery decision, and she and his family provided much support during the hospitalization. There were no postoperative complications, and AP was discharged from care in February 1984.

In September 1986, AP was interviewed at length as part of our follow-up study (Tiefer et al., 1988). He reported that the postoperative pain had been much worse than he expected but that recovery was complete, and the implant functioned properly. In contrast to his sickly appearance in 1983, AP was now feeling physically excellent as a result of a successful renal transplant in June 1984. In fact, he felt so strong, and so many capacities had returned to him, that he wondered if his erectile function might not have returned, too, had he not had the implant. He had indeed lost his earlier job, but he now had a better one and was supervising other professionals. He felt the prosthesis had helped him accept and act on his vocational ambitions.

However, from the point of view of sexual activity, the picture was less rosy. The patient had had sex with his woman friend sporadically, and that relationship had ended within a year. He had had intercourse with three prostitutes and with a sex surrogate recommended by a sex therapist who specializes in working with the disabled. The patient had gone to her on referral from an Orthodox Jewish therapist, whose name had been given to him as someone who might be able to help him and his woman friend improve their relationship. He had necked and petted with three other women. He masturbated once every other week but reported that he had been unable to achieve ejaculation most of the time in masturbation or with partners. The patient was satisfied with the implant and the erection it provided, but he was very frustrated about his sexual life. He felt that his sexual drive was very high since the renal transplant had renewed his sense of well-being and vigor.

We next heard from the patient in May 1988, when he came with a complaint that his prosthesis had begun malfunctioning. His life was tremendously different. Shortly after the 1986 interview, the patient had been introduced to a young (22), blind (mother had had rubella during pregnancy), Orthodox Jewish woman visiting a relative and had fallen in love. After much discussion with many rabbis, the couple married in February, 1987 and commenced a happy marital life, including frequent sexual intercourse. The patient reported that he had regained his ability to ejaculate, that he no longer masturbated or consorted with prostitutes, and that he was sexually satisfied. He and his wife had ceased using contraception and were expecting their first child in September 1988. "A fairy tale," he said, "a genuine fairy tale." But, then, the tubing in his prosthesis sprung a leak, and inflation was no longer possible. He chose reoperation, and despite again finding the surgical aftermath very painful, he reported himself pleased with the results and ready to resume his sexual life. The patient's wife, briefly interviewed on the telephone, confirmed these facts.

One small countertransferential note is added to close this extraordinary case. This patient bore a significant physical and verbal likeness to the psychologist's younger brother, which caused her much emotional anguish with the case, particularly when the patient's health was so poor and he was so depressed. (Perhaps this overinvolvement extends even to choosing this case to write up!) At any rate, the patient's fortitude in dealing with his physical afflictions, his determination to remain a man (as he defined it in terms of erectile function), and his ironic New York sense of humor have endeared him to us for the almost 6 years he has been our patient.

REFERENCES

Althof, S. E., Turner, L. A., Levine, S. B., Risen, C. B., Bodner, D., Kursh, D., & Resnick, M. I. (1988). *Why do so many people drop out from injection therapy for impotence? The view after two years.* Paper presented at the Society for Sex Therapy and Research, New York, NY.

American Psychiatric Association. (1987). *Diagnostic and statistical manual of mental disorders* (3rd ed., rev.). Washington, DC: Author.

Barbach, L. G. (1975). *For yourself: The fulfillment of female sexuality.* New York: Doubleday.

Byrne, D. (1986). Introduction: The study of sexual behavior as a multidisciplinary venture. In D. Byrne & K. Kelley (Eds.), *Alternative approaches to the study of sexual behavior* (pp. 1-12). Hillsdale, NJ: Erlbaum.

Condra, M., Morales, A., Surridge, D. H., Owen, J. A., Marshall, P., & Fenemore, J. (1986). The unreliability of nocturnal penile tumescence recording as an outcome measurement in the treatment of organic impotence. *Journal of Urology, 135,* 280-282.

D'Emilio, J., & Freedman, E. B. (1988). *Intimate matters: A history of sexuality in America.* New York: Harper & Row.

Duffy, L. M., Sidi, A. A., & Lange, P. H. (1987). Vasoactive intracavernous pharmacotherapy: The nursing role in teaching self-injection therapy. *Journal of Urology*, *138*, 1198–1200.

Ebbehoj, J., & Wagner, G. (1979). Insufficient penile erection due to abnormal drainage of cavernous bodies. *Urology*, *13*, 507–510.

Elliott, M. L. (1985). The use of "impotence" and "frigidity": Why has "impotence" survived? *Journal of Sex and Marital Therapy*, *11*, 51–56.

Fisher, C., Gross, J., & Zuch, J. (1965). Cycle of penile erection synchronous with dreaming (REM) sleep. *Archives of General Psychiatry*, *12*, 29–45.

Harvey, J. H., & Weary, G. (Eds.). (1985). *Attribution: Basic issues and applications*. Orlando, FL: Academic Press.

Heiman, J. R. (1983). Women and sexuality. In G. W. Albee, S. Gordon, & H. Leitenberg (Eds.), *Promoting sexual responsibility and preventing sexual problems* (pp. 7–38). Hanover, NH: University Press of New England.

Kaplan, H. S. (1979). *Disorders of sexual desire*. New York: Brunner/Mazel.

Karacan, I., Goodenough, D., Shapiro, A., & Starker, S. (1966). Erection cycle during sleep in relation to dream anxiety. *Archives of General Psychiatry*, *15*, 183–189.

Kinsey, A. C., Pomeroy, W. B., & Martin, C. E. (1948). *Sexual behavior in the human male*. Philadelphia. W. B. Saunders.

Lewis, R. W. (1988). Venous surgery for impotence. *Urologic Clinics of North America*, *15*, 115–121.

LoPiccolo, J. (1985). Diagnosis and treatment of male sexual dysfunction. *Journal of Sex and Marital Therapy*, *11*, 215–232.

Marshall, P. G., Earls, C., Morales, A., & Surridge, D. H. (1982). Nocturnal penile tumescence recording with stamps: A validity study. *Journal of Urology*, *128*, 946–947.

Martin, C. E. (1981). Factors affecting sexual functioning in 60–79-year-old married males. *Archives of Sexual Behavior*, *10*, 399–420.

Masters, W. H., & Johnson, V. E. (1966). *Human sexual response*. Boston: Little, Brown.

Masters, W. H., & Johnson, V. E. (1970). *Human sexual inadequacy*. Boston: Little, Brown.

Melman, A., Tiefer, L., & Pedersen, R. (1988). Evaluation of the first 406 patients in a urology department based center for male sexual dysfunction. *Urology*, *32*, 6–10.

Metz, P. (1986). *Arteriogenic erectile impotence. Thesis*. Copenhagen: Laegeforeningens Forlag.

Michal, V., Kramar, R., Popsichal, J., & Hejhal, L. (1977). Arterial epigastricocavernous anastomosis for the treatment of sexual impotence. *World Journal of Surgery*, *1*, 515–520.

Morales, A., Condra, M. S., Owen, J. E., Fenemore, J., & Surridge, D. M. (1988). Oral and transcutaneous pharmacologic agents in the treatment of impotence. *Urologic Clinics of North America*, *15*, 87–93.

Mueller, S. C., & Lue, T. F. (1988). Evaluation of vasculogenic impotence. *Urologic Clinics of North America*, *15*, 65–76.

Ohlmeyer, P., Brilmeyer, H., & Hullstrung, H. (1944). Periodische vorgange im schalf. *Pfluegers Archiv*, *248*, 559–560.

Pedersen, B., Tiefer, L., Ruiz, M., & Melman, A. (1988). Evaluation of patients and partners one to four years following penile prosthesis surgery. *Journal of Urology*, *139*, 956–958.

Person, E. S. (1980). Sexuality as the mainstay of identity: Psychoanalytic perspectives. *Signs*, 5, 605–630.

Reckless, J., & Geiger, N. (1978). Impotence as a practical problem. In J. LoPiccolo & L. LoPiccolo (Eds.), *Handbook of sex therapy* (pp. 295–321). New York: Plenum Press.

Schiavi, R. C., & Fisher, C. (1982). Assessment of diabetic impotence: Measurement of nocturnal erections. *Clinics in Endocrinology and Metabolism*, 11, 769–784.

Schiavi, R. C., & Schreiner-Engel, P. (1988). *Healthy aging and male sexual arousal*. Paper presented at the Society for Sex Therapy and Research, New York, NY.

Schmidt, G. (1983). Introduction: Sexuality and relationships. In G. Arentewicz & G. Schmidt (Eds.), *The treatment of sexual disorders* (pp. 3–8). New York: Basic Books.

Schover, L. R., & von Eschenbach, A. C. (1985). Sex therapy and the penile prosthesis: A synthesis. *Journal of Sex and Marital Therapy*, 11, 57–66.

Segraves, R. T., Schoenberg, H. W., Zairns, C., Camic, P., & Knopf, J. (1981). Characteristics of erectile dysfunction as a function of medical care system entry point. *Psychosomatic Medicine*, 43, 227–234.

Sidi, A. A. (1988). Vasoactive intracavernous pharmacotherapy. *Urologic Clinics of North America*, 15, 95–101.

Smith, A. D. (1988). Psychologic factors in the multidisciplinary evaluation and treatment of erectile dysfunction. *Urologic Clinics of North America*, 15, 41–51.

Strage, M. (1980). *The durable fig leaf: A historical, cultural, medical, social, literary, and iconographic account of man's relations with his penis*. New York: William Morrow.

Tiefer, L. (1986). In pursuit of the perfect penis: The medicalization of male sexuality. *American Behavioral Scientist*, 29, 579–599.

Tiefer, L., & Melman, A. (1983). Interview of wives: A necessary adjunct in the evaluation of impotence. *Sexuality and Disability*, 6, 167–175.

Tiefer, L., & Melman, A. (1987). Adherence to recommendations and improvement over time in men with erectile dysfunction. *Archives of Sexual Behavior*, 16, 301–309.

Tiefer, L., Pedersen, B., & Melman, A. (1988). Psychosocial follow-up of penile prosthesis implant patients and partners. *Journal of Sex and Marital Therapy*, 14, 184–201.

Virag, R., Legman, M., Zwang, G., & Dermange, H. (1979). Utilization de l'erection passive dans l'exploration de l'impuissance d'origine vasculaire. *Contraception Fertilité Sexualité*, 7, 707–720.

Wein, A. J., & Van Arsdalen, K. N. (1988). Drug-induced male sexual dysfunction. *Urologic Clinics of North America*, 15, 23–31.

Witherington, R. (1988). Suction device therapy in the management of erectile impotence. *Urologic Clinics of North America*, 15, 123–128.

9

Psychogenic Impotence: Treatment of Men and Couples

STANLEY E. ALTHOF

As Althof describes in this chapter, erectile failure invariably elicits great consternation in men of all ages who typically view the disorder as a blow to their masculine adequacy. Treatments for psychogenic erectile insufficiency run the gamut from behavioral to psychodynamic. The Case Western Reserve treatment perspective elaborated in this chapter includes a blend of psychodynamic, object-relations, self-psychology, and behavioral interventions within a short-term psychotherapy framework. A guiding principle of this treatment approach is the clarification of meaning of the erectile difficulty within the interpersonal context in which it occurs.

Althof suggests that primary impotence is best treated by means of individual psychotherapy, since it frequently suggests conflicts regarding gender, sexual orientation, or paraphilic interests. Often, major early conflicts need to be resolved for a successful outcome of the impotence. If secondary impotence exists, the couple is usually seen together, and the focus is on the resolution of a particular conflict or event that may be interfering with the couple's sexual life. Sensate-focus exercises are prescribed along with educational information and suggestions. Althof emphasizes the importance of engendering hope and providing empathy for both partners in a relationship.

Althof cautions therapists to be aware of too "rapid" cures since they are often illusionary, and he reminds readers of the power of the sexual equilibrium established between sexual partners. He reminds patients that "the penis is attached to the heart." He also suggests that the symptom of erectile failure may represent an adaptive as well as a pathological solution to a problem. Investigation of both possibilities is often recommended.

The model espoused by Althof in this chapter is an eclectic one which includes the prescription of behavioral tasks and sensate-focus exercises as well as the analysis of transference, where appropriate. But Althof is also a realist and notes that psychotherapy has its limitations and that treatment is not always successful. In such cases, referral to other resources or a trial of

medical intervention by means of autoinjection therapy or an external
vacuum pump device is sometimes suggested.

Stanley E. Althof, Ph.D., is Director of the Male Sexual Health Center
at University Hospitals of Cleveland and is Assistant Professor of Psychol-
ogy in the Department of Psychiatry at Case Western Reserve University
School of Medicine.

INTRODUCTION

Initial Clinical Presentations of Impotence

A distinguished 55-year-old man enters the office, slowly seats himself, and says, "I'm impotent. I've lost my manhood. I'm no good, useless. I can no longer perform. My wife will probably have an affair and leave me." His partner laments, "He no longer loves me; I'm not attractive. Maybe he's involved with another woman!"

A stooped, sad, tired-looking, retired 65-year-old grandfather declares, "My wife sent me to you because we are no longer affectionate." His short, gray-haired 63-year-old wife confides, "I'm very sad. It's ended our sex life. Now he won't even touch me."

An anxious, stylishly dressed, recently divorced, 38-year-old vice-president rhetorically asks, "What woman would want to go out with a man who can't get it up?"

An Old Concern

Man has been concerned with his sexual prowess since the dawn of civiliza-tion. Treatments, rituals, folk remedies, advice, and sex manuals have been discovered among the writings of the ancient Greek physicians, the Islamic and Talmudic scholars, and the Chinese and Hindu practitioners. Cross-cultural rituals to ensure potency run the gamut from elaborate circumcision ceremonies to having pubertal adolescents fellate and swallow sperm of mature warriors. In ancient Greece, impotent men were treated in the Temples of Aphrodite by prostitute–priestesses who functioned as religious surrogate therapists (Kaplan, 1974). The venerable Indian text *The Kama Sutra* (Vatsayana, 1964) offered sage advice and illustrated the varied coital positions. Even today, folk remedies for impotence include ginseng, rhinoc-eros horn, and vitamin E. Promoters of "impotence cures" prey on the desperation of men deprived of their potency. A patient brought in the following ad:

Say goodbye to impotence, soft erections, weak ejaculations and sexual
disability. Say goodbye to the heartbreaking feeling of never being able to

satisfy a woman—or yourself—with the pleasure and intimacy of sexual intercourse. Instead, say hello to [product name].

[Product name] is the impotence remedy whose active ingredient has been used in countless laboratory tests with men and animals. This exact same formula has been recommended by board certified M.D. specialists for their important [sic] patients. There is no other impotence formula, no other sexual stimulant considered as potent and effective as the active ingredient in [product name].

The formula has an impressive record as a male sexual stimulant and aphrodisiac. Its active ingredient works in the sexual centers of the brain and in the muscle tissues of the penis to arouse sexual desire and a full, hard erection. . . . Potency and performance satisfaction guaranteed.

The Goals of Psychotherapy for Psychogenic Impotence

Psychotherapy aims to restore men's potency to the optimal level possible, given the limits of physical well-being and life circumstances. Treatment seeks to overcome the psychological barriers that preclude mutual sexual satisfaction. In order to accomplish these goals, the patient(s) and therapist embark on an intrapsychic and interpersonal journey to discover and demystify the meaning of the impotence. On this journey the psychosomatic symptom of impotence is transformed into cognitive and emotional experiences. The therapist understands the patient's symptom of impotence as a metaphor, one that contains a compromised solution to one of life's dilemmas.

Psychogenically impotent men often feel puzzled, disgraced, weakened, and frightened. They have lost their hope and confidence and wonder, "Why me?" Their "failure" is attributed to physical illness, psychological concerns, interpersonal disturbance, or religious retribution. They can overcome the psychogenic impotence by understanding their responses to their dilemmas, integrating previously unacknowledged feelings, seeking new solutions to old problems, increasing communication, surmounting the barriers to intimacy, and restoring sexual confidence.

Although this chapter focuses on psychogenic erectile dysfunction, psychotherapy can also be beneficial to men who suffer from organic or mixed (a blending of organic and psychogenic factors) impotence. In these cases, the primary treatment goal is to help men function at the optimum level consistent with their physiological capability. Additional goals are to decrease performance anxiety, resolve the psychological aspects of the dysfunction, and broaden a couple's sexual repertoire. Treatment may also assist couples in gaining comfort with the implantation of a penile prosthesis, adjunctive utilization of intracavernosal injection, or a suction pump device.

An Overview of the Various Treatment Approaches

Historically, the psychoanalytic understanding of symptom formation linked discrete, unresolved, unconscious conflicts occurring during certain developmental periods with specific symptoms. Therefore, identical symptoms were retrospectively traced to a designated constellation of conflicts occurring in childhood. Consistent with this universal pathogenesis theory, Freud (1912/1957b) ascribed impotence to a man's failure to resolve his Oedipal struggle. He believed impotent men confused their mothers with their lovers. Being sexual with one's lover, now an incestuous love object, was unconsciously taboo. His view persists today as the "deep" explanation for impotence among many analytically trained therapists. In this tradition, men entered psychoanalysis and were seen up to five times weekly for several years. Treatment of the couple was not undertaken.

Current psychodynamic understanding views impotence as the end-product of multiple converging past and present influences. Oedipal dynamics sometimes account for the symptom, but not for everyone. Examples of other past influences contributing to adult impotence include preoedipal separation–individuation conflicts or adolescent masturbatory guilt. The more commonly seen present influences are relationship deterioration, widowhood, health concerns, and aging.

Performance anxiety—the fear of future sexual failure based on a previous failure—is a universal experience seen in almost all impotent men. Behavior therapy (LoPiccolo & LoPiccolo, 1978; Obler, 1973) seeks to eliminate the anxiety or performance demands that interfere with sexual arousal. Systematic desensitization, the pairing of relaxation with a hierachy of anxiety-provoking sexual scenes, is the most common behavioral method employed to treat erectile disturbances. Like psychoanalysis, however, behavior therapy concentrates on individual rather than couples treatment.

Cognitive therapy focuses on uncovering the scripts (Gagnon, Rosen, & Leiblum, 1982) or irrational beliefs (Ellis, 1980) that interfere with the erectile response. Therapy helps men and couples to shed these beliefs and learn more adaptive cognitive strategies.

Masters and Johnson (1970) and Masters, Johnson, and Kolodny (1982) revolutionized the treatment of sexual problems by working with couples to overcome the obstacles that impede natural function. They developed a highly structured 2-week treatment model employing male and female co-therapy teams. The multiple facets of their treatment include physical examination, history taking, individual and couple psychotherapy, and prescription of behavioral tasks. They briefly used sexual surrogates to treat some impotent men without partners.

Treatments for psychogenic impotence have evolved into blends of psychodynamic, behavioral, and cognitive therapies utilizing individual, couples, and group formats (Cooper, 1972; Kilmann & Auerbach, 1979; Kilmann et al., 1987; Levine, 1985; McCarthy & McCarthy, 1984; Zilbergeld, 1975, 1978). The best-known integrated approach is Helen Kaplan's (1974) *New Sex Therapy*. Incorporating Masters and Johnson's methods with more modern-day psychodynamic theory, she eliminated the necessity for male and female co-therapy teams. Her method emphasizes the intrapsychic and interpersonal aspects of each partner's contribution to the sexual dysfunction.

Hypnosis (Araoz, 1982) and medications (Morales, Condra, Owen, Fenemore, & Surridge, 1988) are occasionally employed as supplements to the above treatment methods. Finally, specialized treatment regimens have been developed for homogeneous populations of impotent men who are elderly (Schover, 1984) or have had myocardial infarction (Kolodny, Masters, & Johnson, 1979), cancer (Schover, Evans, & von Eschenback, 1987), or diabetes (Schiavi, 1980).

The Case Western Reserve University Medical School Perspective

This chapter describes one practitioner's method for conducting psychotherapy with individuals or couples who present with psychogenic impotence. These ideas represent an integration of psychodynamic, object-relations, self-psychology, and behavioral theory within a short-term psychotherapy model. This method further extends Masters and Johnson's as well as Kaplan's approaches by emphasizing the sexual equilibrium and the importance of context. This model for treating and understanding sexual problems is an outgrowth of many years of work with my colleagues Stephen Levine, M.D., Candace Risen, L.I.S.W., and Louisa Turner, Ph.D., at Case Western Reserve University School of Medicine/University Hospitals of Cleveland; it is not mine alone.

Such an integrative model risks being misunderstood as a prescription for undisciplined eclecticism. Although techniques from different schools of thought are utilized, treatment is not an impressionistic mosaic of interventions. Rather, the guiding principle of the treatment model is to clarify the meaning of the symptom and to understand the context in which it occurs.

EARLY TREATMENT CONSIDERATIONS

The Therapist's Illusion: Evaluation Is Not Treatment

The previous chapter by Melman and Tiefer describes the methods for conducting a comprehensive, state-of-the-art evaluation of the patient and partner who present for treatment of potency disorders. Three diagnostic aims of evaluation are to (1) delineate all the medical and psychological factors that contribute to the initiation and maintenance of the symptom, (2) communicate the clinician's understanding of the impotence to the patient in a clear and empathic fashion, and (3) discuss all possible medical and psychological solutions, allowing the patients time to reach a decision that fits their psychological, economic, and aesthetic needs. If individual or conjoint treatment is recommended, the patients are given a tentative formulation that serves as a blueprint for initiating psychotherapy.

Although clinicians conceptually separate evaluation and treatment processes, patients do not. For them, the cure begins with the first encounter. The patient is, of course, correct; the attentive therapist is aware that the psychotherapeutic relationship and all its transference ramifications are initiated with the handshake and entry into the consulting room.

Attend to the Relationship before Attending to the Data

The establishment of a respectful, comfortable, and healing relationship is the primary goal of the evaluation. Too often, the secondary goal of gathering data displaces the more human process of relating to one another. The man and woman are likely to be anxious and uncomfortable; they are about to share aspects of their intimate life with a stranger.

Talking about sexual matters does not come naturally to most people. The therapist must first set them at ease before plunging into the more difficult material. When couples desire immediate work, one can ask, "What brings you in?" Others may need more soothing, so asking, "How is it for you to come in today and talk with me?" may be helpful. For the very anxious patient, it may be advisable to start by asking, "Did you have any trouble finding the office?"

Look for the Early Resistances

There are first meetings at which sexual issues are not discussed. This is significant and challenges the therapist to assess whether the resistance belongs to the patient or the therapist. I still remember my reluctance to ask an elderly man about his sexual life because he very much reminded me of my father. When I realized the problem, I laughed to myself and was able to proceed. This gentleman was quite willing to discuss his sexual life and in so doing helped to settle me down.

Patients' reluctance to share sexual material may be the result of a number of factors. The old analytic maxim, "resistance before conflict," is good advice. The task shifts from asking about sexual life to understanding what prevents the man or woman from discussing this subject. When the first hour passes without directly addressing the sexual problem, begin the next session by inquiring about the patient's reluctance to talk about sexual matters.

Even in the most ordinary clinical interview, sociocultural and religious prohibitions against talking about sexual life are encountered. "In our family, such matters were never discussed. I grew up thinking it was wrong to talk about sex with anyone." Sometimes the gender of the interviewer is the focus of the resistance. "I can't talk about this with a male doctor." Acknowledging the patient's discomfort and giving permission and reassurance often helps overcome resistance stemming from these sources. If gender continues to be an unyielding source of resistance, referral can be made to an opposite-sexed colleague. The following vignette demonstrates how cultural ignorance and the patient's resistance can contribute to the avoidance of sexual material in a first hour:

> A middle-aged Arabic woman and her American husband sought consultation about his impotence. She was unable to look at me or discuss her sexual life. Yet, this was an extremely articulate woman, a published poet, who understood erotic life and demonstrated a wide range of emotion. During our second meeting, I asked why she looked away from me and did not discuss sexual issues. She explained that it was disrespectful to look directly at male authority figures and that she was unaccustomed to discussing sexual matters with strangers. With some encouragement, she was able to talk about her sexual life, but she never once looked at me. While I found the lack of eye contact disconcerting, I respected her need to avoid it, and the evaluation and treatment proceeded with a positive outcome.

Patients' expectations regarding treatment also contribute to resistance. Couples do not know what to expect. Some are afraid that the therapist will physically examine them or watch them engage in sexual behavior. Others may have concerns about the therapist being sexual with them or asking them to engage in sexual behaviors that they consider unconventional. The following vignette illustrates one couple's fear:

> My office is located on the second floor of a five-story psychiatric facility. In addition to a number of outpatient offices, the second floor houses a child inpatient unit. Because the ward was being painted, the furniture had been moved into the outpatient hallways, and a hospital bed had been placed outside my office. I walked a new couple from the waiting room to the office without noticing the bed. Obviously they had. They seemed unusually frightened, and I asked how they felt about coming to see me. They coyly asked if I planned to watch them have sex. Puzzled, I asked what had given them that impression? They pointed to the bed outside the door. Their anxiety evaporated after a brief explanation that ended with laughter.

The Secret: Pitfalls from Collusion

A stronger, more persistent source of resistance stems from patients' wishes not to reveal aspects of themselves that are embarrassing, shameful, or hurtful to their partner. These secrets from the therapist may have their origins in fragments of traumatic childhood sexual experiences, awareness of unconventional fantasies, extramarital relationships, or conflictual young-adult life events that have not been shared with others such as an abortion, periods of sexual promiscuity, a visit to a prostitute, or a homosexual encounter.

Levine (1988) lists three categories of secrets: (1) secrets from oneself; (2) secrets from the partner; and (3) secrets known to both partners but kept from the therapist. Secrets from the self are caused by repression or suppression and often emerge during the course of treatment. Some examples are: "I had an inkling that my sexual attractions were to men, but I tried to push this out of my mind and live a straight life"; "I think I really never loved my partner." Secrets from the partner or secrets from the therapist are of a different order and almost always lead to therapeutic impediments— ongoing affairs, alcoholism.

Some patients rationalize that these events, feelings, or fantasies are unrelated to the current problem; therefore, they do not need to be shared. Conversely, others are keenly aware of the impact of this secret on their psychological and sexual life; unfortunately, they lack sufficient trust, courage, or motivation to address these problematic life dilemmas.

Honesty between therapist and patient(s) is the cornerstone of treatment. Conscious avoidance and withholding of information compromise the therapeutic process. My current policy is not to begin couples treatment if one partner asks me not to talk about a certain topic. Earlier in my career, when I agreed to such arrangements in an attempt to be "flexible," therapeutic catastrophes often resulted.

During the course of an evaluation with just the woman, she revealed an incident of childhood abuse. She begged me not to tell her husband and not to "touch on" this subject in treatment. I responded that I had no intention of telling her husband something she did not wish him to know, but I shared my uneasiness about not being able to talk about anything and everything in therapy. She pleaded with me to see them, stating that she did not think her abuse had anything to do with her husband's impotence. My initial formulation agreed: I saw his dysfunction as a response to traumatic events at work. I acquiesced and agreed to see them in conjoint treatment and avoid the issue of her childhood abuse. The first few conjoint sessions went very well. He was beginning to recover his potency, and she was a supportive and helpful partner. In the fourth session, the couple reported that they had avoided sexual activity during the previous week. I asked, "What do you think this is about?" In an angry, accusatory manner she blurted out, "You promised we did not have to talk about that and now you are telling him." Before I could say anything, she proceeded to spill the secret and ran out of the session. Although I attempted to salvage the therapy through phone contacts, the couple refused to return to treatment. When I asked my question, I was looking for present-day events that had disrupted their progress. I incorrectly and naively assumed that because she had had no difficulty being sexual with her partner prior to his dysfunction, resumption of sexual life would not lead to a resurgence of the memory of the abuse. Clearly, the secret needed to come out.

The First Decision: Individual or Couples Work

The evaluation concludes with the therapist offering the patient(s) his or her treatment recommendations. There are several distinct psychotherapy possibilities: individual therapy for one or both partners, conjoint or couples treatment, separate group psychotherapies for one or both partners, or a mixture of all of the above.

Treatment recommendations are primarily influenced by a therapist's values and prejudices regarding ideology and treatment modality. Current research data are not sophisticated enough to predict that a given patient with a specific disorder will do best with a particular therapist of a distinct therapeutic ideology who engages in a specialized form of treatment. There is significant overlap among practitioners of different orientations who purport to engage in specialized forms of treatment. Many patients are just as likely to do well in an individual treatment as they are in a conjoint treatment, or with an analytic or behavioral therapist.

This does not imply that we should not be thoughtful about offering alternatives to patients because it really makes no difference. Rather, we should recognize the limitations of our knowledge and appreciate that some of what we do is intuitive, rather than scientific. Given this caveat, some suggestions for treatment planning follow. These are not intended to be hard and fast rules. And ultimately, it is the patient who makes the final decision to accept or reject our offerings.

Guidelines for Recommending Treatment

If the erectile dysfunction is primary—that is, there has never been a period in the man's life when he has been able to achieve or maintain good-quality erections for intercourse—I generally recommend individual therapy. This decision is based on the assumption that primary impotence is an intrapsychic developmental failure, rather than an interpersonal problem. These men tend to have severe character pathology. Individual treatment lends itself to the intensive exploration of early life events and allows understanding and working through of the obstacles in the way of establishing a comfortable sexual self. Our experience has demonstrated that primary impotence is often the end result of unresolved gender identity, sexual orientation, or paraphilic conflicts. These issues are more difficult to explore and resolve in couples or group treatment. Not only does the presence of others dilute the focus, but patients are often reluctant to share these concerns with others.

However, when a man with primary impotence has limited psychological reflectiveness, is markedly inarticulate, and/or is estranged from his emotional life, individual treatment is ill-advised. In these situations, I ask the partner to join us to help me. She is often aware of his family events or can help the patient more quickly talk about aspects of himself that would remain obscured in individual treatment.

I recommend conjoint treatment for patients with secondary impotence who have viable relationships. Secondary impotence suggests that the patient has successfully traversed developmental hurdles to establish a comfortable sexual self. Moreover, the symptom is generally rooted in the present or recent past; it is not simply an outgrowth of early childhood issues. The dysfunction often represents the couple's shared solution to some aspect of their relationship.

The exceptions to the guideline of "conjoint treatment for secondary impotence" are the single man without a partner, the single man with an uncommitted partner, and the couple whose relationship has deteriorated so much that they cannot productively work with one another. Obviously, the man without a partner will be seen in individual treatment. Years ago, there were some therapists who would have demanded the patient first become involved with a partner and then seek treatment. Although the lack of involvement in a relationship does present clear limitations for therapy, the patient can nonetheless benefit. The stickier decision is how to determine whether a single man has a "committed" partner. Meeting with each partner alone is helpful in deciding how committed the partners are to one another. I generally attempt to see dysfunctional couples in a conjoint format first, but employ more structure than usual. If this proves unworkable, I can refer one or both for individual treatment.

Every now and then we see married men who have no desire to make love to their wives but wish to be sexual with a lover. These situations represent ethical dilemmas for therapists. My comfort level allows me to see these men in individual treatment but not in conjoint therapy with their lovers.

THE FOUNDATION AND FRAMEWORK OF PSYCHOTHERAPY

Psychotherapy, like housebuilding, requires a foundation and frame. The foundation is built on the clinician's theoretical base for understanding behavior and on the strength of the patient–therapist relationship. The frame is formed by the therapeutic contract, which includes the ground rules, expectations, and foci of treatment.

A Model for Understanding Sexual Life

Primary erectile dysfunctions are often the end-product of disturbances in gender identity, object choice, or intention. Figure 9.1 illustrates the CWRU model for understanding sexual life. This is an extension of Masters and Johnson's two-part model of arousal and orgasm and Kaplan's tripartite

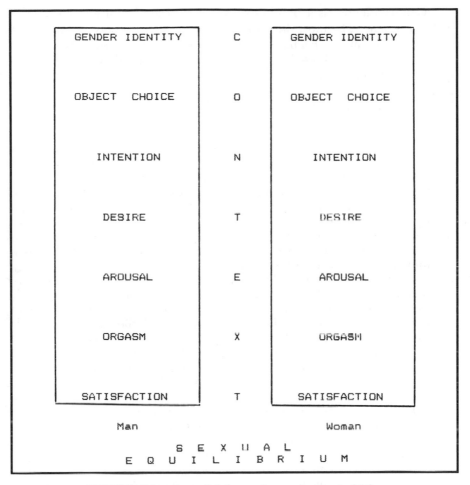

FIGURE 9.1.   A model for understanding sexual life.

model of desire, arousal, and orgasm. The concepts of gender identity, object choice, and intention are elaborated below. Desire and orgasm are not elaborated on, as they are discussed elsewhere in this book. The contextual elements of sexual life are symbolized by the white space between the two figures. The context is composed of all the interpersonal and social elements that contribute to the couple's relationship, such as children, retirement, finances, and health concerns. These life events enhance or interfere with sexual functioning. Context is, therefore, given a major focus in the treatment of impotence.

The sexual equilibrium describes the ever-shifting dynamics between the couple. Assuming that sexual life operates as a closed system, any change in one partner affects the other. Sexual dysfunction affects both partners, and neither partner is able to change without influencing the other.

Gender identity is a person's subjective sense of himself or herself as male or female. The most dramatic form of gender identity disturbance is transsexualism, in which a male patient might describe himself "as a woman trapped in a man's body." More subtle and disguised forms of gender identity disturbance are often seen in cases of primary impotence and paraphilias. The following vignette describes a case of primary impotence based on gender identity disturbance:

A burly, gruff, 35-year-old electrical engineer dressed in a Cleveland Indians' windbreaker consulted me because he wished a sex-change operation. I met his wife of 2 years, a plain-looking, 42-year-old teacher who supported his cross-gender aspirations. This couple had met through a church social group; each had had very limited dating experience. Their marriage was unconsummated because of Mr. G's primary erectile dysfunction. Mrs. G was a virgin with little sexual desire and was tolerant of her husband's cross-dressing. She planned to live with him after he had sex-reassignment surgery.

Mr. G's childhood had been marred by his father's violent behavior secondary to head injury. He recalled episode upon episode of the father's unprovoked violent outbursts. As punishment for misbehavior, the father would make him wear his sister's clothes and stand in the corner. He did well academically, but he felt socially isolated. Although he discovered his homoeroticism in adolescence, he made feeble attempts to date girls. He remained staunchly homophobic.

He began cross-dressing and having fantasies of himself as a woman being made love to by a man. After high school, he enlisted in the Army and was sent to Vietnam. He stopped cross-dressing out of fear of being caught, drank heavily, and unsuccessfully attempted to have intercourse with prostitutes. On return to the States, Mr. G seldom dated and resumed cross-dressing. He was fired from several jobs because of his inability to get along with others.

The couple legally divorced but continued to live together, with Mr. G beginning to cross-dress full time. The patient once attempted to become sexually involved with another male-to-female transsexual. The nature of his attraction was never clear—male-to-male, female-to-female, or male-to-female attraction.

After several years of treatment, the patient had settled on a non-surgical solution to his gender conflict. He lived and worked full-time as a woman apart from his ex-wife, although they remained close friends. Four years after treatment ended, I saw Mr. G dressed as a male. He had given up full-time cross dressing but on weekends worked as a make-up artist for "female impersonators." His primary impotence had not abated in infrequent attempts with his ex-wife or male friends.

Object choice describes the source of personal attraction—to whom or what one is attracted, and/or with whom or what one behaves sexually. This construct goes beyond the traditional one-dimensional concept that erotic life and sexual behavior can be categorized along the continuum of hetero-erotocism/heterosexuality to homoerotocism/homosexuality. In addition to characterizing a person along this continuum, the concept can also be used to describe attractions to and/or behaviors with children, animals, or inanimate objects. The following vignette describes a case of secondary impotence based on inappropriate object choice:

> Jim, a 39-year-old corporate executive, was "sent in to be fixed" by his fiancee of 4 months. He had no trouble achieving an erection, but would mysteriously lose it during intercourse. Jim knew it was a mistake to have proposed to Beth and did not want to go through with the wedding. This man had a secret: He was attracted to men, not women. He had waged a lifelong war against this "dark side of himself." As a youngster, he had set up an altar in his room and prayed for God to remove these "evil" impulses. He also developed a handwashing compulsion. Jim had given in to his homosexual impulses on only a few occasions by hiring young male prostitutes. He had no erectile problems with them.
>
> Jim loved Beth as a friend but had little desire to be sexual with her. He rationalized that marriage would help him contain his homosexual urges. I told the patient that his lack of desire and impotence helped solve his life crisis; that is, they provided him with a way out of the marriage and highlighted his struggle with being gay. I also asked him how it felt to be dishonest with someone he truly loved. Over six sessions, Jim told Beth his secret, and the wedding plans were canceled. Jim became more accepting of his homosexuality and "came out." He found several gay professionals who admitted him to their support group.

Intention refers to what one wishes to do with a sexual impulse. Is the aim to share warmth and intimacy, or is it to shock, dominate, hurt, or humiliate? Intention disorder is the name we use to characterize paraphilic (perverse) behavior. Stoller (1975) observes that all sexual behavior includes some aggression, but that perversion represents an erotic form of hatred. Thus, what separates paraphilic and nonparaphilic behavior is the degree to which aggression dominates the totality of an individual's sexual life.

> A large, 48-year-old physicist, with closely cropped gray hair and out-of-style clothing, sought treatment for primary impotence. After an unconsummated first marriage that had ended in divorce, he was now faced with the prospect of another divorce by his angry second wife. His early childhood had been spent in poverty-stricken rural portions of South America with his physician–missionary parents. As a youngster, he had endured facial surgery without anesthesia at the hands of his parents. When the family returned to the states, they lived in a religious community. Mr. Z believed he was intellectually gifted but socially retarded.

Mr. Z's second wife became increasingly upset as he spent more and more time watching R-rated movies that were both violent and sexual. It was not the movies that she objected to per se but, rather, a certain mesmerized look that came over his face as he sat watching these images. Steadfastly, he maintained that his only interest in these movies was to admire the beautiful bodies of the young women; the violence was gratuitous.

I asked to see this couple in conjoint treatment because Mr. Z seemed very estranged from his emotional life. The aim of psychotherapy was to help Mr. Z recognize the impact of his parents' early cruelty, his anger toward women for making him feel socially awkward, and the impact of his religious indoctrination. Within 4 months, Mr. and Mrs. Z had consummated their marriage. Initially, he was able to give up the need for the violent porn movies; unfortunately this need returned over time.

The Therapeutic Contract

The therapeutic contract is a negotiated agreement between the patient(s) and clinician describing fees, frequency of meetings, rules for canceling sessions, anticipated length of treatment, what the patient can expect from the therapist, what the therapist expects from the patient(s), and, finally, the foci of treatment.

Treatment for sexual problems is generally conducted within a short-term psychotherapy model. The short-term model differs from traditional long-term treatment in the selection of a focus, a higher level of therapist activity, careful patient selection, and special attention to the termination phase of treatment (Mann, 1973; Sifneos, 1972).

The foci are the therapist's initial formulations of the intrapsychic and interpersonal dynamics that contribute to the initiation and maintenance of the erectile dysfunction. Although the focus is offered by the clinician, there must be a mutual agreement to explore the suggested topics. The focus is a starting point for beginning the treatment; it also structures the therapy so that the agreed-on areas are intensively scrutinized. The focus may shift as treatment proceeds, thereby enabling an understanding of the important themes that contribute to the sexual problem. By employing a short-term psychotherapy model, the therapist departs from the traditional stance that all conflicts, especially those from early childhood, require exploration, insight, and resolution. Symptom resolution may be achieved by working with a conflict in the present and sometimes in only a superficial way. The following vignettes demonstrate the usefulness of choosing a focus:

A 62-year-old elegantly dressed investment banker and his 60-year-old cultured, artistic spouse of 35 years came in for treatment. Both partners enjoyed good health. Up until October 1987, they shared a frequent, satisfying sexual relationship. Darcy characterized Seymour as "preoccupied, depressed, and more irritable than usual; he had also lost his self-confidence." He agreed with her assessment and worried that their sexual life was over.

Given the specific onset of the symptom, I asked what happened in October 1987. "What do you think happened in October?" replied the testy investment banker, "The market crashed, and I lost a million and a half dollars." Although upset over the loss, he assured (or impressed) me that it would not affect their style of living or their children's future in the slightest. He tearfully stammered, "I feel so stupid. You know, there's no fool like an old fool."

Given this trauma, I suggested that treatment focus on his injured narcissism, with the goal of restoring his previously held sense of competency. In eight conjoint sessions, his self-worth was rejuvenated, and so was his potency.

Mr. Y provides another illustration of the usefulness of a focus. Married just 2 years, he divorced Mrs. Y after finding out that she was involved in numerous extramarital affairs. He said his friends all knew but were reluctant to tell him. Following the divorce, he encountered erectile problems with all partners—even those to whom he felt close. We chose to focus on his anger at his wife for her betrayals and his subsequent difficulty in trusting new partners. Over 6 months of constantly reworking this theme, his potency returned.

Therapist Activity Level

Short-term psychotherapy requires a higher level of therapist activity than long-term, insight-oriented treatment. In traditional therapy, the clinician maintains a more receptive, passive therapeutic stance. "Activity" in sex therapy refers not only to the frequency of one's comments, but also to the type of intervention offered. Because the short-term model requires a focus, the therapist is active in terms of keeping the patient's attention directed toward the identified conflicts. He or she also gives patients permission to be sexual, provides educational information, dispels myths, offers advice, and prescribes specific sexual exercises, for example, sensate focus. The therapist is also active in terms of making sure each person can "hear" the other's concerns.

Importance of Empathy

Self-psychology (Ornstein & Ornstein, 1984) stresses the therapeutic role of empathy and failures in empathy. As a therapist, I endeavor to "stand inside my patient's shoes" to see how he or she experiences the world. Time after time, patients remark on how important it is for them to be understood. Thus, many of my early comments are clarifications of or reflections on what I think they are experiencing.

In conjoint treatment, I try to understand each partner's unique experience and strive to enable each partner to hear and see, but not necessarily agree with, his or her partner's perspective. That is, I want each person to have a sense of the other's experience. This perspective allows partners to recognize differences in feelings and helps them understand why each person has his or her unique experiences. Patients may try to use the therapist as a judge to rule on issues of fact, for instance, what actually happened. I use these moments to point out that the manner in which a person experiences an event is, for that individual, the way it happened.

Engendering Hope

Men or couples may be demoralized and hopeless when they come for therapy. The infusion of realistic hope by an "expert" creates a positive therapeutic climate that by itself fosters progress. Couples who are wallowing in sadness and frustration cannot make progress. Follow-up studies lend credence to our belief that psychotherapy helps most patients regain their potency (Kilman & Auerbach, 1979). Even if treatment is unable to completely restore potency, the knowledge patients acquire about themselves and each other may help them get along better in the world.

Too Much Too Soon

Too much affect, argumentativeness, confrontation, or new information early in treatment threatens the therapeutic process. Highly charged early sessions typically result in the disruption of treatment. It takes time to forge an empathic bond between therapist and patient that is strong enough to contain and withstand highly charged affect or revelation of difficult material.

Therefore, the clinician should cut off "spilling" or overly intense interactions in the early sessions. The therapist needs to interrupt couples who begin to verbally assault one another, to modulate the degree of affect, and to help patients to suppress early revelation of highly charged material that is inappropriate at that time. Group therapy research (Lieberman, Yalom, & Miles, 1972) supports the fact that negative outcomes are associated with "too much too soon." Emotionality without some cognitive understanding or framework is not beneficial. Also, honesty in therapy is sometimes confused with sadism; instead of sharing and promoting intimacy, the intent of "honesty" can be to hurt and drive a wedge between one another.

The Illusion of Rapid Cure

When I was a youngster, I remember watching a grade-B movie in which a patient in psychotherapy dramatically recalled a long-forgotten memory and was suddenly cured. I call this powerful fantasy of psychotherapy "Hollywood Freud." This notion of a one-time, dramatic, derepression leading to cure is very misleading. Healing actually occurs slowly, as a result of a process called "working through." Insight or affect alone is rarely curative. "Working through" is the process of psychologically integrating and assimilating the previously conflictual aspects of oneself into new cognitive and emotional schemata. In concrete terms, this process is the ongoing, repetitive discussion of specific issues or themes that ultimately result in the patient's achieving a new cognitive and emotional perspective.

> Mr. M is a fast-talking, high-energy, 50-year-old, never-married sports car enthusiast. He has lived in life's fast lane, flying jet planes, gambling, drinking, and palling around with the guys. He also is very attached to his 85-year-old mother, whom he visits daily in a nursing home. Mr. M says that his mother has never considered any woman he dated good enough for him to marry. When he recently became engaged to a 48-year-old divorced mother of two, he developed impotence. He has not told his mother about his engagement and is concerned because his fiancee does not approve of his sports cars, thrice-weekly poker games, or male friends. Mr. M says he's ready to settle down and give up his bachelor life.
>
> Psychotherapy has focused on whether or not Mr. M can really settle down to a conventional life style. We spend the hours working through his attachment to his mother and lifelong avoidance of settling down. He is afraid his mother will die if he does not visit her daily. Also, he feels she would not approve of his engagement. By tediously rehashing these issues, the patient achieved these new perspectives: Regardless of whether he visits or tells her of the engagement, his mother might die; his mother should be pleased that he has finally found somebody with whom he wishes to spend his life; his fiancee can help him to care for his mother. He has come to feel less guilty about his mother and less hostile toward his fiancee. Now he is able to decrease the frequency of his visits to his mother and assert himself with his fiancee regarding "his need to be with the boys." As he has begun to make these changes, his potency has started to return.

The time needed to work through issues is dependent on the intensity and depth of conflict. In general, secondary erectile dysfunction, especially cases of recent onset, are more amenable to brief treatment than primary impotence. Sometimes, only one or two sessions prove beneficial.

WORKING WITH THE SEXUAL EQUILIBRIUM: VALUING THE CONTEXT

The Sexual Equilibrium

The sexual equilibrium is the balance among forces that promote sexual health or initiate or maintain the sexual dysfunction. Sexual life operates in a closed system in which change in one partner influences the other. The erectile disturbance affects both partners, but serves different psychological functions for each. For instance, the impotence may be a passive-aggressive expression of the man's anger. His wife welcomes the impotence as it helps her avoid feeling vulnerable and inadequate each time they make love.

The power of the sexual equilibrium surprises many therapists. Often couples seem to take one step back for each step forward. For example, as a man begins to get firmer erections, his partner suddenly loses her sexual desire. This trading of symptoms between partners occurs with such frequency that we refer to it as the "hot potato syndrome." Like a sexualized version of Newton's second law of motion, the sexual equilibrium implies that any change in one partner will produce a change in the other.

The experienced clinician anticipates the resistances engendered by the sexual equilibrium and uses them to point out the need for some symptoms in the couple's sexual life. Slowly, each partner's contribution to the initiation and maintenance of the impotence is understood and worked through. The following vignette illustrates the power of the sexual equilibrium:

> The sexual life of a demure, young professional couple who had been married for 2 years was impeded by John's psychogenic impotence. His difficulties began shortly after they were married. Susan felt she was entitled to a satisfying sexual life and was distressed by John's lack of concern about his continued problem and avoidance of any form of sexual play. They had not touched one another for 6 months prior to seeking consultation.
>
> Both John and Susan had attended parochial schools; currently, however, he was more invested in Catholicism. Prior to marriage, they had dated for 2 years and had engaged in premarital intercourse.
>
> Unfortunately, Susan became pregnant and underwent an abortion. During the evaluation, John said, "It was like dragging her down the sewer. I forced her to have sex with me, and look what happened." Susan responded that he didn't force her, that she very much wanted to be sexual, and had enjoyed it. She regretted the abortion but thought it was the right decision under the circumstances.
>
> I suggested that treatment focus on their premarital sexual life. They agreed, and John's potency returned during the following week. John seemed pleased, but Susan had suddenly lost her desire. As John was talking about "robbing Susan of her virginity," she seemed increasingly uncomfortable. When I asked what was troubling her, she "confessed" that John had not been the first. We then shifted the focus to why she had allowed John to believe she was a virgin. She explained that she felt very guilty about her past behavior and feared John would not love her if she told him about the others. Although John felt angry and betrayed by Susan's "secret," he also felt relieved that he was not the only one who had done something wrong sexually prior to their marriage. The couple began to appreciate their need for some sexual symptom to alleviate their guilt. Over the next two sessions, Susan's

desire returned, and John's potency remained intact. At 2-month follow-up, the sexual gains had persisted.

Cognitive Aspects of Treatment

Cognitive beliefs and expectations are viewed by some clinicians as the primary cause of erectile dysfunction (Ellis, 1980). Whereas patients' beliefs clearly contribute to their dysfunctions, I generally do not view them as the sole or primary cause. Although this point of view may be controversial, emphasis is given to contextual and emotional factors rather than cognitive ones.

Two brief clinical examples illustrate how cognitive factors can compromise erectile functioning. A widower is puzzled to find himself impotent as he ventures out to date just 3 months after his wife's death from a debilitating illness. A middle-aged man recounts episode after episode of mutual marital cruelty in his on-again, off-again marriage. In the next breath this man turns to the therapist asking why he is unable to perform. These men share the belief that the penis is a machine—that it should work any time, anywhere, under any circumstances, and with any partner. For such men, the context in which they make love seems irrelevant. Sadly, many women also share this myth that the penis is a machine.

Therapy helps both the man and the couple appreciate the importance of the context of lovemaking. The therapist points out what is obvious to him or her. For instance, the clinician suggests that the recently widowed man is still quite psychologically attached to his wife. The symptom is really his "friend" in that it serves two purposes: It reminds him of his old attachment, and it prevents him from another attachment that he is not yet ready for emotionally. As regards the embittered couple, one could simply say, "I don't know how anyone could possibly make love with so much hatred in the air." Treatment stresses the importance of the context and attempts to help patients to understand that lovemaking does not occur in an emotional vacuum.

Other frequently encountered male myths include: (1) it is the function of the male to satisfy the woman; (2) size and firmness are necessary determinants of the female partner's satisfaction; (3) a woman's favorite part of sex is intercourse; (4) a man always wants and is always ready to have sex; (5) once a woman learns to like sex, she will become insatiable; (6) with age, all men lose their ability to achieve erections (Cooper, 1978; Schover, 1984; Zilbergeld, 1978). The myth most often held by a partner of an impotent man is that the failure to achieve erection indicates a diminution of affection for her and suggests the man's involvement with another woman.

Alienation from the Self

At CWRU, we often suggest to patients that "the penis is attached to the heart." As corny as this phrase sounds, it conveys the often unappreciated concept that a man's feelings can enhance or interfere with lovemaking. The feelings that reside in the hearts of the men and their partners contribute to the context and influence sexual performance. We explain that the context becomes more and more important as a man gets older. Who he is with, how he feels about his partner, the circumstances under which he makes love, the overall quality of his relationship, and the influence of other life events all affect the quality of erection.

The Dysfunction as Friend or Solution

Ego psychology (Blanck & Blanck, 1974) teaches that symptom formation has both an adaptive and a pathological context. A modern way of viewing adaptive context is that the erectile dysfunction is a creative and unique solution for some life dilemma. In accordance with this less pathological perspective, we suggest to the man or couple that the symptom may be his or their friend. Couples seem willing to embrace this explanation for their difficulty because it sounds more hopeful. Couples come to appreciate that, perhaps unconsciously, they have chosen the least destructive of many possible alternatives; for some, this choice may prevent the behavioral expression of a less acceptable impulse.

> Immediately after his divorce, Mr. C, a 55-year-old very European and aristocratic gentleman, became involved with a 25-year-old unwed mother of a 5-year-old boy. Mr. C felt cheated by the divorce agreement, which required him to sell his condominium as well as give a significant portion of his annual income to his wife. He claimed that Mrs. C did not need such a generous settlement as she earned more money from her trust than he made in his vocation. She insisted on the settlement "to make him pay for his freedom." Mr. C feared that he would quickly become involved with another woman, remarry, and "live to regret it." He described his young friend as very supportive and good company. He knew, however, that he could never marry her because of the difference in their ages and backgrounds. Also, he was not accustomed to dating several people or to having casual sexual liaisons.
>
> I suggested that his erectile dysfunction was a creative solution to the dilemma of not wanting to get too involved and being uncomfortable about sexual behavior with a partner to whom he was not committed. By being impotent, he prevented himself from either being sexual or becoming attached to another person. His impotence slowly got better as we continued to talk about his life crisis.

> Another example of symptom as friend occurred in the treatment of a paraphilic man who harbored sadistic fantasies toward women. I suggested that his dysfunction was very useful. It allowed him to relate against his wife, while it simultaneously protected her from his more troubled side. He was referred for psychotherapy, but declined the offer.

The Three Requirements for a Good Sexual Life

We often tell patients about the three requirements for having a good sexual life. These are: (1) you have to be willing to make love; (2) you have to be relaxed; (3) you have to concentrate on sensation. Willingness comes from working through conflictual intrapsychic and interpersonal issues. Relaxation and concentration on sensation can be enhanced through sensate-focus exercises.

TRANSFERENCE

"Transference is the experiencing of feelings, drives, attitudes, fantasies, and defenses toward a person in the present which do not befit that person but are a repetition of reactions originating in regard to significant persons of early childhood, unconsciously displaced onto figures in the present" (Greenson, 1967, p. 171). Freud brought this phenomenon to the world's attention in his 1912 paper, "The Dynamics of Transference" (Freud, 1912/1957a). Merton Gill's (1982) scholarly thesis *The Analysis of Transference* traces the evolution of this concept from its classical roots to more current views of theory and technique.

A person's response to another has multiple origins. In simple terms, transference is one of the many influences that determine how an individual thinks, feels, or behaves. People are generally unaware of how this phenomenon works.

Psychotherapy seeks to make transference paradigms conscious for patients. Transference can be positive or negative. It is the positive transference to the therapist that promotes the healing process. The negative transference fuels hostile and sadistic feelings toward others.

Therapists occasionally remark that the room feels full of other people—two sets of parents, four sets of grandparents, brothers, sisters, and previous lovers. Each partner benefits from the analysis of transference, but for different reasons. If we are analyzing a man's transferential responses to his partner, we focus on past and present factors that account for the way in which he experiences her. The insight thus garnered promotes change. In listening to, and participating in, the analysis, the woman begins to appreciate how and why he responds to her.

Lee is a brilliant, 42-year-old, never-married attorney. As a child, he lived in fear of his father's frequent temper outbursts. His parents' marriage was less than adequate, and his mother turned to him for consolation. She was a gifted musician who encouraged his love of music and literature. Together they often played duets, read books, and maintained a protracted, overly close relationship. The patient developed clear fantasies about wanting to marry mother, believing his brother was mother's and his child, and feeling that father intruded on their relationship by coming home from work.

At a literary society to which Lee and his mother belong, he met Leonore. She is a talented musician who is 10 years his senior and has a fiery temper. Initially, they maintained a strictly platonic relationship based on their mutual interests in music and literature. When the relationship evolved into being sexual, it was marred by Lee's low sexual desire and episodic impotence.

In conjoint treatment, Lee described a pattern of developing platonic relationships with older women whose favor he curried. It also seemed important that these women not be available to him as sexual partners. Lee assiduously avoided any potential conflicts with his colleagues and clients to the extent that he was often taken advantage of.

Analysis of the transference demonstrated that Leonore was perfect for him. He related to her as both the precocious child who wished to please his mother and as the fearful, guilty child who did not have the psychological wherewithal to stand up to father. Moreover, Lee thought that he would somehow cause father to die by being sexual. He knew that this idea had no basis in reality but was unable to shake it. It became clear to Lee and Leonore that the powerful, silent, transferential themes embedded in their relationship were making their sexual relationship problematic. Leonore's angry outbursts were also transference-based responses to her father, who had ignored her in favor of her sister.

In individual treatment, transference is traditionally analyzed in terms of the patient's relationship to the therapist. Classically, transference to others has not been interpreted. My position has been that the therapist should actively interpret all transferences to himself and to others. In conjoint treatment, the therapist helps each partner to understand the transferential portion of his or her interpersonal responses.

The eroticized or sexualized transference, in which a patient falls in love with and/or becomes sexually attracted to the therapist, poses special problems. It occurs most frequently when a female therapist treats an impotent man in individual psychotherapy. Conjoint treatment dilutes the transference of either partner to the therapist.

The eroticized transference requires active setting of limits, interpretation of the erotic and hostile components of the transference, and awareness of one's countertransferential responses. The following case was provided by my colleague, Dr. Louisa Turner:

For the past 3 years, Mr. N, a 52-year-old, married business consultant, had been experiencing impotence and inhibited sexual desire. He asked to be seen in insight-oriented individual psychotherapy, and the clinician agreed.

During the evaluation sessions, he reported a history of several intense, nonsexual, idealized, "obsessive attachments" to blonde women; his wife was a redhead. These attachments would last for years at a time, and thoughts of the women would fill his days.

In the first therapy hour, he told the therapist that she immediately fit the "light-haired woman" image, which made him feel comfortable and close to her. By the fourth session, the attachment had become sexualized. He spoke of wanting to quit therapy in order to have a sexual relationship with her. Mr. N sought to find out personal aspects of the therapist's life and was unreceptive to any interpretations of his intrusiveness or the defensive nature of the sexual transference.

One of the important themes that emerged much later in treatment concerned his father's promiscuity and encouragement of his young teenage son to follow in his footsteps. His father had told him, "If you don't get her in bed by the fourth date, you're not a man." Together the therapist and patient remembered that it had been in the fourth session that Mr. N had sexually approached the therapist.

THE PRESCRIPTION OF BEHAVIORAL TASKS

Insight has traditionally been viewed as the most powerful agent of change in psychotherapy. This idealized perspective is both incorrect and excessively narrow in scope. Insight is useful, but not sufficient in overcoming impotence. The judicious integration of carefully selected behavioral tasks augments and facilitates treatment.

Behavioral tasks are employed to (1) overcome performance anxiety (Masters & Johnson, 1970), (2) aid with diagnostic assessment and clarification of underlying dynamics, (3) alter the previously destructive sexual system, (4) confront resistances in each partner, (5) alleviate couples' anxiety about physical intimacy (Kaplan, 1974), (6) dispell myths and educate patients regarding sexual function and anatomy, (7) counteract negative body image concerns (Hartman & Fithian, 1972), and (9) heighten sensuality.

In the early days of sex therapy, clinicians routinely prescribed behavioral tasks at the beginning of treatment. They hoped these exercises would rapidly resolve the sexual dysfunction. Rather than cure, the tasks sometimes precipitated unexpected resistances in one or both partners. This was not all bad, however, as the astute therapist was able to make use of these resistances as part of the ongoing treatment process (Levine, 1976). Currently, therapists are apt to delay the prescription of behavioral tasks until after some of the major therapeutic issues have been worked through.

Behavioral exercises early in treatment are reserved for men whose erectile dysfunction is primarily the result of performance anxiety. This condition is a fear of future failure that stems from an initial difficulty in achieving or maintaining an adequate erection. After this first failure, some men burden themselves with increasing demands to perform ("I'd better make up for last time") and worry that they will fail again. Their fears cause them to become preoccupied with sexual performance. They begin to observe, rather than participate. They attempt to "will" an erection rather than abandon themselves to sensation. Ultimately, they fail again. After several failures, these men tend to avoid sexual situations and feel sapped of their sexual self-confidence.

Sensate Focus: Days I and II

Sensate focus is one behavioral exercise frequently employed to help patients achieve the three requirements necessary for a good sexual life—willingness, relaxation, and sensuality. Masters and Johnson developed these structured exercises to heighten sensuality and arousal while minimizing performance demands.

Sensate focus ensures couples of a successful sexual encounter. The therapist enters into a contract with the couple that requires them to abstain from attempting sexual intercourse while doing the exercises. The therapist also negotiates the frequency with which couples believe they can perform the tasks during the week. Care must be taken to ensure that couples achieve their goal.

In designing sensate-focus exercises, the therapist must be both creative and sensitive to both partners' anxieties regarding sexual intimacy. It may be necessary for the clinician to have couples begin the exercises at a very rudimentary level, such as holding hands in the dark, in bed, with both partners dressed in pajamas. Others may start by taking a bubble bath and washing each other's backs.

What follows are the instructions for Day I sensate focus, given in Helen Kaplan's book *The New Sex Therapy*. Remember, these instructions need to be modified to fit the needs of each couple. Also, I suggest having the couple negotiate who goes first and how many times they will engage in the exercises.

I'd like you both to get ready for bed—to take your clothes off, shower, and relax. I want you [the woman] to lie on your belly. Then you [the man] caress her back as gently and sensitively as you can. Move your hands very slowly. Begin at the back of her neck, caress her ears, and work your way down to her buttocks, legs, and feet. Use your hands and/or your lips. Concentrate only on how it feels to touch her body and her skin.

In the meantime, I want you [the woman] to focus your attention on the sensations you feel when he caresses you. Try not to let your mind wander. Don't think about anything else, don't worry about whether he's getting tired, or whether he is enjoying it—or anything. Be "selfish" and just concentrate on your sensations; let yourself feel everything. Communicate with him. Don't talk too much or it will interfere with your responses—and his. But remember that he can't possibly know what you are feeling unless you tell him. Let him know where you want to be touched and how, and where his caresses feel especially good; and let him know if his touch is too light or too heavy, or if he is going too fast. If the experience is unpleasant, tell him so. Try to identify those areas of your body that are especially sensitive or responsive.

When you have both had enough of this, I want you [the woman] to turn over on your back, so that you [the man] can caress the front of her body. Start with her face and neck and go down to her toes. But this first time don't caress her sexual organs. Skip her nipples, her vagina, and clitoris. Again, both of you are to concentrate only on what it feels like to caress and to be caressed. Stop when this becomes tedious for either of you. Now it's your [the man's] turn to receive. I want you [the woman] to do the same to him. Do either of you have any questions about this procedure? (Kaplan, 1974, p. 209)

After couples can comfortably and regularly engage in Day I sensate focus, they are moved on to Day II. Sensate focus Day II directs couples to include breast and genital stimulation as part of the pleasuring exercise. The aforementioned nondemand characteristics and the need for communication are reiterated. Following successful completion of Day II, couples are instructed to attempt vaginal penetration without active thrusting. As the couple develops sexual confidence, intercourse without any prohibition is prescribed. Couples' reactions to the exercises are carefully monitored and discussed in therapy.

Although Masters and Johnson are credited with developing sensate-focus exercises, a physician named Dr. John Hunter (1788) wrote in 1788 that impotence could be cured by patients having "six amatory experiences without coital connexion." In the following vignette, the Hunter–Masters and Johnson technique was employed to resolve a case of impotence in which the culprit appeared to be performance anxiety.

Mr. M, a 53-year-old successful insurance agent, and his wife, a 50-year-old nutritional counselor, had been happily married for 28 years. With the exception of time spent on vacation, Mr. M had a 7-year history of erectile dysfunction. The frequency of their lovemaking had gradually declined to its current level of once every 4 months. Mr. M reported considerable performance anxiety, enhanced by his competitive personality style. He summed up his dilemma: "When you have a life full of successes, you don't get much practice at how to deal with inadequacy."

During the first hour, sensate-focus exercises were suggested, with instructions to engage in sensual nongenital touching. They returned in a week, noting how difficult it had been to find time to pleasure one another. Their mutual avoidance was discussed and understood as a means of warding off feelings of inadequacy. Working through the resistance allowed the Ms to engage in the exercises three times over the course of the next week. With the pleasuring, Mr. M was able to achieve good, long-lasting erections.

Therapy now progressed to include genital touching, Day II sensate focus. When they returned, they talked about their problem of "silliness." They realized that humor had been used to cope with the impotence; now, however, joking in bed seemed to inhibit sexual closeness. Mr. M's good erections were maintained, although he was having trouble concentrating on sensation. Further exploration revealed that he was focusing his attention in a driven, intense manner. To counter this, the therapist redirected him to maintain a relaxed awareness akin to meditation. Mr. M found this analogy very helpful, and the couple felt ready to proceed with intercourse. During the following week, they were able to have mutually satisfying intercourse. They scheduled one more session because they feared a recurrence of the problem. It did not return, and the time was spent talking about their sexual life. Despite otherwise good communication, they had never been able to broach this topic with one another.

Other Behavioral Tasks

Other behavioral exercises that are useful in the treatment of impotence are aimed at helping the man achieve confidence in his erection. This is done by having him purposely become flaccid only to have him re-erect. Some therapists suggest that the woman squeeze the man's penis until he is flaccid. I simply ask patients to stop pleasuring one another. "Quiet vagina" is an exercise utilized with couples who have significant anxiety about resuming intercourse. In this exercise, the man is on his back with the woman astride him. She gently lowers herself onto his penis and, initially, does not move. Movement is added to the task by first asking the woman to gently and rhythmically move her hips; finally, the man is instructed to thrust. Guided explicit fantasy is often helpful for men who have difficulty becoming aroused, or those who are preoccupied with obsessive thoughts of failure.

FINAL THOUGHTS

There Are Some Men/Couples Who Cannot Be Helped

In spite of our most diligent efforts, it is not possible to help everyone who presents for treatment of impotence. For some, talking therapy alone is insufficient to overcome severe early trauma, the aftermath of years of destructive interactions, or limited psychological resources in the man or couple (Levine, 1985).

There are instances in which patients achieve profound psychological gains, yet their potency does not return. Similarly, a couple's relationship may improve, but their sexual life does not.

Mr. M, a reserved 45-year-old author, was urged to seek treatment for his erectile dysfunction by his wife. She was an ambitious, powerful professional woman who had become increasingly distressed regarding her husband's failure to seek help for his difficulty. He attributed the impotence to rage toward his wife for undermining his authority at home. Three years ago one of his two adolescent sons began to have serious school and behavior problems compounded by drug abuse. The boy had gotten over his drug problem, but the relationship between him and Mr. N became strained. Conversely, Mrs. N's relationship to her son deepened. Mr. N resented feeling excluded. One of the outcomes of this family crisis was Mr. N's development of impotence. Given the temporal relationship between the sexual symptom and the family crisis, therapy initially focused on the new equilibrium among family members. Mrs. N was able to stop undermining her husband, and he was able to develop a better relationship to the boy. However, his potency did not return.

As treatment increasingly focused on the couple's sexual life, Mr. N's resistance heightened. He refused to share the content of his sexual fantasies, insisting that it was none of my business and that they were irrelevant to his problem. He began to appear late for treatment hours but without any sense that his behavior could have any meaning. I sensed that there was something in the content of his sexual fantasies that might hold the key to understanding the sexual problem. Mr. N continued to refuse to discuss his fantasy life, stating that he would rather be impotent than look at this part of himself. He recognized he did not want to make love to his wife, although he did not want to disrupt their marriage. Mrs. N felt stymied; she also did not want to disrupt the marriage, but did not know how long she could tolerate a nonsexual relationship. Treatment was terminated because Mr. N did not want to continue working to restore his potency. I reluctantly respected his conviction that treatment might be worse than a cure. They were not interested in seeing another therapist or pursuing nonpsychological interventions.

Psychotherapy has its limitations. The therapist cannot help everyone. Some patients may do better with another therapist, but there are some who will not benefit with any treatment or therapist. At these times, the therapist should discuss the limitations of his or her method of psychotherapy, as well as any and all other options for restoration of potency. One might consider referral to another professional who employs different methods or a conjoint medical/psychological intervention. When I have patients who have not regained their potency after what seems like a reasonable period of time, I discuss the benefits and limitations of autoinjection therapy (injections of papaverine and phentolamine) or the use of an external vacuum pump device (Osbon's ErecAid System). Preliminary studies (Althof et al., 1987, Turner et al., 1988) demonstrate that the majority of patients are able to make use of these interventions without symptom substitution or major disruption to the couple's equilibrium. I continue to see such patients in therapy to help them adapt to these interventions.

Acknowledgment. The author wishes to thank Ms. Barbara Juknalis for her editorial assistance in the preparation of this manuscript.

REFERENCES

Althof, S., Turner, L., Levine, S., Risen, C., Kursh, E., Bodner, D., & Resnick, M. (1987). Intracavernosal injection in the treatment of impotence; A prospective study of sexual, psychological, and marital functioning. *Journal of Sex and Marital Therapy, 13*(3), 155–167.

Araoz, D. (1982). *Hypnosis and sex therapy.* New York: Brunner/Mazel.

Blanck, G., & Blanck, R. (1974). *Ego psychology: Theory and Practice.* New York: Columbia University Press.

Cooper, A. (1972). The causes and management of impotence. *Postgraduate Medical Journal, 48,* 549–552.

Cooper, A. (1978). Treatment of male potency disorders: The present status. In J. LoPiccolo & L. LoPiccolo (Eds.), *Handbook of sex therapy* (pp. 323–326). New York: Plenum Press.

Ellis, A. (1980). Treatment of erectile dysfunction. In S. Leiblum & L. Pervin (Eds.), *Principles and practice of sex therapy* (pp. 235–260). New York: Guilford Press.

Freud, S. (1957a). The dynamics of transference. In J. Strachey (Ed.), *Standard Edition, Vol. 12* (pp. 99–108). London: Hogarth Press. Original work published in 1912.

Freud, S. (1957b). On the universal tendency to debasement in the sphere of love. In J. Strachey (Ed.), *Standard Edition, Vol. 11* (pp. 177–190). London: Hogarth Press. Original work published in 1912.

Gagnon, J., Rosen, R., & Leiblum, S. (1982). Cognitive and social aspects of sexual dysfunction: Sexual scripts in sex therapy. *Journal of Sex and Marital Therapy, 8*(1), 44–56.

Gill, M. (1982). *Analysis of transference: Volume I: Theory and technique.* New York: International Universities Press.

Greenson, R. (1967). *The theory and practice of psychoanalysis: Vol. I.* New York: International Universities Press.

Hartman W., & Fithian, M. (1972). *The treatment of the sexual dysfunctions.* Long Beach: Center for Marital and Sexual Studies.

Hunter, J. (1788). *Treatise on the venereal disease.* London: Mr. G. Nicol and Mr. J. Johnson.

Kaplan, H. (1974). *The new sex therapy.* New York: Brunner/Mazel.

Kilmann, P., & Auerbach, R. (1979). Treatments of premature ejaculation and psychogenic impotence: A critical review of the literature. *Archives of Sexual Behavior, 8*(1), 81–100.

Kilmann, P., Milan, R., Boland, J., Nankin, H., Davidson, E., West, M., Sabalis, R., Caid, C., & Devine, J. (1987). Group treatment of secondary erectile dysfunction. *Journal of Sex and Marital Therapy, 13*(3), 168–182.

Kolodny, R., Masters, W., & Johnson, V. (1979). *Textbook of sexual medicine.* Boston: Little, Brown.

Levine, S. (1976). Marital sexual dysfunction: Introductory concepts. *Annals of Internal Medicine, 84,* 448–453.

Levine, S. (1985). The psychological evaluation and therapy of psychogenic impotence. In R. T. Segraves & H. W. Schoenberg (Eds.), *Diagnosis and treatment of erectile disturbances: A guide for clinicians* (pp. 87–104). New York: Plenum Press.

Levine, S. (1988). *Sex is not simple*. Columbus: Ohio Psychology Publishing Company.

Lieberman, M., Yalom, I., & Miles, M. (1972). *Encounter groups: First facts*. New York: Basic Books.

LoPiccolo, J., & LoPiccolo, L. (Eds). (1978). *Handbook of sex therapy*. New York: Plenum Press.

Mann, J. (1973). *Time limited psychotherapy*. Cambridge: Harvard University Press.

Masters, W., & Johnson, V. (1970). *Human sexual inadequacy*. Boston: Little, Brown.

Masters, W. M., & Johnson, V., & Kolodny, R. (1982). *Masters and Johnson on sex and human loving*. Boston: Little, Brown.

McCarthy, B., & McCarthy, E. (1984). *Sexual awareness: Sharing sexual pleasure*. New York: Carroll & Graff.

Morales A., Condra, M., Owen, J., Fenemore, J., & Surridge D. (1988). Oral and transcutaneous pharmacologic agents in the treatment of impotence. *Urologic Clinics of North America, 15*(1), 87–93.

Obler, M. (1973). Systematic desensitization in sexual disorders. *Journal of Behavior Therapy and Experimental Psychiatry, 4*, 93–101.

Ornstein, A., & Ornstein, P. (1984). *Empathy and the therapeutic dialogue*. Paper presented at the Fifth Annual Psychotherapy Symposium on Psychotherapy and the Therapeutic Dialogue. Harvard University, The Cambridge Hospital, Boston.

Schiavi, R. (1980). Psychological treatment of erectile disorders in diabetic patients. *Annals of Internal Medicine, 92*, 337–339.

Schover, L. (1984). *Prime time: Sexual health for men over fifty*. New York: Holt, Rinehart & Winston.

Schover, L., Evans, R., & von Eschenback, A. (1987). Sexual rehabilitation in a cancer center: Diagnosis and outcome in 384 consultations. *Archives of Sexual Behavior, 16*(6), 445–462.

Sifneos, P. (1972). *Short term psychotherapy and emotional crisis*. Cambridge: Harvard University Press.

Stoller, R. (1975). *Perversion: The erotic form of hatred*. New York: Pantheon.

Turner, L., Althof, S., Levine, S., Risen, C., Kursh, E., Resnick, M., & Bodner, D. (1988). Self-injection of papaverine and phentolamine in the treatment of psychogenically impotent men. Paper presented at the Society for Sex Therapy and Research Annual Meeting. New York.

Vatsayana. (1964). *The kama sutra*. New York: Grove Press.

Zilbergeld, B. (1975). Group treatment of sexual dysfunction in men without partners. *Journal of Sex and Marital Therapy, 1*(3), 204–214.

Zilbergeld, B. (1978). *Male sexuality*. Toronto: Bantam Books.

Special Populations
IV

10

Sex Therapy with Lesbians, Gay Men, and Bisexuals

MARGARET NICHOLS

In order to understand the special issues associated with conducting sex therapy with gay and bisexual men and women, Margaret Nichols suggests that it is important to understand their unique life styles, identity issues, and personal values. Moreover, one must be cognizant of the value differences between gay men and gay women. As Nichols points out, for many gay men, sexual freedom used to mean the opportunity to engage in high-frequency, casual, and even anonymous "high-tech" sex. A premium was placed on sexual experimentation, diversity, and novelty. For gay women, on the other hand, sexual activities that seemed even remotely patriarchal were frowned upon, whether they be sexual practices involving vaginal penetration or stereotypic female roles. For lesbians during the 1970s, the "personal was political," and "politically incorrect" sex was avoided. One unfortunate side effect of this ethic was sexual avoidance.

There have been considerable changes in homosexual values and sexual behaviors in the last decade, and Nichols suggests that gay men have begun to make sex less of the central focus of their lives, while lesbians have become more sexually interested and experimental. Gay women are moving away from the belief that their sexual scripts must be quintessentially female, that is, gentle, egalitarian, and loving, and are investigating more genitally explicit and even, at times, "kinky" sexual practices. Because of the fear of AIDS, gay men are showing increasing interest in committed relationships and "safe" sexual practices. Courses in "Dating 101" are being directed at gay men so that they can learn the fundamentals of dating and courtship before becoming sexually involved.

Nichols suggests that gay men and women often experience considerable sexual identity confusion, and she describes several forms it may take, for example, the "heterosexual bisexual" who experiences bisexual arousal but is fearful of exploring gay relationships. She also reminds

*readers that many homosexuals experience an internalized homophobia
that must be addressed. Nichols also notes the high incidence of alcohol
abuse often found in gay communities and observes that some of the
sexual dysfunctions experienced by gay men and women may be related
to alcoholism.*

*Although the sexual problems of gay men and women are not dissim-
ilar to those found in heterosexuals, there is a difference in prevalence.
Lesbian women tend not to complain of dyspareunia or vaginismus but
are concerned about an aversion to oral sex. Gay men are dealing with
many AIDS-related anxieties.*

*Loss of sexual desire and fear about becoming HIV infected, for
example, are widespread. Helping gay men establish more "monogamous" relationships and safer sexual scripts is important. For both gay
men and women, lifestyle issues and relationship dynamics are an intrinsic part of sex therapy.*

*Dr. Nichols provides a wide variety of clinical examples to illustrate
the sexual-identity and life-style concerns of gay and bisexual individuals. She addresses the impact of AIDS on sexual behavior and sexual
therapy. In this chapter, Dr. Nichols describes in depth the special issues
and dilemmas of working with gay individuals and couples.*

*Margaret Nichols, Ph.D., is Director of the Institute for Personal
Growth in New Brunswick, New Jersey. She has written widely about sex
therapy with gay and bisexual individuals and is the founder of The
Hyacinth Foundation, an organization devoted to meeting the social and
psychological needs of persons with AIDS.*

Fortunately, the days when psychiatry labeled homosexuality a disease
and when the only professional writing on the subject dealt with "curing"
this pathology are over. These days countless journal articles and books
discuss homosexuality as a normal variation of sexual orientation and
focus, not on homosexual pathology per se but rather on the special
therapeutic issues attendant to this population.

It is appropriate that this literature proliferates. For although it is
true that homosexuals are not automatically "mentally ill" by virtue of
their sexual orientation, neither is it true that gay people are "just like
everyone else."

In fact, the form homosexuality has taken in our culture in the latter
part of the 20th century is probably a new and unique phenomenon in
history. In most Western industrialized nations, homosexuality constitutes not just a preference of gender of love object or sexual partner; it
also represents an identity, a life style, a subculture (Boswell, 1980).
Homosexuality can be compared to race or ethnic background and shares

many characteristics of a racial or ethnic subgroup, but it differs in that the inclination is not necessarily passed from one generation to the next, and gays cannot count on a family-of-origin network to help buttress them against prejudice or hostility from the mainstream culture. Moreover, gayness, unlike skin color, can be hidden, and thus individual gay people have the option of "passing" for straight with all the psychological issues attendant to that choice. In this regard, many gays could be compared to, for example, Jews who change their names and try to assimilate, or light-skinned blacks who "pass" for whites.

In any case, the enlightened mental health professional who wishes to work with a gay or bisexual clientele needs to have more than just an accepting attitude; at times the professional must be able to be *more* positive about homosexuality than a self-hating gay client. The clinician needs to appreciate the cultural milieu within which the client lives as well as the special psychological issues attendant to homosexuality. It is well worth the time the clinician must take to learn about "the gay life style": From Kinsey (1948) to the present, estimates of the number of gays or lesbians in the population run from 2% to 10%, and the numbers of Americans who are behaviorally bisexual as adults are much larger, perhaps as high as 25% (Hyde, 1982).

Accordingly, the first part of this chapter is a brief overview of "gay culture" as it has existed since 1969, focusing particularly on the 1980s. Next, the chapter discusses some of the psychological dynamics of gayness that are relevant to sex therapy and illustrates the ways in which sex therapy with gay, lesbian, and bisexual individuals differs from sex therapy with heterosexuals. Next, the author's own methods are described, and finally, case examples are given to illustrate important points.

THE GAY COMMUNITY AND GAY ISSUES

To understand what it is like to be gay or bisexual in contemporary society, it is useful to have some understanding of the gay political movement that received major impetus in 1969,[1] the date of the "Stonewall Rebellion," a protest rebellion that marked the start of gay liberation. Before the 1970s, there was a nearly universal consensus among Americans that homosexuality was an illness, a sin, or both. Most importantly, gay people themselves joined in this consensus. Even the most self-accepting gay people of these times seemed to perceive their homo-

---

[1] Throughout this section in particular I speak primarily of the gay community built by predominantly white educated gays who lived in "gay ghettos." Life for gays outside a gay ghetto has always been closer to the mainstream. Nevertheless, the impact of gay ghetto culture has spread in part even to the farthest regions of the country.

sexuality as a disability that made them inherently inferior to hetero-sexuals. Indeed, the political efforts of homosexuals to obtain tolerance from heterosexuals were to convince the public that homosexuality was a congenital disability for which the homosexual was blameless and over which he or she had no control. There was not even a concept of "coming out of the closet"; gay people did their best to "pass" for straight and suppress or at least hide their gay feelings. Moreover, it could be danger-ous to act on one's gay attractions: Parents psychiatrically hospitalized even their adult children if homosexuality was discovered, and police raids on gay bars and other social gatherings were frequent and terrifying to patrons leading a "double life" (Katz, 1976).

From a psychological point of view, the major effect of the gay liberation movement was to help gays affirm the soundness and positive aspects of their orientation: "Gay is good" became a rallying cry just as "black is beautiful" had been in the 1960s. In certain "gay ghettos" in urban areas of the country, gay people "came out" and built communities that could support them as families of origin often could not. The gay liberation movement helped replace shame with pride.

During the 1970s, gay men and lesbians "came out"—went public with their orientation—in ways that made it impossible for many Ameri-cans to dismiss homosexuality as something "out there" that happened to "others." The communities that grew so rapidly had spheres of influence that extended far beyond their geographic boundaries. Whereas before the gay movement homosexuals could scarcely find information about their orientation, and what they did find was negative, by the end of the 1970s, virtually everyone had been exposed to some version of the "gay and proud" theme, if only via watching gay people on television talk shows. This has had an enormous impact, particularly on gay adolescents who previously felt dismally trapped and alone, not only in their teen peer environment but also in the larger world outside their own commu-nities. Most individuals who lived gay lives before the 1970s remember adolescence as a time of alienation. Although still common, that expe-rience has been greatly mitigated by the emergence of a visible gay culture and media coverage of gays.

Gay men and lesbians developed their communities in quite differ-ent ways, however. In large urban centers, gay men seemed to embark on an orgy of celebration of freedom, and that celebration often included the proliferation of opportunities for multiple casual and even anony-mous sexual encounters. For gay men the freedom to have sex seemed to be the cornerstone of gayness. To an extent many gay men acted out one aspect of a rather traditional masculinity: Their appearance changed to become hypermasculine (e.g., leather jackets, Levis and boots, short hair, and moustaches). Free of the commitments and constraints of finan-cially supporting a family, gay men had the highest disposable income of any men in America. They spent that money on tasteful clothes and furnishings, travel, concerts, opera, and plays—in other words, had lives that centered around having fun. Most notably, gay men had more sexual opportunities than anyone else—they could act on the traditional male fantasy (lots of sex, little commitment), unfettered by the traditional female fantasy (lots of intimacy and commitment) with which heterosexuals still had to contend. The concept of the "zipless fuck," ironically introduced into American culture by a woman, Erica Jong, became a reality for many gay men.

When Bell and Weinberg (1978) published their study of gay men and lesbians in the San Francisco area, many people were shocked to learn that some gay men had had 500 to 1,000 *different* sexual partners during adulthood. But in fact, accumulating so many different partners was not so difficult for a gay man in San Francisco in the 1970s. With the abundance of bath houses and "back rooms" where sex might occur in "orgy" style, one man could have several different partners in one night.

It would be a mistake, however, to characterize this behavior as pathological, although certainly some few men did become compulsive sexual "addicts." Nor was this behavior a flight from intimacy: As McWhirter and Mattison (1984) point out in their groundbreaking book on gay couples, most gay men eventually became partners, often for extremely long periods, a finding corroborated by Blumstein and Schwartz's (1983) study comparing gay, lesbian, and heterosexual couples. But gay men tended to couple in a manner distinctly geared to their life styles: Most had open mutually consensual nonmonogamous relationships. How prevalent this pattern was is illustrated by the fact that of McWhirter and Mattison's sample of male couples *100%* were nonmonogamous by their fifth year.

Another aspect of gay male sexuality as it evolved in the 1970s was the development of "high-tech sex." Not only did gay men have more sex than anyone else, they also experimented with forms of sexuality previously associated only with fetishists. For example, Jay and Young (1979) report that 37% of gay men had experiences with sadomasochistic practices, 23% with "water sports" (urination), and 22% with "fist fucking" (insertion of hand into partner's anus). Specialized clubs sprang up for aficionados of a particular practice, and guide books for different practices were written, such as *The Leatherman's Handbook* (Townsend, 1972) (about sadomasochism) and *Anal Pleasure and Health* (Morin, 1981) (including information about analingus, use of enemas, etc.). Sex therapists inexperienced with the gay male community often equate these practices with fetishism. True fetishism is quite different from the sex practiced by "fast lane" gay men in the 1970s. Most fetishists have an extremely narrow sexual script and can only become sexually aroused by their particular fetish. Gay male sexuality in the 1970s was an *expansion* of sexuality boundaries to include a wide range of sometimes rather exotic sexual techniques, not a rigidification of sexual repertoire.

At the same time that gay men were building a community emphasizing sexual experimentation, novelty, and diversity, lesbians were
building communities based on feminist principles. For many gay
women, feminism became the foundation of their orientation. In the
following excerpt, Faderman (1984) describes the emergence of the
"new gay" lesbians:

> Women who have come to lesbianism reject the notion that *lesbian* is a
> *sexual* identity. . . . Sexual activity is for them, generally, only one as-
> pect, and perhaps a relatively unimportant aspect, of their commitment
> to a lesbian life style . . . . Lesbianism in this context . . . is defined as a
> political choice more than a sexual preference . . . less a personal choice
> about whom to sleep with than a uniting of women against patriarchal
> power. (p. 86)

Many lesbians in the 1970s seemed to see men—including gay men—
as oppressive, and if they acted politically, they were apt to do so in
feminist or lesbian-only organizations rather than in a "gay rights" context. Many lesbians were interested in "reclaiming" areas of life—spiritu-
ality, history, family structure, the arts—that had been male dominated
and that had ignored women's needs and voices. Not only was sex not the
focus of lesbianism, it was actually quite a problematic issue. Until
recently, most feminist (including lesbian feminist) analyses of female
sexuality focused on the sexual exploitation of women. Rape, incest, and
pornography occupied center stage; women's sexual pleasure was much
less discussed or explored. The extremes of this view were that having
sex with men was by definition colluding with the enemy or that, as
Andrea Dworkin has said, the "missionary position" is by its nature
oppressive to women (Echols, 1984). Within the lesbian community, the
"sexual exploitation" focus on sex probably caused some damage. Because feminism itself has been founded, in part, on the thesis that "the
personal is political," women's sexual lives were subjected to scrutiny by
themselves and peers. Anything associated with stereotypic heterosexual
sex was viewed automatically as "patriarchal," even when practiced by
two women. Thus, many lesbians came to define as politically incorrect
(p. i.) such behaviors as the attraction to or desire to wear "feminine"
clothing, make-up, etc.; any sexual act that involved a more "active" and
more "passive" partner; "rough" sex; fantasies involving domination/
submission, overpowerment, etc.; and sometimes even the desire to
penetrate a partner or be penetrated oneself. As one can imagine, this
attitude toward sex proved stifling for many women. To make matters
worse, whereas gay men usually defined their orientation as a visceral
sexual attraction over which they had no control, lesbians tended to
define their orientation as a political or relationship choice and not
necessarily an indication of where their exclusive or even strongest sexual
attraction lay. Thus, many self-defined lesbians were in essence bisexual

women who, for various reasons, choose not to act on their heterosexual sexual attractions. A great many of these women felt guilty about or frightened of their heterosexual fantasies or attractions, just as a primarily heterosexual person might feel frightened by his or her homosexual fantasies and attractions.

It should be clear by now that gay male and lesbian life styles, behaviors, identities, and values evolved in quite different ways following the early gay liberation and feminist movements. In the recent past, however, this has changed enormously.

The Impact of AIDS

For gay men, AIDS has been substantially responsible for effecting major changes in life styles. Within a few years, the kind of sexual activity that had previously seemed "liberating" and "life affirming" became a potential death sentence. This has changed gay male life styles in several ways. There is a markedly reduced incidence of casual and anonymous sex among gay men. Anal sex has been largely abandoned, and when it does occur, condoms are used. Oral sex is performed with condoms or without ejaculation into the mouth. Finally, gay male couples are more monogamous. AIDS has also had a profound impact on how gay men view their sexuality. Many gay men believe that their penises and ejaculate are "toxic" or that other men's organs are dangerous. Inhibited sexual desire (ISD) and sexual aversion, problems once rarely encountered among gay men, are more widespread.[2] Some gay men are learning the rudiments of dating and courtship behavior for the first time. As adolescents, their relationships often were initiated with sexual activity on the first encounter, and they may have never enjoyed a dating or courtship phase in any of their relationships. Some gay men engage in what Shernoff (personal communication, May 10, 1988) has termed the "binge–purge" syndrome. That is, their depression and hopelessness about changing their sex lives leads to long periods of abstinence until sexual needs build to a crescendo, and they "binge" on unsafe sex.

Younger gays, just "coming out," are presented with a new set of sexual difficulties: They are more likely to have been exposed to positive images of gayness than in previous times, but they are "coming out" into a community that is literally dying. Many gay men are re-experiencing "internalized homophobia"—feelings of guilt or shame over their gayness—that appeared to have been resolved earlier but now resurface in the face of the superstition that perhaps gays have "brought this on themselves" or that AIDS really is God's punishment.

But although AIDS has affected gay male sexuality in devastating ways, gay men have not reacted so extremely as to embrace fully the heterosexual

---

[2] Some ISD may be caused by the virus itself in men who are seropositive or ill. The AIDS virus seems to decrease testosterone levels and diminish sex drive.

ideal of lifelong monogamous marriages. Instead, they have modified their behavior and are creating yet another type of sexual liberation. Nonmonogamous couples may be less commonplace, and sexual contact outside a primary relationship may be less frequent, but there are still a substantial number of sexually nonexclusive male relationships. Gay organizations are conducting workshops for their members and teaching them how to eroticize safe sex or the rudiments of "Dating 101." Although in many cities bathhouses and back rooms have been shut down, other private clubs have emerged in which safe sex is the norm. For example, "jerk off" (J.O.) clubs have proliferated, as have private clubs where penetration is not allowed. Telephone sex has become more widespread. Thus, gay men have greatly modified their sexual and relationship behavior, but they are hardly mimicking the heterosexual norm.

At the same time that gay men have made sex less of a focal point of their lives, lesbians have become more interested in sex. The "mainstream" lesbian/feminist community of the 1970s was primarily concerned with the sexual oppression of women, and when woman-to-woman sex was described or delineated, there was general agreement that truly "female" expression of sexuality would celebrate gentleness, egalitarianism, sensuality (as opposed to a genital focus), tenderness, and other warm and loving but not necessarily orgasmic aspects of sex. During the late 1970s, however, another group of lesbians became increasingly vocal: Women who wanted to produce female pornography. Tastes in erotica became more varied and not limited to "warm" sex, and many women began to prefer sex that included activities heretofore considered to be outside the boundaries of "normal" female sexuality: rough sex, "dirty" sex, role-polarized sex, "promiscuity," anonymous sex, sex without love, and sadomasochistic sex. By the mid-1980s, some women were producing pornographic magazines for lesbians such as *On Our Backs* (a takeoff on a well-known feminist newspaper called *Off Our Backs*), audiotapes like the *Hot Women Talk Tape* series, and lesbian video porn that included scenes with dildoes, vaginal "fist fucking," and explicit sadomasochism. Other lesbians created support organizations for women who enjoyed unusual or kinky sex: for example, sex parties and group sex, casual sex, bisexual sex, sadomasochistic or fetishistic sex, etc. The two best known of these groups were Samois in California and the Lesbian Sex Mafia in New York. Many of these lesbians had been influenced by the gay male sexuality of the 1970s that included "uncommon" techniques.

Because feminism considers one's personal life to be the ultimate expression of one's politics, it is not surprising that the "lesbian sex radical" trend became a major issue of political debate within the gay women's community. The lesbians who have most vocally criticized the sex radicals tend to be allied with the antipornography movement and consider many of the radical lesbians' approach to sex to be violent and degrading and to be woman-to-woman replicas of male sexual oppression of heterosexual women. The sex radicals feel that *all* expressions of female sexuality except those that are *clearly* physically coercive (e.g., rape) must be accepted and supported by other women. They tend to consider much of sexuality to be outside the bounds of feminist analysis.

> It is essential to separate gender and sexuality analytically to more accurately reflect their separate existence. This goes against the grain of much contemporary feminist thought, which treats sexuality as a derivation of gender . . . . Feminist conceptual tools were developed to detect and analyze gender-based hierarchies. To the extent that these overlap with erotic stratifications, feminist theory has some explanatory power. But as issues become less those of gender and more those of sexuality, feminist analysis becomes irrelevant and often misleading. (Rubin, 1984, p. 308)

Although the lesbian sex radicals are still quite controversial, their influence has been widespread. Younger lesbians now are much less likely to eschew a traditionally feminine appearance as did their early 1970 feminist counterparts: The so-called "lipstick lesbian" dresses and adorns herself with as much concern for physical attractiveness as her heterosexual counterpart. Perhaps more importantly, there has been a loosening of sexually rigid standards, and lesbians feel freer to express their sexuality in any way they like without considering themselves, or being judged, as "politically incorrect." Finally, many lesbians have, as a result of the sex radical movement, been exposed to a greater variety of sexual techniques. The average lesbian is probably much more likely to know about "kinky" sex than is her heterosexual sister.

Contemporary Bisexuality

Gay and lesbian norms are changing in one other important way: A "bisexual pride" movement is beginning within the gay community. Bisexuality is one of the least understood aspects of sexual orientation. So strong is the tendency to dichotomize sexual orientation that many people simply do not believe it exists. Many gays themselves view the bisexual as no more than a gay person who is too afraid to "come out." And indeed, up until recently the only type of bisexual that had been studied was the married man who had furtive, clandestine sexual encounters with other men. Many of these "bisexuals" may have been exclusively or predominantly gay men who used marriage as a way to hide their preferred sexual orientation, although others were probably genuinely attracted to both sexes. But within the recent past, researchers have noted both the many forms of bisexuality and the apparent ability of some individuals to *change* orientation (including erotic feelings, behavior, and even fantasy) at various points in their lives (Klein & Wolf, 1985; Herdt, 1987). There are increasing numbers of individuals who identify themselves as gay or lesbian, often in quite open and political ways, for some time, and only later come to label themselves as bisexual. These individuals consider their bisexuality as an expansion of their sexuality rather than as a "return to heterosexuality." Although bisexuals really do not yet have a community or much support from either gays or heterosexuals, many seek acceptance from within the gay culture, reasoning that this culture can have an inclusive, rather than an exclusive, definition of sexual orientation. In New York, for example, there are two bisexual support groups that meet at the Lesbian and Gay Community Center and march in the Gay Pride Parade despite some hostility from other participants.

Ironically, in the 1980s gay male sexuality has become more "lesbian," while lesbian sexuality has become more "gay male." Both men and women, however, exhibit the effects of their sexual orientation and of the subculture of gayness in ways that distinguish their sexuality not only from each other but from heterosexuality. Although much sex therapy is not sexual-orientation-specific, there are some important differences that the sex therapist wishing to work with gay clients must understand.

SEX THERAPY WITH GAYS, LESBIANS, AND BISEXUALS

Sexual Identity Issues

Sex therapy with gay clients differs from that with heterosexuals in many respects. This section explores some of these differences, both in content of problems brought to treatment and techniques used with this population.

Although not really a sexual dysfunction, sexual identity issues are often seen in gay clients. Often the client complaining of identity confusion has an unambiguous homosexual sexual orientation but finds this orientation unacceptable to himself or herself. Other individuals are genuinely attracted to both men and women and have some "choice" in selecting the object of their romantic and sexual fantasies. Still other clients have lived their lives within the gay community and only recently are experiencing heterosexual attraction. This creates considerable confusion and conflict for them.

Because the average sex therapist is more likely to see more cases of sexual identity confusion than actual sexual dysfunction among gays, it is worth devoting some time to describing the various forms in which such confusion may manifest itself.

The "Frightened Homosexual"

By far the majority of "confused" clients are individuals whose erotic and romantic attractions are overwhelmingly same-sex and whose confusion is a defense against accepting this reality. Interestingly, many of these clients seek a heterosexual therapist because openly gay therapists appear too threatening. In working with these people (as with others described in this section), the therapist must keep in mind that the resolution of *personal identification* is the primary issue and that the conflicts that must be addressed center around alienation versus acceptance within a community, loss of previously held ideals and self-concept, and the taking on (or casting off) of a stigmatized social status. The Australian psychologist Vivien Cass has aptly described the process of identity formation in gay individuals in a six-stage model (1979). In Stage 1, "identity confusion," the individual realizes that feelings, thoughts, or behavior can be defined as homosexual, and this realization injects an incongruous element into a previously stable situation in which both the individual and the environment assumed the person to be heterosexual. This first stage can occur very early in life (and is often described by adults as "feeling different" from others of their own gender as young children), or it may not appear until adulthood. The initial realization—"my feelings/attractions *may* be gay"—is usually greeted with horror by the individual, who then proceeds, secretly at first, to go through what is often a long process of denying, defending against, or repressing homosexual feelings, redefining homosexual behavior or attractions as "not really gay," constructing a facade of heterosexuality, and, finally, if successfully resolved, not only integrating his or her orientation into identity but accepting and ultimately feeling pride in this identification. Much of what this client must confront is what has often been termed "internalized homophobia," that is, the internalization of social stigma against homosexuality in a form that results in self-hatred, just as, for example, some blacks have internalized racism and feel a pervasive sense of being "less than" whites. Some case vignettes can illustrate some of the varieties of ways this process can take place:

> Georgia was a 30-year-old suburban housewife, mother of two young children, whose entry into therapy was precipitated by heavy alcohol use and suicidal gestures. Georgia had been aware of attractions to women since early adolescence but had pushed them out of her mind, had never had a homosexual experience, and had rationalized them in various ways. She married young and, although she experienced little sexual pleasure with her husband, for many years simply accepted a relationship with no romantic or sexually enjoyable aspects for her. Then she fell in love with a neighborhood housewife and had a sexual experience that was intense, powerful, and romantic.
>
> Georgia felt trapped: She could no longer be satisfied with her marriage but felt that life as a lesbian was impossible. She presented her initial problem as "identity confusion," and in a sense that was true: Her desires were overwhelmingly homosexual, but she needed help to assume a gay identity and life style—or to choose to never express that side of herself again. Eventually, Georgia left her husband, retaining custody of their children; found a lover; and joined Alcoholics Anonymous and "gay AA" groups.
>
> Stacey was a 16-year-old brought by her parents to treatment because of Stacey's suicidal threats. A "model adolescent," Stacey was popular,

bright, well-behaved, and a star female athlete. Alone in session, she very quickly revealed that since age 13 she had been aware of powerful attractions exclusively to women, and this seemed to her a nightmare beyond belief. Stacey was seen by the author, at the time a young and naive psychology intern. I promptly told Stacey that she was gay, that "gay was good," and that she had to accept this fact about herself. Thinking me a crazy woman, Stacey immediately terminated therapy and asked for a referral to someone who would "cure" her of her homosexuality.

Michael had entered a seminary to become a Catholic priest at age 18. As he later described it, "I thought I must have had a calling from God to the priesthood and celibacy because I experienced no sexual attractions of any kind as a teenager." His repressive mechanisms, less common in men than women, worked until his third year in the seminary, when his erotic attractions surfaced in this all-male atmosphere. After 2 years of personal struggle and much guilt, he left the seminary and spent several years trying to drink away his feelings. After joining AA and attaining 3 years of sobriety, he finally had the courage to seek help, with a large portion of therapy focusing on the conflict between his sexual/romantic feelings and his religious feelings.

Jeff was a 16-year-old who asked his parents to bring him for therapy; he was profoundly depressed. Although he initially presented himself as unsure of his orientation, a sexual history of attractions and fantasies suggested very clearly that he was nearly entirely homosexual in his orientation. Jeff experienced the positive, supportive attitude of his therapist as a huge relief and in this atmosphere came to embrace a gay identity rather easily. Unfortunately, in the flush of his emerging "gay pride," Jeff "came out" precipitously to his parents, who promptly threw him out of their home. Jeff was helped to set up an independent living situation and, although deeply wounded by his parents' rejection, maintained himself well, eventually putting himself through college and, many years later, reconciling with his parents.

Several points should be made about treatment with the "frightened homosexual." First, it is usually fairly easy to assess (unless your client has been coerced into treatment and conceals data) simply by getting a detailed history of sexual attractions, romantic attractions, behavior, and fantasy life. Usually the clinician will find little or no attraction to the opposite sex, although clients may often report that they "feel more like" or "feel more comfortable with" the opposite sex. Second, viewed essentially as an identity issue, one must realize that the client is struggling not only with "internalized homophobia" but also with the potential loss of many of the important structures of life that contribute to self-identity for all of us: family, friends, future life plans, religion, etc. With these people in particular, the therapist must be more positive about homosexuality than the client. Moreover, the therapist should be able to provide the client with models and mechanisms to replace the social structures that may be lost. This can be done by giving clients information about local gay organizations and recommending gay-positive books. The therapist must be able to support and guide the "frightened homosexual" through identity development to gay pride but must be sensitive to the fears and not go too fast for the client (the obvious mistake made in the second case vignette). It is often useful to point out to clients the distinction between *feelings* and *behavior* and to remind them that although they may not be able to control the former, they can almost certainly control the latter.

The "Heterosexual Bisexual"

This term has been chosen to delineate those people who, although genuinely bisexual to some degree, have never developed or explored gay relationships. It is useful to think of these people as having two "parts": one "heterosexual" and one "gay." It is also useful to frame the problem this way for the client. A "heterosexual bisexual" case is presented in more detail later in this chapter, but some general principles of treatment can be outlined here. These clients presumably have some "choice" in how to act out their desires, but they are not really free to choose and are often aware of feeling constrained and unfulfilled. To the extent that discomfort with homosexuality and internalized homophobia exists, the treatment issues resemble those for the "frightened homosexual." When the "gay part" is healthy and free, the whole person is free. At this point, most people gravitate to one orientation or the other, so strong is the dichotomous view of sexual orientation in this culture. Generally, individuals gravitate toward whichever attraction they are experiencing most strongly at that period in their lives, but this is not necessarily true, especially among women.

> *Joyce* was a 40-year-old successful business woman having problems in her 18-year marriage. She was motivated in part to enter therapy because she was clearly aware of her lesbian attractions and had in fact acted them out occasionally in "three-way" sexual interactions with her husband and another woman. She feared that perhaps her lesbian attractions were stronger than she realized and might be a source of her marital problems. After working on her internalized homophobia concerns, she felt freer to choose and decided that she was indeed more strongly attracted to men than women. She ended her marriage and sometime later became involved with another man.

> *Ben* was a young man in his 20s who felt paralyzed by sexual identity confusion. Careful sexual assessment revealed that he was bisexual but had acted on few attractions, either heterosexual or homosexual. His attitudes about homosexuality were intensely negative. Ben was encouraged to initiate both homosexual and heterosexual relationships at the same time that he tried to resolve his hatred for the gay part of himself.

Eventually, Ben decided that he was "more gay than straight" and chose a gay identity and life style.

Alice left a 15-year, physically abusive marriage to a man and soon afterwards, at the age of 35, became involved with a woman. Alice was aware that her purely erotic attractions were stronger for men but felt that her relationships with women were more intimate, more egalitarian, and more satisfying. She consciously chose to assume a lesbian identity and appears to have integrated her heterosexual attractions into her fantasy life with little discomfort.

Nina consciously decided to explore her lesbian attractions, of which she had been previously dimly aware, after the breakup of an 8-year relationship with a man. She answered ads in the *Village Voice* and soon had her first lesbian sexual relationship, which she experienced as very pleasurable. She soon had a steady female lover. She came to therapy in part because she knew she still retained negative feelings about the "gay part" of herself and did not want these feelings to interfere with current relationships. For Nina, it was important that she retain a strong *bisexual* identity: She reported that the terms "gay" and "straight" both felt inappropriate to her.

As these examples suggest, many of the issues faced by "heterosexual bisexuals" are similar to those of "frightened gays." The major differentiating variable is *choice* and whether the person feels comfortable with a fluid, open-ended sexual identity or feels compelled to "choose up sides."

The "Gay Bisexual"

For unknown reasons, perhaps simply as a manifestation of the continued evolution of the gay and lesbian community, a number of previously gay-identified individuals are exploring heterosexual attractions. Some are simply acknowledging the existence of heterosexual attractions. When these clients seek help, it is usually because their attractions cannot be fit into a dichotomous framework. Often, merely explaining sexual orientation as a continuum and emphasizing the difference between feelings and behavior (the latter can be controlled) alleviates the "heterosexual panic" of the clients.

But some gay-identified individuals are choosing to experiment with heterosexual sex and relationships, and this often causes them great discomfort. The major problem these individuals face is the absence of a bisexual community; they feel they do not "fit in" any place. Just as the person just beginning to acknowledge a gay identity faces the loss of cherished social supports, so does the gay who is grappling with a bisexual identity have to contend with potential rejection by the gay community they have felt so much a part of. This dilemma is particularly poignant because many of these people already incurred loss when they made the transition from heterosexually identified to gay. They now face a second loss, this time with no alternative structures or community to replace the gay community that often rejects them nearly as often as do heterosexuals. Moreover, the more politically conscious of these individuals feel a sense of guilt and betrayal: They now have the option of some of the heterosexual privileges (e.g., marriage) denied to their gay friends.

Sharon was a 26-year-old woman who for 8 years had been an outspoken, politically active lesbian. To her dismay, she fell in love with a male colleague. She was plagued with guilt and a sense that she had "defected from the movement." Moreover, she did indeed experience rejection from many of her lesbian friends. She was particularly upset that her parents accepted her boyfriend as a lover, because the parents did not know that she had been gay for many years. Her discomfort was alleviated only when she "came out" to her parents as bisexual and told them of her previous lovers. She eventually came to accept that she would always be something of an outsider, belonging neither to the heterosexual nor the gay world.

This type of alienation is similar to that experienced by multiracial couples, who must often build their own personal support networks to buffer themselves from rejection by both whites and blacks.

Steven had suppressed his gay impulses, known to him since early adolescence, until his early 30s. After 12 years of marriage and a conventional heterosexual life style, he left his wife, "came out" as gay, settled down with a male lover, and became quite active in the gay community. Four years later he fell in love with a woman who also identified herself as gay and had been a colleague in gay political organizations. Steven, who had lost a great deal during his gay "coming out"—his family rejected him, and he was fired from his job—had a very difficult time acknowledging his bisexuality. He often experienced it as "going backwards," and it brought up renewed feelings of sorrow over his "coming out" losses and doubts about why he had ever come out as gay. Eventually he came to feel that his "exclusively gay" period had been important to him as an acknowledgment of the powerful gay component within him, and his bisexuality became more palatable to him.

Internalized Homophobia in Gay-Identified Clients

Related to the issue of identity confusion is the impact of internalized homophobic feelings on sexual function. Sex therapists are well aware of how negative messages received and internalized can interfere with joyful sexual expression. In the same way, incorporation of antihomosexual messages from parents, peers, or culture can impede sexual functioning in the gay clients even if they have acknowledged their gay identities on most other levels. Until recently this was particularly true for lesbians, since for them the antigay messages were merely an overlay of repressive antisexual attitudes with which all women are socialized.

> *Claudia* came to therapy reporting arousal and desire difficulties. She appeared to be completely comfortable with her gay identity, and her relationship seemed stable and satisfying. During a hypnotherapy session, she remembered and relived an early adolescent incident during which she was discovered in a sexual encounter by the mother of the girl with whom she was involved. She came to realize that that experience had registered with her as a "body memory" despite the fact that she had long ago stopped consciously feeling shame about her lesbianism. After repeated work on these early antigay messages, she was able to be more sexually responsive.

> *Marie* was confused about the negative feelings she had about having sex because she felt otherwise so good about being a lesbian. In therapy, she spent a good deal of time recounting her mother's disapproval of her lesbianism, and eventually she was able to "kick her mother out of the bedroom."

In recent years, AIDS has added such a stigma to sex for many gay men that their sexual functioning is also greatly impaired, not only from the association of AIDS, sex, and toxicity but also because AIDS has caused a recurrence of earlier homophobic feelings. For example, nearly all of the gay men with AIDS I have counseled eventually express self-hating and antigay feelings, usually connected with religious teachings and feelings about an afterlife. Many of these men were open and proud of their sexuality until they became ill.

> *Gene*, a client in an AIDS support group for 2 years, seemed to be a model of healthy gay pride. He overcame the feelings of toxicity he experienced shortly after his diagnosis and his fears of rejection from other gay men and eventually was able to have "safe sex" encounters with other gay men with AIDS. On his deathbed, he asked for counseling and only at this point poured out a torrent of fears that he would go to hell after his death, punished by God for his "perversion" and "promiscuity."

> *Don's* sexual drive diminished greatly after he learned of his HIV antibody-seropositive status. He felt dirty, unclean, and full of shame. He became unable to have one-to-one sex and only frequented group sex "J.O." clubs, although he greatly missed the intimacy of one-to-one encounters. At one J.O. party, he was asked for a date by a man he later learned was seronegative. Don was so moved by the discovery that this man still considered him sexually desirable despite his "contamination" that his sense of sexual self-worth blossomed, and he again was able to lead a more fully expressive sexual life.

Gay Couples

Therapists who work with gay, lesbian, and heterosexual couples are often struck by the *absence* of gender-specific roles among gay and lesbian couples and, therefore, the absence of some clinical issues related to these roles. Before the advent of the gay liberation movement, gay couples often tried to mimic heterosexual marriage. For example, in the "butch–femme" lesbian relationships that at one time were prevalent but are now rarely encountered, the "femme" dressed in feminine ways and was subservient to the more masculine-appearing butch, and she stayed home while the butch supported both of them financially. Now, even in couples where the partners seem role stereotyped in physical appearance, these apparent roles rarely hold up in actual behavior. The partner who looks masculine may be the one who enjoys children and keeping house, whereas the woman who loves lipstick and high heels may also be the one who does household plumbing repairs. Most importantly, it is rare to find one member of a gay or lesbian couple totally financially dependent on the other, and it is less common for a gay or lesbian household to contain children. Thus, gay couples obviously are less likely to stay together because one person is financially dependent on the other or "for the sake of the kids." These differences make the power dynamics in gay couples somewhat different and, interestingly, make the quality of their sexual/intimate relationship assume a higher priority than in many more traditional heterosexual marriages.

However, even if roles in same-sex relationships tend to be a bit more variable and fluid, in general, roles in the bedroom may get rigidified. This problem is a bit easier to deal with in same-sex couples. For one thing, same-sex partners are not dealing with opposing sexual role expectations (e.g., male must initiate, female must be submissive) as are heterosexual partners.

Gay men and lesbians tend to have a more varied sexual repertoire than heterosexuals; penetration is not the main focus of sexual activity for either men or women. Lesbians, and especially gay men, often have a knowledge of sexual technique that may surpass that of the therapist, and because there is nothing in gay sex comparable to the heterosexual emphasis on vaginal intercourse, they may be more willing to experiment with new sexual approaches. Gay male couples (and some lesbian couples) often have sexually nonexclusive relationships. Both men and women in gay relationships sometimes request help in successfully conducting nonmonogamous relationships within the context of a primary commitment to one partner. In these cases most nongay therapists have to examine their own beliefs about nonmonogamy. Most people, including sex therapists, are raised to regard nonmonogamy as sinful or destructive and are reluctant to acknowledge that sexual openness can work quite well for many couples provided that conflicts arising from jealousy, etcetera, are adequately dealt with.

Often the therapist can help the couple construct "rules of conduct" for nonmonogamy that will minimize pain and strife, and when nonmonogamy works it often actually enhances the sexual relationship of the primary partners. For example, with the aid of a counselor, Joe and Harold, monogamous partners for 2 years, negotiated a transition to nonmonogamy that began with joint expeditions to J.O. parties, moved to "three-ways," and eventually permitted both Joe and Harold to have independent sexual contacts provided that these contacts were "one-night stands." Sally and Jessica were in conflict because Sally felt unable to commit to monogamy, and Jessica was doubtful about her ability to handle her jealousy. In therapy, the two women negotiated an agreement in which Sally was permitted outside affairs as long as Jessica never knew about them; that is, Sally could not see women who were mutual acquaintances and must conduct her affairs so that Jessica would not find out. Nonmonogamy tends to be more common among gay male couples and also tends to be more successful. In large part, this is because gay men (like their heterosexual counterparts) can often separate sex and love quite easily and are satisfied with extramarital encounters that are purely sexual. By contrast, lesbians (like most women) fuse sex and love and tend to want not casual sexual encounters but "affairs" that are potentially more threatening to the primary relationship.

Just as nonmonogamy is a common issue for many gay male couples, lesbian couples often suffer from fusion or the existence of such intense closeness and intimacy that the individual identities of the two women become completely submerged in the couple (Nichols, 1988). Fusion is often an underlying cause of inhibited sexual desire in lesbian couples, the most frequent sexual complaint among gay women. Female couples tend to have less frequent sex than either heterosexuals or gay men (Blumstein & Schwartz, 1983).

Incest is often implicated in the sexual dysfunction of lesbians (and sometimes gay men) and is discussed in detail in Chapter 11 of this volume. Herman (1982) has speculated that incest may be more common in the childhood experiences of gay as opposed to heterosexual women. Herman speculates that for women with a bisexual potential, the choice to relate to women as opposed to men may be an adaptive mechanism on the part of the victim, whose perpetrator was almost always male. It may be an attempt to compartmentalize the incest trauma by associating the incest behavior with only men, not women. Unfortunately, this often does not work; incest memories may not be so easily contained. In the author's experience, one of the worst effects of incest on adult sexual functioning is that often the incest experiences and the perpetrator himself were indelibly eroticized for the victim, so that she may not only be plagued by memories of the experience but find, usually to her horror, that fragments of these experiences may emerge as sexual fantasies during masturbation or lovemaking. This can be doubly disturbing to a lesbian because it is not only the incest that has been eroticized but the *male* perpetrator. Moreover, in attempting to avoid the unwanted emergence of these erotic images, many women repress *all* sexual desires or simply avoid sex. This effect is discussed in more detail in a case example later in this chapter.

Other Issues: Specific Techniques

There is some speculation that alcoholism may be more prevalent within the gay community than among heterosexuals because of the dependence many gays still have on gay bars to give them social outlets. To the extent that this is true, the impact of alcoholism, and sobriety in those whose sexual functioning was previously linked to alcohol, is encountered more frequently among gay clients. Gays in the initial stages of sobriety, like heterosexuals, often find that their sexual response has become so linked to drinking that they must literally "relearn" how to become aroused. In addition, gays often encounter homophobic responses from the staff of alcohol treatment facilities or among members of Alcoholics Anonymous. This can make them feel that their sobriety is in conflict with their sexual orientation. Fortunately, the proliferation of gay AA groups in recent years has eased this conflict somewhat.

Finally, sex therapists must remember that the types of sexual dysfunctions will be different among gay and lesbian clients. Vaginismus and dyspareunia are almost never presenting problems with lesbians; women who suffer from these dysfunctions usually avoid penetration. An aversion to oral sex, however, is a frequent complaint of both lesbians and gay men, since oral sex tends to be an important component of the sexual repertoires of both. And although less frequent nowadays, gay men still sometimes seek help for difficulty performing anal sex.

Some specialized sex therapy techniques may be helpful in working with gay, lesbian, and bisexual clients. For example, with gay and bisexual clients I use a special questionnaire that traces the development of sexual orientation identity, detects discrepancies in orientation that may be potentially ego-dystonic (e.g., high levels of heterosexual sexual fantasy in a lesbian-identified woman), and probes for the existence of internalized homophobia. Another questionnaire includes questions about participation in such activities as "water sports" or enemas. When I probe for a history of sex-negative messages, I also probe for a history of gay-negative messages and am sensitive to the ways in which early gay sexual experiences, which are frequently more conflict-ridden and furtive than early heterosexual experiences, may affect current sexual function. For example, some gay men, as adolescents and young adults, "warded off" a gay identity while engaging in homosexual behavior by, for example, only having sex with strangers and never engaging in acts of intimacy and affection like kissing. Later on, such men may have difficulty experiencing erotic feelings toward an intimate partner or accepting such feelings from another.

Many lesbians avoided a gay identity when young by having close affectionate relationships with other women but never engaging in genital sex. Some of these women may be extremely affectionate and sensual in their partner relationships but have difficulty in genitally focused sex. One female client never allowed herself to be touched, although she was quite happy to make love to her partner. She finally revealed that she had been particularly influenced by religious injunctions against homosexuality and had developed her touch aversion because she reasoned that God might forgive her for her homosexuality if she herself did not desire any sexual pleasure from her lesbian relationships. Another gay male client had had so many years of "tea-room" sex (public toilets) while fighting a homosexual identity that he had difficulty having sex lying down on a bed.

As the examples indicate, much of the differences in the way gay clients are treated in sex therapy derive from the special dynamics of being gay in a homophobic society or from various aspects of gay and lesbian culture. I recently worked with a lesbian couple who, at the start of their relationship, used many sadomasochistic sexual techniques but were currently having very infrequent sexual contacts. On questioning, both women revealed some ambivalence about the normalcy of their S/M practices, which mostly involved dominance/submission and light spankings. In addition, the women had fairly inflexible "top–bottom" roles, but the "top" had wanted to engage in sexual acts normally recognized as "bottom," such as being spanked. Therapeutic interventions included giving "permission" for their S/M sex and helping them devise creative S/M "scenes" that would provide mutual pleasure, such as having the "top" *order* her partner to spank her.

Another client, Danny, a gay man of 26, had never had a sexual experience of any kind and was afraid to approach men at bars or gay organizations. He was convinced that his lack of experience would be obvious to any partner, and he feared ridicule and rejection. Treatment included getting him to agree to buy the sexual services of a "male escort" for his first encounter and then teaching him, step by step, how to do this. Danny was told which gay magazines to buy, how to interpret the escort ads, what to ask when he called these men, and so on. Danny's fear of rejection was so great that he insisted on telling the "escorts" he called that he was a virgin, and he arranged to buy the services of a man who, Danny felt, responded warmly and empathetically to him on the phone. Danny's encounter was a success; not only did Danny enjoy the sex, but the "escort" proved as warm in person as he had been on the phone, cuddling Danny afterwards and assuring Danny that his sexual technique was competent. This experience gave Danny the self-confidence to begin to approach gay men in social situations.

With many gay men, the advent of AIDS has fostered the development of sex therapy techniques that help to overcome the fears of contagion and that literally teach men new, safer sexual repertoires. Quite naturally, many men fear *getting* infected. Ironically, fear of transmission often seems greater among men who are seropositive or have been diagnosed with AIDS or ARC; these men fear *giving* the virus to others. Often, the first response of frightened men is to avoid all sexual practices, even those that are completely safe such as frottage or mutual masturbation. With some men, therapy that is primarily educational can be very helpful. A knowledgeable clinician can explain carefully the mechanisms of AIDS transmission; typically, people need to hear this repeated several times before they assimilate it fully. There are now a number of safe-sex erotic videos available for gay men, and the therapist can recommend these or show them in the office. These videos often quite effectively portray, for example, the use of condoms in a way that is erotic, or nonpenetrative sex that is attractive and stimulating. The therapist can role play with the client the negotiating of safe sex with a potential partner or teach a client how to "date" without having to have a sexual encounter immediately. In many large cities, gay organizations regularly conduct open seminars on eroticizing safe sex, negotiating safe sex, and "Dating 101," and it can be very affirming for a client to participate in these workshops with other gay men.

At other times, education is not enough, because AIDS fears are actually bringing to the surface more deep-seated problems. John came for treatment because he compulsively engaged in anonymous unsafe sex despite his fears of contagion. One day he brought in his personal journal, which was replete with passages in which John concluded that he deserved to die for the "sin" of being gay. Another gay man, Philip, had spent 15 years using "fast food sex" as a staple of his life. Although he gave this up out of fear of AIDS, he subsequently entered a deep depression. Therapy helped him realize that for years, most of his social and intimacy needs had been met by his casual sexual encounters, helping him avoid other, more threatening kinds of intimacy. AIDS forced Philip to learn new, nonsexual ways of becoming intimate. Peter entered treatment because his sexual script was very rigid and limited to performing fellatio and swallowing the semen of his partner. Therapy included a behavioral program in which he not only experimented with new techniques but also changed his old script by increments: first, to swallow only some semen, then to have ejaculation into his mouth but not swallow at all, and finally, to enjoy having his partner ejaculate on him, not in him.

In summary, with the advent of AIDS, therapists must be able to help gay men develop new sexual scripts and repertoires (Gagnon, Rosen, & Leiblum, 1982) while they are grieving the loss of sexual behaviors that are no longer viable. Although gay men have the advantage of having rather varied repertoires to begin with, such re-education may be difficult for those men whose scripts are limited and unsafe, for example, men whose primary activity has been anal receptive or swallowing semen. Help is needed as well to teach gay men an entirely new way of approaching sex with new sexual partners. Many gay men, reluctant now to jump into bed with every new person they meet, must be taught courtship and dating skills, skills that heterosexual men learn in adolescence. As one newly single gay male commented: "It's all entirely different. Before, I met a man, went to bed with him, and if the sex was good, I'd decide to see him again. Now, I'm learning to date and get to know someone before I decide whether or not to have sex. This way is much more personal and intimate." And, one might add, much more anxiety-inducing for men who are accustomed to having their sex without intimate, vulnerable self-exposure.

Finally, and sadly, sex therapists must learn to deal with a new cause of inhibited sexual desire in gay men: depression resulting from grief over the loss of their age mates, multiple bereavements, fears of their own mortality, and from seeing a whole generation of their peers wiped out by AIDS.

CASE EXAMPLES

In order to illustrate more completely some important issues in sex therapy with gay/lesbian/bisexual clients, four cases are presented.

Diane and Kathleen: A Case with a Positive Outcome

Diane and Kathleen were a lesbian couple who had lived together for 4 years when they contacted the author for sex therapy. They complained of a drastic reduction in the frequency of sexual activity over the course of their relationship. Whereas, initially, they had enjoyed sex at least twice a week, in the last 2 years sexual exchanges occurred only once every 2 or 3 months. In other respects, they had few complaints about their relationship.

In talking with this couple, it became apparent that both of them perceived Diane to be responsible for the sexual problems in their relationship. Diane had been seen in therapy previously because of a history of depression resulting from father–daughter incest. Two individual sessions with Diane seemed to substantiate this hypothesis. For instance, during hypnotic age regression, she recalled that, as a child, her father used to approach her for sex by coming up behind her. With her current lover, Diane was very distressed if Kathleen approached her from behind and put her arms around her waist. Similarly, some of Diane's conflicts about sex were clearly related to her guilt about having enjoyed some of the incest experiences and to the fact that she still had sexual fantasies about men and sometimes even about her father. However, after two individual sessions with Diane, I insisted that Kathleen accompany her, and it quickly emerged that Kathleen was contributing to the problem.

Kathleen's first lesbian relationship had ended in a slow, agonizing way when her first lover left her for a man after deceiving her and denying her attractions to men for over a year. The first signs of the demise of this relationship had been the lover's increasingly frequent sexual rejection of Kathleen. Consequently, Kathleen was extremely threatened by Diane's fantasies about men, and Diane's sexual rejection of Kathleen seemed to her a repeat of her earlier loss. Diane was able to detect Kathleen's fears despite Kathleen's efforts to be supportive, and this merely increased Diane's sense of hopelessness and depression.

From that point on therapy consisted of a combination of couple sessions and individual sessions with both partners. In couple sessions, homework assignments were given, and results were discussed. Individual sessions with Kathleen focused on helping her resolve the feelings about her first lover so that she, finally, could not only understand but really feel that her current situation was different. Individual sessions with Diane were primarily hypnotherapy sessions in which she uncovered and attempted to resolve memories of her incest experiences.

Homework assignments included traditional sensate-focus exercises as well as other behavioral exercises tailored to the couple. Exercises were used not only to "recondition" the couple's sexual relationship but also to pinpoint and uncover sources of anxiety. For example, one exercise was designed to deal with the anxiety Diane experienced when Kathleen was physically affectionate without Diane expecting it, for example, when Kathleen approached her from behind and touched her. I assigned Kathleen the task of deliberately approaching Diane this way several times a week, taught Diane a rapid self-hypnosis technique, and then instructed Diane to use this technique to relax herself when Kathleen touched her and she became anxious. At the same time I worked with Kathleen individually to help her cope with the overwhelming feelings of rejection she experienced during this exercise when she sensed Diane's "tightening up" with anxiety. In another instance, a sensate-focus exercise resulted in Diane's developing stomach pains when Kathleen touched her anywhere near her abdomen. In an individual trance session, Diane recovered memories of her father slipping into her room at night, putting his hand under the covers, and caressing her abdomen and genitals.

Therapy with this couple lasted for 8 months, at the end of which time they were having regular sexual exchanges that were mutually enjoyable. It should be noted, however, that therapy in this kind of situation, where part of the problem involves an earlier severe trauma such as incest, can often take much longer. The fact that the couple relationship was so strong and loving in nonsexual areas speeded the course of treatment considerably.

Stephanie and Chris: An Unsuccessful Case

Stephanie and Chris, coupled for 2 years, also requested therapy because of the absence of sex in their relationship. In the first interview, they looked more like "loving roommates" than lovers. Stephanie reported never experiencing sexual desire for Chris. Nevertheless, the relationship was important to both of them, and they feared that the lack of sex would signal the demise of the partnership. After the first joint interview, I saw first Chris and then Stephanie alone for individual sessions. In Chris's interview, it became apparent that she had a history of becoming attached to women who were emotionally or sexually unavailable to her. The reasons for this pattern were not clear.

Stephanie's interview was more unusual. She was in her mid-30s and had been in individual therapy for 8 years, primarily because she had a long history of becoming involved with men for whom she felt great passion but who usually abused and then eventually abandoned her. Quite consciously, she decided she *wanted* to be a lesbian because she no longer wanted to deal with the problems encountered in her relationships with men. She did experience occasional erotic attractions to women, although not nearly as intense as those she felt for men. She had met Chris in a women's "coming out" group; Chris was Stephanie's first female lover. In the individual interview, Stephanie revealed that even in the initial phases of their relationship she had felt only mild sexual desires for Chris. This frightened her because she feared both the end of her relationship with Chris and being forced to face the fact that she was not "really" a lesbian. She felt she had "given up" on men and that lesbian relationships represented her only chance of having a nurturing, successful relationship. In this session, I acknowledged that indeed there did not seem to be much evidence that Stephanie felt strong desire for women, that she might never feel strong desire for *any* woman, and that she could be faced with two alternatives: having warm, close, but basically nonsexual relationships with women or having passionate but difficult relationships with men.

Later that week Stephanie called to inform me angrily that they would not be returning to therapy. She was furious about my statements about her sexual orientation and accused me of "putting thoughts into her head."

In looking at this case retrospectively, two mistakes seem obvious. First was my haste in judging the limits of Stephanie's sexual desires for women. Perhaps Stephanie's erotic attractions to women were to an extent being inhibited by, for example, some internalized homophobia, or perhaps Stephanie feared really confronting intimacy now that she finally had a partner who would be loving rather than abusive. Her lack of sexual desire might have been a distancing technique. Perhaps the couple needed to be taught sexual enhancement skills to supplement an overly narrow repertoire. Second, even if my first assessment had been accurate, it was clear that my timing was terrible. Stephanie was unable to tolerate my message, but, if the message was accurate, she might have been able to reach a similar conclusion herself later in therapy.

Raymond: A Successful Case

Raymond, a 27-year-old bisexual married man, had developed erectile problems with his wife during the preceding year. Prior to contacting the author, he had been in therapy with two other therapists for a total of nearly

6 months of treatment. The first therapist had used exclusively behavioral techniques to overcome the erectile failure, but without success. The second therapist saw his bisexuality as a pathological symptom of his fear of intimacy with his wife and tried to analyze Raymond's bisexual feelings from that perspective. In the first interview with Raymond (his wife did not come initially), I suspected that his impotence was tied to his bisexuality, specifically to his fears that his gay impulses would "overwhelm" him and cause him to destroy his relationship with his wife, Sandra.

An extensive, detailed sex history convinced me that Raymond was, indeed, bisexual (what I have labeled a "heterosexual bisexual" earlier in this chapter) rather than a gay man trying to repress his homosexuality. His first attractions and sexual experiences were with girls in early adolescence, and by midadolescence he had become conscious of gay attractions as well. He loved his wife very much, and his sexual attraction to her seemed genuine. However, he had never really understood or accepted the "gay part" of himself, although his wife knew of his gay feelings and experiences before their marriage. He tried to repress his attractions to men, but shortly before his impotence problem began he had begun to have occasional homosexual fantasies during masturbation or during sex with his wife. During the last 6 months, he had, without his wife's knowledge, rented a gay pornographic movie and become aroused watching it. He had also unwittingly stumbled on two men having sex in a public bathroom and masturbated while watching them.

Treatment consisted of eight sessions, six alone with Raymond and two with him and his wife. Behavioral techniques were not used in therapy. Rather, Raymond was helped to accept the gay part of himself. He dealt with his internalized homophobia and recognized that accepting his homosexual erotic attraction did not mean that he needed to act on it. With this realization, Raymond began to be able to maintain erections during sexual activities with his wife. Following two sessions, Raymond's wife, Sandra, was invited to join him in order to deal with her feelings about his bisexuality. Sandra was very uncomfortable accepting that her husband was bisexual and worried that he would begin to have homosexual extramarital relations. It was suggested to Sandra that Raymond's guilt over his homosexual attractions had reached an obsessive level and that, at this point, his guilt and concomitant sexual dysfunction were more likely to destroy the marriage than was his bisexuality. Sandra accepted this reframing, and her acceptance reduced pressure on Raymond. Raymond has not experienced any other instances of erectile dysfunction since this brief treatment ended.

Several points are salient in this case. First is the obvious ineffectiveness of purely behavioral techniques in a situation with such psychological complexity. Second, the failure of Raymond's first two therapists to confront his bisexuality directly is an indication of how difficult it is even for clinicians to conceptualize a continuous, rather than dichotomous, view of sexual orientation. Third is the importance of helping bisexuals accept both "parts" of themselves even if they choose only to act on one constellation of attractions. Indeed, Raymond's difficulty in accepting his "gay self" may have made his same-sex attractions assume far more importance than they would have had otherwise.

But finally, I would like to suggest that I have oversimplified this case both in this presentation and in my feedback to Raymond and Sandra. Although in the short run treatment was effective, the final chapter on the story of Raymond's sexual orientation has yet to be written. In fact, Raymond consulted with me recently to tell me that although his sexual functioning was still satisfactory and pleasing to him, he had been speculating that someday he might have a much stronger desire to act on his gay attractions; did I think this was likely? I responded that although I could not predict the likelihood of that occurring, sexual orientation for some people was somewhat fluid and changeable, and it was certainly possible that someday he might want and need to have the experience of having a gay lover or even assuming a gay identity.

Tom and Phillip: An Unsuccessful Case

Tom and Phillip, both in their early 40s, had ended their relationship of 10 years a year earlier and were presently consulting the author in order to attempt a reconciliation. Their sexual problem involved discrepant sexual desire, a difficulty that had been problematic throughout their years together.

This case seemed very complex right from the beginning. Both men agreed that Tom had lost desire for Phillip but that Phillip still wanted sex with Tom. Their previous relationship had been nonmonogamous, and it seemed possible that jealousy and hurt feelings might have harmed their relationship. Tom had been addicted to cocaine during several years of the relationship, and his recovery may have been implicated in his loss of desire. Phillip appeared to have a drinking problem. Tom had been physically and sexually abused by his father during childhood. Because Phillip in some ways represented a fatherlike image for Tom, the incest memories might have had a negative impact on Tom's desire.

After an initial joint assessment interview and individual assessment sessions with both men, I began sensate-focus assignments. Because both men had incorporated S/M practices in their sex life and found S/M "scenes" to be their best sex, I began to discuss with Tom and Phillip designing "homework" that incorporated S/M into the activities.

At this point, Tom asked for a session with me alone. During this session, he revealed that he had only agreed to try to restore the couple relationship because several months earlier Phillip had been diagnosed with ARC. Tom and Phillip had remained good friends after the breakup, which had been initiated by Tom and never fully accepted by Phillip. Tom felt such warm devotion to Phillip that he decided to restore the couple so that he could care for Phillip during his illness and possible death. However, Tom reported that he had lost desire for Phillip long before the relationship ended. Since sex therapy began, Tom had increasingly come to feel that his plan, although altruistic, was not feasible. After this session Tom revealed his decision to Phillip, and the two men once again parted.

It is difficult to assess why treatment with these men was unsuccessful, in part because it was difficult to determine when the desire discrepancy began and what caused it. Tom, who had been tested and was seronegative for HIV antibodies, was undoubtedly aware long before the relationship originally ended of Phillip's risk factors. Perhaps Tom's original decision to leave—and/or his second decision to leave—was in part precipitated by a fear of contracting AIDS from Phillip. Perhaps Tom's straightforward explanation that he was unable to carry out his altruistic plan was accurate. It is possible that he could not carry out his plan because of low sexual desire, but it is even more plausible that he feared the prospect of caretaking Phillip throughout the course of a disease that is often gruesome and painful not only for the victim but also for those who observe the dying process. In another, similar case, the "well" lover ceased having sex with his sick partner immediately after the partner's AIDS diagnosis, broke off the relationship three times because he could not tolerate watching his lover die, and returned three times out of guilt. Ultimately, in that case, the "well" man had his lover institutionalized so that his suffering was out of sight. One important factor the clinician must keep in mind when dealing with sexual dysfunction in couples where one or both partners have AIDS, ARC, or are seropositive is that in addition to dealing with "ordinary" factors that might cause sexual difficulties, one is potentially contending with a host of issues revolving around fear of death and dying.

SUMMARY AND CONCLUSIONS

The prevailing wisdom about psychological treatment of gay men, lesbians, and bisexuals has changed enormously over the past few decades. From considering homosexuality an illness itself, we have progressed to the more liberal but not entirely accurate view that gay people are "normal" and "just like everyone else." Finally, we have begun to see nonheterosexual sexual orientations as "equal but different." This chapter attempts to support the view that gayness is not simply a difference in choice of gender of love or sexual object but, in fact, constitutes an *identity* not dissimilar to ethnic or racial identity. From this perspective, clinicians who want to be effective with gay, lesbian, and bisexual clients must familiarize themselves with gay culture, movies, and trends.

In no clinical area is this more true than in sex therapy, in part because even same-sex sexual acts are by nature different from heterosexual sexual acts. Within gay culture, sexuality carries with it different meanings for gay men and gay women, and is constantly evolving as gay identity, a relatively new phenomenon, evolves and changes. It is hoped that this chapter provides a context from which the nongay (and gay) sex therapist can more readily interpret the behavior of gay clients. Early in the chapter, a historical overview described the changes in gay male sexuality from liberation to AIDS, and in lesbian sexuality from feminism to an expanded sexual repertoire. Specific issues in sex therapy have been described with examples that I hope are illuminating and instructive.

Because this is a book for sex therapists, not sex historians, this chapter has of necessity focused on what is problematic and dysfunctional. Unfortunately, what is lacking is an exposition of how much the sex therapist's own understanding of sex can be enhanced by working with gay clients. We have all been raised with a heterosexual model of sexuality, and it is sometimes hard to see just how narrow and restrictive the heterosexual model is. In part because gay sex *cannot* precisely duplicate the physical acts of heterosexual sex, gay men and lesbians have literally invented new methods of "doing sex." The gay man who takes his partner through a 5-hour "bondage trip" has invented an altered-state sexual experience. The lesbian sex radical who penetrates her lover's vagina with her entire hand has taken female sexuality beyond boundaries few women ever cross.

Recently, the author of this chapter has begun to treat more heterosexual couples for sexual dysfunction, and her background in gay and lesbian sex therapy has provided valuable assistance. From this background, it is striking to note how pervasively heterosexual sex is focused on penile-vaginal penetration with intravaginal ejaculation—a very narrow script indeed. Activities that might in and of themselves constitute a fully satisfying sexual experience for a gay or lesbian couple are devalued by being labeled "foreplay" in a heterosexual context. The net result of this for heterosexuals is a greatly limited sexual repertoire. This can be corroborated by anyone attempting to do AIDS prevention work with heterosexuals. This task is made more difficult by the narrow focus of most heterosexuals on orgasm-centered, penile–vaginal sex. The clinician who chooses to do sex therapy with gay, lesbian, and bisexual clients will probably discover that his or her own sexual awareness is increased manyfold. In this situation, the helper is truly being taught by the helped.

REFERENCES

Bell, A. P., & Weinberg, M. S. (1978). *Homosexualities: A study of diversity among men and women.* New York: Simon & Schuster.

Blumstein, P., & Schwartz, P. (1983). *American couples.* New York: William Morrow.

Boswell, J. (1980). *Christianity, social tolerance, and homosexuality.* Chicago: University of Chicago Press.

Cass, V. (1979). Homosexual identity formation: A theoretical model. *Journal of Homosexuality*, *4*, 219–233.

Echols, A. (1984). The taming of the id: Feminist sexual politics 1968–1973. In C. S. Vance (Ed.), *Pleasure and danger: Exploring female sexuality* (pp. 50–72). Boston: Routledge & Kegan Paul.

Faderman, L. (1984). The "new" gay lesbian. *Journal of Homosexuality*, *10*(3/4), 85–96.

Gagnon, J. H., Rosen, R. C., & Leiblum, S. R. (1982). Cognitive and social aspects of sexual dysfunction: Sexual scripts in sex therapy. *Journal of Sex and Marital Therapy*. *8*, 44–56.

Herdt, G. (1987). *The Sambia: Ritual and gender in New Guinea*. New York: Holt, Reinhart and Winston.

Herman, J. (1982). *Father–daughter incest*. Cambridge: Harvard University Press.

Hyde, J. S. (1982). *Understanding human sexuality*. New York: Thomas Y. Crowell.

Jay, K., & Young, A. (1979). *The gay report*. New York: Summit Books

Katz, J. (1976). *Gay American history*. New York: Thomas Y. Crowell.

Kinsey, A. (1948). *Sexual behavior in the human male*. Philadelphia: W. B. Saunders.

Klein, F., & Wolf, T. J. (Eds.). (1985). Bisexualities: Theory and research. *Journal of Homosexuality*, *11*(1/2).

McWhirter, D., & Mattison, A. (1984). *The male couple*. Englewood Cliffs, NJ: Prentice-Hall.

Morin, J. (1981). *Anal pleasure and health*. Burlington, CA: Down There Press.

Nichols, M. (1988). Low sexual desire in lesbian couples. In S. Leiblum & R. Rosen (Eds.), *Sexual desire disorders* (pp. 387–412). New York: Guilford Press.

Rubin, G. (1984). Thinking sex. Notes for a radical theory of the politics of sexuality. In C. S. Vance (Ed.), *Pleasure and danger* (pp. 267–319). Boston: Routledge & Kegan Paul.

Townsend, L. (1972). *The leatherman's handbook*. New York: Modernismo Publications

11

Impact of Sexual Abuse
on Sexual Functioning

JUDITH V. BECKER

The number of female survivors of sexual coercion is staggering, and it is not surprising that victims of coercive, intrusive, and often terrifying sexual assaults experience sexual problems as adults. In this chapter, Judith Becker, one of the foremost researchers and clinicians in this area, reviews the common sequelae of incest and stranger sexual abuse on sexual response. She suggests that sexual inhibitions and anxieties may endure for many years post-assault because they do not get disclosed or discussed with helping professionals.

Becker suggests that it is essential that clinicians inquire about whether new patients have ever been the recipient of unwanted sexual acts. The use of the term "unwanted" is deliberate, since many women do not identify early sexual violations from boyfriends, lovers, or even husbands as rape, believing that rape is only committed by strangers. Drawing the connection between present sexual difficulties and past assault experiences is important. Interestingly, Becker does not recommend intensive probing for the details of vague recollections of previous sexual assault. Rather, she suggests that it is more important to determine the specific stimuli or behaviors that are maintaining the present sexual problem.

In treatment, Becker recommends the use of a multicomponent 10-session group program that can be adapted to various programs and individuals. The goal of treatment is to assist women in regaining control of their sexuality through gradual exposure to fear-inducing sexual situations, behaviors, and interactions. The program consists of a number of behavioral interventions including systematic desensitization, assertion training, and body-image and sensuality exercises. This program has been quite successful in facilitating anxiety reduction in both heterosexual and homosexual survivors. Although considerable success is achieved in creating greater feelings of autonomy and control, Becker notes that some women continue to have problems in relating sexually to their partners.

The most successful outcomes are typically achieved with women who have had positive sexual experiences prior to the sexual assault and who currently have supportive and loving partners. As might be expected, less positive outcomes are achieved with women who have had extensive histories of negative sexual experiences and are presently living in a nonsupportive interpersonal situation.

Judith V. Becker, Ph.D., is Professor of Psychology in Psychiatry at the College of Physicians and Surgeons at Columbia University and is Director of the New York State Psychiatric Institute. She has worked extensively with sex offenders and victims for more than a decade and has published widely in this area.

Rape and child molestation are major problems in American society. Studies indicate that from 5% to 22% of adult women have been sexually assaulted (Kilpatrick, Best, & Veronen, 1984; Koss, 1983). Prevalence studies of child molestation indicate that between 6% and 62% of females and 3% to 31% of males have been sexually abused as children (Finkelhor, 1986). Over the past 18 years, a considerable amount of literature and numerous clinical research studies have been published on the impact of child sexual abuse and rape (for reviews see Finkelhor, 1986; Steketee & Foa, 1987). Both long- and short-term responses to child sexual abuse and rape have been described. These include fear and anxiety, depression, impaired social functioning, sleep disturbance, somatic disturbances, and sexual dysfunctions (Finkelhor, 1986; Steketee & Foa, 1987).

Research with sexual abuse/assault survivors has demonstrated that sexual problems may be an immediate consequence of an assault and may endure for many years post-assault (Becker, Skinner, Abel, & Cichon, 1986; Feldman-Summers, Gordon, & Meagher, 1979; McGuire & Wagner, 1978).

In a retrospective study of 372 sexual assault survivors and 99 women with no history of sexual assault, Becker et al. (1986) found that 58.6% of the sexual assault survivors experienced sexual dysfunctions compared to 17.2% of the nonassaulted women. Of the 219 sexually dysfunctional assault survivors, 69.4% reported that the development of sexual problems was related to their assaults. Furthermore, multiple sexual problems were common among the survivors. Two or more sexual problems were reported by 66.4% of these women, with 30.9% having two problems, 23% having three, 19% having four, and 26.5% having five.

Based on the type of assault experienced, each woman was classified in a category such as a rape (vaginal, oral, and/or anal penetration or attempted penetration by a stranger, husband, or partner), incest (sexual abuse as a child by a relative), or mixed-category (both rape and incest survivors) victim. A comparison of the incidence of sexual problems across the three subgroups indicated that women whose assault history included incest were more likely to experience assault-related sexual problems than were survivors with no history of incest. The most common sexual dysfunctions (88.2% of women) involved response-inhibiting reactions including fear of sex, arousal dysfunctions, and desire dysfunctions. Only 25.2% of the survivors reported orgasmic dysfunctions; 12.7% experienced intromission problems; and 19.3% reported other sexual problems (Becker, Skinner, Abel, Axelrod, & Cichon, 1984).

This chapter addresses clinical issues in working with sexual assault survivors and describes a time-limited multicomponent treatment program for sexual assault survivors with sexual problems.

CLINICAL ISSUES

A considerable number of sexual assault survivors seen by sex therapists experience an acute, chronic, or delayed posttraumatic stress disorder (PTSD). Consequently, the sex therapist should be familiar with symptoms and diagnostic criteria for this disorder. The diagnostic criteria for PTSD can be found in the *Diagnostic and Statistical Manual of Mental Disorders* (DSM-III-R; American Psychiatric Association, 1987).

When a sexual assault survivor is engaging in sexual activity, she may experience intrusive thoughts about the sexual abuse. Some women will avoid sexual activity because the sexual assault might be recalled. For those women who dealt with the assault by dissociating, the dissociation may occur when they are engaging in lovemaking with a consensual partner.

Kilpatrick, Veronen, and Best (1985) present an excellent description of major rape-induced problems from a PTSD perspective as well as a learning-theory model of the etiology of rape-induced problems. These authors state:

> We believe that rape victims' fear and anxiety problems are largely acquired through classical conditioning, stimulus generalization, and second-order conditioning. Victims perceive rape as a situation in which their physical well-being and even their lives are in jeopardy. . . . Any stimuli associated with the rape become conditioned stimuli that acquire the capacity to evoke fear and anxiety as well. (pp. 118–119)

Since sexual stimuli are present in all rapes, it is not unusual for a woman to develop fear, anxiety, and avoidance responses to sexual stimuli.

The behavioral treatment for PTSD has included systematic desensitization (Frank & Stewart, 1983a), cognitive therapy (Frank & Stewart, 1983b), and stress inoculation (Kilpatrick, Veronen, & Resick, 1982).

An important issue for therapists in treating clients is learning whether the client has brought a criminal or civil suit against the assailant; in such cases therapy notes may be subject to subpoena. It is important to advise the client of this before recording any information. The client then can request that certain material not be recorded if she feels it is not in her best interest.

For example, I had evaluated and treated a woman who had been victimized by a stranger and who later brought a civil suit. In taking her sexual history, I had obtained information regarding her previous sexual activity. In criminal cases in many states, prior sexual history would not be admissible. However, in this civil case, my therapy notes were subpoenaed as part of the discovery process. The client was understandably upset about the thought of this material being presented in a courtroom. Fortunately, the case was settled out of court, and the client was spared that unpleasant experience. The client's involvement in court proceedings may also increase her fear levels (Kilpatrick, Veronen, & Resick, 1979).

It is common for clients to have seen other counselors or therapists previously. Historically, therapists have not been trained routinely to question clients as to whether they have been sexual assault victims. The client may not have discussed her assault in detail with other mental health professionals and may welcome the opportunity to do so at this time. Unfortunately, in some cases where clients have disclosed the abuse/assault to a therapist, the therapist has served to further traumatize her by either overtly or covertly suggesting that she had initiated or invited the abuse/assault. In other instances, therapists have suggested that the client engage in sex with the therapist to assist her in overcoming her sexual problem. In such cases a second abuse/assault occurs, and the client may have difficulty in trusting any therapist.

When taking a sexual history from a client, the clinician needs to inquire as to whether the client has been the recipient of unwanted sexual acts. It is important to use the term "unwanted" because a client may not feel comfortable labeling himself or herself as a rape victim or incest victim (particularly male clients). Consequently, when you ask a young woman if she has been raped, she may reply that she has not, when in fact her boyfriend, husband, or lover may have forced sex on her; she doesn't conceptualize it as a rape because she may believe one is "raped" only by strangers.

In taking a sex history, it is also important to inquire whether the client has been involved in sexual acts with relatives (other than spouse) and, if so, to ask her specifically with whom: brother, sister, cousin, aunt, uncle, father, and/or mother.

Because clients have difficulty discussing this material, they may not disclose such behaviors unless the therapist makes the inquiry. Once a disclosure is made to the therapist, he or she should attempt to learn as much about the abuse as possible, including the duration, the activity that took place, how the client felt about the behavior, and what impact she feels it has had on her emotionally and sexually.

Explain to the client that the sexual problem she is experiencing may be related to these unwanted sexual experiences and that any exploration of what occurred will help the therapist to identify what element of the abuse may presently affect sexual functioning. The therapist needs to be gentle and sensitive in probing such feelings and experiences and to recognize that it may take many sessions before the client feels comfortable sharing this information.

In some cases the client may not recall specific details of the abuse but may have vague recollections that "something sexual" happened to her when she was a child. If the client requests help in recalling such memories, the therapist may decide to work with the client to overcome the repression. My experience has been that the majority of clients do not ask for assistance in helping to uncover these vague recollections.

What is important in treating the sex dysfunctions is determining what stimuli or behaviors are maintaining or reinforcing the sex problem. If there was a past event that is recurring in the present sexual scene, then it should be addressed. However, if the patient does not have specific recall of an event, then it may or may not have relevance to her present sexual activity.

SEX DYSFUNCTION THERAPY

The major goal of sex dysfunction therapy with abuse/assault survivors is to facilitate their regaining control of their bodies and their sexuality. Assault survivors routinely feel that they have lost control of their bodies as a result of the abuse or assault. The sexual offender "invaded" and used her body, and she was unable to stop the attack. Consequently, she feels out of control.

A multicomponent treatment program for sex abuse/assault-related sexual problems was evaluated at the New York State Psychiatric Institute (specifically the Sexual Behavior Clinic). The therapeutic intervention utilized was based on previous work with sexually dysfunctional women as well as with women who had been victims of coercive or uninvited sex acts. A time-limited, behaviorally oriented sexual dysfunction treatment program was developed. The major goal was to help the woman regain control over her sexuality through gradual exposure to fear-inducing sexual situations, behaviors, and interactions. Consequently, women become able to restore their beliefs about functional sexual interaction. The treatment package and therapy outcome data are described in detail by Becker and Skinner (1984) and Becker et al. (1986).

The sexual dysfunction treatment package is based on the PLISSIT model, a framework of sex therapy involving a number of different levels of intervention (Annon, 1976). Components from a variety of other treatment programs (Masters & Johnson, 1970; Barbach, 1975; Deutsch, 1968; Dodson, 1974; Heiman, Lo Piccolo, & Lo Piccolo, 1976; Kegel, 1952; Lobitz & Lo Piccolo, 1972; Zeiss, Rosen, & Zeiss, 1978) were incorporated within the PLISSIT model in the development of the treatment package. For research purposes, the package was designed to be applied across ten 1-hour therapy sessions. Clinically, the number and length of sessions can be modified to meet the needs of the woman. In addition to the treatment sessions, a major emphasis is placed on exercises and assignments that women can perform at home. The therapy was conducted with the survivors only (again for research purposes), since some women may not have regular sexual partners. The treatment package can be implemented in either an individual or group therapy format.

The focus of the ten sessions was as follows:

Session 1

Since a major goal is to help the woman regain control, it is important that the therapist not place himself or herself in a position of control or power. Rather, the therapist should inform the client that he or she is a consultant to the patient and will provide an objective perspective as well as make specific suggestions and recommendations that the client is free to accept or reject. It is not uncommon for a sexual assault survivor to believe that she is the only woman to be experiencing the type of symptoms and sexual problems that can occur after an assault. Some women think that something is wrong with them because they are experiencing sexual difficulties, and this increases their already heightened feelings of guilt and self-blame.

Educating the client during the first session can help dispel these beliefs. It is important that the client know that sexual problems are frequently seen in sex abuse/assault survivors. The therapist then discusses how sexual problems can develop postassault or how an assault may exacerbate preexisting problems. Specifically, it should be noted that any sexual stimuli may evoke memories of the assault and that people usually tend to avoid anxiety-provoking situations.

Session 2

The second therapy session focuses on body image. Many women in our society have been socialized to be highly critical and rejecting of their bodies. This is understandable because women often compare themselves to standards of beauty set by Hollywood movies, fashion magazines, or centerfolds in sexually explicit magazines.

Sexual abuse/assault may have a significant impact on a client's body image. Women often feel "dirty or invaded." Abuse or assault directed at the client's breasts and/or genitals may cause the development of negative feelings about these areas.

On occasions women gain weight post abuse/assault; for some women this "layering" or "padding" is an effort to desexualize and thus protect themselves from further abuse.

The major goal of the second session is to assist the client in developing a positive attitude and a feeling of mastery over her body. Body-image exercises are given as homework assignments. The client is asked to set aside 30 minutes each day during which time, in the privacy of her home, she carefully examines her nude body from head to toe before a full-length mirror. As she focuses on each body part she is to make a positive statement.

Session 3

When the client returns for the third session, the body-imagery assignment is discussed. Generally, the client will have been able to make some positive statements about her body, although negative feelings may still persist. Several therapeutic techniques are useful in dealing with persistent negative thoughts. These include "thought stopping" (Geisinger, 1969), where the client learns to interrupt the negative cognitions. A client can also be requested to write down positive body aspects and review the list five times each day. Also, the importance of the functional abilities of the body can be stressed for women who deny any appreciation of their physical assets.

A second focus of this session is to assist the client in learning what is arousing to her. The client is instructed to incorporate touch into the homework assignment. This exercise involves having the client explore her body tactually for 3 minutes from head to toe. The client is instructed to vary the touch and pressure in order to discover what is arousing for her.

Session 4

Because sexual stimuli can trigger flashbacks of the abuse/assault, clients frequently find their minds wandering during sexual experiences, and they have difficulty staying focused. Session 4 addresses this issue. The two major goals of session 4 are to increase the client's ability to focus on her sexual behavior and to utilize sexual fantasies to facilitate arousal. One of the homework assignments for this session includes the reading of fantasy material. Therapists need to exercise caution in what they recommend as reading material. Although the fantasy material should cover a broad spectrum of behavior, clients can be further traumatized if the material contains coercive or incestuous sex. Consequently, the therapist should not recommend material unless she or he has screened it for appropriateness.

For example, one client had reported that she no longer had sexual fantasies. It was recommended that she read a book that collected a sample of women's sexual fantasies. When she returned for her next session she indicated she was upset because one woman had described a man forcing her to be sexual as erotic. This client found it difficult to believe that anyone could find such a thought erotic.

During this session specific suggestions are made for women who have specific dysfunctions. For example, women with arousal or orgasmic dysfunctions are instructed in Kegel (1952) exercises. Masturbatory training is outlined for women who are nonorgasmic (Barbach, 1975; Lobitz &

Lo Piccolo, 1972). Women with vaginismus are instructed in the use of dilators (Annon, 1976).

Session 5

During the fifth therapy session, problems with the use or development of fantasies are discussed. If the client describes difficulty in generating a fantasy of her own, she should be encouraged to modify those fantasies that she liked from her reading in order to facilitate arousal.

Two homework assignments are given: the first involves writing an original fantasy; the second is continuing to do the specific sexual dysfunction exercises given in the previous session.

Some women who are abused/assaulted have difficulty recognizing the physiological and emotional components of pleasurable sexual stimulation or orgasm. Specifically, they may mislabel sexual touches or behaviors as negative or unpleasant because they are actually generalizing from the abuse/assault situation to the present consensual one.

Session 6

Session 6 focuses on a discussion of the physiological components of sexual arousal and orgasm. This helps to demystify sex. Cognitive restructuring is also addressed in this session. Basically, the client learns to apply new labels to certain behaviors. For example, a client who is anorgasmic because she has labeled the experience of orgasm as "being out of control" learns that in fact she can allow herself to have an orgasm or not, and consequently that it is she who controls her sexuality. The issue of control is a critical one for abuse/assault survivors. It is also helpful to have the client, in the privacy of her home, role play what she anticipates her behavior would be during an orgasm.

The homework assignments for this session involve practicing the cognitive restructuring exercises and continuing the specific sexual dysfunction exercises given in session 4.

Session 7

The anxiety sexual assault survivors experience during the assault may generalize and interfere with sexual pleasure. Session 7 focuses on anxiety reduction. Systematic desensitization is a useful therapeutic technique to assist in anxiety reduction. Systematic desensitization, developed by Wolpe (1958), is a popular behavioral technique. The procedure consists of teaching the client progressive relaxation, construction of a hierarchy of fearful stimuli, and teaching the client to associate relaxation with the fearful stimuli. Women who need desensitization begin practicing it during this session.

Session 8

The preceding sessions have focused on teaching the client to feel comfortable with her body and to regain a sense of control over her sexuality. Because most clients are relating to sexual partners, it is essential that they be able to tell partners their sexual needs and desires. Successful communication enables the client to avoid stressful situations, experience increased sexual pleasure, and improve overall functioning.

Communication skills are taught through behavioral rehearsal (Lazarus, 1966). Clients are also taught how to deal with their partner's reaction to their requests. During this session, sensate-focus exercises (Masters & Johnson, 1970) are explained as a method of improving sexual communication. Assignments include implementing the sensate-focus exercises and readings on assertiveness (Phelps & Austin, 1975).

Session 9

Session 9 reviews the sensate-focus assignments. Because women often feel uncomfortable or guilty when they begin to assert themselves, this issue is addressed, and women are encouraged to aim for gradual changes as opposed to immediate global ones. Homework assignments involve continued sensate focus and assertion.

Session 10

The 10th therapy session involves a review of each woman's therapy goals and progress on each.

Outcome

A detailed description of the effectiveness of this program with 68 women is presented elsewhere (Becker et al., 1984). The outcome with this behavioral program appears to be good. Fewer than 4% of the women reported that they had made "no progress" in achieving their sexual goals. However, treatment tends to be most effective for sexual goals that do not involve a partner, such as self-stimulation assignments or controlling rape flashbacks. In the research protocol, women were assigned to either a group or individual therapy format. Stability of treatment effect was greater for women who participated in group therapy. In all probability this finding is related to two factors: (1) women had the opportunity to share their experiences with other survivors, and (2) some of the women would adjourn to coffee shops or restaurants after a group meeting and continue discussions.

Clinically, group treatment appears to be efficacious in that the women see that they are not alone in having developed sexual problems. They also receive feedback and support from other group members. In general, it may be advantageous to establish homogeneous groups, since the issues for women who are incest survivors are somewhat different from those for women who were raped.

The treatment format outlined above can and should be altered for clinical practice. The clinician should conduct a thorough assessment and tailor the treatment to the client's specific problems. In clinical practice, the clinician has the advantage of including the woman's sexual partner in the therapy. It is imperative that the partner be supportive of the woman receiving therapy and available and willing to carry out the assignments. If the partner is at all opposed to the therapy, the clinician can work through this opposition in the sessions. Some partners are concerned that reinstituting sex might retraumatize the woman; others may have "blamed" the woman for her assault or believed that she may have enjoyed it. These beliefs and concerns need to be processed in therapy.

A comment needs to be made regarding lesbian women who have been sex abuse victims and present with a sexual dysfunction. Nichols (1988), in discussing low sexual desire in lesbian couples, notes that since women are more likely to be abused than men, the probability that one of the partners in a lesbian relationship has been abused is much higher than in a heterosexual relationship. She also reports that lack of sexual desire is the most common complaint of lesbian couples who seek sex counseling.

Both lesbian and heterosexual women were treated within our research protocol. The treatment issues were basically similar. If a lesbian woman in a relationship presents with low sex desire, the clinician is advised to read Nichols's chapter (Chapter 10) in which she discusses causes as well as therapeutic interventions.

CASE STUDIES

Three cases of women who participated in the treatment project are now presented.

Case 1: Success

The first case involves a 25-year-old single female who was the victim of a date rape. Laura presented the following circumstances surrounding the assault. Two years ago she had been traveling abroad. She was invited to a party where she met a man 10 years her senior. Laura accepted a ride home from him. Instead of immediately taking her home, he brought her to his apartment, where he proceeded to rape her vaginally. Initially, she attempted to "talk him out of it," and when that failed, she physically resisted. He threatened to "beat her up" if she didn't stop resisting. He also stole her jewelry.

Following the rape, she received medical attention. Both VD and pregnancy testing proved negative. Laura reported the incident to the police, but she felt that they did not handle the situation very well. The man was never prosecuted.

Immediately following her assault, Laura experienced sleep and appetite difficulties. She was afraid of being alone and became distrustful and fearful of men. Laura experienced depressive symptomatology. She also felt guilty and engaged in self-blame because she had accepted the ride from the man. Six months after the rape, she saw a therapist weekly for a 5-month period to deal with her rape trauma.

Laura felt that the following sexual problems resulted from the rape: She was "easily turned off" during sexual activity, she would be distracted, and she found it difficult to refuse sexual invitations or overtures.

Laura presented the following sexual history. Her first nongenital sexual experience occurred at age 14, and she had intercourse at age 18½. Prior to the rape, Laura had had sexual relations with five partners. Following the rape, she had a nonsexual relationship with a man for 1 year. Six months prior to beginning therapy at our clinic, Laura had begun a new relationship. In the evaluation session, Laura set the following goals: (1) not to be distracted sexually, (2) to be more assertive, and (3) to become more orgasmic. In the first therapy session, Laura described what occurred sexually with her partner. During foreplay, her mind would start to wander, and she would either begin humming a tune or have a nonsexual fantasy. Laura was orgasmic with her present partner only when she had several alcoholic drinks. She wanted to give up this "crutch" and enjoy lovemaking without reliance on alcohol.

During the first session, the therapist explained to Laura the likely genesis of her present sexual problems. Specifically, she was able to distract herself from flashbacks of the rape by "allowing her mind to wander" during sexual activities. Laura trusted her current boyfriend and was able to be relaxed during sex with him. She drank to facilitate relaxation, and the more relaxed she became, the easier it was for her to lubricate and achieve orgasm. Laura reported that she was orgasmic in about 10% of her sexual encounters with her partner.

Because Laura was concerned about her ability to concentrate during lovemaking, she was given the following assignment. She was asked to "concentrate" during a sensate-focus exercise; if she found her mind wandering, she was to say "stop" and check the time to see for how long she had drifted.

During the second session, Laura reported that she had done the exercise, and that it had proven very helpful. Laura and her partner had intercourse following the sensate-focus exercise, and she was orgasmic.

During the session, Laura revealed that she had changed since the rape. Prerape she would become very upset if she didn't have a date; postrape she realized that the only person she could depend on was herself. She felt that the experience had made her more independent and distrustful of people.

Laura was given a body-awareness exercise for a homework assignment and was requested to continue the sensate-focus exercises.

When Laura returned for her third therapy session, she reported that she and her partner had gone away for a 3-day weekend. She related that they had had intercourse several times, and she had been distracted only once. Further, the distraction had been external (people in another room making noise) as opposed to internal. She also reported that she did not drink and had been able to relax and enjoy sex without alcohol.

Laura was seen for three more sessions. She reported that she was comfortable with her body and that she had communicated to her partner what her erogenous areas were. During the last session, Laura said that she was no longer distracted during lovemaking and that she almost always had orgasms during penile vaginal intercourse. She also related that therapy had helped her to more effective in communicating sexual wishes to her partner.

At a 3-month follow-up, Laura was still dating her partner, was happy with the relationship, and indicated that she was now orgasmic with every occurrence of intercourse.

Obviously, not all cases go as smoothly as this one. Factors that facilitated the treatment success were that Laura had not been pressured or persuaded to have sex immediately postassault. She did have a nonsexual relationship postassault that allowed her to feel comfortable with men again, since she had become distrustful. When she met a man with whom she wanted to be sexual and experienced some difficulty, she decided to seek help. Consequently, Laura had begun the process of regaining control. The therapist offered her specific suggestions and support for her to communicate her needs to her partner.

Case 2: Partial Success

Sue, a 30-year-old married woman, had been sexually abused by her stepfather from age 8 to 17. She was unable to recall how many times her stepfather had abused her over this period. The sexual abuse involved genital fondling and digital penetration of the vagina. The stepfather had not been physically violent toward her. She recalled that the only affection he showed her was when he sexually fondled her. The stepfather cautioned her not to disclose the abuse to her mother because her mother would be "hurt" if she heard he was "having sex" with her. She felt unable to tell her mother about the abuse because her mother had once cautioned her not to do anything that would cause her stepfather to leave.

Sue was married and had a young daughter. She related a number of nonsexual problems that she felt were related to the incest, including anger toward her mother, fear of men, poor communication skills, difficulty being an effective parent, and the lack of a support system. She had been unemployed for many years even though she had a college degree and had been previously employed.

Sexually, Sue experienced an arousal dysfunction (specific to her husband) that was exacerbated by an incident that occurred with her husband.

Her husband wanted her to perform fellatio on him, and he had attempted verbally to persuade her on a number of occasions. One day he attempted to place her head in a position to facilitate oral sex. Sue became very upset, and her husband reacted with anger and frustration. Over the years, sex occurred less frequently. When Sue did have intercourse, she was orgasmic 50% of the time. She masturbated weekly and had no difficulty achieving orgasm with self-stimulation.

Sue reported that extended periods of caressing (60–90 minutes) were required for her to experience any arousal. If her husband attempted to touch her genitals before she was "ready," she would feel invaded. Sue and her husband had extremely limited premarital sexual experiences, and she felt that they were both "inept." She reported that she had been anorgasmic during the first year of their marriage.

Prior to entering therapy, Sue and her husband had been in treatment for 8 months at a sex therapy clinic at a local medical center. Sue characterized the therapy as having been "useless." She described the male therapist as insensitive, unknowledgeable about incest, and as always siding with her husband.

Sue set the following goals for herself: (1) to stop the recurring thoughts of incest that occurred during lovemaking, (2) to learn what was sexually arousing for her, (3) to improve communication with her husband, and (4) to be freer sexually, specifically, to be more of a participant and to feel comfortable touching her husband's body.

Because Sue had had some prior therapy, it was important to determine if there had been anything about the treatment that was helpful, in order to incorporate it into the present treatment. Sue indicated that she did find the sensate-focus exercises helpful. Because Sue was somewhat comfortable with her own body and was able to achieve orgasm in masturbation, the first session reviewed sensate-focus exercises. Sue was asked to explain the exercises to her husband and to try them two times a week without engaging in penile–vaginal intercourse.

During the first session, the issue of control was also discussed. Sue's husband made most of the decisions for the family, and he also tried to be the sexual initiator. I suggested to Sue that perhaps she felt little control in the relationship in general and perhaps felt overpowered by her husband as she had by her stepfather. Sue responded to this interpretation by revealing that she had never wanted to have a child and did so only at her husband's insistence. She was resentful of the fact that her husband accepted very little responsibility for their child. It became apparent that Sue was angry at her husband and felt that their relationship was "one-sided" (she put in most of the effort to make the relationship work). I suggested to Sue that she might find it helpful to express her feelings to her husband, noting that perhaps her anger toward him was interfering with her sexual responsiveness.

During the second session, Sue reported that she had spoken with her husband about her feelings of lack of control in their relationship and told him that this mirrored the relationship she had had with her stepfather. She felt affirmed that her husband understood her feelings. Sue initiated the next sensate-focus exercise with her husband. Rather than alternating within a session, the exercises were done over a 2-day period. She caressed him the first day, and he caressed her the second day. This was an important step for Sue, since she had been so uncomfortable initiating and caressing her husband's body.

During the second session, Sue wanted to focus on the issue of control. She offered the interpretation that perhaps she had been unable to make progress in her previous sex therapy because she had experienced that therapist as being controlling. Sue also asserted that she wanted her relationship with her husband to become more egalitarian.

Sue was requested to continue the sensate-focus exercises. During the fourth session, Sue reported that she and her husband had intercourse and it was quite pleasurable. She indicated that she was feeling more in control and less guilty with her husband. Apparently Sue would feel guilty if her husband did not have a "terrific" orgasm. She realized that he was responsible for his orgasm, and this self-statement allowed her to focus more on her own pleasure.

Sue reported no longer having intrusive thoughts about the incest. Although this had not been directly targeted during the initial sessions, the thoughts ceased as she gained more control in the relationship.

The remaining sessions focused on helping Sue attain her goal of becoming more creative in lovemaking. I recommended the book, *The Joy of Sex*, to Sue and suggested that she and her husband read it together and use it as a guide to creative lovemaking. Whereas Sue's husband thoroughly enjoyed the book, Sue found the suggestions of bondage disturbing. Therapists working with rape and incest survivors should forewarn clients about passages in books that might prove to be upsetting.

This was not a major setback for Sue, and she was able to continue with her assignments. At a 3-month follow-up visit, Sue was asked to evaluate whether she had made any progress in achieving her initial treatment goals. Regarding her goals to increase arousal and sexual activity, she felt she had totally accomplished them; regarding her goal to reduce orgasmic latency and engage in alternate forms of lovemaking, she felt that she had achieved them in part.

At the completion of the time-limited therapy, Sue asked to remain in therapy to continue working on other life problems. Specifically, she wanted help with her child who was a discipline problem, she wanted her husband to become more involved in parenting, and she wanted to explore returning to work.

In this case, the time-limited therapy had been effective in addressing sexual arousal. Sue, however, was still not totally satisfied with her orgasmic latency, and she continued to feel limited in her ability to be more "creative" in lovemaking.

As Sue's communication with her husband improved, and as the relationship became more egalitarian, Sue became more sexually responsive. I continued to see Sue in more intensive therapy and had some conjoint sessions with Sue and her husband.

This case was more than a "single" sex dysfunction case. Sue's sexual experience prior to marriage had been limited. Her anger at her husband and her difficulty in expressing her feelings and making requests of him, both sexually and nonsexually, appeared to interfere with her arousal. The better their communication became, the better able Sue was to inform her husband what she wanted sexually.

At the conclusion of the therapy Sue returned to work, her relationship with her child improved, and she and her husband were functioning well in their relationship.

Case 3: Failure

This client, age 26, came from an unstable home that necessitated placing her in foster care when she was 36 months old. When Carole was 9 years of age, her oldest foster brother began to sexually abuse her. He would have her masturbate him. Three years later, her foster father began to force her to perform fellatio. Carole revealed the abuse to a case worker, who subsequently removed her from the home. Carole was placed in a group home and lived there until age 20.

Carole was participating in individual therapy as well as a support group when she entered treatment at our clinic. She related the following problems resulting from the incest experience: inability to engage in oral sex, flashbacks of the incest experience, fear of letting people have "power" over her, and inability to achieve orgasm in intercourse. Carole's prior sexual experiences had involved sexual intercourse with two male sexual partners and one female sexual partner. When she masturbated 75% of her fantasies were lesbian, and 25% were heterosexual. Carole masturbated by rubbing her genitals against a pillow. She was repulsed by the thought of touching her genitals. Carole reported that she had been taught that she was not attractive, and she felt that she kept herself unattractive by becoming obese and staying unkempt. She was afraid that if she were attractive and appealing, she would be inviting sexual abuse.

Carole's first assignment was a body-awareness exercise. She indicated that she did not have a mirror but would purchase one. When she returned for the next session, she said that she had purchased a mirror but had not done the exercise because a friend had promised to help her install the mirror, and he had not kept his word. Carole's failure to do the homework suggested how much revulsion she felt toward her body. During the session, rather than discussing sexual issues, Carole wanted to discuss her desire to become pregnant. She indicated that she wanted to become pregnant in order to overcome feelings of loneliness.

By the fourth therapy session, Carole had looked at her naked body in a mirror and felt the assignment was "sensuous." Whenever she touched a part of her body she would say "my body's okay," but then felt compelled to say "my body's ugly." Carole was unable to touch her genital area because she felt it would be "dirty" to do so.

Because she had experienced difficulty in touching the genital area, it was suggested that she consider touching one of her genital "parts" on a daily basis, beginning with the mons area. By the fifth session, Carole reported that she was able to complete the exercise. She was then requested to stimulate the genital area manually.

The following session, Carole revealed that she had masturbated on two occasions using the pillow but on each occasion had inserted a finger vaginally. She was orgasmic on both occasions. Even though Carole had been able to stimulate her genitals and achieve orgasm, she was not excited by these events. She began to cry during the session. On questioning, she revealed a number of depressive symptoms including suicidal ideation.

When questioned as to whether her other therapist knew about the extent of her depression, Carole indicated that her therapist was on vacation and would not be returning for several days. Unfortunately, my vacation coincided with her therapist's, and Carole was referred to a colleague until I returned.

When Carole was seen for her next session, she appeared less depressed. She had not engaged in any masturbatory exercises, nor had she followed through on a recommendation to explore expanding her social contacts. During this session, I discussed her pattern of not following through with established goals.

Carole did not appear for her next session. An attempt was made to contact her, but her home telephone number had been changed to an unlisted number. Six weeks later she contacted the clinic. She indicated that she had dropped out of therapy because she had been depressed. A desire to return was related to the issue that for most of her life she would begin projects and not complete them. She wanted to feel a sense of completion.

During her absence from the clinic, Carole had had intercourse with a man who had been a close friend for a number of years. Although the sexual act was not described as pleasurable, she did indicate that it had felt good to have someone close to her. Carole had stopped masturbation because she felt a mass in her vagina. I recommended that she set up an appointment with a gynecologist.

When Carole returned for her next session she reported that she had made an appointment to see a gynecologist. Carole had wanted to discuss nonsexually related material in the session. She was informed that since she was seeing an individual therapist who worked with her on those issues, it would be more appropriate to discuss them with her. I recommended that we delay another appointment until after her gynecological consultation. Carole never recontacted the clinic. Follow-up data are not obtainable.

Although Carole had made some progress in therapy, her problems were many and long-standing. In retrospect, Carole should probably not have been entered into a short-term sex therapy program even though she had continued to receive long-term individual therapy. Her depression and her negative self-evaluation interfered with her being able to make progress. Carole was in need of a total cognitive–behavior therapy treatment that would focus on altering her self-image and target her depression and social isolation. Once that had been accomplished, the sex therapy could be initiated. Carole wanted so much to complete a task and experience success. Although she was able to bring herself to orgasm, she didn't feel happy about this. Understandably, the discovery of the vaginal mass increased her fear and avoidance of her body. It may also have increased her guilt over touching her body.

If Carole had had a sexual partner, she might have had more motivation to remain in therapy. Her social contacts were limited, however, and Carole had never had a "sustained" sexual relationship.

DISCUSSION

In the beginning of this chapter, several issues were raised regarding therapy with sexual abuse/assault survivors. Those issues are discussed in terms of the three cases presented. Control clearly is the major issue in all three cases. In the second case history, Sue felt her relationship was nonegalitarian, and these feelings brought back memories of her controlling father. She had experienced her first therapist as controlling and unsupportive, consequently found it difficult to make progress, and ultimately terminated the therapy. When Sue shared her feelings with her husband and associated her lack of power with the sexual problem, her husband had been able to relinquish some control, which facilitated her being more sexually responsive and willing to give to him sexually.

In the third case history, Carole had a fear that people would gain "power" over her. This fear was a product of her early life experiences. Her biological parents had been neglectful, and in the foster placement she had been abused by two family members. Carole felt that in general she had little ability to exercise any control over her environment. She even feared touching her own body. Because she had experienced so little caring in her life and was not exposed to functional parental or peer models, Carole had little opportunity to learn to care for herself physically or emotionally. She found herself to be an unattractive and unworthy person. It is understandable that she had difficulty initiating and maintaining social–sexual relationships. It is impossible to extrapolate how much of Carole's problems were related to the abuse per se or to the emotionally deprived home environments she experienced. In a number of incest situations this appears to be the case. In some cases, children learn that they cannot trust, because the very people they had relied on to love, nurture, and protect them abuse their innocence. Maltz and Holman (1987, p. 9), in describing treatment for incest survivors, note that in order for incest survivors to have positive healthy sexual experiences, five conditions must be met. They label these CERTS:

1. *Consent*—the ability to choose to be sexual.
2. *Equality*—with a partner.
3. *Respect*—a feeling of positive regard for oneself and one's partner.
4. *Trust*—in a partner.
5. *Safety*—a feeling of security within the sexual setting.

It was quite clear that these conditions had not been met for the two incest survivors.

The women described in these case examples had attempted to cope with the abuse/assault by dissociating themselves from the event as it was occurring. During the assault, dissociation serves the purpose of giving the woman a sense of control and power. Dissociation helped separate them from the experience. However, this phenomenon was also occurring in nonabuse situations. Laura found herself humming a tune or having nonsexual fantasies during lovemaking, and this behavior then inhibited her sexual pleasure. It is helpful for survivors to be able to identify what mechanism they used to cope during the abuse/assault and how these mechanisms may have been adaptive during the assault but may currently be maladaptive.

Because a conditioning of sexual stimuli with anxiety can occur during abuse/assault situations, it is understandable that women experience flashbacks of the abuse. One can hypothesize that the more the sexual stimuli resemble that abuse/assault, the more likely the women will experience flashbacks of the event. The flashbacks then interfere with arousal, and such women may begin to avoid sexual interaction.

When a woman has experienced sexual abuse as a child by a family member, the experience(s) can impact negatively on the formation and maintenance of relationships. For some women, the more intimate the relationship becomes, the greater they fear being used, abused, or hurt. These unresolved issues of betrayal can be destructive to relationships and have both sexual and nonsexual impacts.

Sexual partners of abuse/assault survivors often face a difficult task. Although the partner was not responsible for the past and cannot change it, unresolved issues or sexual problems are brought into the relationship. Partners may feel resentful of having to suppress their sexual needs or desires to lend total support to the survivor. Consequently, it is imperative that the survivor and her partner be able to discuss these issues. In cases 1 and 2, both women felt that therapy had helped them to express their feelings, and consequently, they learned to encourage their partners to express theirs. The mutuality and attending to each other's needs enhanced their relationships. This was particularly true for Laura, whose partner came from a different ethnic and cultural background from hers. His expectations regarding the role of women were very different from her own. With therapy, they were able to negotiate these issues.

CONCLUSION

For many years the sexual component of sexual abuse/assault had been downplayed, and consequently little attention had been paid to the sexual problems that were assault related. Research has demonstrated that a considerable number of women develop sexual dysfunctions that are indeed assault related. Treatments are now available that can help sexual abuse survivors to enjoy sexually fulfilling lives.

Future research with sex abuse/assault survivors who have developed sexual dysfunctions needs to focus on a number of issues, including (1) abuse patterns associated with treatment success or failure, (2) the relevance of the client's present relationship in effecting a favorable outcome, (3) the desirability of couples' therapy in facilitating a successful treatment result.

My clinical experience suggests that if the woman had positive sexual experiences preassault and has supportive partners and social environment, outcome is extremely favorable.

The more negative sex experiences a woman had preassault, and the more negative her present interpersonal situation, the more likely the outcome will be less successful.

Whatever the factors influencing treatment outcome, therapists must not undervalue the important role they play in the facilitation of healing.

REFERENCES

American Psychiatric Association. (1987). *Diagnostic and statistical manual of mental disorders* (3rd ed., rev.). Washington, DC: Author.

Annon, J. (1976). *The behavioral treatment of sexual problems: Brief therapy.* New York: Harper & Row.

Barbach, L. (1975). *For yourself: The fulfillment of female sexuality.* New York: Doubleday.

Becker, J., Skinner, L., Abel, G., Axelrod, R., & Cichon, J. (1984). Sexual problems of sexual assault survivors. *Women and Health, 9*(4), 5–20.

Becker, J., Skinner, L., Abel, G., & Cichon, J. (1986). Level of postassault sexual functioning in rape and incest victims. *Archives of Sexual Behavior, 15*(1), 37–49.

Deutsch, R. (1968). *The key to feminine response in marriage.* New York: Random House.

Dodson, B. (1974). *Liberating masturbation.* New York: Body Sex Designs.

Feldman-Summers, S., Gordon, P., & Meagher, J. (1979). The impact of rape on sexual satisfaction. *Journal of Abnormal Psychology, 88,* 101–105.

Finkelhor, D. (1986). *Sourcebook on child sex abuse.* Beverly Hills, CA: Sage.

Frank, E., & Stewart, B. D. (1983a). Physical aggression: Treating the victims. In E. A. Blenchman (Ed.), *Behavior modification with women* (pp. 245–272). New York: Guilford Press.

Frank, E., & Stewart, B. (1983b). Treatment of depressed rape victims: An approach to stress-induced symptomatology. In P. J. Clayton & J. E. Barrett (Eds.), *Treatment of depression: Old controversies and new approaches.* New York: Raven Press.

Geisinger, D. (1969). Controlling sexual interpersonal anxieties. In J. D. Krumboltz & C. E. Thoreson (Eds.), *Behavioral counseling: Cases and techniques.* New York: Holt, Rinehart & Winston.

Heiman, J., LoPiccolo, J., & LoPiccolo, L. (1976) *Becoming orgasmic: Sexual growth program for women.* Englewood Cliffs, NJ: Prentice-Hall.

Kegel, A. (1952). Sexual functions of the pubococcygeus muscle. *Western Journal of Surgery, 60,* 521–524.

Kilpatrick, D., Best, C., & Veronen, L. (1984). *Mental health consequences of criminal victimization: A random community survey.* Paper presented at the meeting of the American Psychological Association, Toronto, Canada.

Kilpatrick, D., Veronen, L., & Best, C. (1985). Factors predicting psychological distress among rape victims. In C. R. Figley (Ed.), *Trauma and its wake* (pp. 113–141). New York: Brunner/Mazel.

Kilpatrick, D., Veronen, L., & Resick, P. (1979). *The aftermath of rape: One year follow-up.* Paper presented at the meeting of the Association for the Advancement of Behavior Therapy, San Francisco.

Kilpatrick, D., Veronen, L., & Resick, P. (1982). Psychological sequelae to rape: Assessment and treatment strategies. In D. M. Daleys & R. L. Meredith (Eds.), *Behavioral medicine: Assessment and treatment strategies* (pp. 473–497). New York: Plenum Press.

Koss, M. (1983). The scope of rape: Implications for the clinical treatment of victims. *The Clinical Psychologist, 36,* 88–91.

Lazarus, A. (1966). Behavioral rehearsal vs. non-directive therapy vs. advice in effecting behavior change. *Behavior Research and Therapy, 4,* 209–212.

Lobitz, W., & LoPiccolo, J. (1972). New methods in the behavioral treatment of sexual dysfunctions. *Journal of Behavior Therapy and Experimental Psychiatry, 3,* 266–271.

Maltz, W., & Holman, B. (1987). *Incest and sexuality: A guide to understanding and healing.* Lexington, MA: Lexington Books.

Masters, W., & Johnson, V. (1970). *Human sexual inadequacy.* London: J. A. Churchill.

McGuire, L., & Wagner, N. (1978). Sexual dysfunction in women who were molested as children: One response pattern and suggestions for treatment. *Journal of Sex and Marital Therapy, 4,* 11–15.

Nichols, M. (1988). Low sexual desire in lesbian couples. In S. R. Leiblum & R. C. Rosen (Eds.), *Sexual desire disorders* (pp. 387–412). New York: Guilford Press.

Phelps, S., & Austin, N. (1975). *The assertive woman.* San Luis Obispo, CA: Impact Publishers.

Steketee, G., & Foa, E. (1987). Rape victims: Posttraumatic stress responses and their treatment. *Journal of Anxiety Disorders, 1*, 69–86.

Wolpe, J. (1958). *Psychotherapy by reciprocal inhibition.* Stanford: Stanford University Press.

Zeiss, A., Rosen, G., & Zeiss, R. (1978). Orgasm during intercourse: A treatment strategy for women. In J. LoPiccolo & L. LoPiccolo (Eds.), *Handbook of sex therapy* (pp. 219–225). New York: Plenum Press.

12

Sexual Problems in Chronic Illness

LESLIE R. SCHOVER

Despite the fact that sexual problems are so common in individuals with chronic illnesses, it is only recently that sex therapists and physicians have begun to address the sexual complaints of this population. Regrettably, a typical reaction to the patient's presentation of a sexual problem is reassurance or dismissal. But, as Leslie Schover notes, patients are often quite distressed and worried about changes in their sexual performance following an illness or surgery and can benefit greatly from brief, problem-focused sexual interventions.

Nevertheless, sexual counseling with patients having a chronic illness does differ from more traditional sexual therapy. Often, counseling occurs in a medical setting in which both time and privacy are at a premium. Consequently, interventions must be brief, and treatment goals must be modest. At times, physiological as well as psychological interventions are necessary.

Schover observes that certain problems are quite common in individuals having chronic illness. Reduced sexual desire is often a result of depression, loss of self-esteem related to the illness, fears about the consequences of sexual activity, and a decrease in marital intimacy. Erectile problems are especially prevalent since the hormonal, vascular, and neurological mechanisms underlying erection are easily impaired. Problems with arousal in women are typical as well. Interestingly, Schover notes that orgasm is the most robust aspect of sexual response and tends to be less of a problem for most men and women with chronic illness.

Schover offers a useful guide to assessment in which the special issues related to interviewing patients in a medical setting are discussed. She notes that it is not uncommon for individuals to have more than one sexual difficulty. Her treatment approach is a skillful combination of sex education and attitude-change techniques coupled with behavioral suggestions and ideas for resuming sex. Dr. Schover is both practical and realistic in her recommendations for working with chronically ill individuals, as well as sensitive and humane. Her chapter offers an extremely useful guide to working with this most deserving and challenging of treatment populations.

Leslie R. Schover, Ph.D, is a member of the Center for Sexual Function at The Cleveland Clinic Foundation. She is the author of Prime Time *(1984), a book exploring male sexuality during the second half of life, as well as a new book co-authored with Søren Buus Jensen entitled* Sexuality and Chronic Illness: A Comprehensive Approach *(1988). She is regarded as an authority on the sexual sequelae of chronic illness.*

Sexual problems are common in the general population, but they occur even more frequently in men and women with a chronic illness. Decreased sexual activity and high rates of sexual dysfunction have been documented in patients with cardiovascular disease, cancer, neurological disease, diabetes, end-stage renal disease, chronic obstructive pulmonary disease, and chronic pain (Schover & Jensen, 1988).

How concerned are people about their sexuality when survival itself is at issue? In a classic survey of terminally ill cancer patients, although sexual intercourse was not a high priority, the intimacy of touch was rated as very important (Lieber, Plumb, Gerstenzang, & Holland, 1976). Numerous studies have documented that patients with disabilities related to diabetes, myocardial infarctions, or strokes do want information about sexual function from their primary-care team but rarely solicit or receive sex education relevant to their medical problems (House & Pendleton, 1986; Jensen, 1981; Papadopoulos, Beaumont, Shelley, & Larrimore, 1983; Papadopoulos, Shelley, Piccolo, Beaumont, & Barnett, 1986; Sikorski, 1985; Sjögren, 1983).

Typically, the patient's medical care occurs in a busy clinic. Initial history taking and follow-up appointments do not include routine questions about sexual health. Only the patient who is concerned and assertive enough to initiate a discussion of sex receives any information. Sadly, many physicians and other health care professionals lack enough knowledge about the sexual impact of illness, even within their specialty area, to answer patients' questions. Despite medical schools' efforts in the 1970s to include sex education in their curricula, most now offer only an elective course or a few days of lectures crammed into a psychiatry module. Graduate programs in psychology are even more remiss in offering training in sexual health care (Nathan, 1986). The one factor that may be increasing attention to sexual health in medical settings is the AIDS epidemic (Trubo, 1987). The need to assess AIDS risk factors is motivating clinicians to take sexual histories. Techniques described in this chapter should be relevant to heterosexual or gay couples who are adjusting to a diagnosis of AIDS, but the major focus is on more common chronic diseases.

Even within that minority of patients whose sexual concerns are identified, only a few ever see a sex therapist. Having spent the last 7 years as a practicing sex therapist in medical settings, I have gotten the impression that a majority of physicians use reassurance or dismissal as tactics when chronically ill patients bring up sexual problems. Typical comments to patients have included: "It's normal not to feel desire after this surgery. Just be glad you're alive." "Are you really worrying about sex at your age?" "Maybe you're bored with your wife. Why don't you try someone new?" "If you're still having a problem in 6 months, we'll talk about it." It is the exception, rather than the rule, for the physician to offer a referral to a sexuality specialist.

An example of the type of case that frustrates a sex therapist is the following history, elicited when Roger, a 62-year-old businessman, was seen with his 58-year-old wife, Anita. The sex therapist was consulted to provide education and advice on sexual rehabilitation during Roger's recovery from an abdominoperineal resection—surgery to remove a rectal malignancy and create a colostomy. In obtaining a history of the couple's sexual relationship, the therapist discovered that Anita had had two mastectomies, the first at age 45 and the second at 50. Since that time, the couple had sex much less frequently. Anita avoided situations in which her husband could see her nude. Even genital caressing as a part of foreplay had decreased. Anita had postmenopausal vaginal dryness, so that intercourse had become painful and was often followed by urinary tract irritation. Because of her cancer history, she could not take replacement estrogen to alleviate these problems. Anita was quite reticent in discussing sex and had never brought up these issues with her physicians. She did not know about available vaginal lubricants and had never before disclosed to Roger her thoughts about losing her breasts.

He was surprised but very supportive when Anita began crying during the interview. He expressed his own wish that they could improve their sexual communication. The therapist compared his feelings about his colostomy to his wife's reaction to mastectomy. A productive discussion about breast reconstruction followed. Anita had considered reconstruction but had been afraid that Roger would regard her as vain or frivolous if she sought a plastic surgery consulation. Roger was enthusiastic about exploring the idea, however. Anita had a chance to reciprocate by supporting Roger's interest in having a penile prosthesis implanted if his erections failed to return to normal in the months after cancer surgery. Anita's comment was, "Why wasn't there someone like you to talk with us after my mastectomies?"

Unlike Roger and Anita, many patients referred for sex therapy react with disappointment or dismay. Patients envision help for a sexual problem as something medical, like a pill or a hormone shot. A suggestion to try sex therapy is seen as an attempt to label the problem as "all in your head." As difficult as it is to persuade men or women to see a sex therapist individually, setting up a couple evaluation is even more challenging. The identified patient may insist that the spouse is too embarrassed to discuss sex or is hostile to the idea of counseling. Sometimes one partner is having an affair and is afraid the other will discover it if the couple talks with a sex therapist.

Despite all of these barriers, a sex therapist can develop a diverse and thriving practice in a medical setting. It is wise to remain aware, however, that the men and women we see are a very special group. In a study of 160 diabetic patients interviewed about their sexuality, only 14% were interested in having sex therapy (Jensen, 1981). In 384 consultations performed as part of a sexual rehabilitation service in a cancer center, only eight cases were eventually treated with full-scale sex therapy (Schover, Evans, & von Eschenbach, 1987).

COMMON SEXUAL PROBLEMS RELATED TO CHRONIC ILLNESS

Although the whole spectrum of sexual dysfunctions can be seen in chronically ill populations (Schover, Friedman, Weiler, Heiman, & Lo-Piccolo, 1982), some problems are especially common. A clinician should be alert for multiple sexual dysfunctions across the phases of the response cycle and for problems in the partner as well as in the identified patient. As I review the most usual symptom pictures, I will discuss emotional and physiological risk factors related to chronic illness.

Low Sexual Desire

Low sexual desire is one of the most typical complaints in men or women with a chronic illness. Although lack of interest in sex sometimes predates the onset of a disease, the more usual picture is a global decrease in desire associated with diagnosis or treatment of a medical problem. Certainly fatigue, stress, and chronic pain detract from sexual energy. Extreme weight loss, the stress of an operation, or acute illness can transiently decrease serum testosterone in men (Woolf, Hamill, McDonald, Lee, & Kelly, 1985). Physiological causes of low sexual desire can also include generalized dementia or some specific brain lesions (Hawton, 1984; Wise, 1983); elevations of the hormone prolactin that are related to a pituitary tumor, end-stage renal disease, or to medications such as opiate pain relievers or phenothiazines (Schover & Jensen, 1988); or reduced androgen levels in men or women subjected to hormone therapy for cancer of the prostate, breast, or uterus (Schover, Schain, & Montague,

1989). Other medications can reduce sexual desire by acting as a central nervous system depressant (for example β blockers or minor tranquilizers) or interfering with the hypothalamic–pituitary–gonadal axis (cimetidine for ulcers or spironolactone for cardiac disease).

Psychological factors also play an important role in reducing sexual desire during a chronic illness. The incidence of depression does increase in chronically ill populations (Bukberg, Penman, & Holland, 1984). A man or woman may ask for help for a loss of desire, unaware that the sexual problem is just one facet of a major affective disorder. Clinicians need to screen carefully for other signs of depression when low desire is the presenting complaint.

Herbert, a 45-year-old carpenter, was evaluated for sexual dysfunction. He had several episodes of losing erections around the time he was diagnosed with scleroderma, a progressive autoimmune disease of the connective tissue. He was told he might have only 5 to 10 years to live because his heart was enlarged, and his lungs were becoming fibrotic as part of the illness. Not only was he experiencing shortness of breath, but he was losing the hand dexterity he needed for his work because of loss of flexibility in his skin and joints.

Herbert had lost all desire for sex, so that he and his wife had not even attempted lovemaking for several months. On further questioning, the clinician discovered that Herbert was depressed in mood, had lost 10 pounds because of poor appetite, was awakening each morning at 3 or 4 a.m., and was feeling absent-minded and indecisive. He became tearful during the session when discussing his failures to fulfill his sexual and occupational roles.

Loss of self-esteem related to illness is another factor that can decrease sexual desire. Men often base their self-worth on traditional male roles of wage earner and sexual performer. If an illness threatens to interfere with job skills or erections, it is experienced as an assault on masculinity itself (Liss-Levinson, 1982.) Men also tend to withdraw emotionally and sexually if they feel ashamed at being dependent on a wife because of their illness. Women seem to focus more on changes in physical appearance than on sexual performance. Although mastectomy is often seen as the epitome of changed attractiveness, body image is even more impaired in women with gynecologic cancers that can interfere with sexual function directly than in women with breast cancer (Andersen & Jochimsen, 1985). Perhaps because of our youth-oriented ideal of female sexuality, older women seem to be far less concerned with staying sexually active than are groups of elderly men with comparable medical problems (Althof, Coffman, & Levine, 1984; Schreiner-Engel, Schiavi, Vietorisz, & Smith, 1987; Schover et al., 1987). This gender difference may well diminish, however, when future cohorts of women with greater expectations for sexual pleasure reach their 50s or 60s.

An illness may evoke specific fears about sexual activity. Patients or partners sometimes worry that cancer could be sexually transmitted (Schover et al., 1987). After a heart attack or stroke, a common fear is that sex could provoke another cardiovascular episode (Derogatis & King, 1981). Guilt about past sexual behavior such as an affair, premarital sex, sex with a prostitute, or an abortion can evoke a fear that a disease is the punishment for sin. Because our society generally labels sex as unclean, many patients have a vague notion that intercourse is unhealthy and could interfere with medical treatment. Some even use a kind of religious "bargaining," vowing to give up sex altogether if only they can get well or survive longer.

Finally, loss of desire for sex may reflect a decrease in a couple's intimacy. The illness often cuts down on private time for relaxing, talking, or making love because both spouses are scrambling to take care of children, finances, and daily life tasks. If each partner tries to keep up a cheerful facade, the result is two lonely people, each burdened with a secret load of fear and sadness. The person who is ill can become increasingly self-centered and angry at the world, thereby alienating significant others.

Erectile Dysfunction

Difficulty in achieving or maintaining erections is the most common sexual presenting complaint in men with a chronic illness. The hormonal, vascular, and neurological mechanisms of erection are vulnerable to damage. Men often feel more comfortable seeking help for erection problems than for other sexual dysfunctions because they see the loss of erectile capacity as a medical problem. Because Chapter 7 discusses organic causes of erectile dysfunction in detail, Table 12.1 briefly summarizes the chronic illnesses that can damage the erection reflex and the basic mechanisms usually affected. Life-style habits that impair general health, including smoking (Condra, Morales, Owen, Surridge, & Fenemore, 1986), alcohol abuse (Fahrner, 1987), and a high-fat diet (Virag, Bouilly, & Frydman, 1985), also increase a man's risk of sexual dysfunction with aging because of their effects on the mechanisms underlying erection.

Nevertheless, some men with a chronic illness have purely psychological causes for an erection problem. For example, Jensen (1986) found a 36% rate of spontaneous remission of sexual dysfunction in a group of 51 men with Type I diabetes followed for 6 years. Many of the men whose problem improved had found new, more satisfying relationships. Psychological factors that play a role in decreased desire for sex, particularly performance anxiety related to the traditional male role, can also impair erections. The clinician should be alert for signs of a psychogenic dysfunction, including preserved nocturnal erections, satisfactory erections during masturbation or erotic stimulation, better function with a particular partner, or a sudden onset of the problem that does not coincide with any new physical factor.

TABLE 12.1   Diseases Associated with Organic Erectile Dysfunction

Disease	Frequent mechanisms of impairment
Cardiovascular disease	Pelvic arteriosclerosis Medication side effects (antihypertensives, β blockers, lanoxin, spirolactone)
Cancer	Damage to prostatic nerve plexus in radical pelvic surgery Neurotoxic chemotherapy Vascular damage from pelvic irradiation Hormonal effects of opiates and antiemetics Hormone therapy for metastatic prostate cancer
Diabetes	Pelvic arteriosclerosis Autonomic neuropathy
End stage renal disease	Pelvic arteriosclerosis Autonomic neuropathy Hyperprolactinemia and other hormonal abnormalities Medication side effects (antihypertensives, β blockers, etc.)
COPD	Pelvic arteriosclerosis Autonomic neuropathy Hormonal abnormalities
Multiple sclerosis	Damage to spinal cord centers mediating sexual function

Female Arousal-Phase Dysfunctions

In women, too, the arousal phase is easily disrupted by illness (Schover et al., 1987). Because rates of cardiovascular disease, cancer, arthritis, and other medical problems increase with age, many patients are postmenopausal. The major sexual impact of decreased estrogen is a thinning of the genital mucosa, with decreased vaginal expansion and lubrication (Leiblum, Bachmann, Kemmann, Colburn, & Swartzman, 1983; Semmens, Tsai, Semmens, & Loadholt, 1985). Some women experience only slight changes in sexual function, but others have dryness and pain with intercourse as well as spotting, genital soreness, or urethral irritation for days after sexual activity. Although an underlying mechanism of postmenopausal changes is probably decreased genital vascularity, researchers have not been able consistently to measure changes in vaginal blood flow with current technology (Myers & Morokoff, 1986). Perhaps risk factors for pelvic arteriosclerosis, such as heavy smoking, hypercholesterolemia, or diabetes, determine the severity of postmenopausal vaginal atrophy just as they affect men's erectile capacity. Several studies have found reduced vaginal lubrication with sexual arousal in diabetic women (Jensen, 1981, 1986; Schreiner-Engel et al., 1987;

Tyrer et al., 1983). Another possible mechanism for the diabetic woman's problems could be autonomic neuropathy.

Premature menopause related to end-stage renal disease, pelvic irradiation, or cancer chemotherapies that damage ovarian function can cause especially severe symptoms. If women with premature menopause do not have estrogen replacement therapy, they are also at increased risk for osteoporosis and cardiovascular disease with aging. Pelvic radiotherapy as a cancer treatment not only impairs sexual arousal by destroying the ovaries but also can have direct effects on the vagina, causing the mucosa to become thin and the vaginal barrel to shrink and lose elasticity. Pain with intercourse is not unusual after such treatment (Schover, Fife, & Gershenson, 1989).

Women who lack desire for sex or who are distracted by fears of dyspareunia may also have difficulty becoming subjectively and physiologically aroused if they try to engage in sex. Another emotional factor inhibiting arousal is a reminder during lovemaking of a physical defect. For example, some women after a mastectomy no longer enjoy the caressing of their remaining breast.

Male Orgasmic Dysfunction

For both men and women, orgasm is a more robust part of the sexual response than arousal. With chronic illness, orgasm-phase dysfunctions are less common than impairment of the excitement phase. Few physical conditions other than central nervous system damage from a stroke (Bray, De-Frank, & Wolfe, 1981; Sjögren, 1983) or spinal cord injury (Yalla, 1982) actually prevent men from reaching orgasm. Although only 14% of men attain the sensation of orgasm after spinal cord injury (Yalla, 1982), men continue to have orgasms after amputation of the penis for cancer or after radical pelvic cancer surgery that removes the semen-producing prostate and seminal vesicles (Schover, 1987). The sensory nerves that control the muscular contractions of ejaculation and the sensation of orgasmic pleasure are protected near the sidewall of the pelvis so that they are rarely damaged. Premature ejaculation also seems unrelated to chronic illness (Schover et al., 1987).

A number of conditions can decrease the intensity of orgasmic pleasure, however (Schover & Jensen, 1988). Men who reach orgasm without a firm erection, for example after impairment of the circulation to the penis, may complain that the duration or strength of their orgasmic sensation is decreased. "Dry" orgasms that occur without ejaculation of semen after a transurethral prostatectomy (Murphy & Lipschultz, 1987), radical prostatectomy or cystectomy (Schover, Evans, & von Eschenbach, 1986), or surgery that damages the nerves that regulate the first, emission phase of male orgasm (Schover & von Eschenbach, 1985b) also sometimes are less intense than normal. Some psychotropic medications, particularly the phenothiazines, interfere with emission or the sensory experience of orgasm as well (Schover & Jensen, 1988). High doses of these same medications, or of alcohol, may delay or prevent orgasm.

Occasionally men with a chronic illness may have difficulty reaching orgasm or experience reduced pleasure with orgasm because of psychological factors. One of the most common scenarios is a man with organically impaired erections who simply gives up on sex, not even experimenting with masturbation or penile stimulation from a partner to see if orgasm would be possible without a full erection. A few men inhibit themselves from reaching orgasm because of specific fears, such as the anxiety that orgasm would cause a heart attack or that semen could contain cancer cells harmful to a partner.

Female Orgasmic Dysfunction

Surveys about sexual function in groups of medical patients often focus on ease of reaching orgasm as a measure of women's sexual satisfaction. Orgasm is certainly an important dimension of female sexuality, but sometimes researchers may overlook the impact of chronic illness on desire and arousal because orgasm is so much easier to assess. As in men, isolated orgasm-phase dysfunctions are less common than decrements in desire or arousal for chronically ill women. Most studies of diabetic women have found that orgasmic capacity is no different than in age-matched healthy samples (Jensen, 1981, 1986; Newman & Bertelson, 1986; Tyrer et al., 1983). One recent paper reported deficits in desire, arousal, and orgasm in older, Type II diabetic women compared to controls (Schreiner-Engel et al., 1987). The problems in reaching orgasm were not an isolated dysfunction, however, but rather part of an overall decrease in sexual responsiveness. Female sexual dysfunction in end-stage renal disease also appears to affect all phases of the response cycle (Mastrogiacomo et al., 1984). The survey by Schover et al. (1987) of cancer patients who were undergoing sexual counseling revealed a high prevalence of problems reaching orgasm for women even before cancer. Thus, after cancer treatment, the increase in inorgasmia was less pronounced than the changes in sexual desire or dyspareunia.

Some antidepressant drugs apparently do prevent orgasm in a sizable minority of women (Shen & Sata, 1983). The mechanism for the change is not clearly defined, but patients report feeling normal levels of sexual desire and arousal. Paradoxically, the same drugs seem more likely to impair erection, rather than orgasm, in men.

Like men, women can undergo loss of portions of the genital tissue or pelvic organs and still retain a normal capacity for orgasm. Orgasm occurs after radical vulvectomy (Anderson & Hacker, 1983a; Moth, Andreasson, Jensen, & Bock, 1983), simple or radical hysterectomy (Dennerstein & Burrows, 1982; Schover, Fife, & Gershenson, 1989), or anterior (Schover & von Eschenbach, 1985c) or total exenteration (Andersen & Hacker, 1983b).

Although clinicians have theorized that sensations from the uterus or cervix add to orgasmic pleasure, few prospective studies exist of orgasmic changes in women undergoing hysterectomy alone, without oophorectomy and its accompanying hormonal changes (Dennerstein & Burrows, 1982). One prospective case series of 26 women having radical hysterectomy for cervical cancer did not find reduced orgasmic intensity or capacity after hysterectomy (Schover, Fife, & Gershenson, 1989).

Surprisingly little is known about orgasm in spinal-cord-injured women (Schover & Jensen, 1988, pp. 100–101). Anecdotal reports suggest that some women experience orgasms even though genital sensation has been lost, but no psychophysiological recordings of such phenomena are available (Levin & Wagner, 1987). Our understanding of the mechanisms of orgasm, even in healthy women, remains limited (Rosen & Beck, 1988, Chapter 6).

Women may have trouble reaching orgasm because of lack of sexual desire or arousal. Dyspareunia, chronic fatigue, or anxiety about physical attractiveness are frequent culprits interfering with orgasm in women with chronic illness.

Chronic Pain

Men or women can have sexual problems related to chronic pain. Low back pain or arthritis can impair range of motion or make vigorous movement difficult during sexual activity (Schover & Jensen, 1988). Pain can produce fatigue or depression, reducing sexual desire. Genital pain is a common sexual problem for women with gynecologic cancer (Schover et al., 1987). Any syndrome associated with postmenopausal vaginal atrophy can also produce dyspareunia. Men sometimes develop pain with ejaculation or syndromes of prostatic, testicular, or penile pain. The causes for these symptoms are not always organic, although prostatitis and the penile curvature of Peyronie disease are frequent factors in male genital pain. Opiate pain medications also can interfere with sexual function by central nervous system depression or by elevating the pituitary hormone prolactin.

Overview of Diagnostic Issues

To summarize, all of the sexual dysfunctions may be seen as a consequence of chronic illness, but for men and women, sexual desire and arousal appear to be more vulnerable to disruption than orgasm. Many patients have multiple sexual problems involving more than one phase of the sexual response cycle. Depression, chronic pain, and iatrogenic effects of medications or surgical therapies frequently complicate an already intricate pattern of emotional and organic factors. The next section describes a plan for assessing these multidimensional problems to arrive at a comprehensive treatment plan.

ASSESSMENT TECHNIQUES

The most important tool for assessing a sexual problem is the interview (Schover & Jensen, 1988). If the patient has a committed relationship, it is preferable to see both partners jointly. Scheduling a conjoint interview communicates the message that sexuality is a couple issue, setting the stage for treatment. If time permits, or if the clinician feels that some issues are not being elicited, spending a few minutes alone with each partner is helpful. Some questionnaires also aid the assessment process, including the Sex History Form (Schover & Jensen, 1988), Dyadic Adjustment Inventory (Spanier, 1976), Brief Symptom Inventory (Derogatis & Melisaratos, 1983), and Psychosocial Adjustment to Illness Scale (Derogatis, 1983). Because some patients may not have the stamina to fill out long batteries of paper-and-pencil inventories, clinicians who work in medical settings become very aware of the need to limit questionnaires to those with the highest clinical utility.

Some special issues arise in evaluating patients in a medical hospital or clinic setting. The majority of patients referred to the sex therapist have never seen a mental health professional before. They may view psychotherapy as stigmatizing or fear that the referral means that their problems are viewed as psychogenic. Rather than beginning by asking for a definition of the sexual dysfunction, as a clinician would in a sex therapy clinic, it can be helpful to start by discussing the purpose of the sexual evaluation. The clinician can explain that sexual problems are common after a chronic illness and that the purpose of the interview is to find out how the patient and partner have coped with the disease and its sexual effects and to determine whether sex education or counseling could be helpful.

Another patient concern is confidentiality. Sexual information is very private, yet in a hospital setting, the medical chart is accessible to many, including clerks, nurses, and the patients themselves. It is important to keep chart notes brief, limiting them to a thumbnail sketch of the history, a diagnosis, and a treatment plan. More detailed information can be kept in a private file. If the hospital will allow this arrangement, it reassures patients to know privacy is protected. Occasionally, the interview must be conducted in a hospital room with another patient in the neighboring bed and nurses walking in and out. If there is no reasonable alternative, the clinician can ask the patient if he or she feels comfortable before proceeding. Sometimes leaving a television or radio on can provide some masking background noise.

Referring health professionals vary in their wish for information from the assessment. Some see the referral as a way to avoid dealing with an unsettling topic. Others are very interested and want to discuss the details of the case. The sex therapist should ask patients' permission to share the "private file" evaluation note with the referral source. If the assessment could have an impact on medical care, the clinician can call the referring clinician directly to discuss the issues.

Whether practicing in a medical setting or a private office, the sex therapist who treats chronically ill patients should have close contact with medical specialists who collaborate in the evaluation process. Most men with erectile dysfunction need specialized examinations to determine whether vascular, neurological, or hormonal abnormalities contribute to the problem (Montague, 1988; Schover & Jensen, 1988, Chapter 6). Women with dyspareunia are another group that should be referred to a specialist, in this case a gynecologist with expertise in assessing sexual dysfunction (Fordney, 1978). Other sexual problems may require input from an endocrinologist, internist, diabetologist, oncologist, or other specialist before a mental health professional can prescribe treatment responsibly.

The Assessment Interview

A comfortable way to begin an assessment interview is to review background material from the chart, such as age, occupation, years of marriage, number of children, and medical history. Going over these facts briefly gives the clinician a chance to communicate caring and understanding of the patient or couple's viewpoint before asking about more emotionally laden issues. It is also a good time to ask about emotional coping mechanisms used by each partner in reacting to the illness and about their ability to live a healthy life style, that is, compliance with medical care, smoking, diet, and use of substances.

The clinician can then turn to the marital relationship or, for an unmarried patient, to a history of intimate dating relationships and previous marriages. One way to organize the questions is to try to assess the relationship strengths that can help a couple cope with a chronic illness. From clinical and research experience, couples with a good relationship often feel closer as they deal with an illness (Rieker, Edbril, & Garnick, 1985; Schover & von Eschenbach, 1985b; Schover, Gonzales, & von Eschenbach, 1986). Couples do well when partners communicate caring openly, can share other feelings, especially fear and sadness, can temporarily switch some of their marital roles as the illness demands, can negotiate to resolve disagreements, and have similar needs for intimacy. Table 12.2 suggests questions that assess these areas. For unmarried patients, the interviewer can focus on whether social relationships meet similar criteria.

One can also define sexual skills that help patients stay sexually active despite debilitating medical problems. These include flexibility in terms of who initiates lovemaking, clear sexual communication, a focus on the pleasure of the lovemaking process versus on a goal of performance, comfort with each partner reaching orgasm through noncoital stimulation as an alternative to intercourse (Schover, Evans, & von Eschenbach, 1986, 1987), agreement between partners on sexual variety, and an attitude that sexual

TABLE 12.2 Assessing Relationship Strengths

Strengths	Questions to ask
Ability to show caring	Is it easy for each partner to reach out with an affectionate gesture, compliment, or loving statement? How do you show caring to your mate? Has expression of caring changed since the illness began? . . . since the sexual problem began?
Ability to share feelings	How do you let your partner know if you feel . . . (angry, frightened, depressed)? How openly do you show your positive feelings? How much have you discussed this illness together? How much have you discussed this sexual problem?
Role flexibility	If your illness prevents you from managing your usual jobs in the family, how does your mate take over? How do each of you feel about that? How often do the two of you switch jobs, such as child care, household chores, or financial management?
Ability to negotiate about disagreements	How are family decisions made? If you disagree, how does the issue get resolved? Are there disagreements that keep coming up on a chronic basis? How has the illness affected conflict between you?
Similar needs for intimacy	Do the two of you usually agree about the amount of time you like to spend together? Does either of you end up feeling lonely, even when you are together? How has the illness affected each of your needs for togetherness and for time alone?

attractiveness does not consist only of physical perfection. Table 12.3 suggests strategies for assessing these issues.

Of course it is also crucial to get a thorough sense of sexual function for each partner, including problems of desire, arousal, orgasm, or coital pain (Schover et al., 1982; Schover & Jensen, 1988). Patients with a chronic illness often have more than one specific sexual dysfunction. For older women, assessing problems related to menopause is particularly important. Clinicians should be alert for patients, female and male, who panic at small changes in the sexual response related to normal aging. Because the assessment of specific sexual dysfunctions is covered in the references cited above as well as in other chapters of this volume, there is no need to elaborate further here.

Several other issues should be kept in mind during the assessment because they may complicate treatment of sexual problems in the chronically ill. For young couples, fertility may be an even more salient concern than sexual dysfunction. Clinicians should become familiar with causes of infertility related to chronic disease and with emotional reactions to available treatments (Fagan et al., 1986; Leiblum, Kemmann, & Lane, 1987; Schover & Jensen, 1988, Chapter 11). End-stage renal disease and therapy to treat cancer often impair fertility. An illness can also bring an extramarital affair into the open as priorities in life change or the partners panic about the future. Sometimes the healthier spouse begins an affair as a way of punishing a partner for becoming ill or to cope with separation anxiety. In other instances one partner abandons an affair when the illness is diagnosed and undergoes the stress of secretly mourning the loss. Unmarried patients often lack adequate social support to cope with an illness. A sexual dysfunction can prevent them from trying to find a partner or reduce their motivation to socialize in nonromantic contexts.

TREATMENT TECHNIQUES

The clinician should conclude the assessment interview with recommendations for treatment. A number of patients seek reassurance and knowledge about causes of their sexual problems but are not ready to engage in sex therapy or to commit to a medical treatment. For these individuals, perhaps 15 minutes to an hour of education and advice during the assessment session or in one more appointment can suffice. In 384 evaluations of cancer patients referred to a sexual rehabilitation service, 73% of patients were seen only once or twice (Schover et al., 1987).

Another large group of patients would benefit from two to five sessions of brief sexual counseling (Schover & Jensen, 1988, Chapter 7). These couples or individuals are basically healthy psychologically but need help in adjusting to the impact of illness on sexuality and relationships. Perhaps 10% to 20% of patients with a chronic illness need intensive sex therapy. Of course

TABLE 12.3 Assessing Sexual Skills

Skill	Questions to ask
Flexibility in initiating sex	Who usually get things started when you make love? Has there been a change in sexual initiation since the sexual problem began?
Clear sexual communication	If you would like a particular kind of touch during sex, how do you let your partner know (verbal, nonverbal, no cue at all)? How much have the two of you discussed this sexual problem? Have you been able to change your sexual routine to accommodate to your illness?
Focus on pleasure versus performance	How would you define good sex? What aspects of sex are most important to each of you?
Comfort with noncoital orgasms	Do you ever help your partner reach orgasm through manual or oral caressing rather than during intercourse? If your illness or sexual problem makes intercourse difficult, will you sometimes use other lovemaking techniques to reach orgasms together?
Agreement on sexual variety	Do the two of you ever disagree about experimenting sexually, for example, trying oral sex, a new position for intercourse, or a new location for lovemaking?
Feeling sexually attractive despite physical changes	What makes you feel like a sexually attractive person? What do you think makes your partner attracted to you? Has your illness or this sexual problem made you feel less attractive?

333

this group makes up a larger percentage of those ultimately evaluated by a sex therapist, since the more severe problems are the ones most likely to be identified by the primary care team. Criteria for choosing sex therapy include a chronic sexual dysfunction that predated the illness or has not responded to brief counseling, a relationship that is conflicted or destabilized by the illness, sexual dysfunction associated with generally poor psychological coping, or difficulty adjusting to a severe change in sexual self-image such as after facial cancer surgery, radical pelvic cancer surgery, spinal cord injury, stroke, etc.

Brief Sexual Counseling

Brief sexual counseling usually has several components (Schover & Jensen, 1988; Schover, Schain, & Montague, 1989). They include sex education, changing maladaptive sexual attitudes, helping patients resume sex after an illness, overcoming physical handicaps, and dealing with the impact of illness on the dyadic relationship. These therapy elements do not need to be applied in a particular order. Rather, clinicians should consider each of them in constructing a comprehensive treatment plan for a particular case. The distinction between brief sexual counseling and intensive sex therapy is quantitative to a large extent. The techniques described below are also used in an intensive case; they would, however, be supplemented by behavioral techniques to treat specific dysfunctions and by interventions using psychodynamic or systems principles that demand a longer-term approach.

Sex Education

Many patients with a chronic illness are sadly ignorant of the physiological impact on their sexual response. They often harbor unrealistic fears, for example, that a hysterectomy will prevent orgasm, that intercourse is a high-risk situation for heart attacks, or that cancer is contagious through sexual contact. They may not be aware of real risks to their sexual function such as the side effects of antidepressant medications or antihypertensives (Segraves, Madsen, Carter, & Davis, 1985), long-term damage to sexual function from heavy tobacco and alcohol use (Abel, 1985; Condra et al., 1986), or the impact of postmenopausal vaginal atrophy (Leiblum et al., 1983; Semmens et al., 1985). Thus, education is a crucial role for the sexuality specialist.

Most patients benefit from a brief review of male and/or female genital anatomy, the changes that occur during the sexual response cycle, and the causes of any organic impairment related to aging or illness. Three-dimensional models of the external genitals and cross-sectional models of the pelvis are particularly helpful in illustrating this information,[1] but drawings

---

[1] A catalogue of genital models is available from Jim Jackson and Company, 33 Richdale Avenue, Cambridge, Massachusetts 02140.

are a reasonable, low-cost alternative. A variety of educational videotapes are also available.[2] For some specific diseases, patient-education materials have been published (Arthritis Foundation, 1982; Schover & Randers-Pehrson, 1988a, 1988b). Optimally, both partners in a couple should be present for the education session. As the clinician presents material, he or she should elicit questions and discussion (Schover & Jensen, 1988, Chapter 7).

Attitude Change

Some sexual attitudes are quite maladaptive when coping with a chronic illness. Those include the following beliefs:

1. Sexual activity is unhealthy. Because sex is linked in our culture to sin, filth, and disease, many patients believe that having sex will exacerbate an illness or interfere with medical therapy. If these beliefs are not challenged, they lead to unnecessary cessation of sexual activity.

2. Sex should be spontaneous. If lovemaking can only occur on a whim, patients have no way to cope with pain, fatigue, or medication effects except to wait for a better time. During an illness, couples who want to stay sexually active often need to plan sex for the optimal moment. For example, a woman on hemodialysis may only have normal energy levels on one day out of three. A man with a colostomy may prefer sex at a time of day when his bowels are less active. A terminally ill cancer patient can have a small "window" of time when pain medications are effective but drowsiness has not set in.

3. Intercourse is the only sex worth having. Couples who reject the idea of sharing orgasms through manual or oral caressing have no alternative lovemaking available if an erection problem or dyspareunia interferes with intercourse. This belief also can interfere with "safe sex" practices for a couple in which one partner is antibody-positive for HIV. Many people refuse to try condoms or to eliminate sexual practices that involve exchange of body fluids because of narrow views of what is normal or pleasurable.

Attitude change can be fostered by using cognitive–behavioral methods such as constructing arguments to combat false beliefs, substituting positive self-statements for negative ones, providing examples of good sexual coping from peer support groups or patient education materials, and actually assigning new behaviors in a sequence of graduated tasks to increase the chance of a success experience.

[2] A catalogue of sex education videotapes can be obtained from Focus International, Inc., 14 Oregon Drive, Huntington Station, New York 11746.

Resuming Sex

If an illness, debilitating medical treatment, or surgery has interrupted a couple's sex life, the sensate-focus exercises provide a helpful framework for resuming sexual activity. Often affectionate touching has decreased along with sexual caressing so that any intimate contact is fraught with performance anxiety. The structure of the sensate-focus exercise, including explicit planning of how to initiate sexual touch, takes the worry out of making the first move. The focus is on exploring each partner's capacity to enjoy touch. Patients may discover that new ways of caressing can compensate for changes in arousability or even in sensory capacity. These exercises also can desensitize partners to body changes such as a mastectomy scar, ostomy appliance, or limb prosthesis.

Another skill that aids when resuming sex is clear verbal and nonverbal communication. The therapist can ask partners to be quite explicit in telling each other about preferred sexual stimulation, readiness to proceed to intercourse, or even genital pain. Techniques of nonverbal communication can also be suggested. A sexual routine may work well for decades as long as both partners are healthy. An illness that impairs sexual function disrupts old habits, however, so that open communication becomes crucial. Some medical problems also interfere with channels of communication, including a laryngectomy, aphasia, or blindness. In such cases, partners must learn to enhance alternative sensory modes of contacts.

Overcoming Physical Handicaps

An illness may affect genital integrity; for example, radical cancer surgery may remove genital tissue (Schover, 1987). Arthritis (Ferguson & Figley, 1979) or chronic back pain (Sjögren & Fugl-Meyer, 1981) may diminish range of motion during lovemaking. Multiple sclerosis (Valleroy & Kraft, 1984) or spinal cord trauma (Yalla, 1982) may actually create abnormalities of genital sensation. Organic erectile dysfunction is another type of sexual "handicap." Changes in physical appearance such as a mastectomy scar, an ostomy, or a limb amputation may not directly impair sexual function, but they can be devastating to a person's feelings of attractiveness.

The clinician can become familiar with technical problems that patients experience by visiting them in the hospital during recovery and seeing the physical changes, conferring with physical, occupational, or enterostomal therapists, and talking to people who have managed to become sexually active again despite a physical disability. Advice on overcoming physical limitations is often based on creativity and common sense. Patients can (1) time sex to avoid periods of fatigue or pain, (2) use positions that are less strenuous, (3) use pillows to support a body part that is painful or weak, (4) use a vibrator to compensate for decreased genital sensation, (5) wear attractive nightgowns or undergarments to conceal a scar or an ostomy appliance, or (6) prepare for sex by taking a warm bath or a pain medication to decrease discomfort.

Decreasing Marital Conflict

Marital conflict that is related to the stress of illness often responds well to brief counseling. Common situations include confusion or resentment on the part of the healthy spouse at having to assume new marital roles, disagreement in the extended family about the proper management of the disease, difficulty in communicating about sexual needs, fear of dependency or impending death, and anger on the part of one spouse at the other's failure to live a healthier life style.

Some techniques of behavioral marital therapy are particularly helpful with these problems. Assigning couples to increase their expression of caring (Stuart, 1980) often lightens the mood at home, as does focusing attention on the need for intimate time apart from daily life stress. The therapist can suggest going out on planned "dates" or scheduling time routinely just to talk or hold each other. A caretaker spouse also needs to feel entitled to a few private hours for relaxation. Communication and problem-solving skills can be taught to the partners (Jacobson & Holtzworth-Munroe, 1986).

Intensive Sex Therapy

The techniques of sex therapy can easily be applied to a patient whose dysfunction is related to a chronic illness (Schover & Jensen, 1988, Chapter 7). Men and women in medical settings exhibit the entire spectrum of sexual dysfunctions so that the methods described elsewhere in this book are all relevant at times.

Some special issues can arise when practicing in a medical setting, however.

Spacing of Sessions

Originally, Masters and Johnson (1970) tailored sex therapy to patients who lived out of town, with sessions taking place daily over 2 weeks. Heiman and LoPiccolo (1983) compared the effectiveness of daily versus weekly sex therapy and found essentially equal success with either format. Currently, one weekly session is the most common spacing for outpatient sex therapy. In some medical settings, however, such as a regional cancer center, a clinician may need to compress sessions into a brief span of time to minimize traveling expenses for the patient who does not live locally.

Diane wanted help in improving her self-esteem and regaining sexual desire after a renal transplant. She hated her surgical scars and the visible side effects of her prednisone regimen including weight gain, "moon face," and acne. She and her husband lived 200 miles away, however. After an initial couple session coinciding with a postoperative visit to her surgeon, the therapist scheduled several telephone consultations. The couple lived in a rural area that lacked clinicians with expertise in sex therapy. Diana's sexual responsiveness improved, but the therapist believed the progress was probably the result of reassurance, better knowledge of how to cope, a basically good marriage, and "tincture of time."

Including the Partner

In a sex therapy clinic, it is relatively easy to structure treatment as couple's therapy. People often arrive expecting sex therapy to involve both partners. In a medical setting, the ill patient is more clearly labeled as the one with the problem. Although diabetes, for example, can become a couple issue (Jensen, 1985), the relationship between disease and dyad is less intuitive than is the connection between a sexual dysfunction and marital conflict. Thus, the clinician may encounter more resistance to involving the partner. Because the sexual dysfunction often has some medical basis, patients are more likely to reject couple therapy as an appropriate treatment.

Not only is it challenging to reframe the sexual dysfunction as a couple issue, but the partner may not even be available for therapy sessions. If the couple lives far away, the healthy spouse may be at home while the patient stays at the medical center. Even if the couple lives locally, the spouse may be stretched to the limit by assuming work, household, and child-care responsibilities.

Some hospitals facilitate partner involvement because they encourage spouses to participate in learning about an illness and promoting healthier behavior, for example, as part of cardiac rehabilitation or education about coping with diabetes. The sex therapist can take advantage of such programs to entice the partner to come in. Alternatives to couple therapy include working with the patient alone, having the partner come in only periodically for therapy sessions but agreeing to participate regularly in behavioral homework, or developing therapy groups for patients who share similar illness-related sexual problems.

Goals of Sex Therapy

When sexual dysfunction is purely psychogenic, the goal of sex therapy is to reverse the symptom. If a problem has a multifactorial basis, however, treatment goals must be more modest. For example, a couple that has discontinued all sexual activity after a wife's stroke may be glad to resume some gentle lovemaking, even if the frequency never approaches premorbid levels and the patient is orgasmic far less reliably. Some couples are content with learning to vary their sexual routine by focusing on noncoital orgasms instead of intercourse when pelvic cancer surgery has destroyed a man's erectile capacity. They may reject the idea of a more drastic treatment such as a penile prosthesis.

It is important to set realistic goals with partners before beginning sex therapy so that they are not disappointed with a less-than-perfect outcome. Often the organic limitations to sexual function remain ill-defined even after extensive assessment. In those cases the clinician can begin by discussing the uncertainty with the couple. When the couple has made a good effort but progress is slow, it may be time to bring up the possibility of organic limits. The clinician can give the partners the option to discontinue sex therapy if all agree that treatment has gone as far as seems to be possible. It is important to emphasize improvement that has occurred, for example, in having sexual activity more often and with more relaxation and pleasure. The clinician often treads a tightrope between fostering unrealistic hope and becoming discouraged prematurely.

Combining Sex Therapy with Physiological Treatments

Rather than seeing intensive sex therapy as an alternative to a medical or surgical intervention, clinicians need to create integrated treatment plans that combine various modalities (Schover & Jensen, 1988, Chapter 8). Sex therapy can enhance adjustment to treatments such as a penile prosthesis (Schover & von Eschenbach, 1985a) or vaginal reconstruction. Even hormonal therapy for male hypogonadism or for postmenopausal vaginal atrophy may correct a technical problem but fail to restore sexual satisfaction. The organic deficits in sexual function associated with a chronic illness often create a ripple effect, especially in relationships that are already conflicted. Although erections normalize or dyspareunia improves, partners still struggle with deficits in self-esteem, body image, expression of affection, and sense of intimacy and trust.

It is optimal to offer a sex therapy component as part of the initial treatment so that a "package" is created. For example, a home papaverine injection program could be recommended along with a series of couple sessions to work on sexual skills such as initiation, communication, and enhancing emotional intimacy.

The biggest hurdle is working closely with the physician who is providing medical or surgical therapy so that the sex therapist is a full member of the team rather than a peripheral consultant or the person who is called in to mop up after treatment failures. In our institution we have a Center for Sexual Function including a sex therapist, an urologist, a gynecologist, and an internist, but unless we make a special effort, we still often recommend one treatment rather than taking a truly integrative approach. One key is to have frequent case conferences, with the ideal being a weekly meeting to discuss all new evaluations.

CASE STUDIES

A Successful Case

The following case illustrates intensive sex therapy techniques modified for use in a medical setting. The patient was seen individually, but his partner cooperated in behavioral homework exercises. Sessions took place 2 to 4 weeks apart because the patient was undergoing chemotherapy for cancer and suffered periodic debilitation after his treatments. Although the sexual problem had predated his illness, it was unclear whether organic factors now played a minor role in the dysfunction.

James was a 56-year-old never-married accountant diagnosed as having large-cell lymphoma 4 years before his evaluation for sexual dysfunction. He was treated with 15 courses of chemotherapy and had 3 years of remission. A month before the assessment, he was found to have a mass at the dome of his bladder. Surgery revealed a recurrence of the lymphoma and, in addition, a second primary cancer, a small adenocarcinoma in his sigmoid colon. A section of colon was removed, and he began a new regimen of chemotherapy drugs to treat the lymphoma. He took early retirement from his job and rented an apartment near the cancer center, since he lived several hundred miles away.

James asked to see the cancer center's sex therapist because he was having difficulty achieving erections. He was a slight man, always neatly dressed in a suit and tweed hat to conceal the baldness caused by his chemotherapy. Although he appeared on edge during therapy sessions, he was quick to laugh at himself and had a warmth that was appealing.

James had had a long history of sexual dysfunction and marginal psychological coping. He had been raised by a very controlling widowed mother, who had James sleep in bed with her until he was age 12. When he was in his mid-30s, James had 2 years of psychotherapy and medication with meprobamate to treat obsessive thoughts that he was homosexual. In fact his sexual fantasies were about women, and he had never engaged in any activity with a partner of either gender. At that time he did begin a relationship with a woman. It took a number of attempts before he was able to achieve an erection firm enough for intercourse. Several more months of sexual activity took place before he could ejaculate intravaginally, but the couple then had a satisfying sex life for 4 years. James ended the relationship because his girl friend was pressing for marriage. In the ensuing years, he continued to masturbate with normal erections and ejaculation but had no further partner activity until he met a new woman 2 weeks before he came in for evaluation.

Emily was a 66-year-old woman who had been widowed for 8 years before meeting James at a dance. She took an assertive role in initiating their conversation, letting him know that she found him attractive. In fact, she drove him to her house and seduced him. James felt Emily was not very physically attractive but said he could not afford to be picky, given his own poor health. He did like her personality and was able to feel some sexual excitement during their lovemaking.

Although James had continued to masturbate with normal erections and ejaculation after his recent cancer surgery, he could not achieve a full erection with Emily. He tried giving her feedback on how to caress his penis, but she did not seem to understand what he wanted. She was also reluctant when he suggested they try the female superior position for intercourse, but James could not manage to penetrate in any case. James was quite aware of feeling anxious and consciously tried to be less goal-oriented on the couple's second date. Although Emily was shy about communicating any of her own preferences for touch, James managed to bring her to orgasm through manual stimulation. She was upset that James did not have an orgasm himself, but even her prolonged hand caressing of his penis was not effective.

James was particularly concerned about effects of arousal without ejaculation on his health. He denied anxiety that sex would worsen his cancer, but he did have a long history of "chronic prostatitis" and had been told by a urologist that he should masturbate to ejaculation at least twice a week. James never had a documented bacterial infection of his prostate. His only symptom over the years had been a vague congested sensation. The therapist explained that this feeling was related to temporary vasocongestion in the genital area caused by sexual arousal, and even without James reaching orgasm, his genital circulation would routinely normalize so that there were no long-term health risks.

James sought advice on whether to keep seeing Emily. The therapist suggested that if he were enjoying the contacts he might as well get to know Emily a little better. He needed a friend in his new environment and had been honest in explaining his situation to Emily, not fostering any hope of a committed relationship. The therapist pointed out that since James was not highly attracted to Emily, he was not likely to feel traumatized if their dating did not work out. Just to rule out any impact of cancer treatment, serum testosterone and prolactin levels were obtained. Both were in the normal range.

After the first session, the therapist assigned James to begin reading *Male Sexuality* (Zilbergeld, 1978) and to continue dating Emily without attempting intercourse. He returned 2 weeks later after another course of chemotherapy. He and Emily had tried lovemaking with an agreement not to include vaginal penetration. James noticed that his erection became firm at several times during the session, although he did not reach an orgasm. He also had asked Emily for oral sex, but she nonverbally avoided it. The couple did not discuss her reluctance. James was worried about whether sexual activity could damage the catheter implanted in his subclavian vein, just below the shoulder, for delivery of chemotherapy. He was also concerned about the safety of having sex during periods when his immune system was suppressed as a side effect of cancer treatment. After consulting with James's oncologist, the therapist reassured him that his subclavian catheter was safe as long as he avoided hitting, rubbing, or contaminating the site—an unlikely consequence during routine lovemaking. The oncologist also suggested that sex was safe as long as James's blood counts were high enough so that he could be treated as an outpatient. It could be more important to avoid crowds and people with colds or flu. Sexually transmitted diseases were naturally a concern, but Emily had not been sexually active for several years prior to meeting James.

James also wanted to talk about his determination to stay optimistic in fighting his cancer. He was encouraged because his lymph nodes had decreased in size after his first course of chemotherapy. The therapist again suggested that Emily could be a source of companionship and pleasure to James during his stay at the cancer center. James had told Emily about his sex therapy. She agreed to participate in some sensate-focus homework, but neither felt a need to have Emily present at the sessions with the therapist.

James had a total of 13 sessions over a period of 10 months. Spacing the sessions gave him a chance to attempt new behaviors while taking some days off from sex at the time he received chemotherapy. He continued to read *Male Sexuality* and was working on substituting positive self-statements for the distracting thoughts about erectile dysfunction. He told himself, "I can just enjoy this touching and give Emily an orgasm with my hand. It does not matter if I have an erection tonight." In his own masturbation he practiced gaining and losing erections to increase his confidence that he did not need to have an erection at all times during sex. His erections became more reliable during Emily's manual stimulation, although he still could not reach orgasm in her presence. When James became discouraged at his slow progress, the therapist reminded him that it had been 4 years since his last sexual relationship.

It took James 2 months to be able to accomplish the step of penetrating Emily's vagina for a brief moment, first just with a partial erection and then with a full one. Emily became more assertive, too, in telling James how she preferred to be touched. At around this time, James told the therapist that he was feeling pressured by Emily.

JAMES: She keeps saying she loves me.

THERAPIST: How does that make you feel?

JAMES: Well I'm grateful to her for being so good to me while I'm sick and all, and she's a real nice lady, but she *is* 66 and kind of overweight.

THERAPIST: Are you saying you like Emily, but you don't love her?

JAMES: I guess so. Sometimes when I think about getting old and being alone, I've even started to wonder if I should get married.

THERAPIST: Would Emily like to marry you?

JAMES: I'm sure she would, even though I told her from the start I was a confirmed bachelor, and she never mentions the word. But anyway, I wouldn't marry anyone unless I could have normal sex.

THERAPIST: You know in my experience, most women in your age group don't see erections as crucial to that decision.

JAMES: I know, but *I* do.

The therapist realized that James now had made the erection problem the perfect excuse for not marrying Emily. She suspected that his ambivalence about intimacy was a factor in maintaining the sexual dysfunction. Sure enough, after his first successful attempt at vaginal penetration, James came in certain that Emily was expecting marriage and was ready to break off their relationship. The therapist pointed out that James had been honest about his intentions towards Emily from the start. The pressure stemmed more from his own attitudes than from any verbal communication on Emily's part. James agreed to have another talk with Emily, voicing his fears of hurting her and asking her openly to continue dating without any expectations about more commitment. James also decided he needed a self-statement to use during intercourse. He and the therapist came up with the following: "I can have intercourse with Emily because with all our sexual play we are already as close as two lovers can get. Intercourse won't make us any closer."

James was able to progress to thrusting while maintaining his erection but still was unable to ejaculate in Emily's presence. He became more distressed when he began to have difficulty reaching orgasm in his own masturbation. Again he brought up fears that his prostate would be damaged. The therapist discovered that James had a mental image of his prostate getting swollen with semen to the point of bursting. She used a lifelike model of the pelvic organs to correct his ideas and again reassured him that there was no negative health consequence to failure of ejaculation. Over the next several weeks James tried to focus on pleasurable arousal during sex. With Emily, he practiced slow, nondemanding movement during intercourse. He had never had vivid sexual fantasies, so he read a book of men's erotica and watched an X-rated video with Emily, who was much more comfortable than James about lust.

James began to have orgasms easily again through his own masturbation. During intercourse with Emily, he experienced a seepage of semen, without any force or a clear sensation of orgasm. He was practicing further cognitive strategies when he finished his chemotherapy and decided to go home for a while. Emily was sad to see him leave but did not press for any change in their living arrangements. James promised to visit her whenever he returned to the cancer center for follow-up, and on those occasions, they continued to have functional sex, although James never was completely satisfied with the quality of his orgasms.

The sex therapist realized that she had not heard from James for a number of months and asked his oncologist for news. She was saddened to hear that James had had a second recurrence of lymphoma and had died in his home community after a rapid worsening of his disease.

One of the issues in sex therapy with chronically ill patients is setting realistic goals. Quality of life is precious, even if an improvement of sexual function is transient because the underlying disease progresses or becomes fatal. In this case, the therapist felt satisfied that James had achieved a sense of closeness with Emily and had enjoyed a period of renewed sexuality after his years of celibacy. She hoped that his experience might have made life feel a little more meaningful at the end. Her major regret was her own lost chance to say good-bye to James or to offer emotional support during his dying. She had decided to let him initiate contacts, but given his pride and essential isolation, perhaps she might have been more aggressive in scheduling follow-ups. The boundary between anticipating the patient's needs and intrusively serving her own needs was unclear in her clinical judgment.

A Failed Case

This second case was treated under more optimal conditions, since both partners could participate fully and lived in the local area. It points up the limitations imposed by a severe illness as well as the difficulties when a relationship has been conflicted for many years, and the spouses are still influenced by anger and guilt about the past.

Sylvia, a 60-year-old homemaker, was evaluated along with her husband of 42 years, Harry, a retired highway engineer. Two years previously, Sylvia had had a lumbar laminectomy, surgery to repair a herniated disk in her spine. She had had a respiratory arrest postoperatively, resulting in anoxic encephalopathy. Permanent neurological damage included total loss of her hearing, a short-term memory deficit, and myoclonus (episodes of muscle twitches). She could walk with the aid of a cane, but she was unable to carry out most daily household tasks. Harry became a devoted caretaker, bathing and dressing his wife, staying with her at all times, and encouraging her in her rehabilitation. Not only did Harry give up his hobby of sailing, but he no longer could bear to listen to music, knowing that Sylvia could not enjoy it. In session, Harry often reached over to hug his wife or take her hand.

The presenting problem was Sylvia's loss of sexual desire and total inability to reach orgasm since her illness. Both partners agreed that they had had an excellent sex life until her surgery, with only mild interference from back pain. Sylvia had sometimes initiated sex, with lovemaking occurring about twice a week. She had no problem after menopause with vaginal lubrication and had been coitally orgasmic on most occasions. Sexual communication had always been nonverbal, with Harry's only dissatisfaction being his wife's reluctance to try oral sex. Harry and Sylvia wanted to be able to enjoy sex again as part of their efforts to resume a more normal life. At a previous counselor's suggestion, they had tried providing Sylvia with vaginal stimulation from a phallic-shaped vibrator and had watched erotic videos, with no improvement. Sylvia's vagina was dry, and she had no sexual pleasure. In fact, intercourse had become painful.

The evaluation revealed that Sylvia had a posttraumatic stress disorder. Several times a day she had flashbacks of her experiences in the hospital. At these times she became shaky and tearful. She also startled easily, had nightmares, and had early morning awakenings. She was demoralized by her loss of ability to do domestic chores. She repeatedly asked Harry the date and forgot events from earlier in the day. Harry felt his wife coped with her anxiety about the memory deficit by watching TV game shows and consoling herself with her good ability to get the right answers or solve the puzzles. Besides beginning behavioral sex therapy, the therapist referred Sylvia to a psychiatrist who prescribed a tricyclic antidepressant. While the dose was being adjusted, Sylvia was able to learn cognitive techniques including thought-stopping plus evoking a relaxing image to deal with the flashbacks. Her general outlook improved. She slept more soundly and rarely became tearful. Her memory seemed less impaired, although some deficit clearly remained. Flashbacks still occurred, but they were not so disturbing to her.

The couple began sensate-focus exercises. They experimented with ways that Sylvia could prop herself comfortably on pillows while she caressed Harry. Although he found the touching intensely arousing, Sylvia found it only mildly pleasant. She was aware of many thoughts during the touching about her own inability to feel sexual and her failure to give Harry the pleasure he deserved. As the couple discussed their experiences, the therapist pointed out Sylvia's self-defeating cognitions and suggested that she focus instead on her physical sensations. Given Sylvia's memory deficits, it was heartening during the therapy to see her make use of cognitive techniques over the weeks.

Although Sylvia gradually experienced some mild pleasure with Harry's genital caressing, she did not reach high levels of sexual arousal. Over several weeks, the couple experimented with watching more erotic films and stimulating Sylvia's clitoral area with a hand-held vibrator that had several attachments. The therapist discovered that neither partner had much knowledge about female genital anatomy, and clitoral stimulation had not been emphasized in their previous lovemaking. Sylvia did begin to reach higher levels of arousal. The couple used a water-based lubricant to avoid irritating her vulva. They usually ended a session of lovemaking with intercourse because Sylvia wanted to give Harry that pleasure. After three therapy sessions and 6 weeks of effort, Sylvia had an orgasm from vibrator stimulation.

Harry had been calling the therapist every couple of weeks without Sylvia's knowledge, seeking reassurance that he was not a bad husband for

having sexual feelings. The therapist did not discourage the calls completely, because she perceived Harry's need for support. She encouraged
him to begin taking some leisure time for himself, emphasizing that no man
could achieve sainthood, no matter how much he loved his wife. Harry
refused to go sailing or leave Sylvia with anyone else but did feel relieved
when the therapist encouraged him to use masturbation as an outlet for the
sexual feelings that Sylvia could not satisfy. The therapist also reminded
Harry, however, that he and Sylvia were working together as partners. She
asked him to bring up his concerns in the couple's sessions. Harry tended to
infantilize Sylvia, even during the therapy hour. Because Sylvia was dependent on lip reading, the therapist always spoke slowly and distinctly, making sure Sylvia could understand. Harry tended to deliberately add comments that his wife could not catch, talking about her instead of to her. The
therapist halted this process many times.

At the beginning of the next session, Sylvia asked to see the therapist
alone. She spent a half hour expressing her concern that Harry was alienating the couple's two sons and their wives. When Sylvia became ill, Harry
had looked to his daughters-in-law for support, and they had disappointed
him greatly. He believed they did not truly love Sylvia, and he hated them
for their failure to call her and visit her routinely. Sylvia also was disappointed, but was far less angry. Her chief concern was keeping the family
together. In contrast to the rosy picture Harry and Sylvia had jointly painted
of their marriage, Sylvia very articulately described Harry's alcoholism up
until the past 6 or 7 years and his conflicts with her side of the family. She
cried as she mourned her own loss of strength and independence.

The therapist asked permission to bring Harry in to discuss these issues
jointly. It was easier to understand Harry's desperate attempts to shower
Sylvia with love, knowing his guilt over his failures in their earlier years
together. The therapist pointed out that he could be angry at family
members for their lack of caring toward him but that he needed to let Sylvia
use her own ways of handling their neglect of her. Harry agreed to be civil
to the family for Sylvia's sake.

Over the next few weeks, Sylvia had orgasms on several occasions
through Harry's manual caressing of her clitoris. Increasingly, however, she
became handicapped by severe back pain. She was rarely in the mood for
sex but always willing to help Harry reach orgasm. When she could not
endure intercourse, she would caress him with her hands. Finally, her
physicians decided that she must have another back surgery to correct a
narrowing of her spinal canal. Sylvia was frightened to go back to the
hospital but willing to risk surgery in order to reduce her chronic pain and
immobility.

The therapist continued to see Harry and Sylvia once every month or
two after surgery, but the focus of treatment became emotional support
rather than sex therapy. Struggling just to walk again and regain some
ability to perform self-care, Sylvia lost all the gains she had made in sexual

desire and arousability and could not even recall that she had recovered the capacity to reach orgasm. The situation was complicated by family turmoil, with Harry's aged father dying of cancer, and one son divorcing his wife. Even Harry lost interest in sex with these new stresses. The therapist suggested that the partners put aside the work on sexual rehabilitation until some of their daily concerns were under better control.

A major reason for the failure of this case was Sylvia's continued medical deterioration and the other family stresses. Perhaps the therapist could have had a more lasting impact, however, if she had seen Sylvia individually at intervals in addition to the couple sessions. Despite her memory deficits, Sylvia had excellent verbal skills and was able to change her behavior over time. The therapist was impressed, on the occasion that Sylvia requested individual time, with her determination to continue to hold the extended family together.

By spending time with Harry on the phone but restricting Sylvia's treatment to couple sessions, the therapist collaborated with Harry in keeping Sylvia dependent rather than encouraging Sylvia's needs for autonomy. The therapist wondered if Sylvia's lack of sexual desire was part of her frustration at being totally dependent on Harry. Certainly his intense devotion had a controlling aspect to it. Sylvia's difficulty reading lips often slowed the pace of the sessions. The therapist found herself struggling to direct all remarks to Sylvia rather than letting Harry seduce her into talking to him, with Sylvia left out. Individual work with Sylvia would have eliminated that bias.

CONCLUSIONS

Sex therapy with chronically ill patients presents special challenges. The clinician may have to work within an institutional setting where sex therapy is a novelty, juggling treatment techniques to accommodate patients' reduced energy levels and disrupted daily life routines. Most patients need brief sexual counseling rather than formal sex therapy. The goals of treatment may also be limited by the physiological impact of the disease or the treatment on sexual function. Nevertheless, the potential rewards are great because a restoration of sexual pleasure is a victory in the face of sadness and a confirmation of the will to live and be intimate with others.

REFERENCES

Abel, E. L. (1985). *Psychoactive drugs and sex*. New York: Plenum Press.

Althof, S. E., Coffman, C. B., & Levine, S. B. (1984). The effects of coronary bypass surgery on female sexual, psychological, and vocational adaptation. *Journal of Sex and Marital Therapy, 10*, 176–184.

Andersen, B. L., & Hacker, N. E. (1983a). Psychosexual adjustment after vulvar surgery. *Obstetrics and Gynecology, 62,* 457–462.

Andersen, B. L., & Hacker, N. F. (1983b). Psychosexual adjustment following pelvic exenteration. *Obstetrics and Gynecology, 61,* 331–338.

Andersen, B. L., & Jochimsen, P. R. (1985). Sexual functioning among breast cancer, gynecologic cancer, and healthy women. *Journal of Consulting and Clinical Psychology, 53,* 25–32.

Arthritis Foundation. (1982). *Arthritis: Living and loving: Information about sex.* Atlanta: Arthritis Foundation.

Bray, G. P., DeFrank, R. S., & Wolfe, T. C. (1981). Sexual functioning in stroke survivors. *Archives of Physical Medicine and Rehabilitation, 62,* 286–288.

Bukberg, J., Penman, D., & Holland, J. C. (1984). Depression in hospitalized cancer patients. *Psychosomatic Medicine, 46,* 199–212.

Condra, M., Morales, A., Owen, J. A., Surridge, D. M., & Fenemore, J. (1986). Prevalence and significance of tobacco smoking in impotence. *Urology, 27,* 495–498.

Dennerstein, L., & Burrows, G. D. (1982). Hormone replacement therapy and sexuality in women. *Clinics in Endocrinology and Metabolism, 11,* 661–679.

Derogatis, L. R. (1983). *Psychosocial Adjustment to Illness Scale (PAIS and PAIS-SR): Administration, scoring and procedures manual—I.* Baltimore: Clinical Psychometric Research.

Derogatis, L. R., & King, K. M. (1981). The coital coronary: A reassessment of the concept. *Archives of Sexual Behavior, 10,* 325–335.

Derogatis, L. R., & Melisaratos, N. (1983). The Brief Symptom Inventory: An introductory report. *Psychological Medicine, 13,* 595–605.

Fagan, P. J., Schmidt, C. W., Rock, J. A., Damewood, M. D., Halle, E., & Wise, T. N. (1986). Sexual functioning and psychologic evaluation of *in vitro* fertilization couples. *Fertility and Sterility, 46,* 668–672.

Fahrner, E. (1987). Sexual dysfunction in male alcohol addicts: Prevalence and treatment. *Archives of Sexual Behavior, 16,* 247–258.

Ferguson, K., & Figley, B. (1979). Sexuality and rheumatic disease: A prospective study. *Sexuality and Disability, 2,* 130–138.

Fordney, D. S. (1978). Dyspareunia and vaginismus. *Clinical Obstetrics and Gynecology, 21,* 205–221.

Hawton, K. (1984). Sexual adjustment of men who have had strokes. *Journal of Psychosomatic Research, 28,* 243–249.

Heiman, J. R., & LoPiccolo, J. (1983). Clinical outcome of sex therapy: Effects of daily vs. weekly treatment. *Archives of General Psychiatry, 40,* 443–449.

House, W., & Pendleton, L. (1986). Sexual dysfunction in diabetes: A survey of physicians' responses to patients' problems. *Postgraduate Medicine, 79,* 227–235.

Jacobson, N. E., & Holtzworth-Munroe, A. (1986). Marital therapy: A social learning–cognitive perspective. In N. S. Jacobson & A. S. Gurman (Eds.), *Clinical handbook of marital therapy* (pp. 29–70). New York: Guilford Press.

Jensen, S. B. (1981). Diabetic sexual dysfunction: A comparative study of 160 insulin-treated diabetic men and women and an age-matched control group. *Archives of Sexual Behavior, 10,* 493–504.

Jensen, S. B. (1985). Sexual relationships in couples with a diabetic partner. *Journal of Sex and Marital Therapy, 11,* 259–270.

Jensen, S. B. (1986). Sexual dysfunction in insulin-treated diabetics: A six-year follow-up study of 101 patients. *Archives of Sexual Behavior, 15,* 271–284.

Lieber, L., Plumb, M. M., Gerstenzang, M. L., & Holland, J. (1976). The communication of affection between cancer patients and their spouses. *Psychosomatic Medicine, 38*, 379–389.

Leiblum, S. R., Bachmann, G., Kemmann, E., Colburn, D., & Swartzman, L. (1983). Vaginal atrophy in the postmenopausal woman: The importance of sexual activity and hormones. *Journal of the American Medical Association, 249*, 2195–2198.

Leiblum, S. R., Kemmann, E., & Lane, M. K. (1987). The psychological concomitants of *in vitro* fertilization. *Journal of Psychosomatic Obstetrics and Gynecology, 6*, 165–178.

Levin, R. J., & Wagner, G. (1987). Self-reported central sexual arousal without vaginal arousal—Duplicity or veracity revealed by objective measurement. *Journal of Sex Research, 23*, 540–544.

Liss-Levinson, W. S. (1982). Clinical observations on the emotional responses of males to cancer. *Psychotherapy: Theory, Research, and Practice, 19*, 325–330.

Masters, W. H., & Johnson, V. E. (1970). *Human sexual inadequacy.* Boston: Little, Brown.

Mastrogiacomo, T., De Besi, L., Serafini, E., Zussa, S., Zucchetta, P., Romagholi, G. F., Saporiti, E., Dean, P., Ronco, C., & Adami, A. (1984). Hyperprolactinemia and sexual disturbances among uremic women in hemodialysis. *Nephron, 37*, 195–199.

Montague, D. K. (Ed.). (1988). *Disorders of male sexual function.* Chicago: Year Book Medical Publishers.

Moth, I., Andreasson, B., Jensen, S. B., & Bock, J. E. (1983). Sexual function and somatopsychic reactions after vulvectomy. *Danish Medical Bulletin, 30*, 27–30.

Murphy, J. B., & Lipschultz, L. I. (1987). Abnormalities of ejaculation. *Urologic Clinics of North America, 14*, 583–596.

Myers, L. S., & Morokoff, P. J. (1986). Physiological and subjective sexual arousal in pre- and postmenopausal women and postmenopausal women taking replacement therapy. *Psychophysiology, 23*, 283–292.

Nathan, S. G. (1986). Are clinical psychology graduate students being taught enough about sexuality? A survey of doctoral programs. *Journal of Sex Research, 22*, 520–524.

Newman, A. S., & Bertelson, A. D. (1986). Sexual dysfunction in diabetic women. *Journal of Behavioral Medicine, 9*, 261–269.

Papadopoulos, C., Beaumont, C., Shelley, S. T., & Larrimore, P. (1983). Myocardial infarction and sexual activity of the female patient. *Archives of Internal Medicine, 143*, 1528–1530.

Papadopoulos, C., Shelley, S. I., Piccolo, M., Beaumont, C., & Barnett, L. (1986). Sexual activity after coronary bypass surgery. *Chest, 90*, 681–685.

Rieker, P., Edbril, S. D., & Garnick, M. B. (1985). Curative testis cancer therapy: Psychosocial sequelae. *Journal of Clinical Oncology, 3*, 1117–1126.

Rosen, R. C., & Beck, J. G. (1988). *Patterns of sexual arousal: Psychophysiological processes and clinical applications.* New York: Guilford Press.

Schover, L. R. (1987). Sexuality and fertility in urologic cancer patients. *Cancer, 60*, 553–558.

Schover, L. R., & von Eschenbach, A. C. (1985a). Sex therapy and the penile prosthesis: A synthesis. *Journal of Sex and Marital Therapy, 11*, 57–66.

Schover, L. R., & von Eschenbach, A. C. (1985b). Sexual and marital relationships after treatment for nonseminomatous testicular cancer. *Urology, 25*, 251–255.

Schover, L. R., & von Eschenbach, A. C. (1985c). Sexual function and female radical cystectomy: A case series. *Journal of Urology, 134*, 465–468.

Schover, L. R., Evans, R. B., & von Eschenbach, A. C. (1986). Sexual rehabilitation and male radical cystectomy. *Journal of Urology, 136*, 1015–1017.

Schover, L. R., Evans, R. B., & von Eschenbach, A. C. (1987). Sexual rehabilitation in a cancer center: Diagnosis and outcome in 384 consultations. *Archives of Sexual Behavior, 16*, 445–461.

Schover, L. R., Fife, M., & Gershenson, D. M. (1989). Sexual function and treatment for early stage cervical cancer. *Cancer, 63*, 204–212.

Schover, L. R., Friedman, J., Weiler, S., Heiman, J. R., & LoPiccolo, J. (1982). The multiaxial problem-oriented diagnostic system for the sexual dysfunctions: An alternative to DSM-III. *Archives of General Psychiatry, 39*, 614–619.

Schover, L. R., Gonzales, M. O., & von Eschenbach, A. O. (1986). Sexual and marital relationships after radiotherapy for seminoma. *Urology, 27*, 117–123.

Schover, L. R., & Jensen, S. B. (1988). *Sexuality and chronic illness: A comprehensive approach.* New York: Guilford Press.

Schover, L. R., & Randers-Pehrson, M. (1988a). *Sexuality and cancer: For the man who has cancer, and his partner* (Publication No. 4658). New York: American Cancer Society.

Schover, L. R., & Randers-Pehrson, M. (1988b). *Sexuality and cancer: For the woman who has cancer, and her partner* (Publication No. 4657). New York: American Cancer Society.

Schover, L. R., Schain, W. S., & Montague, D. K. (1989). Sexual problems of patients with cancer. In V. T. DeVita, S. Hellman, & S. A. Rosenberg (Eds.), *Cancer: Principles and practice of oncology* (3rd ed.). Philadelphia: J. B. Lippincott.

Schreiner-Engel, P., Schiavi, R. C., Vietorisz, D., & Smith, H. (1987). The differential impact of diabetes type on female sexuality. *Journal of Psychosomatic Research, 31*, 23–33.

Segraves, R. T., Madsen, R., Carter, C. S., & Davis, J. M. (1985). Erectile dysfunction associated with pharmacological agents. In R. T. Segraves & H. W. Schoenberg (Eds.), *Diagnosis and treatment of erectile disturbances: A guide for clinicians* (pp. 23–64). New York: Plenum Medical.

Semmens, J. P., Tsai, C. C., Semmens, E. C., & Loadholt, C. B. (1985). Effects of estrogen therapy on vaginal physiology during menopause. *Obstetrics and Gynecology, 66*, 15–18.

Shen, W. W., & Sata, L. S. (1983). Inhibited female orgasm resulting from psychotropic drugs: A clinical review. *Journal of Reproductive Medicine, 28*, 497–499.

Sikorski, J. M. (1985). Knowledge, concerns, and questions of wives of convalescent coronary artery bypass graft surgery patients. *Journal of Cardiac Rehabilitation, 5*, 74–85.

Sjögren, K. (1983). Sexuality after stroke with hemiplegia II. With special regard to partnership adjustment and fulfillment. *Scandinavian Journal of Rehabilitation Medicine, 15*, 63–69.

Sjögren, K., & Fugl-Meyer, A. R. (1981). Chronic back pain and sexuality. *International Rehabilitation Medicine, 3*, 19–25.

Spanier, G. B. (1976). Measuring dyadic adjustment: New scales for assessing the quality of marriage and similar dyads. *Journal of Marriage and the Family, 38*, 15–28.

Stuart, R. B. (1980). *Helping couples change: A social-learning approach to marital therapy.* New York: Guilford Press.

Trubo, R. (1987). Sexual counseling: Your patients now expect it. *Medical World News*, 28(21), 52–66.

Tyrer, G., Steel, J. M., Ewing, D. J., Bancroft, J., Warner, P., & Clarke, B. F. (1983). Sexual responsiveness in diabetic women. *Diabetologia*, 3, 166–171.

Valleroy, M. L., & Kraft, G. H. (1984). Sexual dysfunction in multiple sclerosis. *Archives of Physical Medicine and Rehabilitation*, 65, 125–128.

Virag, B., Bouilly, P., & Frydman, D. (1985). Is impotence an arterial disorder: A study of arterial risk factors in 440 impotent men. *The Lancet, 8422*, 181–184.

Wise, T. N. (1983). Sexual disorders in medical and surgical conditions. In J. K. Meyer, C. W. Schmidt, Jr., & T. N. Wise (Eds.), *Clinical management of sexual disorders* (pp. 317–332). Baltimore: Williams & Wilkins.

Woolf, P. D., Hamill, R. W., McDonald, J. V., Lee, L. A., & Kelly, M. (1985). Transient hypogonadotropic hypogonadism caused by critical illness. *Journal of Clinical Endocrinology and Metabolism*, 60, 444–450.

Yalla, S. V. (1982). Sexual dysfunction in the paraplegic and quadriplegic. In A. H. Bennett (Ed.), *Management of male impotence* (pp. 182–191). Baltimore: Williams & Wilkins.

Zilbergeld, B. (1978). *Male sexuality*. New York: Bantam.

13

Sex Therapy with Aging Adults

SANDRA R. LEIBLUM AND R. TAYLOR SEGRAVES

> For age is opportunity, no less
> Than youth itself; though in another dress.
> And, as the evening twilight fades away
> The sky is filled with stars.
> Invisible by day.
>
> HENRY WADSWORTH LONGFELLOW

Aging adults constitute the fastest growing segment of our population and represent a group that we, with any luck, will join. Yet, until relatively recently, older individuals were considered asexual and disinterested in pursuing or maintaining intimate physical relationships.

It has only been in the last few decades that greater recognition has been paid to the sexual problems and concerns of mature adults. Initially, the focus was on the impact of illness and medication on sexual response, particularly male erectile function. Recently, more research has been directed at women, particularly changes in sexual interest and behavior accompanying the climacteric and postmenopausal years.

The sexual problems of older adults are not significantly different from those experienced by younger individuals, but greater sensitivity must be paid to the impact of biological and psychological factors in treatment. In aging adults, biological factors require greater attention in both diagnostic evaluation and treatment intervention. Because of the increased prevalence of medical disorders in an aging population, the clinician must be cognizant of biogenic factors that may be instrumental in causing or maintaining sexual difficulties. A meticulous medical and pharmacological history is critical. Erectile difficulties in this population often have some physical basis, and it is recommended that a physical evaluation precede psychotherapy for erectile failure. Although fewer female than male problems have physical causes, estrogen deprivation may heighten complaints of dyspareunia during the menopausal and postmenopausal years.

Both men and women do report reductions in sexual desire in the decades after 50, as well as some changes in the biological capacity to respond to sexual stimuli. The satisfaction and pleasure obtained from physical intimacy can be considerable, however, and many older adults seek therapy if their spouse or partner is no longer sexually interested or functional. It is often necessary to be sensitive to the attitudinal beliefs and cognitive assumptions that these patients hold, since these may need to be challenged or explored in treatment. Sometimes, "sexual script" changes are helpful in assisting couples coping with changing life circumstances and as a means of providing some novelty in long-established relationships. Dealing with the losses associated with aging may be necessary, such as the loss of close friends as well as changes in social and professional status. Retirement may introduce problems for some couples, since it involves adjusting to unstructured time and new leisure with a mate as well as finding new sources of confirmation of self-esteem.

This chapter reviews the physical changes that accompany aging and their impact on the sexual response of men and women. The impact of drugs and illness on sexuality is reviewed insofar as these may affect the sexual functioning of mature adults. Finally, the special issues relevant to an aging population are discussed, with specific attention to their impact on therapy.

Sandra R. Leiblum, Ph.D., is Professor of Clinical Psychiatry and Associate Professor of Obstetrics and Gynecology at UMDNJ-Robert Wood Johnson Medical School in Piscataway, New Jersey. She is particularly interested in the physical and psychosexual changes associated with menopause and has conducted considerable research in this area.

R. Taylor Segraves, M.D., Ph.D., is Associate Director, Department of Psychiatry, Cleveland Metropolitan General Hospital, Cleveland, Ohio and Professor of Psychiatry at Case Western Reserve University Medical School, Cleveland, Ohio. He has published widely in the area of medical and psychological evaluation of erectile disorders.

———————

Despite the preponderance of youthful images in the advertising media, current figures suggest that the "old" will constitute 20% of the population of the United States by the year 2000 (Comfort, 1976). Regrettably, older adults tend to be the victims of negative stereotypes that associate aging with images of fragility, incompetence, and disengagement. Although there are certainly changes in physical capacity and function as individuals grow older, the more distressing consequences of aging are often the sociogenic ones that strip older adults of their dignity and rightful place in society.

Perhaps the most powerful negative image of the older adult is the one that neuters men and women and portrays them as asexual, neither interested in nor capable of physical intimacy. Although the frequency of sexual activity and the percentage of adults engaging in sexual activity tend to fall with increasing age, the truth is that many older adults remain sexually lively and active (Comfort, 1976; Renshaw, 1988). In his large-scale Consumer Union survey of 4,246 adults over 50, Brecher (1984) found that the majority of both married husbands and wives considered the sexual side of their marriages important. The vast majority of respondents were still having marital intercourse, and those who were sexually active were more likely to report happy marriages than those who were not. Moreover, more than three-quarters of the men and women who responded to this survey rated their enjoyment of sex as high. In fact, there was a positive association between satisfaction with one's sexual life and marital satisfaction. Conversely, low enjoyment of marital sex was an important predictor of marital unhappiness.

Not surprisingly, Brecher (1984) also found that older couples experience many of the same sexual dissatisfactions and difficulties as younger couples: problems with sexual desire discrepancy, arousal problems, erectile failure, anorgasmia, early or delayed ejaculation, script incompatibility, and difficulties with sexual communication. Few of the couples complained that they wanted less variety in their sexual lives. Rather, many of the husbands and some of the wives indicated that they would enjoy greater sexual experimentation in their marriage. Although Brecher's study may be nonrepresentative of the elderly population in general, since it comprised a self-selected sample of volunteer respondents, his findings do suggest that if sex was a source of pleasure and gratification during early and middle adulthood, it would probably continue to be an important source of life satisfaction as one aged. On the other hand, there are many elderly individuals who grew up in a post-Victorian society with sexually traditional and proscriptive values. Sex was sanctioned primarily for procreation, and sexual behaviors other than intercourse, such as oral–genital sex and masturbation, were considered either unnatural or immoral. For such individuals, the opportunity to "retire" from sexual exchange may be ardently anticipated and appreciated.

Nevertheless, even within this population, there are many elderly adults who remain sexually "alive" and who experience considerable distress when performance difficulties impede sexual gratification. These individuals constitute a growing segment of the population seeking sex therapy. For example, Renshaw (1988) reports that of the 986 couples requesting sexual counseling at the Loyola Sexual Dysfunction Clinic between 1972 and 1986, 20% of patients were over 50 years of age, and half of these were over 65.

Data from the Sexual Counseling Center at Robert Wood Johnson Medical School indicate that 55% of men seeking services for evaluation and treatment of erectile insufficiency are over 60 years of age. Erectile problems, more than other kinds of sexual difficulty, appear to motivate the request for sex therapy, and older men tend to be seen with greater frequency than elderly women in sexual treatment centers.

MYTHS AND MISCONCEPTIONS ABOUT AGING

When working with an elderly population, both therapists and patients must question some of their assumptions about "aging" adults. For instance, it is often taken as a "given" that older men and women are inflexible and rigid, unwilling or incapable of new learning. Although this may be true for some older individuals, others are quite amenable to suggestions for change. Many have undergone a considerable, although quiet, sexual revolution over the passing years. As one 76-year-old "bride" confided to her therapist, "I never did anything 'fancy' in my first marriage, but if *you* recommend it, I would be willing to try almost anything now!"

Some research suggests that different sexual preferences emerge over time because of changes in sexual physiology and marital status. For example, Turner and Adams (1988), in a study looking at the sexual preferences of a group of 60 to 85-year-old men and women, found that many respondents reported a greater interest in petting and masturbation and less interest in coitus as they grew older. Changes in women's sexual preference appeared to be related to their marital status; wives preferred petting over coitus, whereas unmarried women were more likely to prefer a solitary activity, such as sexual daydreaming. Interestingly, intercourse continued to be the sexual activity most highly correlated with positive sexual experiences and overall life satisfaction.

Regrettably, one of the most significant aspects of growing old is the loss of a partner and the necessity of developing new relationships. It is not surprising that many newly "single" older adults experience many of the same worries as younger individuals. Concerns about personal desirability, attractiveness, and sex appeal are often real and significant worries. How to meet "eligible" partners can be a source of considerable preoccupation. Some older adults worry about the risk of acquiring sexually transmitted diseases. One 72-year-old gentleman called a clinic wanting to know whether it was likely that he had "contacted AIDS" because he had just had sex with an unfamiliar woman in his apartment building. Another 70-year-old woman reported being offended by her gynecologist. She explained that she had asked her doctor, "How do you keep from getting herpes?" and he just laughed at her. She felt humiliated and insulted since it was a real worry to her. It is important to treat the concerns of older adults with respect.

Many older adults are unaware of the normal age-related changes in sexual response that accompany aging and are perplexed or put off by changes in their own or their partner's response. One long-married woman, for example, complained to her therapist that "Nothing happens when I walk around naked. He doesn't even get an erection!" She failed to appreciate that visual stimulation alone was insufficiently arousing to her aging mate and that more direct manual or oral stimulation was necessary to supply the additional arousal "boost" needed to achieve erections.

Whereas we have emphasized the potential for new learning in older adults, there are age-related changes in sexual physiology and response that are important to identify so that erroneous expectations can be confronted, and new realities can be accepted.

FEMALE SEXUAL RESPONSE AND AGING

In women, the menopause, occurring around age 50, represents a clear marker of aging, the beginning of life's second chapter. About this time, most women note changes in their appearance, that is, wrinkles, loss of breast and abdominal elasticity, senile skin changes, etc. The termination of menstruation, a process intimately associated with declining estrogen levels, is such a salient reminder of the aging process that both women and their partners have, historically, tended to attribute any complaints, sexual or physical, occurring around this time as caused by "the change." However, inadequate nutritional and exercise regimens in addition to a history of substance abuse (e.g., alcohol, drugs, tobacco) may be instrumental in causing some of the physical changes accompanying menopause (Leiblum & Bachmann, 1987). Estrogen deficiency does lead to changes in genital appearance. Because vascular supply to the entire pelvis is reduced, genital organs show some atrophy. The labia majora lose fullness, and there is a reduction in pubic hair. The vaginal mucosa becomes thin, friable, and dry, and, in the sexually abstinent woman, the introitus becomes more narrow and the vaginal vault stenotic.

The anatomic changes associated with the climacteric period may affect the ease and comfort of sexual exchange. For instance, as the walls of the vagina become thin and friable, the incidence of dyspareunia increases (although as we shall shortly be discussing, this is by no means inevitable). Atrophy of the Bartholin glands and a decrease in the number and maturity of vaginal cells cause an increased latency of lubrication with sexual stimulation. Vaginal secretions change in both quantity (never quite equaling the amount in the premenopausal woman) and quality. These vaginal-atrophy changes lead to an increased susceptibility to vaginal infection, that is, monilial, trichomonial, etc., which, through inflammatory changes, can interfere with sexual comfort.

It is for this reason that dyspareunia is the most common sexual complaint of older women seeking gynecological consultation (Bachmann, Leiblum, & Grill, 1989). Whereas in younger women, the complaint of painful intercourse is often psychogenic in nature, in older women, it is typically organogenic.

There are some minor changes in the sexual response cycle as well. Most women note that it takes longer to become aroused and lubricated. There tends to be less engorgement of the labia and clitoris, and the vagina is less elastic, especially if there has been a period of sexual abstinence.

Orgasmic response, however, is not significantly impaired. Although the number and intensity of orgasmic and rectal contractions are somewhat reduced, with younger women averaging 5 to 10 vaginal contractions with orgasm, and older women averaging 2 to 3, few women either notice or complain about these changes. In fact, several recent studies have reported that postmenopausal women report little or no changes in subjective sexual arousal (Morrell, Dixen, Carter, & Davidson, 1984; Myers & Morokoff, 1985). Whereas there is clearly less vaginal lubrication during sexual arousal in women not taking estrogen replacement, the psychological experience of sexual excitement is not significantly correlated with physiological measures of arousal and women report considerable subjective arousal when shown erotic material.

Nevertheless, with increasing age, there does tend to be an increase in sexual complaints. Research suggests that among women aged 60 and older, lack of vaginal lubrication and decreased sexual interest are quite common, and orgasmic attainment becomes more difficult (Leiblum & Bachmann, 1988; Bretschneider & McCoy, 1988). Women worry about their partner's inability to achieve or maintain erections, and unmarried women often complain about the lack of opportunity for sexual encounters.

Overall, it appears that most women are quite resilient sexually and show few major alterations in their response to sexual stimulation across the life cycle. Nevertheless, sexual interest does diminish, and the incidence of sexual complaints does increase with aging.

SURGICAL MENOPAUSE AND SEXUAL RESPONSE

Whereas the majority of women experience "menopausal" changes over a protracted period of time beginning in the mid-30s, 35–40% of women are catapulted into early menopause by undergoing hysterectomy with bilateral oophorectomy (CDC Surveillance Summaries, 1981). Such women experience the same genital and sexual response cycle changes as women undergoing natural menopause, but with some important differences. Because aging changes in the vascular system have not yet occurred, blood vessels to the pelvic area, especially those to the external genitalia, are full and not sclerotic. Consequently, oxygen and nutritional supply are unimpaired. Adrenal hormone production is not compromised, and the woman can maintain intrinsic estrogen production, although at lower rates.

More significant than the physical changes accompanying hysterectomy are the psychological sequelae. For most women the operation constitutes a life crisis. It leads them to examine their feelings about their uterus and ovaries and may stir up deeply held beliefs about their sense of "womanliness" (Lalinec-Michaud & Engelsmann, 1988). To the extent that a woman views her uterus as symbolic of her womanhood, she may become depressed following a hysterectomy. For some women, the operation provides a welcome relief from physically uncomfortable symptoms and abnormal bleeding; for others, however, it is experienced as an assault on body image and self-concept. Recent research suggests that the women who are most adversely affected by hysterectomy are those with a lifelong history of depression (Moore & Tolley, 1976; Garth, Cooper, & Day, 1982). Moreover, how the woman's partner reacts to her hysterectomy can have important consequences on how comfortably she deals with the loss of her uterus.

Clinical Example

A 55-year-old insurance salesman consulted his internist because of concerns about his decreased libido. Following an endocrine evaluation, he was referred for a psychological consultation. He reported having coitus three to four times a week without difficulty. However, he complained of a lack of sexual desire. "It's like looking at a dessert tray in a fancy restaurant when you're full. You notice that the pastries are beautiful. You just don't want to eat them!"

The patient was evasive concerning his emotional relationship with his wife, and so a conjoint session was arranged. His wife, an attractive manager of a small restaurant, reported sadly that her husband had "lost interest in her." She did not think he was having an affair. Tears came into her eyes as she related that the change seemed to coincide with her hysterectomy. As she continued to speak, it became apparent that she felt unattractive and doubtful about her femininity. She indicated that she and her husband rarely talked intimately. When she would discuss painful feelings or personal worries, her husband would immediately interrupt her and try to "solve" her problem.

As the couple talked together in the session, it became clear that following his wife's hysterectomy, the husband had increased his frequency of sexual initiation in order to reassure his wife of her appeal for him. This had backfired, since she intuited that his overtures exceeded his ardor. Once he was able to admit that he was initiating sexual encounters out of love rather than passion, his wife could discuss her reactions to her hysterectomy and her fears about aging. The couple were then able to have a frank and intimate discussion about their love and attraction for each other.

Orgasmic Changes following Hysterectomy

There is some controversy as to whether women experience less intense and satisfactory orgasms following hysterectomy. Cutler and Garcia (1984) suggest that women who undergo total abdominal hysterectomies may sustain losses in orgasmic capability. In a study by Kilkku and his colleagues (Kilkku, Gronross, Hirvemen, & Fauramo, 1983), a matched group of post-abdominal-hysterectomy patients were compared with women who had undergone a supravaginal hysterectomy, a procedure in which the proximal vagina and cervix are retained. Results indicated that the postabdominal-hysterectomy patients reported a greater loss in orgasmic capability than the supravaginal hysterectomy patients. Several authors suggest that there is a cervicouterine orgasmic response to deep coital thrusting that is lost with a hysterectomy (Cutler & Garcia, 1984; Zussman, Zussman, Sunley, & Bjornson, 1981). However, other investigators maintain that uterine and cervical sensations do not add significantly to orgasmic pleasure and that hysterectomy does not diminish orgasmic capability or intensity (Dennerstein & Burrows, 1982; Schover & Jensen, 1988). Although the final answer is not yet in, it appears likely that orgasmic responsivity following hysterectomy is experienced differently by different women and is partially dependent on the particular surgical procedure employed and on the woman's general awareness of, and attention to, her orgasmic contractions.

SEXUAL CHANGES IN THE AGING MALE

Whereas there appear to be few substantial biological limitations in sexual response in healthy aging women, there are, unfortunately, substantial changes in the aging male. Although these changes are pronounced, they occur gradually, allowing the man and his partner time to adapt to a shifting pattern of responsiveness. Studies of various parameters of sexual behavior have indicated a gradual decline in sexual activity after age 50, with a more precipitous decline after 70 (Hegeler & Mortensen, 1977; Pfeiffer, 1974; Kinsey, Pomeroy, & Martin, 1948). It is important to stress, however, that age alone does not preclude coitus in healthy males. Some males will remain sexually active into their 80s and 90s, albeit at a lower frequency than in their 40s or 50s. Moreover, there is considerable individual variability in the effects of age on sexual behavior. Whereas most 70-year-old men may have intercourse once a week or less, others will report coitus three times a week. One cannot assume that advanced age alone accounts for diminished activity.

Regrettably, a number of men and their partners fall prey to the psychosocial trap of expecting constancy of sexual performance across the life span and try to "force" a sexual response characteristic of their youth. It is crucial that the clinician be aware of the sexual changes accompanying normal aging. For example, where a young male may achieve a full erection in seconds, an older man may require minutes to achieve the same response. Pre-ejaculatory fluid emission may be decreased or absent, and the aging male may experience less ejaculatory demand. Ejaculation is typically less forceful, and the seminal fluid volume is decreased. The refractory period may extend to days rather than minutes. For some men, there are changes in penile sensitivity (Melman & Laiter, 1983) and decreased frequency of nocturnal erections (Schiavi & Schreiner-Engel, 1988). The force and frequency of desire for sexual release decrease with age. When a parallel reduction in sexual interest does not coexist in the partner, the path is open for misunderstanding, disappointment, and withdrawal. It is for this reason that Masters and Johnson (1977) have emphasized that the older male and his partner should be aware of these changes so that they do not engender unnecessary and avoidable psychological sexual dysfunction.

Case Example

A 65-year-old warehouse foreman contacted a urological service after reading about an experimental pharmacological erection program. His complaint was of intermittent erectile failure. On questioning, he revealed attempting coitus on a daily basis. Careful interviewing suggested that this coital frequency stemmed from his "wish" to be sexually active rather than from an internal urge for sexual release. For example, his masturbation frequency when apart from his wife was considerably less than once daily. He tended to resort to an extensive collection of X-rated VCR films to engender arousal, and he needed considerable manual and occasional vibratory stimulation in order to achieve orgasm. When gently confronted about his sexual frequency, the patient insisted that his internal desire for coitus was, indeed, once daily. The suggestion that he engage in coitus twice weekly and enjoy sexual activities not culminating in orgasm on other occasions was totally unacceptable to him. He did, however, reluctantly agree to bring his wife in for the next session.

In the conjoint session, his wife seemed initially confused by the questions the therapist asked but then said, "Do you mean he's looking for the male equivalent of a menopause baby? He just doesn't like to admit that he's getting older." This led to a discussion of the difficulty many individuals have in accepting age-related changes. Although the man remained quiet during most of the session, he listened closely as the wife discussed her own difficulties in accepting aging. In the next session, the couple reported having fewer but more pleasurable sexual encounters during the preceding week. Although the husband never directly verbalized agreement with the implicit therapeutic message, his behavior changed. He became less compulsive about sexual initiation and more relaxed. His wife was pleased with the change in their relationship. The therapist never pressed the patient to discuss his feelings, but indirectly, therapeutic benefits were achieved by bypassing the patient and exploring the wife's feelings about aging.

Hormonal Changes and Male Sexual Response

Unlike the female, the sex hormone status of the healthy male remains relatively stable from early adulthood until the fifth decade of life. At this point, a gradual decline in androgen production begins, although there is considerable individual variation in the onset of this change (Bancroft, 1983). Typically, the first sign of alteration in endocrine function is a slight elevation of the pituitary stimulating hormones (gonadotrophins), although serum testosterone levels remain within normal limits. This elevation of pituitary gonadotrophins signals the relative inability of the aging testes to efficiently produce testosterone. Subsequently, the serum testosterone levels will gradually fall. By age 80, serum testosterone levels may be only one sixth that of a younger male. In spite of this decline, the serum testosterone levels are usually still within normal limits (Schover, 1984).

The clinical significance of the drop in serum testosterone levels over time is unclear. Because it clearly parallels the decline in sexual function with age, certain investigators have questioned whether declining androgen production is the mechanism underlying decreased libido in older men. From clinical medicine, it is known that disease states associated with low testosterone levels are characterized by decreased libido and lessened ejaculatory demand (Jones, 1985). Although the capacity to respond to sexual stimuli remains, the drive to seek sexual release diminishes. In hypogonadal men, libido and ejaculation are restored by androgen replacement (Bancroft & Wu, 1985). It is also clear that diminished libido may be one of the primary complaints of men with even mild to moderate hypogonadism (Segraves, Schoenberg, & Ivanoff, 1983) and that men with hypoactive sexual desire disorder may have diminished androgen production (Schiavi & Schreiner-Engel, 1988).

In spite of the seeming parallels between the sexual decline noted with normal aging and that in hypogonadal men, there is minimal evidence to date that testosterone replacement therapy augments sexual responsiveness in men whose base-line serum testosterone levels are within normal limits. To dramatize this point, giving an 80-year-old massive androgen replacement will not restore his libido to what it was when he was 18. There appears to be a certain minimal level of testosterone necessary for adequate sexual functioning; additional amounts are without effect. Unfortunately, most elderly men appear to have this minimal level and are not helped by exogenous testosterone. The mechanism by which aging results in diminished libido appears to be more complicated than a simple decline in androgen levels (Davidson, Camargo, & Smith, 1983).

HORMONES AND FEMALE SEXUAL RESPONSE

In general, hormonal influences appear to exercise a greater impact on male sexual behavior than on female sexual behavior (Bancroft, 1983). The majority of women undergoing gonadectomy or menopause do not become sexually dysfunctional, whereas the agonadal or hypogonadal man does (Davidson, Camargo, & Smith, 1983; Davidson, Kwan, & Greenleaf, 1982).

The role of estrogen in stimulating female sexual desire and ensuring satisfactory sexual functioning is not completely understood. Unequivocally, an adequate supply of estrogen is critical for maintaining genital health, ensuring adequate vaginal lubrication, and avoiding insertional dyspareunia. Conflicting data exist on whether estrogen directly stimulates or ensures sexual desire. Recent evidence suggests that a close association exists between declining estrogen levels and declining frequency of intercourse and that serum estradiol levels below 35 mg/ml are associated with reduced coital activity in women when compared to age-matched controls whose levels exceed this value (Cutler, Garcia, & McCoy, 1987). Reduced estrogen supplies may contribute to reduced sexual activity because of the higher incidence of dyspareunia in hypoestrogenic women.

Dennerstein and Burrows (1982) have suggested that although a "deficiency of estrogens may not necessarily be the cause of sexual problems presenting in midlife, they may provide a biological vulnerability which, for some with a somewhat tenuous sexual adjustment, may be enough to tip the balance from just coping to sexual dysfunction" (p. 675).

Brecher (1984), in the previously cited large-scale survey of sexual behavior in men and women over 60, reports that in comparing 408 postmenopausal women taking estrogen with 1,356 women not taking it, 93% of the estrogen users were sexually active as compared with 80% of the nonusers. Furthermore, those women on estrogen replacement reported a high enjoyment of sex, high or moderate sexual frequency, occasional sleep awakening associated with sexual arousal, occasional spontaneous orgasms during the day or night, and good vaginal lubrication. It certainly appears to be the case that adequate estrogen supply facilitates sexual comfort in climacteric women, although it is likely that women electing hormone replacement therapy may be more sexually interested and active to begin with. It is noteworthy that a relatively small percentage of elderly women take estrogen despite evidence of its utility. In part this represents a carryover of fears prevalent in the 1970s that estrogen replacement was associated with an increased risk of endometrial cancer (Swartzman & Leiblum, 1987).

Varying hormone replacement regimens impact on different aspects of sexual response. Whereas estrogen replacement is clearly beneficial in maintaining vaginal integrity and stimulating lubrication, androgen administration appears to be more useful in whetting sexual appetite. In a well-controlled and methodologically sophisticated investigation of the effects of an estrogen–androgen combined preparation, estrogen alone, androgen alone, and placebo on the sexual interest and response of oophorectomized and hysterectomized women, Sherwin, Gelfand, and Brender (1985) reported that exogenous androgen enhanced the intensity of sexual desire and arousal and the frequency of sexual fantasy in their subjects.

"USE IT OR LOSE IT"

Masters and Johnson (1966) were among the early sex physiologists to suggest that the maintenance of an active sexual life retards genital atrophy and helps maintain sexual comfort. In their early physiological studies investigating human sexual response, they reported that out of a sample of 54 women older than 60 years of age, only three responded physiologically to sexual stimulation in a manner comparable to that of younger women, that is, with considerable vaginal lubrication despite thin and atrophic vaginal mucosas. These three women were the only subjects who had remained sexually active throughout and subsequent to menopause.

In an investigation designed to determine the effect of sexual activity on vaginal atrophy, Leiblum, Bachmann, Kemmann, Colburn, and Swartzman (1983) studied two groups of postmenopausal women, those who were sexually active (intercourse frequency three or more times monthly) and those who were sexually inactive. Two gynecologists who were uninformed about the women's sexual activity status examined all the women and completed an index of vaginal atrophy assessing six genital dimensions. Blood samples of circulating estrone, estradiol, androstenedione, testosterone, FSH, and LH were analyzed as well in order to determine the impact of hormones on sexual interest and function. The results of this study provided support for Masters and Johnson's dictum, "Use it or lose it." Those women who were sexually active displayed significantly less vaginal atrophy than their inactive cohorts. Moreover, masturbation appeared to be helpful as well in retarding genital atrophic changes: When masturbation frequency was summated with intercourse frequency to provide an overall measure of sexual activity, the negative correlation with vaginal atrophy became even greater.

In a follow-up study involving a sample of sexagenarian women, Leiblum and Bachmann (1988) confirmed these findings—those sexagenarian women who were maintaining an active sexual life obtained significantly higher ratings of genital health than their coitally abstinent peers. In this study, the hormonal status of the sexually active women was not significantly different from that of the inactive women, and hormones did not appear to be the critical factor differentiating the groups.

In men, there is no comparable study demonstrating the efficacy of continued sexual relations on erectile ability. Nevertheless, it appears likely that regular sexual behavior promotes greater confidence in feelings of sexual competence. Certainly, those men who have refrained from actively engaging in sex following the death of a mate or the loss of a girl friend report more anxiety about their sexual adequacy than men who continue to masturbate successfully. Although it is unlikely that regular sexual engagement ensures erectile rigidity, sexual desire and, indirectly, erectile competency, may be enhanced by increased testosterone production stimulated by sexual activity.

THE IMPACT OF ILLNESS
ON SEXUAL PERFORMANCE

Although the majority of older adults are in good health (Comfort, 1976), increased age is associated with an increased prevalence of many disease states that may contribute to sexual problems. For instance, general malaise or pain may interfere with sexual activity. One 62-year-old man with cardiac disease complained of loss of erection. On questioning, he reported the onset of severe angina during active thrusting. This pain and the attendant anxiety provided the explanation of his erectile difficulties. Modification of his digoxin dose resulted in a relatively straightforward solution to his problem. Other patients may have sexual activity interrupted by arthritic pain. In many cases, altering sexual positions can result in the alleviation of discomfort and permit the continuation of sexual activity. In other patients with chronic diseases such as cardiac failure or respiratory failure, diminished capacity for sexual expression may be an early sign of the worsening of the disease state.

Both surgical and medical treatment of various diseases can have side effects that interfere with sexual performance. For example, lower abdominal surgery, pelvic radiation, and certain types of prostate surgery may interfere with the neurological innervation of the penis and cause erectile problems. Surgical procedures frequently associated with erectile failure are listed in Table 13.1.

Pharmacological agents used to treat various disease states may also be associated with an increased prevalence of sexual problems. The aging male may be especially vulnerable to the impact of drugs on his erectile ability. Although medications used to treat hypertension appear to be the primary offenders, a wide variety of pharmacological agents, including psychiatric drugs, may also be associated with erectile problems. Drugs often associated with erectile dysfunction are listed in Table 13.2.

A number of disease states may interfere with sexual function as a direct consequence of the disease state. For example, the prevalence of cardiovascular disease increases with age (Stephenson & Umstead, 1984). Occlusion of the abdominal aorta or of the iliac arteries may be associated with erectile failure. Arteriosclerotic damage to the small penile arteries is also suspected to be a cause of erectile problems.

TABLE 13.1   Surgery and Erectile Failure

Radical perineal prostatectomy

Radical retropubic protatectomy

Retroperitoneal lymphadenectomy

Sympathectomy

Cystectomy

Proctectomy

Abdominal colon resection

Aortoiliac vascular reconstruction

Abdominal aneurysmectomy

TABLE 13.2   Drugs and Sexual Problems

Methyldopa (Aldomet)
Guanethidine (Esmelin)
Clonidine (Catapres)
Reserpine (Serpasil)
Spironolactone (Aldactone)
Diuretics (e.g., Diuril)
Chlorthalidone (Hygroton)
Prazosin (Minipress)
Clofibrate (Atromid-S)
Methantheline (Banthine)
Cimetidine (Tagamet)
Propranolol (Inderal)
Methadone (Dolophine)
Baclofen (Lioresal)
Ethionamide (Trecator)
Perhexiline (Pexid)
Hexamethonium (Methium Cl)
Mecamylamine HCl (Inversine)
Trimethaphan camsylate (Arfonad)
Propantheline (Pro-Banthine)
Disulfiram (Antabuse)
Digoxin (Lanoxin)
Cancer chemotherapy agents

Diabetes mellitus is associated with erectile problems in approximately 50% to 60% of diabetic men (Ellenberg, 1977; Jensen, 1985). Damage to the nerves mediating erections is the probable mechanism. Interestingly, female diabetics appear to be less compromised by diabetes than male diabetics. They do appear to have more difficulty in obtaining sufficient vaginal lubrication during sexual arousal than control women, but, surprisingly, most women do not show major impairment in either sexual interest or orgasmic attainment (Assalian, 1988). Nevertheless, Schreiner-Engel, Schiavi, Vietorisz, and Eichel (1985) reported that older Type II diabetic women display some decrement in overall sexual responsivity.

A variety of other syndromes may be associated with autonomic neuropathies and are capable of producing erectile problems. These include neuropathies, thyroid disease, alcoholic neuropathy, carcinomatous neuropathy, and inflammatory neuropathies. A partial list of diseases causing erectile problems is presented in Table 13.3.

TABLE 13.3   Diseases Associated with Erectile Problems

Diabetes mellitus
Renal failure
Multiple sclerosis
Hepatic failure
Aortoiliac disease
Alcoholic neuropathy
Inflammatory neuropathy
Peripheral nerve trauma (pelvic fracture)
Spinal cord injury
Temporal lobe lesions
Pituitary adenomas
Hypogonadism
Adrenoleukodystrophy
Priapism
Peyronie disease

In women, gynecologic and breast cancer often lead to unfortunate sexual sequelae. Not only is body image assaulted, but the side effects of radiation or chemotherapy compromise sexual interest and sense of well-being. Although breast surgery for women over 60 may be less traumatic than for reproductively aged women, many elderly women experience mastectomy as both mutilative and life threatening and suffer postsurgical depression and loss of libido.

As stated throughout this chapter, one must not assume that all performance problems in the elderly are caused by medication or physical disease. Usually, psychogenic factors coexist and may be the more salient cause of sexual difficulty, but the patient is reluctant to acknowledge these and focuses on medication as the culprit.

The following case example illustrates how a patient found it more acceptable to blame his antihypertensive medication for erectile difficulties than his feelings of dissatisfaction with his new marriage.

Case Example

A successful 60-year-old lawyer who had been on antihypertensive medication for years lost his wife suddenly and tragically when she died of cardiac arrest. Within 3 months, he began dating, and soon fell in love with, a 41-year-old divorced woman with three young children. His depression seemed to lift, although he was troubled by his inability to sustain an erection during sexual relations. In all other respects, however, he maintained that the relationship was "perfect."

He had initiated the request for individual therapy, saying that the erectile problems were entirely his responsibility. In treatment, it became apparent that all was not well in the courtship. His son as well as his girl friend's three children disapproved of his dating, and at times the patient himself felt panicky about "what he was letting himself in for." Occasionally, he experienced intense feelings of guilt about dating so soon after his wife's death, and images of her haunted him. Despite the therapist's questioning as to why he was becoming so committed so quickly to his new girl friend, the patient married less than 1 year after his wife's death. Although he had occasional encounters with good erectile functioning, his anxiety about being able to "satisfy" his young wife continued.

Nine months later he returned for treatment, complaining that his erectile problems had totally returned. Not surprisingly, domestic relations were more conflicted than ever. He and his 12-year-old stepdaughter were engaged in constant conflict. He felt unsupported by his wife in these squabbles, and he blamed her for being an inadequate disciplinarian. He felt angry and depressed. Nevertheless, he wondered whether his erectile difficulties were caused by his antihypertensive medication and elected to stop taking the medication. His erectile performance improved briefly, only to deteriorate after a new round of battles with his stepdaughter and complaints by his son that he should not have remarried. It was only then that the patient acknowledged that family conflicts and personal misgivings were the primary source of his sexual problems.

This case is a familiar one to sex therapists and illustrates many common dynamics. Men generally tend to blame their erectile problems on physical rather than psychological factors. Moreover, remarriage, even if positively anticipated by all family members, usually stresses a system and creates conflicting loyalties. In second or even third marriages, men and women find themselves inheriting whole families in addition to their chosen partner. When working with these couples, it is important to acknowledge the problems associated with stepparenting (or stepgrandparenting), the jealousies, sensitivities, and needs of all the involved family members, since sexual problems may be the barometer of more basic systemic conflicts.

PSYCHOLOGICAL FACTORS AFFECTING SEXUALITY IN THE ELDERLY

A number of psychological factors can interfere with and complicate the sexual lives of elderly adults. To the extent that both older men and women embrace the widespread societal notion that "sex is for the young," an active interest in sexual pursuits may be viewed as unseemly or undignified. This is a particular problem for older women. "Grandmothers" are not considered to be sexual beings and receive little encouragement from their children to reestablish sexual relationships following the death or loss of a spouse. The shortage of available partners is a real problem for older women. Not only is there a dearth of older men for older women, but many men are sexually disinterested or dysfunctional. Moreover, sexual relationships with younger men are often viewed as unseemly (a striking holdover of the double standard, since December–May unions are often viewed indulgently). Older women tend to be uncomfortable with the thought of sexual relationships with other women, and many older women may find themselves feeling sexually frustrated. Whereas masturbation is a sensible option, long-standing beliefs that masturbation is either unhealthy or "unnatural" prevent women from exploring this outlet. Education and permission from a health professional can be helpful in challenging some of these misconceptions.

For example, an elderly married 75-year-old complaining of insomnia was referred for treatment by her internist. She explained that she would frequently awaken during the night with uncomfortable genital sensations. She did not know what was causing her nocturnal "tension" or how to relieve it. A brief review of her past history revealed that her husband of 38 years was ill with prostate cancer and had been sleeping in a separate bedroom for the last 5 years, which effectively discouraged sexual contact. She missed the physical intimacy as well as the genital release coital activities used to provide. Although she had never masturbated, she indicated receptivity but ignorance regarding effective self-stimulation. She was sent home with an instructional paperback as well as a vibrator. Two weeks later, she returned, delighted with her success. Her sleeping problem was resolved.

THE WIDOWERS' SYNDROME

The "widowers' syndrome" is a common sequela to the loss of a wife or long-standing sexual partner. Following a long period of nursing his mate, she dies, and the husband feels an admixture of guilt, relief, and anger. Before completing the grieving process, however, he is thrust into the dating scene by friends and relatives. Often, he feels coerced or pressured into sexual engagement before he is emotionally ready and then experiences erectile problems that create further anxiety and guilt. Sensitive counseling is necessary in order to help the patient sort out his conflicted feelings and confused cognitions regarding the resumption of life as a single person.

Concerns about physical imperfections can sometimes mar the comfort and ease of physical exchange in the elderly. Scarring, sagging, and surgery can interfere with positive self-esteem about one's body and can lead to increased feelings of modesty. Such concerns need to be addressed directly in treatment. Comfort (1976) reminds us that many older persons, despite their worries, still have good bodies since covered skin ages less rapidly than uncovered skin.

It is obvious that normal age-related physical changes, the impact of drugs and disease, as well as a host of psychological factors may all contribute to the sexual interest and abilities of older adults. It is equally clear that the wish for physical intimacy is lifelong, and sexual counseling can be beneficial with many, if not all, older individuals. Let us now turn to the particular issues that are relevant to sex therapy with elderly adults.

THERAPEUTIC TACTICS IN WORKING WITH ELDERLY ADULTS

Older adults are beset by the same kinds of sexual difficulties and dysfunctions as younger adults, and typically the treatment approach is similar. Nevertheless, there are several issues that should be highlighted when one considers therapy with elderly individuals. These issues can be roughly classified into three major areas: (1) biological changes with age that influence sexual behavior, (2) attitudinal factors in the elderly concerning sexual behavior, and (3) the impact of life events on sexual behavior in this age group.

At all ages, sexual function involves an interplay of both psychological and biological factors. In aging adults, the role of biological factors is more salient in both diagnostic evaluation and treatment planning. One clearly does not wish to overlook a treatable organic difficulty (e.g., erectile or libido problem secondary to hypogonadism or hyperprolactinemia) or to naively begin sex therapy for a difficulty that is irreversible secondary to a biogenic disease process (e.g., severe vasculogenic impotence). Because of the increased prevalence of medical disorders in an aging population, the clinician must be suspicious about the possibility that biogenic factors will be instrumental in causing or maintaining sexual problems. It is essential that a meticulous medical and pharmacological history be obtained with elderly patients, and it is probably good policy to require that all men over 50 be evaluated by a physician prior to starting psychologically oriented sex therapy.

Controversy exists about what should be included in the medical evaluation. Because of the increased frequency of hypogonadism with aging, most patients should probably have at least a serum testosterone and prolactin determination. If nocturnal penile tumescence recording is utilized, one should be certain that the polysomnographer is cognizant of the changes in nocturnal erections that occur with normal aging. Recent work has suggested that some sexually functional older males may not demonstrate nocturnal erections and may be erroneously classified as organogenic (Schiavi, 1988). Many centers routinely include penile blood pressure determination to rule out vascular causes of erectile difficulties. However, there is some disagreement concerning how much of a decrement in penile blood pressure is required before one can confidently conclude that the difficulty is vascular in origin. More recently, injection of a mixture of two drugs— papaverine and phentolamine—directly into the corpora cavernosa to induce erections pharmacologically has been employed as a diagnostic procedure. This drug combination induces vasodilation of the penile vasculature. Theoretically, the pharmacological induction of an erectile response indicates the integrity of the vascular system, and this rules out vasculogenic impotence. It should be emphasized that a good sexual history may obviate the need for such evaluations in many patients. If a patient reports the presence of erections on awakening at least twice a week that last until micturition and are of normal turgidity, one can conclude with some confidence that the difficulty is psychogenic in etiology (Segraves & Segraves, 1987).

Elderly female patients complaining of pain with sexual activity, vaginal discharge, or vaginal bleeding should clearly be referred for physical evaluation. Whether a physical evaluation should be recommended for female patients who are in good health but are complaining of sexual dysfunction is debatable. The lack of certainty regarding the need for physical evaluation of women with sexual complaints reflects our minimal knowledge of the biological underpinnings of female sexuality and the primitive state of our assessment approach to female disorders. Nocturnal vaginal photoplethysmography remains an experimental procedure of questionable clinical utility. Pudendal nerve conduction studies have been done in a small number of female patients and remain primarily an experimental procedure. Endocrine evaluation of female sexual dysfunction has questionable clinical utility since the endocrinological correlates of female sexual response are unclear. Although some evidence suggests that androgens are the "libido" hormones for both women and men, there is, to date, uncertainty concerning the appropriate indications for androgen therapy with women.

In working with elderly patients, the therapist often has to make certain practical suggestions to help couples circumvent physical limitations.

For older women, problems with lubrication are common during the climacteric and postmenopausal years, and the use of external lubrication is highly recommended. For some women, Vaseline® (petroleum jelly) is preferable to water-soluble lubricants that evaporate too quickly. Other women find that topical lubricants such as Astroglide®, Lubrin®, Today® lubricant, or Transilube® are helpful. If hot flushes are frequent and discomforting and if osteoporosis is a concern, hormone replacement therapy may be indicated. The estrogen–progesterone regimen that is currently favored mimics the natural menstrual cycle and is associated with a low risk of endometrial cancer, particularly if Pap testing is regularly performed.

If physical mobility is a problem, as in chronic arthritis, nonsteroidal analgesics taken before sexual activity is started may increase comfort.

Even a hot bath before sex may reduce pain and stiffness. Sexual activities may be undertaken in the early or late afternoon rather than the evening in order to reduce fatigue and, for arthritic individuals, to avoid the pain often felt on awakening.

Sexual positions must be carefully considered when working with older adults. A side-by-side position is often preferable to a male superior position, since it avoids excess weight on the wife. Moreover, husbands may find the missionary position too physically taxing. Sometimes elevation of the upper part of the bed is helpful to avoid lying flat on one's back.

Sensual massage should be considered as an alternative to intercourse or genital sex, as well as mutual nondemand caressing. Often, simply touching and stroking are important and sometimes preferred sources of physical intimacy. Holding hands, fondling, and bathing together are additional ways of expressing closeness.

As mentioned previously, most aging men will eventually experience a gradual decline in the appetitive aspects of sexual function. This may be experienced as a decreased desire for coitus, a decreased ejaculatory demand, and/or a decreased responsivity to previously erotic stimuli. Most aging men and their spouses gradually adapt to these physical changes without the need for medical or psychological consultation. A small number of elderly men may require minimal education and reassurance. Such education may consist of reassurance that such changes are normal as well as suggestions or permission to utilize techniques to augment arousal. For example, one 71-year-old retired New Orleans dockworker was extremely upset when he found that he could only have intercourse twice weekly rather than his previous lifelong pattern of three to four times weekly. He was upset that this might be a sign of the "beginning of the end" of his sexual life. After a thorough evaluation, he was reassured that such changes were normal, that there was no reason to suspect a subsequent rapid decline in function, and that he might require manual stimulation on occasion from his partner. This man was able to assimilate this information, and subsequent sessions were not necessary. In an even smaller number of cases, a more extensive intervention may be required. In certain couples, sexual scripts from an earlier era may preclude the easy assimilation of factual information.

More commonly, age will be associated with a relative decline in the biological capacity to respond. In such situations, attitudinal factors may then interact with the biological changes, interfering with adaptation and healthy function. It is important for the therapist to realize that these attitudinal factors derive from a different era and may have once been adaptive for the couple. Some patients display considerable resistance in reevaluating their sexual beliefs and attitudes, especially when the therapist working with them is the age of their children or even grandchildren. Whereas some elderly adults have silently participated in society's changing sanctions regarding sexuality and have become more "liberal" in their behaviors, others are still firmly anchored to the past. They may have strong feelings about what they consider appropriate gender roles and sexual behaviors. These beliefs often have the emotional significance and tenacity of religious beliefs and may require a similar respect from the therapist if therapeutic rapport is to be maintained. An example is the following case:

> An elderly man sought help because he was having difficulty achieving erections. He was dating an attractive widow of 66, whom he wished to marry. She felt that it would be improper for them to marry so soon after her husband's death. Moreover, women of her social circle did not "shack up" with men. Thus, their sexual activity consisted of her sleeping over one night a week in his beach home outside of the city. His uncertainty concerning her commitment to the relationship plus the lack of frequency of their sexual contact placed considerable performance pressure on him. A compromise solution was achieved in therapy—she would be entertained in his beach home twice a week as long as no one knew that she stayed over. As a sign of her commitment to him, she agreed to allow him to escort her to local charity balls. Once this compromise was reached, he began to regain his composure, and erectile function returned as well.

In this case, the therapist helped the couple to negotiate their interpersonal vulnerability and commitment through a compromise of cultural symbols of commitment. This was done while respecting the widow's symbols regarding proper sexual behavior. In another instance, the male's rigid adherence to his rules of sexual conduct essentially directed the therapist's intervention strategy.

> Raymond, a 70-year-old retired appliance salesman, appeared at a university urology service with the complaint of impotence. The urologist requested a routine psychological evaluation of this man from the psychiatry service. Raymond reluctantly agreed to the psychological evaluation. A history revealed that his wife of 40 years had died 10 years earlier. Prior to her illness, their sex life had been mutually fulfilling and had consisted exclusively of male-superior coitus. Raymond succinctly summarized his life with his wife: "She was a good woman and mother." By this, he meant that he did not feel that sexual experimentation with her was proper. Because of her chronic illness, there had been no sexual activity during the 5 years prior to her death: "She was dying. It would not have been right." He felt that it was improper to date after her death but infrequently sought out prostitutes, thinking that she would have understood. Several months before he consulted the urologist, Raymond began dating a neighbor who had been a friend of his wife's, and he was devastated when he was unable to achieve an erection. Since he had had no erectile difficulties with his wife and several prostitutes, he was perplexed about his loss of function.

The recent erectile failure represented his first sexual contact with a "decent woman" in 15 years. The consultant inquired closely about his infrequent contacts with prostitutes. It appeared that with the prostitutes he had paid "hard-earned money" for services and had no reservations about indulging in oral–genital sex and demanding manual stimulation. However, he did not feel it was right to ask these things of his neighbor. "She's a good woman, a grandmother, and a widow." Likewise, it was not proper to ask her to come to therapy with him—"We're not married."

The therapist pointed out that it had been some 15 years since the patient had had intercourse with a "good" woman and that he might require more stimulation in order to obtain erections at age 70 than he did at 55. The patient agreed to this logic but steadfastly refused to involve the neighbor in therapy with him as "It wouldn't be right." Finding himself at an impasse, the therapist finally asked the patient if the therapist could communicate with the neighbor by telephone. The patient agreed, and the therapist contacted the neighbor, who appeared relieved to be able to speak freely. She told the therapist that she wanted to help her friend but was afraid that he would think she was a bad woman if she were more forward. By a series of interviews with the patient and his partner (by telephone), the therapist was gradually able to help this man engage in a greater number of sexual activities and attain potency with his partner.

With more flexible couples, a careful assessment of the sexual "script," that is, the who, what, when, where, and how of sexual encounters, can be evaluated and, where necessary, modified (Gagnon, Rosen, & Leiblum, 1984; Rosen & Leiblum, 1988). In long-married couples, the script has often become routinized, repetitive, and less consonant with current realities. For example, whereas late-night sex might have been optimal during the child-raising years when private time was at a premium, in later life, nighttime might signal feelings of exhaustion rather than ecstasy. Similarly, whereas sexual exchange over the years may have occurred in the confines of the bedroom behind locked doors, it may now be possible for couples to venture out of the bedroom and into other areas of the house. As one 68-year-old divorcee exclaimed, "The bedroom is boring!"

On the other hand, some long-married couples may have eliminated some positive components of their sexual script over time. For instance, during early courtship, much time is usually spent getting "ready" for a sexual encounter. Taking long baths or showers before sex, anointing oneself with body oils and perfumes, and putting on (or taking off!) sexy underclothes may have been important parts of the sexual encounter. During the preparenting years, sex may have been spontaneous and leisurely, with much sensual stroking and mutual arousal prior to intercourse. Over the course of a 30- to 40-year marriage, a more "no-nonsense" approach to sex may have evolved, without the niceties, thoughtfulness, and just plain zestiness of youth. Unfortunately, there is often a greater need for just such script elements as one grows older.

Case Example

Lou and Louise, a 65-year-old retired couple, complained about Louise's lack of sexual interest. Louise indicated that in addition to the fact that intercourse is often uncomfortable because of her "dry" vagina, Lou is no longer sexually appealing to her. When questioned about this, she confides that Lou has become more "sloppy" about his personal hygiene; he doesn't bathe or shave before sex, and often doesn't change his underwear frequently enough. She finds his body odor offensive and also objects to the fact that he "just expects me to roll over and be ready for him whenever he wakes up with an erection." "I'm not interested in early morning sex, and I refuse to simply go along for the ride!" she angrily declared. The therapist reframed the problem as a "scripting" problem and suggested some changes in sexual initiation, such as giving each other a long, sensual bath and body oil "treatment" prior to sexual exchange, something they had not done since their honeymoon. They agreed to these suggestions and "showered" together for the first time in years. They were encouraged to buy each other a "sexy" present, which they accomplished with some humor. By making minor modifications in *how* and *when* they approached each other, many of Louise's complaints disappeared, and marital harmony was reinstated.

The following case example illustrates the treatment of a couple who came for sexual counseling because a cardiovascular accident had disrupted the somewhat tenuous sexual adjustment they had developed over the years.

A Successful Case: Barbara

Barbara, a 56-year-old married accountant, sought sex therapy because of several concerns. Her husband of 30 years, Bernie, had recently had a heart attack, and he was experiencing intermittent difficulties achieving an erection. Barbara was having sexual arousal problems, caused in part by her postmenopausal status. She also complained that she could not find a comfortable position for sexual intercourse, although she had previously preferred the male-superior position. In order to reduce what she believed was the "work" of sex, they avoided the missionary position, and further, Barbara felt that she had to be the "active" sexual partner. In her new role, she was unable to relax, lubricate, or achieve orgasm, and she felt guilty about her lack of sexual interest.

Past History

Barbara was the older of two children. As a child, she had "adored" her father and tolerated her critical mother. Her family was quite traditional in their beliefs and inculcated their conviction that sexual relations be reserved for marriage. Barbara was an obedient daughter who tried to please her parents. In fact, she described herself as a "goody two-shoes."

She accepted the first offer of marriage she received, feeling that her marital choices would be limited since she felt plain and unattractive. She excelled intellectually, however, and prided herself on her slim figure and quick wit. She was accustomed to "having her way" with her friends.

Both Barbara and Bernie were virgins when they married but slowly evolved a comfortable sexual script. Bernie never pushed Barbara for more sensual exchange than she could tolerate, and she avoided physical affection, saying that she had always disliked touching or being touched. Long evenings of sensual exchange and kissing were disagreable to her. Rather, she preferred "quick" sexual relations, with little foreplay and brief intercourse. Although this script had worked satisfactorily in the past, it was no longer tenable. The antihypertensive medication Bernie was taking as well as the anxiety both Bernie and Barbara felt about precipitating a "coital coronary" made sex a burden rather than a pleasure.

Treatment

Barbara was seen alone for four sessions during which her worries about her husband's health as well as her own sexual inhibitions were explored. Accurate information about the oxygen "cost" of sexual intercourse was provided, and Barbara was advised to consult her husband's cardiologist about the safety of intercourse. She came away from these sessions realizing that she and Bernie had exaggerated the risks associated with coitus. She also learned that the shift in sexual position from missionary to female superior was neither necessary nor desirable. The consequences of her postmenopausal status were discussed, as well as the importance of using either external lubrication or initiating hormone replacement. Barbara's feelings of anger and fear concerning the changes necessitated by her husband's heart attack were validated as "normal." She was assured that with the passage of time, these fears would diminish if not totally disappear.

Because of Barbara's long-standing sexual inhibitions and touch aversion, she was invited to join a time-limited sexual enhancement group for middle-aged women. Although she was initially reluctant to do so, she agreed to "give it a try" and soon reported that she looked forward to these group sessions, exclaiming, "It's more fun than bridge!" She valued the opportunity of discussing sex openly with other women, something she had not done growing up, and benefited from having the other women challenge her traditional and often puritanical sexual assumptions. She began to masturbate and discovered that she was easily orgasmic with self-stimulation. In fact, although she was the oldest woman in the group, she was the most readily and reliably orgasmic, which was a source of pride and pleasure to her. The group suggested a variety of sensual massage exercises, and Barbara reported considerable success with them. In fact, Bernie's erectile performance improved, which increased her sexual receptivity. The use of external lubrication reduced the discomfort she felt during intercourse. Finally, she spontaneously discovered a new pleasurable "position" for coitus. By kneeling on her knees and elbows, Barbara reported that penetration was readily accomplished via rear entry, and she and Bernie both enjoyed the feelings they experienced.

As a result of both the individual and group sessions, Barbara reported considerable improvement in her sexual life. She was more sexually open and orgasmic and was gratified by the increase in sexual comfort and marital intimacy achieved.

Discussion

This case is not atypical. Men and women in their 50s must often deal with medical conditions, treatment, or drugs that impact on sexual functioning. Partners who have been together for decades often develop comfortable but relatively invariant sexual scripts. Changing life circumstances wrought by illness or disease often necessitate sexual script modifications, since what worked in the past no longer works. In this case, Barbara did not realize that her lack of lubrication was as much the result of postmenopausal estrogen deprivation as lack of arousal. When sex became irritating, she became more avoidant of physical intimacy generally. Her husband's heart attack exacerbated an already problematic sexual situation but, in some ways, provoked the crisis that led to therapy.

The fact that Barbara and Bernie loved each other helped supply the necessary motivation for script changes. Although Barbara never had been an enthusiastic lover, she did feel increasingly guilty about her sexual avoidance. She knew her husband valued sexual intimacy, and she was motivated to find a way of making sex palatable to herself. The women's group was especially helpful, since she tended to resist suggestions coming from the therapist but was receptive to the comments of the other women in the sexual enhancement group. Often, they were quite direct in challenging her preconceived notions about sex, which surprised her but provided the impetus to re-examine her sexual beliefs. She was particularly gratified by her orgasmic success since many of the other middle-aged women in the group were struggling with the initial attainment of orgasm. The fact that she became readily orgasmic validated her feelings about her sexual adequacy.

In this, as in other cases involving middle-aged and elderly couples, both partners were having sexual difficulties, and physical factors exacerbated the problem for each of them. Fairly straightforward "sex therapy" interventions were successful in resolving what might have become intractable sexual problems.

Aging is associated with a series of losses and necessary adjustments that may be foreign to the younger therapist (Berman & Lief, 1976). These include such losses as the death of lifelong friends as well as changes in social and professional status. For example, a somewhat upbeat middle-aged psychiatrist who was treating an elderly academic couple in conjoint marital therapy expressed surprise when the husband appeared depressed after an international meeting in molecular biology. His wife, an Emeritus Professor in biochemistry, replied, "It's always hard for us to go to these meetings. Each year, we learn that more of our closest friends have died." Coupled with the loss of treasured friends is the loss of professional and social status. Younger colleagues begin to assume positions of prominence and authority. For those elderly couples fortunate enough to have survived together into advanced age, considerable readjustment is necessary. Their relationship may be strained by new interpersonal demands formerly met in other relationships. Close friends and confidants may have passed away. Retirement may have severed collegial friendships and/or status. Suddenly, a marital relationship that may have been marginally functional for decades is asked to sustain these new interpersonal needs. Retirement may not involve simply adjusting to unstructured time or new leisure with a mate but rather a time when each spouse looks desperately to the other for confirmation of self-worth.

Many couples find their relationship stressed by retirement. A woman who has spent most of her life as a homemaker may resent the sudden intrusion into *her* home of a retired husband. As one woman commented, "I married my husband for better or for worse, but not for lunch!" Another housewife expressed her irritation with her husband's presence following retirement by exclaiming, "men and dust should be out of the house by 9 a.m." She felt angry that her husband wanted her to provide the compensation and companionship that was suddenly absent in his life. One businessman was bewildered by his wife's anger and sexual disinterest. She explained that she was irate because he had shown little interest in her or the family for years. Now that he was retired, he wanted her and the children to make him the center of the universe, much as his secretaries and staff had treated him before his retirement as president of a large corporation.

The following case illustrates how retirement as a life-stage event can impact on sexual functioning.

An Unsuccessful Sex Therapy Outcome

A 64-year-old master cabinetmaker read an article on sex therapy and insisted that his wife of 40 years immediately seek treatment for lifelong low sexual desire. She agreed, reluctantly, to enter treatment and described a chronic absence of sexual fantasies, thoughts, or sexual pleasure. She had been raised to believe that a nice woman should not seek or expect sexual pleasure but should satisfy her husband's sexual needs. In fact, she had lived her life according to these dictates.

The first therapist the couple consulted was skeptical about whether change was possible but referred this 63-year-old woman to an experienced 66-year-old female sex therapist. Self-exploratory and self-pleasuring activities were started. Within 6 weeks, the woman experienced her first orgasm and began calling her husband at work, asking him to come home early for sexual play.

The couple were then seen in couples' therapy. Her husband maintained that he was pleased with his wife's progress but gave excuses as to why he could not participate in the sexual homework assignments. He then began to complain of severe headaches that awakened him from sleep. A check of his blood pressure indicated a significant rise, resulting in a medical referral. The patient never returned for therapy and refused to respond to telephone messages from the sex therapist. His wife, however, agreed to return alone for a follow-up visit. She reported that she was masturbating on a regular basis but that her husband refused to have intercourse with her or to discuss his feelings of sexual avoidance. She also reported that he had discarded his large collection of pornography. On further probing, she said that she thought her husband felt less manly because of his impending retirement and that he was threatened by the changes in her sexual appetite. She remarked, "I guess that it came at the wrong time in his life."

In retrospect, it appears that the husband's preoccupation with his wife's sexuality may have been a displacement of his concern about retirement. His own attitudes about female sexuality were challenged by his wife's new-found ardor. He was unable to cope with her sexuality because he felt emasculated by the prospect of retirement. The therapist may have unwittingly contributed to the husband's loss of self-esteem.

This couple helped to educate the therapist about the necessity of being aware of life stresses faced by the elderly and the difficulties they may have in adjusting to the sexual changes seen in themselves or their partners.

CONCLUSION

Sex therapy with the elderly is both similar to and different from sex therapy with other age groups. In all populations, one must assess the relative contributions of both biological and psychological factors to sexual difficulties. In aged populations, greater care must be taken to exclude biogenic causes of dysfunction. Finally, the therapist must be especially sensitive to the unique life stresses faced by the elderly and appreciate the attitudinal disparity toward sexuality in older as opposed to younger individuals.

Acknowledgments. The authors wish to gratefully acknowledge the helpful suggestions of Drs. Gloria Bachmann and Marian Dunn for this chapter.

REFERENCES

Assalian, P. (1988). Diabetes and female sexual response. *Journal of Clinical Practice in Sexuality, 4*(1), 11–16.

Bachmann, G., Leiblum, S., & Grill, J. (1989). Brief sexual inquiry in gynecologic practice. *Obstetrics and Gynecology, 73*(3), 425–427.

Bancroft, J. (1983). *Human sexuality and its problems.* Edinburgh: Churchill Livingstone.

Bancroft, J., & Wu, F. C. W. (1983). Changes in erectile responsiveness during androgen replacement therapy. *Archives of Sexual Behavior, 12,* 59–66.

Berman, E. M., & Lief, H. I. (1976). Sex and the aging process. In W. W. Oaks, G. A. Melchiode, & I. Fischer (Eds.), *Sex and the life cycle* (pp. 125–134). New York: Grune & Stratton.

Brecher, E. (1984). *Love, sex and aging: A Consumer's Union survey.* Boston: Little, Brown.

Bretschneider, J., & McCoy, M. (1988). Sexual interest and behavior in healthy 80–102 year-olds. *Archives of Sexual Behavior, 17*(2), 109–130.

Centers for Disease Control. (1981, April 24). Surveillance Summaries. Hysterectomy among women of reproductive age. U.S. Update for 1970–1980. *Morbidity and Mortality Weekly Report, 32*(2), 1SS–7SS.

Comfort, A. (1976). *A good age.* New York: Simon & Schuster.

Cutler, W., & Garcia, C. (1984). *The medical management of menopause and premenopause: Their endocrinologic basis.* Philadelphia: J. P. Lippincott.

Cutler, W., Garcia, C. R., & McCoy, N. (1987). Perimenopausal sexuality. *Archives of Sexual Behavior, 16*(3), 225–234.

Davidson, J., Cameron, C. A., & Smith, E. R. (1983). Effects of androgen on sexual behavior in hypogonadal men. *Journal of Clinical Endocrinology and Metabolism, 48,* 955–958.

Davidson, J., Kwan, M., & Greenleaf, W. (1982). Hormonal replacement and sexuality in men. *Clinics in Endocrinology and Metabolism, 11,* 599–623.

Dennerstein, L., & Burrows, G. D. (1982). Hormone replacement therapy and sexuality in women. *Clinics in Endocrinology and Metabolism, 11,* 661–679.

Ellenberg, M. (1977). Sexual aspects of the female diabetic. *Mt. Sinai Journal of Medicine, 44,* 495–500.

Gagnon, J., Rosen, R., & Leiblum, S. (1984). Cognitive and social aspects of sexual dysfunction: Sexual scripts in sex therapy. *Journal of Sex and Marital Therapy, 8*(1), 44–56.

Garth, D., Cooper, P., & Day, A. (1982). Hysterectomy and psychiatric disorder. I: Levels of psychiatric morbidity before and after hysterectomy. *British Journal of Psychiatry, 140,* 335–342.

Hegeler, S., & Mortensen, M. M. (1977). Sexual behavior in elderly Danish males. In C. C. Wheeler (Ed.), *Progress in sexology.* New York: Plenum Press.

Jensen, S. B. (1985). Sexual relationships in couples with a diabetic partner. *Journal of Sex and Marital Therapy, 11,* 259–270.

Jones, T. M. (1985). Hormonal considerations in the evaluation and treatment of erectile dysfunction. In R. T. Segraves & H. W. Schoenberg (Eds.), *Diagnosis and treatment of erectile disturbances* (pp. 115–158). New York: Plenum Press.

Kilkku, R., Gronross, M., Hirvemen, T., & Fauramo, L. (1983). Supravaginal uterine amputation vs. hysterectomy: Effects on libido and orgasm. *Acta Obstetrica et Gynecologica Scandinavica, 62,* 147–152.

Kinsey, A. C., Pomeroy, B., & Martin, C. I. (1948). *Sexual behavior in the human male.* Philadelphia: W. B. Saunders.

Lalinec-Michaud, M., & Engelsmann, F. (1988). Psychological profile of depressed women undergoing hysterectomy. *Journal of Psychosomatic Obstetrics and Gynecology, 8*(1), 53–66.

Leiblum, S., & Bachmann, G. (1987). The sexuality of the climacteric woman. In B. Eskin (Ed.), *The menopause: Comprehensive management* (pp. 165–180). New York: Yearbook Publications.

Leiblum, G., & Bachmann, G. (1988, August). *Sexuality in sexagenarian women.* Paper presented at the Annual Meeting of the International Academy of Sex Research, Minneapolis, MN.

Leiblum, S., Bachmann, G., Kemmann, E., Colburn, D., & Swartzman, L. (1983). Vaginal atrophy in the postmenopausal woman: The importance of sexual activity and hormones. *Journal of the American Medical Association, 249*(16), 2195.

Longfellow, H. W. (1968). *Selected Poems.* New York: Peter Pauper Press.

Masters, W., & Johnson, V. (1966). *Human sexual response.* Boston: Little, Brown.

Masters, W., & Johnson, V. (1977). Sex after sixty-five. *Reflections, 12,* 31–43.

Melman, A., & Leiter, E. (1983). The urological evaluation of impotence (male excitement phase disorder). In H. S. Kaplan (Ed.), *The evaluation of sexual disorders: Psychological and medical aspects.* New York: Brunner/Mazel.

Moore, J. T., & Tolley, D. H. (1976). Depression following hysterectomy. *Psychosomatics, 17,* 86–89.

Morrell, M., Dixen, J., Carter, S., & Davidson, J. (1984). The influence of age and cycling status on sexual arousability in women. *American Journal of Obstetrics and Gynecology, 148,* 66–71.

Myers, L., & Morokoff, P. (1985). *Physiological and subjective sexual arousal in pre- and postmenopausal women.* Paper presented at the American Psychological Association Meeting.

Pfeiffer, E. (1974). Sexuality in the aging individual. *Journal of the American Geriatrics Society, 22,* 481–484.

Renshaw, T. (1988). Sexuality in the later years. *Geriatric Sexual Counseling Mediguide to Aging, 3*(1), 1–6.

Rosen, R. C., & Leiblum, S. R. (1988). A sexual scripting approach to problems of desire. In S. R. Leiblum & R. L. Rosen (Eds.), *Sexual desire disorders.* New York: Guilford Press.

Schiavi, R. (1988). NPT in the evaluation of erectile disorders: A critical review. *Journal of Sex and Marital Therapy, 14,* 83–88.

Schiavi, R. C., & Schreiner-Engel, P. (1988). *Healthy aging and male sexual arousal.* Paper presented at the Annual Meeting of the Society for Sex Therapy and Research, New York.

Schover, L. R. (1984). *Prime time: Sexual health for men over fifty.* New York: Holt, Rinehart & Winston.

Schover, L., & Jensen, S. (1988). *Sexuality and chronic illness.* New York: Guilford Press.

Schreiner-Engel, P., Schiavi, R. C., Vietorisz, D., & Eichel, J. (1985). Diabetes and female sexuality: A comparative study of women in relationships. *Journal of Sex and Marital Therapy, 11,* 165.

Segraves, K. A. B., & Segraves, R. T. (1987). Differentiation of biogenic and psychogenic impotence by sexual symptomatology. *Archives of Sexual Behavior, 16,* 125–137.

Segraves, R. T., Schoenberg, H. W., & Ivanoff, J. (1983). Serum testosterone and prolactin levels in erectile dysfunction. *Journal of Sex and Marital Therapy, 9,* 19–26.

Sherwin, B., Gelfand, M., & Brender, W. (1985). Androgen enhances sexual motivation in females: A prospective, crossover study of sex steroid administration in the surgical menopause. *Psychosomatic Medicine, 47,* 339–351.

Stephenson, J. A., & Umstead, G. (1984). Sexual dysfunction due to anti-hypertensive agents. *Journal of Drug Intelligence and Clinical Pharmacology, 18,* 113–121.

Swartzman, L., & Leiblum, S. (1987). Changing perspectives on the menopause. *Journal of Psychosomatic Obstetrics and Gynecology, 6,* 11–24.

Turner, B., & Adams, C. (1988). Reported change in preferred sexual activity over the adult years. *Journal of Sex Research, 25*(2), 289–303.

Zussman, L., Zussman, S., Sunley, R., & Bjornson, E. (1981). Sexual response after hysterectomy–oophorectomy: Recent evidence and reconsideration of psychogenesis. *American Journal of Obstetrics and Gynecology, 140,* 725–729.

14

Assessment and Treatment of Atypical Sexual Behavior

JOHN P. WINCZE

Deviant or atypical sexual behavior confronts the clinician with a variety of therapeutic dilemmas and conflicts. Beginning with the issue of definition and classification of atypical sexual behavior, Wincze distinguishes between coercive and noncoercive paraphilias. He emphasizes that individuals who practice victimless forms of atypical sexual behavior, such as transvestism and fetishism, rarely enter therapy voluntarily. Where the motivation for treatment is based entirely on external pressure or threat, it may be difficult for the clinician to obtain accurate assessment information or to engage the client in a meaningful therapeutic contract. Furthermore, clinicians may avoid treating clients with atypical sexual behavior because of the negative emotional reactions elicited by these behaviors or because of lack of specialized training on the part of the therapist. On the other hand, Wincze points out that newly developed treatment methods are available that can be used for effective management of atypical sexual behavior.

How does one explain the development of deviant sexual behavior? The author discusses this issue in detail, finding the current evidence for a hormonal or genetic explanation to be unconvincing. By contrasting psychodynamic and behavioral explanations, he suggests that several background factors appear to play a key role in most cases. These include the experience of atypical sexual behavior in childhood (many offenders were victims of sexual abuse themselves), the lack of a consistent parental environment, and sexual ignorance and misinformation. Paraphilic clients are also typically lacking in self-esteem and have poor stress-coping abilities.

A strength of this chapter is the detailed presentation of both the structure and content of early assessment sessions. Wincze emphasizes first the importance of establishing trust and rapport with a new client. Self-monitoring of deviant urges or behavior is also important, as is an in-depth consideration of possible maintaining factors. Psychophysiological procedures are also discussed, as the author emphasizes the value of these proce-

dures in identifying specific patterns of arousal. Laboratory assessment has also been shown to aid in the prediction of recidivism.

Current treatment techniques vary from the use of antiandrogenic drugs, such as medroxyprogesterone acetate (MPA), to psychological interventions, such as aversive therapy or masturbatory satiation. Wincze describes a four-stage model of treatment in which a variety of treatment interventions are prescribed at different stages of therapy. In addition to techniques designed to reduce deviant arousal, he recommends social and sexual skills training, anxiety reduction techniques, and a structured relapse prevention program. Detailed case studies are used to illustrate positive and negative prognostic factors and the role of manipulation in determining treatment outcome.

Although most clinicians continue to have difficulty in treating clients with atypical or paraphilic sexual behavior, the author presents a compelling argument for attempting treatment whenever possible. In addition to assisting these individuals in achieving a more productive and socially desirable life style, there is the important potential for reducing the probability of future victimization.

John P. Wincze, Ph.D., is Professor of Psychology at Brown University and Chief of Psychology at the Providence VA Medical Center. He has conducted extensive research on sexual disorders and paraphilias.

Although the terms deviation and perversion are still applied to sexual behaviors, most professionals who work in the field of human sexuality prefer to use the less pejorative term "atypical." The use of the term atypical connotes that all human sexual behavior falls on a continuum and is defined by the laws and cultural mores of a society. Most human sexuality textbooks describe the enormous variations in sexual practices across cultures in order to reject the concept of abnormality when applied to sexual behavior.

Discussions of atypical sexual behaviors can be divided into two major categories: (1) noncoercive behaviors and (2) coercive victimization. An example of a noncoercive atypical sexual behavior is a man who buys women's underwear and masturbates while wearing the underwear in the privacy of his home. An example of an atypical sexual behavior that involves coercion and a victim would be sexual intercourse between an adult and a child.

Another important concept in the classification of atypical sexual behaviors is "paraphilia." The term paraphilia recognizes the end of a continuum of sexual behavior; that is, it describes an extreme degree of investment in, or consumption by, a sexual behavior that dominates and directs a person's sexual practices. Paraphilic sexual practices are central to a person's sexual excitement. In many cases sexual excitement cannot occur without the paraphilic behavior.

The classification of atypical sexual behaviors into noncoercive and coercive categories and nonparaphilic and paraphilic categories is extremely important for treatment considerations. Very different treatment approaches are indicated depending on these categorizations. For example, if paraphilic behavior includes victimization, then inpatient therapy or antiandrogen medication may be the very first step in therapy in order to control further occurrences. On the other hand, if a client manifests victimless behavior, then therapy may initially ask the client to record the occurrence of the behavior and its stimulus antecedents. Some examples of paraphilic behaviors and nonparaphilic behaviors, and victimless behaviors and victimizing behaviors are given in Table 14.1.

Precise estimates of the incidence and prevalence of atypical sexual behaviors are unavailable. This is especially true of noncoercive victimless behaviors because of the secret nature of the behaviors. Rough estimates are available, however, from surveys such as those achieved by Kinsey and his associates (Kinsey, Pomeroy, & Martin, 1948; Kinsey, Pomeroy, Martin, & Gebhard, 1953). For sexual behaviors in which there is a victim (including exhibitionism, child molestation, and rape), the incidence of sexual offenses can be obtained from crime statistics. However, such figures are considered to be underestimates for several reasons. Victims of sexual offenses are often deterred from reporting the crime because of embarrassment or because the reporting system may bring further trauma to the victim. For example, a child who is victimized by sexual assault may have to explain his or her experience numerous times to those who are helping (police, social workers, child care workers, nurses, doctors, psychologists, and attorneys). Faced with this probability, parents may decide against putting their child through a system that may be viewed as additionally stressful.

Atypical sexual behaviors only come to the attention of a therapist if the behaviors are troublesome to an individual or to society. Rarely does a

TABLE 14.1 Examples of Paraphilic and Nonparaphilic Behaviors

	Paraphilic	Nonparaphillic
Victim (Coercive)	Pedophilia Voyeurism Obscene phone calls Incest Rape Toucherism Exhibitionism Zoophilia	Child abuse Incest Rape
No victim	Sadomasochism (consenting) Transvestism Fetishism	Unusual sexual behaviors that occur infrequently

person who is practicing atypical noncoercive (victimless) sexual behaviors enter therapy voluntarily. It is more common for the person to be pressured into therapy by society or by the legal system. Unfortunately, a large percentage of clients are court referred, and the client's goal is to "beat the charges." Very few clients initially recognize the harm they are causing themselves or others, and consequently, they have difficulty participating in the therapeutic process. Clients who have committed offenses that victimize others are often defensive and may actually blame the victim. Often the therapist is viewed as part of the judicial system and has an extremely difficult time extracting the complete story. For these reasons, many therapists are reluctant to deal with clients presenting with atypical sexual behaviors. Furthermore, many therapists are simply uncomfortable with the nature of the problem or feel poorly trained to deal with it. A nonprofessional person will often advocate jail (that is, punishment) for sexual offenders and view with suspicion and anger the therapist who is "helping" the offender.

For all of the above reasons, few well-trained therapists are available to treat atypical sexual behaviors. Yet, recent evidence supports the claim that well-executed treatment can reduce recidivism for child sex offenders when compared to incarceration only (Freeman-Longo & Wall, 1986; Groth, 1983). Berlin and Meinecke (1981) also point out that the use of antiandrogens such as medroxyprogesterone acetate combined with psychotherapy is an effective treatment for paraphilic behaviors. There is certainly a growing body of evidence to support the use of a psychotherapeutic approach for the treatment of atypical sexual behavior.

ETIOLOGICAL CONSIDERATIONS

There is little certainty about the exact causes of atypical sexual behavior. This is not surprising, since most of our information about atypical sexual behaviors comes from retrospective studies of individuals who have entered therapy. The motivation for participating in atypical sexual behaviors and the circumstances surrounding participation are so diverse that it seems unlikely that common etiological factors exist. To date there are no compelling hormonal or genetic explanations that enhance our understanding of the development of atypical sexual behaviors. Abnormal hormonal or genetic conditions are found no more commonly in individuals displaying atypical sexual behaviors than they are in individuals with typical sexual behaviors.

Psychological theories provide more insight into the etiology of atypical sexual behavior than do the biological explanations, but the former also lack empirical verification. Stoller (1975), speaking from a psychodynamic perspective, postulates that "sexual perversions" are expressions of hostility. Furthermore, they represent revenge for inhibited childhood sexual expression.

It should be noted that specific types of paraphilic behaviors may be viewed as a part of a more specific psychodynamic process. Van de Loo

(1987), for example, points out that exhibitionism may represent an individual's attempt to reduce castration anxiety by the reassurance of the presence of the penis during exposure. It may also be viewed as part of the preoedipal process of the discovery and acceptance of genital differences between the sexes.

Behaviorists look on atypical behaviors as products of a faulty learning environment in which a childhood opportunity to cross normative sexual boundaries was experienced and reinforced. Repeated experiences with the actual behavior or fantasies coupled with sexual arousal and orgasm served to strengthen the atypical behavior. Once normative sexual boundaries are crossed for one behavior, then additional atypical sexual behaviors are likely to be expressed. Abel, Becker, and Skinner (1983) have presented empirical support for this notion by their observation that paraphilics often have multiple types of paraphilic experiences; that is, a single individual may be a pedophile, voyeur, and exhibitionist.

It is often noted that paraphilics and nonparaphilics act out during times of great emotional distress. There are often very specific emotional states that serve as precursors to the sexual behavior and that dissipate once the sexual act occurs. This pattern is consistent with the tension reduction model (Rosen & Fracher, 1983), whereas dynamic therapists view this as a struggle with castration anxiety (Stoller, 1975).

Although an exact etiological explanation of atypical sexual behaviors may be lacking, there are a number of common background factors that seem to be present in individuals who participate in these behaviors:

1. Early crossing of normative sexual boundaries through a direct (for example, sexual abuse by an adult) or indirect (hearing about or observing father's atypical sexual behavior) experience.
2. Lack of a consistent parental environment in which normative sexual behavior and values were modeled.
3. Lack of self-esteem.
4. Lack of confidence and ability in social interactions.
5. Ignorance and poor understanding of human sexuality.

In addition to specific background factors that are often present in individuals manifesting atypical sexual behaviors, specific attitudes may also facilitate such behaviors. This is especially true of men who commit sexual offenses against women. Burt (1980) has identified a number of such attitudes: conservative sexual beliefs, rigid adherence to traditional male/female roles, endorsement of adversarial sexual beliefs, and endorsement of rape myths. Groth (1983) suggests that lack of sensitivity to the impact on a victim is often present in sex offenders. Objectification of the victim is another factor related to this. Thus, not only might an offender lack awareness of the harm he may cause, but he may view the victim as an object rather than as a person with feelings.

A final consideration is that atypical sexual behaviors are often associated with specific emotional states including anger, frustration, and desperation. Feelings of low self-esteem and an attitude of "I don't care" often lead to sexual acting out.

Thus, atypical sexual behaviors appear to be a product of a developmental process that includes early childhood exposure to crossing of sexual boundaries combined with a lack of normative parental guidance. Throughout development, there are influences that formulate attitudes toward sexuality and victimization, influences that facilitate the probability of sexual acting out. Late factors that complete the process are opportunity and emotional distress and, for many, the use of drugs and alcohol.

CLINICAL CONSIDERATIONS

Because threat of incarceration is often present, sex offenders in particular and those involved in atypical sexual behaviors in general are often defensive and reticent in their initial discussions with a therapist. The therapist has to be well trained and knowledgeable about sexual behavior in order to gather meaningful information. Knowledge of gender dysphoria is also important because gender dysphoria is commonly present as an issue and because those presenting as transsexuals often turn out to be transvestites.

The therapist's knowledge and experience will help him or her to focus on therapy issues and avoid becoming a legal pawn. Lawyers and their sexually offending clients usually understand that participation in therapy will help to reduce and sometimes avoid legal consequences. The therapist must define his or her therapeutic role at the onset and gain a commitment for therapy regardless of the legal consequences. At the same time, working with the legal system is important, for without legal coercion, most offenders would never enter therapy and would continue offending unabated.

A very important consideration when working with sex offenders is that certain types of offenses must legally be reported to child welfare authorities or the police. The laws may vary from state to state or country to country, but generally if there is a known victim who is currently being sexually molested, the offense must be reported. The therapist is put in the awkward position of encouraging the offender to be completely open and honest to gain his trust yet warning the client that if he reports certain offenses he will be reported to legal authorities. I feel that a thorough discussion with the client about the need for honesty and the therapist's legal obligations is extremely important at the beginning of the assessment process. The therapist should be completely familiar with his or her local laws and procedures for reporting offenses and should talk to child welfare authorities to understand what obligations and discretionary power he or she has.

One other related issue that therapists are faced with is that therapy may be misconstrued by the client as a "confessional" followed by exoneration. Because sex is often associated with guilt and sin, the analogy to Catholicism is apropos. Abramson and Hayashi (1982) point out that rape behavior is looked on very differently in Japan compared to the United States. In Japan, there is a deep-rooted sense of shame that never leaves an individual who has committed a sexual offense, whereas in the United States, atonement for an offense is possible. This difference, it is speculated, is one important reason that Japan has an incidence of rape about 16 times lower than the United States (Abramson & Hayashi, 1982). Once atonement occurs, then the past is erased, and the potential controlling factors of guilt and of harm to a victim are removed.

One recent paraphilic client of mine who had served 6 months in jail and who had gone through 2 years of therapy, was extremely indignant when new charges were brought against him for a past offense.

"How could they do this? I served my time and did everything I was supposed to in therapy. I'll sue them. They have no right to arrest me because I've paid my dues."

It did not matter to this client that the new charges were related to an offense that had not previously been dealt with. I reminded this client that successfully completing therapy does not remove past sexual offenses, and he must always be vigilant about recurrences. Assessment should be approached with the above clinical considerations in mind. The behavioral model outlined next focuses on antecedents and consequences of offensive sexual behavior. Cognitive, physiological, and medical aspects that may influence the problem are also considered.

ASSESSMENT

Comprehensive and accurate assessment is, of course, crucial to formulating an effective treatment program. Obtaining meaningful information to the assessment process involves more than just asking the right questions. In all areas of clinical practice, the clinician must attend to process issues as well as structure and content of assessment. For example, the clinician must be aware of how he or she is coming across to the client. This is all the more crucial with the client presenting with atypical sexual behaviors, who is often frightened, defensive, and/or hostile. The interview itself must be very carefully planned and should attend to assumptions, goals, process issues, and structure and content.

Assumptions

Assumptions are the "default" attitudes and hypotheses that the clinician makes to help gather the most accurate information without wasting time and effort. Assumptions are the guidelines for a preferred direction of error. For example, it is better for a clinician to assume a low level of understanding on the part of the client so that language is directed to the patient in a clear and concrete manner. Obviously, as the clinician learns more about the patient, assumptions are adjusted to the needs of the specific client.

Goals

Goals are the desired session outcomes and should be established before each session. At times, the goals have to be adjusted to accommodate the needs of the patient as new information is learned.

Process

Process issues include assumptions and goals as well as those factors that facilitate or inhibit the assessment. Rapport, trust, and confidence can facilitate assessment; a therapeutic relationship that includes these characteristics can be achieved if the clinician is friendly and conveys positive regard and competency. It is clear that many clinicians feel uncomfortable dealing with men who perpetrate sexual offenses against women and children or who dress in women's clothing. Personal feelings of anger, disgust, amusement, or even revenge may show through ingenuine attempts to be friendly and accepting. Shock and dismay may be felt inwardly as the offender tells his story. To express these feelings overtly, or even subtly, could be divisive and create a barrier to effective therapy. If a therapist's feelings cannot be concealed, then he or she should not be dealing with this population.

Structure and Content

These are the guidelines for conducting the assessment. Essentially, this is the order in which issues and topics will be approached so that the most meaningful information can be gathered in the briefest time. As in the case of goals, the structure and content must be changed to accompany the needs of the client. Therapist experience and skill are important in knowing when to follow a prescribed structure and when to allow digression.

THE ASSESSMENT INTERVIEW

The first interview with a new client is crucial for establishing a comfortable, trustworthy therapeutic environment. It may be assumed that the client will be defensive and underreport or even deny problematic sexual behavior. It is also quite likely that the client will not trust the therapist, and that he may be highly anxious or severely depressed and suicidal. The goals of the first interview are to establish rapport, gather preliminary information about the client's background, and help the client deal with his "crisis."

An important process issue is to help the client build confidence and trust in the therapist. To do this, the therapist must convey his or her experience and comfort in treating a wide range of sexual behaviors. Another process issue in the first interview is to set the limits of the therapeutic relationship. The client should be confronted with any attempts at "boundary crossing" such as calling the therapist by a first name or asking personal questions.

As a part of the process of helping to reduce the client's anxiety and at the same time build rapport, it is helpful to begin the interview structure with an overview of the therapy procedure and then ask nonthreatening questions regarding age, employment, household composition, etc. Following this, a general question such as "What brings you here today?" is an effective way of probing the client's willingness to discuss his behavior. If possible, the first interview should obtain general information about the client's current problem, past psychosocial history, current medical problems, and past medical history. The interview should end on an encouraging note with comments about how helpful the client has been in reporting information. The therapist should again acknowledge that it might have been difficult for the client. The client should be reminded that successful treatment depends on honest reporting of information and accurate record keeping. Clients should then be asked to keep a diary of urges and actual occurrences of the atypical behavior in order to understand the circumstances under which it occurs.

Each assessment session should continue to attend to assumptions, goals, process issues, and structure and content. The first interview should focus a great deal on building rapport and gathering general information, whereas the second and third sessions attempt to gather more detailed information about the parameters of the sexual problem. Psychological testing may be a useful adjunct to the assessment procedure. Although there are no tests that are able to discriminate the paraphilic from the nonparaphilic, or the sex offender from the nonoffender, psychological tests may help to identify areas of pathology. Questionnaires such as the Derogatis Sexual Functioning Inventory (DSFI; Derogatis & Meyer, 1979) or the Rape Myth Scale (Burt, 1980) can supplement interview information.

The fourth session is typically the time to introduce the therapy based on the information gathered. It can be assumed that most clients will have a great deal of difficulty in accepting any therapy plan, since they do not wish to relinquish their participation in atypical sexual behavior.

The details of the plan and the efforts needed to carry it out successfully should be discussed in detail with the client. The session should end on an optimistic note, and the client should be reminded of the importance of honesty and the importance of daily efforts outside of the therapy sessions.

The above discussion is intended to give the reader a reasonable assessment approach for clients presenting with atypical sexual behaviors. The interview will serve as the most comprehensive and valuable source of information and has been presented in a session-by-session plan to maximize its efficiency and effectiveness.

One other supplement to the interview is the use of psychophysiological assessment. Psychophysiological assessment most typically uses a mercury-in-rubber strain gauge placed on the penis while the client is exposed to a series of auditory or video sexual vignettes. The vignettes typically present a wide array of stimuli so that the relative strength of responses can be compared. The resulting "pattern" of responding will reveal the stimuli that elicit the most responding. Earls and Marshall (1983) point out that psychophysiological assessment has been applied to a wide variety of atypical sexual behaviors; however, the validity and reliability of the procedure have often been brought into question. Attempts have been made to strengthen the utility of this measure (Earls & Marshall, 1983), but it should still only be used as a supplement to the interview and not as a definitive statement. Abel, Mittelman, and Becker (1985) have reported that the debriefing period immediately following the stimuli presentation is a valuable source of additional information. A significant proportion of men undergoing the procedure report additional information when discussing their psychophysiological records. Overall, psychophysiological procedures are limited but have some utility in corroborating other data gathered and in eliciting new information.

A number of research studies have demonstrated that psychophysical procedures can differentiate subgroups of individuals with atypical sexual behaviors. Abel, Barlow, Blanchard, and Guild (1977) demonstrated that the degree of dangerousness in terms of physical harm to the victim could be identified to men who rape. In another example, Buhrich and McConaghy (1979) were able to differentiate three subgroups of male cross-dressers based on measures of penile volume changes during exposure to a variety of erotic stimuli. The psychophysiological methodology has added to our knowledge to assist in differential diagnosis.

In addition to refining differential diagnosis, theoretical hypotheses have been tested using this methodology. For example, Freund (1967) challenged the psychoanalytic concept that homosexuality in men results from a "horror feminae" or aversion to females. By using measures of penile volume change, Freund (1967) demonstrated that homosexual men showed more physiological arousal to female adults than to female children. There was not an aversion to women in general; it was a matter of degrees of arousal.

One final application of psychophysiological assessment has been in the prediction of recidivism in child sex offenders (Marshall, 1975). Marshall (1975) has demonstrated that men who continue to show sexual arousal to deviant stimuli, as measured by penile volume change, are more likely to offend in the future.

THERAPY

Therapy emanates directly from assessment and, in fact, is a part of assessment. In cases in which a victim may potentially be involved, the client must be given immediate short-term strategies to control the behavior. Part of the initial assessment session can be set aside to discuss the issue of immediate control. If there is a trusted "significant other" in the client's life, this person may be incorporated into the therapeutic process as a contact person in a time of need. The "significant other" is someone to whom urges can be reported, someone who can spend time with the client, and someone who can help monitor accountability. Ideally, the "significant other" should be someone who knows the client's daily routine and who is easily accessible to the client. In addition to including a "significant other" in treatment, immediate cessation of offending behavior can be facilitated by the following:

1. Self-monitoring of urges using a written record (diary).
2. Discussion of immediate high-risk situations and immediate and necessary changes to reduce risks, such as arranging to stay with someone, ceasing activities that bring the client into risk.
3. Planning activities to occupy time and interfere with risk.

Although the above procedures do not guarantee compliance, they can be helpful in many cases. A client entering therapy is usually in a crisis. He has been mandated by either court action or public pressure. Certainly the crisis issue must be attended to immediately during assessment because the crisis overwhelms the client and focuses his attention on resolution of the crisis. Often during the crisis period, the client is unusually open and responsive to change. The therapist should take advantage of this time to commit the client to substantial changes—open discussion with family and friends and changes in activities and work in order to reduce his contact with potential victims. There also has to be a concrete discussion during this time to outline commitment to therapy after the crisis has been resolved. Therapy goals must be established at this time to go beyond the crisis,and the client has to be alerted to the possibility of a waning interest in therapy once a legal resolve is reached. Risk of suicide is enhanced at this time, and the offender must be encouraged to report suicidal feelings. The therapist must be reachable and let the client know he can call at all times. Once the initial assessment period is over and the focus has shifted more toward therapy per se, a number of considerations must be met. Therapy is approached much like assessment with a set of assumptions, goals, process issues, and a planned structure and content.

Assumptions for Therapy

As in the case of assessment, assumptions for therapy are the guesses that a therapist makes about the client in the direction that will create the least amount of error. Some helpful assumptions for therapy are as follows:

1. The client does not wish to give up the atypical sexual behavior and will do everything possible to continue practicing the behavior.
2. The client does not appreciate the need for therapy and will try to avoid sessions and confrontation of issues.
3. The client is *always* at risk for relapse.

Goals for Therapy

1. Arrest the atypical sexual behavior.
2. Make the client aware of all the factors that lead to risks for the occurrence of the offensive behavior.
3. Help the client to develop a sensitivity to the impact that his sexual behavior has on others.
4. Improve client's overall well-being.

Process Issues

A client's participation in atypical sexual behavior often crosses sexual boundaries and also often crosses social boundaries. The client may also cross boundaries with the therapist. Very often the client will call the therapist by the first name and ask personal questions. The therapist must use good clinical judgment and prevent "too much familiarity." This is, of course, a process issue in any therapy situation but seems to happen more commonly in therapy with these clients.

Therapy relies on trust and openness, and these points must be discussed with the client. There can be no secrets, and all urges and offenses must be reported even though the offender will try to hide them. The client must be prepared to discuss urges when they occur and not feel he is letting the therapist down.

Structure and Contact

The therapy structure proceeds through various stages depending on a client's needs. The most usual sequence is described by the four stages shown in Table 14.2.

THERAPEUTIC PROCEDURES

There are a variety of therapeutic procedures that may be employed with a client depending on the client's needs. This section focuses specifically on the procedures that are useful in the treatment of individuals with atypical sexual behaviors and does not focus on other procedures (for example, anxiety reduction) that may apply to this population but may also commonly apply to individuals experiencing other problems.

TABLE 14.2   Therapeutic Procedures Applied in Progressive Stages of Therapy

Stage	Target problem	Possible therapeutic procedures
Stage 1	Crisis	Crisis intervention counseling Support
	Decreasing inappropriate sexual arousal	Stimulus control Aversion procedures Victim awareness Group therapy Satiation and orgasmic reconditioning Depo-Provera
Stage 2	Increasing appropriate sexual arousal	Social skills training Sexual skills training Assertiveness
Stage 3	Ancillary problems that affect well-being: anxiety, depression, self-image	Anxiety reduction Improving self-image Depression management
Stage 4	Lifelong maintenance of control of atypical sexual behavior	Relapse prevention Therapy booster sessions

Stimulus Control

For individuals experiencing atypical sexual behavior, there are usually very specific overt and covert stimuli that precede the unwanted behavior. Knowledge of the antecedents leading up to the urges and atypical behavior is crucial to controlling the behaviors. The stimulus control procedure begins with the behavioral records and with other information obtained during the assessment procedure. Each client is asked to keep a record of all urges and actual occurrences of the atypical behavior during the week. An urge is defined as a fantasy or actual behavior that results in any sexual arousal. The antecedents include emotions, activities, thoughts, and situations that have been associated with the atypical behavior in the past and that put the client at risk for the occurrence of the atypical behavior. The therapist helps the client identify all aspects of the stimulus antecedents through careful questioning and review of the behavioral record. The following discourse between a therapist and child sex offender is an example of the process of identifying stimulus antecedents:

THERAPIST: What contacts have you had with children during the past week?
CLIENT: I was out picking blueberries, minding my own business, and two kids came along. I did very well though. We talked for a long time. They were very interested in what I was doing. Nothing

happened though, and after talking for a half hour, they went on
their way and I went on mine.

THERAPIST: How did you begin talking to the children in the first place?

CLIENT: Well, they started talking to me. As I said, they were very
interested in what I was doing.

THERAPIST: Let's go over the whole incident very carefully. Why did
they start talking to you in the first place?

CLIENT: I don't know. I guess they were interested in what I was doing.

THERAPIST: Did you see them approaching you?

CLIENT: Yes, I saw them coming down the path, and I watched them as
they approached.

THERAPIST: Did you smile at them or act friendly?

CLIENT: Yes. I guess I did. I'm a friendly person. Do you think I should
be rude?

The client was seemingly unaware that his body posture, his smile, and
his eye contact were all important precursors to the ensuing conversation
with the children. Furthermore, he had placed himself on a pathway fre-
quented by children. All of these antecedents that led to involvement with
the children were identified and discussed with the client. The therapist also
role played alternative ways to avoid involvement with the children. Stimulus control procedures involve identification of *all* stimulus antecedents and
development of alternative responses to avoid risk.

Aversion Procedures

The use of aversion therapy in dealing with sexually offensive behavior has
an infamous past. In fact, some of the early aversion therapy procedures
remind one of torture and have been maligned in the cult film *A Clockwork
Orange*. The focus of early aversion therapy in the treatment of male
homosexual behavior adds to the negative image of aversion therapy given
today's more accepting attitude toward homosexuality. Additionally, Quinsey and Marshall (1983) point out that there is a lack of research evidence
supporting a viable theoretical explanation of why aversion therapy works.
A study by James (1962) is an excellent example of an early use of aversion
therapy that would make any of today's Research Ethics Boards shudder in
fear. James's (1962) subject was a homosexual who was injected with
synthetic drugs in the name of therapy and asked to view pictures of nude
males while nausea set in. The "therapy" was interrupted twice because the
client was suffering from acetonuria. He was also given alcohol to drink and
awakened throughout the night as part of the therapy procedure.

More contemporary use of aversion therapy procedures has relied on
covert sensitization (Cautela, 1987) and assisted covert sensitization (Maletzky, 1974). In covert sensitization, coversive stimuli and the desired

(although forbidden) sexual behaviors are presented in imagination. In assisted covert desensitization, a foul odor such as valeric acid is presented along with the covert imagery, theoretically to potentiate the conditioning value of the procedure. Quinsey and Marshall (1983), however, point out the paucity of research evidence to support the effectiveness of either procedure.

Victim Awareness

Clinicians working with clients who have victimized others have observed in these clients a distinct lack of sensitivity to the experience of their victims. Because child sex offenders, exhibitionists, and voyeurs typically do not physically injure their victims, there is often the distortion that the victim was unharmed or even enjoyed the experience. I have even heard child sex offenders report indignantly that they were actually seduced by the child or that they were really helping the child.

The beliefs of offenders who victimize others must be challenged and put into perspective. Both short-term and long-term effects on the victim must be discussed. The offender must become aware that a victim may be very frightened but not show it, have nightmares, and may not be able to trust or develop close relationships with people because of the sexual offense. Furthermore, the offender must be made aware of centers to help victims and understand why victims need help. Reading literature on victims, seeing timely films that depict the suffering of victims, and reviewing incidents in their own lives when they were victimized may help to sensitize the offenders to the victims' peril.

I ask the offenders to review what one of their victims was thinking during a sexual assault. I review actual past experiences (as well as hypothetical ones) and challenge attitudes that minimize any negative impact by reminding the offender of hidden damages and long-term consequences. It is also important to use the names of victims (when known) and challenge the offender's use of terms that objectify the victim. For example, offenders may use terms like "broads" or refer to the body parts of victims (for example, "she had a nice ass"). Such objectification makes it easier to offend, since objects are not thought of as having feelings.

Freeman-Longo and Wall (1986) report an innovative procedure for sex offenders in prison settings in which victims of sexual assault are brought into group therapy sessions with the offenders. Such confrontations require great courage on the part of the victims but, it is hoped, may lead to increased sensitivity to the victims' feelings and reduced recidivism for sex offenders.

Group Therapy

Group therapy for sex offenders exists in prison settings (Groth, 1983) as well as in the community (Geller, Devlin, Flynn, & Kaliski, 1985). The structure and content of group therapy procedures may vary from setting to setting, but confrontation or denial by one's peers is crucial to the group therapy process. Geller et al. (1985) point out that confrontation or denial by his peers can be a very powerful and emotional experience, one that facilitates overall change.

Satiation and Orgasmic Conditioning

Orgasmic conditioning is a procedure for increasing arousal to "appropriate" stimuli. It is typically used in cases of pedophilia or fetishism when little or no arousal is present for adult-oriented stimuli. The procedure instructs the client to masturbate to imagery or pictures of his preferred but unwanted stimulus and then, at the point of orgasm, switch his imagery or pictures to the "appropriate" sexual stimuli. This strategy is based on a classical conditioning model in which a previously neutral stimulus (that is, the fetish object) becomes a conditioned stimulus eliciting the unconditioned response (sexual arousal). As a client repeats the procedure, he gradually shifts the greater percentage of time masturbating from his preferred stimulus (for instance, children) to his conditioned stimulus (adults). Finally, the masturbation is completed entirely in the presence of the conditioned stimulus. Although early work by Conrad and Wincze (1976) failed to verify that any conditioning occurred as a result of this procedure, Kantorowitz (1978) and Abel et al. (1985) have presented data that suggest that a conditioning effect does occur.

Marshall (1979) has also described a variation of the masturbating procedure that he has termed satiation. In this procedure, a client is instructed to masturbate to his preferred but unwanted stimulus *after* orgasm. Masturbating occurs during the refractory period, and nonarousal is associated with the preferred but unwanted stimulus. I have found this to be an effective clinical procedure with my clients, but verification with a larger sample is indicated.

Chemical Procedures

Medroxyprogesterone acetate (MPA) and cyproterone acetate are two chemical compounds with antiandrogen effects that have been used for over 20 years in the treatment of sex offenders (Money, 1968; Laschet & Laschet, 1975; Berlin & Meinecke, 1981). A recent study by Wincze, Bansal, and Malamud (1986) has demonstrated that MPA does effectively reduce testosterone levels and erectile responding when taken in sufficient amounts. Although effective, there are some potential side effects and contraindications that must be taken into consideration before using this drug. Antiandrogen medication affects sexual arousal and therefore should be used only in cases where sexual arousal has clearly been associated with the atypical behavior. It is not an appropriate medication to use with juvenile offenders whose bone growth plate may be adversely affected by a hormone-altering drug. Potential dose effects include exacerbation of depression and obesity. One final cautionary note is that MPA may elevate glucose levels and therefore may be inappropriate for use with diabetic patients (Berlin, 1983).

All other therapeutic interventions listed under the structure and content of therapy are not unique to the treatment of atypical sexual behavior and are not discussed in this chapter. Therapeutic procedures for increasing appropriate arousal and decreasing inappropriate arousal must be applied with careful attention paid to proper timing. Therapy is often difficult for the client since he is being asked to give up behavior that is highly reinforcing and to replace it with behavior that is often nonrewarding or even stressful. The challenge for the therapist is to know when to apply what procedures and to understand the needs of the client and the needs of society. The case illustrations that follow are intended to yield a better understanding of the issues that are faced in treating individuals with atypical sexual behavior.

CASE STUDIES

Case 1: Successful Treatment of Chronic Exhibitionism

Presenting Problem

Robert was 22 years old when he first entered treatment on referral from a private psychiatric hospital. He had been working as a janitor at a mental health facility while living at home with his mother, father, and older brother. Robert reported a history of chronic exhibitionism that began when he was 11 years old. He grew up in a home with little or no structure, and his life was characterized by a total lack of direction; he found making plans not only strange but aversive. Robert's sexual development was without boundaries or direction, and sexual urges were allowed to be freely expressed.

He learned at a young age that exposing himself was a quick means of sexual gratification without the encumberment of a relationship. Although he always knew that exhibitionism was wrong in the eyes of the law, his own lack of moral guidance permitted such behavior without guilt. The behavior went unchecked for many years and grew to obsessive–compulsive proportions; Robert's rate of exposure increased in spite of social and legal problems. At his most compulsive point, Robert estimates that he was exposing himself about four times a day for several weeks. He described himself as waking up with urges and being so obsessed with the urges that at times he would break down and cry. He stated that he could masturbate as many as 15 times a day without abatement of his sexual urges. Although it is difficult to explain the exact reason for the compulsive nature of his behavior, several factors seemed to be present that exacerbated his problem. As his teen-age sexuality was emerging, his exhibitionism seemed to provide him with a sense of relieving frustration and gaining control or power over females who would surely reject him. In addition, the seriousness of his offenses had not yet impacted on him, and every opportunity to expose himself was acted on.

Robert had a very poor self-image and described himself as unattractive, unhandy, and unathletic. Both parents were preoccupied with their own problems and spent no time with Robert.

Etiology

The important etiological factors in this case seem to be related to the total lack of structure during the subject's development and the early crossing of sexual boundaries. He had been molested by an older man when he was 10 and was repeatedly witness to open sexual expression by his parents in their living room. Robert's poor self-image was also important since he felt insecure with friends his own age and was unsuccessful in dating. A final important factor was that he felt very stressed most of the time and found exposing himself not only sexually arousing but a tension-reducing mechanism. Exhibitionism was thus more rewarding than seeking acceptable sexual outlets, and it was easier to do.

Therapy Plan

The immediate need for Robert was to control his sexual behaviors. He had been arrested several times and was facing the possibility of a jail term. Robert agreed to sequester himself voluntarily as much as possible in his home while he underwent Depo-Provera® treatment. At the same time, he was asked to keep a record of his urges and rate his emotional state on a daily basis. Because of the unusually high frequency of urges, I felt that no therapy was possible until he was controlled. He reported exposing himself twice immediately after the first evaluation session because "the discussion made me sexually aroused." Once he was under control, then other problems and procedures could be addressed in the following order:

1. Stimulus control.
2. Victim sensitivity.
3. Responsibility for his own behavior.
4. Tension reduction.
5. Social skills.
6. Self-esteem.
7. Stabilized life plan.
8. Relapse prevention.

Therapy Results

Robert responded very well to the Depo-Provera® treatment, and within 2 weeks was reporting that for the first time in his life he did not wake up with "those terrible urges." He kept a very detailed daily record, and stimulus control procedures began with a description of the emotional and behavioral antecedents to exposing. Although he had described his exhibitionism as pervasive throughout every day, the behavioral record revealed that tension and riding in his car were precursors to most episodes.

Unfortunately, Robert went to trial and was incarcerated for 8 months after only 6 weeks of therapy. He was not allowed to continue Depo-Provera® in prison and received no therapy. On release, he exposed himself three times within the first 2 days and was arrested again. Fortunately, he was mandated to treatment instead of jail by the Court this time and was once again put on Depo-Provera®. He again responded very well to this and was able to progress through the other stages of therapy. Robert was very compliant throughout the whole therapy program, which consisted of weekly sessions for 1 year and then a maintenance program for 4 years. He has not exposed himself once in the past 5 years and is now married and expecting his first child. He was weaned off the Depo-Provera® 2 years ago, and although he occasionally has urges to expose himself, he has always been able to follow the relapse prevention plan consisting of early identification of risk, tension reduction, and communication of urges to his wife.

The therapy program was successful because Robert was the ideal candidate for Depo-Provera® therapy, and he was very compliant with psychotherapy instructions. He "felt" the difference on undergoing Depo-Provera® therapy, and this provided the basis for trust in the therapist. He also noticed the change in his feelings once stimulus control focuses were identified and he was given concrete instructions on how to avoid high-risk situations. A positive prognostic indicator was that Robert identified himself as having a problem and needing help. This is not always the case with sex offenders, and unsuccessful cases often stem from poor motivation for therapy on the part of the client.

Case 2: Unsuccessful Treatment of Pedophilia

Presenting Problem

Lee entered therapy very depressed and in a panic state because his wife was very suspicious of his relationship with his 16-year-old stepson. Lee was a school teacher and had been sexually abusing his stepson for approximately 2 years. He would take the boy to a motel where he supposedly worked on weekends and sexually molested the boy while he (Lee) "slept." Lee was never quite sure if the boy really knew that he was awake since he told the boy he suffered from somnambulism. The wife became suspicious when large gifts were purchased for her son without reasonable explanation. This was presumably out of guilt on Lee's part.

Background

Lee grew up in an upper-middle class family and described himself as a loner. He did not interact much with peers but felt at ease with adults. He had been sexually molested at age 11 by a man who was a "good" friend of the family. Lee does not look on this with anger, and, in fact, speaks fondly of the man.

Lee never felt comfortable with females, and when he started teaching, he became sexually involved with two students whom he was tutoring. His pattern was to get close to a family, gain their trust, and then get involved sexually. Involvement sometimes came a year or more after getting to know a boy. He married his wife after tutoring her son. Sexual involvement with him came after 2 years of marriage.

Etiology

A key factor in Lee's background seems to be his own sexual molestation. His parents had a very tumultuous relationship and were very strict with him. The man who molested him was perceived as a very calm and wonderful man in contrast to his own punishing father. In addition, Lee was a very tall, awkward boy who was nicknamed "praying mantis" and was rejected by girls. Behaviorally speaking, a man–boy sexual relationship was very rewarding to him in contrast to other punishing relationships.

Therapy Plan

Since Lee did not evidence a strong sexual drive, and since his involvement with boys always came after a long nonsexual involvement, Depo-Provera® treatment was not indicated. Therapy focused initially on stimulus control, victim sensitization, and acceptance of responsibility for his behavior. Although Lee seemed to be cooperative with therapy, he resisted considering a change out of the teaching profession. It was agreed as a condition of therapy that he could not get involved with families, and he could not tutor students.

Lee attended therapy faithfully and on the surface seemed to be responsive. However, there was always a distance from me in therapy, and I always had the feeling that he was holding back. As part of a relapse prevention program, it was agreed to inform his family of the details of his therapy to help monitor his program.

Therapy Outcome

After 1 year of therapy, it was decided to reduce sessions to once very 2 months. Six months after this, I received a call from his brother who informed me that he had currently visited Lee and learned that Lee had deceived everyone and was still tutoring students in his apartment. Lee was confronted, and since he had violated the treatment contract he was terminated from therapy.

In retrospect, therapy should have focused more on "not getting involved with tutoring." The desire to tutor and the tendency to rationalize involvement in tutoring should have been addressed early in therapy. Setting up a "contract" not to tutor inhibited discussion of this very important behavior and closed the channels of communication around this issue.

PARTING THOUGHTS

In any therapy program, the client's motivation and reasons for entering therapy are important factors in predicting therapeutic success. The motivation of clients who demonstrate atypical sexual behavior is often very dubious. Such clients often believe that their behavior is acceptable and that they are entering therapy only because of societal, family, or legal pressures. Furthermore, therapy is aimed at eliminating behaviors that are highly reinforcing and deeply ingrained in their life style. For some clients, changing behavior may also involve confronting intense fears (especially adult social and sexual relations). The combination of the above factors overwhelms some people and undermines therapy motivation.

Finally, clients who cannot describe internal reasons for being in therapy are likely to show poor progress. For example, a client who focuses predominantly on the legal issues may have difficulty in complying with a therapy program aimed at changing his behavior. This is especially true once the threat of legal action is past. On the other hand, a client who focuses on his own shame and on the hurt he feels he has caused others is a good candidate for positive change.

Manipulation is another therapy problem with this population. Patterns of involvement with children and their families often require a great deal of manipulation on the part of the perpetrator. In Case 2, presented above, years of manipulations occurred before and throughout the sexual involvement. The degree of the manipulation was very sophisticated and quite extensive and persistent during therapy. The extension of a manipulative approach by a client within therapy bodes very poorly for therapy outcome. When manipulation is detected as part of a client's pattern, regardless of the type of atypical sexual behavior, the manipulation should be identified as a target behavior for change. Manipulation is commonly found in other appetitive disorders such as overeating, smoking, alcohol abuse, and drug abuse, and it is commonly agreed that the manipulation must be dealt with openly in order for therapy to progress.

In conclusion, treating people with atypical sexual behaviors is often thought of as impossible and undesirable; for these reasons few clinicians make themselves available to these clients. Although this is a difficult population, it is not an impossible one to treat. Therapists who are aware of some of the major impediments to therapy and who know of the effective assessment and therapy procedures should be successful in treating clients with atypical sexual behaviors. The rewards of working with this population are that the therapist can experience the satisfaction of directly reducing the incidence of coercive sexual crimes while helping an individual achieve a more productive life style. The therapist is not only helping the client, but in many cases, other potential victims are helped as well. I hope that this chapter has demystified this area and has encouraged therapists to tackle these problems.

REFERENCES

Abel, C., Barlow, D., Blanchard, E., & Guild, D. (1977). The components of rapists' sexual arousal. *Archives of General Psychiatry, 34*, 895–903.

Abel, G., Becker, J., & Skinner, L. (1983). Treatment of the violent sex offender. In L. Roth (Ed.), *Clinical treatment of the violent person: Crime and delinquency issues* (pp. 100–123). Bethesda, MD: NIMH.

Abel, G., Mittelman, M., & Becker, J. (1985). *The effects of erotica on paraphiliacs' behavior.* Paper presented at the 11th annual meeting of the International Academy of Sex Researchers, Seattle, Washington.

Abramson, P., & Hayashi, H. (1982). Pornography in Japan: Cross-cultural and theoretical considerations. In N. M. Malamud & E. Donnerstein (Eds.), *Pornography and sexual aggression* (pp. 145–169). New York: Academic Press.

Berlin, F. (1983). Sex offenders: A biomedical perspective and a status report on biomedical treatment. In J. Greer & I. Stuart (Eds.), *The sexual aggressor: Current perspectives on treatment* (pp. 83–127). New York: Van Nostrand Reinhold.

Berlin, F., & Meinecke, C. (1981). Treatment of sex offenders with antiandrogenic medication: Conceptualization, review of treatment modalities, and preliminary findings. *American Journal of Psychiatry, 138*(5), 601–607.

Buhrich, N., & McConaghy, N. (1979). Three clinically discrete categories of fetishtic transvestism. *Archives of Sexual Behavior, 8*(2), 151–157.

Burt, M. (1980). Cultural myths and supports for rape. *Journal of Personality and Social Psychology, 38*, 217–230.

Cautels, J. (1967). Covert sensitization. *Psychological Reports, 20*, 459–468.

Conrad, W., & Wincze, J. (1976). Orgasmic reconditioning: A controlled study of its effects upon the sexual arousal patterns and behavior of adult male homosexuals. *Behavior Therapy, 7*, 155–166.

Derogatis, L., & Meyer, J. (1979). A psychological profile of the sexual dysfunctions. *Archives of Sexual Behavior, 8*(3), 201–223.

Earls, C., & Marshall, W. (1983). The current state of technology in the laboratory assessment of sexual arousal patterns. In J. Greer & I. Stuart (Eds.), *The sexual aggressor: Current perspectives on treatment* (pp. 336–362). New York: Van Nostrand Reinhold.

Freeman-Longo, R., & Wall, R. (1986). Changing a lifetime of sexual crime. *Psychology Today, 20,* 58–64.

Freund, K. (1987). Diagnosing homo- or heterosexuality and erotic age-preference by means of a psychophysiological test. *Behaviour Research and Therapy, 5,* 209–228.

Geller, M., Devlin, M., Flynn, T., & Kaliski, J. (1985). Confrontation of denial in a father's incest group. *International Journal of Group Psychotherapy, 35*(4), 545–567.

Groth, N. (1983). Treatment of the sexual offender in a correctional institution. In J. Greer & I. Stuart (Eds.), *The sexual aggressor: Current perspectives on treatment* (pp. 160–176). New York: Van Nostrand Reinhold.

James, B. (1962). Case of homosexuality treated by aversion therapy. *British Medical Journal, 1,* 768–770.

Kantorowitz, D. (1978). An experimental investigation of preorgasmic reconditioning and port-orgasmic deconditioning. *Journal of Applied Behavior Analysis, 11,* 23–34.

Kinsey, A., Pomeroy, W., & Martin, C. (1948). *Sexual behavior in the human male.* Philadelphia: W. B. Saunders.

Kinsey, A., Pomeroy, W., Martin, C., & Gebhard, P. (1953). *Sexual behavior in the human female.* Philadelphia: W. B. Saunders.

Laschet, V., & Laschet, L. (1975). Antiandrogens in the treatment of sexual deviations in men. *Journal of Steroid Biochemistry, 6,* 821–826.

Maletzky, B. (1974). Assisted covert sensitization in the treatment of exhbitionism. *Journal of Consulting and Clinical Psychology, 42,* 34–40.

Marshall, W. (1975). *The prediction of treatment outcome with sexual deviants based on changes in erectile responses to deviant and nondeviant stimuli.* Unpublished report, Queens University, Kingston, Ontario.

Marshall, W. (1979). Satiation therapy: A procedure for reducing deviant sexual arousal. *Journal of Applied Behavior Analysis, 12,* 10–22.

Money, J. (1968). Discussion on hormonal inhibition of libido in male sex offenders. In R. Michael (Ed.), *Endocrinology and human behavior* (pp. 325–338). London: Oxford University Press.

Quinsey, V., & Marshall, W. (1983). Procedures for reducing inappropriate sexual arousal: An evaluation review. In J. Greer & I. Stuart (Eds.), *The sexual aggressor: Current perspectives on treatment* (pp. 267–292). New York: Van Nostrand Reinhold.

Rosen, R., & Fracher, J. (1983). Tension reduction training in the treatment of compulsive sex offenders. In J. Greer & I. Stuart (Eds.), *The sexual aggressor: Current perspectives on treatement* (pp. 144–159). New York: Van Nostrand Reinhold.

Stoller, R. (1975). *Perversion: The erotic form of hatred.* New York: Pantheon Books.

Van de Loo, E. (1987). *Genital exposing behavior in adult human males: A clinical study of a coping mechanism.* Thesis, Rijksuniversiteit Leiden, The Netherlands.

Wincze, J., Bansal, S., & Malamud, M. (1986). Effects of medroxyprogesterone acetate on subjective arousal, arousal to erotic stimulation, and nocturnal penile tumescence in male sex offenders. *Archives of Sexual Behavior, 4*(15), 293–306.

Index